T0093527

Praise for the Previous Edition

"*Game Design Workshop* is a truly great book, and has become, in my opinion, the de facto standard text for beginner to intermediate level game design education. This updated new edition is extremely relevant, useful and inspiring to all kinds of game designers."

– Richard Lemarchand, *Interactive Media and Games Division, School of Cinematic Arts, University of Southern California*

"This is the perfect time for a new edition. The updates refresh elements of the book that are important as examples, but don't radically alter the thing about the book that is great: a play-centric approach to game design."

–Colleen Macklin, *Associate Professor, Parsons The New School for Design*

"Tracy Fullerton's *Game Design Workshop* covers pretty much everything a working or wannabe game designer needs to know. She covers game theory, concepting, prototyping, testing and tuning, with stops along the way to discuss what it means to be a professional game designer and how to land a job. When I started thinking about my game studies course at the University of Texas at Austin, this was one book I knew I had to use."

–Warren Spector, *Creative Director, OtherSide Entertainment*

"This is a break-through book, brimming with battle-tested 'how-to's.' Aspiring game designers: you will 'break through' to the next level when you learn to set, and then test, experience goals for your game players."

–Bing Gordon, *former Chief Creative Officer, Electronic Arts*

"*Game Design Workshop* is without a question the most important (and best book) on the topic of game design. Its unique approach is both deep and practical and draws students into the very heart of what game design is all about. The emphasis on paper-and-pencil prototyping encourages students to think, quite literally, "outside the box," and stretch themselves to innovate beyond simply rehashing commercially successful game genres. If the author's students are any indication, this method has a proven track record of producing both original and successful games. *Game Design Workshop* is ideal for those starting new educational programs as the book is structured around a design curriculum that can be easily implemented by instructors with no prior game design experience."

–Celia Pearce, *Professor of Game Design, Northeastern University and Festival Chair, IndieCade*

Game Design Workshop

"Create the digital games you love to play".

Discover an exercise-driven, non-technical approach to game design without the need for programming or artistic experience with *Game Design Workshop, Fifth Edition*.

Tracy Fullerton demystifies the creative process with clear and accessible guidance on the formal, dramatic, and dynamic systems of game design. Using examples of classic and popular games, illustrations of design techniques, and refined exercises to strengthen your understanding of how game systems function, this book gives you the skills and tools necessary to create a compelling and engaging game.

This updated 5th edition brings deeper coverage of playcentric design techniques, including setting emotion-focused experience goals and managing the design process to meet them. It includes a host of new diverse perspectives from top industry game designers.

Game Design Workshop puts you to work prototyping, playtesting, and revising your own games with time-tested methods and tools. These skills will provide the foundation for your career in any facet of the game industry including design, producing, programming, and visual design.

Tracy Fullerton is an award-winning game designer and educator with over 25 years of professional experience, including winning the Games for Change Game of the Year Award for her independent game Walden, a game. She has also been awarded the **2016 GDC Ambassador Award**, the **2015 Games for Change Game Changer Award**, and the **IndieCade 2013 Trailblazer award** for her pioneering work in the independent games community. Tracy is a Professor of Interactive Media & Games ad the USC School of Cinematic Arts and the founding Director (emeritus) of the USC Games Program, which has regularly been ranked the #1 game design program in North America by the Princeton Review.

Game Design Workshop

A Playcentric Approach to Creating Innovative Games

Fifth Edition

Tracy Fullerton

CRC Press
Taylor & Francis Group
Boca Raton London New York

CRC Press is an imprint of the
Taylor & Francis Group, an **informa** business

AN A K PETERS BOOK

Fifth edition published 2024
by CRC Press
2385 NW Executive Center Drive, Suite 320, Boca Raton FL 33431

and by CRC Press
4 Park Square, Milton Park, Abingdon, Oxon, OX14 4RN

CRC Press is an imprint of Taylor & Francis Group, LLC

© 2024 Tracy Fullerton

First edition published by CMP Books 2004
Fourth edition published by A K Peters/CRC Press 2018

Names: Fullerton, Tracy, author.
Title: Game design workshop : a playcentric approach to creating innovative games / Tracy Fullerton.
Description: Fifth edition. | Boca Raton, FL : CRC Press, 2024. |
Includes bibliographical references and index.
Identifiers: LCCN 2023043761 (print) | LCCN 2023043762 (ebook) |
ISBN 9781032607016 (hardback) | ISBN 9781032607009 (paperback) |
ISBN 9781003460268 (ebook)
Subjects: LCSH: Video games—Programming. | Video games—Design. |
Computer graphics.
Classification: LCC QA76.76.C672 F84 2024 (print) | LCC QA76.76.C672 (ebook) |
DDC 794.8/3—dc23/eng/20231026
LC record available at https://lccn.loc.gov/2023043761
LC ebook record available at https://lccn.loc.gov/2023043762

ISBN: 978-1-032-60701-6 (hbk)
ISBN: 978-1-032-60700-9 (pbk)
ISBN: 978-1-003-46026-8 (ebk)

DOI: 10.1201/9781003460268

Typeset in Josefin Sans
by codeMantra

Contents

Part 3   Working as a Game Designer 411

Chapter 12   Team Structures 413

Chapter 13   Stages and Methods of Development 447

Chapter 14   Communicating Your Designs. 469

Foreword

No matter what game we create, no matter how well we are able to play it, it is our game, and we can change it when we need to.

— Bernie De Koven

There is magic in games.

Not magic like a level 19 fireball spell is magic. Not the kind of magic you get when you purchase a trick in a magic store. And not the kind of mystical experience that organized religion can go on about. No, games are magic in the way that first kisses are magic, the way that finally arriving at a perfect solution to a difficult problem is magic, the way that conversation with close friends over good food is magic.

The magic at work in games is about finding hidden connections between things, in exploring the way that the universe of a game is structured. As all game players know, this kind of discovery makes for deeply profound experiences. How is it possible that the simple rules of chess and Go continue to evolve new strategies and styles of play, even after centuries and centuries of human study? How is it that the nations of the entire world, and even countries at war with each other—at war!—can come together to celebrate in the conflict of sport? How do computer and videogames, seemingly so isolating, pierce our individual lives, and bring us together in play?

To play a game is to realize and reconfigure these hidden connections—between units on a game board, between players in a match, between life inside the game and life outside—and in so doing, create new meaning. And if games are spaces where meaning is made, game designers are the meta-creators of meaning, those who architect the spaces of possibility where such discovery takes place.

Which is where this book comes in. You are reading these words because you are interested in not just playing games, but making them. Take my word for it: *Game Design Workshop* is one of the very few books that can truly help you to make the games that you want to make. Those games bursting from your heart and your imagination. The ones that keep you up at night demanding to be designed. Games that are brimming with potential for discovery, for meaning, for magic.

Game Design Workshop presents, with sharp intelligence and an eye to the importance of the design process, tried-and-true strategies for thinking about and creating games. More than just fancy notions about how games work, *Game Design Workshop* is a treasury of methods for putting game design theories into practice. Tracy Fullerton has real experience making games, teaching game designers, and writing about game design. And she has personally taught me a great deal about games. In the ambition of its scope and the value of its insights, you hold in your hands a unique text.

Why do we need a book like *Game Design Workshop*? Because despite the fact that games are so very ancient, are part of every culture, and are increasingly important in people's lives, we hardly know anything about them. We are still learning. What makes games tick? How do we create them? How do they fit into culture at large? The explosion of computer and videogames in recent decades has multiplied the complexity and the stakes of such questions. For better or worse, questions like these don't have simple answers. And *Game Design Workshop* won't give them to you. But it can help you figure out how to explore them on your own, through the games you design.

We are living through the rebirth of an ancient form of human culture. Just as the 19th century ushered in mechanical invention, and the 20th century was the age of information, the 21st will be a century of play. As game designers, we will be the architects, the storytellers, and the party hosts of this playful new world. What a wonderful and weighty responsibility we have. To bring meaning to the world. To bring magic into the world. To make great games. And to set the world on fire through play.

Are you with me?

Eric Zimmerman

Preface

So much has changed in the game industry since I wrote the first edition of this book twenty years ago. There has been an explosion in new platforms of play and an emergence of exciting new markets and genres of games. Today, it seems that everyone plays games, everywhere. The one constant I see in this world of change is the need for innovative game designers to realize the potential for play in all of these new platforms and places.

And so I offer this updated twentieth anniversary edition, with its strong focus still on learning the playcentric process of design and iteration, but enhanced with updated techniques and ideas that have sprung from today's industry, and filled with the perspectives of new designers who are on the front lines of facing today's design challenges and opportunities—designers such as Jane McGonigal, Ian Dallas, Dan Cook, Wren Brier, Derek Yu, Shawn Alexander Allen, Elizabeth LaPensée, Mary Flanagan, Bruce Straley, Neil Jones, Anna Anthropy, Christina Norman, and more. This edition includes sidebars on using AI in the creative process, designing game and narrative beats for impactful moments of play, building inclusive teams, designing innovative mobile games and virtual reality content, on art games and social games, and on techniques for tuning games and using metrics to get the best player experience.

Back when I wrote the first version of this book, there was a sense in the field that game design was not something that could be taught. You either had a "knack" for games or you didn't. Needless to say, I didn't agree. Fast-forward twenty years and the sense is completely different. Now, game design programs, such as the one that I created at USC, are seen as incubators for innovative ideas and people. The training that students get in such programs is coalescing into a set of best practices that turn out creative people who are able to work well on diverse teams, and who have strong design skills and understanding of how to create interesting game mechanics. Some of these programs have arisen in technical schools, some in art schools, and others in a staggering variety of disciplines that cross the humanities, arts, and sciences. Game design is everywhere.

Not only is everyone learning game design, but everyone is doing it. Today's schoolchildren are using construction games like Minecraft or Roblox to learn everything from art and coding, to history and environmental awareness. Their love of games is leading them to learn critical skills like systems thinking and procedurality. They are modding and making and playing and learning and the boundaries between these things are no longer clear or important. What will the world look like in another twenty years, when the children who grew up learning from and thinking in game systems become adults? What games will they want to play then? What systems will they engage with to learn more about the world? I can hardly wait to see.

The students who studied game design with me while I wrote the earlier editions of this book have completely stunned me with their talent and vision. They have set new levels of aesthetic expectations for the field as a whole and are deeply embedded in the changes that will define the next generation of play. The games that I see coming out of the industry today, especially in the world of experimental and independent designs, make me believe that this is only the beginning of the evolution of play that we will see, culturally, creatively, and commercially.

I am so thrilled to be part of this change, and to know that this book has inspired so many to follow the path of innovative game design. I can only hope that the students and designers who read this new edition will do so with the same passion and commitment as those who have done in the past twenty years.

Play on!

Acknowledgments

I'd like to thank the many game designers, producers, executives, and educators who have provided invaluable ideas, information, and insights during the writing of the several editions of this book. These talented individuals include:

Steve Ackrich, Activision
Phil Adam, Intellivision
Shawn Alexander Allen, NuChallenger
Anna Anthropy
Graeme Bayless, NetherRealm Studios (WB Games)
Ranjit Bhatnagar
Seamus Blackley, Pacific Light & Hologram
Jonathan Blow
Chip Blundell
Wren Brier, Witch Beam
Ian Bogost, Washington University
Chris Brandkamp, Cyan
Jeff Chen, Activision
Jenova Chen, thatgamecompany
Stan Chow, Centrix Studio
Doug Church
Dino Citraro, Periscopic
Dan Cook, Spry Fox
Don Daglow, Daglow Entertainment
Elizabeth Daley, USC School of Cinematic Arts
Ian Dallas, Giant Sparrow
Rob Daviau, IronWall Games and Restoration Games
Bernie DeKoven
Jason Della Rocca, Execution Labs
Dallas Dickinson, Crystal Dynamics

Neil Dufine
Peter Duke, Duke Media
Troy Dunniway
Greg Ecker
Glenn Entis, Google Research
James Ernest, Cheapass Games
Noah Falstein, The Inspiracy
Dan Fiden, Signia Venture Partners
Matt Firor, Zenimax Online Studios
Scott Fisher, USC School of Cinematic Arts
Nick Fortugno, Playmatics
Mary Flanagan, Resonym
Tom Frisina, Tilting Point
Bill Fulton, Insomniac Games
Richard Garfield
John Garrett
Jeremy Gibson, University of Michigan Ann Arbor
Chaim Gingold
Greg Glass
Susan Gold
Bing Gordon
Sheri Graner Ray
Bob Greenberg, R/GA Interactive
Michael Gresh
Gary Gygax
Justin Hall
Brian Hersch, Hersch and Company
Richard Hilleman
Kenn Hoekstra
Steven Hoffman, Founders Space
Leslie Hollingshead, Vivendi Universal Games
Josh Holmes, Octopus Panic Games

Adrian Hon, Six to Start
Robin Hunicke
Steve Jackson, Steve Jackson Games
Michael John, UC Santa Cruz
Neil Jones, Aerial_Knight
Matt Kassan
Kevin Keeker, Sony PlayStation
Heather Kelley, Carnegie Mellon University
Scott Kim, GameThinking.io
Naomi Kokubo, LavaMind
Matt Korba, The Odd Gentlemen
Vincent Lacava, Pop and Co.
Lorne Lanning, Oddworld Inhabitants
Frank Lantz, NYU Game Center
Nicole Lazzaro, XEODesign
Elizabeth LaPensée, Twin Suns Corp.
Marc LeBlanc, Riot Games
Elan Lee, Expoding Kittens
Timothy Lee, USC Game Innovation Lab
Nick Lefevre, Konami of America
Richard Lemarchand, USC School of Cinematic Arts
Tim LeTourneau, Fortis Games
Ethan Levy
Stone Librande, Riot Games
Rich Liebowitz, EP1TOME STUDIOS
Starr Long, GigStan and Stellar Effect
Sus Lundgren, PLAY Research Group
Laird Malamed, Meta
Michael Mateas, UC Santa Cruz
Don Mattrick, Prometheus Ventures
American McGee, Mysterious
Jane McGonigal, SuperBetter
Jordan Mechner
Nikita Mikros, BumbleBear Games
Scott Miller, 3D Realms
Peter Molyneaux, 22Cans
Alan R. Moon
Minori Murakami, Namco
Janet Murray, Georgia Institute of Technology
Ray Muzyka, Threshold Impact
Christina Norman, Elodie Games
Dan Orzulak, Sucker Punch Productions
Trent Oster, Beamdog

Rob Pardo, Bonfire Studios
Celia Pearce, Northeastern University
David Perry, GetCarro.com
Sandy Petersen, Petersen Games
Chris Plummer, Activision
Rhy-Ming Poon, Activision
Nathalie Pozzi
Kim Rees, Periscopic
Stephanie Reimann, Epic Games
John Riccitiello
Erin Reynolds, Disney Consumer Products
Sam Roberts, USC School of Cinematic Arts and IndieCade
Neal Robison, Western Governors University
John Rocco
Brenda Romero, Romero Games
Bill Roper, Lunacy Games
Kate Ross, Wizards of the Coast
Rob Roth
Jason Rubin
Chris Rubyor, Microsoft
Susana Ruiz
Katie Salen, UC Irvine
Kellee Santiago
Jesse Schell, Carnegie Mellon University
Carl Schnurr
Steve Seabolt
Nahil Sharkasi, Cliffhanger Games
Bruce C. Shelley
Tom Sloper, Sloperama Productions
Randy Smith, Tiger Style
Warren Spector, OtherSide Entertainment
Phil Spencer, Microsoft
Jen Stein, USC School of Cinematic Arts
Bruce Straley, Wildflower Interactive
Michael Sweet
Steve Swink, Flashbang Studios
Keita Takahashi
Chris Taylor, kanoogi.com
Brian Tinsman, Predixa
Eleanor Todd, Orange Monkey Games
Kurosh ValaNejad
Jim Vessella, Respawn Entertainment
Jesse Vigil, Psychic Bunny

XXIV   Acknowledgments

Asher Vollmer
Jeff Watson
Steve Weiss, Sony Online Entertainment
Jay Wilbur, Epic Games
Dennis Wixon
Will Wright, Stupid Fun Club
Richard Wyckoff, Reverge Labs
Derek Yu, Mossmouth
Eric Zimmerman, NYU Game Center

I would also like to thank my editors and agents at CRC Press, Elsevier, Morgan Kaufmann, CMP, and Waterside Productions:

Rick Adams, CRC Press
Will Bateman, CRC/Taylor & Francis
Dorothy Cox, CMP Books
Danielle Jatlow, Waterside Productions
Georgia Kennedy, Elsevier
Laura Lewin, Elsevier
Carol McClendon, Waterside Productions
Jamil Moledina, CMP Books
Dawnmarie Simpson, Elsevier
Paul Temme, Elsevier

And, of course, all of my students and colleagues at the University of Southern California.

Image Credits and Copyright Notices

Cover design by Ala' Diab

Playtesting and prototyping photos by Tracy Fullerton and Chris Swain unless otherwise noted

Diagrams and illustrations by Tracy Fullerton unless otherwise noted

Images from You Don't Know Jack™ courtesy of Jellyvision—© Jellyvision, Inc.

Image from Beautiful Katamari © 2007 Namco Bandai Games

Chess Grand Master Nodirbek Abdusattorov in 2023 courtesy of Frans Peters.

Image of professional eSports players courtesy of lincconf.com.

Image from Darfur is Dying © 2006 Susana Ruiz

Images from Life is Strange series © Square Enix

Image from World of Warcraft™ © 2007 Blizzard Entertainment®

Image from City of Heroes © 2007 NCsoft

PAC-MAN™ © 1980 Namco Ltd,. All Rights Reserved. Courtesy of Namco Holding Corp.

Image from 7th Guest © Virgin Interactive Entertainment

Image from Tomb Raider courtesy of Eido Interactive. © Eidos Interactive Ltd.

Image from Slingo courtesy of Slingo, Inc. © Slingo

SOUL CALIBER II™ © 1982 Namco Ltd. All Rights Reserved. Courtesy of Namco Holding Corp. SOULCALIBUR II® & © 1995 1998 2002 2003 NAMCO LTD., ALL RIGHTS RESERVED.

Scotland Yard © Ravensburger

Scrabble, Monopoly, Milton Bradley's Operation, Lord of the Rings board game, Connect Four, and Pit © Hasbro

Images from Dark Age of Camelot courtesy of Mythic Entertainment. Copyright © 2003 Mythic Entertainment, Inc. All rights reserved. www.darkageofcamelot.com

Images from Maximum Chase™ courtesy of Microsoft Corporation. Screenshots reprinted by permission of Microsoft Corporation

POLE POSITION™ © 1982 Namco Ltd,. All Rights Reserved. Courtesy of Namco Holding Corp.

MotoGP™ © 1998 2000 Namco Ltd., All Rights Reserved. Courtesy of Namco Holding Corp.

MotoGP3 © 1998 2000 2001 2002 NAMCO LTD., ALL RIGHTS RESERVED. Licensed by Dorna.

Image from Halo 3 © 2007 Microsoft Game Studios

Introduction

One of the most difficult tasks people can perform, however much others may despise it, is the invention of good games.

—C.G. Jung

Games are an integral part of all known human cultures. Digital games, in all their various formats and genres, are just a new expression of this ancient method of social interaction. Creating a good game, as noted in the Jung quote above, is a challenging task, one that requires a playful approach but a systematic solution. Part engineer, part entertainer, part mathematician, and part social director, the role of the game designer is to craft a set of rules within which there are means and motivation to play. Whether we are talking about folk games, board games, arcade games, or massively multiplayer online games, the art of game design has always been to create that elusive combination of challenge, competition, and interaction that players just call "fun."

The cultural impact of digital games has grown to rival television and films as the industry has matured over the past half century. Game industry revenues have been growing at a double-digit rate for years and have long eclipsed the domestic box office of the film industry, reaching 56.6 billion dollars in the U.S. in 2022.[1] According to a Pew Internet report, 97% of all American teens age 12-17 play computer, web, console, or mobile games. That's nearly *all* teens. Nearly one-third of those play games every day,

and another one in five play games three to five days a week.[2] This may not be surprising behavior among teenagers, but the Entertainment Software Association also reports that the average age of game players is now 36 years old and that the average U.S. household owns at least one dedicated game console, PC, or mobile gaming device.[3]

As both sales and cultural reach of games have increased, interest in game design as a career path has also escalated. Similar to the explosion of interest in screenwriting and directing that accompanied the growth of the film and television industries, creative thinkers today are turning to games as a new form of expression. Degree programs in game design are now available in major universities all over the world in response to student demand. The International Game Developers Association, in recognition of the overwhelming interest in learning to create games, established an Education SIG in 2003 to help educators create curriculum that reflects the real-world process of professional game designers. There is a Game Education Summit held every year at the Game Developers Conference where best practices in teaching game design are shared. And GameCareerGuide.com provides information on schools, jobs, and student games to connect the study of game development to the practice of it. On their website, the Higher Education Video Game Alliance lists over 140 programs that offer game design courses or degrees in North America alone. There are over 200 programs listed worldwide. This does not include game design courses in high schools or middle schools; after school; summer programs; or programs like Girls Make Games or Girls Who Code, which offer summer programs for girls and non-binary kids from eight to 18.

In addition to my experience designing games for companies such as Microsoft, Sony, MTV, and Disney, I have spent over 25 years teaching the art of game design to students from a variety of different backgrounds and experience levels and have established a world-renowned game design curriculum for the USC Games program at the University of Southern California. In this time, I have found that there are patterns in the way that beginning designers grasp the structural elements of games, common traps that they fall into, and certain types of exercises that can help them learn to make better games. This book encapsulates the experience I have gained by working with my students to design, prototype, and playtest hundreds of original game concepts.

My students have gone on to jobs in all areas of the game industry, including game design, producing, programming, visual design, marketing, and quality assurance. A number of them have gone on to become prominent independent game developers, such as the team at thatgamecompany, which developed the hit downloadable title flOw from a student research project created at USC and then went on to create the critically acclaimed games Flower and Journey. Many more of them have gone to work for established companies, from Microsoft and Electronic Arts to Riot and Zynga. They have worked on games as varied as Bioshock 2, Zynga Poker, League of Legends, What Remains of Edith Finch, and Kinect Star Wars. I have seen the method I present here prove to be successful over and over again with a wide variety of students. Whatever your background, your technical skills, or your reasons for wanting to design games, my goal with this book is to enable you to design games that engage and delight your players.

My approach is exercise driven and extremely nontechnical. This might surprise you, but I do not recommend implementing your designs digitally right away. The complexities of software development often hamper a designer's ability to see the structural elements of their system clearly. The exercises contained in this book require no programming expertise or visual art skills and so release you from the intricacies of digital game production while allowing you to learn what works and what does not work in your game system. Additionally, these exercises will teach you the most important skills in game design: the process of setting compelling experience goals, prototyping, playtesting, and revising your system based on player feedback.

There are three basic steps to my approach:

Step 1

Start with an understanding of how games work. Learn about rules, procedures, objectives, etc. What is a game? What makes a game compelling to play? Part I of this book covers these game design fundamentals.

Step 2

Learn to ideate, prototype, and playtest your original games. Create rough physical or digital prototypes of your designs that allow you to separate the essential system elements from the complexities of full production. Put your playable prototype in the hands of players and conduct playtests that generate useful, actionable feedback. Use that feedback to revise and perfect your game's design. Part II, starting on page 175, covers these important design skills.

Step 3

Understand today's rapidly changing industry and the place of the game designer in it. The first two steps give you the foundation of knowledge to be a literate and capable game designer. From there you can pursue the specialized skills used in the game industry. For example, you can pursue producing, programming, art, or marketing. You might become a lead game designer or perhaps one day run a whole company. Part III, starting on page 411, of this book covers the place of the game designer on a design team and in the industry.

The book is full of exercises intended to get you working on game design problems and creating your own designs. When you reach the end, you will have prototyped and playtested many games, and you will have at least one original playable project of your own. I emphasize the importance of doing these exercises because the only way to really become a game designer is to make games, not just play them or read about them. If you think of this book as a tool to lead you through the process of design, and not just a text to read, you will find the experience much more valuable.

So if you are ready to get started, it's your turn now. Best of luck!

END NOTES

1. Entertainment Software Association, "Essential Facts about the U.S. Video Game Industry," July 2023.
2. Pew Internet, "Teens, Video Games and Civics," September 16, 2008.
3. Entertainment Software Association, "Essential Facts about the Computer and Game Industry," June 2017.

Part 1
Game Design Basics

Since there have been games, there have been game designers. Their names might have been lost to history, but at some point the first clay dice were thrown, and the first smooth stones were placed in the pits of a newly carved mancala board. These early inventors might not have thought of themselves as game designers—perhaps they were just amusing themselves and their friends by coming up with competitions using the everyday objects around them—but many of their games have been played for thousands of years. And although this history stretches back as far as the beginnings of human culture, when we think of games today, we tend to speak of the digital games that have so recently captured our imaginations.

These digital games have the capacity to take us to amazing new worlds with fantastic characters and fully realized interactive environments. Games are designed by teams of professional game developers who work long hours at specialized tasks. The technological and business aspects of these digital games are mind-boggling. And yet, the appeal of digital games for players has its roots in the same basic impulses and desires as the games that have come before them. We play games to learn new skills, to feel a sense of achievement, to interact with friends and family, and sometimes just to pass the time. Ask yourself, why do you play games? Understanding your own answer, and the answers of other players, is the first step to becoming a game designer.

I bring up this long history of games as a prelude to a book primarily about designing digital games because I feel that it's important for today's designers to "reclaim" that history as inspiration and for examples of what makes great gameplay. It's important to remember that what has made games such a long lasting form of human entertainment is not intrinsic to any technology or medium but to the experience of the players.

The focus of this book will be on understanding and designing for that player experience, no matter what platform you are working with. It is what I call a "playcentric" approach to game design, and it is the key to designing innovative, emotionally engaging game experiences. In the first chapter of this section, I'll discuss the special role played by the game designer throughout the process: the designer's relationship to the production team, the skills and vision a designer must possess, and the method by which a designer brings players into the process. Then I will look at the essential structure of games—the formal, dramatic, and dynamic elements that a designer must work with to create that all-important player experience. These are the fundamental building blocks of game design, and they provide an understanding of what it takes to create great games.

DOI: 10.1201/9781003460268-1

Chapter 1

The Role of the Game Designer

The game designer envisions how a game will work during play. She creates the objectives, rules, and procedures; thinks up the dramatic premise and gives it life; and is responsible for planning everything necessary to create a compelling player experience. In the same way that an architect drafts a blueprint for a building or a screenwriter produces the script for a movie, the game designer plans the structural elements of a system that, when set in motion by the players, creates the interactive experience.

As the impact of digital games has increased, there has been an explosion of interest in game design as a career. Now, instead of looking to Hollywood and dreaming of writing the next blockbuster, many creative people are turning to games as a new form of expression.

But what does it take to be a game designer? What kinds of talents and skills do you need? What will be expected of you during the process? And what is the best method of designing for a game? In this chapter, I'll talk about the answers to these questions and outline a method of iterative design that designers can use to judge the success of gameplay against their goals for the player experience throughout the design and development process. This iterative method, which I call the "playcentric" approach, relies on inviting feedback from players early on and is the key to designing games that delight and engage the audience because the game mechanics are developed from the ground up with the player experience at the center of the process.

AN ADVOCATE FOR THE PLAYER

The role of the game designer is, first and foremost, to be an advocate for the player. The game designer must look at the world of games through the player's eyes. This sounds simple, but you'd be surprised how often this concept is ignored. It's far too easy to get caught up in a game's graphics, story line, or new features and forget that what makes a game great is solid gameplay. That's what excites players. Even if they tell you that they love the special effects, art direction, or plot, they won't play for long unless the gameplay hooks them.

DOI: 10.1201/9781003460268-2

As a game designer, a large part of your role is to keep your concentration focused on the player experience and not allow yourself to be distracted by the other concerns of production. Let the art director worry about the imagery, the producer stress over the budget, and the technical director focus on the engine. Your main job is to make sure that when the game is delivered, it provides superior gameplay.

When you first sit down to design a game, everything is fresh and, most likely, you have a vision for what it is that you want to create. At this point in the process, your view of the game and that of the eventual new player are similar. However, as the process unfolds and the game develops, it becomes increasingly difficult to see your creation objectively. After months of testing and tweaking every conceivable aspect, your once-clear view can become muddled. At times like this, it's easy to get too close to your own work and lose perspective.

Playtesters

It is in situations like these when it becomes critical to have playtesters. Playtesters are people who play your game and provide feedback on the experience so that you can move forward with a fresh perspective. By watching other people play the game, you can learn a great deal.

Observe their experience and try to see the game through their eyes. Pay attention to what objects they are focused on, where they touch the screen or move the cursor when they get stuck or frustrated or bored, and write down everything they tell you. They are your guides, and it's your mission to have them lead you inside the game and illuminate any issues lurking below the surface of the design. If you train yourself to do this, you will regain your objectivity and be able to see both the beauty and the flaws in what you've created.

Some game designers don't involve playtesters in their process until it's too late to change the essential elements of the design. Perhaps

1.1   Playtest group

they are on a tight schedule and feel they don't have time for feedback. Or perhaps they are afraid that it's too early in the design process — that they don't have enough working features in their game to get useful feedback. Maybe they think that getting a playtest group together will cost too much money. Or they might be under the impression that testing is something only done by large companies or marketing people.

What these designers don't realize is that by divorcing their process from this essential feedback opportunity, they probably cost themselves considerable time, money, and creative heartache. This is because games are not a form of one-way communication. Being a superior game designer isn't about controlling every aspect of the game design or dictating exactly how the game should function. It's about building a *potential* experience, setting all the pieces in place so that everything's ready to unfold when the players begin to participate.

In some ways, designing a game is like being the host of a party. As the host, it's your job to get everything ready—food, drinks, decorations, music to set the mood—and then you open the doors to your guests and see what happens. The results are not always predictable or what you envisioned. A game, like a party, is an interactive experience that is only fully realized after your guests arrive. What type of party will your game be like? Will your players sit like wallflowers in your living room? Will they stumble around trying to find the coatroom closet? Or will they laugh and talk and meet new people, hoping the night will never end?

Inviting players "over to play" and listening to what they say as they experience your game is the best way to understand how your game is working. Gauging reactions, interpreting silent moments, studying feedback, and matching those with specific game elements are the keys to becoming a professional designer. When you learn to listen to your players, you can help your game to grow.

In Chapter 9 on page 293, when I discuss the playtesting process in detail, you'll learn methods and procedures that will help you hold professional-quality playtests and make the most of these tests by asking good questions and listening openly to criticism. For now, though, it's just important to know that playtesting is the heart of the design process explored in this book and

that the feedback you receive during these sessions can help you transform your game into a truly enjoyable experience for your players.

Like any creative design, games transform throughout their development cycle. Guiding your design process requires you to set a direction for the team and be open to ideas that lead you towards your goal. If you understand how to listen to both your players and your team, you can mold your early ideas into the desired experience through repeated testing and careful observation. As a game designer, it's up to you to set innovative goals, but be open to evolve your game into more than you originally envisioned with the help of this process. That's the art of game design. It's not locking things in place; it's giving birth and parenting. No one, no matter how smart, can conceive and produce a sophisticated game from a blank sheet of paper and perfect it without going through this process. And learning how to work creatively within this process is what this book is all about.

1.2 More playtest groups

Exercise 1.1: Become a Tester

Take on the role of a tester. Go play a game and observe yourself as you play. Write down what you're doing and feeling. Try to create one page of detailed notes on your behaviors and actions. Then repeat this experience while watching a friend play the same game. Compare the two sets of notes and analyze what you've learned from the process.

Throughout this book, I've included exercises that challenge you to practice the skills that are essential to game design. I've tried to break them down so that you can master them one by one, but by the end of the book, you will have learned a tremendous amount about games, players, and the design process. And you will have designed, prototyped, and playtested at least one original idea of your own. I recommend creating a folder, either digital or analog, of your completed exercises so that you can refer to them as you work your way through the book.

PASSIONS AND SKILLS

What does it take to become a game designer? There is no one simple answer, no one path to success. There are some basic traits and skills I can suggest, however. First, a great game designer is someone who loves to create playful situations. A passion for games and play is the one thread all great designers have in common. If you don't love what you're doing, you'll never be able to put in the long hours necessary to craft truly innovative games.

To someone on the outside of the process, making games might seem like a trivial task—something that's akin to playing around. But it's not. As any experienced designer can tell you, testing your own game for the thousandth time can become work, not play. As the designer, you have to remain dedicated to that ongoing process. You can't just go through the motions. You have to keep that passion alive in yourself, and in the rest of the team, to make sure that the great gameplay you envisioned in those early days of design is still there in the exhausting, pressure-filled final days before you lock production. To do that, you'll need to develop some other important skills in addition to your love of games and your understanding of the playcentric process.

Communication

The most important skill that you, as a game designer, can develop is the ability to communicate clearly and effectively with all the other people who will be working on your game. You'll have to "sell" your game many times over before it ever hits the store shelves: to your teammates, management, investors, and perhaps even your friends and family. To accomplish this, you'll need good language skills, a crystal-clear vision, and a well-conceived presentation. This is the only way to rally everyone involved to your cause and secure the support that you'll need to move forward.

But good communication doesn't just mean writing and speaking—it also means becoming a good listener and a great compromiser. Listening to your playtesters and to the other people on your team affords fresh ideas and new directions. Listening also involves your teammates in the creative process, giving them a sense of authorship in the final design that will reinvest them in their own responsibilities on the project. If you don't agree with an idea, you haven't lost anything, and the idea you don't use might spark one that you do.

1.3   Communicating with team members

What happens when you hear something that you don't want to hear? Perhaps one of the hardest things to do in life is compromise. In fact, many game designers think that compromise is a bad word. But compromise is sometimes necessary, and if done well, it can be an important source of creative collaboration.

For example, your vision of the game might include a technical feature that is simply impossible given the available time and resources. What if your programmers come up with an alternative implementation for the feature, but it doesn't capture the essence of the original design goals? How can you adapt your idea to the practical necessities in such a way as to keep the gameplay intact? You'll have to compromise. As the designer, it's your job to find a way to do it elegantly and successfully so that the game doesn't suffer.

Teamwork

Game production can be one of the most intense collaborative processes you'll ever experience. The interesting and challenging thing about game development teams is the sheer breadth of types of people who work on them. From the hardcore computer scientists, who might be

1.4   Team meeting

designing the AI or graphics tools, to the talented illustrators and animators who bring the characters to life, to the market-focused executives and business managers who deliver the game to its players, the range of personalities is incredible.

As the designer, you will interact with almost all of them, and you will find that they all speak different professional languages and have different points of view. Overly technical terms may not translate well to artists or the producer, while the subtle shadings of a character sketch might not be instantly obvious to a programmer. These are generalizations, of course, and many team members will come from multidisciplinary backgrounds, but you can't always count on that. So a big part of your job, and one of the reasons for your documents and specifications, is to serve as a sort of universal translator, making sure that all of these different groups are, in fact, working toward the same goals.

Throughout this book, I often refer to the game designer as a single team member, but in many cases, the task of game design is a team effort. Whether there is a team of designers on a single game or a collaborative environment where the visual designers, programmers, or producer all have input to the design, the game designer rarely works alone. In Chapter 12 on page 413, I will discuss team structures and how the game designer fits into the complicated puzzle that is a development team.

Process

Being a game designer often requires working under great pressure. You'll have to make critical changes to your game without causing new issues in the process. All too often, a game becomes unbalanced as attempts are made to correct an issue because the designer gets too close to the work and, in the hopes of solving one problem, introduces a host of new problems. But, unable to see this mistake, the designer keeps making changes, while the problems grow worse, until the game becomes such a mess that it loses whatever magic it once had.

Games are fragile systems, and each element is inextricably linked to the others, so a change in one variable can send disruptive ripples throughout. This is particularly catastrophic in the final phases of development, where you run out of time, mistakes are left unfixed, and portions of the game may be cut in order to ship the project on time. Alternatively, teams may try to "crunch," working around the clock to finish features. And when we work under pressure like this, mistakes are made and team member's health and wellness is put at risk.

The one thing that can rescue a game team from these kinds of issues is instilling the need for good processes from the beginning. Production is a messy business; it is where ideas can get convoluted and objectives can disappear in the chaos of daily crises. But good process, using the play-centric approach of playtesting, and controlled, iterative changes, which I'll discuss throughout this book, can help you stay focused on your goals, prioritize what's truly important, and avoid the pitfalls of an unstructured approach.

Exercise 1.2: Inspiration

Seek out inspiration for a game by doing something new: go to play, read a new genre of book, watch a documentary, follow the news, or go for a walk and look at your neighborhood with "beginners eyes." What did you find that might be the basis for a playful system?

Inspiration

A game designer often looks at the world differently from most people. This is in part because of the profession and in part because the art of game design requires someone who is able to see and analyze the underlying relationships and rules of complex systems and to find inspiration for play in common interactions.

1.5   Systems all around us

When a game designer looks at the world, he often sees things in terms of challenges, structures, and play. Games are everywhere, from how we manage our money to how we form relationships. Everyone has goals in life and must overcome obstacles to achieve those goals. And, of course, there are rules. If you want to win in the financial markets, you have to understand the rules of trading stocks and bonds, profit forecasts, IPOs, and so forth. When you play the markets, the act of investing becomes very similar to a game. The same holds true for winning someone's heart. In dating and other relationships, there are different types of rules that you should follow, and it's in understanding these rules and how you can work within them to succeed that makes these systems playful and, sometimes, fun.

If you want to be a game designer, try looking at the world in terms of its underlying systems. Try to analyze how things in your life function. What are the underlying rules? How do the mechanics operate? Are there opportunities for challenge or playfulness? What about older technologies that might seem strange and playful – like a payphone or paper maps? Objects like these sometimes hold great inspirations for game mechanics or challenges. Write down your observations and analyze the relationships inherent in these systems. You'll find there is potential for play all around you that can serve as the inspiration for a game. You can use these observations and inspirations as foundations for building new types of gameplay.

Why not look at other games for inspiration? Well, of course, you can and you should. I'll talk about that in just a minute. But if you want to come up with truly original ideas, then don't fall back on existing games for all your ideas. Instead, look at the world around you. Some of the things that have inspired other game designers, and could inspire you, are obvious: personal relationships, buying and selling, competition in the workplace, and on and on. Take ant colonies, for example: They're organized around a sophisticated set of rules, and there's competition both within the colonies and between competing insect groups. Well-known game designer Will Wright made a game about ant colonies in 1991, SimAnt. "I was always fascinated by social insects," he says. "Ants are one of the few real examples of intelligence we have that we can study and deconstruct. We're still struggling with the way the human brain works. But if you look at ant colonies, they sometimes exhibit a remarkable degree of intelligence."[1] The game itself was something of a disappointment commercially, but the innate curiosity about how the world works that led Wright to ant colonies has also led him to look at ecological systems such as the Gaia hypothesis as inspiration for SimEarth or psychological theories such as Maslow's Hierarchy of Needs as inspiration for artificial intelligence in The Sims. Having a strong sense of curiosity and a passion for learning about the world is clearly an important part of Wright's inspiration as a game designer.

What inspires you? Examine things that you are passionate about as systems; break them down in terms of objects, behaviors, relationships, and so forth. Try to understand exactly how each element of the system interacts. This can be the foundation for an interesting game. By practicing the art of extracting and defining the games in all aspects of your life, you will not only hone your skills as a designer, but you'll open up new vistas in what you imagine a game can be.

Exercise 1.3: Your Life as a Game

List five activities in your life that might make interesting game systems. What seems playful about them? Do they have rules or objectives? Describe the "verbs" that make up these activities. Briefly describe a possible game based on several of these verbs.

Becoming a Better Player

One way to become an advocate for players is by being a better player yourself. By "better," I don't just mean more skilled or someone who wins all the time—although by studying game systems in depth, you will undoubtedly become a more skilled player. What I mean is using yourself and your experiences with games to develop

an unerring sense for good gameplay. The first step to practicing any art form is to develop a deep understanding of what makes that art form work. For example, if you've ever studied a musical instrument, you've probably learned to hear the relationship between the various musical tones. You've developed an ear for music. If you've studied drawing or painting, it's likely that your instructor has urged you to practice looking carefully at light and texture. You've developed an eye for visual composition. If you are a writer, you've learned to read critically. And if you want to be a game designer, you need to learn to play with the same conscious sensitivity to your own experience and critical analysis of the underlying system that these other arts demand.

The following chapters in this section look at the formal, dramatic, and dynamic aspects of games. Together, the concepts in these chapters form a set of tools that you can use to analyze your gameplay experiences and become a better, or more articulate, player and creative thinker. By practicing these skills, you will develop a game literacy that will make you a better designer. Literacy is the ability to read and write a language, but the concept can also be applied to media or technology. Being game literate means understanding how game systems work, analyzing how they make meaning, and using your understanding to create your own game systems.

I recommend writing your analysis in a game journal. Like a dream journal or a diary, a game journal can help you think through experiences you've had and to remember details of your gameplay long afterwards. As a game designer, these are valuable insights that you might otherwise forget. It is important when writing in your game journal to try to think deeply about your game experience—don't just review the game and talk about its features. Discuss a meaningful moment of gameplay. Try to remember it in detail—why did it strike you? What did you think, feel, do, and so forth? What are the underlying mechanics that made the moment work? The dramatic aspects? Perhaps your insights will form the basis for a future design, perhaps not. But, like sketching or practicing scales on a musical instrument, the act of writing and thinking about design will help you to develop your own way of thinking about games, which is critical to becoming a game designer.

Exercise 1.4: Game Journal

Start a game journal. Don't just try to describe the features of the games you play, but dig deeply into the choices you made, what you thought and felt about those choices, and the underlying game mechanics that supports those choices. Go into detail; look for the reasons why various mechanics of the game exist. Analyze why one moment of gameplay stands out and not another. Commit to writing in your game journal every day.

Creativity

Creativity is hard to quantify, but you'll definitely need to access your creativity to design great games. Everyone is creative in different ways. Some people come up with lots of ideas without even trying. Others focus on one idea and explore all of its possible facets. Some sit quietly in their rooms thinking to themselves, while others like to bounce ideas around with a group, and they find the interaction to be stimulating. Some seek out stimulation or new experiences to spark their imaginations. Great game designers like Will Wright tend to be people who can tap into their dreams and fantasies and bring those to life as interactive experiences.

Another great game designer, Nintendo's Shigeru Miyamoto, says that he often looks to his childhood and to hobbies that he enjoys for inspiration. "When I was a child, I went hiking and found a lake," he says. "It was quite a surprise for me to stumble upon it. When I traveled around the country without a map, trying to find my way, stumbling on amazing things as I went,

I realized how it felt to go on an adventure like this."[2] Many of Miyamoto's games draw from this sense of exploration and wonder that he remembers from childhood.

Think about your own life experiences. Do you have memories that might spark the idea for a game? One reason that childhood can be such a powerful inspiration for game designers is that when we are children, we are particularly engrossed in playing games. If you watch how kids interact on a playground, it's usually through gameplaying. They make games and learn social order and group dynamics from their play. Games permeate all aspects of kids' lives and are a vital part of their developmental process. So if you go back to your childhood and look at things that you enjoyed, you'll find the raw material for games right there.

Exercise 1.5: Your Childhood

List ten games you played as a child, for example, hide and seek, four square, and tag. Briefly describe what was compelling about each of those games.

Creativity might also mean putting two things together that don't seem to be related—like Shakespeare and the Brady Bunch. What can you make of such a strange combination? Well, the designers of the classic trivia game You Don't Know Jack used silly combinations

1.6 You Don't Know Jack

of high- and low-brow knowledge like this to create questions that challenged players to be equally proficient in both. The result was a hit game with such creative spark that it crossed the usual boundaries of gaming, appealing to players old and young, male and female. You Don't Know Jack has gone on to inspire a whole line of irreverent party games based on this simple creative strategy.

Sometimes creative ideas just come to you, and the trick is to know when to stand by a game idea that seems far-fetched. Keita Takahashi, designer of the quirky and innovative hit game Katamari Damacy, was given an assignment while working at Namco to come up with an idea for a racing game. The young artist and sculptor wanted to do something more original than a racing game, however, and says he just "came up with" the idea for the game mechanic of a sticky ball, or katamari, that players could roll around, picking up objects that range from paper clips and sushi to palm trees and policemen. Takahashi has said inspiration for the game came from sources as wildly different as the paintings of Pablo Picasso, the novels of John Irving, and Playmobil brand toys, but it is also clear that Takahashi has been influenced by Japanese children's games and sports such as tamakorogashi (ballroller) as a designer and is thinking beyond digital games for his future creations. "I would like to create a playground for children," he said. "A normal playground is flat but I want an undulating one, with bumps."[3]

Another example is my own game about Henry David Thoreau's time at Walden Pond. I was inspired by his writings and by the thought that underlying his philosophical experiment was an interesting set of rules that he was "playing by" when he set out to "live deliberately."

1.7   Beautiful katamari and tamakorogashi

The game took ten years to make and required a deep commitment to the original idea over those years. When we started making it, the idea of an indie game "about" something like a philosopher's experiment in living was considered somewhat strange and new. Today, personal games, and games about ideas or experiences, are relatively common, especially in the indie space.

Our past experiences, our other interests, our relationships, and our identity all come into play when trying to reach our creativity. Great game designers find a way to tap into their creative souls and bring forth the best parts in their games. However you do it, whether you work alone or in a team, whether you read books or climb mountains, whether you look to other games for inspiration or to life experiences, the bottom line is that there's no single right way to go about it. Everyone has a different style for coming up with ideas and being creative. What matters is not the spark of an idea but what you do with that idea once it emerges, and this is where the playcentric process becomes critical.

A PLAYCENTRIC DESIGN PROCESS

Having a good solid process for developing an idea from the initial ideation process into a playable and satisfying game experience is another key to thinking like a game designer.

The playcentric approach I will illustrate in this book focuses on involving the player in your design process from conception through completion. By that I mean continually keeping the player experience in mind and testing the gameplay with target players through every phase of development.

Setting Player Experience Goals

The sooner you can bring the player into the equation, the better, and the first way to do this is to set "player experience goals." Player experience goals are just what they sound like: goals that the game designer sets for the type of experience that players will have during the game. These are not features of the game but rather descriptions of the interesting and unique situations in which you hope players will find themselves. For example, "players will have to cooperate to win, but the game will be structured so they can never trust each other," "players will feel a sense of happiness and playfulness rather than competitiveness," or "players will have the freedom to pursue the goals of the game in any order they choose."

Setting player experience goals up front, as a part of your brainstorming process, can also focus your creative process. Notice that these descriptions do not talk about how these experience goals will be implemented in the game. Features will be brainstormed later to meet these goals, and then they will be playtested to see if the player experience goals are being met. At first, though, I advise thinking at a very high level about what is interesting and engaging about your game to players while they are playing and what experiences they will describe to their friends later to communicate the high points of the game.

Learning how to set interesting and engaging player experience goals means getting inside the heads of the players, not focusing on the features of the game as you intend to design it. When you're just beginning to design games,

one of the hardest things to do is to see beyond features to the actual game experience the players are having. What are they thinking as they make choices in your game? How are they feeling? Are the choices you've offered as rich and interesting as they can be?

Prototyping and Playtesting

Another key component to playcentric design is that ideas should be prototyped and playtested early. I encourage designers to construct a playable version of their idea immediately after brainstorming ideas. By this I mean a physical prototype of the core game mechanics. A physical prototype can use paper and pen or index cards or even be acted out. It is meant to be played by the designer and her friends. The goal is to play and perfect this simplistic model before a single line of code or art asset is ever made. This way, the game designer receives instant feedback on what players think of the game and can see immediately if they are on track to achieve their player experience goals.

This might sound like common sense, but in the industry today, much of the testing of the core game mechanics comes later in the production cycle, which can lead to disappointing results. Because many games are not thoroughly prototyped or tested early on, flaws in the design aren't identified until late in the process—in some cases, too late to fix. People in the industry now realize that this lack of player feedback means that many games don't reach their full potential, and the process of developing games is evolving to solve this issue. The work of professional user research experts like Nicole Lazzaro of XEODesign and Dennis Wixon of Microsoft (see their sidebars on pages 299 and 320) is becoming more and more important to game designers and publishers in their attempts to improve game experiences, especially with the new, sometimes inexperienced, game players that are being attracted to platforms like smartphones

DESIGNERS YOU SHOULD KNOW

The following is a list of designers who have had a monumental impact on digital games. The list was hard to finalize because so many great individuals have contributed to the craft in so many important ways. The goal was not to be comprehensive but rather to give a taste of some designers who have created foundational works and who it would be good for you, as an aspiring designer yourself, to be familiar with. I'm pleased that many designers on the list contributed interviews and sidebars to this book.

Shigeru Miyamoto

Miyamoto was hired out of industrial design school by Nintendo in 1977. He was the first staff artist at the company. Early in his career, he was assigned to a submarine game called Radarscope. This game was like most of the games of the day—simple twitch-game play mechanics, no story, and no characters. He wondered why digital games couldn't be more like the epic stories and fairy tales that he knew and loved from childhood. He wanted to make adventure stories, and he wanted to add emotion to games. Instead of focusing on Radarscope, he made up his own beauty-and-the-beast-like story where an ape steals his keeper's girlfriend and runs away. The result was Donkey Kong, and the character that you played was Mario (originally named Jumpman). Mario is perhaps the most enduring character in games and one of the most recognized characters in the world. Each time a new console is introduced by Nintendo—starting with the original NES machine—Miyamoto designs a Mario game as its flagship title. He is famous for the wild creativity and imagination in his games. Aside from all the Mario and Luigi games, Miyamoto's list of credits is long. It includes the games Zelda, Starfox, and Pikmin.

Will Wright

Early in his career, in 1987, Wright created a game called Raid **on** Bungling Bay. It was a helicopter game where you attacked islands. He had so much fun programming the little cities on the islands that he decided that making cities was the premise for a fun game. This was the inspiration for SimCity. When he first developed SimCity, publishers were not interested because they didn't believe anyone would buy it. But Wright persisted, and the game became an instant hit. SimCity was a breakout in terms of design in that it was based on creating rather than destroying. Also, it didn't have set goals. These things added some new facets to games. Wright was always interested in simulated reality and has done more than anyone in bringing simulation to the masses. SimCity spawned a whole series of titles, including SimEarth, SimAnt, SimCopter, and many others. His game The Sims is one of the bestselling game of all time, and Spore, possibly his most ambitious project, explores new design territory in terms of user-created content. See "A Conversation with Will Wright by Celia Pearce" on page 196.

Sid Meier

Legend has it that Sid Meier bet his buddy, Bill Stealey, that within two weeks he could program a better flying combat game than the one they were playing. Stealey took him up on the offer, and together they founded the company Micro Prose. It took more than two weeks, but the company released the title Solo Flight in 1984. Considered by many to be the father of PC gaming, Meier went on to create groundbreaking title after groundbreaking title. His Civilization series has had a fundamental influence on the genre of PC strategy games. His game Sid Meier's Pirates! was an innovative mix of genres—action, adventure, and role-playing—that also blended real-time and turn-based gaming. His gameplay ideas have been adopted in countless PC games. Meier's other titles include Colonization, Sid Meier's Gettysburg!, Alpha Centauri, and Silent Serv.

Warren Spector

Warren Spector started his career working for board game maker Steve Jackson Games in Austin, Texas. From there, he went on to the paper-based role-playing game company TSR, where he developed board games and wrote RPG supplements and several novels. In 1989, he was ready to add digital games to his portfolio and moved to the developer ORIGIN Systems. There, he worked on the Ultima series with Richard Garriott. Spector had an intense interest in integrating characters and stories into games. He pioneered "free-form" gameplay with a series of innovative titles, including Underworld, System Shock, and Thief. His title Deus Ex took the concepts of flexible play and drama in games to new heights and is considered one of the finest PC games of all time. See his "Designer Perspective" interview on page 29.

Brenda Romero

Brenda Romero began her career at Sir-tech Software as part of the Wizardry role-playing team, where she worked her way up from testing to designer for Wizardry 8. While at Sir-tech, she also worked on the Jagged Alliance and Realms of Arkania series before moving to Atari to work on Dungeons & Dragons. Throughout her career, she has been a passionate advocate for diversity in the industry and was awarded the Ambassador Award from the Game Developers Conference as well as a special British Academy for Film and Television Arts award for her contributions to the industry. On page 93, she discusses her groundbreaking analog game series The Mechanic Is the Message.

Richard Garfield

In 1990, Richard Garfield was an unknown mathematician and part-time game designer. He had been trying unsuccessfully to sell a board game prototype called RoboRally to publishers for seven years. When yet another publisher rejected his concept, he was not surprised. However, this time the publisher, a man named Peter Adkison doing business as Wizards of the Coast, asked for a portable card game that was playable in under an hour. Garfield took the challenge and developed a dueling game system where each card in the system could affect the rules in different ways. It was a breakthrough in game design because the system was infinitely expandable. The game was Magic: The Gathering, and it singlehandedly spawned the industry of collectible card games. Magic has been released in digital format in multiple titles. When Hasbro bought Wizards of the Coast in 1995 for $325 million, Garfield owned a significant portion of the company. See his article "The Design Evolution of Magic: The Gathering" on page 236.

Amy Hennig

Amy Hennig began her career in the game industry working as an artist and animator on games for the NES. While she was working at Electronic Arts as an artist on Michael Jordan: Chaos in the Windy City, the lead designer left the project and Hennig landed the job. Later, she moved to Crystal Dynamics, where she was director, producer, and writer for Legacy of Kain: Soul Reaver. She is well known for her work as a game director and writer on some of the most successful titles in the industry, including the Uncharted series for Naughty Dog and Sony. She has been awarded two Writers Guild of America Video Game Writing Awards in addition to numerous other awards for her work on the Uncharted games. She describes her writing work on this series as being on the "bleeding edge" of the genre of cinematic video games.

Peter Molyneux

The story goes that it all started with an anthill. As a child, Peter Molyneux toyed with one—tearing it down in parts and watching the ants fight to rebuild, dropping food into the world and watching the ants appropriate it, and so on. He was fascinated by the power he had over the tiny, unpredictable creatures. Molyneux went on to become a programmer and game designer and eventually the pioneer of digital "god games." In his breakout title, Populous, you act as a deity lording it over tiny settlers. The game was revolutionary in that it was a strategy game that took place in real time, as opposed to in turns, and you had indirect control over your units. The units had minds of their own. This game and other Molyneux hits had a profound influence on the real-time strategy (RTS) games that were on the horizon. Other titles he has created include Syndicate, Theme Park, Dungeon Keeper, and Black & White.

Gary Gygax

In the early 1970s, Gary Gygax was an insurance underwriter in Lake Geneva, Wisconsin. He loved all kinds of games, including tabletop war games. In these games, players controlled large armies of miniatures, acting like generals. Gygax and his friends had fun acting out the personas of different pieces on the battlefield such as commanders, heroes, and so forth. He followed his inclination of what was fun and created a system for battling small parties of miniatures in a game he called Chainmail. From there players wanted even more control over and more character information about the individual units. They wanted to play the role of single characters. Gygax, in conjunction with game designer Dave Arneson, developed an elaborate system for role-playing characters that was eventually named Dungeons & Dragons. The D&D game system is the direct ancestor of every paper-based and digital RPG since then. The system is directly evident in all of today's RPG's and spin-off genres.

Richard Garriott

Richard Garriott—a.k.a. "Lord British"—programmed his first game right out of high school in 1979. It was an RPG called Akalabeth. He sold it on his own through a local computer store in Austin, Texas. The packaging for this first version was a Ziploc bag. Akalabeth later got picked up by a publisher and sold well. Garriott used what he learned to create Ultima, one of the most famous game series of all time. The Ultima titles evolved over the years—each successive one pushing the envelope in terms of both technology and gameplay—eventually bringing the world of the game online. Ultima Online, released in 1997, was a pioneering title in massively multiplayer online worlds.

Dona Baily

Dona Baily was a young programmer in 1981 who, along with Ed Logg, created the classic arcade video game Centipede. At the time, when Baily joined Atari's coin-op division, she was the only woman employed there. When given a notebook of ideas for possible games to program, all of which involved "lasering or frying things," she chose a short description of a bug winding down the screen because, she said, "it didn't seem bad to shoot a bug." Centipede went on to become one of the most commercially successful games from the arcade era's golden age.

Gerald Lawson

Gerald Lawson was an electronic engineer known for his work in the 1970s, designing the Fairchild Channel F video game system and inventing the video game cartridge. The Fairchild Channel F console, while not a commercially successful product, introduced the idea that game software could be stored on swappable cartridges for the first time. Prior to the Channel F, most game systems had the game software programmed into the architecture of the hardware, so games could never be added to or updated. Lawson's invention was so novel that every cartridge he produced had to be approved by the FCC before distribution as new product. Quickly, his invention became the standard for all future game consoles. Lawson was one of the few African-American engineers working in the industry at that time.

Carol Shaw

Carol Shaw, the first widely recognized female designer and programmer, is most recognized for her best-selling game River Raid (1982), published by Activision for the Atari 2600 home console. The award-winning game, which sold more than one million copies, was a vertically scrolling shooter where the player flies a fighter jet over the River of No Return in a raid behind enemy lines. As the daughter of a mechanical engineer, Shaw became interested in electronics at an early age. She started programming in BASIC during high school and went on to earn a bachelor's degree in Electrical Engineering and Computer Science at the University of California, Berkeley, in 1977. When she donated a collection of her professional papers and materials to The Strong Museum of Play in 2017, the press announcement noted that they "serve as tangible evidence that women were involved in the creation of home video games from their inception. Her design documents, many of which contain advanced mathematical calculations, demonstrate her proficiency in an industry still stereotyped as being heavily dominated by men. It also serves as an excellent representation of early Atari home console games and the process by which they were developed."[4]

Danielle Bunten Berry

Danielle Bunten Berry was a pioneering game developer who created M.U.L.E., one of the first successful multiplayer games on the Atari platform, which required players to both compete and cooperate. The unique game took advantage of the four joystick ports of the Atari 400 and 800 to allow four-player simultaneous play and was one of the first five games published in 1983 by new company Electronic Arts. Although the game only sold about 30,000 copies, it was loved by reviewers and became a cult classic and an inspiration for many game designers including Shigeru Miyamoto, Will Wright, and Tracy Fullerton. Bunten Berry (credited as Dan Bunten), found inspiration in childhood memories of playing games with her family. "When I was a kid," she said, "the only times my family spent together that weren't totally dysfunctional were when we were playing games. Consequently, I believe games are a wonderful way to socialize." Although many of Berry's titles were not commercially successful, they were widely recognized by the industry as being ahead of their time. In 1998, Berry was awarded the Lifetime Achievement Award by the Computer Game Developers Association.[5]

or tablets. You don't need to have access to a professional test lab to use the playcentric approach. In Chapter 9, I describe a number of methods you can use on your own to produce useful improvements to your game design.

I suggest that you do not begin production without a deep understanding of your player experience goals and your core mechanics. This is critical because when the production process commences, it becomes increasingly difficult to alter the software design. Therefore, the further along the design and prototyping are before the production begins, the greater the likelihood of avoiding costly mistakes. You can ensure that your core design concept is sound before production begins by taking a playcentric approach to the design and development process.

Iteration

By "iteration" I simply mean that you design, test, and evaluate the results over and over again throughout the development of your game, each time improving upon the gameplay or features, until the player experience meets your criteria. Iteration is deeply important to the playcentric process. Here is a detailed flow of the itera-tive process that you should go through when designing a game:

- Player experience goals are set.
- An idea or system is conceived.
- An idea or system is prototyped. (This may mean a physical or digital prototype, or even storyboards or an animatic for an idea that can be presented to players.)
- The idea or system is playtested or shown to potential players for response and feedback.
- Results are evaluated against player experi-ence goals.
- Issues are prioritized and addressed by mak-ing changes to the prototype.
- The prototype is retested and the results are evaluated against experience goals again.
- This process is repeated until solutions are found and the design is deemed to meet the goals.

As you will see, this process is applicable during every aspect of game design, from initial concep-tion through final quality assurance testing. Figure 1.8 shows how the player experience goals provide a touchstone for the entire iterative process.

Step 1: Ideation

- Set player experience goals.
- Come up with game concepts or mechanics that you think might achieve your player experi-ence goals.
- Narrow the list down to the top three.
- Write up a short, one-page description for each of these ideas, sometimes called a concept document. You can also write a longer three- to six-page treatment at this phase if you are confident in your mechan-ics. This process is described in Chapter 6 on page 206.
- Test your written concepts with potential players (you might also want to create rough visual mock-ups of your ideas at this stage to help communicate the ideas).

Step 2: Physical Prototype

- Create a playable prototype using pen and paper or other craft materials.
- Playtest the physical prototype using the process described in Chapters 7 and 9.
- When the physical prototype demonstrates working gameplay that achieves your player

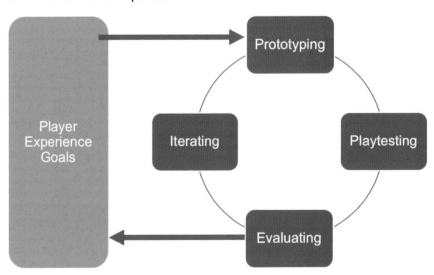

1.8   Playcentric process diagram

experience goals, write a three- to six-page gameplay treatment describing how the game functions.

Step 3: Presentation (Optional)

- A presentation is often made to secure funds to hire the prototyping team. Even if you do not require funding, going through the exercise of creating a full presentation is a good way to think through your game and introduce it to team members and upper management for feedback.

- Your presentation should include draft artwork and a solid gameplay treatment.

- If you do not secure funding, you can either return to step 1 and start over again on a new concept or solicit feedback from your funding sources and work on modifying the game to fit their needs. Because you have not yet invested in extensive artwork or programming, your costs so far should be pretty reasonable, and you should have a great deal of flexibility to make any changes.

Step 4: Software Prototype(s)

- When you have your prototyping team in place, you can begin creating rough digital models of the core gameplay. Often, several software prototypes are made, each focusing on different aspects of the system. Digital prototyping is discussed in Chapter 8 beginning on page 257. (If possible, try to do this entirely with temporary graphics that cost very little to make. This will save time and money and speed up the process.)

- Playtest the software prototype(s) using the method process described in Chapter 9.

- When the software prototype(s) demonstrate working gameplay that achieves your player experience goals, move on to develop plans for the full feature set and levels of the game.

Step 5: Design Documentation

- While you have been prototyping and working on your gameplay, you have probably been compiling notes and ideas for the "real" game. Use the knowledge you've gained during this prototyping stage to develop a full list of goals for the game, which are documented in a way that is useful and accessible for the team.

- Recently, many designers have moved away from creating large static documents for this purpose, moving instead toward online groupware like wikis and smaller, as-needed forms of documentation because of the flexible, collaborative nature of modern design processes. The design documentation that comes out of your production process should be thought of as a collaboration tool that changes and grows with production. Chapter 14 discusses various types of design documentation that you may do for your project, including flowcharts, wireframes, one-page design documents, a macro, or control map.

Step 6: Production

- Work with all team members to make sure your goals are clear and achievable and that the team is on board with the priorities for these goals.

- Staff up with a full team and plan a set of development "sprints" for each of the goals in your plan. Evaluate your game as a team after each sprint to make sure you are still on target with your player experience goals.

- Don't lose sight of the playcentric process during production—test your artwork, gameplay, characters, and so forth as you move along. As you continue to perform iterative cycles throughout the production phase, the problems you find and the changes you make should get smaller and smaller. This is because you resolved your major issues during the prototyping phases.

THE ITERATIVE DESIGN PROCESS

by Eric Zimmerman, game designer and Arts Professor, NYU Game Center

Eric Zimmerman is a game designer and a thirty-year veteran of the game industry. Eric cofounded Gamelab, an award-winning New York City-based studio that helped invent casual games with titles like Diner Dash. Other projects range from the pioneering independent online game SiSSYFiGHT 2000 to tabletop games like the strategy board game Quantum and Local No. 12's card game The Metagame. Architect Nathalie Pozzi and Eric have designed installations that have been exhibited in museums and festivals around the world. He is the coauthor with Katie Salen of Rules of Play, the author of The Rules We Break, and is a founding faculty and Arts Professor at the NYU Game Center. Also see his article with Nathalie Pozzi on playtesting methods on page 310.

The following excerpt is adapted from a longer essay entitled "Play as Research," which appears in the book Design Research, edited by Brenda Laurel (MIT Press, 2004). It appears here with permission from the author. Iterative design is a design methodology based on a cyclic process of prototyping, testing, analyzing, and refining a work in progress. In iterative design, interaction with the designed system is the basis of the design process, informing and evolving a project as successive versions, or iterations, of a design are implemented. This sidebar outlines the iterative process as it occurred in one game with which I was involved—the online multiplayer game SiSSYFiGHT 2000.

What is the process of iterative design? Test, analyze, refine. And repeat. Because the experience of a player cannot ever be completely predicted, in an iterative process design, decisions are based on the experience of the prototype in progress. The prototype is tested, revisions are made, and the project is tested once more. In this way, the project develops through an ongoing dialogue between the designers, the design, and the testing audience.

In the case of games, iterative design means playtesting. Throughout the entire process of design and development, your game is played. You play it. The rest of the development team plays it. Other people in the office play it. People visiting your office play it. You organize groups of testers that match your target audience. You have as many people as possible play the game. In each case, you observe them, ask them questions, then adjust your design and playtest again.

This iterative process of design is radically different from typical retail game development. More often than not, at the start of the design process for a computer or console title, a game designer will think up a finished concept and then write an exhaustive design document that outlines every possible aspect of the game in minute detail. Invariably, the final game never resembles the carefully conceived original. A more iterative design process, on the other hand, will not only streamline development resources, but it will also result in a more robust and successful final product.

Case Study: SiSSYFiGHT 2000

SiSSYFiGHT 2000 is a multiplayer online game in which players create a schoolgirl avatar and then vie with three to six players for dominance of the playground. Each turn, a player selects one of six actions to take, ranging from teasing and tattling to cowering and licking a lolly. The outcome of an action is dependent on other players' decisions, making for highly social gameplay. SiSSYFiGHT 2000 is also a robust online community. You can play the game at www.sissyfight. com. In the summer of 1999, I was hired by Word.com to help them create their first game. We initially worked to identify the project's play values: the abstract principles that the game design would embody. The list of play values we created included designing for a broad audience of nongamers, a low technology barrier, a game that was easy to learn and play but deep and complex, gameplay that was intrinsically social, and, finally, something that was in line with the smart and ironic Word.com sensibility.

These play values were the parameters for a series of brainstorming sessions interspersed with group play of computer and noncomputer games. Eventually, a game concept emerged: little girls in social conflict on a playground. While every game embodies some kind of conflict, we were drawn toward modeling a conflict that we hadn't seen depicted previously in a game. Technology and production limitations meant that the game would be turn based, although it could involve real-time chat.

When these basic formal and conceptual questions had begun to be mapped out, the shape of the initial prototype became clear. The very first version of SiSSYFiGHT was played with Post-it Notes around a conference table. I designed a handful of basic actions each player could take, and acting as the program, I "processed" the actions each turn and reported the results back to the players, keeping score on a piece of paper.

Designing a first prototype requires strategic thinking about how to most quickly implement a playable version that can begin to address the project's chief uncertainties in a meaningful way. Can you create a paper version of your digital game? Can you design a short version of a game that will last much longer in its final form? Can you test the interaction pattern of a massively multiplayer game with just a handful of players?

In the iterative design process, the most detailed thinking you need at any moment is that which will get you to your next prototype. It is, of course, important to understand the big picture as well: the larger conceptual, technical, and design questions that drive the project as a whole. Just be sure not to let your design get ahead of your iterative research. Keep your eye on the prize, but leave room for play in your design, for the potential to change as you learn from your playtesting, accepting the fact that some of your assumptions will undoubtedly be wrong.

The project team continued to develop the paper prototype, seeking the balance between cooperation and competition that would become the heart of the final gameplay. We refined the base rule set—the actions a player can take each turn and the outcomes that result. These rules were turned into a specification for the first digital prototype: a text-only version on IRC, which we played hot-seat style, taking turns sitting at the same computer. Constructing that early, text-only prototype allowed us to focus on the complexities of the game logic without worrying about implementing interactivity, visual and audio aesthetics, and other aspects of the game.

While we tested gameplay via the text-only iteration, programming for the final version began in Director, and the core game logic we had developed for the IRC prototype was recycled into the Director code with little alteration. Parallel to the game design, the project's visual designers had begun to develop the graphic language of the game and chart out possible screen layouts. These early drafts of the visuals (revised many times over the course of the entire development) were dropped into the Director version of the game, and the first rough-hewn iteration of SiSSYFiGHT as a multiplayer online game took shape, inspired by Henry Darger's outsider art and retro game graphics.

As soon as the web version was playable, the development team played it. And as our ugly duckling grew more refined, the rest of the Word.com staff was roped into testing as

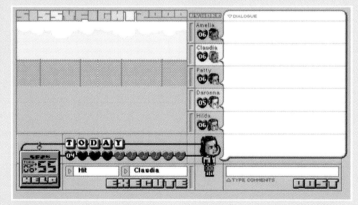

SiSSYFiGHT 2000 Interface

well. As the game grew more stable, we descended on our friends' dot-com companies after the workday had ended, sitting them down cold in front of the game and letting them play. All of this testing and feedback helped us refine the game logic, visual aesthetics, and interface. The biggest challenge turned out to be clearly articulating the relationship between

player action and game outcome: Because the results of every turn are interdependent on each player's actions, early versions of the game felt frustratingly arbitrary. Only through many design revisions and dialogue with our testers did we manage to structure the results of each turn to unambiguously communicate what had happened that round and why.

When the server infrastructure was completed, we launched the game to an invitation-only beta tester community that slowly grew in the weeks leading up to public release. Certain time slots were scheduled as official testing events, but our beta users could come online anytime and play. We made it very easy for the beta testers to contact us and e-mail in bug reports.

Even with this small sample of a few dozen participants, larger play patterns emerged. For example, as with many multiplayer games, it was highly advantageous to play defensively, leading to standstill matches. In response, we tweaked the game logic to discourage this play style: Any player that "cowered" twice in a row was penalized for acting like a chicken. When the game did launch, our loyal beta testers became the core of the game community, easing new players into the game's social space.

In the case of SiSSYFiGHT 2000, the testing and prototyping cycle of iterative design was successful because at each stage we clarified exactly what we wanted to test and how. We used written and online questionnaires. We debriefed after each testing session. And we strategized about how each version of the game would incorporate the visual, audio, game design, and technical elements of the previous versions, while also laying a foundation for the final form of the experience.

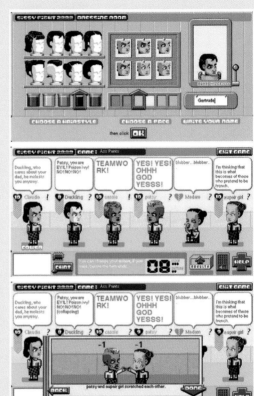

SiSSYFiGHT 2000 Game Interfaces

To design a game is to construct a set of rules. But the point of game design is not to have players experience rules—it is to have players experience play. Game design is therefore a second-order design problem in which designers craft play, but only indirectly, through the systems of rules that game designers create. Play arises out of the rules as they are inhabited and enacted by players, creating emergent patterns of behavior, sensation, social exchange, and meaning. This shows the necessity of the iterative design process. The delicate interaction of rule and play is something too subtle and too complex to script out in advance, requiring the improvisational balancing that only testing and prototyping can provide.

In iterative design, there is a blending of designer and user, of creator and player. It is a process of design through the reinvention of play. Through iterative design, designers create systems and play with them. They become participants, but they do so in order to critique their creations, to bend them, break them, and refashion them into something new. And in these procedures of investigation and experimentation, a special form of discovery takes place. The process of iteration, of design through play, is a way of discovering the answers to questions you didn't even know were there. And that makes it a powerful and important method of design. SiSSYFiGHT 2000 was developed by Marisa Bowe, Ranjit Bhatnagar, Tomas Clarke, Michelle Golden, Lucas Gonze, Lem Jay Ignacio, Jason Mohr, Daron Murphy, Yoshi Sodeka, Wade Tinney, and Eric Zimmerman.

- Unfortunately, this is the time when most game designers actually wind up designing their games, and this can lead to numerous problems related to time, money, and frustration.

Step 7: Postproduction and Quality Assurance

- In this phase, you will be polishing your game and making sure all the details are right. By this point, you should be very sure that your gameplay is solid, though you may be making small tweaks to levels and such just to be sure that everything is working as intended.
- By the time the project is ready for quality assurance testing, there may still be some issues, so continue playtesting with an eye to usability. Now is the time to make sure your game is accessible to your entire target audience.

As you can see, the playcentric approach involves player feedback throughout the production process, which means you'll be doing lots of prototyping and playtesting at every stage of your game's development. You can't be the advocate for the player if you don't know what the player is thinking, and playtesting is the best mechanism by which you can elicit feedback and gain insight into your game. I cannot emphasize this fact enough, and I encourage any designer to rigorously build into their production schedule the means to continually playtest all aspects of their game as thoroughly as possible.

Prototypes and Playtesting in the Industry

In the game industry today, designers often skip the creation of a physical prototype altogether and jump straight from the ideation stage to writing up the design. The problem with this method is that the software coding has commenced before anyone has a true sense for the game mechanics. To be frank, the reason this is possible is because many games are simply variations on standard game mechanics, so the designers have a good idea of how the game will work because they've played it, or a variation of it, as another game.

It's important to remember that the game industry is just that: an industry. Taking risks and spending a lot of time and money creating new gameplay mechanics are difficult to reconcile with a bottom line. However, the game industry is changing and growing rapidly, with new platforms that demand innovative designs. This means that you will likely be asked to design for different types of players outside the traditional gaming audience. New platforms like VR, AR, smartphones, tablets, gestural and multitouch interfaces, and breakout hits like *Pokémon* Go have proven that there is demand from new audiences if the right new kind of gameplay is offered.

While the industry as a whole is extremely skilled at maintaining steady technological innovation and cultivating core audience demand for those innovations, the same isn't true when it comes to developing original ideas in player experience. To meet the demands of new players using game devices in wildly different contexts than a traditional game audience, we are seeing the need for breakthroughs in player experience just as surely as there has always been a need for breakthroughs in technology to drive the industry forward. But it is difficult to design an original game if you skip the physical prototyping process. What happens is that you are forced to reference existing games in the design description. This means your game is bound from the outset to be derivative. Breaking away from your references becomes even more difficult as the production takes off. When your team is in place, with programmers coding and artists cranking out graphics, the idea of going back and changing the core gameplay becomes very difficult.

That is why a number of prominent game designers have begun to adopt a playcentric approach. Large companies such as Electronic Arts have in-house training in preproduction (see sidebar in Chapter 6, page 188) originally run by Chief Visual Officer Glenn Entis. This workshop included physical prototyping and playtesting as part of the initial development stage. The workshop runs development teams through a series of exercises, one of which is coming up with a quick physical prototype. Entis' advice is make it "fast, cheap, public, and physical. If you don't see people on the team arguing," he says, "you can't know if they are sharing ideas. A physical prototype gets the team talking, interacting."[6]

Chris Plummer, SVP and Co-Head of Mobile at Activision, says, "Paper prototypes can be a great tool for low-cost ideation and playtesting of game features or systems that would otherwise cost a lot more to develop in software. It's much easier to justify spending the resources to realize a game in software after the game framework is developed and refined through more cost-effective means, such as analog prototypes."[7]

Some companies engage in "game jams," events where local independents and students come together for a weekend to generate prototypes for new game projects. The Global Game Jam is an annual worldwide event that brings together tens of thousands of participants to develop innovative game prototypes. By leveraging their local community of independent game designers, small groups and companies are able to jump-start their new ideas in a collaborative environment.

1.9 Angry Birds Star Wars and Pokémon Go—unconventional markets and players

1.10 USC Games students at work at weekend game jam

DESIGNING FOR INNOVATION

As I mentioned earlier, today's game designers have the challenge—and opportunity—to produce breakthroughs in player experience as part of their basic job description. They will have to do this without taking too many risks in terms of time and money. By innovation, I mean:

- Designing games with unique play mechanics—thinking beyond existing genres of play
- Appealing to new players—people who have different tastes and skills than hard-core gamers
- Designing for new platforms such as smartphones, tablets, and gestural and multitouch interfaces
- Creating games that integrate into daily life, real-world spaces, and the systems around us
- Embracing new business models for games such as free-to-play or subscription
- Trying to solve difficult problems in game design such as:

  ◊ The integration of story and gameplay
  ◊ Deeper empathy for characters in games
  ◊ Creating emotionally rich gameplay
  ◊ Discovering the relationships between games and learning

- Asking difficult questions about what games are, what they can be, and what their impact is on us individually and culturally

The playcentric approach can help foster innovation and give you a solid process within which to explore these provocative, unusual questions about gameplay possibilities, to try ideas that might seem fundamentally unsound but could have within them the seed of a breakthrough idea, and to craft them until they are playable. Real innovation seldom comes from the first spark of an idea; it tends to come from long-term development and experimentation. By interacting with players throughout the design process, experimental ideas have time to develop and mature.

CONCLUSION

My goal in this book is to help you become a game designer. I want to give you the skills and tools you'll need to take your ideas and craft them into games that aren't mere extensions of games already on the market. I want to enable you to push the envelope on game design, and the key to doing this is process. The approach you will learn here is about internalizing a playcentric method of design that will make you more creative and productive, while helping you to avoid many of the pitfalls that plague game designers.

The following chapters in this first section will lay out a vocabulary of design and help you to think critically about the games you play and the games you want to design. Understanding how games work and why players play them is the next step to becoming a game designer.

DESIGNER PERSPECTIVE:
CHRISTINA NORMAN

President, Elodie Games

Christina Norman is an experienced game designer whose credits include League of Legends: Wild Rift (2020), League of Legends (2009), Mass Effect 3 (2012), Mass Effect 2 (2011) and Mass Effect (2007).

How did you become a game designer?

I would say I became a game designer at age 9. I was playing Dungeons & Dragons with some kids at school, and our dungeon master moved away. I'd already memorized all the rules, so I was a natural to replace him. This was the starting point of a nine-year-long D&D campaign, and the moment I became a game designer.

The story of how I became employed as a game designer is, of course, entirely different. That story starts with... depression. I had a successful career programming e-commerce web sites, but I felt deeply unfulfilled. I didn't care about what I was doing, so I asked myself—what do you care about? What do you really want to do? The answer was: make games.

I had three things going for me: I was a hardcore gamer, I had created several successful Warcraft 3 mods, and I was a programmer. I applied for a game design job at BioWare and...they rejected me. I applied again as a programmer and they said, okay! After I had been there for a few years I was able to convince the lead designer to give me a shot at game design. Since then it's been all flowers, bunny rabbits, and joy!

On games that have inspired her:

Dungeons & Dragons: This, along with other great pen-and-paper role-playing games, taught me the fundamentals of system design. It was my unquenchable thirst for more Dungeons & Dragons that drove me to CRPGs (what we used to call "computer RPGs").

Nethack (honorable mention to Diablo 2): Nethack is one of the early "roguelike" games. In this vast procedurally generated world, I endlessly pursued the fabled amulet of Yendor. As I descended through the seemingly endless dungeon levels, I marveled at the intricate and complex systems and their many interactions. Years later, Diablo 2 was the first mainstream game I played that captured much of Nethack's strengths, improving it with AAA production values and addictive multiplayer.

Baldur's Gate 2: This game taught me that games can be an exceptional storytelling medium that really makes you feel. Through my adventures I came to truly care for my party members—I wanted to help them achieve their goals! On top of all this, BG2 remains a mastery of systems design and in my opinion is the best realization of D&D in a video game to date.

Master of Orion 2 (honorable mention to Civilization): This was the first 4X (explore, expand, exploit, extermi- nate) game that completely captivated me. The idea of starting at a single planet, developing the technology of space flight, and ultimately ruling the entire universe was mind blowing.

Soulslikes: Bucking the industry trend toward broad appeal and low difficulty, Demon Souls put forth a masterful love letter to challenge and mastery in RPGs, while simultaneously defining the genre mechanics of modern third person Action-RPGs and defining a new genre.

Honorable Mentions: Hollow Knight, Slay the Spire, and Helldivers.

What is the most exciting development in the recent game industry?

In the earlier editions of this book I spoke with great excitement about the opportunities in the market for smaller game developers to produce innovative and successful titles that could also become financially successful. Even League of Legends started as a small title.

More recently we've seen tighter control of the market by publishers and other large, established, players. The indus- try has grown significantly, and the cost of developing new titles has increased dramatically; this has created a more chal- lenging forum for new developers and fresh ideas to find their place in the market.

At the same time, game development tools and tutorials are better than they have ever been, online game devel- opment communities are more prevalent than ever before, and social media continues to drive discovery of innovative games. It remains an exciting time to be a novice game developer or game designers.

On her design process:

"Design depends largely on constraints" - Charles Eames, 1972

As I have matured as a game designer so has my design process. I've adopted a fairly formal design model which I shared more broadly in my 2017 GDC talk - Embrace Radical Constraints, which I will summarize below.

When tackling difficult design problems, clearly articulate: the problem the design seeks to solve, hard constraints the design must satisfy, soft constraints that are seen as desirable, and the pillars that inspire and guide the design process. These criteria define the solution space of your designs.

Express your design simply and clearly in a written or diagrammatic form that can be evaluated against the solution space. When iterating, feel free to change the constraints that define this space when they feel too restrictive. This process will generate insights.

In evaluating a design, evocatively imagine how a player will experience the design through actual play. When a design is implemented, evaluate the actual play experience, and contrast that with your expectations. This process will generate insights.

Do you use prototypes?

I'm a programmer, so code is my paintbrush. When I want to try an idea out, I code it fast and dirty. From there it's test, iterate, test, iterate, test...and when the design works...build it properly. When I do code-based prototyping, I use whatever tools will let me test ideas the quickest.

I'm also a big fan of building physical prototypes. Sometimes it's just faster to build something as a card game, or board game, than to code it.

On a particularly difficult design problem:

Mass Effect was essentially a hardcore RPG dressed as a shooter. Whether you hit enemies or not was determined by an invisible die roll. This meant that even if you aimed perfectly, you could miss, so guns felt weak and unreliable.

For Mass Effect 2 we wanted guns to feel accurate, powerful, and reliable. We disabled the to-hit rolls, but aiming still felt sub-par. This was my unruly introduction to combat design—I learned that making something work a certain way is different than making it feel great. My team studied the great shooters, learned from them, and then we polished our guns until they felt great.

But it wasn't that simple. Making firing guns feel great required adjusting the pacing of gameplay, which required... reinventing pretty much every system in Mass Effect. By the time we were done, we had an entirely different game than the first one, but the results were worth it.

I spoke about this experience in my 2010 GDC talk "Where did my Inventory Go? Refining Gameplay in Mass Effect 2".

What are you most proud of in your career?

Bringing the full League of Legends game experience to a phone was a problem that was thought for many years to be impossible to solve. When I took on this challenge for Riot Games I didn't know if it was possible, but I believed that phone gamers would love a more compelling PvP experience. The result was League of Legends: Wild Rift, which was recognized as the 2021 Game of the Year by Apple and achieved global success.

On advice to designers:

Play many games. Play them hardcore. If you get into the game industry, you'll have less time to play games, and so many insights come from your experience as a player.

Go beyond your own insights. Learn to be a better designer by listening to other players. Just watching someone play a game can teach you a great deal about game design.

Listen to your team. Just because someone's title doesn't include the word "designer" doesn't mean they don't have valuable design insights. Some of the best designers I have worked with have producer, programmer, or QA in their title.

Designer Perspective: Warren Spector

Studio Director, OtherSide Entertainment

Warren Spector is a veteran game designer and producer whose credits include Ultima VI (1990), Wing Commander (1990), Martian Dreams (1991), Underworld (1991), Ultima VII (1993), Wings of Glory (1994), System Shock (1994), Deus Ex (2000), Deus Ex: Invisible War (2003), Thief: Deadly Shadows (2004), Disney Epic Mickey (2010), and Disney Epic Mickey: The Power of Two (2012).

On getting into the game industry:

I started out, like most folks, as a gamer, back in the day. Back in 1983, I made my hobby my profession, starting out as an editor at Steve Jackson Games, a small board game company in Austin, Texas. There, I worked on TOON: The Cartoon Roleplaying Game, GURPS, several Car Wars, Ogre, and Illuminati games and learned a ton about game design from people like Steve Jackson, Allen Varney, Scott Haring, and others. In 1987, I was lured away by TSR, makers of Dungeons & Dragons and other fine RPGs and board games. 1989 saw me homesick for Austin, Texas, and feeling like paper gaming was a business/art form that had pretty much plateaued. I was playing a lot of early computer and video games at the time, and when the opportunity to work for Origin came up, I jumped at it. I started out there as an associate producer, working with Richard Garriott and Chris Roberts before moving up to full producer. I spent seven years with Origin, shipping about a dozen titles and moving up from associate producer to producer to executive producer.

On game influences:

There have probably been dozens of games that have influenced me, but here are a few of the biggies:

- Ultima IV: This is Richard Garriott's masterpiece. It proved to me (and a lot of other people) that giving players power to make choices enhanced the gameplay experience. And attaching consequences to those choices made the experience even *more* powerful. This was the game that showed me that games could be about more than killing things or solving goofy puzzles. It was also the first game I ever played that made me feel like I was engaged in a dialogue with the game's creator. And that's something I've striven to achieve ever since.

- Super Mario 64: I was stunned at how much gameplay Miyamoto and the Mario team managed to squeeze into this game. And it's all done through a control/interface scheme that's so simple that, as a developer, it shames me. Mario can do maybe ten things, I think, and yet the player never feels constrained—you feel empowered and liberated, encouraged to explore, plan, experiment, fail, and try again, without feeling frustrated. You have to be inspired by the combination of simplicity and depth.

- Star Raiders: This was the first game that made me believe games were more than just a fad or passing fancy, for me and for, well, humanity at large. "Oh, man," I thought, "we can send people places they'll never be able to go in real life." That's not just kid stuff—that's change-the-world stuff. There's an old saying about not judging someone until you've walked a mile in their shoes, you know? Well, games are like an experiential shoe store for all mankind. We can allow you to walk in the shoes of anyone we can imagine. How powerful is that?

- Ico: Ico impressed me because it proved to me how powerfully we can affect players on an emotional level. And I'm not just talking about excitement or fear, the stuff we usually traffic in. Ico, through some stellar animation, graphics, sound, and story elements, explores questions of friendship, loyalty, dread, tension, and exhilaration. The power of a virtual touch—of the player holding the hand of a character he's charged to protect, even though she seems weak and moves with almost maddening slowness—the power of that touch blew me away. I have to find a way to get at some of that power in my own work. Interestingly, some recent games, like Last of Us and The Walking Dead, have exploited the human need to make contact with and protect another. Clearly, this is an idea games can exploit exceptionally well—an idea that allows us to move people, emotionally, in ways many nongamers and even some gamers thought impossible.

- Suikoden: This little PlayStation role-playing game showed me new ways of dealing with conversation. I had never before experienced Suikoden's brand of simple, straightforward, binary-choice approach—little things like "Do you fight your father or not? Y/N" or "Do you leave your best friend to almost certain death so you can escape and complete your critically important quest? Y/N" will blow you away! But it wasn't just the simplicity of the conversation system that made those choices special. It was the idea that the player had to make choices — ethical choices — at all. The choices were false, but I remember wondering "what if we could make those choices real?" Critically important to me moving forward as anyone who's played the games I've worked on knows. In addition, the game featured two other critical systems: a castle-building mechanic and a related player-controlled ally system. The castle-building bit showed me the power of allowing players to leave a personal mark on the world—the narcissistic aspect of game playing. The ally system, which affected what information you got before embarking on quests, as well as the forces/abilities available to you in mass battles, revealed some of the power of allowing each player to author his or her own unique experience. It is a terrific game that has a lot to teach even the most experienced RPG designers in the business.

- One game that inspired me, though perhaps not in the way I expected or the creators of the game intended, was The Walking Dead. Playing that game, I was drawn into a narrative, into an experience, that felt more emotionally compelling than maybe any other game I've played. As an experience, the game was magnificent. As a game? I'm not so sure. I think The Walking Dead worked as well as it did because it was unabashedly cinematic—the creators of the game knew exactly where every player would be at all times, what each player would do, exactly how they would do it...In a sense, that meant The Walking Dead was "just" a movie—but a movie that gives an incredibly convincing illusion of interactivity. As a player, I was charmed by it. As a developer, I was aghast that anyone would make a game where developers would never be surprised by anything players did and where no player would ever do anything the creators didn't intend, plan for, and implement. I'm still working through the contradiction inherent in the idea of a game I loved as a player but felt disappointed in as a developer. Any game that is as enjoyable and, albeit inadvertently, thought provoking is worth including on a list of influences!

On free-form gameplay:

I guess I'm pretty proud of the fact that free-form gameplay, player-authored experiences, and the like are finally becoming not just common but almost expected these days. From the "middle" Ultimas (4-6), to Underworld, to System Shock, to Thief, to Deus Ex, there's been this cadre of us arguing, through our work, in favor of less linear, designer-centric games, and, thanks to the efforts of folks at Origin, Looking Glass Studios, Ion Storm, and others - even, with some of the Zelda games, Nintendo. And it isn't just the hardcore gamers—the mass market is waking up, too. That's pretty cool.

I'm hugely proud of having had the privilege of working alongside some amazingly talented people. It's standard practice in all media to give one person credit for the creation of a product, but that's nonsense. Nowhere is it more nonsensical than in games. Game development is the most intensely collaborative endeavor I can imagine. It's been an honor to work with Richard Garriott, Paul Neurath, Doug Church, Harvey Smith, Paul Weaver, Chase Jones, and many others (who will now be offended that I didn't single them out here!). I know I've learned a lot from all of them and hope I've taught a little bit in return.

Advice to designers:

Learn to program. You don't have to be an ace, but you should know the basics. In addition to a solid technical foundation, get as broad-based an education as you can. As a designer, you never know what you're going to need to know—behavioral psychology will help you immensely, as will architecture, economics, and history. Get some art/graphics experience, if you can, so you can speak intelligently with artists even if you lack the skills to become one yourself. Do whatever it takes to become an effective communicator in written and verbal modes. And most importantly, make games. Get hold of one of the many free game engines out there and build things. Get yourself on a mods team and build some maps, some missions, anything you can. Heck, make something amazing in Minecraft! You can do all of this on your own or at one of the many institutions of higher learning now (finally!) offering courses, even degrees, in game development and game studies. It doesn't really matter how you get your training and gain some experience—of life as much as game development—just make sure you get it. Oh, and make sure you really, really, really want to make games for a living. It's gruelingly hard work, with long hours and wrecked relationships to prove it. There are a lot of people who want the same job you do. Don't go into it unless you're absolutely certain it's the career for you. There's no room here for dilettantes!

FURTHER READING

Hiwiller, Zack The Game Designer's Playlist: Innovative Games Every Game Designer Need to Play. Sydney: Pearson Education, Limited, 2018.

Kelley, Tom. The Art of Innovation: Lessons in Creativity from IDEO, America's Leading Design Firm. New York: Random House, 2001.

Moggridge, Bill. Designing Interactions. Cambridge: The MIT Press, 2007.

Schell, Jesse The Art of Game Design: A Book of Lenses. Boca Raton: Taylor & Francis, 2019.

The Imagineers. The Imagineering Way. New York: Disney Editions, 2003.

Tharpe, Twyla The Creative Habit: Learn it and use it for Life. New York: Simon & Schuster, 2006.

Tinsman, Brian. The Game Inventor's Guidebook. New York: Morgan James Publishing, 2008.

Zimmerman, Eric The Rules We Break: Lessons in Play, Thinking, and Design. New York: Princeton Architectural Press, 2023.

END NOTES

1. Phipps, Keith, "Will Wright Interview by Keith Phipps" A.V. Club. February 2, 2005. https://www.avclub.com/will-wright-1798208435

2. Sheff, David. Game Over: How Nintendo Conquered the World. New York: Vintage Books, 1994, p. 51.

3. Hermida, Alfred. "Katamari Creator Dreams of Playground." BBC News.com November 2005. http://news.bbc.co.uk/2/hi/technology/4392964.stm

4. Symonds, Shannon."Preserving Carol Shaw's Trailblazing Video Game Career" The Strong National Museum of Play, July, 19, 2017. https://www.museumofplay.org/blog/preserving-carol-shaws-trailblazing-video-game-career/

5. Wikipedia, "Danielle Bunten Berry" accessed December 21, 2023. https://en.wikipedia.org/wiki/Danielle_Bunten_Berry

6. Entis, Glenn. "Pre-Production Workshop." EA@USC Lecture Series. March 23, 2005.

7. Plummer, Chris. E-mail interview, May 2007.

Chapter 2
The Structure of Games

Exercise 2.1: Think of a Game

1. Think of a game, any game. Now write down a description of the how the game works. Be detailed. Describe how to play the game as if to someone who has never played a game like it before.

2. Now think of another game—a completely different type of game. The more different this game is from the first one, the better. Describe how the game works.

3. Compare your descriptions. Which elements were different and which were similar? Dig deep and really think about the underlying elements of each game.

There is no wrong answer to this exercise. The goal is simply to get you to begin thinking about the nature of games and to realize that games, no matter how dissimilar they might seem, do share some common elements. Those common elements are why we recognize certain experiences, and not others, as games, and throughout this book they will form the basis for our study of games and game design.

GO FISH VERSUS QUAKE

Do all games share the same exact structure? Of course not. A card game has a very different format from a board game; a 3D action game is not at all the same as a trivia game. There is something, however, that they must share because we clearly recognize them all as games.

Take Go Fish and Quake. They must have some similarities because if I asked you if each was a game, you'd say, "Yes!" In other words, if these games don't share the same structure, then what do they share that makes them games and not two different forms of entertainment?

Before venturing to say what the similarities between them might be, it would help to look more closely at each of the two example games.

Go Fish

This is a game for three to six players using a standard 52-card deck. The dealer deals five cards to each player. The rest of the cards are placed face down in a draw pile. The player to the dealer's left starts.

A turn consists of asking a player for a specific rank. For example, if it's your turn, you might say, "Chris, please give me your Jacks." You must already hold at least one card of the requested rank, so you must hold at least one Jack to say this. If Chris has cards of the named rank (Jacks in this case), he has to give you all his cards of this rank. You then get another turn and can again ask any player for any rank that you hold.

If Chris does not have any cards of the named rank, he says, "Go fish!" You must then draw the top card from the draw pile. If the drawn card is the rank you asked for, you show it and get another turn. If the drawn card is not the rank you asked for, you keep it, but the turn now passes to the player who said, "Go fish!"

As soon as a player collects a book of four cards of the same rank, this must be shown and

discarded face down. The game continues until either someone has no cards left in their hand or the draw pile runs out. The winner is the player who then has the most books.

Quake

In single-player Quake,[1] the player controls a character within a 3D environment. Your character can walk, run, jump, swim, shoot, and pick up stuff, but you have a limited amount of armor, health, and ammo.

In the game there are eight types of weapons: axe, shotgun, double-barreled shotgun, nail gun, perforator, grenade launcher, rocket launcher, and thunderbolt. Each weapon uses a specific type of ammo: Shells are for both types of shotguns, nails are for nail guns and perforators, grenades are for grenade launchers and rocket launchers, and cells are for thunderbolts. There are also power-ups within the game that will boost your power; protect you; heal you; or render you invisible, invulnerable, or able to breathe underwater.

Your enemies include rottweilers, grunts, enforcers, death knights, rotfish, zombies, scrags, ogres, spawn, fiends, vores, and shamblers. Hazards you might find in the environment are explosions, water, slime, lava, traps,

2.1   Quake and Go Fish

and teleporters. Your main enemy, codenamed Quake, is using "slip-gates" (transporter devices) to insert death squads inside your bases to kill, steal, and kidnap. There are four episodes in the game; the first level of each episode ends in a slip-gate—these signify that you've entered another dimension. When you complete an entire dimension (five to eight levels), you encounter another slip-gate, which returns you to the start. The goal of Quake is to stay alive while you work your way through each level, killing all enemies in your way.

Comparison

At first glance, the descriptions of these two experiences could not be more dissimilar: One is a turn-based card game; the other is a real-time 3D action shooter. One requires a piece of commercial software and a personal computer capable of running it; the other can be played with a common deck of cards. One is a copyrighted product; the other is a public domain set of rules, which can be transferred verbally from person to person, generation to generation. And yet we call them both games and agree, even if we cannot at first verbalize it, that they are similar experiences at some deep level.

If we look closely, though, and try not to ignore ideas that seem self-obvious, there are enough similarities between the experience of Quake and the experience of Go Fish for us to begin to understand what underlying requirements we are looking for when we judge whether or not something is a game.

Players

The most obvious similarity in these two descriptions is that both describe experiences designed for players. This sounds like a simple distinction, but what other forms of entertainment are designed to demand active participation by their consumers? Music is one example; musicians participate in creating the experience of music, but the primary consumers are the audience, not the

2.2 Players

players. Similarly, dramatic actors participate in the experience of a play, but again, the experience is primarily created for the audience.

In single player Quake, the design calls for a lone player working against the game system, while Go Fish requires a group of at least three players challenging each other. These are very different scenarios, but what the term "player" implies in each situation is the notion of a voluntary participant who both partakes in and consumes the entertainment. Players are active, they make decisions, they are invested, they are potential winners—they are a very distinct subset of people. To become a player, one must voluntarily accept the rules and constraints of a game. This acceptance of a game's rules is part of what author Bernard Suits has called the "lusory attitude" ("lusory" derives from the Latin word for "game").

The lusory attitude of the players is the "curious state of affairs wherein one adopts rules which require one to employ worse rather than better means for reaching an end."[2] For example, Suits describes the game of golf: "Suppose I make it my purpose to get a small round object into a hole in the ground as efficiently as possible. Placing it in the hole with my hand would be a natural means to adopt. But surely I would not take a stick with a piece of metal on one end of it, walk three or four hundred yards away from the hole, and then attempt to propel the ball into the hole with the stick."[3] But, of course, players do just this when they play golf because they have accepted the rules of golf as constraints on their attempts to achieve the objective of the game.

This attitude, this voluntary acceptance of the rules of a game, is part of the psychological and emotional state of players that we need to consider as part of the playcentric process of game design.

Exercise 2.2: Players

Describe how players might join or start a game of Go Fish versus single-player Quake. What steps do they need to take in each case—social, procedural, or technical? There will clearly be differences in the beginning of a multiplayer card game versus a single-player digital game, but are there also similarities? If so, describe them.

Objectives

The next clear distinction is that both descriptions lay out specific goals for the players. In Go Fish, the goal is to be the player who makes the most books. In Quake, it's to stay alive and complete the level of the complex you are in.

This is very different from other experiences in which we can participate in general. When you watch a film or read a book, there is no clear-cut objective presented for you to accomplish during the experience—of course, there is one for the characters, but we're talking about the players here. In life, we set our own objectives and work as hard as we feel necessary to achieve them. We don't need to accomplish all of our objectives to have a successful life. In games, however, the objective is a key element without which the experience loses much of its structure, and our desire to work toward the objective is a measure of our involvement in the game.

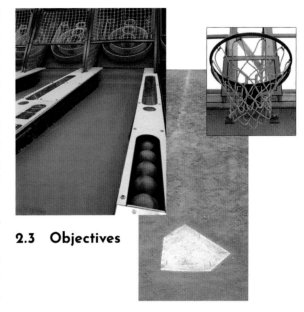

2.3   Objectives

Exercise 2.3: Objectives

List five games, and in one sentence per game, describe the objective in each game.

Procedures

Both descriptions also give detailed instructions on what players can do to achieve the game objectives. For example, in Go Fish, some of these instructions include: "The dealer deals five cards to each player," or "A turn consists of asking a specific player for a specific rank." In Quake, the description states that "Your character can walk, run, jump, swim, shoot, and pick up stuff." The directions also provide a set of controls for doing so. These controls are the method by which the player accesses the basic procedures of the game. If we played Go Fish on a computer, we'd have to create controls for dealing or asking a player for a card of a certain rank.

Procedures, the actions or methods of play allowed by the rules, are an important distinction of the experiences we call games. They guide player behavior, creating interactions that

2.4   Procedures

2.5   Rules

would probably never take place outside the authority of the game.

For example, if you wanted to create a set of four cards of like rank, you wouldn't necessarily ask one player at a time for these cards. You might use a more efficient means, like asking all of the players at once, or simply looking through the draw deck for the cards you need. Because games, by their nature, have procedures that must be followed, you don't take these more efficient actions. Instead, you follow the procedures, and in doing so, you confirm that these required actions are indeed an important distinction that sets games apart from other behaviors and experiences.

Rules

Both descriptions spend a great deal of time explaining exactly what objects the game consists of and what the players can and cannot do. They also clarify what happens in various situations that might arise. In Go Fish, "The cards are placed face down in a draw pile," or "If Chris has cards of the named rank, he must give me all his cards of this rank." And from Quake, "There are eight types of weapons," and "Shells are for both types of shotguns, nails are for nail guns and perforators, etc."

Some of these rule statements define game objects and concepts. Objects, like the deck of cards, draw pile, and weapons, are the building blocks of each of these systems upon which the rest of the design depends. Other rules limit player behavior and prescribe reactive events. For example, if nails are for nail guns, you can't use nails in the thunderbolt. If you have a Jack when you're asked for one, you have to give it up; you can't keep it, or you're breaking the rules of the game. Who will stop you from breaking the rules? Your own sense of fair play? The other players? The underlying code of a digital game?

The concepts of both rules and procedures imply authority, and yet there is no person or body named in either description with whom to associate that authority. The authority of the rules stems from an implicit agreement by the players to submit themselves to the experience. If you don't follow the rules, in a very real way, you are no longer playing the game.

So our next distinctive quality of games is that they are experiences that have rules that define game objects, prescribe principles, and limit behavior within the game. These rules are respected because the players understand that they are a key structural element of the game, and without them, the game would not function.

Exercise 2.4: Rules

Can you think of a game that has no rules? If so, describe it. How about one rule? Why is this exercise difficult?

Resources

In the discussion of each of these games, I have mentioned certain objects that seem to hold a rather high value for the players in reaching their objectives. In Go Fish, the cards of each rank are valued, and in Quake, the weapons, their ammunition, and the power-ups mentioned in the rule set are valued. These objects, made valuable because they can help the players achieve their goal, but which are made scarce in the system by the designer, are what we call resources.

Finding and managing resources is a key part of many games, whether those resources are cards, weapons, time, units, turns, or terrain. In the two examples we see here, one depends on a direct exchange of resources (Go Fish), while the other offers resources fixed in place by the game designer (Quake).

Resources are, by definition, items made valuable by their scarcity and utility. In the real world, and in game worlds, resources can be

used to further our aims; they can be combined to make new products or items; and they can be bought and sold in various types of markets.

Conflict

As noted previously, both experiences as described lay out specific objectives for their players. And, as also noted, they dictate procedures and rules that guide and limit player behavior. The problem for the players is that the procedures and rules of games tend to deter them from accomplishing goals directly; and, in the case of multiplayer games like Go Fish, can also make players work against each other to accomplish these goals. For example, as mentioned earlier, you cannot simply ask everyone at the table to give you the other three Jacks all at once when you're playing Go Fish. You have to ask each player one at a time, risking that you might not get a card and lose your turn, while revealing to the other players that you have a card of the rank you asked for.

Similarly, in Quake, if you could just leave the level of the complex you're on, that would solve the objective, but it's not that easy. To find the exit, you're forced to make it through a mazelike obstacle course of enemies and hazards. In both cases, the relationship between the objectives of the players and the rules and procedures limiting and guiding behavior creates another distinctive element of games: conflict, which the players work to resolve in their own favor.

Exercise 2.5: Conflict

Compare and contrast the conflict in football to the conflict in poker. Describe how each game creates conflict for the players.

Boundaries

Another similarity between these two experiences, one that is not referred to directly in either description but is, however, implied, is that the rules and goals that are driving the players apply

2.6   Resources

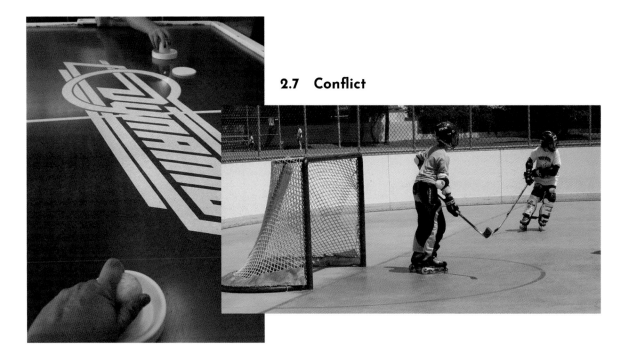

2.7 Conflict

only within the game and not in "real life." In the case of Quake, the architecture of the 3D space forms a virtual boundary. Players are precluded from moving their characters out of these boundaries by the underlying code.

In the case of Go Fish, the boundaries are more conceptual than physical. Players are not precisely bound in a physical sense by any of the rules, except that they need to be able to speak to one another and trade cards back and forth. They are, however, conceptually bound by the social agreement that they are playing the game and that they will not leave the game with some of the cards or add extra cards to the deck.

In his foundational book *Homo Ludens*, theorist Johan Huizinga (see Further Reading) describes the temporary world in which a game takes place as the "magic circle," a temporary world where the rules of the game apply, rather than the rules of the ordinary world. He writes: "All play moves and has its beginning within a playground marked off beforehand either materially or ideally ... the arena, the card-table, the

magic circle, the temple, the stage, the screen, the court of justice, etc. are all in form and function playgrounds, i.e., forbidden spots, isolated, hedged round, within which special rules obtain. All are temporary worlds within the ordinary world, dedicated to the performance of an act apart."[4]

2.8 Boundaries

The idea that these experiences are somehow set apart from other experiences by boundaries is yet another distinction we can make about the structure of games.

Outcome

One last similarity between both of these experiences is that for all their rules and constraints, the outcome of both experiences is uncertain, though there is the certainty of a measurable and unequal outcome of some kind—a winner, a loser, etc. For example, in Go Fish, the player who achieves the objective of making the most books by the end of the game wins. In Quake, a player can either win (stay alive) or lose (be killed).

The outcome of a game differs from the objective in that all players can achieve the objective, but other factors within the system can determine which of them actually win the game. For example, in Go Fish, a number of players can accomplish the objective of creating books, but only one player will create the most books, unless there's a tie, and that type of special case is usually addressed in the rules of a game.

The aspect of uncertainty in outcome is an important one for the playcentric process because it is a key motivator for the players. If players can anticipate the outcome of a game, they will stop playing. You have probably been in this situation before—when one player is so far ahead that no one will be able to catch up. At this point, everyone generally agrees to end the game. In chess, a player who has calculated that she cannot win will often concede the game without playing it to the conclusion.

Unlike favorite movies or books, which can remain entertaining even if we already know the ending, games depend on uncertainty of outcome in every play for their dramatic tension. And players invest their emotions in that uncertainty, making it the job of the game designer to craft a satisfying resolution to the game, usually in the form of a measurable and unequal outcome.

2.9   Outcome

Formal Elements

The games you described in Exercise 2.1 might also have other elements I have not mentioned here: perhaps special equipment, digital environments, complex resource structures, or character definitions. And of course Go Fish and Quake each have their own unique elements that I haven't touched upon, such as the turn structure in Go Fish or the real-time element of Quake. But what we're interested in right now are elements that all games share—elements that make up the essence of games.

A number of scholars from different fields have examined this same question from other perspectives. Some of the most influential have been those looking at games in terms of studying conflict, economics, behavioral psychology, sociology, and anthropology. Katie Salen and Eric Zimmerman do an excellent job of synthesizing these various points of view about the nature of games in their book *Rules of Play* (see Further Reading). But our perspective here is not strictly scholarly, and our purpose here is not to provide a definitive taxonomy. Rather, it is to provide a useful context, a set of conceptual tools, and a vocabulary for us to discuss the playcentric process of designing games.

The distinctive elements of games that are described above are important concepts for the game designer to understand because they provide structure (and form), which can help a beginning designer make choices in the design process and understand problems that arise in the play-testing process. However, as with any art form,

one of the reasons to understand and master the traditional structures is so that you can experiment with alternatives. (See sidebar on page 268 on the development of the experimental game Cloud.) The innovation designers seek in today's game industry might very well require going beyond well known combinations of these elements and exploring new forms of interactivity that lie at the edge of what we call "games." Because they play an essential structural function in traditional game systems, however, I call these the "formal elements" of games. I will look at each of these formal elements in more detail in Chapter 3 and discuss how you can use them in various combinations to achieve your player experience goals.

Engaging the Player

If the formal elements described above provide structure to the experience of games, then what gives these elements meaning for the players? What makes one game capture the imagination of players and another fall flat? Certainly, some players are engaged by pure abstract challenges, but for most players, there needs to be something else that draws them in and allows them to connect emotionally with the experience. Games are, after all, a form of entertainment, and good entertainment engages us and moves us both intellectually and emotionally.

This sense of engagement comes from different things for different players, and not all games require elaborate means to create it. Next I list some elements that allow a player to make an emotional connection with a game.

Challenge

I said that games created conflict that the players had to work to resolve in their own favor. This conflict challenges the players, creating tension as they work to resolve problems and varying levels of achievement or frustration. Increasing the

challenge as the game goes on can cause a rising sense of tension, or, if the challenge is too great, it can cause frustration. Alternatively, if the challenge level remains flat or goes down, players might feel that they have mastered the game and move on. Balancing these emotional responses to the amount of challenge in a game is a key consideration for keeping the player engaged with the game.

Exercise 2.6: Challenge

Name three games that you find particularly challenging and describe why.

Play

The relationship between games and play is a deep and important one. To engage with a game system is to play it, but play itself is not necessarily a game. Salen and Zimmerman define play as "free movement within a more rigid structure" using the example of "free play" of a car's steering wheel. "The 'play' is the amount of movement

2.10   Chess Grand Master Nodirbek Abdusattorov in 2023, left. Image credit: Frans Peters. And professional eSports players, right. Image credit: lincconf.com.

that the steering wheel can move on its own within the system, the amount the steering wheel can turn before it begins to turn the tires of the car. The play itself exists only because of the more utilitarian structures of the driving-system."[5] While this is a somewhat abstract definition, it is useful because it points out the way in which the more rigid systems of games can provide opportunities for players to use imagination, fantasy, inspiration, social skills, or other more free-form types of interaction to achieve objectives within the game space, to play within the game, as well as engage the challenges it offers.

Play can be serious, like the pomp and circumstance surrounding a Grand Master match in chess, or it might be charged and aggressive, like the marathon play environment of an eSports tournament. It might also be an outlet for fantasy, like the rich online worlds of World of Warcraft and Guild Wars 2. Designing for the type of play that will appeal to your players, and also designing the freedom for a bit of free play within the more rigid game structures, are other key considerations for engaging players in your game.

Premise

A basic way that games create engagement is with their overarching premise, which gives context to the formal elements. For example, the premise in Monopoly is that the players are landlords, buying, selling, and developing valuable pieces of real estate in an effort to become the richest player in the game. This premise was quite appealing to down-and-out players during the Great Depression when the game was invented. It remains a favorite to this day, and one reason for that continued appeal is its premise—players enjoy the fantasy of being powerful, land-grabbing landlords with plenty of money to wheel and deal.

Many digital games have even richer premises. Our earlier example of Quake, for instance, places the game play in an immersive environment, filled with violent, militaristic imagery. The premise of World of Warcraft is that players are characters in a rich fantasy world filled with archetypal quests and adventures. The base-level effect of the premise is to make it easier for players to contextualize their choices, but it's

WHAT IS A PUZZLE?

by Scott Kim

Scott Kim has been a fulltime puzzle designer since 1990 with his company GameThinking.io. His work includes puzzles for Tetris, Bejeweled, and Moshi Monsters, as well as game design for computer games Heaven & Earth and Obsidian, the brain game web site Lumosity, and educational games for ABCmouse.com. He has written a monthly puzzle column for Discover magazine, and has designed many games, including Railroad Rush Hour, for the toy company ThinkFun. He has degrees in music and computers & graphic design from Stanford University, and lectures widely on puzzle design and math education.

From casual games to 3D action games, puzzles are an important part of many electronic games. Whether you are designing or producing games for mobile, web, computer, or console, you need to know how to create good puzzles. In this article, I define what a puzzle is, explain how it differs from other types of games, and offer suggestions for how to design good puzzles.

What is a puzzle?

The Random House dictionary defines a puzzle as "a toy or other contrivance designed to amuse by presenting difficulties to be solved by ingenuity or patient effort." A humorous but insightful definition is "a simple task with a bad user interface" – twisting the faces of a Rubik's Cube is a bad user interface for the simple task of turning all the faces solid colors.

My favorite definition of "puzzle" came out of a conversation with puzzle friend Stan Isaacs:

1. A puzzle is fun,
2. And it has a right answer.

Part 1 of the definition says that puzzles are a form of play. Part 2 distinguishes puzzles from other forms of plays, such as games and toys.

This deceptively simple definition has some interesting consequences. For instance, here's the first puzzle I invented. The figure below is a letter of the alphabet that has been cut of paper and folded just once. It is not the letter L. What letter is it?

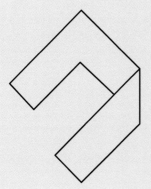

Figure 1   What letter has been folded once to make this shape?

Take a moment to solve this puzzle if you like. The answer is given at the end of this article. Now let's see how well our definition applies.

Is it fun?

There are several things that help make this puzzle fun.

- *Novel*: Puzzles are a form of play. And play starts by suspending the rules of everyday life, giving us permission to do things that are not practical. Folded letters certainly don't have any practical value. They take something familiar and give it a novel twist—a good way of inviting you to be playful.

- *Not too easy, not too hard*: Puzzles that are too easy are disappointing; puzzles that are too hard are discouraging. You know there are only 26 letters in the alphabet, so it seems that this puzzle can't be too difficult. In fact this puzzle is hard enough that many people never get the answer. Nonetheless, the perceived lack of difficulty helps keeps you interested.

- *Tricky*. To solve this puzzle, you must change how you interpret the picture. Personally, I enjoy puzzles that involve such perceptual shifts.

But, like beauty, fun is in the eye of the beholder. What may be fun for one person may be torture for another. For instance, some people prefer word puzzles and won't touch visual or logical puzzles. Puzzles that are too easy for one person may be too hard for another. Chess puzzles are fun only if you know how to play chess.

Consequently, my first job as a puzzle designer is to tailor puzzles to the interests and abilities of my audience. For instance, my monthly puzzles for *Discover* magazine all revolved around science and math themes. To reach both scientific lay people and experts, I broke each puzzle into several questions, ranging from very easy to very hard. Finally, I include three puzzles in each column—usually a word puzzle, a visual puzzle, and a mathematical puzzle—to reach readers who prefer various types of puzzles.

Another consequence of the subjective nature of fun is that what may seem like an everyday problem to you may seem like a delightful puzzle to someone else. Is washing the dishes a chore or a game? That depends on whom you ask. It tickles me to think that for every problem in the world, no matter how tedious, there is someone who would leap at the chance to figure it out.

If fun is a state of mind, then you can make your life more enjoyable by finding ways to turn work into play. When I was in school, I used to hate to take notes. Then I learned about mind-mapping, a technique of capturing ideas in diagrams and cartoons, instead of transcribing every word the teacher says. Not only were my notes more useful, taking notes became an enjoyable game of translating words into pictures.

On the flip side, even the best game can be ruined if the players do not play it with a spirit of fun. Game designer and philosopher Bernie Dekoven recommends in his book *The Well-Played Game* that players be willing to alter the rules to keep the game fun for everyone. For instance, an expert chess player playing with a beginner can level the playing field by starting with fewer pieces or letting the other player take back moves.

Does it have a right answer?

So does my letter puzzle have a right answer? It does in the sense that when shown the answer, most people will agree that this is the best answer. But there are several loopholes.

First, exactly what shape constitutes a letter is a subjective matter. For instance, in a squarish typeface, the following shapes could be interpreted as a lowercase R or a capital J:

I could plug this leak in my puzzle by showing the particular alphabet of letters I have in mind:

Figure 2   These shapes could be the letters R and J

ABCDEFGHIJKLM NOPQRSTUVWXYZ

Figure 3   The answer comes from this typeface

Another subtlety is that my definition doesn't insist that there be only one right answer. If you interpret the diagram differently, there are many other possible answers. For instance, the following shapes, which could be interpreted as the letters J and G, can all be unfolded from Figure 1, if we interpret the edges a bit differently:

Figure 4   Other ways to unfold Figure 1

Puzzles vs. Games

The purpose of "has a right answer" is to distinguish puzzles from games and other play activities. Some game designers categorize puzzles as a subspecies of games. I prefer a finer-grained definition from Chris Crawford, veteran game designer and author of *Chris Crawford on Game Design*.

Chris distinguishes four types of play activities, ranging from most interactive to least:

- **Games** are rule-based systems in which the goal is for one player to win. They involve "opposing players who acknowledge and respond to one another's actions. The difference between games and puzzles has little to do with mechanics; we can easily turn many puzzles and athletic challenges into games and vice versa."
- **Puzzles** are rule-based systems, like games, but the goal is to find a solution, not to beat an opponent. Unlike games, puzzles have little replay value.
- **Toys** are manipulable, like puzzles, but there is no fixed goal.
- **Stories** involve fantasy play, like toys, but cannot be changed or manipulated by the player.

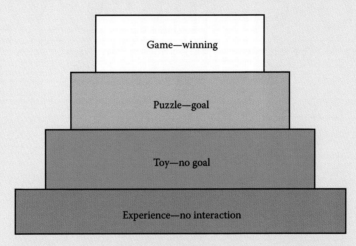

Figure 5   Four types of play, each built on the previous

For instance,

- **The Sims** (PC) is a toy, which players make more puzzle-like by setting their own goals.
- **Half-Life 2** (console/PC) is a first-person shooter, which includes some puzzles.
- **Portal** (console/PC) is a puzzle game built on a first-person shooter engine, with a strongly integrated story, and innovative cooperative puzzles.
- The **Professor Layton** (handheld) series is a nicely told adventure game that wraps a medley of diverse puzzles in a loose story.
- **Cut the Rope** (mobile) is a series of puzzles with a compelling character, which requires both logical problem solving and precise timing.
- **Boggle**™ (physical/mobile) is a multiplayer game in which players race to find the most solutions to a randomly generated puzzle.

This hierarchy leads me to a useful rule of thumb for puzzle designers: To design a good puzzle, first build a good toy. The player should have fun just manipulating the puzzle, even before reaching a solution. For instance, players can enjoy rotating and manipulating blocks in the action puzzle game Tetris even if they don't understand the goal.

The card game Solitaire is an interesting borderline case between game and puzzle. We normally call Solitaire a single-player game, but in fact it is a kind of puzzle, since any given deck has a definite solution (or sometimes no solution). Shuffling the cards is a way to randomly generate a new puzzle.

Other types of puzzles that walk the line on the issue of right answers include trivia questions (which require knowledge of the world), dexterity puzzles (which could be classified with sports), puzzles involving chance (in which the players do not completely control their own fate), and poll-based questions (in which the rightness of the answer depends on what everyone else answers).

Designing puzzles

Here are some tips for designing good puzzles.

First, there are two aspects of puzzle design. Level design, as it applies to puzzles, is crafting a particular puzzle configuration within a fixed set of rules. For instance, composing a crossword puzzle is a form of level design. The level designer's challenge is to craft a puzzle with a distinct sense of drama and coherence, tailored to a particular difficulty level.

The other type of puzzle design is rule design: inventing the overall rules, goal, and format of a puzzle. For instance, Ernö Rubik was a rule designer when he invented Rubik's Cube. Generally speaking, rule design is harder than level design. Note that some rule sets, like that of Sudoku, yield thousands of good levels, while other rule sets yield only one interesting level.

Second, puzzle design has the same goal as game design in general: to keep the player in a pleasurably challenging state of flow. That means capturing the player's interest with an attractive goal, teaching the player the rules in a seamless interesting way, giving feedback during gameplay that keeps the player engaged, and rewarding the player appropriately at the end.

Finally, be creative. Don't limit yourself to imitating the puzzles you have seen. There is an infinite universe of puzzles waiting to be invented. Puzzles can be as varied and expressive as songs, movies, or stories. For inspiration, look beyond other computer games to puzzle books, mystery stories, physical puzzles, science, mathematics, and anything else that captures your imagination.

Exercise: Invent a puzzle

Your challenge is to invent a computer-based puzzle inspired by a headline from today's news. After you have invented the rules, craft at least two levels for your game: one easy and one hard. Remember that you are designing a puzzle, not an action game, so the puzzle must have a precisely defined solution, preferably unique.

Make a paper prototype of your puzzle and test it on other people. Be sure to explain what the goal of the puzzle is, what the rules are, and how the player controls the action. What do your testers enjoy? Where do they get stuck or confused? How can you change the puzzle or the rules to make the game better?

Answer to the letter puzzle

Just to make things more exciting, the answer to the quiz above is the only letter in the alphabet that does not appear in this sentence.

2.11   Monopoly

also a powerful tool for involving players emotionally in the interaction of the formal elements.

Exercise 2.7: Premise

What are the premises for the games Risk, Clue, Pit, and Guitar Hero? If you don't know these games, pick games that you are more familiar with.

Character

With the advent of role-playing and digital games, designers began to utilize another potential tool for engagement, and that is the notion of character. In traditional storytelling, characters are the agents through which dramatic stories are told, and they can function this

way in games as well, providing a way for us to empathize with the situation and live vicariously through their efforts. But characters in games can also be vessels for our own participation, entry points for us to experience situations and conflicts through the guise of a mask we create and direct. Character is a rich area for dramatic engagement in games, and many games, especially digital games, have explored this area of potential.

Story

Lastly, some games engage players emotionally by using the power of story within or surrounding their formal elements. Story differs from premise in its narrative qualities. A premise need not go anywhere from where it begins, while stories unfold with the game. How story is created in games continues to evolve and grow as the form expands. Game stories may be driven by branching choices as in the narrative adventures of the Life is Strange series. Or they may emerge from player-created characters and situations like those found in role-playing games. There is no one best way to think about story and games, but it's clear from the interest of both players and designers that dramatic narratives integrated with play can create powerful emotional results.

2.12   The Evolution of Mario

Choose carefully. This action will have consequences

ATTACK ⬛   ● RUN

2.13   Life is Strange series: clockwise from top left, Life is Strange 2, Life is Strange, True Colors, Before the Storm. (Images © Square Enix)

Exercise 2.8: Story

Have any stories within a game ever gripped you, moved you emotionally, or sparked your imagination? If so, why? If not, why not?

Dramatic Elements

The games you picked in Exercise 2.1 on page 33 almost certainly have one or more of the elements described previously as a part of their design. I call these the "dramatic elements" of games because they engage the players emotionally by creating a dramatic context for the formal elements. In Chapter 4 on page 101, I'll look at each of these more closely and discuss how you can use dramatic elements to create rich experiences for your players.

THE SUM OF THE PARTS

One thing that might not be immediately apparent from your game descriptions or from our examples of Go Fish and single-player Quake is the depth to which each of the elements I've discussed relies on the others. This is because games are systems, and systems, by definition, are groups of interrelated elements that work together to form a complex whole.

An important idea to consider when thinking about games as systems is the old saying that the whole is greater than the sum of its parts. What is meant by this is that a system, because of the interrelationship of its elements, takes on new dimensions when it is set in motion. As an example, think of a system you are familiar with, such as the engine in your car. You can examine and understand the physical makeup of each element in the engine. You can understand their functions and even predict how they will respond in interaction with other elements. But unless you set the system in motion, you cannot observe certain important qualities of the engine as a whole—namely, its primary function of producing motive power. When the system is started, however, these qualities emerge as a consequence of the interaction of all the elements.

Game systems are much the same. All of the elements I have laid out previously form a potential that remains nascent until the game is played. What emerges in play is something that cannot be predicted from examining each of the elements separately. The game designer needs to be able to look at a game system not only as separate elements but also as a whole in play. Chapter 5 will look at games as dynamic systems and describe a number of key concepts for working with the system elements in your own games.

DEFINING GAMES

Now that we've thought about some of the various aspects of games, it seems a good time to try to pull it all together and answer the question I posed at the beginning of this chapter: What is a game? What makes Go Fish, or Quake, or any other game that you can play a game and not some other type of experience?

I have said that games are given structure by their *formal elements*, that they also have *dramatic elements* that make them emotionally engaging experiences. I have also said that games are *dynamic systems* and that their elements work together to produce a complex whole. I can expand my definition by pulling out some of the most important elements from the earlier discussion.

When I talked about boundaries, I mentioned the physical and the conceptual because this is what most games deal with in their rules. What I did not mention is the emotional boundary between the rest of life and a game. When you play a game, you set the rules of life aside and take up the rules of the game instead. Conversely, when you finish playing a game, you set aside the incidents and outcome of that game and return to the trappings of the outside world. Within the game, you might have slaughtered your best friend, or she might have slaughtered you. But that was within the game. Outside the game, these actions have no real consequences. What I am emphasizing here is the fact that game systems are separate from the rest of the world; they are closed.

I said that games are formal systems—that they are defined as games, and not some other type of interaction, by their formal elements. Also, I know that it is key to my definition of games to show that these elements are interrelated, so I should include the concept that a game is a system. So the first statement I can make confidently about games is that *they are closed, formal systems*.

I have talked at length about the fact that games are for players, that the entire purpose of games is to engage players. Without players, games have no reason to exist. How do games engage players? By involving them in a conflict that is structured by their formal and dramatic elements. Games challenge players to accomplish their objectives while following rules and procedures that make it difficult to do so. In single-player games, this challenge can come from the system itself, while in multiplayer games it can come from the system, from other players, or from both. So the second statement I can add to my definition of games is that *they engage players in structured conflicts.*

Lastly, *games resolve their uncertainty in unequal outcomes.* A fundamental part of gameplay is that it is uncertain. However, it promises to end that uncertainty, by producing a winner or winners. Games are not experiences designed to prove we are all equal. In fairness to the great breadth of game systems, some games are not exacting in their sense of closure or in the measure of their outcome. However, even if you are playing a game like World of Warcraft that goes on and on ad infinitum, or a game like The Sims, which has no specified objective, these games find ways to provide both moments of resolution and measurable achievement to their players.

Drawing these concepts together, I can come to this working conclusion about the nature of games. A game is:

- A closed, formal system, that
- Engages players in structured conflict, and
- Resolves its uncertainty in an unequal outcome.

BEYOND DEFINITIONS

Now that I have created a definition, the first thing I want to do is look beyond it. There is a realm of possibilities for game designers that exists on the edges of what we consider to be games. I have already mentioned online worlds such as World of Warcraft and simulations such as The Sims, but there are also emerging genres of play that move games beyond entertainment into the areas of education, training, political action, health and wellness, art, architecture, and other important areas of society.

For example, there is a very large community of design around "serious games" or games for learning. These games are being designed to engage students playfully around educational concepts. Some have called this "gamification" and have extended the idea to include just about any aspect of life that we usually need motivation to engage with. For example, a gamification project might give you a badge for completing a history project, or running five miles. As a game designer, I'm not fond of the term gamification because it insinuates that layering game features over any system will make it fun. Players realize immediately that this isn't true. While they might be motivated for a while by shiny prizes, real engagement requires a much stronger lure. That means a deeper, more interesting system design must be developed.

The impulse behind the idea, however, which is to make playful experiences that engage us with important ideas, is a good one. And there are examples of excellent designs that use playful activities and games to create learning moments. Examples such as Darfur is Dying, a game about the genocide in Darfur, or September 12th, a simulation about the futility of direct militaristic response to terrorism, take on serious themes and use some of the formal and dramatic elements of games to engage players with those themes. More recently, we have seen the power of games like That Dragon Cancer, about a family facing cancer in their infant son. The Games for Change Festival has developed a large community around this growing trend in game design and highlights many good examples on its website at www.gamesforchange.org.

In addition to serious and learning games, there is also a growing community around experimental and art games. These games, as you might expect from experimental projects, wildly differ from one another. For example, there is the beautiful and contemplative Dear Esther, in which the player explores a mysterious narrative woven into the landscape of a remote island. Or, there is the collective cinematic experience of Renga, a game where a theatrical audience of one hundred players armed with laser pointers

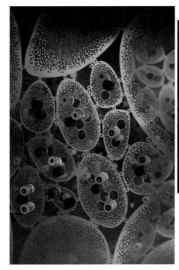

2.14   Interference and The Night Journey

Interference image © Maxime Dufour Photographies. The Night Journey image © Bill Viola Studios and The Game Innovation Lab.

must collaborate to marshal their resources and bring their space ship home. There are art games like my own The Night Journey, a collaboration with media artist Bill Viola, which explores the spiritual journey in a surreal game space. And there are installation pieces like Interference by Eric Zimmerman and Nathalie Pozzi, a physical game commissioned for museum exhibition by la Gaîté Lyrique, Paris. Richard Lemarchand gives more examples of experimental games in his sidebar on page 209.

The range of experimental and art game pieces is expanding rapidly, as is the number of venues where such games can be played. The IndieCade Festival of Games and the Independent Games Festival at the Game Developers Conference are two such venues for experimental and art games. These are both open to student participants as well as professionals and are a wonderful way to gain exposure and experience. Festival director Sam Roberts goes into more detail on the opportunities for independent designers available at festivals such as IndieCade in his sidebar on page 463.

Some people would not call these examples games, but as the commercial market for games diversifies, I believe that it is communities of innovation such as these that will drive new ideas and point new ways to new forms of play and interactivity.

___

Exercise 2.9: Applying What You Have Learned

For this exercise, you will need a piece of paper, two pens, and two players. First, take a moment to play this simple game[6]:

1. Draw three dots randomly on the paper. Choose a player to go first.
2. The first player draws a line from one dot to another dot.
3. Then that player draws a new dot anywhere on that line.

4. The second player also draws a line and a dot:
   - The new line must go from one dot to another, but no dot can have more than three lines coming out of it.
   - Also, the new line cannot cross any other line.
   - The new dot must be placed on the new line.
   - A line can go from a dot back to the same dot as long as it doesn't break the "no more than three lines" rule.
5. The players take turns until one player cannot make a move. The last player to move is the winner.

Identify the formal elements of this game:

- *Players*: How many? Any requirements? Special knowledge, roles, etc.?

- *Objective*: What is the objective of the game?
- *Procedures*: What are the required actions for play?
- *Rules*: Any limits on player actions? Rules regarding behavior? What are they?
- *Conflict*: What causes conflict in this game?
- *Boundaries*: What are the boundaries of the game? Are they physical? Conceptual?
- *Outcome*: What are the potential outcomes of the game?

Does the game have dramatic elements? Identify them:

- *Challenge*: What creates challenge in the game?
- *Play*: Is there a sense of play within the rules of the game?
- *Premise/Character/Story*: Are these present?

What types of dramatic elements do you think might add to the game experience?

CONCLUSION

Notice that although I have arrived at a working definition, I have come to no grand conclusion on the absolute nature of games. In fact, I have said that it is clear that the next generation of game designers is already looking beyond the traditional definition of games and exploring new territories. The areas of structure I have mapped out are important to the process of design, and as such they need to be clear. The areas left in shadow are just as interesting, and I encourage you to think about aspects of games that interest and inspire you.

My goal in this taxonomy exercise is to provide a starting point. It is not meant to constrict you as a designer. Having said that, terminology is key. The lack of a shared design vocabulary is one of the largest problems that faces every new game team as they begin to work together. The terms I have suggested here are just that—suggestions. I use them consistently throughout this book so that I can have a common language with you with which to discuss the design process and to help you evaluate and critique your designs.

After you have gained experience with this process, it is up to you as a designer to move beyond any limitations you find with it. Consider everything you read here a starting point from which you can jump off—a launch pad for your expedition into the world of designing games that will hopefully push the envelope and transport players to places they didn't imagine possible.

DESIGNER PERSPECTIVE: JANE MCGONIGAL

Inventor, SuperBetter

Jane McGonigal, PhD, is a game designer and bestselling author of "Reality is Broken: Why Games Make Us Better and How They Can Change the World." Her games include Cruel 2 B Kind (2006), World Without Oil (2007), The Lost Ring for the 2008 Olympic Games (2008), SuperStruct for the Institute for the Future (2008), CryptoZoo for the American Heart Association (2009), EVOKE for the World Bank (2010), Find the Future for the New York Public Library (2011), and SuperBetter (2012).

Jane McGonigal at Find the Future for the New York Public Library

How did you become a game designer?

I was in graduate school studying theater when location-based gaming started to become a thing; it was 2001. I thought my stage management experience in off-Broadway theater would be useful for games being played in real spaces, so I got myself hired as a writer and mission designer by the first location-based gaming company in the United States, the Go Game.

On games that have inspired her:

I was inspired to start working in reality-based games by the 2001 alternate reality game The Beast, created by Microsoft Game Studio for Steven Spielberg's movie, *Artificial Intelligence*. It was the first 100% co-operative, collective intelligence-based game. The project lead, Elan Lee, said he wanted to turn all the players into the world's first true artificial intelligence, a hive mind made up of tens of thousands of gamers working together. Pretty much every game I've created since then has tried to build on this idea.

On exciting developments in the industry:

I'm thrilled by all innovations that link games and physical activity. As an industry, I think we need to be a part of helping people lead happier, healthier lives. For most gamers, that means trying to get an hour of physical activity every day—and if we can use physical interfaces to do that, we're playing a positive role in society. GPS, motion detection, sensors that we wear like the Nike Fuelband. These are all amazing ways to create games that help us feel good about gaming. I'm less thrilled by the development of 3D virtual reality headsets, because that seems like a step backwards to me. Give me more physical input, and less escaping reality.

On design process:

To be honest, most of my game design begins with me taking long walks or running with my husband. I spend the whole run or walk talking out loud about different game ideas, and he helps me figure out which ones are worth testing. I've been designing this way for a decade. I think it's important to talk out loud with someone who can make your ideas better before you get started on a prototype. For me it's particularly important because I'm often trying to make a game that does something no game has tried to do before—a game that when you win, you've written a book that can be printed on demand and added to a real physical library collection. A game that helps you getting funding for a social enterprise that you hadn't even imagined before you started playing. A game that teaches you a "lost" Olympic Sport so you can go to Beijing and win a gold medal even though you don't think of yourself as an athlete. When you have ideas that crazy, I guess it's good to talk them through with someone you trust before you go too far down the road of design!

On prototyping:

I use prototypes, but they're often more thought experiments than anything else. I don't usually prototype with software. I will say to someone, "Do you think you could do this?" "Would it be fun to try this?" "If your goal were X, what strategy would you adopt?" In fact, this is my new favorite design strategy, very early stage. I call it the Twitter virtual playtest. I tweet a goal and rule set that I am considering, and I ask my followers, "What strategy would you adopt?" and "How confident do you feel you could achieve this?" I did this recently with a game I'm designing for an outdoor freshman convocation at a university. Four thousand incoming students, and I'm going to have them make paper planes and we're going to fly them at the same time. I'm working on the game part now—how do I make it more of a challenge, something that will require creativity and teamwork to get all 4000 planes in the air at the same time?

On a difficult design problem:

For the 2008 Olympic Games, I had the opportunity to invent a sport that we would train players to become great at in the six months leading up to the games. We would hold gold-medal finals during the final day of the Olympic Games. (We actually did this, by the way! We ran them on the Great Wall of China; it was amazing.) I knew I wanted to invent a new kind of team sport that didn't require athleticism so much as teamwork and dedication. I was inspired by ancient Greece and their love of labyrinths, so I was playing with different ideas. I worked out an idea I was really excited about: a blindfolded runner trying to escape from the center of a labyrinth. But how could people all over the world make a labyrinth from scratch? I wanted it to be like basketball or Frisbee or soccer: you show up on a court or field and you can play without special equipment. But I couldn't figure it out. Could they lay out string? If so, what would keep the string in place? I was thinking about this while I was doing yoga. I always work on game design problems when I'm exercising. I was doing a pose called "triangle pose," with my feet planted on the ground and my body turned sideways. And suddenly I saw in my mind: Players could stand on the string. And then I realized: Players could BE the walls of the labyrinth. They could come together and physically form the walls. If I hadn't been doing yoga, I'm not sure I would have thought of this. That idea led to the best idea, which is that players hum to help the blindfolded runner navigate his or her way out. The runner must run with his or her arms folded across the chest to avoid feeling the way out—they have to trust their teammates to show them the way with their voices. All of this is to say that I use physical activity a lot in my creative process. I think better while moving.

What are you most proud of in your career?

I think I have successfully demonstrated something new with each game, something new about what games or gamers are capable of. Gamers can solve real-world problems or change their own lives just by playing. My most recent project, SuperBetter, has probably been the most personally satisfying. I invented it to help me heal from a traumatic brain injury. Now, a quarter of a million people have played it to achieve goals like losing weight or recovering from surgery to battling diagnoses of diabetes, asthma, ALS, and cancer. The University of Pennsylvania ran an independent, controlled, randomized trial of the game for depression. The results, with 250 participants, showed that the game helped players eliminate six symptoms of depression from their lives in six weeks of gameplay. I get letters every day from players who say they have really improved their own lives with this game. I love that game designers have the power to change or even save lives!

Advice to designers:

Seek to have a real-life or real-world positive impact with every game you make. You can strengthen relationships by designing multiplayer games, especially if they have co-op. You can improve players' physical health by having physical activity as a part of the gameplay. You can improve cognitive function with action games or puzzles games. You can teach empathy with different kinds of people through just about any kind of adventure game. You can simply focus on a single positive emotion, like curiosity or surprise, and try to give players as much of that emotion as possible. In my dream world, every game designer can speak intelligently and passionately about the real impacts their games have on players.

DESIGNER PERSPECTIVE: RANDY SMITH

Creative Director, Tiger Style

Randy Smith is a game designer whose credits include Thief: The Dark Project (1998), Thief II: The Metal Age (2000), and Thief: Deadly Shadows (2004). In 2009, Smith started Tiger Style and released the award-winning Spider: The Secret of Bryce Manor for the iPhone, followed by Waking Mars (2012) and Spider: Rite of the Shrouded Moon (2015).

How did you become a game designer?

When I attended college in 1992, gaming degrees weren't offered. I majored in computer science with minors in philoso-phy and media arts, which turned out to be a great substitute, even by today's standards. I had a normal computer-y job the summer after college, and in my spare time I compiled a list of every video game company that might be hiring, sorted by my interest in working for them. The very top of the list was Looking Glass Studios, whose work I deeply respected based on System Shock, a seminal immersive sim, which to this day is one of my all-time favorite games. Looking Glass's web-site at the time was an incredibly evocative teaser, all tone and mood with no details, for a game known only as The Dark Project. I wanted to work on it more than anything, so I looked up the information for project director, Greg LoPiccolo, and cold called the phone sitting on his desk. I would not recommend this approach today, but Greg didn't hang up on me, and he entertained my request to drive myself down to Cambridge, Massachusetts, for an interview. After a couple of interviews and some homework assignments to prove my potential, I was hired on as a hybrid designer/programmer on the game that would become Thief. Eventually the senior staff pushed me into a pure design role, due to more confidence in those skills than my iffy programming abilities.

On games that have inspired him:

The Ultima games, especially IV and V, for crafting enormous, believable worlds and enabling a personal and spiritual journey through them, thereby demonstrating that games can have resonance and substance. System Shock, for present-ing a seamlessly immersive experience and going far beyond even most modern games in giving ownership of it back to the player. Rogue and its descendants, especially ADOM, for using procedural generation to make game systems the foundation of the player experience, not designer-authored content. And Zelda, for showing how much powerful player control you can cram in without complicating the interface or making the gameplay fussy.

What is the most exciting development in the recent game industry?

The democratization of game development. Even five years ago, it felt like the major studios had a chokehold on the games industry and were forcing their risk-averse, hits-driven agenda. It was a sad period of cultural homogeny and regurgitated formulas. A number of recent developments including more powerful authoring tools, digital distribution, and platforms that enable self-publishing have turned things around and made it very possible for small studios and risky ideas to survive and even excel. All of this has contributed to the fantastic rise of indie games and their active audience. Today indies in gaming play a role similar to what we see in film and music: a viable and self-sustaining alternative to the offerings of the mainstream. This is huge and has contributed profoundly to the evolution of gaming, essentially freeing us from where we were stuck less than a decade ago.

On his design process:

I use a multilateral process where ideas can come from any direction and gradually inform an amorphous vision until it coheres. The top-down direction can include plot structure, product vision, central game mechanics, and the major themes of the work, both interactive and fictional ones. So, for example, Waking Mars is all about "ecosystems" and their role in our lives, so the majority of the gameplay, environments, story beats, and dialog were crafted with that in mind. Spider deals with relatable domestic dramas and spaces that are overlaid with a larger mystery, all seen through the unsympathetic eyes of a spider who leaves the place covered in cobwebs, so each level's design plays a role in presenting those ideas. The bottom-up direction is isolated moments that might have a place in the work, including specific locations, interactions, story beats, and scenes. One of the early images from Spider was a heart-shaped locket thrown down a well: an emotionally moving set piece very appropriate to the project's goals, so much so that I knew I had to figure out how it fit into the higher-level story. For Waking Mars, I really liked the idea that dead life forms would decay and leave something useful behind, since that's representative of what makes real ecosystems fascinating, but we had to figure out what that object would be and how it connected to the rest of the gameplay. I feel there are numerous "lateral" directions, too, ideas that come seemingly at random from a stray comment, the right kind of brainstorm meeting, being inspired by happenstance, or research. Waking Mars required months of research into how planets form, the history of Mars, and the evolution of life on Earth, and much of that was passed into the project as realistic details or top-down constraints.

Generally I try to assemble ideas from all directions, far more than can possibly fit into one project, then treat it as a constraints problem where multiple solutions exist but the ideal solution assembles as many of the best ideas as possible in a harmonious way that nails the project goals and ideally isn't too difficult to implement. The top-down direction of the game solidifies out of this approach; at first it might be any of a few possibilities, and then the stars start to fall into alignment and either you realize which vision will return the best results or it sort of imposes itself on you as something you had been unknowingly working toward all along.

What are you most proud of in your career?

I founded Tiger Style with a couple things in mind. One, I wanted to show that the casual audience is ready for sophisticated interactive concepts. Just because they don't devote dozens of hours per week gaming and don't want to read enormous stat sheets doesn't mean they won't understand Spider's environmental storytelling or be able to manage Waking Mars's emergent interactions. Two, and more importantly, I wanted to create engaging action games that don't rely on violence. The "action drawing" of Spider and the "ecosystem gameplay" of Waking Mars were inventions of the Tiger Style teams, and both are completely non-violent. It's not that we are against violence per se; our issue is that it's been unfathomably overdone and is typically handled in a way that makes our art form appear emotionally stunted. I'm proud that our studio has joined others that eschew convention and push themselves into uncharted design frontiers, something I believe is necessary for the continued evolution of the interactive medium.

On advice to designers:

Don't do what everyone else is doing. Don't accidentally make a career out of being a fan, paying homage to your favorite games. Don't implement combat, racing, and platforming gameplay just because that's what's already been done, solved, and expected by the audience. Really think about your subject matter and how your game can convey it. Treat the interactive medium like an art form. Notice dogmas and challenge them. Games don't have to be fun, fair, balanced, clear, and certainly not "addictive." Games can have meaning and resonance like any other art form, and we are just starting to explore all the ways that's possible. The day will come when everyone will have forgotten about the Black Ops clones, but the games pushing the medium boundaries will be remembered as classics. Strive to design one of those!

FURTHER READING

DeKoven, Bernie. *The Well-Played Game: A Player's Philosophy*. Cambridge: The MIT Press, 2013.

Huizinga, Johan. *Homo Ludens: A Study of the Play Element in Culture*. Boston: The Beacon Press, 1955.

Salen, Katie and Zimmerman, Eric. *Rules of Play: Game Design Fundamentals*. Cambridge: The MIT Press, 2004.

Suits, Bernard. *The Grasshopper: Games Life and Utopia*. Boston: Godine, 1990.

Sutton-Smith, Brian. *The Ambiguity of Play*. Cambridge: Harvard University Press, 1997.

END NOTES

1. It can be argued that single- and multiplayer Quake are completely different games, or at least they provide very different player experiences. For the sake of this discussion, I have chosen to look at the single-player version to establish a greater contrast between it and the multiplayer card game Go Fish.
2. Suits, Bernard. *The Grasshopper: Games, Life and Utopia*. Boston: Godine, 1990. p. 23.
3. Ibid, p. 38.
4. Huizinga, Johan. *Homo Ludens: A Study of the Play Element in Culture*. Boston: The Beacon Press, 1955. p. 10.
5. Salen, Katie and Zimmerman, Eric. *Rules of Play: Game Design Fundamentals*. Cambridge: The MIT Press, 2004. p. 304.
6. Conway, John and Patterson, Mike, Sprouts, 1967.

Chapter 3

Working with Formal Elements

Exercise 3.1: Gin Rummy

Let's take the classic card game gin rummy. If you don't know how to play, you can find the rules here: https://bicyclecards.com/how-to-play/gin-rummy. There are two basic procedures to a turn in gin rummy: drawing and discarding. Take away the discard procedure and try to play the game. What happens?

Now take away both the discard procedure and the draw procedure, and then play the game. What's missing from the game?

Put the drawing and discarding procedures back, but take out the rule that says that an opponent can "lay off" unmatched cards to extend the knocker's sets. Is the game still playable with this change?

Now put back the original rules, but take away the objective and play the game again. What happens this time?

What does this exercise tell us about the formal elements of games?

Formal elements, as I've said, are those elements that form the structure of a game. Without them, games cease to be games. As you saw in the opening exercise of this chapter, a game without players, without an objective, without rules or procedures is not a game at all. Players, objective, procedures, rules, resources, conflict, boundaries, and outcome: These are the essence of games, and a strong understanding of their potential interrelationships is the foundation of game design.

After you grasp these basic principles, you can use the knowledge to create innovative combinations and new types of gameplay for your own games. This chapter will delve more deeply into each of the formal elements discussed in Chapter 2 and break them down into conceptual tools that you can use to analyze existing games or help make design decisions in your own games.

PLAYERS

We've determined that games are experiences designed for players and that players must voluntarily accept the rules and constraints of the game in order to play. When players have

DOI: 10.1201/9781003460268-4

accepted the invitation to play, they are within Huizinga's "magic circle," as discussed in Chapter 2. Within the magic circle, the rules of games take on a certain power and a certain potential. Bound by the rules of play, we perform actions that we would never otherwise consider—shooting, killing, and betrayal are some. But we also perform actions we would like to think ourselves capable of and have never had the chance to face—courage in the face of untenable odds, sacrifice, and difficult decision-making. Somehow, through a strange and wonderful paradox, those restrictive and binding statements that are game rules, when put into motion within the safety of the magic circle, mysteriously create the opportunity for play.

Invitation to Play

Other arts also create their own temporary worlds: the frame of a painting, the proscenium of a stage, a motion picture screen. The moments of entry into these worlds are ritualized in recognizable moments: the dimming of the lights, the drawing back of the curtains, and, for games, the invitation to play. One of the most important moments in a game is this invitation. In a board or card game, the invitation is part of the social makeup of the game—players invite each other to play. The offer is accepted and the game is begun. In a digital game, the process is much more technical. Usually there is a start button or an entry screen. But some games make an extra effort to extend a more visceral invitation. One of the best examples of this is the Guitar Hero controller. A small plastic mock-up of a guitar, when strapped on by a player, suddenly becomes an excuse to *act* like a guitar player, not just play the game, but play the fantasy of the game. Crafting this invitation to play, making it visceral and compelling to your target audience is an important part of playcentric design.

It might seem obvious that you need to create an engaging invitation to get players interested in playing your game. But there are other decisions you'll need to make about players in your game. For example, how to structure their

3.1   Costumed players at Comi-Con

participation: How many players does the game require? How many total players can the game support? Do various players have different roles? Will they compete, cooperate, or both? The way you answer these questions will change the overall player experience. To answer them, you'll need to look back to your player experience goals and think about what structure will support your goals.

Number of Players

A game designed for one player is essentially different from a game designed for two, four, or 10,000 players. And a game designed for a specific number of players has different considerations than a game designed for a variable number of players.

Solitaire and tic-tac-toe are games that require an exact number of players. Solitaire, obviously, supports only one player. Tic-tac-toe requires two players—no more, no less. The system will not function without the exact number of players. Many single-player digital games support only one player. This is because, like solitaire, their structure supports one player competing against the game system.

On the other hand, there are games that are designed to be played with a range of players. Parcheesi is a game designed for two to four players, while Monopoly is designed for two to eight players. Massively multiplayer games like EVE Online and World of Warcraft are designed to function for a variable number of players, ranging into the tens of thousands; however, a single player can be alone in World of Warcraft, and many of the formal elements of the system will still function.

Exercise 3.2: Three-Player Tic-Tac-Toe

Create a version of tic-tac-toe that works for three players. You might need to change the size of the board or other elements of the game to do this.

Roles of Players

Most games have uniform roles for all players. In chess and Monopoly, there is only one role for all players. But some games have more than one role for players to choose between. In Mastermind (described on page 145), one player chooses to be the code-maker, while the other chooses to be the code-breaker. The system requires both roles to be filled, or it will not work. Also, many team games, like football, have different player roles that make up the full team. Role-playing games, as the name implies, have a variety of roles for players to choose between. Players can take on

the role of healers or fighters or magic wielders. These roles define many of the player's basic abilities, and often players will create more than one character in an online world so that they will have the opportunity to play several different roles.

In addition to roles that are defined within the game rules, however, you might also want to consider other potential play styles as types of roles when you are designing your game. Richard Bartle, creator of the first multiuser dungeon (MUD), wrote a widely referenced article describing the four basic player types he found in his MUD. These were: achievers, explorers, socializers, and killers.[1] Bartle posits that players often have a primary play style and will only switch if it suits their purposes. Social Scientist Nick Yee of Quantic Foundry has expanded this model to include 12 "motivation models" grouped into six correlated pairs. Action-oriented players enjoy destruction and excitement. Socially oriented players enjoy competition and community. Mastery-focused players enjoy challenge and strategy. Achievement-oriented players enjoy completion and power. Immersion-focused players enjoy fantasy and story. And creativity-seeking players enjoy design and discovery.[2] Using data science methods, Yee and the team at Quantic Foundry have developed nine gamer

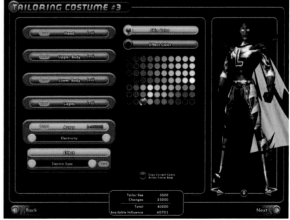

3.2   Create character screens: World of Warcraft and City of Heroes

motivation profiles that can help you to understand what types of gameplay your players may prefer. You can take their gamer motivation profile test here to find your own profile and explore others: https://quanticfoundry.com/. So as you design the roles for your players, or if you provide the opportunity for players to define their own roles, think about what motivates each type of role your design and the different types of players that will be engaged by these roles.

Player Interaction Patterns

Another choice to consider when designing your game is the structure of interaction between a player, the game system, and any other players. The following breakdown of interaction patterns is adapted from the work of E. M. Avedon in his article "The Structural Elements of Games."[3] You'll see that many digital games fall into the pattern "single player versus game," and, more recently, "multilateral competition." There's a lot of potential in the other patterns that is rarely taken advantage of, and I offer these ideas to you in the hopes that they can inspire you to look at new combinations and possibilities of player interactions to use in your designs.

1. Single player versus game

This is a game structure in which a single-player competes against a game system. Examples include solitaire, Pac-Man, and other single player digital games. This was once the most common pattern for digital gaming, though today most single-player games also include a multiplayer mode. You'll find this pattern in mobile games, console games, and PC games. Because there are no other human players in this pattern, games that use it tend to include puzzles or other play structures to create conflict. It is perhaps because of the success of this pattern that we now refer to digital games that have more than one player as "multiplayer" games when, in fact, analog games were multiplayer by definition for thousands of years.

2. Multiple individual players versus game

This is a game structure in which multiple players compete against a game system in the company of each other. Action is not directed toward each other, and no interaction between participants is required or necessary. Examples include bingo, roulette, and Farmville. This is a pattern that became very popular during the early days of Facebook because of the asynchronous aspect to many of its social games. Essentially, this pattern is a single-player game that is played in the company (virtual or real) of other players who are also playing the same game. This pattern works well for noncompetitive players who enjoy the activity and the social arena, for example, casino games.

3. Player versus player

This is a game structure in which two players directly compete. Examples include checkers, chess, and tennis. This is a classic structure for strategy games and works well for competitive players. The one-on-one nature of the competition makes it a personal contest. Two-player fighting games such as Soul Calibur II, Mortal Kombat, and others have employed this structure successfully. Again, the intense competition marks this pattern for focused, head-to-head play.

4. Unilateral competition

This is a game structure in which two or more players compete against one player. Examples include tag, dodge ball, Among Us and the Scotland Yard board game. A highly undervalued structure, this pattern works as well with "free-for-all" games like tag as it does with intensely strategic games like Scotland Yard or social deception games like Among Us. As does tag and Among Us, Scotland Yard pits one player, Mr. X, against all the other players.

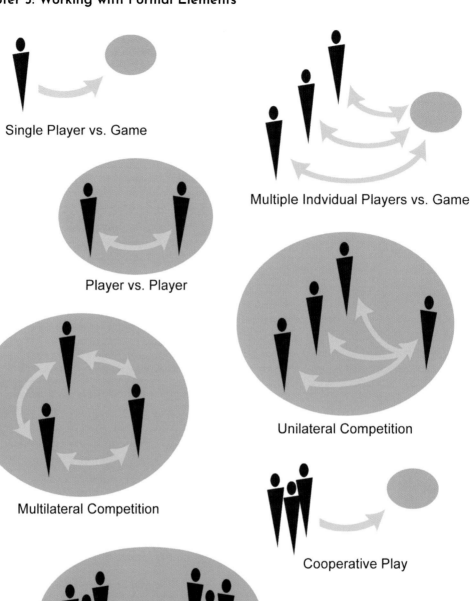

Single Player vs. Game

Multiple Indvidual Players vs. Game

Player vs. Player

Unilateral Competition

Multilateral Competition

Cooperative Play

Team Competition

3.3   Player interaction patterns

3.4 Single player versus game examples: Pac-Man, The 7th Guest, and Tomb Raider

Pac-Man © 1980 Namco Ltd. All Rights Reserved. Courtesy of Namco Holding Corp.

However, unlike tag, Scotland Yard has the larger group (the detectives) trying to catch the singled-out player (the criminal). This game balances between the two forces because the criminal has full information about the state of the game, while the detectives have to work together to deduce the state from clues left by the criminal. Similarly, Among Us has the larger group (the crew) working together to complete tasks on a spacecraft before one or more impostors can kill everyone else aboard. These examples show how unilateral play is a very interesting model for combining cooperative and competitive gameplay.

5. Multilateral competition

This is a game structure in which three or more players directly compete. Examples include poker; Monopoly; multiplayer games like Call of Duty: Black Ops, StarCraft II, and Halo 4; etc. This is the pattern that most players think of when they refer to "multiplayer" gaming. Nowadays, the trend is to think of multiplayer in terms of massive numbers of players, but as the thousands of years of predigital multiplayer game history supports, there's still plenty of room for innovative thinking in terms of smaller, directly competitive groups. Board games with this pattern of player interaction have been "tuned" for generations for groups of between three to six players; clearly there's a social force at work that makes this an ideal group size for direct competition. Want to do something fresh in digital gaming? Try tuning your multiplayer game to encourage the same high level of social interaction that occurs with a three- to six-person board game.

3.5   Multiple individual players versus game: Farmville 2

3.6   Player vs. Player: Boxing for Atari 2600 (right) and Soul Calibur II for Xbox (left)

Soul Calibur II © 2003 Namco Ltd. All Rights Reserved. Courtesy of Namco Holding Corp.

3.7 Unilateral competition: Scotland Yard

6. Cooperative play

This is a game structure in which two or more players cooperate against the game system. Examples include Left 4 Dead 2, Journey, Portal 2, and Fortnight: Save the World. This pattern has seen a lot of innovation lately, including the minimalist design of Journey. Designer Jenova Chen created a vast mysterious world in which two travelers meet along their respective paths.

Only able to communicate by singing out a single note, players used creative methods to convey ideas, forming deeply meaningful relationships with their fellow travelers. Portal 2's cooperative campaign required players to work together creatively to solve levels in a very rewarding fashion and Fortnite: Save the World has four players collaborating to survive as they work toward common mission objectives. It is very exciting to see more designers experiment with this interaction structure.

7. Team competition

This is a game structure in which two or more groups compete. Examples include soccer, basketball, charades, Defense of the Ancients, and Team Fortress 2. Team sports have proved the power of this pattern of player interaction over and over, not only for the players but for a whole other group of participants— the fans. As if responding to the need for this particular multiplayer pattern, teams (called clans or guilds) sprang up almost immediately upon the introduction of multiplayer and massively multiplayer digital games. The team- and class-based features in Team Fortress 2 allow for an incredible range of play styles

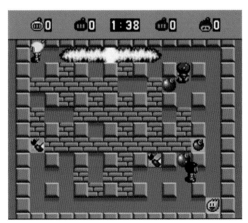 

3.8 Multilateral competition: Super Bomberman and Mario Party

3.9   Cooperative play: Journey

and modes of competition. Think about your own experiences with team play—what makes team play fun? What makes it different from individual competition? Is there an idea for a team game that comes from your answers to those questions?

Exercise 3.3: Interaction Patterns

For each of the interaction patterns, create a list of your favorite games in each pattern. If you can't think of any games in a particular pattern, research games in that area and play several of them.

3.10   Team competition: Team Fortress 2

Persuasive Games

by Ian Bogost

Ian Bogost is the Barbara and David Thomas Distinguished Professor in Arts & Sciences and Professor of Computer Science and Engineering at Washington University in St. Louis. He is also founding partner at Persuasive Games LLC. Bogost is the author of numerous books, including *Persuasive Games: The Expressive Power of Videogames, How to Do Things with Videogames,* and *Play Anything.*

How do video games express ideas? Without understanding how games can be expressive in a general sense, it is hard to understand how they might be persuasive. And how do video games make arguments? Video games are different from oral, textual, visual, or filmic media, and thus when they try to persuade, they do so in a different fashion from speech, writing, images, or moving images.

How Video Games Express Ideas

Video games are good at representing the behavior of systems. When we create video games, we start with some system in the world—traffic, football, whatever. Let's call this the "source system." To create the game, we build a model of that source system. Video games are software, so we build the model by authoring code that *simulates* the behavior we want to focus on. Writing code is different from writing prose or taking photographs or shooting video; code models a set of potential outcomes, all of which conform to the same general rules. One name for this type of representation is *procedurality* (Murray 1997); procedurality is a name for a computer's ability to execute rule-based behaviors. Video games are a kind of procedural representation.

Consider some examples: Madden Football is a procedural model of the sport of American football. It models the physical mechanics of human movement, the strategy of different sets of plays, and even the performance properties of specific professional athletes. Sim City is a procedural model of urban dynamics. It models the social behavior of residents and workers, as well as the economy, crime rate, pollution level, and other environmental dynamics.

So, in a video game, we have a source system and a procedural model of that source system. A player needs to interact with the model to make it work—video games are interactive software; they require the player to provide input to make the procedural model work. When players play, they form some idea about the modeled system and about the source system it models. They form these ideas based on the way the source system is simulated; that is to say, there might be many different ways of proceduralizing a system. One designer might build a football game about the strategy of coaching, while another might build one about the duties of a particular field position, such as a defensive lineman. Likewise, one designer might build a city simulator that focuses on public services and new urbanism (Duany, Plater-Zyberk, & Alminana 2003), while another might focus on Robert Moses-style suburban planning. This is not just a speculative observation: It highlights the fact that the source system never really exists as such. One person's idea of football or a city or any other subject for a representation of any kind is always *subjective.*

The inherent subjectivity of video games creates dissonances, gaps between the designer's procedural model of a source system and the players' subjectivity, their preconceptions and existing understanding of that simulation. This is where video games become expressive: They encourage players to interrogate and reconcile their own models of the world with the models presented in a game.

How Video Games Persuade

Most of the time, video games create procedural models of fantasy lives, like that of the pro ballplayer (Madden), or a blood elf (World of Warcraft), or a space marine (DOOM). But we can also use this facility to invite the player to see the ordinary world in new or different ways. One way to use video games in this fashion is for persuasion, to make arguments about the way the world works.

Consider a game we created at my company, Persuasive Games. Airport Insecurity (Persuasive Games 2005) is a mobile game about the Transportation Security Administration (TSA). In the game, the player takes the role of a passenger at any of the 138 most trafficked airports in the United States. The gameplay is simple: The player must progress through the security line in an orderly and dignified fashion, taking care not to lag behind when space opens in front of him, as well as to avoid direct contact with other passengers. When he reaches the x-ray check, the player must place his luggage and personal items on the belt. The game randomly assigns luggage and personal items to the player, including "questionable" items like lighters and scissors, as well as legitimately dangerous items like knives and guns.

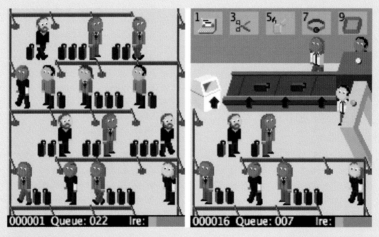

Airport Insecurity

For each airport, we gathered traffic and wait time data to model the flow of the queues, and we also gathered as much as we could find in the public record on TSA performance. Government Accountability Office (GAO) analysis of TSA performance used to be reported publicly, but the agency reportedly started classifying the information after it became clear that it might pose a national security risk. The upshot of such tactics is that the average citizen has no concept of what level of security they receive in exchange for the rights they forego. While the U.S. government wants its citizens to believe that increased protection and reduced rights are necessary to protect us from terrorism, the effectiveness of airport security practices is ultimately uncertain. The game made claims about this uncertainty by modeling it procedurally: The player got to choose if they would dispose of their dangerous items in a trash can near the x-ray belt or if they would test the limits of the screening process by carrying them through.

Consider another example, this one a live-action game played via text messaging on mobile phones in a real-world environment. Cruel 2 B Kind, which ubiquitous game researcher and designer Jane McGonigal and I created, is a modification of games like Assassin where players attempt to surreptitiously eliminate each other with predetermined weapons like water pistols. But in Cruel 2 B Kind, players "kill with kindness." Each player is assigned a "weapon" and "weakness" that corresponds with a common, even ordinary pleasantry. For example, players might compliment someone's shoes or serenade them. While Assassin is usually played in closed environments like college dorms, Cruel 2 B Kind is played in public on the streets of New York City or San Francisco or anywhere in the world.

Cruel 2 B Kind

Players not only don't know who their target is, they also don't know who is playing. In these situations, players are forced to use guesswork or deduction to figure out who they might target. As a result, players often "attack" the wrong groups of people or people who are not playing at all. The reactions to such encounters are startling for all concerned; after all, exchanging anonymous pleasantries is not something commonly done on the streets of New York. Cruel 2 B Kind asks the player to layer an alternative set of social practices atop the world they normally occupy. Instead of ignoring their fellow citizens, the game demands that players interact with them. This juxtaposition of game rules and social rules draws attention to the way people do (or more properly, don't) interact with one another in everyday life.

Disruptive and Strange

Persuasive games model ideas about the world and how it works in the subjective opinion of the game's designer. As players, we come to a video game with an idea of the world and how it works. A game presents a model of that same world, but that model has its own properties that likely differ from the player's. When we put the two models together, we can see where they converge and diverge—this is what we do when we play games critically. Procedural arguments can do just this: produce player deliberation, not by making those arguments seamless and comfortable, but rather by making them disruptive and strange.

REFERENCES

Bogost, I. *Persuasive Games: The Expressive Power of Videogames*. Cambridge: MIT Press, 2007.

Bogost, I. *Unit Operations: An Approach to Videogame Criticism*. Cambridge: MIT Press, 2006.

Duany, A., Plater-Zyberk, E. and Alminana, R. *The New Civic Art: Elements of Town Planning*. New York: Rizzoli Publications, 2003.

Murray, J. *Hamlet on the Holodeck: The Future of Narrative in Cyberspace*. New York: Free Press, 1997.

OBJECTIVES

Objectives give your players something to strive for. They define what players are trying to accomplish within the rules of the game. In the best-case scenario, these objectives seem challenging—but achievable—to the players. In addition to providing challenge, the objective of a game can set its tone. A game in which the objective is to capture or kill the opponent's forces will have a very different tone from a game in which the objective is to spell more or longer words.

Some games are constructed so that different players have different objectives, while other games allow the player to choose one of several possible objectives, and still others allow players to form their own objectives as they play. Additionally, there might be partial objectives, or mini-objectives, in a game that help the players to accomplish the main objective. In any case, the objective should be considered carefully because it affects not only the formal system of the game but also the dramatic aspects. If the objective is well integrated into the premise or story, the game can take on strong dramatic aspects.

Some questions to ask yourself about objectives as you design your own games are:

- What are some objectives of games you have played?
- What impact do these objectives have on the tone of the game?
- Do certain genres of play lend themselves to certain objectives?
- What about multiple objectives?
- Do objectives have to be explicit?
- What about player-determined objectives?

Here are some examples of objectives from games you might have played:

- *Connect Four*: Be the first player to place four units in a contiguous line on the playing grid.

- *Battleship*: Be the first player to sink all five of your opponent's battleships.
- *Mastermind*: Deduce the secret code of four colored pegs in as few steps as possible.
- *Chess*: Checkmate your opponent's king.
- *Clue*: Be the first player to deduce who, where, and how a murder was committed.
- *Super Mario Bros.*: Rescue Princess Toadstool from the evil Bowser by completing all eight worlds (32 levels) of the game, each of which has its own miniobjectives.
- *Spyro the Dragon*: Rescue your fellow dragons who have been turned to stone, and defeat the evil Gnasty Gnorc by completing all six worlds of the game, each of which has its own miniobjectives.
- *Civilization*: Option 1: conquer all other civilizations on the board, or Option 2: colonize the star Alpha Centauri.
- *The Sims*: Manage the lives of a virtual household; as long as you can keep your household alive, you can set your own goals for the game.
- *Katamari Damacy*: Gather enough material by rolling the sticky katamari ball to create stars that can repopulate the sky.
- *Gone Home*: Explore the Greenbriar family home and discover what has happened to them.
- *Pokémon Go*: Catch as many Pokémon in and around the real world as you can.

Are there any generalizations we can make about the types of objectives that might help us in our design process? A number of game scholars have made attempts to categorize games by their objectives. Here are some of the categories they defined.[4]

1. Capture

The objective in a capture game is to take or destroy something of the opponent's (terrain,

3.11 Capture or kill: SOCOM II and DOOM

units, or both), while avoiding being captured or killed. Examples of this type of game are strategy board games like chess and checkers, as well as action games like Quake, SOCOM II, and their brethren. Also in this category are real-time strategy games like the WarCraft series and Command & Conquer. There are, in fact, so many examples of games with this type of objective that it is difficult to make any generalizations. Suffice to say that the concept of capture or killing the opponent's forces is one that is deeply ingrained in games today and has been since antiquity.

2. Chase

The objective in a chase game is to catch an opponent or elude one, if you are the player being chased. Examples of chase games include tag, Fox & Geese, Assassin, and Need for Speed: Rivals. Chase games can be structured as single player versus game, player versus player, or unilateral competition. For example, tag and Fox & Geese are unilateral competitions, or one player versus many. Assassin is player versus player with each player chasing and being chased simultaneously. Need for Speed has an innovative social system that allows players to transition seamlessly between playing alone against the computer and playing online with friends. Chase games can be determined by speed or physical

dexterity, as in tag and Need for Speed, or by stealth and strategy, as in Assassin. Also, a game like Scotland Yard, discussed on page 63, is a chase game that is determined by logic and deduction. There is clearly a wealth of possibilities for games using this type of objective.

3. Race

The objective in a race game is to reach a goal—physical or conceptual—before the other players. Examples could be a footrace, a board game like Uncle Wiggly or Parcheesi, or a simulation game like Virtua Racing. Race games can be determined by physical dexterity (such as with the footrace and, to some extent, Virtua Racing) or chance (such as with Uncle Wiggly and Parcheesi). They can also be determined by a mix of strategy and chance, such as in backgammon.

4. Alignment

The objective in an alignment game is to arrange your game pieces in a certain spatial configuration or create conceptual alignment between categories of pieces. Examples include tic-tac-toe, solitaire, Connect Four, Othello, Tetris, and Bejeweled. Alignment games are often somewhat puzzle-like in that they involve solving spatial or organizational problems to achieve the goal. They can be determined by logic

3.12 Chase games: Need for Speed Rivals

Need for Speed: Rivals trademark Electronic Arts.

3.13 Race games: Pole Position and Gran Turismo 4

Pole Position © 1982 Namco Ltd. All Rights Reserved. Courtesy of Namco Holding Corp.

and calculation, as in Othello and Pente, or by chance opportunity combined with calculation, as in Tetris and Bejeweled. Conceptual alignment is used in many games that require the players to make matches or sets of game pieces.

5. Rescue or escape

The objective in a rescue or escape game is to get a defined unit or units to safety. Examples are Super Mario Bros., Prince of Persia 3D, Emergency Rescue: Firefighters, and Ico. This objective is often combined with other partial objectives. For example, in Super Mario Bros., the overall objective, as mentioned previously, is

to rescue the Princess. But each of the game levels also has their own objectives that are more puzzle-like (see Solution on page 77).

6. Forbidden Act

The objective in a forbidden act game is to get the competition to break the rules by laughing, talking, letting go, making the wrong move, or otherwise doing something they shouldn't. Examples include Twister, Operation, Ker-Plunk!, and Don't Break the Ice. This is an interesting game type that isn't often found in digital games, perhaps because of its lack of direct competition or the difficulty in monitoring fair play. From the examples, it is clear to see that there is often a physical component to games with this objective, sometimes involving stamina or flexibility, and sometimes just plain chance.

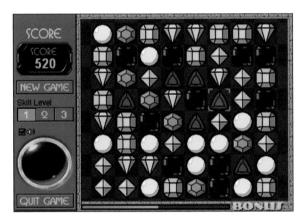

3.14   Alignment: Bejeweled

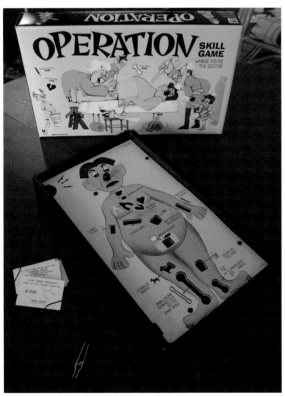

3.15   Rescue or escape: Prince of Persia 3D

3.16   Forbidden act: Milton Bradley's Operation

One interesting experimental game that has a forbidden act objective is Johan Sebastian Joust (see image on page 209 in Richard Lemarchand's sidebar on Experimental Gameplay), a physical game in which players try to hold their Sony Move controller still, while bumping and interacting with their opponents to get them to move their controllers too quickly. Anything goes, including kicking and pushing and the winner is the last player standing.

Not included in the work of the scholars mentioned previously, but interesting nonetheless, are objectives such as the following items.

7. Construction

The object in a construction game is to build, maintain, or manage objects; this might be within a directly competitive or indirectly competitive environment. This, in many instances, is a more sophisticated version of the alignment category. Examples of this type of game are simulation games like Animal Crossing, Minecraft, SimCity, or The Sims, or board games like Settlers of Catan. Games with a construction objective often make use of resource management or trading as a core gameplay element. They are usually determined by strategic choice making rather than chance or physical dexterity. Also, construction games can often be left open to player interpretation as to what ultimate success is within the game; for example, players choose what type of city to build in SimCity or household to encourage in The Sims.

8. Exploration

The object in an exploration game is to explore game areas. This is almost always combined with a more competitive objective. In the classic game of exploration, Colossal Cave Adventure, the objective is not only to explore Colossal Cave but also to find treasure along the way. In games like the Zelda series, the objectives of exploration, puzzle solving, and sometimes combat intertwine to form multifaceted gameplay. Open-world adventure games like The Elder Scrolls V: Skyrim and Grand Theft Auto V also use exploration as one of several objectives in their game structures, as do experimental games like Dear Esther or narrative games like Gone Home.

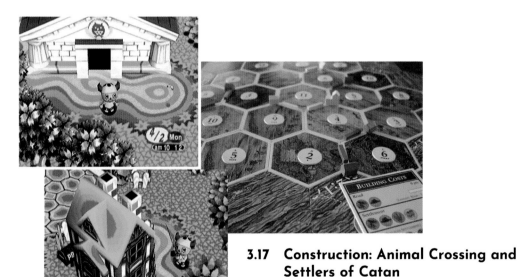

3.17   Construction: Animal Crossing and Settlers of Catan

3.18 Exploration: Dear Esther and
The Legend of Zelda: The
Wind Waker

9. Solution

The object in a solution game is to solve a problem or puzzle before (or more accurately) than the competition. Examples include graphic adventures like the Myst series, text adventures like the classic Infocom titles, and many games that fall into other categories but have puzzle qualities. These include some I have mentioned already: the Mario and Zelda games, Tetris, and The Sims. Some games of pure strategy fall into this puzzle-like category as well: Connect Four and tic-tac-toe.

3.19 Solution: Day of the Tentacle

10. Outwit

The object in a game of wits is to gain and use knowledge in a way that defeats the other players. Some games of this type focus on having extra-game knowledge, like in Trivial Pursuit or Jeopardy! Others focus on gaining or using in-game knowledge, such as Survivor and Diplomacy. This second type of game provokes interesting social dynamics, which have yet to be truly explored in digital games, though a number of real-world games use this type of objective, such as Area/Code's Identity and Ian Bogost and Jane McGonigal's Cruel 2B Kind.

3.20 Outwit: Diplomacy

Summary

This list is by no means exhaustive, and one of the most interesting things about objectives in games is when they are somewhat mixed. For example, the genre of real-time strategy mixes war with construction, forming a split focus that appeals to gamers who might not be interested in either pure war games or pure construction games. What you can do with a list like this is use it as a tool to look at the types of objectives you like in games, as well as those you do not like, and see how you might use these objectives in your own game ideas.

Exercise 3.4: Objectives

List ten of your favorite games and name the objective for each. Do you see any similarities in these games? Try to define the type or types of games that appeal to you.

PROCEDURES

As discussed in Chapter 2, procedures are the methods of play and the actions that players can take to achieve the game objectives. One way to think about procedures is: Who does what, where, when, and how?

- Who can use the procedure? One player? Some players? All the players?
- What exactly does the player do?
- Where does the procedure occur? Is the availability of the procedure limited by location?
- When does it take place? Is it limited by turn, time, or game state?
- How do players access the procedure? Directly by physical interaction? Indirectly through a controller or input device? By verbal command?

There are several types of procedures that most games tend to have:

- *Starting action*: How to put a game into play.
- *Progression of action*: Ongoing procedures after the starting action. This includes the "core loop," discussed on page 80, which is a set of activities that repeat to move the game forward.
- *Special actions*: Available conditional to other elements or game state.
- *Resolving actions*: Bring gameplay to a close.

In board games, procedures are usually described in the rule sheet and put into action by the players. In digital games, however, they are generally integrated into in the control section of the manual because they are often accessed by the player via the controls. This is an important way in which procedures differ from rules because rules might actually be hidden from the player in a digital game, as I'll discuss on page 81. Here are some examples of procedures from both a board/tabletop game and a digital game.

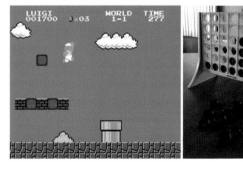

3.21   Super Mario Bros. and Connect Four

Connect Four

1. Choose a player to go first.
2. On their turn, each player drops one of their color checkers down any of the slots in the top of the grid.
3. The play alternates until one of the players gets four checkers of his color in a row. The four in a row can be horizontal, vertical, or diagonal.

Super Mario Bros.[5]

Select button: Use this button to select the type of game you wish to play.

Start button: Press this button to start the game. If you press it during play, it will pause/unpause the game.

Left arrow: Walk to the left. Push button B at the same time to run.

Right arrow: Walk to the right. Push button B at the same time to run.

Down: Crouch (Super Mario only).

A Button

Jump: Mario jumps higher if you hold the button down longer.

Swim: When in water, press this button to bob up.

B Button

Accelerate: Press this button to run. If while holding B, you press A to jump, you can jump higher.

Fireballs: If you pick up a fire flower, you can use this button to throw fireballs.

Comparison

Notice that both Connect Four and Super Mario Bros. specify a starting action. The progression of action in Connect Four is clearly shown in steps 2 and 3, while in Super Mario Bros., which is a real-time game, the progression is implied by the left and right walk commands, which move the player through the game. Connect Four doesn't have any special actions, but Super Mario Bros. has commands that are only applicable in certain situations: that is, "when in water press this button to bob up," and "if you pick up a fire flower, you can use this button to throw fireballs." Connect Four also states the resolving action: when one player gets four checkers in a row. Super Mario Bros. does not state the resolving action; this is because the resolution is adjudicated by the system, not the players.

Exercise 3.5: Procedures for Blackjack

List the procedures for blackjack. Be specific. What is the starting action? The progression of action? Any special actions? The resolving action? If you're not familiar with Blackjack, pick another traditional card game.

System Procedures

Digital games can have much more complex game states than nondigital games. They can also have multifaceted system procedures that work behind the scenes, responding to situations and player actions. In a role-playing combat system, character and weapon attributes can be used as part of a system calculation determining whether a particular player action succeeds, and if so, how much damage it causes. If the game were to be played on paper, as many role-playing games are, these system procedures need to be calculated by the players, using dice to generate random numbers. If the game is played digitally, the same system procedures are calculated by the program rather than the players.

Because of this, digital games can involve more sophisticated system procedures and process them more quickly than nondigital games. This does not mean that digital games are more complex than nondigital games. When I discuss system structures in Chapter 5 on page 134, I'll look at systems that have simple procedures, which lead to extremely complex results. For

3.22   SSX Tricky: Learn the trick procedures to score "Tricky Points"

example, games like chess or Go are nondigital systems that have intrigued players for thousands of years with their innate complexity, all of which stems from the relationship of very simple game objects and the procedures for manipulating them.

Defining Procedures

When you are defining the procedures for your game, it's important to keep in mind the limitations of the environment in which your game will be played. Will your game be played in a nondigital setting? If so, you will want to make sure the procedures are easy for players to remember. If your game will be played in a digital setting, what type of input/output devices will that setting have? Will players have a keyboard and

mouse, or will they have a proprietary controller? Will they sit close to a high-resolution screen or several feet from a low-resolution screen?

It is especially important to consider the "core loop," which, as mentioned earlier, is a special set of procedures that repeat throughout play to move the game forward. So, for example, roll the dice, move your piece, and do what it says on the square you land on is a simple core loop for a board game. In a digital game, the core loop may include checking many conditions of the game state, such as where players are in the world and if they are colliding with anything important. The core loop also checks for player input so that the system knows how to proceed—whether to move a particular player or take action on an object in the world. In an analog game, players must adjudicate the outcome of actions themselves during each cycle, so designing your core loop in such a way that players can grasp it quickly and process all of its steps easily and keep the game moving forward is important in both digital and analog games. Dan Cook discusses game loops in more detail in his sidebar on page 161.

Procedures are, by nature, affected by these constraints. As a designer, you need to be sensitive to constraints and find creative and elegant solutions so that the procedures are intuitive to access and easy to remember. These types of questions will be addressed in more detail in Chapter 8, when I discuss the prototyping of interfaces and controls for digital games.

RULES

I said in the last chapter that rules define game objects and define allowable actions by the players. Some of the questions you might ask yourself about rules are: How do players learn the rules? How are the rules enforced? What kinds of rules work best in certain situations? Are there patterns to rule sets? What can we learn from those patterns?

Like procedures, rules are generally laid out in the rules document of board games. In digital games, they can be explained in the manual or they can be implicit in the program itself. For example, a digital game might not allow certain actions without explicitly stating that fact; the interface might simply not provide controls for such an action, or the program might stop a player from performing that action if it is attempted.

Rules can also close up loopholes in the game system. One classic example of this is the famous rule from Monopoly: "Do not pass go, do not collect $200." This rule is applied when a player is sent to jail from any spot on the board. It is important because if it was not stated, a player could make the argument that moving past "go" all the way to jail entitled him to collect $200, transforming the intended punishment into a reward.

When you are designing rules, as when you are designing procedures, it's important to think of them in relation to your players. Too many rules might make it difficult for the players to manage their understanding of the game.

Leaving rules unstated or poorly communicating them might confuse or alienate players. Even if the game system (in the case of a digital game) is tracking the proper application of rules, the players need to clearly understand them so that they do not feel cheated by the consequences of certain rules.

Here are some sample rules from several different types of games that we can use as reference for the following discussion:

- *Poker*: A straight is five consecutively ranked cards; a straight flush is five consecutively ranked cards of the same suit.
- *Chess*: A player cannot move her king into check.
- *Go*: A player cannot make a move that recreates a previous state of the board—this means an exact replication of the whole board situation.
- *WarCraft II*: To create knight units, a player must have upgraded to a keep and built a stable.
- *You Don't Know Jack*: If a player answers a question incorrectly, the other players get a chance to answer.
- *Jak and Daxter*: If a player runs out of green mana, they are "knocked out" and return to the last checkpoint of the level.

Even from this short list, there are some generalities that start to emerge concerning the nature of rules, which are discussed below.

Rules Defining Objects and Concepts

Objects in games have a unique status and meaning that is totally different from objects in the real world. These game objects, defined as part of the game's rule set, can be completely fabricated, or they can be based on real-world objects. But even if they are based on familiar objects, they are only abstractions of those objects and still need to be defined in the rules as to their nature in the game.

Think about the poker rule regarding the concept of a straight or a straight flush. This is a concept unique to the game. There is no straight outside of the realm of poker. When you learn the rules of poker, one of the key concepts to learn is the makeup and values of certain hands—a straight being one of these hands.

Then again, there is chess. We know that chess has objects in its system called kings, queens, bishops, etc., all of which have counterparts in the real world. But this is misleading; the king in a chess game is an abstract object with explicit rules defining its nature. A king outside of the game bears little resemblance to this abstract game object. The rules of chess have simply used the notion of a king to give dramatic context to the behavior and value of this important piece.

Board games and other nondigital games generally define their objects explicitly as a part of their rule sets. Players must read and understand these rules, and then they have to be able to adjudicate the game themselves. Because of this, most nondigital games limit themselves to fairly simple objects, with only one or two possible variables or states for each, usually denoted by some physical aspect of the equipment, board, or other interface elements. In a board game like chess, the only variables for each piece are color and position, both of which the player can easily track visually.

Digital games, on the other hand, can have objects such as characters or fighting units that

are made up of a fairly complex set of variables that define their overall state. Players might not be aware of this entire state because, unlike a board game, the program can track the variables behind the scenes. For example, here are the default variables underlying both knights and ogres in the digital strategy game WarCraft II:

- *Cost*: 800 gold, 100 lumber
- *Hit Points*: 90
- *Damage*: 2-12
- *Armor*: 4
- *Sight*: 5
- *Speed*: 13
- *Range*: 1

While these variables are important to how the play proceeds, and they are in fact available to players via the interface, they are not something that players must directly manage and update. Even the most advanced player probably does not consistently calculate their strategy using these mathematical variables. Rather, they gain an intuitive knowledge of the knight's cost, strength, power, range, etc., versus the other units on the board through their play experience.

3.23   WarCraft II–Unit properties

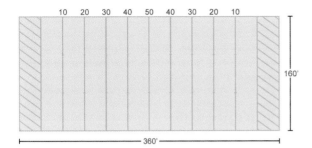

3.24   Dimensions of a football field

When defining your game objects and concepts, an essential thing to keep in mind is how players will learn the nature of these objects. If the objects are complex, will the players have to deal with that complexity directly? If the objects are simple, will players feel they are differentiated enough from each other to make an impact on the gameplay? Do the objects evolve? Are they only available under certain circumstances? How will players learn the nature of each object in the game? One interesting point to note is the way in which the laws of the physical world allow many nondigital games to compress a lot of complexity in their description of game objects. For example, the way in which the effect of gravity in Connect 4 is used to create an implicit rule about how players can place pieces on the board.

Rules Restricting Actions

The next general rule concept we can see reflected in my list of sample rules is the idea of rules restricting actions. In chess, the rule that "a player cannot move their king into check" keeps players from losing the game by accident. The example from Go where "a player cannot make a move that recreates a previous state of the board" keeps the players from becoming locked in a never ending loop of play. Both of these address potential loopholes in the game systems. Additionally, rules restricting actions can take the form of basic delimitations: "the play

3.25   Jak II—Almost out of mana

takes place on a field of 360 × 160 feet" (football) or "a team shall be composed of not more than 11 players, one of whom shall be the goalkeeper" (soccer). In both of these cases, we can see that the rules overlap with other formal aspects—namely the number of players and the boundaries of the game. This is actually true of all formal aspects, which will be represented in either the procedures or the rules in some way.

Another example of rules that restrict actions is in the type of rules that keep gameplay from becoming imbalanced in one or more players' favor. Think about the effects of the rule from WarCraft II where "in order to create knight units, a player must have upgraded to a keep and built a stable." What this means is that one player cannot simply choose to use their resources early in the game to create knights, while other players are still creating lower-level fighting units. All players must progress along a fairly similar path of resource management to gain more powerful units.

Exercise 3.6: Rules Restricting Actions

There are many types of rules that restrict action. Here is a list of games: Twister, Pictionary, Scrabble, Operation, and Pong. What rules within these games restrict player actions?

Rules Determining Effects

Rules also can trigger effects based on certain circumstances. For example, "if" something happens, there is a rule that "xyz" results. In our list of sample rules, the condition from You Don't Know Jack falls into this type of rule: "If a player answers a question incorrectly, the other players get a chance to answer." Also, this rule from Jak and Daxter is of the same quality: "If a player runs out of green mana, they are 'knocked out' and return to the last checkpoint."

Rules that trigger effects are useful for a number of reasons. First, they create variation in gameplay. The circumstances that trigger them are not always applicable, so it can create excitement and difference when they come into play. The example from You Don't Know Jack shows this quality. In this case, the second player gets a chance to answer the question, already having seen the results of the first player's guess. Because of this, they have an advantage, a higher percentage chance of answering correctly.

Additionally, this type of rule can be used to get the gameplay back on track. The rule from Jak and Daxter shows this. Because the game is not competitive in the sense that it is a single-player adventure, there is no reason for the player to "die" when they lose all their mana. However, the designers want the player to be penalized in some way so that they will take care with their actions and try to keep from losing mana. Their

solution is the previous rule: Players are penalized, but not badly, for losing all their mana. This gets the game back on track, incentivizing the players to work harder to keep their mana loss in check.

Defining Rules

As with procedures, the way in which you define your rules will be affected by your play environment. Rules need to be clear to players, or, in the case of digital games that adjudicate for players, they need to be intuitively grasped so that the game seems fair and responsive to given situations. In general, it is important to keep in mind that the more complex your rules are, the more demands you will place on the players to comprehend them. The less well that players understand your rules, whether rationally or intuitively, the less likely they will be able to make meaningful choices within the system and the less sense they will have of being in control of the gameplay.

Exercise 3.7: Rules for Blackjack

In the same way that you wrote down the procedures for blackjack in Exercise 3.5, now write down the rules. It is harder than you think. Did you remember all the rules? Try playing the game as you have written it. You might realize that you have forgotten something. What rules did you forget? How did those missing rules affect the play of the game?

RESOURCES

What exactly is a resource? In the real world, resources are assets (i.e., natural resources, economic resources, human resources) that can be used to accomplish certain goals. In a game, resources play much the same role. Most games use some form of resources in their systems, such as chips in poker, properties in Monopoly,

and gold in WarCraft. Managing resources and determining how and when to control player access to them is a key part of the game designer's job.

How does a designer decide what resources to offer to players? And how does a player control access to those resources to maintain challenge in the game? This is a hard question to answer in the abstract. It is easier if I take an example that you are probably familiar with.

Think of a role-playing game like Diablo III. What are some of the resources you might find in such a system: money, weapons, armor, potions, magic items? Why don't you find things like paper clips or pieces of sushi? While it might be fun to find such random items, the truth is, a piece of sushi won't help you to achieve the goals of the game. The very same items might actually have useful value in another game. For example, in Katamari Damacy, which was discussed in Chapter 1 on page 12, paper clips and sushi are just two of the quirky types of game resources you need to deal with. In this game, the main value of these resources lies in their size relative to your katamari, or "sticky ball." In each of these examples, the designers have carefully planned how you can find or earn the very resources that you need to accomplish the goals they have put before you. You might not find or earn as much as you would like, but if you meet the challenges the game presents, you will gain enough resources to allow you to move forward. If you did not gain these resources, the game system would be unbalanced.

By definition, resources must have both utility and scarcity in the game system. If they do not have utility, they are like our example of sushi in Diablo III: a funny and strange thing to find, but essentially useless. On the same note, if the resources are overly abundant, they will lose their value in the system.

Exercise 3.8: Utility and Scarcity

What are the resources in the games Scrabble and Call of Duty? How are they useful to players? How are they made scarce by the game system?

Many designers fall into the trap of copying existing games when it comes to resource management. One way to break your game away from

the tried and true is to think about resources in a more abstract sense. Look at the basic functions of resource types and try to apply them in new and creative ways. To illustrate what I mean, let's review some abstract examples that you should consider when designing your game.

Lives

The classic scarce resource in action games is lives. Arcade games are built on the management of this primary resource. Examples of this are games like Space Invaders or Super Mario Bros., where you have a certain number of lives to accomplish the goals of the game. Lose your lives, and you have to start over. Do well, and you earn more lives to work with. Lives as a resource type are usually implemented as part of a fairly simplistic pattern: More is always better, and there's no downside to earning lives.

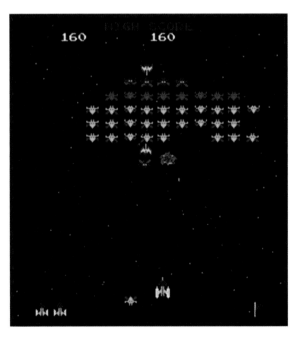

3.26 Galaxian: Two lives left

Galaxian © 1979 Namco Ltd., All Rights Reserved. Courtesy of Namco Holding Corp.

Units

In games in which the player is represented in the game by more than one object at a time, they generally have unit resources to manage rather than lives. Units can be all of one kind, as in checkers, or a number of different types, as in chess. Units can keep the same values throughout the game, or they can upgrade or evolve, as in real-time strategy games. Units can be finite (i.e., when they are lost, they are lost for good), or they can be renewable, as in games that allow players to build new units over time. When units are renewable, they often have an associated cost per unit. Determining this cost per unit and how it balances with the rest of the resource structure can be tricky. Playtesting is the one good way to determine if your cost per unit is balanced.

Health

Health can be a separate resource type, or it can be an attribute of an individual life in a game. No matter how it is thought of, when health is used as a resource, it helps to dramatize the loss or near loss of lives and units. Using a resource like health usually means that there is some way to increase health, even as it is lost as part of gameplay.

How might players raise health levels in a game? Many action games place medical kits around their levels—picking one up raises a player's health. Some role-playing games force players to eat or rest to heal their characters. Each of these methods has its uses in a particular genre. The action game uses a method that is very fast, while being somewhat unrealistic. The role-playing example is more realistic within the story aspect of the game, but it is slow and potentially frustrating to players.

Currency

One of the most powerful resource types in any game is the use of currency to facilitate trade. As we'll see in Chapter 5 on page 146, currency is one of the key elements of an in-game economy.

3.27 Checkers: Simple units

3.28 Diablo—Low health meter on lower left of screen

It is not the only way to create an economy—many games also use barter systems to accomplish the same goals. Currency in games plays the same role it does in real life: It greases the wheels of trade, making it easier for players to trade for what they need without having to barter using only the goods they have on hand. Currency need not be limited to a standard bank note system, however.

Actions

In some games, actions, such as moves or turns, can be considered resources. An example of this is the game of 20 Questions. Your questions have utility and scarcity in this system, and you have to ration them carefully to guess the answer within your limit. Another example is the phase structure of the turns in Magic: The Gathering. Each turn is made up of phases; some specific actions can be performed in each phase. Players must plan their turns carefully not to waste any potential actions.

Even real-time games can restrict actions that are too powerful, and by doing so, these actions become resources that need to be managed by the players. An example of this can be seen in Enter the Matrix, where the "focus" feature allows players to enter "bullet time," a feature that slows down the action so they can move more quickly relative to their opponents. You have only so much time to focus, however,

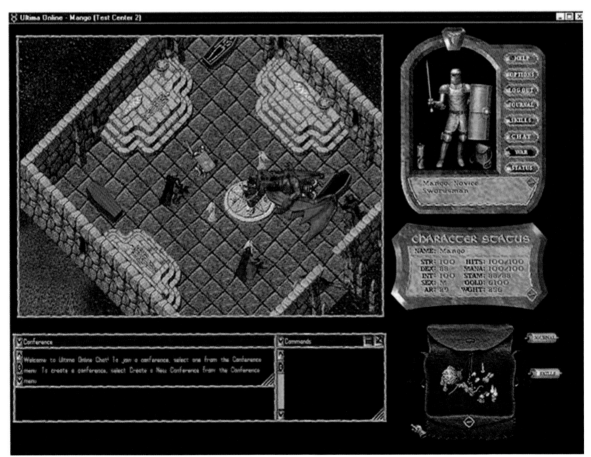

3.29 Ultima Online—Player knapsack with sack of gold

before you return to normal time. Managing the use of your focus time is a key part of gameplay.

Power-Ups

One classic type of resource is the power-up. Whether it is magic mushrooms in Super Mario Bros. or blue eco in Jak and Daxter, power-ups, as their name implies, are generally objects that give a boost of some sort to the player. This boost can increase size, power, speed, wealth, or any number of game variables. Power-up objects are generally made scarce, so that finding them doesn't make the game too easy. Power-ups are also generally temporary, limited in number, available for only a short time, or useful only in certain game states.

Inventory

Some game systems allow players to collect and manage game objects that are not power-ups or units. As a generic term, I am calling these game objects "inventory" after the way in which they are usually managed. I've already mentioned the armor, weapons, and other objects found in role-playing games such as Diablo III. These objects help players to accomplish game objectives, and they are made scarce by their high price at purchase or by the opportunity cost of finding them in dungeons guarded by more and greater monsters. The concept of an inventory of game objects is not limited to role-playing games: trading-card games like Magic: The Gathering ask players to manage their inventory

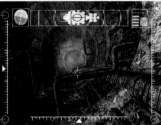

3.30   Enter the Matrix—Focus

of cards, limiting the number of cards they can have in their playing deck. Additionally, objects like ammunition or weapons can also be thought of as inventory. Like all of the other types of resources mentioned above, inventory objects must have utility and scarcity so that players are making meaningful choices when managing these objects.

Special Terrain

Special terrain is used as a resource in an important part of some game systems, especially those that are map-based systems, such as strategy games. In games like WarCraft III, the currency of the game (wood, gold, oil) is extracted from special areas of the terrain, so these areas become important primary resources. Other types of games can also use terrain as a resource in ways you might not have thought of. The triple letter squares in Scrabble are important resources found on the terrain of the game board, as are the bases on the diamond of a baseball field.

Time

Some games use time as a resource—restricting player actions by time or phases of the game in periods of time. A good example of time used as a resource can be seen in speed chess,

3.32 Scrabble—Triple letter score

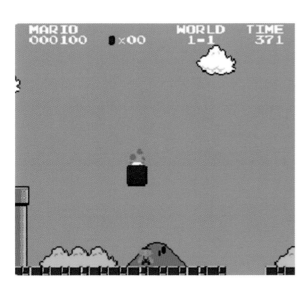

3.31 Super Mario Bros.—Magic mushroom

3.33 Chess clock

where players have a total amount of time (e.g., 10 minutes) to use over the course of a game. Players alternate turns as normal, but a game clock keeps track of each player's used time. Other examples of time as a resource are the children's games hot potato and musical chairs. In each of these cases, players struggle not to be "it," whether that means holding the hot potato or being the only one without a chair, when the time is up. Time is an inherently dramatic force when used as a resource. We are all familiar with the tension of a countdown deadline or the anticipation caused by a ticking bomb in an action movie. When used as a resource that players must ration or work against, time can add an emotional aspect to a game design.

Exercise 3.9: Resource Types

For each of the resource types just described, create a list of your favorite games that use resources of that type. If you can't think of any games that use a particular type of resource, research games that do and play several of them.

These are just some of the resource types that you should think about using when designing your own games. Challenge yourself to both create your own original types of resources and take resource models from one genre and adapt them to games where they're seldom, if ever, used. You might be surprised with the results.

CONFLICT

Conflict emerges from the players trying to accomplish the goals of the game within its rules and boundaries. As I have already mentioned, conflict is designed into the game by creating rules, procedures, and situations (such as multiplayer competition) that do not allow players to accomplish their goals directly. Instead, the procedures offer fairly inefficient means toward accomplishing the game objective. While inefficient, these means challenge the players by forcing them to employ a particular skill or range of skills. The procedures also create a sense of competition or play, which is enjoyable in some way, so that players will submit themselves to this inefficient system to gain the ultimate sense of achievement that comes from participating.

3.34   Pong and Quake III opponents

Here are some examples of things that cause game conflicts to emerge:

- *Pinball*: Keep the ball from escaping the field of play using only the flippers or other devices provided.
- *Golf*: Get the ball from the tee to the hole, past any obstacles on the course, in as few strokes as possible.
- *Monopoly*: Manage your money and your properties to become the richest player in a tightly constrained real estate market.
- *Quake*: Stay alive while player or nonplayer opponents try to kill you.
- *WarCraft III*: Maintain your forces and resources while using them to command and control the map objectives.
- *Poker*: Outbid opponents based on your hand or your ability to bluff.

These examples point to three classic sources of conflict in games: obstacles, opponents, and dilemmas. Let's look at each of these more closely to see what they offer in terms of various types of gameplay.

Obstacles

Obstacles are a common source of conflict in both single- and multiplayer games, though they play a more important role in single-player games. Obstacles can be physical or conceptual in nature. And they can require different types of skills or resources to overcome. Examples of physical obstacles would be the sack in a sack race, the water on a golf course, or the bumpers on a pinball table. Examples of conceptual obstacles would be rules that constrain our behavior, like not speaking the answer aloud in charades or not moving our golf ball from a bad location in golf. Overcoming obstacles may require very specific actions, like a double jump in a platforming game, or unique skills like the mental acuity to solve the puzzles in an adventure game.

Opponents

In multiplayer games, other players are typically the primary source of conflict. In the previous examples, Quake uses other players in addition to nonplayer opponents and physical obstacles to create conflict in the game. Also, Monopoly's conflict comes from interactions with other players.

Dilemmas

As opposed to physical or mental obstacles and conflict from direct competition with other players, another type of game conflict can come from dilemma-based choices that players have to make. An example of a dilemma in Monopoly is the choice of whether to spend money to buy a property or use that money to upgrade a property that is already owned. Another dilemma would be whether to stay in or fold in poker. In both cases, players have to make choices that have a range of potential consequences. A dilemma can be a powerful source of conflict in both single- and multiplayer games.

Exercise 3.10: Conflict

Explain how conflict is created in the following games: Tetris, Frogger, Bomberman, Minesweeper, and solitaire. Does the conflict in these games come from obstacles, opponents, dilemmas, or a combination of these?

BOUNDARIES

Boundaries are what separate the game from everything that is not the game. As discussed on page 38, the act of agreeing to play, to accept the rules of the game, to enter what Huizinga calls the "magic circle" is a critical part of feeling safe that the game is temporary, that it will end, or that you can leave or quit if you don't want to play anymore. As a designer, you must define the boundaries of the game and how players will enter and exit the magic circle. These boundaries can be physical—like the edges of an arena, playing field, or game board—or they can be conceptual, such as a social agreement to play. For example, ten people can be physically sitting in a room where Truth or Dare is being played, but two of them might not have agreed to play and are therefore outside the boundaries of the system.

Why are boundaries an important aspect of game design to consider? Think about what might happen if there were no boundaries in a familiar game system. Imagine a game like football. What if you tried to play football (either in a physical setting or on a computer) without boundaries? Players could run anywhere they wanted to; they could run as far as they could physically get without being tackled by the other team or blocked by random objects like buildings or cars. What does this do to the strategy of football? What about the abilities necessary for play? Apply this line of thinking to other games you know. Can you see how they would be intrinsically different if their boundaries were not closed? What if you could add real money to the bank in Monopoly? Or if you could add cards to the deck in poker? What if the edges of a chess board were infinitely expanding? It is clear without even playing these games that without their boundaries, they would become totally different games. This is not necessarily a bad thing—an interesting design exercise would be to take a familiar game and change its boundaries to see how it affects the play experience.

3.35   Boundaries of a tennis court

In addition to the purely formal aspect for game boundaries, however, there's also an emotional one. The boundaries of the game serve as a way to separate everything that goes on in the game from daily life. So while you might act the part of a cutthroat opponent facing off against your friends within the boundaries of a game (taking over their civilizations or destroying their forces), you can shake hands at the end of the game and walk away without any real damage to your relationships. In fact, you might feel closer to them, having met in this game-world competition.

As designers, boundaries are another tool we have in crafting the player experience. Some games are very free form and do not require strictly defined boundaries to work. For example, tag is usually played with loosely defined boundaries with no detriment to the overall experience. Recent game designers have begun playing with the idea that interaction with outside elements is an interesting design choice for their systems. The genre of games called alternate reality games (ARGs) use a combination of real-world and online interaction to create their game play.

THE MECHANIC IS THE MESSAGE

by Brenda Romero

Brenda Romero is an award-winning game designer, artist, writer and Fulbright scholar who has worked in the game industry since 1981. As a designer, she has contributed to many seminal titles, including the Wizardry and Jagged Alliance series and titles in the Ghost Recon and Dungeons & Dragons franchises. Her analog series of six games, The Mechanic is the Message, has drawn national and international acclaim and is housed in the National Museum of Play.

The Mechanic is the Message is a collection of seven analog games designed to answer a question, "Can game mechanics capture and express difficult emotions like photographs, paintings, music, and books?" The answer may seem an obvious and resounding, "Yes!" but in video games, we often communicate deeper meaning through text, cut scenes, and other graphical means. In this series of games, and taking a formalist view, I wanted the meaning to arise from the mechanics instead. After all, mechanics are the one thing that makes a game a game.

The series began in February 2007 when my daughter Maezza, then 7, came home from school and discussed her day with me. "What did you learn about today?" I asked her. "The Middle Passage," she replied. I stopped what I was doing and focused on her exclusively. Maezza's father is half black, half Irish, and as such, the Middle Passage is an important part of her personal history. "How did you feel about that?" I asked. She went on to discuss the Middle Passage with a memory that would have made any parent or teacher proud, naming names and citing key moments in abolition. What was missing, however, was any sense of emotion or connection. She was only 7, so I wasn't expecting her to fall apart, but still, some sense of connection, of empathy, seemed appropriate given the gravity of the topic. When she finished her list of buzzwords, she looked toward her game console and asked, "Can I play a game, Mommy?"

"Sure," I said. Impulsively, I grabbed a bunch of wooden pawns, some paint and a few brushes and set them in front of her. As a game designer, I often prototype my games in the analog, so am fortunate to have a home loaded with all kinds of game-making goods. "Make me some families. Use different colors," I said. So, she started. She made a blue family, a pink family, a yellow family. Nearly an hour had passed when I approached her, grabbed some of the pawns and put them on a boat (an index card). Next to the boat, I placed a pile of pennies that would serve as food. "Wait," she said. "You forgot the mommy." She picked it up and put it on the boat. See, I'd grabbed people at random, and as such, I'd neglected to grab every member of the affected families. I put the pawn back. "She wants to go," said Maezza, returning the mommy to the boat. I was insistent. "No one wants to go," I told her. "This is the Middle Passage." She looked at me in a way that only a game designer's child can look, as if to say, "Your prototype is broken. Your rules don't make sense, but okay. I'll go along."

The rules of the game were simple: It takes 10 turns to cross the ocean. Each turn, we roll a die to see how much food we use. We were about halfway through the trip, and Maezza was rolling high. "I don't think we're going to make it," she said. "What do we do?" She had reached a turning point.

"We can keep going and hope we make it, or we can put some people in the water," I answered. She was seven, so I didn't want to hit her over the head with it, but I didn't want to hide the reality from her either. She understood precisely what I meant. She stared at the boat for a bit, the opposing shores on the opposite sides of the table and finally asked, "Did this really happen, Mommy?"

After Black History Month at school, after movies, after books, after posters, after lectures, it was finally the mechanics of a simple and spontaneous game and the time she took to experience it (the time in the "magic circle") that brought the connection home. That day ended with our family discussing the Middle Passage at length and on a very personal level.

I was determined to repeat the experience, and decided to make a series of six games, each of which focused on a different difficult moment in human history. I've covered the Cromwellian Invasion of Ireland (Síochán Leat), the Trail of Tears (One Falls for Each of Us), Mexican immigration (Mexican Kitchen Workers) and daily life in Haiti (Cité Soliel). The game that is perhaps the best known of the series is Train.

Train

Train is a three-player game in which you are tasked with getting passengers from the start of the rail line to its terminus. The game consists of 3 tracks (one for each player), 60 pawns and 6 train cars. Each turn, you may roll a die to add passengers or to move the train that many spaces, or you may select or play a card. Players typically roll the die and add passengers on their first turn before beginning their trek down the track on their next roll. The cards allow players to speed up or slow down the movement of the trains. The rules for Train, however, are not quite so black and white. There is ambiguity written into them on purpose. For instance, if the player opts to play the Derail card, it forces them to return half the passengers to the beginning station, and further says the others refuse to re-board. What does the player do with those pawns? The game doesn't say. The players have to figure it out for themselves.

Some players have declared them dead; others have left them there at the side of the track only to add them via die roll later. Still others have grabbed them, declared them "free" and announced that they were going to Denmark. As the game's designer, I was acutely aware of the possibility space surrounding the game. Every line in the rules permitted or prohibited some behavior, and I considered each line again and again. I wanted players to explore that possibility space ("The rules don't say I *can't* do it!"), find their way within it and thus find their own complicity or salvation. At the end of the tracks, at the terminus, the player draws a card, which tells them where they've delivered their passengers. Each is labeled with the name of a Nazi extermination camp. It's a grim and jarring moment for players. Some have cried. Many gasp. Others recognize the symbolism in the game (the tracks rest atop a broken window with smashed glass which symbolizes Kristallnacht), the pawns are yellow and the trains are boxcars, and realize these trains are going nowhere good. They begin to derail their own cars to free people, puzzling their fellow players.

For me, the key design moment in games comes in finding the system I want to represent. Systems are inherent in everything around us, from how we get to school to the classes we take to the grades we receive. With my games and particularly my games that focus on difficult subjects, I look for the systems that allow the event to happen in the first place, and human-on-human tragedy at such a scale always requires such a system. Then, I decide how I want that person to feel as a direct result of interacting with the system. This is, perhaps, the most important decision I make.

In Síochán Leat, for instance, I want the player to feel the powerlessness of the English onslaught while gradually being forced to turn on their fellow Irish countrymen in order to survive. Train questions the player's complicity. Will we blindly follow the rules even if we pull those rules from a Nazi typewriter? Will we stand by and watch when we know that what's being done is inherently evil? In One Falls for Each of Us, my game about the Trail of Tears, I want the player to feel the power of systems to overtake us, to envelop our thinking. The game features 50,000 individual pieces (one for Each of Us), and at a single glance, the player is both overwhelmed and systemic in their thinking, "How will I ever move all this?" The mechanics that I choose reinforce the player's role in the system. In fact, the role creates the mechanics for me. If you're transporting passengers, the rules of doing that suggest themselves. I never force mechanics or accept mechanics that compromise the larger system. They integrate naturally, controlling the player's behavior and giving meaning to the role the game dictates they play. Mechanics also allow the player room to find their own emergent way, imparting tremendous meaning. With Train, for instance, one player wanted to find peace with his family's past. The game, he told me, allowed him to do that. I don't know what his family's past was, but the rules, being only rules, allow the player to fill the game with their own meaning instead of just the one dictated by the designer. Mechanics, when integrated in such a way, do not need cut scenes to tell players how to feel.

Why is it important to make games with meaning in their mechanics? Why is the mechanic the message? For me, pure mechanic is pure player. There is nothing else—no story, no cut scene, no text, no outside influence—to accept responsibility for what has happened. The player followed the rules and the result and resultant meaning is theirs alone. To the exact extent that the rules allow them, they accept their role and change the world state as a result. There are no procedural gaps for exposition—the metaphorical equivalent of a driver jumping into the backseat for someone else (the cut scene) to take over for a while. Instead, the player drives the game from beginning to end.

An early example of this was I Love Bees, an ARG created to promote the release of Halo 2. The game, which was accessed at the website www.ilovebees.com, sent players to real-world locations to find ringing pay phones where they would receive further information and instructions. See Elan Lee's comments on the design of I Love Bees in his Designer Perspective on page 290. Other games that break physical and conceptual boundaries are sometimes called "big games," large-scale games that take over public spaces for playful interactions. Games like the Big Urban Game by Frank Lantz, Katie Salen, and Nick Fortugno; Humans vs. Zombies by Chris Weed and Brad Sappington; or the viral folk game Ninja, which has been popularized on college campuses and indie game festivals, are examples of this type of boundary-breaking play. Also, mobile games like Zombies, Run!, discussed in Adrian Hon's sidebar in Chapter 15 on page 502, are able to use information about the player's location and movement to integrate gameplay with real-world interaction.

The way that these experimental games treat the boundaries of their systems are exciting innovations, though they are something of an exception at this time. Most games are typically closed systems. These games clearly define that which is within the game versus that which is outside the game, and they purposefully keep the in-game elements from interacting with outside forces. But it is up to you as the game designer to determine just where and how these boundaries are defined and when or if to ever breach them, and it is an interesting challenge in game design to consider how your game might be enhanced by opening its boundaries, or making them semi-permeable to real-world information or actions.

Exercise 3.11: Boundaries

What are the boundaries in the tabletop role-playing game Dungeons & Dragons? Can you think of physical and conceptual boundaries?

© Doug Jaeger, 2004 - doctorjaeger.com

3.36   Big Urban Game and PacManhattan—Turning cities into game boards

OUTCOME

As described previously, the outcome of a game must be uncertain to hold the attention of the players. That uncertainty is generally resolved in a measurable and unequal outcome, though this is not always necessary: Many massively multiplayer online worlds do not have the concept of a winner or even an end state. Also, simulation games might not have a predetermined win condition. Some games are designed to be played indefinitely. These games are built to reward players in other fashions than by winning or finishing the game. Though some people might not call these games because they differ from the basic definition, I don't find it useful to remove these powerful experiences from our consideration of games. Rather, I believe that expanding our definition or exploring the border cases makes for a more interesting and useful stance.

For traditional game systems, however, producing a winner or winners is the end state of a game. At defined intervals, either the players (in the case of a nondigital game) or the system check to see if a winning state has been

achieved. If it has, the system resolves and the game is over.

There are a number of ways to determine outcome, but the structure of the final outcome will always be related to both the player interaction patterns discussed on page 63 and the objective. For example, in pattern one, single player versus game, the player might either win or lose, or the player might score a certain amount of points before ultimately losing. Examples of this outcome structure are solitaire, pinball machines, or a number of different arcade games.

Additionally, the outcome is determined by the nature of the game objective. A game that defines its objective based on points will most certainly use those points in the measure of the outcome. A game that defines its objective as capture, like chess, might not have a scoring system—rather, chess games are won or lost based solely on meeting the primary objective, capturing the king.

Chess is what is called a "zero-sum" game. By this I mean that if we count a win as +1 and a loss as a −1, then the sum for any outcome is zero. In chess, one player wins (+1), and one player loses (−1). No matter which player wins, the sum is always zero.

But many games are not zero-sum games; a non-zero-sum game is one in which the overall gains and losses for the players can be more than or less than zero. Games such as World of Warcraft are not zero sum because the overall outcome of this complex, ongoing game world is never equal to zero. Cooperative games, such as the Lord of the Rings board game by Reiner Knizia, are also non-zero sum because a gain by one player does not mean a loss by the others. Narrative games, such as Gone Home, are also non-zero sum because they are not competitive in nature. Non-zero sum games often have more subtle gradations of reward and loss than zero-sum games, for example, ranking systems, player statistics, multiple objectives, or even player-created objectives, all of which can create

measurable outcomes without the finite judgment of a zero-sum game.

On page 382, I discuss the way in which non-zero-sum games can create interesting player dilemmas and complex, interdependent risk/reward scenarios that can make for interesting gameplay. Look at the games you play: What types of outcomes are most satisfying? Does that answer change in different situations, for example, mobile social games versus sporting events? When you determine the outcome for a game that you are designing, be sure to keep these types of considerations in mind.

Exercise 3.12: Outcome

Name two zero-sum games and two non-zero-sum games. What is the main difference in the outcomes of these games? How does this affect gameplay?

CONCLUSION

These formal elements, when set in motion, create what we recognize as a game. As we have seen throughout this chapter, there are many possible combinations of these elements that work to create a wide variety of experiences. By understanding how these elements work together and thinking about new ways of combining these elements, you can invent new types of gameplay for your games. A good practice for a beginning game designer is to use these formal elements to analyze games that you play. Use the game journal you began in Chapter 1 to start a record of your analysis of the games you

play. This will increase both your understanding of gameplay and your ability to articulate complex game concepts.

Exercise 3.13: Revise Rules and Procedures

The rules and procedures of backgammon are fairly simple. Change them so that they are not dependent on chance. You will need to design a new system for defining player movement in order to do this. Play your new design. How does this affect the player experience?

DESIGNER PERSPECTIVE: DEREK YU

President, Mossmouth

Derek Yu is an indie game developer and artist notable for developing Spelunky 2 (2020), Spelunky (2012), Spelunky Classic (2008), Aquaria (2007), and Eternal Daughter (2002) and for editing the indie developer website TIGSource.

How did you become a game designer?

As a kid, I spent many hours designing games on paper with my friends and I like to think that those were my first steps as a game designer! Eventually, I started to bring my ideas to life with DOOM editors, BASIC programming, Klik & Play, graphing calculators... whatever I could work with. By continuing to make games and sharing them online, I met other game developers and got involved with indie game communities like TIGSource. That's what led to me pursuing it full time after I graduated college.

On games that have inspired him:

Nintendo's games have influenced me a lot as a designer. I'm always inspired by how tactile their games feel, as well as the creative connections they make between themes and mechanics. On the other hand, as I've gotten older, I've come to realize that I prefer games that are less forgiving of mistakes, because my participation as a player feels more meaningful to me when the consequences are larger. So that's an area where I've been inspired by them to move in a different direction.

To be honest, though, I'm inspired by many games, big and small, and I never know where an interesting idea will come from. Spelunky is partly inspired by the classic roguelike NetHack, which I was fascinated by as a kid, but it's also inspired by a relatively obscure Japanese game I've only read about, called Kagirinaki Tatakai. Kagirinaki Tatakai was an early example of destructible terrain in side-view action games and the description alone stirred my imagination.

But the process of making games is as important to design as the designs themselves, and in that regard, I've been most inspired by other small developers, from the early shareware pioneers like id Software to my peers in the indie scene today.

On exciting developments in the industry:

I'm most excited by the growth of streaming, content creation, and the preservation of video game history. This obviously helps me learn about as many games as possible as a designer, but I also love just being a fan of the artform, especially its niche corners. These days, I almost always have a stream or video on in the background as I work.

On design process:

Ideas can hit at any time and from any direction. It can be something that interests me thematically or a game mechanic that seems promising. I have a document that I jot ideas onto, no matter how silly or fleeting they may seem. Sometimes it's just a fragment of an idea or a word I like the sound of.

Most of the time, I have a big project that I'm committed to working on for several years, but whenever I need a break from that, I'll go into my brainstorming document and play in there a bit. I might, for example, add some details somewhere or consolidate similar concepts into a single section. I think of the ideas as little amoebas that can stick together to become something bigger. So, the document is like a primordial spawning ground for games in that sense!

Working on the document has the added benefit of preparing me for post-release so there's no "back to the drawing board" moment after my current game comes out. I also use it as a way to "flush out" new game ideas from my head so that I can focus on the task at hand.

On prototypes:

I don't set out to make prototypes — I set out to make complete games! However, like most designers, I still end up abandoning a lot of projects because the ideas don't work well in practice or because I don't enjoy the development process. Only then do I call them prototypes.

This way of thinking about prototypes is probably a consequence of my development style, which I'd describe as intuition-based and action-oriented. I'm wary of overthinking designs and losing the personality of ideas by over-polishing them.

On a difficult design problem:

A type of design problem that I face a lot is when a player has found a too-powerful exploit and the obvious solution is to simply prevent them from doing it by adding a proverbial (or sometimes literal) lock to the door. The lock "solves" the problem, but at the cost of the player's feeling of freedom and agency. There are times when I've had to lock the door, but in general I'd rather retain the exploit and add trade-offs that make it less clear when it's useful.

What are you most proud of in your career?

I'm proud that I've worked on games that have brought people together to play, laugh, create memories, and form communities. This includes the players, of course, but also the other great people I've worked with over the years. I couldn't ask for anything more as a creator and I'm grateful for all these opportunities!

Advice for designers:

My advice to aspiring designers is to practice breaking the things they enjoy into components and try to understand how those components connect. It's easy to be inspired by only one or two games and not understand which connections truly work well together and which connections are more of a stylistic choice. Once you learn how to break things down and separate the pieces, you can start putting them together in ways that are unique to you, which maybe no one else has done before.

FURTHER READING

Adams, Ernest and Dormans, Joris. *Game Mechanics: Advanced Game Design.* Berkeley: New Riders, 2012.

Callois, Roger. *Man, Play and Games.* Urbana: University of Chicago Press, 2001.

Church, Doug. Formal abstract design tools. *Game Developer Magazine.* August, 1999.

Dhule, Maithili. *Exploring Game Mechanic: Principles and Techniques to Make Fun, Engaging Games.* Berkeley: Apress L.P.

Hunicke, Robin, LeBlanc, Marc and Zubek, Robert. MDA: A Formal Approach to Game Design and Game Research. *AAAI Game AI Workshop Proceedings.* July 25-26, 2004. Available online at http://www.cs.northwestern.edu/~hunicke/pubs/MDA.pdf

Salen, Katie and Zimmerman, Eric. *The Game Design Reader: A Rules of Play Anthology.* Cambridge: The MIT Press, 2006.

END NOTES

1. Bartle, Richard. "Hearts, Clubs, Diamonds, Spades: Players who Suit MUDS." April 1996. http://www.mud.co.uk/richard/hcds.htm

2. Yee, Nick et al. "Quantic Foundry Motivational Model." Quantic Foundry, accessed 8/23/2023, https://quanticfoundry.com/#motivation-model

3. Avedon, E.M., "The Structural Elements of Games," *The Study of Games.* New York: Robert E. Krieger Publishing, Inc. 1979. pp. 424-425.

4. Adapted from the work of Fritz Redl, Paul Gump, and Brian Sutton-Smith, "The Dimensions of Games," *The Study of Games.* New York: Robert E. Krieger Publishing, Inc., 1979., pp. 417-418; David Parlett, The Oxford History of Boardgames. New York: Oxford University Press, 1999.

5. Nintendo, Super Mario Bros. Manual, 1986.

Chapter 4
Working with Dramatic Elements

Exercise 4.1: Making Checkers Dramatic

The game of checkers is very abstract: There is no story, no characters, and no compelling reason why you would want to capture all of your opponent's pieces, except for the fact that it's the objective of the game.

For this exercise, devise a set of dramatic elements for checkers that make the game more emotionally engaging. For example, you might create a backstory, give each piece its own name and distinctive look, define special areas on the board, or whatever creative ideas you can think of to connect the players to this simple, abstract system. Now play your new game with friends or family and note their reactions. How do the dramatic elements improve or detract from the experience?

We have seen how formal elements work together to create the experience we recognize as a game, but now let's turn to those elements that engage the players emotionally with the game experience and invest them in its outcome—the dramatic elements of games. Dramatic elements give context to gameplay, overlaying and integrating the formal elements of the system into a meaningful experience. Basic dramatic elements, like challenge and play, are found in all games. More complicated dramatic techniques, like premise, character, and story, are used in many games to explain and enhance the more abstract elements of the formal system, creating a deeper sense of connection for the players and enriching their overall experiences.

One way to create more engaging games is to study how these elements work to create engagement and how they've been used in other games—as well as other media. Your exploration of these dramatic elements and traditional tools can help you think of new ideas and new situations for your own designs.

Exercise 4.2: Dramatic Games

Name five games that you find dramatically interesting. What is it about those games that you find compelling?

DOI: 10.1201/9781003460268-5

CHALLENGE

Most people would agree that one thing that engages them in a game is challenge. What do they really mean by challenge, though? They don't simply mean that they want to be faced with a task that is hard to accomplish. If that were true, the challenge of games would hold little difference from the challenges of everyday life. When players talk of challenge in games, they're speaking of tasks that are satisfying to complete, that require just the right amount of work to create a sense of accomplishment and enjoyment.

Because of this, challenge is very individualized and is determined by the abilities of the specific player in relationship to the game. A young player who is just learning to count might find a game of Chutes and Ladders particularly challenging, while an adult who mastered that skill long ago would probably find it boring.

In addition to being individualized, challenge is also dynamic. A player might find one task challenging at the beginning of a game, but after becoming accomplished in the task, they'll no longer find it challenging. So the game must adapt to remain challenging and hold the interest of the more accomplished player.

Is there a way to look at challenge that is not defined by individual experience? One that can give us some general ideas to keep in mind when designing a game? When you set out to create the basic challenge in your game, you might start by thinking how people really enjoy themselves and which types of activities make them happy. As it turns out, the answer to this question is directly related to the concept of challenge and the level of challenge presented by an experience.

The psychologist Mihaly Csikszentmihalyi set out to identify the elements of enjoyment by studying similarities of experience across many different tasks and types of people. What he found was surprising: Regardless of age, social class, or gender, the people he talked to

described enjoyable activities in much the same way. The activities themselves spanned many different disciplines, including performing music, climbing rocks, painting, and playing games, but the words and concepts people used to describe their enjoyment of them were similar. In all these tasks, people mentioned certain conditions that made the activities pleasurable for them:

First, the experience (of enjoyment) usually occurs when we confront tasks we have a chance of completing. Second, we must be able to concentrate on what we are doing. Third and fourth, the concentration is usually possible because the task undertaken has clear goals and provides immediate feedback. Fifth, one acts with a deep but effortless involvement that removes from awareness the worries and frustrations of everyday life. Sixth, enjoyable experiences allow people to exercise a sense of control over their actions. Seventh, concern for the self disappears, yet paradoxically the sense of self emerges stronger after the flow experience is over. Finally, the sense of the duration

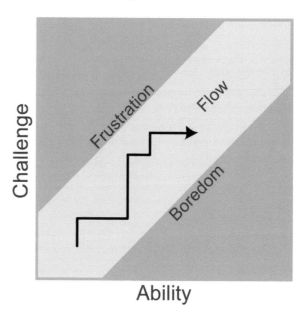

4.1   Flow diagram

of time is altered; hours pass by in minutes, and minutes can stretch out to seem like hours. The combination of all these elements causes a sense of deep enjoyment that is so rewarding people feel like expending a great deal of energy is worthwhile simply to be able to feel it.[1]

Based on his findings, Csikszentmihalyi created a theory called "flow," which is illustrated in Figure 4.1. When a person begins performing an activity, they usually have a low level of ability. If the challenge of the activity is too high, they will become frustrated. As they continue on, their ability rises, however, and if the challenge level stays the same, they will become bored. Figure 4.1 shows a path of rising challenge and ability balanced carefully between frustration and boredom, which would result in an optimal experience for a user.

If the level of challenge remains appropriate to the level of ability, and if this challenge rises as the ability level rises, the person will stay in the center region and experience a state that Csikszentmihalyi calls "flow." In flow, an activity balances a person between challenge and ability, frustration and boredom, to produce an experience of achievement and happiness. This concept is very interesting for game designers because this balance between challenge and ability is exactly what we are trying to achieve with gameplay. Let's look more closely at the elements that help to achieve flow.

A Challenging Activity That Requires Skill

According to Csikszentmihalyi, flow occurs most often within activities that are "goal-directed and bounded by rules...that could not be done without the proper skills."[2] Skills might be physical, mental, social, etc. For a person who does not have any of the skills a task requires, it is not challenging, but meaningless. For a person who has the skills but is not completely assured of the outcome, a task is challenging. This is particularly important to game design.

4.2   An activity that requires skill: Tony Hawk Pro Skater

Exercise 4.3: Skills

List the types of skills required by the games you enjoy. What other types of skills do people enjoy that you could incorporate into the games you design?

The Merging of Action and Awareness

"When all of a person's relevant skills are needed to cope with the challenges of a situation, that person's attention is completely absorbed by the activity," Csikszentmihalyi goes on to say. "People become so involved in what they're doing that the activity becomes spontaneous, almost automatic; they stop being aware of themselves as separate from the actions they are performing."[3]

Clear Goals and Feedback

In everyday life, there are often contradictory demands on us; our goals are not always clearly defined. But in flow experiences, we know what needs to be done, and we get immediate feedback on how well we're achieving our goals. For

4.3   Merging action and awareness: Metal Gear Solid 3

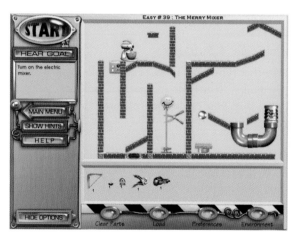

4.4   Clear goals and feedback: Incredible Machine: Even More Contraptions

example, musicians know what notes to play next and can hear when they make mistakes; the same is true whether it's playing tennis or rock climbing. When a game has clearly defined goals, the players know what needs to be done to win, to move to the next level, to achieve the next step in their strategy, etc., and they receive direct feedback for their actions toward those goals.

Exercise 4.4: Goals and Feedback

Pick three games and list the types of feedback generated in each. Then describe how the feedback relates to the ultimate goal of each game.

Concentration on the Task at Hand

Another typical element of flow is that we are aware only of what's relevant here and now. If a musician thinks of his health or tax problems when playing, he is likely to hit a wrong note. If a surgeon's mind wanders during an operation, the patient's life is in danger. In game flow, the

4.5   Concentration on the task: League of Legends

players are not thinking of what is on television or how much laundry they have to do; they are focused entirely on the challenges presented in the game. Many game interfaces take over the entire screen of the PC or build impressive audio-visual worlds to focus our attention. Here is a quote from a mountaineer describing a flow experience (but these might as well be the words of an League of Legends player): "You're not aware of other problematic life situations. It becomes a world unto its own, significant only to itself. It's a concentration thing. Once you're in the situation, it's incredibly real, and you're very much in charge of it. It becomes your total world."[4]

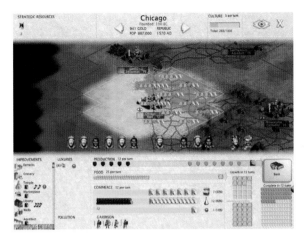

4.6 Paradox of control: Civilization 3

The Paradox of Control

People enjoy the sense of exercising control in difficult situations; however, it is not possible to experience a feeling of control unless the outcome is unsure, meaning that the person is not actually in complete control. As Csikszentmihalyi says, "Only when a doubtful outcome is at stake, and one is able to influence that outcome, can a person really know she is in control."[5] This "paradox of control" is a key element of the enjoyment of game systems. How to offer meaningful choices to players, without offering complete control or an assured outcome, is a subject I will return to many times throughout this book.

The Loss of Self-Consciousness

In everyday life, we are always monitoring how we appear to other people and protecting our self-esteem. In flow, we are too involved in what we're doing to care about protecting the ego. "There is no room for self-scrutiny. Because enjoyable activities have clear goals, stable rules, and challenges well matched to skills, there is little opportunity for the self to be threatened."[6] Although the flow experience is so engrossing that we forget our self-consciousness while we

4.7 Loss of self-consciousness: Dance Dance Revolution

are engaged in it, after a flow activity is over, we generally emerge with a stronger self-concept. We know that we have succeeded in meeting a difficult challenge. So, for example, the musician feels at one with the harmony of the cosmos; the athlete moves at one with the team; the game player feels empowered by the efficacy of her strategies. Paradoxically, the self expands through acts of self-forgetfulness.

The Transformation of Time

"One of the most common descriptions of optimal experience is that time no longer seems to pass the way it ordinarily does," says Csikszentmihalyi. "Often hours seem to pass by in minutes; in general, most people report that time seems to pass much faster. But occasionally the reverse occurs:

Ballet dancers describe how a difficult turn that takes less than a second in real time stretches out for what seems like minutes."[7] Digital games are notorious for sucking players in for hours on end because they involve players in flow experiences that distort the passage of time.

Experience Becomes an End in Itself

When most of these conditions are present, we begin to enjoy whatever it is that produces such an experience and the activity becomes auto-telic, which is Greek for something that is an end in itself. Most things in life are exotelic. We do them not because we enjoy them but to achieve some goal. Some activities such as art, music, sports, and games are usually autotelic: There is no reason for doing them except to enjoy the experience they provide.

These elements of enjoyment are not a step-by-step guide to creating enjoyable, challenging game experiences; you need to work out for yourself what these ideas mean in the context of your own games. But the focus that Csikszentmihalyi places on goal-oriented, rule-driven activities with clear focus and feedback are clues that might point you in a beneficial direction.

Think about questions like these as you design your game:

- What skills does your target audience have? What skill level are they at? Within that knowledge, how can you best balance your game for your players' abilities?

- How can you give your players clear, focused goals, meaningful choices, and discernible feedback?

- How can you merge what a player is doing physically with what they need to be thinking about in the game?

- How can you eliminate distractions and fear of failure; that is, how can you create a safe environment where players lose their sense of self-consciousness and focus only on the tasks at hand?

- How can you make the game activity enjoyable as an end in itself?

4.8   Transformation of time: World of Warcraft

Answering these questions is a good first step toward creating an environment where challenge becomes a central attraction rather than a feature that is too off-putting, or too simplistic, to engage players' emotions.

PLAY

The potential for play is another key dramatic element that engages players emotionally in games. As discussed in Chapter 2, play can be thought of as freedom or movement within a more rigid structure. In the case of games, the constraints of the rules and procedures are the rigid structure, and the play within that structure is the freedom of players to act within those rules—the opportunity for emergent experience and personal expression.

The Nature of Play

The Promise of Play, a documentary film investigating the subject, queried a number of people about the nature of play. Here are some of their responses: "Play is boisterous." "It's non-directed." "It's spontaneous." "It's not scripted." "Play is loud." "Not work." "It's physical." "It's fun." "An emotional state when you're having a good time." "Play actually is meaningless behavior. You do it for its intrinsic value to you, but play can have utility. That is, you end up developing skills, and those skills can then be used in other arenas." "I think play is one of the ways that we get a feel for the shape of the world." "Play is the central item in children's lives. It's like work is to grown-ups. They play to learn." "Play is child's work. It's all that young children do to learn about the world that they're in."[8]

It's clear from these responses that play has many faces: It helps us learn skills and acquire knowledge, it lets us socialize, it assists us in problem solving, it allows us to relax, and it makes us see things differently. Play is not too serious; it induces laughter and fun, which is good for our health. On the other hand, play can be somewhat serious: Play as a process of experimentation—pushing boundaries and trying new things—is an area of common ground for artists and scientists, as well as children. In fact, it is one of the few areas where children are seen as experts with something to teach adults. Play is recognized as a way of achieving innovation and creativity because it helps us see things differently or achieve unexpected results. The one thing that stands out from these meditations on play is that play is not any one thing but rather a state of mind, a type of approach to an activity. A playful approach can

	Freeform play (*paida*)	Rule-based play (*ludus*)
Competitive play (*agôn*)	Unregulated athletics (foot racing, wrestling)	Boxing, billiards, fencing, checkers, football, chess
Chance-based play (*alea*)	Counting-out rhymes	Betting, roulette, lotteries
Make-believe play (*mimicry*)	Children's initiations, masks, disguises	Theater, spectacles in general
Vertigo play (*ilinx*)	Children "whirling," horseback riding, waltzing	Skiing, mountain climbing, tightrope walking

4.9   Examples taken from *Man, Play and Games* (diagram based on *Rules of Play* by Salen and Zimmerman)

be applied to even the most serious or difficult subjects because playfulness is a state of mind rather than an action.

Play theorist Brian Sutton-Smith, in his book *The Ambiguity of Play*, describes a number of activities that could be considered play, including: mind play like daydreaming, solitary play such as collection or handicrafts; social play such as joking around or dancing, performance play such as playing music or acting, contest play such as board games or video games, and risky play such as hang gliding or extreme sports.[9] Playful activities such as these were categorized by sociologist Roger Callois in his 1958 book *Man, Play and Games*, into four fundamental types of play:

- Competitive play, or *agôn*
- Chance-based play, or *alea*
- Make-believe play, or *mimicry*
- Vertigo play, or *ilinx*

Callois modifies these categories further with the concepts of *ludus*, or rule-based play, and *paida*, or free-form, improvisational play. Figure 4.9 shows examples of types of play within each of these categories. What is interesting for game designers about this classification system is that it allows us to talk specifically about some of the key pleasures of the types of play associated with different types of game systems. For example, strategy games like chess or Warcraft III are clearly competitive, rule-based play, while role-playing games involve both mimicry and competition in a rule-based environment. Examining the pleasures of each of these types of play can help you reach the player experience goals for your game system.

Types of Players

After categorizing play itself, we can also identify the various types of players, each of whom comes to a game with different needs and agendas. Similar to the basic player types described by Richard Bartle in Chapter 3 on page 62,

these categories address the pleasures of play from the point of view of the player.[10]

- *The Competitor*: Plays to best other players, regardless of the game
- *The Explorer*: Curious about the world, loves to go adventuring; seeks outside boundaries—physical or mental
- *The Collector*: Acquires items, trophies, or knowledge; likes to create sets, organize history, etc.
- *The Achiever*: Plays for varying levels of achievement; ladders and levels incentivize the achiever
- *The Joker*: Doesn't take the game seriously—plays for the fun of playing; there's a potential for jokers to annoy serious players, but on the other hand, jokers can make the game more social than competitive
- *The Artist*: Driven by creativity, creation, design
- *The Director*: Loves to be in charge, direct the play
- *The Storyteller*: Loves to create or live in worlds of fantasy and imagination
- *The Performer*: Loves to put on a show for others
- *The Craftsman*: Wants to build, craft, engineer, or puzzle things out

This list is not exhaustive, but it provides a good starting point for thinking about what type of players you are designing for. As noted in Chapter 3, Social Scientist Nick Yee and the team at Quantic Foundry have also created a list of nine player types associated with their player motivation profiles. Some interesting new player types from this list include The Gardner, for players who love to nurture virtual characters or creations. The Gardener's top motivation is completion and examples of games they like to play include Candy Crush and Animal Crossing. Also, The Architect, similar to The Artist listed above, are players motivated by completion, design, and creation. There are a number of different lists and taxonomies for defining player types, but specific language is not the important quality of these lists. What is important is that you are clear on the player type(s) you are designing for and that you engage those players in your process as early as possible to make sure you understand how to reach them with gameplay that truly motivates them.

Exercise 4.5: Player Types

For each player type described above, list a game you know that appeals to that variety of player. What type of player do you tend to be?

4.10 Peacemaker

Levels of Engagement

In addition to thinking about categories of play and types of players, the level of engagement can also vary; not all players need to participate at the same level to find the same enjoyment. For example, spectators might find watching sports, games, or other events more satisfying than playing them. We don't tend to think of designing games for spectators, but the truth is, many people enjoy games in this way. How many times have you sat and watched a friend make their way through the level of a console game, waiting for your turn at the controls? Is there a way as a designer to take this spectator mode into account when designing the play?

Participant play is, of course, the most common way to think about play. As opposed to spectator play, where risk is minimal, participant play is active and involved. It is also the most directly rewarding for all the reasons I've already talked about. Sometimes participants

experience transformational play: This is a deep level of play that actually shapes and alters the player's life. Children experience this level when they learn life lessons through play; in fact, it is one of the reasons they engage in play naturally.

Some games in the emerging genre of serious games attempt to access this level of transformational play as a key goal of their player experience. For example, the game Peacemaker, in which players take on the role of a leader trying to bring peace to the Middle East, is an example of a game that attempts to educate players through direct experience with the intricate problems involved in that real-world situation.

It is an interesting area to think about if games are to advance as an art form. Certainly other forms of art inspire transformation and deep learning through their experience. Perhaps finding ways to create this level of play can raise the bar for games as an art form as well.

PREMISE

In addition to challenge and play, games also use several traditional elements of drama to create player engagement with their formal

systems. One of the most basic is the concept of premise, which establishes the action of the game within a setting or metaphor. Without a

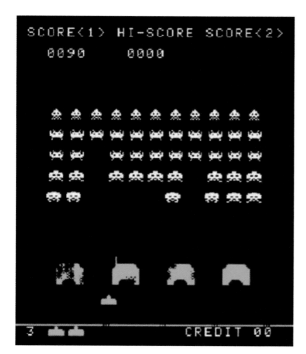

4.11   Space Invaders

dramatic premise, many games would be too abstract for players to become emotionally invested in their outcome.

Imagine playing a game in which you are a set of data. Your objective is to change your data to increase its values. To do this, you engage other sets of data according to complex interaction algorithms. If your data wins the analysis, you win. This all sounds pretty intangible and rather boring, but it is a description of how a typical combat system might work from a formal perspective. To connect players to the game emotionally, the game designer creates a dramatic premise for the interaction that overlays the formal system. In the previous example, let's imagine you play a dwarf named Gregor rather than a set of data. You engage an evil wizard, rather than an opposing set of data, and you attack him with your broadsword, rather than initiating that complex interaction algorithm. Suddenly, the interaction between these two sets

of data takes on a dramatic context over and above its formal aspects.

In traditional drama, premise is established in the exposition of a story. Exposition sets up the time and place, characters and relationships, the prevailing status quo, etc. Other important elements of story that can be addressed in the exposition are the problem, which is the event that upsets the status quo and creates the conflict, and the point of attack, which is the point at which the problem is introduced and the plot begins. While there is not a direct one-to-one relationship, these last two elements of exposition are mirrored in our definition of formal game elements by the concepts of objective and starting action discussed in the previous chapter.

To better understand premise, let's look at some examples from well-known stories from films and books rather than games:

In *Star Wars Episode IV*, the story is set in a far-away galaxy. The protagonist, Luke Skywalker, is a young man who wants to get away from his uncle's remote farm and join the interstellar rebellion, but responsibility and loyalty hold him back. The story begins when his uncle buys two droids carrying secret information that is critical to the rebellion.

In *The Fellowship of the Ring*, the story is set in Middle-earth, a fantasy world of strange races and characters. The protagonist, Frodo Baggins, is a young Hobbit who is happy right where he is—at home. The story begins when Frodo inherits a ring from his uncle, which turns out to be a powerful artifact, the existence of which threatens the safety of all of Middle-earth.

In *Die Hard*, the story is set in a modern office tower in downtown Los Angeles. The protagonist, John McClane, is an off-duty New York City police officer who is in the building trying to make amends with his estranged wife. The story begins when the building is taken over by terrorists and McClane's wife is taken hostage.

These are each examples of how premise is defined in traditional stories. As can be seen, the premise sets the time and place, the main

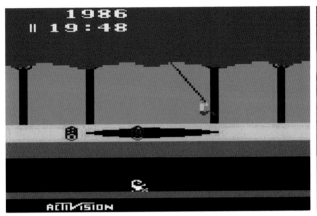

4.12   Pitfall and Diablo

character(s), and the objective, as well as the action that propels the story forward.

Now let's look at examples of premise from games that you might have played. In a game, the premise might be as complex as those previous, involving characters with dramatic motivations, or a game's premise can simply be a metaphor overlaying what would otherwise be an abstract system.

First, here is a very simple game premise: in Space Invaders, the game is set on a planet, presumably Earth, which is attacked by aliens. You play an anonymous protagonist responsible for defending the planet from the invaders. The story begins when the first shot is fired. Clearly this premise has none of the richness that we see in the earlier stories. It does, however, have a simplicity and effectiveness that made it very powerful as a game premise. No player needed to read the backstory of Space Invaders to feel the tension of the steadily approaching aliens.

Now, let's look at some historical games that have attempted to create somewhat more developed premises. In Pitfall, the game is set in the "deep recesses of a forbidden jungle."[11] You play Pitfall Harry, a "world famous jungle explorer and fortune hunter extraordinaire." Your goal is to explore the jungle and find hidden treasures while surviving various hazards like holes, logs, crocodiles, quicksand, etc. The story begins when you enter the jungle.

In Diablo, you play a wandering warrior who arrives in the town of Tristram, which has been ravaged by Diablo. The townspeople ask for your help in defeating Diablo and his undead army, which is ensconced in the dungeon beneath the church. The story begins when you accept the quest.

In Myst, the game is set on a strangely deserted island filled with arcane mechanical artifacts and puzzles. You play an anonymous protagonist with no knowledge of Myst Island or its inhabitants. The story begins when you meet Sirrus and Achenar, two brothers trapped in magical books in the island's library. The brothers, who accuse each other of betrayal, each need you to find some missing pages of their books to help them escape, but both warn you not to help the other brother.

Exercise 4.6: Premise

Write out the premise for five games that you've played and describe how this premise enhances the game.

4.13   Myst

The first task of a premise is to make a game's formal system playable for the user. Rather than shooting at abstract blocks on a screen, players shoot at aliens in Space Invaders. Rather than searching for a generic resource worth 5000 points, players look for diamond rings in Pitfall. Beyond simply concretizing abstract system concepts and making the game playable, a well-thought-out premise can also create a game that appeals to players emotionally.

For example, the premise of Myst not only sends the player on a quest to find the missing pages of one or both of the brothers' magical books, but it also implies that the brothers are not to be trusted and one or both of them might be duping the player. This makes the experience richer for the player, who must determine, by clues found in each age (or level), which, if either, brother to help.

Creating a premise that unifies the formal and dramatic elements is another opportunity for the game designer to heighten the experience of players. As digital games have evolved, more and more designers have begun to make use of more elaborate premises in their designs, which, as we'll see, have evolved to the point where they can be considered fully realized stories.

4.14   Digital game characters (clockwise from top left): Duke Nukem, Guybrush Threepwood, Abe, Link, Sonic the Hedgehog, Lara Croft, and Mario

Guybrush Threepwood image courtesy of LucasArts, a division of Lucasfilm Entertainment Company Ltd.

CHARACTER

Characters are the agents through whose actions a drama is told. By identifying with a character and the outcome of her goals, the audience internalizes the story's events and empathizes with its movement toward resolution.

There are several ways to understand fictional characters in stories. The first, and probably most common, is psychological—the character as a mirror for the audience's fears and desires. However, characters can also be symbolic, standing for larger ideas such as Christianity, the American dream, democratic ideals, etc. Or they can be representative: standing for a segment of people, such as socioeconomic or ethnic groups, a gender, etc. Characters can also be historic, depicting real-world figures. How characters are used

in a story depends greatly on the type of story being told. An action-adventure story might deal only with stereotypical characters who represent certain cultural clichés. Or perhaps it is an action story told as a metaphor or allegory. Perhaps the main character of this action story is symbolic of a larger idea, like truth, justice, and the American way.

The main character of a story is also called the protagonist. The protagonist's engagement with the problem creates the conflict that drives the story. Working against the main character is the antagonist, who opposes the main character's attempts to solve the problem. The antagonist can be a person or some other force that works against the main character. Characters can be major or minor—major characters have a significant impact on the story's outcome, while minor characters have a small impact.

Characters are defined within the story by what they say, what they do, what they look like, or what others say about them. These are called methods of characterization. In addition to function and impact on the story, characters can vary in the complexity of their characterization. If a character has well-defined traits and a realistic personality or undergoes a significant change in personality during the story, they can be thought of as a "round" character. Examples of round characters would be Humphrey Bogart's Rick Blaine from *Casablanca*, Hamlet, or Scarlet O'Hara from *Gone with the Wind*. Characters who have few (if any) defined traits and a shallow personality are considered "flat." Flat characters show little or no change in personality, and they are often used as foils to show off the elements of another character. They are also usually recognizable as stereotypes: the lazy guard, the evil stepmother, the jolly doorman, etc.

No matter what level of complexity a character is written with, the there are four key questions to ask when writing to make sure you have really thought through the character's presence in your story:

- What does the character want?
- What does the character need?
- What does the audience/player hope?
- What does the audience/player fear?

These questions are applicable to game characters as well as characters in traditional media. In fact, game characters have many of the same characteristics and functions as traditional characters, and they are often created using the same techniques of characterization.

Game characters also have some unique considerations. The most important of these is the balance between "agency" and "empathy." Agency is the practical function of a character to serve as a representation of the player in the game. Agency can be completely utilitarian, or it can include aspects of creativity, role-playing, and identification. Empathy is the potential for players to develop an emotional attachment to the character, to identify with their goals and, consequentially, the game objectives.

Agency and empathy must be considered at every level of the game design that involves characters. For example, are characters predesigned? Do they have an existing backstory and motivations? Or are they player-created characters? Do they allow customization and growth? Early game characters were completely defined by how they looked, with little or no attempt at characterization. Mario, in his first appearance in Donkey Kong, was defined by his funny nose and signature cap and overalls. While his motivation, rescuing Pauline, was integrated into

Characters vs. Avatars

Pre-designed characters; backstories, motivations.

Player-created characters; role-playing, growth, customization.

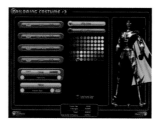

4.15   Characters versus avatars

both the formal and dramatic aspects of the game, he was ultimately a flat, static character who did not change or grow over the course of the game. More importantly, Mario would not do anything to accomplish his goal without the player's control.

Today, many game characters have deep backstories and rich characterizations that affect the player's experience of the game. For example, Kratos, the main character of God of War, is a Spartan general who is sent to kill the god Ares. His duty is intertwined with fate, and

as the game progresses, we discover his motivation to be much deeper than a simple order; he blames Ares for the death of his family, and this mission is one of revenge. Another example is Wander, the protagonist of Shadow of the Colossus. Wander is motivated by his desire to resurrect Mono, a girl who has been sacrificed. We don't know much about the relationship between Wander and Mono or much about Wander himself. But his character is rounded by his actions and demeanor, and the changes that take place in him over the course of the game

4.16   God of War II and Shadow of the Colossus

Free Will vs. Player Control

"Free will"
AI-controlled
character.

Mixture:
Player-controlled
characters w/elements
of simultion that
provide"character."

"Automaton"
Player-controlled
character.

**4.17   Free will versus
player control**

as he gradually transforms into the form of his own enemy, the Colossi he has been ordered to destroy.

Avatars, however, in games like World of Warcraft or Baldur's Gate 3 are player created, often with great investment of time and money. Player-created characters have as great a potential for empathy (if not more) as story-driven characters. The question is not which method is better but which is best for your game's design and player experience goals.

Another question for the designer in the creation of game characters is in regards to "free will" versus player control. Game characters that are controlled by the player do not always have the opportunity to act on their own. The player is assuming agency for the character's actions, which limits the degree to which characters can demonstrate their own personality and inner thought processes. But sometimes game characters are not entirely in the control of the player. Sometimes the character is controlled by artificial intelligence. AI-controlled characters exhibit a sense of autonomy that creates an interesting potential tension between what the player wants and what the character wants.

An early, primitive version of this autonomy is the character of Sonic the Hedgehog—Sega's answer to Mario. If the player stopped interacting with Sonic, the little hedgehog let the player know of his dissatisfaction by crossing his arms and tapping his feet impatiently. Impatience was central to Sonic's character: He did everything fast and had no time to spare. Unlike the blazingly fast actions controlled by the player, however, the toe-tapping routine was Sonic's own, and it established him as a unique character.

Of course, Sonic's toe tapping had no impact on gameplay, but the tension between player-controlled action and character-controlled action is an interesting area that was explored to great effect in games like The Sims, Oddworld: Munch's Oddysee, and Black & White. If the free will feature is turned on in The Sims, characters will decide on their own course of action

(assuming the player hasn't given them anything specific to do). Players can stop a character from performing an action at any time, but with this feature on, the game usually unfolds as a complicated dance between what the player desires and what the character "wishes." This sophisticated model produces dramatic results that the player feels both responsible for and yet surprised by.

Believable artificial intelligence (AI) for characters like The Sims is a hot topic these days — especially for nonplayer characters. Believable AI behavior and dialogue may make for more naturalistic interactions, as well as, replayable game levels. Using what is called "generative AI" designers are looking at ways for players to simply talk to non-player characters conversationally, rather than choosing from a set of options. Technologies like NVIDIA ACE are making it possible for game characters to have natural, flowing conversations with players, rather than being limited to a set of pre-programmed responses. This could make narrative games more immersive and engaging, as players feel like they are interacting with real people within the game world. Figure 4.18 shows Jin, the owner of a ramen shop, who converses realistically with

4.18 *Kairos* demo: NPC converses using natural language processing. @2023 NVIDIA Corporation

players using natural language processing via NVIDIA ACE. Characters using generative AI might be more unpredictable or challenging to interact with, making game levels feel more fresh and replayable. Generative AI might also be used to to create realistic and detailed facial expressions and body language for game characters, which could make them feel more lifelike and believable. For simulation games like The Sims, or role playing games, generative AI has the potential to revolutionize the way game characters are created and interacted with.

Even as we acknowledge the exciting developments in technologies like generative AI to help us develop more realistic interactions, it is still important to consider what it means for a character to be a rounded, dynamic individual within a game story. A good understanding of how to create engaging characters using both traditional dramatic tools and supported by artificial intelligence technologies can add to the effectiveness and believability of characters in your games.

Exercise 4.7: Game Characters

Name three game characters that you find compelling. How are these characters brought to life within the game? What allows you to identify with them? Are they rounded or flat, dynamic or static?

STORY

I've said that the outcome of a game must be uncertain—that this is part of the formal structure of the game. This true of a story as well. The outcome of a story is also uncertain (at least the first time we experience it). Plays, movies, television, and games are all media that involve storytelling and narratives that begin in uncertainty and that are resolved over the course of time. However, the uncertainty in a film or a play is resolved by the author, while the uncertainty of a game is resolved by the players. Because of this, it is very difficult to integrate traditional storytelling methods into games.

In many games, story is actually limited to backstory: sort of an elaborate version of premise. The backstory gives a setting and context for the game's conflict, and it can create motivation for the characters, but its progression from one point to the next is not affected by gameplay. An example of this is the practice of inserting story chapters into the beginning of each game level, creating a linear progression that follows a traditional narrative arc interspersed with gameplay that does not affect how the story plays out. Games like the WarCraft or StarCraft series follow this model in their single-player modes. In these games, the story points are laid out at the beginning of a level, and the player must succeed to move on to the next level and the next story point. Failure means playing the level again and again until you succeed; only then will the story progress, like a gameplay version of the Bill Murray film *Groundhog Day*.

However, there are many game designers who are interested in allowing the game action to change the structure of the story so that choices the player makes affect the eventual outcome. There are a number ways of accomplishing this. The first, and simplest, is to create a branching story line. Player choices feed into several possibilities at each juncture of a structure like this, causing predetermined changes to the story. The diagram in Figure 4.19 shows an example of this type of story structure using a simple fairy-tale story we are all familiar with.

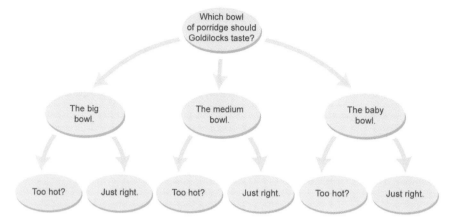

4.19   Branching story structure

One example of a branching game narrative is Heavy Rain, in which you play several characters over the course of a mystery thriller adventure. The game mechanics of Heavy Rain range from daily tasks such as shaving and eating to action mechanics like fighting, and epic choices such as whether to cut off your character's finger to save a child's life. Each of these choices plays into the unfolding of the branching narrative, and the game has a number of extremely different possible ending scenarios. Heavy Rain is something of an exception, as one of the key problems with branching story lines is usually their limited scope. Player choices can be severely restricted in such a structure, causing the game to feel simplistic and unchallenging. In addition, some paths can create uninteresting outcomes. Many game designers believe that there is better potential for use of story in games if the story emerges from gameplay rather than from a predetermined structure. For example, in The Sims, players use the basic elements provided by the formal system to imagine innumerable stories involving their game characters. The system provides features that support this emergent storytelling, including tools for taking snapshots of the gameplay, arranging the snapshots in a captioned scrapbook, and uploading the scrapbook to the web to share with other users.

The most prevalent form of narrative in games, however, is the use of story to propel adventure games along their mainly single-player campaigns. Two interesting games of this vein to compare are The Walking Dead and The Last of Us. Both games are about surviving a zombie-like apocalypse, but have very different story arcs and structures. The Last of Us has a linear narrative focused on the relationship between main characters Joel and Ellie. Ellie is a young girl who has survived infection and is a potential source of a cure, while Joel, who lost his own daughter at the start of the apocalypse, takes on the task of safely bringing Ellie to a group who can generate a vaccine. The story does not change based on the player's actions, and yet it is richly developed and the relationships have depth and importance in regards to the gameplay. Game Director Bruce Straley discusses the development of the narrative arc of The Last of Us on page 129.

The Walking Dead is also an adventure game, but one that focuses on character development rather than action or puzzle solving. As in The Last of Us, The Walking Dead focuses on a parental-like relationship. In this case, escaped prisoner Lee Everett protects a little girl named Clementine, who is separated from her parents. Lee offers to help her find them, and their travels form the arc of the story. In

Directing Games for Emotion

by Ian Dallas

Ian Dallas is the creative director at Giant Sparrow, the studio behind The Unfinished Swan and What Remains of Edith Finch. He's interested in creating experiences that help people see the world in new ways and in making the world a stranger place.

Games tend to focus on a narrow band of emotions: joy, desire, and triumph. These feelings are so common because most games also share the same underlying goal of creating an experience that is fun and those are all fun emotions.

This has started changing recently with the rise of emotionally driven games, including my own studio's game What Remains of Edith Finch. Rather than fun, these games focus on conveying and exploring a mood.

Because emotionally driven games have a different goal, they also have a different path to make them. Games that focus on fun tend to evolve by exploring a system or game mechanic. For example, if the player can run and shoot, you might experiment with different kinds of guns, or targets, or run speed modifiers to find variations that feel the most fun. Emotionally driven games, on the other hand, evolve by exploring a mood or feeling.

Let me give an example. With What Remains of Edith Finch, our overall goal was to evoke a sense of the sublime. For us, the sublime meant a moment that was simultaneously beautiful and overwhelming. The inspiration I personally kept coming back to was a memory from when I was 14 years old, scuba diving in the Pacific Northwest, at the bottom of the ocean and seeing the ground slope away into a seemingly infinite darkness. It was aesthetically beautiful but also a powerful reminder of how small, and fragile, and out of my element I was. When we started working on the game, that's the feeling we were trying to create for players.

We began in a literal way, creating a scuba diving simulator to try to replicate what it felt like to scuba dive. That didn't work so well. We made a rough prototype and if you squinted, it did kinda look like you were scuba diving but emotionally it was very flat. It felt like you were playing a game. Players ended up being very focused on basic issues like how can I move, what can I interact with, and what's my objective?

Questions like these are present in almost any prototype but since scuba diving is a relatively novel and clumsy form of interactivity we found the questions were more pressing and, given that everything was happening underwater, harder to communicate elegantly for various reasons including that divers don't usually talk underwater, body language is hard to read, more degrees of freedom make it harder to focus player attention, etc., etc. These are solvable problems, but finding so much trouble so early gave us pause.

So we put the scuba diving simulator aside and looked at what we felt was necessary to communicate the emotion we were after. There was no reason it had to happen underwater, for example. But the natural world felt important. For whatever reason, sublime experiences tend to happen outdoors. We brainstormed alternative locations like being in the middle of a dense forest, or the beach on a windy day, or anywhere in a rainstorm. It also felt important that the characters seem like specific, believable human beings so there'd be a clear contrast between the fragile individual and the vast landscape they were surrounded by.

Our next step was discussing our own memories of the natural world, ideally ones from childhood (a time when we're at our most fragile) and that involved a family (a source of protection and a way of emphasizing the human element). Ideas that came out of this included: swinging on a tire swing your parents set up, a father-daughter camping trip, outdoor weddings, and flying a kite at the beach. Over time, many of these ideas made their way into the game in various forms. For example: in a sequence about flying a kite at a beach wedding.

As a creative director it's my responsibility to provide direction to the rest of the team. Primarily, this involves answering two questions:

- Where are we going? (Or, what's the feeling we're ultimately trying to achieve?)
- What's most broken? (Or, what's currently ruining the overall experience the most?)

The question of "where are we going" is especially challenging because even if you know exactly what you want it can be quite hard to communicate it. If you're working in an established genre targeting familiar emotions this process is a lot more straightforward. Existing games provide a common language ("it's like game X + game Y, mixed with...") and help everyone imagine what these novel combinations might feel like. But if you're making an experience that's more personal and emotionally driven, there won't be many other games to look at so you'll need to go elsewhere.

What you have in your head is a good start but usually not enough. Finding other media that express the feeling you're after makes it easier for you to see your subject from other angles and to find things you're subconsciously drawn to that just "feel right." I've found the easiest place to start is by searching for images. Asking the Internet to offer up a selection of images on a subject is an invitation to randomness that can be especially helpful early on when many possible directions look appealing. If you're exploring "gloomy forest" images, you may find yourself attracted to puddles, or crows, or a thicket full of discarded washing machines. Images are an easy way to start making abstract ideas concrete. This comes in handy when team members start having increasingly specific questions like "What time of year is it?" or "How hard should the edges of the shadows be?"

What Remains of Edith Finch

Music can also be helpful in narrowing in on an emotional tone. A quick shortcut here is to start with soundtracks for movies that feel tonally similar to your game, since they've already done the work of finding or creating sounds that evoke that feeling. Whether or not you share the music with the rest of the team, listening to it in the background while you work is a good way to nudge yourself into an appropriate frame of mind. Loops of ambient sound recordings (e.g. a forest in the rain, or seagulls at the beach) can be similarly useful.

Beyond images and music there is, of course, a whole world out there for reference, either primary (i.e., experiencing it yourself) or constructed. For example, when making Edith Finch, we found a genre of literature from the 1930s called Weird Fiction that was particularly good at evoking the sublime. We noticed that our favorite works in the genre were all short stories, which gave us the idea of transforming the game itself into a collection of short stories.

After you figure out the direction, the next challenge is communicating this to your team. This can be tricky because most game teams are composed of individuals with a wide range of perspectives and sensibilities. My experience has been that team members in each discipline speak a slightly different language. As a broad but useful generalization, artists like visual references, programmers want to know what new features might be needed, and designers prefer diagrams and prose. A verbal walkthrough and chance to ask questions can help everyone, but even after hours of discussion it's not uncommon to discover days later that each side came away with a very different understanding.

The clearest, least ambiguous form of communication for everyone is an interactive prototype. Seeing things move and being able to interact with them answers many, many questions but unfortunately can be prohibitively difficult to create early in the process. In practice, we rely on a mix of reference types and communication styles since it's easier than finding or making one perfect example and highlights the ambiguity inherent in any emotionally rich subject.

Once the team is on board, the last step is communicating all of this to the player. Here, the production of emotionally driven games starts to look increasingly similar to other kinds of games. Standard problems include making the player's goals clear, the controls intuitive, and having the world respond in satisfying ways to the player's actions. If anything, these nuts-and-bolts issues are even more important in an emotionally driven game because if players get hung up on technical hurdles (e.g., frustrating controls), they're unlikely to be receptive to, or even notice, the emotional goals of the experience. Creating an emotional experience is delicate, a bit like a dream—if anything knocks you out of it, it's nearly impossible to get back in.

This is why, early on, we focus on reducing player frustration even though our ultimate goal is conveying a feeling. I've found that short, frequent playtests are the fastest way to identify what's frustrating. Often one issue will mask or cause another (e.g., players may fail to notice a note on the fridge, but only because they spent 20 minutes floundering in a previous area and are now impatient). It helps to work iteratively, fixing a few issues at a time and then testing again. Fixing these issues also gives us time to explore the emotional effects of what we're working on, even though for much of development the nuances of feelings will be nearly invisible to players.

It's incredibly difficult to predict how an interactive experience is going to feel until you've built it. Your sense of what aspects will be compelling, or confusing, or difficult rarely matches up with what you'll see in playtests. This goes both ways. Usually it's negative, like players getting stuck on something that seems glaringly obvious. But then sometimes, players will be enchanted by a tiny interaction you carelessly tossed into the scene. It's easier to make progress when you stay flexible and listen to what your team, your technology, and your prototypes are already doing well, then do more of THAT. Working with the grain is faster, more effective, and more enjoyable than the alternative, trying to force an idea into the game that sounded good in theory but isn't connecting with players.

This is what makes emotionally driven design such a useful tool even if your game isn't primarily focused on feelings. Emotions are powerful and specific but they're also flexible. There are many ways you could communicate the pain of losing a child or the awkwardness of walking into a party where you don't know anyone. With so much about and within the game constantly evolving, having an emotional core gives you an anchor. It's like a lighthouse that you and the rest of the team can keep sailing toward no matter how many turns you have to make along the way.

this game, unlike the tightly controlled narrative of The Last of Us, player dialogue choices and actions have an effect on the story. This can lead to certain characters being killed, or shifts in a character's attitude towards Lee. The game is structured episodically, and the changes made by a player in one episode carry through to later episodes.

Each of these examples is part of a growing trend of game designers to not only consider narrative in their work, but to experiment with new ways to integrate and expand the depth of their storytelling without sacrificing gameplay.

Exercise 4.8: Story

Pick a game that you feel successfully melds its story line with the gameplay. Why does this game succeed? How does the plot unfold as the game progresses?

WORLD BUILDING

While the integration of story structure itself is a difficult problem for games and interactive media, there is an aspect of story creation that is a natural complement to game design, and that is world building. World building is the deep and intricate design of a fictional world, often beginning with maps and histories, but potentially including complete cultural studies of inhabitants, languages, mythologies, governments, politics, economies, etc. The most famous fictional world, and perhaps the most complete, is J.R.R. Tolkien's Middle-earth. Tolkien began by creating languages, then the people (elves) who spoke them, and later the stories that took place in the world. Many games and films are created using world-building techniques, which, though not as detailed as Middle-earth, give them a sense of depth and story potential that keeps players interested over long periods of time. The World of Warcraft universe is a good game-based example, as are the Star Trek and Star Wars universes, which both span films, games, novels, animated series, and vast universes of fan-created material.

Media theorist Henry Jenkins writes, "more and more storytelling has become the art of world building, as artists create compelling environments that cannot be fully explored or exhausted within a single work or even a single medium. The world is bigger than the film, bigger than even the franchise—since fans speculations and elaborations also expand the world in a variety of directions."[12]

There are many examples of deep world building in the science fiction and fantasy genres, and more and more, world building is becoming integral to the creation of all media properties. The economics of media today make it important that new properties have the depth to expand, not just in terms of sequels, but also in gameplay on new platforms, in both linear and participatory structures. One great example of world-building can be found in the Marvel Cinematic Universe (MCU), which is a shared "universe" of superhero stories based on the characters and stories of comic book writer Stan Lee. The universe, which includes films, television series, games, books, toys, and themed entertainment, was created by crossing over common plot elements, settings, cast, and characters between its more than 32 films, 14 television series, and more. As with the original comics, the MCU is growing and changing, establishing new characters and themes as it resolves and retires older storylines.

There are many different creative aspects to consider when world-building for games. Some of the most important include:

- Setting: What is the physical environment of the game world? Is it a fantasy world, a science fiction world, or something else entirely?

- History: What is the history of the game world? How did it come to be the way it is?
- Cultures: What are the different cultures that exist in the game world? What are their customs, beliefs, and values?
- Geography: What are the different physical features of the game world? What are the mountains, rivers, forests, and other natural wonders?
- Creatures: What kinds of creatures inhabit the game world? Are they friendly, hostile, or something in between?
- Story: What is the story (or stories) that players will experience in the game world? What are the challenges they will face and the rewards they will reap? Does the game world convey a theme?

World-building is an ongoing process, and it is often iterative. As game designers develop the game, they may need to make changes to the world to accommodate new gameplay mechanics or story elements. However, a well-developed world can provide a solid foundation for a game or series of games, and it can help to create a truly immersive experience for players that could launch a franchise that extends to other media. A great example of a game world that is so well designed that it has spawned multiple games and a television series is The Last of Us series, which explores a post-apocalyptic world filled with undead monsters and rich relationship drama.

When you are thinking about getting started with world-building for games, start with a small world. Don't try to create a vast and complex world like the ones that you admire all at once. You can also use existing works as inspiration – I often do an exercise with my game design students that challenges them to create game worlds around various Shakespeare plays. You would be amazed at some of the clever worlds and stories they have come up with using this prompt! Don't be afraid to experiment. The best way to grow your skills in world-building is to start with an idea that captures your interest. One of my students was fascinated with the intelligence exhibited by crows and created an entire world around sentient bird-like creatures.

As with characters and story, world-building is an emerging field that may also benefit from the use of AI. We can imagine procedurally created cultures in games that change and grow with the activities of massive numbers of players in the world. As, I've said though, you can start small at first. Start with the kernel of your world concept and grow it slowly. Think of the way that Gene Roddenbery first conceived of the Star Trek universe: a world filled with a huge variety of sentient species to discover and interact with. He did not define the entire world, but he set up the basic parameters that have launched now thousands of stories and games.

World-building is a challenging but rewarding process. By taking the time to create a rich and immersive world, you can help to make your game a truly memorable experience for players.

THE DRAMATIC ARC

I have introduced a number of key dramatic elements that can help to create player engagement with the game system. But the most important of these elements is actually one that I have talked about already in my discussion of formal elements, and that is conflict.

Conflict is at the heart of any good drama, and, as we have seen in our discussion of formal elements, it is also at the heart of game systems. Meaningful conflict is not only designed to keep players from accomplishing their goals too easily, but it also draws players into the game emotionally by creating a sense of tension as to the

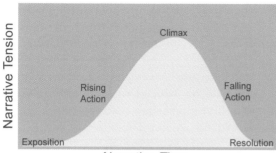

4.20   Classic dramatic arc

Traditional dramatic conflict can be broken down into categories such as character versus character, character versus nature, character versus machine, character versus self, character versus society, or character versus fate. As game designers, we might overlay another group of categories, which are player versus player, player versus game system, player versus multiple players, team versus team, etc. Thinking about game conflict in this way helps us to integrate a game's dramatic premise and its formal system, deepening the players' relationships to both.

When the conflict is set in motion, it must escalate for the drama to be effective. Escalating conflict creates tension, and in most stories, the tension in a story gets worse before it gets better, resulting in a classic dramatic arc. This arc describes the amount of dramatic tension in the story as it progresses in time. Figure 4.20 shows how tension rises and falls during various stages of a typical story. This arc is the backbone of all dramatic media, including games.

As the figure shows, stories begin with exposition, which introduces the settings, characters, and concepts that will be important to the rest of the action. Conflict is introduced when the

outcome. This dramatic tension is as important to the success of a game as it is to a great film or novel.

In traditional drama, conflict occurs when the protagonist faces a problem or obstacle that keeps her from accomplishing her goal. In the case of a story, the protagonist is usually the main character. In the case of a game, the protagonist can be the player or a character that represents the player. The conflict that the player encounters can be against another player, a number of other players, obstacles within the game system, or other forces or dilemmas.

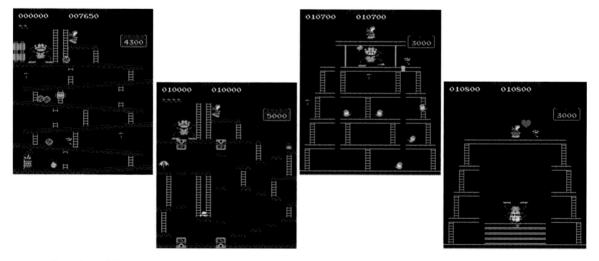

4.21   Donkey Kong

protagonist has a goal that is opposed by their environment, an antagonist, or both. The conflict, and the protagonist's attempt to resolve it, causes a series of events that lead to a rising action. This rising action leads to a climax, in which some sort of deciding factor or event is introduced. What happens in the climax determines the outcome of the drama. The climax is followed by a period of falling action in which the conflict begins to resolve, and the resolution, or dénouement, in which it is finally resolved.

To better understand the classic arc, let's look at it in terms of a simple story you are probably familiar with. In the movie *Jaws*, Sheriff Brody is the protagonist. His goal is to keep the people of Amity safe. The antagonist is the shark, who opposes Brody's goal by attacking the people of Amity. This creates a conflict between Brody and the shark. Brody, who is afraid of the water, attempts to keep the people safe by keeping them out of the water, but this plan fails. The tension rises as the shark attacks more people, even threatening Brody's own children. Finally, Brody must face his fear and go out on the water to hunt down the shark. In the climax of the story, the shark attacks Brody. The story resolves when Brody kills the shark and returns the story to the status quo. Simple, right? You can look at any story you know and you will see the dramatic arc reflected in its structure.

Now, let's look at the arc again, this time in terms of a game. In a game, the rising action is linked to both the formal and dramatic systems. This is because games are usually designed to provide more challenge as they progress. Games that also have well-integrated dramatic elements will intertwine those elements with the formal system so that as the challenge rises, the story develops. Here is an example from a classic game: In Donkey Kong, Mario is the protagonist. Mario's girlfriend, Pauline, has been kidnapped by the giant ape, Donkey Kong, and taken to the top of a building under construction. Mario's goal is to save Pauline before time runs out. To do so, he must climb the levels of the building,

traversing girders, elevators, and conveyer belts, while avoiding flames, barrels, and bouncing rivets thrown at him by Donkey Kong. Each time Mario reaches Pauline, Donkey Kong grabs her and carries her off to the next higher level. Each level builds in difficulty, creating rising tension for the player. Finally, in the climax of the game, Mario must not only avoid Donkey Kong's attacks but also fight him directly by removing all the rivets on every floor of the level. After the rivets are removed, Donkey Kong falls head first onto a stack of girders and is knocked out, allowing Mario to rescue Pauline and resolve both the formal and dramatic tension.

It is clear from even these simple descriptions that the story in *Jaws* is more developed as to character and story—Brody has a fear that he must overcome to solve the problem, and his character changes in motivation as he goes from protecting all the people of Amity, to saving his own family, to defending himself from the shark. While Mario has a goal, and he is certainly vulnerable to attacks from Donkey Kong, he does not have any internal conflict that keeps him from completing his goal, and his goal never wavers. The jeopardy that Pauline is in never increases either, a touch that would have made the formal and dramatic systems of the game better integrated.

What Mario has that Brody does not, however, is that his success or failure is in the hands of the player. It is the player who must learn how to avoid the attacks, moving closer and closer to the goal. And in the climax of the game, it is the player who must figure out how to topple Donkey Kong from his perch and knock him out. So while our response to the climactic moment in *Jaws*, when Brody figures out how to finally kill the shark, is a release of tension built up by our empathy for his character and the character's struggles over the course of the story, our response to the climatic moment in Donkey Kong is quite different.

In the case of Donkey Kong, we are the ones who have figured out the crucial action needed to resolve the tension, and that tension has built

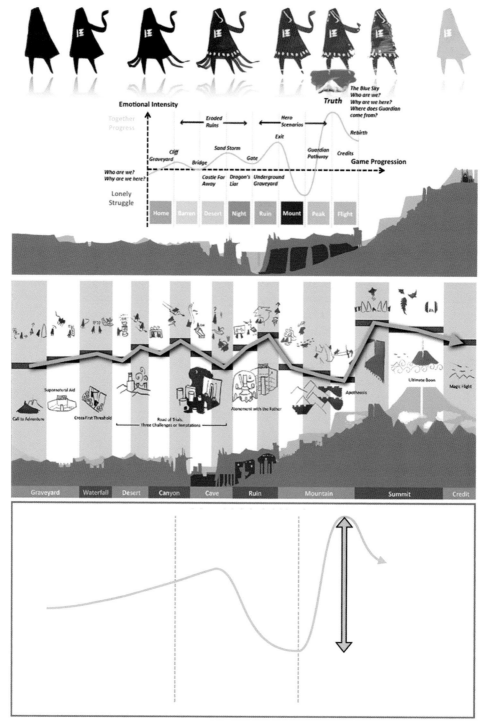

4.22   Emotional Arc Designs from Journey

up over a number of levels of play. When we finally resolve that tension, there's a sense of personal accomplishment on top of any sympathetic response that we might have to the resolution of Mario and Pauline's story. This integration of conflict in the formal and dramatic systems can clearly provide a powerful combination for the players in a game experience.

Donkey Kong is a classic game that exhibits a fairly simple dramatic arc. More recent games, as I noted on page 117 when I discussed story, often deal with richer backstories, deeper characters, and more meaningful themes. Game designers are expanding their roles to include in-depth planning of the emotional journey of their games. A good example of this kind of design can been seen in Jenova Chen's articulate explanation of his design of such an arc for the game Journey. Chen was inspired by Joseph Campbell's monomyth, or Hero's Journey, a basic pattern of heroic stories around the world, and also by the visual storytelling structures of Bruce Block, author of *The Visual Story*. In Campbell's monomyth, a hero responds to a call to action, and heads off into the unknown. The first threshold is the limits of the normal world, which the hero must leave to go into dangerous and unknown territory. The journey includes many trials, including temptation, confrontation with whatever holds power over him, and at the lowest moment, the abyss, which includes a form of death and rebirth. In the end, the hero returns to their starting point, transformed and free from fear.

When Chen set out to design Journey, his goal was to create an emotional arc for the player that followed the Hero's Journey in spirit. While the specifics of the journey are very abstract in the game, the sensibility of each phase is articulated using color, architecture, sound, music, and, most importantly, a subtle shifting of the game mechanics. As can be seen in Figure 4.22, Chen's original design of the game's arc plots each level of the game against a measure of emotional intensity. As his designs progress, this intensity

is mapped against the literal moments of the Hero's Journey. During the playtesting process, Chen found that his final climax, moving from the lowest point of the abyss, or apotheosis, to the point of revelation and transformation was not a big enough change. He and his team had to redesign the game to increase that emotional leap to be twice as extreme in order to achieve their goals. It is this kind of attention to detail in terms of a dramatic arc that made this abstract, experimental game such a surprising success.

Game director Bruce Straley walks through the emotional beats of The Last of Us in his sidebar on page 129, showing how the team carefully planed their world and characters in order to set up the dramatic emotional crisis at the climax of the game. They integrated their story and gameplay to increase the impact of that emotional experience goal.

As designers, we can integrate and apply our understanding of the classic dramatic arc in terms of gameplay as such:

1. Exposition: This is the introduction of the characters, setting, and conflict. The player learns who they are playing as, where they are, and what they need to do.

2. Rising action: This is the stage where the conflict escalates and the stakes get higher. The player faces challenges and obstacles that they must overcome in order to progress.

3. Climax: This is the high point of the story, where the conflict reaches its peak. The player must make a difficult decision or overcome a major challenge.

4. Falling action: This is the stage where the conflict is resolved and the story comes to a close. The player achieves their goal and the story ends with a sense of satisfaction and, if a meaningful story has been told, an understanding of its theme.

As we've seen, the dramatic arc can be used to create a sense of tension and suspense in a game. By gradually increasing the stakes and challenges, the player is kept engaged and eager to see what happens next. The climax of the story should provide a meaningful crisis and conclusion that leaves the player feeling fulfilled by the story they have created or participated in.

When you are thinking about how to use the dramatic arc in your games, think about these creative strategies:

- Introduce the conflict early: The conflict should be introduced early in the game so that the player has a clear goal to work towards.
- Gradually increase the stakes: The stakes should gradually increase throughout the game so that the player feels a sense of urgency.
- Create memorable characters: The characters should be relatable and believable so that the player can connect with them. We should care about the characters and what they are trying to achieve.
- Give the player meaningful choices: The player should be given meaningful choices that affect the outcome of the story. We'll discuss the idea of meaningful choices more in Chapter 11 beginning on page 378.
- End the story on a satisfying note: The ending should be satisfying and leave the player feeling fulfilled and, if possible, thinking about the larger theme of the story.

The dramatic arc can be an important emotional tool for game designers. By studying traditional methods of meaningful storytelling, and applying those techniques to our game designs, we can create games that use the dramatic arc to tell stories that are engaging, suspenseful, and memorable.

Exercise 4.9: Plotting a Story, Part 1

Choose a game that you've played all the way through. Make certain it is a game with a story involved. For example Mass Effect 3, Deus Ex,

BioShock Infinite, and Star Wars: Knights of the Old Republic might be good choices. Now, plot the story against the dramatic arc.

- How is the exposition handled? Who is the protagonist? What is the main conflict, and when is it introduced?
- What does the protagonist do to resolve the conflict?
- What causes the tension in the story to rise? What deciding factor brings the story to a climax?
- What happens in the resolution?

Exercise 4.10: Plotting a Story, Part 2

Now take the same game and plot the gameplay against the dramatic arc.

- What elements of gameplay, if any, support each of these points?
- How is the exposition of gameplay handled? Are controls and mechanics clearly explained? Are they integrated with the dramatic premise? Is the goal clearly stated and integrated with the main conflict of the story?
- How does the gameplay cause the dramatic tension to rise?
- What deciding factor in the gameplay brings the game to a climax?
- What happens in the resolution? Do the dramatic elements and gameplay elements help or hinder each other?
- How might they be better integrated to make the game work from an emotional standpoint?

Exercise 4.11: Plotting a Story, Part 3

Take the same game and come up with three changes to the story or gameplay that you believe would make the two better integrated.

CRAFTING EMOTIONAL BEATS IN THE LAST OF US

By Bruce Straley

Bruce Straley is a designer, artist and director in the video game industry with over 32 years of experience and 15 titles shipped. He was the co-Art Director of Uncharted: Drake's Fortune, the Game Director of Uncharted 2: Among Thieves, the co-creator and Game Director of The Last of Us and founded the company Wildflower Interactive in 2021. Bruce is in a constant pursuit to advance the medium's concepts around interactivity and storytelling.

There are many things we set out to accomplish when making The Last of Us, but I'd like to focus on just one here. Specifically, the moments when we switched the player controls from Joel to Ellie then back to Joel. I'll share why we thought it was important to play as both characters, how we went about crafting the emotional beats that led up to the switch, what made it work dramatically, and then extrapolate a few takeaways for you to consider when planning and creating your own impactful moments.

Why switch characters?

Switching playable characters isn't a novel concept unto itself. Games had done it before The Last of Us. But early on we were convinced that if we could motivate the change "at the right time" story-wise and gameplay-wise, then the switch would have more meaning – hopefully creating a greater emotional impact – than the games that had done it before us.

Gameplay-wise we knew that switching to Ellie, a less powerful character, could be a nice way to progress the gameplay arc. Because tactically speaking it would challenge the player's skills, since playing as Ellie would inherently be more difficult. This meant players would have to have "been Joel" for a long while to emphasize the contrast in controls.

Story-wise, we had the notion that switching to Ellie could be a powerful storytelling device. We believed that if players played as Ellie, rather than just playing alongside her, it could help them see the world through her eyes and in turn build more empathy for her character. Dramatically, it would be an unexpected twist in these characters' relationship. But this meant the switch moment couldn't come at some random spot just to make the gameplay feel different. We knew we had to build toward the change narratively and make it happen at a major story event in order to generate the emotional impact we were after.

So, knowing that we had compelling gameplay and story reasons to motivate switching playable characters, it then became our job to develop the dramatic beats that would come prior in order to generate the strongest possible impact.

Setting expectations: being Joel

We set out to make a unique version of a post-apocalyptic game where the characters take the world, their situations and each other seriously – so in turn the player could take them seriously as well. We wanted the experience to feel personal and grounded, which was novel for the genre (in games) at that time.

The player starts the main story as Joel, an emotionally unavailable protector figure. A survivor who's carrying the unprocessed trauma from the death of his daughter Sarah, who players played-as during the prologue. He's been burdened with the task of protecting and escorting Ellie, a fourteen-year old who's never left the safety of the military city, out to the Fireflies who are based somewhere beyond the walls. Joel wants nothing to do with Ellie.

It was important for us to establish a rhythm of what it's like to be Joel and have the player as aligned with "Joel the Protector" as much as we could. This meant that in gameplay we had to put the player in the shoes of a survivor. We needed our world to apply the necessary pressure that would allow the player to feel what a survivor would feel like. Our hand-to-hand brawling had to feel consequential, heavy, and impactful. We made ammo scarce so that players had to improvise strategies on the fly. Patching yourself up was essential. Keeping the backpack live during gameplay meant you couldn't pause the experience while crafting your items. And deaths were always shockingly brutal. Every decision was made to reinforce what Joel and Ellie were going through and in turn align the player with these characters as survivors.

Character-wise, our premise for Joel's arc was, "Can we take an emotionally broken man and get him to love again?" Which meant each chapter needed to examine the struggle of Joel trying to sort through his feelings of being with Ellie. We meet Bill, who is a reflection of Joel's inner thoughts, "Don't open your heart or you'll get hurt." In Pittsburgh, Ellie gets a chance to shine and show her capabilities and the potential of a trusting relationship. This cracks Joel open just enough so when we introduce Henry and Sam, a mirror of Joel and Ellie's future relationship, we can feel Joel emotionally shut down again after the tragic end of that chapter. And then we meet up with Joel's brother Tommy, with every intention of dropping Ellie off and giving up the burden. But Tommy sees Joel, being the only person that knows what Joel's been through with Sarah. And this interaction convinces Joel to finish the task and take Ellie to the university, where the Fireflies were last known to be stationed. For the sake of humanity.

Each of these narrative beats has led us, hours of gameplay later, to a place where we believe this is Joel's story and we're going to play out our protector trope like a good video game does. We've put in the work to align the player with Joel the survivor and have thoroughly invested them in Joel's emotional struggle. Now, having laid the groundwork for our switch, we were ready to upend the players' expectations of the story.

The crisis: Joel is injured

The two are on horseback exploring the university where the Fireflies were last known to be. Their bond is tight. But unfortunately for them the Fireflies have moved on. What they thought was going to be there isn't – when the Hunters show up.

As the two stealth and fight their way out of the facility, in the middle of the fight at an average door – that's like any other door the player has opened in the game before – it swings open sending Joel into a grapple with the Hunter against the second-floor railing. The force of either winning or losing the struggle breaks the weathered railing and sends the two flying off the ledge. A piece of rebar impales Joel's abdomen on impact.

We take a quick moment to acknowledge how dire this situation is, but there are more Hunters closing in. Time for us to give the player hope. Ellie helps Joel up, but he's severely injured. We compromise the controls to accentuate the desperation by giving Joel an injured walk cycle. We added tech to dynamically detect if the player walks close to a counter and have Joel lean on it for support while moving. And if the player tries to sprint – Joel collapses. The player might make it out of there, but it's going to be difficult.

Simultaneously, we start to align the player with Ellie as her fear sets in. She's powerless over this situation. Her fear launches out as anger. She yells at Joel not to die. She's denying the reality of what's happening before her eyes. She might lose Joel. We might lose Joel.

It's important to note that we could have made this entire sequence a cutscene. But we felt it was dramatically important to play through these events rather than just watch them. It's a critical integration of narrative beats and gameplay design. And these technical changes only feel important because of all the work we did to lead up to this moment. Because the player has been Joel for hours at this point. They have fully embraced that they are Joel. They know how powerful Joel is and what he's capable of. But now he's actively dying as the player is trying to keep him alive. Which allows Ellie to become a mirror for the player's feelings as she starts cussing at Joel to get up. The player is desperately pushing forward on the stick with both the hope and fear of the unknown. "Are we going to be ok? What happens if Joel dies? That wouldn't happen. Games don't kill their protagonists. This is Joel's story, right?"

The player makes it out alive – but Joel has given everything he's got. He falls off the back of the horse as he passes out. We cut to black.

We hold on black for an exceptionally long time. A chapter card reading "WINTER" appears.

The payoff: being Ellie

When we cut back, the first person we see is Ellie. We leave the player wondering what's happened to Joel while simultaneously experiencing for the first time, through gameplay, what it's like to be Ellie. There's probably a mix of emotions as the player processes the moment. We ease the player into the change by putting her in a quiet forest as she hunts a deer. Controls-wise, it was important for us to map the control scheme exactly as it was while playing Joel, so the player could stay present for the emotional beats of the transition and not get distracted with relearning controls. Two successful arrows later and she's tracking the bleeding prey, which leads her to David – which is also when we finally reveal that Joel might be alive as Ellie asks for medicine. But a horde of infected surround Ellie and David and they will need to cooperate to survive.

Now that we are playing as Ellie the camera is lower – the world looks different – more imposing. Her movement speed is scaled down due to her size. And when she faces the same enemies that Joel has had to face for hours, we emphasize that it's not going to be as easy for Ellie. She'll need to be even craftier. But the shift in perspective is profound. The player is so used to playing as Joel. Even in small moments, like when David boosts Ellie up to some scaffolding, up to that point in the game it's always been Joel doing the boosting. But it all adds up to create a new sensation in the player.

And now we play as Ellie for a good chunk of time. Beats need time to resonate with players. We get the player comfortable playing as Ellie. Things went south with David, and Ellie has escaped a cage she was being held in only to have him catch up to her and trap her in an abandoned cafe. And in the final moments in the showdown with David, while Joel is fighting his way back to her, we toy with the idea, "Surely Joel will come to rescue her." But upend that trope. Ellie is left to defend herself. And in a brutal climax, Ellie takes everything out on David. All of her frustrations. All of her despair. All of the disgusting realizations of what humanity is capable of. And Joel finally arrives only to hold her.

Now we're all starting to understand what it must've been like to be Ellie the whole time.

Resolution: a new perspective

It's SPRING. We switch the controls back to playing as Joel. But Ellie's not her normal, quippy self. She's been upset before in the game, but the difference now is the player knows what she must be dwelling on – because they WERE HER – and played as and dealt with what she had to deal with. Joel didn't make it in time to rescue her. Ellie had to rely on herself and commit horrible acts in order to survive. How does a fourteen year old process this? And she's supposed to be saving the world? For this? We're seeing Ellie through a new lens now. Our feelings for her are different because we WERE her. We experienced those harrowing moments AS HER, not alongside her. And because of that, she feels like a new character in the game.

And through all of this, Joel has a new appreciation for Ellie. Ellie saved his life. And he knows what horribleness Ellie had survived, because he's had to commit horrible acts himself. Through all the sequences that led up to this moment, Joel has finally let his guard down. Inside his heart, he now loves Ellie like his daughter. We still have to see that play out in his actions, but the inner transformation has happened.

Takeaways

It's easy to read retrospectives like this one and get the impression the creators had it all figured out from the beginning. But that's never the case. But what we did know was there was potential to create something emotionally resonant by switching characters, if we pursued that goal mindfully. It then became our job to work on all the beats — in gameplay and in story — that led up to the switch in order to accomplish that goal.

Emotionally impactful moments in games do not come for free. We have to invest the time and effort to earn the player's trust in order to then do something with it. We can all get enamored with those cool, impactful moments from other games, stories and movies we've experienced. But I'd posit that it's not the moment itself that made the beat work, but all the work that went in building toward the big moment that allowed it to have impact.

And lastly, it's my belief — and what was new for production at that time and still is at some companies — that we could have only made these beats as impactful as we did because the story and gameplay were both being created at the same time. Story was not written in a black box or slapped onto the gameplay after the fact. And gameplay wasn't created without the desire to land story beats. It was a shared goal between the story and gameplay disciplines to deliver an interactive experience, which required understanding, collaboration, and compromise between the two throughout production. Creating a video game is a journey. There is no blueprint for how to make a game experience land. We learn things and discover things as the game takes shape. But if we're honest with ourselves throughout development, and the people in charge of major story decisions and major gameplay decisions are in constant communication throughout, then the common goal to create 'the most impactful experience possible,' is achievable.

CONCLUSION

The elements of drama that we have looked at form the basis of a tool set that the game designer can use to elicit powerful emotional reactions from players. From integral game concepts like challenge and play, to complex integration of premise, characters, and story, these tools are only as powerful as the inspiration behind their use. The media palette of game design has grown to rival film and television, and the emotional impact of games is also beginning to rival the depths of these more traditional dramatic art forms.

We are seeing game designers reach for more sophisticated goals in terms of their narrative tone, significance of theme, character depth, and overall dramatic intent. And, we are seeing the dramatic worlds of games expanding to other media such as films, television, and theme parks. Game designers today must think about creating characters, stories, and worlds that will move us in ways we have yet to imagine.

What new areas of dramatic possibility do you see? What stories do you want to play? What worlds do you want to live in? To answer these questions, you must have a strong grasp of the tools of traditional drama and understanding of good gameplay and the process by which it can be achieved. Before going on to read about system dynamics in games, spend some time with the exercises in this chapter if you have not already done so because they are designed to help you practice with some of these traditional tools.

FURTHER READING

Block, Bruce. *The Visual Story: Creating the Visual Structure of Film, TV, and Digital Media.* New York: Routledge, 2021.

Campbell, Joseph. *The Hero with a Thousand Faces.* New York: Pantheon Books, 1949.

Csikszentmihalyi, Mihaly. *Flow: The Psychology of Optimal Experience.* New York: Harper & Row Publishers, Inc., 1990.

Hench, John. *Designing Disney: Imagineering and the Art of the Show.* New York: Disney Editions, 2003.

Howard, David. *How to Build a Great Screenplay.* New York: St. Martin's Press, 2004.

Isbister, Katherine. *Better Game Characters by Design: A Psychological Approach.* San Francisco: Morgan Kaufmann, 2006.

McCloud, Scott. *Understanding Comics: The Invisible Art.* New York: HarperCollins Publishers, 1994.

Murray, Janet. *Hamlet on the Holodeck: The Future of Narrative in Cyberspace.* Cambridge: The MIT Press, 1997.

Vogler, Christopher. *The Writer's Journey - 25th Anniversary Edition: Mythic Structure for Writers.* Studio City: Michael Wiese Productions, 2020.

Wolf, Mark J.P. *Building Imaginary Worlds: The Theory and History of Subcreation.* New York: Taylor & Francis, 2012.

END NOTES

1. Csikszentmihalyi, Mihaly. *Flow: The Psychology of Optimal Experience.* New York: Harper & Row Publishers, Inc., 1990. p. 49.
2. Ibid.
3. Ibid, p. 53.
4. Ibid, pp. 58-59.
5. Ibid, p. 61.
6. Ibid, p. 63.
7. Ibid, p. 63.
8. Brown, Stuart and Kennard, David, Executive Producers. *The Promise of Play.* Institute for Play and InCA Productions, 2000.
9. Sutton-Smith, Brian. *The Ambiguity of Play.* Cambridge: Harvard University Press, 1997. pp. 4-5.
10. *The Promise of Play.* The Institute for Play and InCA, 2008.
11. Activision, Pitfall instruction manual, 1982.
12. Jenkins, Henry. *Convergence Culture: Where Old and New Media Collide.* New York: New York University Press., 2006. p. 114.

Chapter 5

Working with System Dynamics

In the previous two chapters, I discussed games in terms of their formal and dramatic elements. Now let's look at how the elements of games fit together to form playable systems and how designers can work with system properties to balance the dynamic nature of their games.

A system is defined as a set of interacting elements that form an integrated whole with a common goal or purpose. General system theory, the idea that the interaction among elements of systems can be studied across a wide variety of disciplines, was first proposed by the biologist Ludwig von Bertalanffy in the 1940s. Variations of system theory have evolved over time, each focusing on different types of systems. My goal here is not to examine all the various disciplines of system theory but rather to investigate how we can use an understanding of basic system principles to control the quality of interactions within our game systems as well as the growth and change of those systems over time.

GAMES AS SYSTEMS

Systems exist throughout the natural and human-made world wherever we see complex behavior emerging from the interaction between discrete elements. Systems can be found in many different forms. They can be mechanical, biological, or social in nature, among other possibilities. A system can be as simple as a stapler or as complex as a government. In each case, when the system is put in motion, its elements interact to produce the desired goal, for example, stapling papers or governing society.

Games are also systems. At the heart of every game is a set of formal elements that, as we have seen, when set in motion, create a dynamic experience in which the players engage. Unlike most systems, however, it is not the goal of a game to create a product, perform a task, or simplify a process. The goal of a game is to entertain its participants. When I discussed formal and dramatic elements, I showed how games do this by creating a structured conflict and providing an entertaining process for players to resolve that conflict. How the interaction of the formal and dramatic elements is structured forms the game's underlying system and determines a great deal about the nature of the game and the experience of the players.

As I mentioned earlier, systems can be simple or complex. Systems can produce precise,

DOI: 10.1201/9781003460268-6

predictable results, or they can produce widely varied, unpredictable effects. What type of system is best for your game? Only you can determine this. You might want to create a game in which there is a certain amount of predictability, in which case you might design a system with only one or two possible outcomes. On the other hand, you might want to create a very unpredictable system, in which there are countless possible outcomes determined by the choices of the players and the interactions of the game elements.

To understand why it is that systems act in such different ways and be able to control the type of system elements that affect the outcome of your own games, we need to first identify the basic elements of systems and look at what factors within these elements determine how a system acts in motion.

The basic elements of systems are objects, properties, behaviors, and relationships. Objects within the system interact with each other according to their properties, behaviors, and relationships, causing changes to the system state. How those changes are manifested depends on the nature of the objects and interactions.

Objects

Objects are the basic building blocks of a system. Systems can be thought of as a group of interrelated pieces called objects, which can be physical, abstract, or both, depending on the nature of the system. Examples of objects in games might be individual game pieces (such as the king or queen in chess), in-game concepts (such as the bank in Monopoly), the players themselves, or representations of the players (such as the avatars in an online environment). Areas or terrain can also be thought of as objects: the squares on a grid board or the yard lines on a playing field. These objects interact with other game objects in the same way that playing pieces do, and they need to be defined with the same amount of consideration.

Objects are defined by their properties and behaviors. They are also defined by their relationships with other objects.

Properties

Properties are qualities or attributes that define physical or conceptual aspects of objects. Generally, these are a set of values that describe an object. For example, the attributes of a bishop include its color (white or black) and its location. The properties of a character in a role-playing game can be much more complex, including variables such as health, strength, dexterity, experience, level, as well as its location in the online environment, and even the artwork or other media associated with that object.

The properties of objects form a block of descriptive data that can be essential to determining interactions of objects in a game system. The simplest types of game objects have very few properties, and those properties do not change based on gameplay. An example of this type of object would be the checkers in a checker game. Checkers have only three properties: color, location, and type. While the location of checkers changes, their color never does. The type of checker can change from "normal" to "king" if it reaches the other side of the board. These three properties completely define the state of each checker within a game.

The concept of "state" is an important one to game systems. The state of all the properties of all the game objects at any particular moment in a game makes up the current state of the game and the potential of these objects to change state, based on the rules of the game, makes up the full possibility space of the game.

What would be an example of a game object with more complex properties than the checker piece? How about a character in a role-playing game? Figure 5.1 shows the main properties of a character from Diablo. As you can see, this list defines an object of much greater complexity than

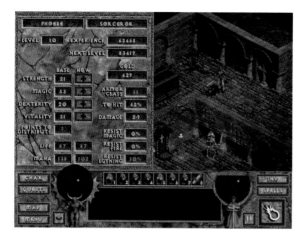

5.1 Diablo: character properties

our first example. Also, the properties of this object change over the course of the game, and not in a simple binary way, like the checker. Because of its greater complexity, the object in this case will probably have less predictable relationships with other objects in the system than would a simple object like a checker. And the game world of Diablo, based on the potential states of all of its game objects, also has a much larger possibility space than the game of checkers.

Exercise 5.1: Objects and Properties

Choose a board game you have at home in which you are able to clearly identify the objects and their properties. Strategy board games often have objects with properties that are easy to identify. Make a list of all of the objects and their properties in the game you have chosen.

Behaviors

The next defining characteristics of objects in a system are their behaviors. Behaviors are the potential actions that an object might perform in a given state. The behaviors of the bishop in chess include moving along any of the diagonals radiating from its current position until it is

blocked by or captures another piece. The behaviors of the role-playing character described previously might include walking, running, fighting, talking, using items, etc.

As with the sheer number of properties, the more potential behaviors an object has, the less predictable its actions within the system and the larger the possibility space of the overall game system. For example, let's take the checkers example again. A "normal" checker has two potential behaviors: It can move diagonally one space or jump diagonally to capture another piece. Its behavior is restricted by the following rules: It can only move toward the opponent; if it can jump an opponent's piece it must do so; and if possible, it can make multiple jumps in a turn. A "king" has the same behaviors, but it does not have the rule regarding moving toward the opponent; instead it can move forward or backward on the board. This comprises all the potential behaviors of the checker objects in the game (obviously, a very limited set of behaviors, which result in a small possibility space and predictable game pattern).

Now, let's look at the Diablo character again. What are the behaviors of this character? It can move: running or walking. It can attack using weapons in its inventory or skills like magic spells. It can pick up objects, converse with other characters, learn new skills, buy or trade objects, open doors or boxes, etc. Because of the range of behaviors available, the progression of this object through the game is much less predictable than the poor checker.

Does this make the game inherently more fun, however? I discuss this in the sidebar "Deconstructing Set" on page 139 when I analyze the system of Set, a simple, yet compelling, card game; the fact is, a greater complexity of gameplay does not always equate to a more enjoyable experience for the player. For now it is simply important to note that the addition of more potential behaviors tends to increase the possiblity space of the game and lessen the predictability of the outcome.

Exercise 5.2: Behaviors

Take the list of objects and properties you created in Exercise 5.1 and add a description of the behaviors for each object. Consider all behaviors in different game states.

Relationships

As I mentioned earlier, systems also have relationships among their objects. This is a key concept in design. If there are no relationships between the objects in question, then you have a collection, not a system. For example, a stack of blank index cards is a collection. If you write numbers on the cards or mark them in several suits, then you have created relationships among the cards. Removing the "3" card from a sequence of 12 will change the dynamics of a system that uses those cards.

Relationships can be expressed in a number of ways. A game played on a board might express relationships between objects based on location. Alternatively relationships between objects might be defined hierarchically, as in the numerical sequence of cards described previously. How relationships between objects in a system are defined plays a large part in how the system develops when it is put in motion.

The hierarchy of cards is an example of a fixed relationship: The numerical values fix a logical relationship between each of the cards in the set. An example of a relationship that changes during gameplay is the movement of the checkers on our checkerboard: Pieces move toward the other side of the board, jumping and capturing the opponent's pieces along the way. As they do so, their relationship to the board and to the other pieces on it continually changes.

Another example of a relationship is the progression of spaces on a board game like Monopoly. This is a fixed, linear relationship that constrains gameplay within a range of possibilities. On the other side of the spectrum, objects might have only loose relationships with other objects, interacting with them based on proximity or other variables. An example of this would be The Sims, where the relationships of the characters to other objects are based on their current needs and the ability of the objects in the environment to fulfill those needs. These relationships change as the characters' needs change; for example, the refrigerator is more "interesting," or ranked more highly in the game AI, to a character who is "hungry," or has a low hunger property, than a character who has just eaten a huge meal and has a high hunger value.

Change in relationships can also be introduced based on choices made by the players. The checkers game exhibits such change: Players choose where to move their pieces on the board. There are other ways to introduce change into game relationships. Many games use an element of chance to change game relationships. A good example of this is seen in most combat algorithms. Here is an explanation of how the combat algorithm works in WarCraft II, the classic real-time strategy game.[1]

Each unit in the game has four properties that determine how effective it is in combat.

- Hit Points: These indicate how much damage the unit can take before dying.
- Armor: This number reflects not only armor worn by the unit, but also its innate resistance to damage.
- Basic Damage: This is how much normal damage the unit can inflict every time it attacks. Basic damage is lowered by the target's armor rating.
- Piercing Damage: This reflects how effective the unit is at bypassing armor. (Magical attacks, like dragon's breath and lightning, ignore armor.)

When one unit attacks another, the formula used to determine damage is: (Basic Damage − Target's Armor) + Piercing Damage = Maximum Damage Inflicted. The attacker does a random

5.2 WarCraft II: going up against an ogre

amount of damage from 50-100% of this total each attack. To see how this algorithm tends to introduce chance into the relationship between objects, or units as we have been calling them, let's look at an example from the strategy guide on Battle.net:

An ogre and a footman are engaged in combat. The ogre has a Basic Damage rating of 8 and a Piercing Damage rating of 4. The footman has an Armor value of 2. Every time the ogre attacks the footman, it has the potential to inflict up to (8 − 2) + 4 = 10 points of damage, or it could inflict as little as 50% damage, or 5 points. On average, the ogre will kill the 60 Hit Point footman in about 8 swings.

The poor footman, on the other hand, with a Basic Damage of 6 and a Piercing Damage of 3, will only inflict 3 to 5 points of damage each time he attacks the ogre, which has an Armor value of 4 (that's (6−4) + 3 = 5). Even if the footman is extremely lucky and does the maximum amount of damage with every attack, it will take 18 swings to kill that 90 Hit Point ogre. By that time, the ogre will have pounded him into mincemeat and moved on.

This example actually shows two ways of determining relationships: chance and rule sets. As can be seen by the calculation, there is a basic rule set determining the range within which damage can fall. Within that range, however, chance determines the final outcome. Some games tend more toward chance in their calculations, while others tend more toward rule-based calculations. Which method is best for your game depends on the experience you want to achieve.

Exercise 5.3: Relationships

Take the list of objects, properties, and behaviors you created in Exercises 5.1 and 5.2 and describe the relationships between each object. How are these relationships defined? By position? By power? By value?

SYSTEM DYNAMICS

As I have noted, the elements of systems do not work in isolation from each other. If you can take components away from a system without affecting its functioning and relationships, then you have a collection, not a system. A system, by definition, requires that all elements be present for it to accomplish its goal. Also, a system's components must typically be arranged in a specific way for it to carry out its purpose, that is, to provide the intended challenge to the players. If that arrangement is changed, the results of the interaction will change. Depending on the nature of the relationships in the system, the change in results might be unnoticeable, or it might be catastrophic, but there will be a change to some degree.

Let's say that my example above of the ogre and the footman from WarCraft II was changed; instead of using the properties of basic damage, piercing damage, and target's armor to determine the range of potential damage from an attack, let's assume the damage dealt by each

DECONSTRUCTING SET

Set is a card game designed by Marsha Falco in 1988. At the time, Falco was studying as a population geneticist in Cambridge, England, trying to understand if German shepherds that get epilepsy actually inherit it. To help her understand the variables, she wrote information about each dog on file cards; she drew a symbol to represent a block of data, indicating different gene combinations. One day she found her kids playing with her research cards—they had made a game out of them. The game was so fun that they went on to publish it as a family business. The game became an instant classic, winning a number of awards, including the Mensa award.

The Rules of Set

The system of Set is quite elegant. The game is played with a special card deck made of 81 unique cards. The cards are the basic objects in the game, and each has a set of symbols with four properties: shape, number, pattern, and color; there are three options for each property. The diagram below shows how the number of properties and the options for each adds complexity to the deck, which is measured by the number of unique cards.

The procedures of Set are also quite simple. The deck is shuffled; 12 cards are then dealt out, as shown in the next diagram. The players all look at the cards, searching for "sets." A set consists of three cards in which each property is either all the same **or** all different. For example, in this layout, A1, A2, and A3 are a set because (1) shape = all the same, (2) number = all different, (3) pattern = all different, and (4) color = all different. A1, A4, and C1 are also a set because (1) shape = all different, (2) number = all the same, (3) pattern = all different, and (4) color = all different.

When a player sees a set, she calls out, "Set!" and points out which cards she believes make a set. If she is correct, she takes the cards; three more cards are dealt and play begins again. If she is incorrect, she must give back one of her sets to the discard pile. When there are no more cards, the player with the most sets wins.

	1	2	3	Unique cards
Shape	Oval	Diamond	Squiggle	3
Number	1	2	3	9
Pattern	Solid	Clear	Striped	27
Color	Green	Red	Purple	81

Elements of Set and how they contribute to complexity

Analyzing Set

As I have said, the design of Set is quite elegant. If you look closely at the cards in the figure at right, you will see that for any two cards you choose, you can describe the third card you would need to create a set. For example, look at B2 and C4. What card would need to create a set including these two cards? First, these cards have different shapes, so you would need another card with a different shape: an oval. Second, these cards have different numbers, one and three, so you need a card with two ovals. Third, these cards have different patterns, so you need a card with a different pattern: solid. Fourth, these cards have the same color, red, so you need another red. To make a

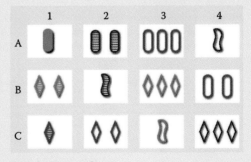

Set playing cards

set with B2 and C4, you need a card with two solid red ovals—there is only one such card in the deck, and it is not shown, so we cannot make a set with these two cards.

Now, how did Marsha Falco decide on this system configuration for the game of Set? Why not more properties? Or fewer? Why not more options for each property? As discussed in the analysis of Mastermind and Clue on page 144, the complexity of a system is greatly affected by the underlying mathematical structures. In Set, a deck of 81 cards provides a challenging, yet playable, number of possibilities. When learning to play Set, players often will remove the property of color to make the experience simpler. Without the property of color, the deck consists of only 27 cards, and it is much easier to find a set. After new players get the hang of it, they add back the remaining cards and the additional complexity that comes with a deck of 81 cards.

	1	2	3	Unique cards
Shape	Oval	Diamond	Squiggle	3
Number	1	2	3	9
Pattern	Solid	Clear	Striped	27
Color	Green	Red	Purple	81
Background	White	Black	Grey	243
Border	Silver	Gold	Onyx	729
Animation	Still	Blinking	Rotating	2187

Elements of Set with added properties

Imagine adding one more property—a background color, for example. As shown in the figure at top, this would create a deck of 243 cards. If we add a background border, our deck has 729 cards. Let's say we are making a digital version of Set. Now we can add animation! Should we? Well, that would mean there are 2187 cards in our digital game of Set. For a player trying to apply the rules of the game, there are now seven properties to consider and about 30 times less probability that the card you need to make a set will be dealt to the current display. You can see that adding this level of complexity has probably **not** improved your player experience. In fact, it is likely that this version of Set is unplayable.

	1	2	3	4	Unique cards
Shape	Oval	Diamond	Squiggle	Square	4
Number	1	2	3	4	16
Pattern	Solid	Clear	Striped	Hatched	64
Color	Green	Red	Purple	Yellow	256

Elements of Set with added option to original properties

The next figure shows another possibility—adding another option to each of the original properties. This does not change things quite as much; at least the deck is only 256 cards, only 3 times more complex than the original game system. But the game is already quite difficult. If you want to see what this change does to the player experience, build your own Set deck with the new option and playtest it.

Conclusion

This analysis deals with a game that is, compared to many digital games, quite simple. However, as you can see, changing just a few of the system elements can exponentially change the complexity of that simple system and the player experience. It is critical to understand the mathematical structures of your own game design and to test differing levels of complexity by adding to or deleting from your properties. One way to do this is the way we have done here with Set: build a matrix and calculate the level of complexity mathematically. And always keep in mind: A more complex mathematical solution might not offer the most satisfying gameplay result. The goal is always to build a system that is complex enough to delight and surprise your players, but not to confound or frustrate them.

unit was just a random number between 1 and 20. How would this change the outcome of each individual battle? How would it change the overall outcome of the game? What about the value of resources and upgrades?

If you said that the element of chance in the game would increase in both individual combat encounters and overall outcome, you are right. Also, the value of resources and the upgrades available via those resources would disappear because upgrades to units and armor would mean nothing in terms of determining outcome. The only strategy open to players in this game would be to build as many units as possible because sheer numbers would still statistically overwhelm in battle. So by changing the relationship between units in combat, we have changed the overall nature of the WarCraft II system.

On the other hand, if we changed the original damage calculation by removing the random element at the end and assuming that all units would deal maximum damage, how would that change the outcome of each battle? In this case, a player would be able to predict exactly how many attacks would be necessary for any one unit to destroy another. This sense of predictability would affect not only strategy but also player engagement. While in the first example of a completely random damage system, player decisions lose much of their strategic value, the example of a completely nonrandom damage system would diminish the unpredictability of individual encounters and the overall game as well. By taking all randomness out of the combat system, we would, in effect, remove the "play" from our system. Player input would be reduced to whether or not they made perfect or imperfect choices about which units to send into battle.

In some games, such as pure strategy games like chess or Go, this level of calculation is part of the game's challenge. Can you calculate your moves deeper and better than your opponent? But in a game like WarCraft II, the balance of calculated strategy against the randomized possibility of success in an attack is at the dramatic heart of the system's possibility space. In Chapter 4, I discussed play within a system as free movement on the part of players within a more rigid structure, but this applies to other objects in the system as well. The less rigid our rules are about potential outcomes, the more play each object has. Play within a system can be resolved by rules, by randomness, or by player choices. None of these are better options than the others in the abstract, but as a designer, you need to understand and judge how that play is affecting your gameplay experience. You can always tighten up a loose system that has too much play to engage your participants, or loosen up a tight system that doesn't have enough play to make participants feel involved. The key is to be able to see how your system elements are affecting each other, and which ones need to be tuned.

This concept of "tuning" a system leads us to the important idea that game systems are greater than the sum of their parts. By this I mean that studying all of the individual qualities of each system element in isolation does not equal studying these elements in relationship to each other. This is important for game designers to realize because games can only be understood during play when their dynamics become evident. Katie Salen and Eric Zimmerman call game design a "second-order" problem because of this,[2] meaning that when we design a game, we cannot directly determine the player experience—we cannot determine exactly how the rules will play out. We have to craft what I've been calling a "possibility space" as best we can, and playtest it as rigorously as possible, but in the end, we just do not know how each and every play of the game will go. The possibility space of many digital games is so complex that we really can't predict all of the potential outcomes of every interaction. We do our best to playtest as many as possible, but in modern design, we also sometimes need to use automated testing methods to test as many permutations as possible, as we will discuss in Chapter 9 Playtesting.

Exactly how the dynamics of any given game system are affected by the properties, attributes, and relationships of its objects is difficult to generalize. A good way to understand how these elements can affect each other is to look at some example systems—ranging from very simple to fairly complex—that exhibit various types of dynamic behavior.

Tic-Tac-Toe

The objects in tic-tac-toe are the spaces on the board. There are nine of them, and they are defined by their properties, behaviors, and relationships. For example, their properties, are "null," "x," or "o." Their relationships are defined by location. There is one center space, four corners, and four sides. When the game begins, the relationship between the spaces is such that there are only three meaningful choices for the first player: center, corner, or side.

The second player has between two and five meaningful choices, depending on where the first player put an "x." You can see by the diagram of potential moves that playing the first "x" in the center reduces the amount of significant next moves to two. Playing the first "x" in a corner or on a side creates up to five next moves.

If I continued this diagram of tic-tac-toe out to its conclusion, you would see that the tree of possibilities is not very large. In fact, when you learn the best possible moves to make, you can always win or tie at this game because of its ultimate simplicity. What is it about tic-tac-toe that makes its system so easy to learn?

First, you can see that the game objects themselves are simple: They have only three properties and one behavior. Also, their relationships to each other are fixed: The locations of the spaces on the board do not change. Because

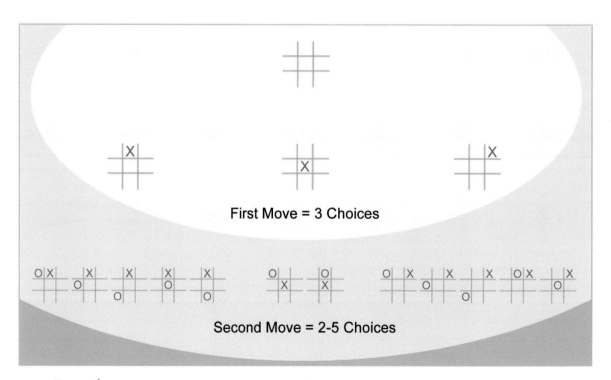

First Move = 3 Choices

Second Move = 2-5 Choices

5.3   Partial tic-tac-toe game tree

of both the number of objects (i.e., the size of the board) and their relationships, the system has only a few possible outcomes, and these are all completely predictable. And as a result of its limited possibilities for play, tic-tac-toe tends to lose the interest of players after they learn the optimal moves for any given situation.

Chess

An example of a system that has more than one type of object, and more complex behaviors and relationships between objects, is chess. First, let's look at the objects in chess: There are six types of units plus 64 unique spaces on the board.

Each unit has several properties: color, rank, and location, as well as a set of behaviors. For example, the white queen has a beginning location of D1 (the space at the intersection of the fourth rank of the first file). The movement behavior of the queen is that it may move in any straight line horizontally, vertically, or diagonally, as long as it is not blocked by another piece. Alone, these properties and behaviors do not make the objects in chess more complex than the spaces on the tic-tac-toe board. However, the varied behaviors of the objects and relationships between them do make the emergent gameplay more complex. Because each unit has specific behaviors in terms of movement and capture, and because those abilities create changes to their locations on the board, the relationships between each unit are effectively changed as a result of every move.

At the start of a game, the queen, as described above, as well as most of the other major pieces, are always blocked, so the opening moves of a chess game are limited to pawns and knights, which can move over other pieces. In fact, there are 20 potential opening moves in chess – 16 for the pawns and four for the knights. Even on the first move, this clearly is a much larger possibility space than the three potential opening moves in tic-tac-toe. So, while it is theoretically possible to create a tree similar to the one I drew for the

opening moves of tic-tac-toe, it quickly becomes clear that the complexity of potential outcomes beyond the first few moves makes this a useless and physically impossible process. This is not the way players tend to approach the game, and it is not even the way that computer chess applications have been programmed to decide the best move. Instead, both players and successful programs tend to use pattern recognition to solve problems, calling up solutions from memories of previously played games (or a database in the case of the computer) rather than plotting out a set of optimal solutions for each move. This is because the elements of the game system, when set in motion, create such a large range of possible situations that the tree becomes too complex to be useful. If you are interested in seeing how a chess engine works, you can read about them at Chess.com. Stockfish, currently considered the most powerful chess engine, is an open source engine that you can play against or use to analyze your own games.

Why does chess have such a vast number of possible outcomes as opposed to tic-tac-toe? The answer lies in the combination of the simple, but varied, behaviors of the game objects and their changing relationships to each other on the board. Because of the extremely varied

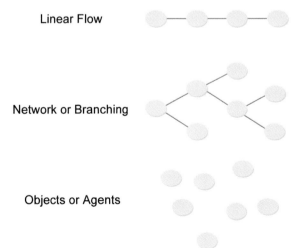

Linear Flow

Network or Branching

Objects or Agents

5.4 Various game structures

possibility set, chess remains challenging and interesting to players long after they have mastered its basic rule set. Even today, when powerful chess engines have beaten even the best grand masters, chess is still enjoying a renaissance of interested due to popular streamers like GothamChess (International Master Levy Rozman) and GMHikaru (Grand Master Hikaru Nakamura). These entertaining streamers deconstruct games and play out potential scenarios for viewers, explaining the possibilities for each player and helping them improve their understanding of the game.

One of the most important aspects of a game is the sense of possibility that is presented to the players at any given time. As I discussed in the previous chapter when talking about challenge, the goal of the designer is to present a situation that is equal to the abilities of the players and yet grows in challenge over time with their abilities. It is clear from the examples of tic-tac-toe and chess described above that how a system is constructed dramatically changes the dynamics of that system over time and the range of possibilities that face the player at any given point.

The range and type of possibilities within the system is not a situation where more is better in all situations. Many successful games have a somewhat constrained set of possibilities, and yet they still offer interesting gameplay. For example, a linear board game like Trivial Pursuit has a very small possibility space in terms of outcome, but the overall challenge of the game is not affected by this. Some digital games games, like side-scrollers, have a similarly small range of possibilities: Either you successfully navigate the challenge or you are stuck. But this range of action works for these types of games. Story-based adventure games often have branching structures with a limited number of outcomes. For players of these games, navigating that defined set of possibilities is part of the challenge.

On the other hand, some games have attempted to create larger spaces of possibility for their systems. The way in which they do

this is to introduce more objects into the system with defined relationships to each other. Open-world games like the Grand Theft Auto series, real-time strategy games, and massively multiplayer worlds all use such an approach to creating increased possibilities. The desired effects of a larger possibility space are a greater scope of choice for the player, opportunities for creative solutions to game problems, and enhanced replayability, all of which are an advantage to capturing players who are motivated by these potentials. Also, as described in the example of chess, games with large possiblity spaces make great subjects for streamers, who can show off interesting gameplay situations and discuss how they made their way through them. If your goal is to design a viral game, then thinking about how gamers might stream your game might be a part of your design goals.

These are all interesting thoughts, especially for bigger game teams, but before we get too far, let's look at some smaller systems as examples of how system complexity can be managed meaningfully as part of your design process. The following example shows how two fairly simple games with very similar objectives and related system designs can provide extremely different ranges of possibilities, and they therefore create completely different player experiences.

Mastermind versus Clue

The game of Mastermind is quite simple. In case you are not familiar with the game, Mastermind is a two-player puzzle game in which one player is the puzzle-maker and the other is the puzzle-breaker. The puzzle is made up of four colored pegs (from a possibility of six colors), and the object of the puzzle-breaker is to solve the puzzle in as few guesses as possible. The procedures are also simple: On each turn, the puzzle-breaker makes a guess, and the puzzle-maker gives him feedback by showing how many pegs are: (1) the correct color and (2) how many are the correct color *and* correct placement in the sequence. The

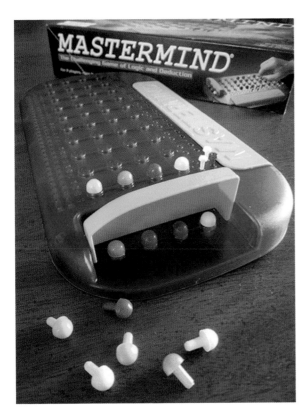

5.5   Mastermind

add such an exponentially greater number of possibilities that it would make the game potentially unplayable—or at least a lot harder. Adding another color would not be as great a change, but it would still double the number of potential puzzles and make the game significantly harder. The designers of Mastermind undoubtedly playtested these various combinations of the system before settling on four pegs and six colors.

Now let's look at Clue, or Cluedo as it is called in Europe. Clue has a similar puzzle-breaking objective, but that objective has a slightly different mathematical structure, and it is couched in a different set of procedural elements, resulting in an entirely different player experience.

Clue is also a game of logic and deduction in which the objective is to solve a puzzle. But Clue is a game is for three to six players, and there are no special roles—all players are trying to deduce the answer to the puzzle. The game maps the premise of solving a murder onto the puzzle system and adds an element of chance into the procedures via the board and movement system.

puzzle-breaker uses a process of elimination and logically attempts to narrow the possibilities and thereby solve the puzzle in as few guesses as possible.

Now let's look at the system structure. The objects in the game are the pegs, the properties are the colors, and the relationships are set by the puzzle-maker when they create the puzzle sequence. In the common version of Mastermind, the puzzle uses four pegs and six colors of pegs; repeated colors are allowed, so there are 6^4, or 1296, unique codes that can be made. If you added one more peg to the length of the code, you would have 6^5, or 7776, possibilities. If you added another color, you would have 7^4, or 2401. These choices are part of the game's system structure and define the possibility set for the players.

Even if you aren't a mathematician, you can see that adding another peg to the code would

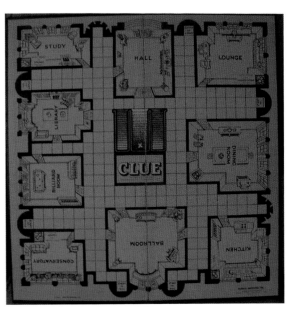

5.6   Clue board, circa 1947

In terms of its mathematical structure, the puzzles in Clue have a much smaller possibility set. There are six possible suspects, six possible weapons, and nine possible rooms, or $6 \times 6 \times 9 = 324$ possible combinations. The puzzle is mathematically simpler to solve, but players are hindered in their ability to guess the answer by the fact that they must roll the die and move around the board to gain information and make accusations. This addition of chance evens the playing field for those who might not have the best deduction skills (i.e., children) and makes Clue more accessible to a wider range of players. Also, the addition of the mystery premise and colorful characters provides a more compelling experience for some types of players, ergo a "family game."

If we compare Mastermind and Clue we see that both have similar objectives (i.e., solve a puzzle). Both puzzles are combinatorial (i.e., they use combinations of existing sets to create a "random" puzzle for each play). Mastermind has many more possible puzzle combinations, so the puzzle is harder to deduce. Clue has more ways of finding information: a social structure of asking for information, reading other players' faces, etc. Mastermind uses logic and deduction. Clue also uses logic and deduction, but it adds more chance to the system (dice and movement), as well as story (characters and setting).

This comparison is not meant to suggest that there is any one correct way to design a game system, just as there is no one type of game player. But you might find, upon analyzing some of your favorite games, that they share successful system designs in terms of the properties, behaviors, and relationships of their objects. Studying how the dynamics of these systems work can help focus your own thoughts and explorations and help you meet your own player experience goals.

Exercise 5.4: System Dynamics

Now let's take the game you have been working with in Exercises 5.1, 5.2, and 5.3 and see how we can change the system dynamics by experimenting with the properties, behaviors, or relationships of its core objects.

1. For example, if you chose a game like Monopoly, change the prices, placement, and rent of every property on the board or change the rules for movement. How you change these things is up to you, but make significant changes.

2. Now play the game. What happens? Did your changes affect the balance of the game? Is the game still playable?

3. If the system is still playable, make another change. For example, take out all the "positive" Chance cards in Monopoly and leave in only "negative or neutral" cards. Play the game again. What happens?

4. Continue doing this exercise until the game is no longer playable.

What was the crucial change you made? Why do you think that change finally broke the game?

One important type of system structure often found in games is an economy. I am going to look at this structure in more detail because it involves dynamics surrounding the resources in a game, one of the fundamental formal elements of games.

Economies

What is an economy? As I touched on briefly in my discussion of the utility and scarcity of resources in Chapter 3, some games also allow for the exchange of resources—either with the system (i.e., the bank in Monopoly) or among players. When a game allows exchanges of this kind, the system of trade forms a simple economy. In more complex systems, the rules of real-world economies might apply, but more often, games have severely controlled economies that only vaguely resemble real-world markets. Even so, there are some basic concepts of economic theory that we can use as a barometer for the feasibility of our game economies.

First of all, to have an economy, a game must have items of exchange, such as resources or other barterable items; agents of exchange, such as players or the system bank; and methods of exchange, such as markets or other trading opportunities. Also, an economy may or may not have currency, which helps to facilitate trade. As in the real world, the methods by which prices are set in an economy depend on what type of market controls are in place. Prices of market items in games can be free, fixed, or subject to a mixture of controls, depending on the design of the system. Also, the opportunities players have for trade can range from complete freedom to controls on prices, timing, partners, amount, etc. Here are some basic questions a designer should ask before building a game economy:

- Does the size of the economy grow over the course of the game? For example, are resources produced, and if so, is the growth controlled by the system?
- If there is a currency, how is the supply of that currency controlled?
- How are prices set in the economy? Are they controlled by market forces or set by the game system?
- Are there any restrictions on opportunities for trade among participants, for example, by turn, time, cost, or other constraints?

To get a sense for how games handle these economic variables, let's look at some examples ranging from classic board games to massively multiplayer online worlds.

Simple Bartering

Pit is a simple card game in which players barter for various commodities to "corner the market." There are eight suits of commodities, nine cards in each suit. The commodities are worth

5.7   Pit

a varying number of points from 50-100. For example, oranges are worth 50 points, oats are 60 points, corn is 75, wheat is 100, etc. You start with the same number of suits in the deck as there are players—from three to eight.

The cards are shuffled and dealt out evenly to all the players. During each round, players trade by calling out the number of cards they want to trade but not the name of the commodity on the cards offered. Trade continues until one person holds all nine cards of a single commodity—a "corner" on that market.

There are several features to note in this simple barter system. First, the amount of product (i.e., cards) in the system is stable at all times—cards are not created or consumed during play. Additionally, the value of each card never changes relative to the other cards in the deck. The value is fixed by the printed point value set before the game begins. Also, the opportunity to trade is only restricted by number—all trades must be for an equal number of cards. Other than this, trade is open to all players at all times.

In this simple barter system, the in-game economy is so restricted by the rules of the game that there is no opportunity for economic growth, no fluctuation of prices based on supply and demand, no chance for market competition, etc. However, the trading system serves its purpose as an excuse for creating a frenetic, social trading atmosphere without any of the complexities of a real-world economy. To recap the features of this system:

- Amount of product = fixed
- Money supply = n/a
- Prices = fixed
- Trading opportunities = not restricted

Complex Bartering

Settlers of Catan is a German board game by designer Klaus Teuber in which players compete as pioneers developing a new land. During the course of the game, players build roads and settlements that produce resources such as brick, wood, wool, rock, and wheat. These resources can be traded with other players and used to build more settlements and upgrade settlements to cities, which in turn produce more resources.

As in Pit, the bartering of resources is a central part of the gameplay, and the trade in this game is also fairly unrestricted, with the following exceptions:

- You may only trade with a player on their turn.
- Players can only trade resources, not settlements or other game objects.
- A trade must involve at least one resource on each side (i.e., a player cannot simply give a resource away). However, trades can be made for unequal amounts of resources.

Other than these constraints, players can wheel and deal as they like for the resources they need. For example, if there is a scarcity of brick in the economy, players can trade two or three of another resource, such as wheat, for one brick.

As you can probably judge already, the economy of Settlers of Catan is much more complex than the simple barter system of Pit. One of the key differences is the fact that the relative values of the resources fluctuate depending on market conditions, an interesting and unpredictable feature that changes the experience of the game from play to play. If there is a glut of wheat in the game, the value of wheat falls immediately. On the other hand, if there is a scarcity of ore, players will trade aggressively for it. This simple example of the laws of supply and demand adds a fascinating aspect to gameplay that we did not see in the Pit example.

Another key difference from the simple bartering in Pit is that in Settlers of Catan, the total amount of product in the economy changes over the course of the game. Each player's turn has a production phase, the results of which are determined by a roll of the dice and the placement of player settlements. Product enters the system during this phase. Product is then traded and "consumed" (used to purchase roads, settlements, etc.) during the second phase of the player's turn.

To control the total amount of product in the system at any time, the system includes a punishment for holding too many resources in your hand. If a player rolls a seven during the production phase of their turn, any player holding more

5.8   Barterable resources from Settlers of Catan

than seven cards has to give half of their hand to the bank. In this way, players are discouraged from hoarding and are encouraged to spend their resources as they earn them.

Another aspect of the economy that is interesting to note is the fact that while the barter system is fairly open, there is a control on price inflation. The bank will always trade 4:1 for any resource; this effectively caps the value of all resources. And, as we also noted, while the trading system itself is quite open, the opportunity to trade is restricted by player turn.

The last difference between these two barter systems is their information structures. In Settlers of Catan, players hide their hands, but the production phase is an open process, so by simply paying attention to which players are getting certain resources on each turn, an

attentive player can remember some, if not all, of the game state.

- Amount of product = controlled growth
- Money supply = n/a
- Prices = market value with cap
- Trading opportunities = restricted by turn

Exercise 5.5: Bartering Systems

For this exercise, take the simple barter game of Pit and add a new level of complexity to its trading system. One way to do this might be to create the concept of dynamically changing values for each of the commodities.

Simple Market

The first two examples we have looked at have both been barter systems (i.e., they did not employ currency). The next type of system we will look at is the simple market system of Monopoly. In Monopoly, players buy, sell, rent, and improve real estate in an attempt to become the richest player in the game. The real estate market in the game is finite—there are 28 properties in the market (including railroads and utilities) at all times. Although properties are not sold until a player lands on their board space, they are still active in the sense that they are available for purchase.

Each player begins the game with $1500 from the bank, which they can use to purchase properties or pay rent and other fees. The growth of the economy is controlled by the rate at which players can circle the board, passing "go" to collect $200. According to the official rules, the bank never goes broke; if it runs out of money, the player acting as banker can create new notes out of slips of paper.

In terms of trading opportunities, the rules state that buying and trading of properties between players can occur at any time, although "etiquette suggests that such transactions occur only between the turns of other players."[3]

5.9   Monopoly money and property

Values of properties in the game are set in two basic ways. First, there is the face value on the title deed; if a player lands on a property, she may purchase it for this amount. If she fails to purchase the property, it goes up to auction and sells to the highest bidder. The auction is not limited by the face value, and the player who passed up purchasing it may bid in the auction. After a property is purchased, it can be traded between players at any price they agree upon. So the second and more important value of properties in the game is a true market value set by the competition of the players.

- Amount of product = fixed
- Money supply = controlled growth
- Prices = market value
- Trading opportunities = not restricted

Complex Market

For examples of complex market economies, we'll look at two historically interesting online games: Ultima Online and EverQuest. These games helped establish the genre of massively multiplayer online role-playing games. The two economies have much in common overall, but different emphases in their designs have created unique situations for each system. The key similarity in these and other online worlds is the fact that they have persistent economies that surpass a single game session by any one player. This immediately puts them in a category of complexity far beyond all the other examples we have looked at so far. The assumption often is that real-world economies apply directly to their systems because of the persistence of economy in these games and because they strive to create a sense of an alternate world.

In both games, players create characters, or avatars, that begin the game with a small number of resources—a little gold in Ultima or platinum in EverQuest, some minimal armor, and a weapon. Now players must enter the "labor market" to gain more resources. In both games, players begin at the lowest level of the labor market—killing small

animals or doing other menial work to earn money. They can sell the results of their labor to system agents (in the form of shopkeepers) or to other players, if they can find interested buyers. In addition to the labor market, players can find, make, buy, or sell more complex items than those gained by labor. Items like weapons, armor, and magic items are part of a complex "goods" market.

In both games, goods and labor are traded in two ways: player to player and player to system. In both games, player-to-system trade, controlled by the game designers, exists to keep low-level "employment" steady while encouraging the player-to-player trade in scarce items. For example, shopkeepers will generally buy anything a player wants to sell, even if there is a glut of the object in the market. This keeps newbies steadily "employed." On the other hand, the shopkeepers' offers to buy on higher-level items will not be as competitive as the player-to-player market, encouraging players to seek out higher prices from one another.

In this way, the games create markets that mimic real-world situations in important ways and contradict real-world expectations in others. Supply and demand is a factor for players dealing at higher levels of commerce, with scarce or unique items, but it is not a factor for a newbie just trying to get ahead.

The amount of product in the system is controlled by the game designers, although Ultima at first tried to create a self-regulating flow in which resources were recycled through the system, available to respawn as new creatures and other materials as they were "spent" by the players. This was quickly changed to a system in which the flow of resources into the economy could be directly controlled by the designers. There were several reasons for this, one of which was a tendency for players to hoard game objects, restricting the total amount of products circulating in the game.

In these games and modern games of this genre, a meta economy often emerges separate from official gameplay in which characters and game objects are sold between players in real-world markets. Characters have been offered on sites such as eBay sometimes sell for hundreds of dollars, depending on the level and inventory offered. While these meta economies are not a planned feature of these role-playing games, there are games that have included the concept of a meta economy in their designs.

- Amount of product = controlled growth
- Money supply = controlled growth
- Prices = market value with base
- Trading opportunities = not restricted

Meta Economy

Magic: The Gathering, is another historically interesting game because it was the genesis for the collectible card game genre of play. It is somewhat different from the other example games we have looked at, in that the game itself does not include a trading or exchange component. The main system of Magic is a dueling game in which players use custom-designed decks of cards to battle each other. These cards, purchased by

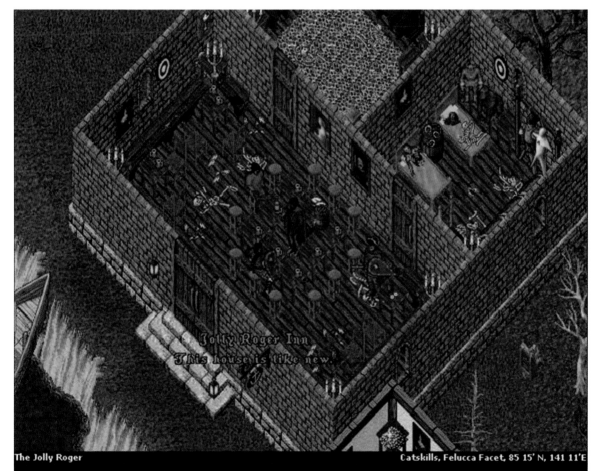

The Jolly Roger   Catskills, Felucca Facet, 85 15' N, 141 11'E

The Jolly Roger Tavern, a dirty but legendary tavern, is the heart of the town of Red Skull Bay and home to fighting contests and some of the best ale in all Britannia. Landlubbers and sailors alike are invited to have a look at this unique bay, and raise a bottle of ale or two with the residents of Red Skull Bay.

5.10   Player-run establishment in Ultima Online

individual players, form the central resource in a meta economy surrounding the game itself.

Magic: The Gathering was designed by Richard Garfield and released by Wizards of the Coast, a Seattle-based game company, in 1993. At the time, Garfield was a mathematics professor at Whitman College as well as a part-time game designer. Wizards asked him to design a card game that was quick, fun, and playable in under an hour. But Garfield imagined a game that had the collectible nature of trading cards or marbles, combined with the qualities of Strat-O-Matic Baseball, in which players draft and compete their own teams. The result was a collectible card game that has been likened to "gaming crack." See Garfield's sidebar on the evolution of the game on page 219.

As mentioned, the game Garfield designed is a two-player dueling game with a fantasy theme. Each player has a deck of cards that consists of various spells, monsters, and lands. Land provides mana, which powers spells. These spells summon monsters that you use to attack your opponent. This would seem pretty straightforward except for the fact that a basic deck of game cards does not include all the cards in the system. In fact, it contains a mere fraction of the cards available. Players are encouraged to buy booster sets and to upgrade their deck as new revisions are released. And, important to our discussion of game economies, players can also buy and trade cards from each other, which they do aggressively. The market for Magic cards, and other similar collectible card game cards, is worldwide, greatly facilitated by the Internet.

The publisher of the game has control of the overall shape of this economy, in that it gauges how many cards to release—some cards are very rare, some are just uncommon, and others are not valuable at all because there are simply far too many of them available. But the publisher has no control over where and how these cards are traded after they have been purchased, and, other than rarity, it has no control over the prices set for these game objects.

In addition to the collectible nature of Magic and the meta economy formed by the trade of its game objects, there is an in-game aspect to this meta economy. Players choose cards from their collection to build decks, adjusting the amount of land and the types of creatures and spells to strike a winning balance.

This process of building and testing decks for effectiveness is similar to the process a game designer would go through when testing the balance of their system, and, of course, the designers of Magic work hard to make sure that any single card or combinations of cards are not so overpowered as to imbalance the game. But the final decisions regarding resource balance are left in the hands of the player and are highly affected by the meta economy surrounding the game.

The openness of the Magic system, and its success as a business as well as a game, has spawned a whole genre of trading games. As with online

5.11   Magic: The Gathering cards

worlds, it is clear that much of the success of these games depends on how their in-game and metagame economies are managed over time.

- Amount of product = controlled growth
- Money supply = n/a
- Prices = market value
- Trading opportunities = not restricted

Meta economies for games have recently become an even greater factor in design with the rise of the somewhat ironically named "free-to-play" model for games. In these games, players can engage with the basic gameplay for free, but are encouraged, through the game structure, to purchase upgrades that can include extra resources, characters, or other items that speed up or improve their gameplay. A good example of this model is Clash of Clans, which is a social strategy game driven by a base resource of green "gems." Players begin with 500 of these gems, 250 of which they will use to complete the entry tutorial. They can earn more gems by meeting in-game goals or by using real-world currency to purchase them. As with the Magic meta economy discussed earlier, this means that players willing to invest money in these kinds of micro transactions can significantly increase their playing power. Today's mobile game industry relies heavily on this model of low-barrier-to-entry game combined with a design structure that encourages players to pay as they go.

As you can see, there are a wide variety of economies, ranging from simple bartering to complex and even real-world markets. The task of the designer is to wed the economic system with the game's overall structure and make sure that it supports satisfying gameplay. The economy must tie directly into the player's objective in the game and be balanced against the comparative utility and scarcity of the resources it involves. Every action players perform in relation to the economic system should either advance or hinder their progress in the game. In the case of free-to-play games, this is an important consideration to think about when or whether players should feel the need to make purchases in the game.

A great example of how a thoughtful designer thinks about their game economy can be found in this quote from Derek Yu, designer of the Spelunky, a unique roguelike/platformer game with procedurally generated levels. Yu's Designer Perspective can be found on page 98. "The shopkeeper has become the most notorious character in Spelunky, equally feared and beloved by his patrons. His shop, which appears 100% of the time in level 2 and has a decreasing chance of appearing in later levels (2/3 chance in level 3, 2/4 in level 4, 2/5 in level 5, and so on), is the most consistent source of life-saving items as you spelunk your way downward. Given the utility of the items, they carry hefty price tags that increase with each level: A sack of extra bombs will cost upwards of $2,500, and more exotic tools like the jetpack can reach into the tens of thousands of dollars."[4] What can be seen from this quote is the way that Yu thought about his resource economy in terms of the player experience. Experienced players, reaching lower levels, will find it increasing difficult to find and afford the resources they need – challenging them to think of creative ways to get what they need.

In general, economies have the potential to transform rudimentary games into complex systems, and if you are creative, you can use them as a way to get players to interact with one another or the system in clever ways. There is nothing better for community building than an underlying economy, which can promote discussion and socializing both in and outside of the game.

Developing new types of in-game economies is one of the areas in which modern game design has just begun to explore the potential. With the success of games like Clash of Clans and interesting new economic models for mobile games that bridge game economies with real-world economies, we are just beginning to understand the power of these systems. The fusing of economic models and social interaction has been of the most active areas of recent game experimentation, and in the next decade, we will see new types of game economies emerge that will certainly challenge our conception of what a game can be.

Emergent Systems

I have mentioned that game systems can display complex and unpredictable results when set in motion. But this does not mean that their underlying systems must be complex in design. In fact, in many cases, very simple rule sets, when set in motion, can beget unpredictable results. Nature is full of examples of this phenomenon, which is called "emergence." For example, an individual ant is a simple creature that is capable of very little by itself and lives its life according to a simple set of rules. However, when many ants interact together in a colony, each following these simple rules, a spontaneous intelligence emerges. Collectively, the drone ants become capable of sophisticated engineering, defense, food storage, etc. Similarly, some researchers believe that human consciousness might be a product of emergence. In this case, millions of simple "agents" in the mind interact to create rational thought. The topic of emergence has spawned dozens of books that explore links between previously unconnected natural phenomena.

One experiment in emergence, which is interesting for game designers, is called the Game of Life. (No, it is not related to Milton Bradley's board game The Game of Life.) This experiment was conducted in the 1960s by a mathematician at Cambridge University named John Conway. He was fascinated with the idea that rudimentary elements working together according to simple rules could produce complex and unpredictable results. He wanted to create an example of this phenomenon so simple that it could be observed in a two-dimensional space like a checkerboard.

Building on the work of mathematicians before him, Conway toyed with rules that would make squares on the board turn "on" or "off" based on their adjacency to the other squares around them. Acting very much like a game creator, he designed, tested, and revised different sets of rules for these cells for several years with several associates in his department at Cambridge.

Finally, he arrived at this set of rules:

- *Birth*: If an unpopulated cell is surrounded by exactly three populated cells, it becomes populated in the next generation.
- *Death by loneliness*: If a populated cell is surrounded by fewer than two other populated cells, it becomes unpopulated in the next generation.
- *Death by overpopulation*: If a populated cell is surrounded by at least four other populated cells, it becomes unpopulated in the next generation.

Conway and his associates set Go pieces on a checkerboard to mark populated cells, and they administered the rules by hand. They found that different starting conditions evolved in vastly different ways. Some simple starting conditions could blossom into beautiful patterns that would fill the board, and some elaborate starting conditions could fizzle into nothing. An interesting

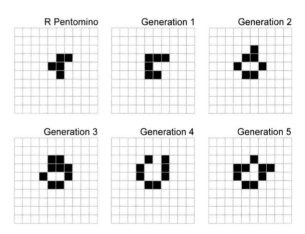

5.12   R Pentomino over several generations

discovery was made with a configuration called R Pentomino. Figure 5.12 shows the starting position for the R Pentomino, followed by several generations.

One of Conway's associates, Richard Guy, kept experimenting with this configuration. He administered the rules for a hundred generations or so and watched a mishmash of shapes appear. Then suddenly a set of cells emerged from the group and appeared to "walk" on its own across the board. Guy pointed out to the group, "Look, my bit's walking!"[5] Guy worked on the configuration until it walked across the room and out the door. He had discovered what the group would call a "glider." A glider is a configuration that cycles through a set of shapes and moves along the board as it goes. Figure 5.13 shows what several generations of Guy's glider look like.

Conway's system was dubbed the Game of Life because it showed that from simple beginnings, life-form-like patterns could develop. There are a number of emulators online that you can download and experiment with. You will see that some use different rules and allow you to create your own starting conditions.

Emergent systems are interesting to game designers because games can employ emergent techniques to make more believable and unpredictable scenarios. Games as different as The Sims, Grand Theft Auto 3, Halo, Black & White, Pikmin, Munch's Oddysee, and Metal Gear Solid 2 have all experimented with emergent properties in their designs.

One interesting example is the character AI in the Halo series. Nonplayer characters have three simple impulses that drive them: (1) perception of the world around them (aural, visual, and tactile), (2) state of the world (memories of enemy sightings and weapon locations), and (3) emotion (growing scared when under attack, etc.).[6] These three sets of rules interact—each consulting the other—as a decision-making system in a character. The result is semirealistic behavior within the game. The nonplayer characters do not follow a script written by a designer but rather make their own decisions based on the situation they are in. For example, if all of their friends have been killed and they are facing overwhelming firepower from the enemy, they tend to run away; otherwise, they stay and fight.

Different games utilize different methods for creating emergent behavior. The Sims embeds simple rules in both the characters and in items in the environment. Will Wright, creator of The Sims, built the household items in the game to have values. When a character gets near an

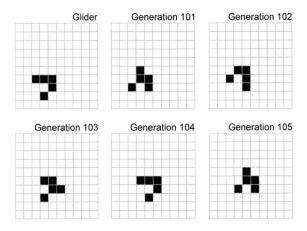

5.13   Glider "walk" cycle

5.14   The Sims

item—such as a bed, refrigerator, or pinball machine—the rules in the character interact with the rules in the item. So if a character's rules say he is sleepy, then an item that provides comfort, such as a bed, might attract his attention.

All of the previous examples share the same basic concept that simple rules beget complex behavior when interacting within a system. This concept is an exciting and fast-moving aspect of games and generative AI today, and it is wide open to experimentation and innovation.

INTERACTING WITH SYSTEMS

Games are designed for player interaction, and the structures of their systems are integrally related to the nature of that interaction. Some of the things that need to be considered when designing for interaction are:

- How much information do players have about the state of the system?
- What aspects of the system do players control?
- How is that control structured?
- What type of feedback does the system give the players?
- How does this affect the gameplay?

Information Structure

For players to make choices about how to proceed in a game, they need information about the state of the game objects and their current relationships to each other. The less information players have, the less informed their choices will be. This affects the sense of control they have over their progress. It can also add to the amount of chance in the system and allow space for misinformation or deception as a part of the gameplay.

To understand the importance of information in a game system, think about what types of information you are given in some of the games that you like to play. Do you know the effect of every move you make? What about the other players? Is there information that you only have access to some of the time?

How information is structured in a game has a large influence on how players come to their decisions. In classic strategy games like chess and Go, the players have complete information about the game state. This is an example of an open information structure. An open structure emphasizes player knowledge and gives full disclosure on the game state. It will generally allow for more calculation-based strategy in the system. If this is the type of play you want to encourage in your system, you need to make sure that important information is available to your users.

On the other hand, if you want to create play situations built around guessing, bluffing, or deceiving, you might want to consider hiding information from players. In a hidden information structure, players do not receive certain data about their opponent's game state. A good example of this is the 5-card stud variation of poker in which all cards are dealt facing down. In this game, the only information players have about their opponents' hands is how many cards they are dealt and the way in which they bet. This hidden information structure allows for a different type of strategy to develop—one based on social cues and deception rather than calculation. It tends to appeal to an entirely different type of player.

Exercise 5.6: Hidden Information

Many strategy games have open information structures that allow the players access to perfect information about the game state. Examples are chess, checkers, Go, mancala, etc. Take a game with an open information structure and change the system so that there is an element of hidden information. You might need to add new concepts to the game to accomplish this. Test your new design. How does adding hidden information change the nature of the strategy? Why do you think this is so?

Many games use a mixture of open and hidden information so that players are given some data about the state of their opponent's game, but not all. An example of such a mixed information structure might be the 7-card stud variation of poker where several cards are dealt down and several up over the course of the betting cycle, giving players only partial information about their opponents' hands. Another example of a mixed information structure is blackjack, for the same reasons.

The amount of information that players receive about their opponents' states often changes during the course of the game. This might be because they have learned information by interacting with their opponents, or it might be because the concept of a dynamic information structure is built into the game. For example, many real-time strategy games, like the classic WarCraft series, use the concept of "fog of war" to provide dynamically changing information to players about their opponents' status. In this game, players can see the state of their opponents' territory if they move a unit into that territory. When they move the unit out of the territory, the information freezes until another unit ventures back to the territory.

A dynamically changing information structure provides an ever-shifting balance between strategy based on knowledge and strategy based on cunning and deceit. For the most part, this type of advanced information structure has only been possible since the advent of digital games and the computer's ability to orchestrate the complex interactions between players.

Exercise 5.7: Information Structures

What type of information structures are present in Unreal Tournament, Age of Empires, Jak II, Madden NFL, Lemmings, Scrabble, Mastermind, and Clue? Do they have open, hidden, mixed, or dynamic information structures? If you do not know one of the games, pick a game that I have not mentioned and substitute it.

Control

The basic controls of a game system are directly related to its physical design. Board games or card games offer control by direct manipulations of their equipment. Digital games might use a keyboard, mouse, joystick, gesture, multi-touch, speech, or other alternative types of control devices. Platform games usually provide a proprietary controller. Arcade games often use game-specific controls. Each of these types of controls is best suited to certain types of input. Because of this, games that require specific input types have been more successful in some game platforms than others. For example, games that require text entry have never been as popular on consoles as they have been on PCs. Today's designers have a wide range of control options to consider, and each brings with it different potential play situations. For example, gestural controls like the now-defunct Kinect system offered the potential for full-body input. They are useful for prompting big, physical actions in games that are more about the emotion and experience of movement than precise input. Recently, we have been seeing more use of speech controls in mobile and alternative platforms. Generative AI characters, combined with speech controls, promise a whole new type of interaction with non-player characters.

One type of control system is not inherently better than another. What matters is whether the control system is well suited for the game experience, and it is the job of the designer to determine this. I encourage you to think about the games you like to play. What type of controls do you enjoy? Do you prefer to have direct control over the game elements, such as you might have when moving your character through a 3D shooter? Or indirect control, as in a game like SimCity? Do you prefer touch controls, as in Angry Birds, or gestural controls like Kinect Star Wars? These decisions will have a huge impact on what type of game you design and how you go about structuring it.

Direct control of movement is a clear-cut way for players to influence the state of the game. Players can also have direct control over other types of input, like selection of items, directly presented choices, etc. Some games do not offer direct control, however. For example, in a simulation game like Rollercoaster Tycoon, players do not have direct control over the guests at their theme park. Instead, players can change ride variables, trying to make certain rides more attractive by lowering price, increasing throughput, or improving the ride design. This indirect control offers ways for players to influence the state of the game that is one step removed from the desired changes and provides an interesting type of challenge within certain game systems.

When the designer chooses what type of control to offer to players, he is deciding a very

5.15   Indirect control: Rollercoaster Tycoon

important part of the game. This decision forms the top-level experience that players will have with the system. Control often involves a repetitive process or action performed throughout a game – the core loop we discussed in Chapter 3 on page 80. If this basic action is hard to perform, unintuitive, or just not enjoyable, the player might stop playing the game altogether.

In addition to deciding the level of control, the designer also needs to consider restricting control of some elements completely. As I discussed when I talked about designing conflict, games are made challenging by the fact that the players cannot simply take the simplest route to a solution. This is true in terms of designing controls as well. Some games allow a high degree of freedom in terms of player control. For example, a 3D shooter allows for spontaneous, real-time movement throughout the environment. Other games restrain player control tightly, using this structure to provide part of the challenge. An example of this would be a turn-based strategy game, like Go or chess.

How do you decide what controls to allow players and what not to allow? This is a central part of the design process. You can see the impact that different levels of input have on games if you look at a familiar game and imagine how it would work if you took away some of the player input.

For example, let's look at a real-time strategy game like StarCraft: Remastered. In this game, the player selects certain units to mine minerals, others to harvest gas, etc. How many units are doing these tasks at any given time is a function of availability, but it is basically under the player's control. What if this opportunity for control were taken away? Imagine how the system would work if the designer determined that system would always assign 50% of the available units to mine minerals and 50% to harvest gas. How would taking this input away from the player affect the system? Would it create too much balance between various players' resources? Would it take away some tedious parts of gameplay?

Or would it take away critical resource management? These are questions a designer faces when thinking about how much and what type of control to give players in the system.

Exercise 5.8: Control

For the same games mentioned in Exercise 5.7, describe the methods of control they use: direct or indirect, real time or turn based. Are there any cases in which these distinctions are mixed?

Feedback

Another aspect of interaction with the system is feedback. When we use the word "feedback" in general conversation, we often are just referring to the information we get back during an interaction, not what we do with it. But in system terms, feedback implies a direct relationship between the output of an interaction and a change to another system element. Feedback can be positive or negative, and it can promote divergence or balance in the system.

5.16   Positive and negative feedback loops

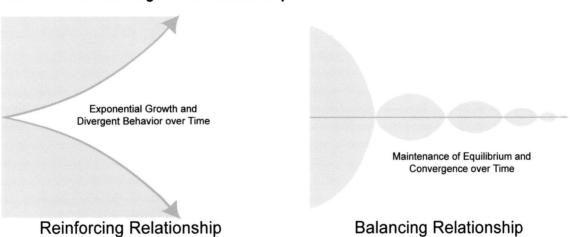

5.17   Reinforcing and balancing relationships over time

Figure 5.16 shows example feedback loops for two different types of game scoring systems. In the first example, if a player scores a point, they get a free turn. This reinforces the positive effects of the scored point, creating an advantage for that player. A negative feedback loop, on the other hand, like that on the right, works against the effect of the point. In this example, every time a player scores a point, they must pass the turn to the other player. This has the effect of balancing the system between the two players rather than allowing one player to get a larger advantage over the other.

"Positive" and "negative" are somewhat loaded terms, and some systems theories use the terms "reinforcing" and "balancing" instead. Generally, reinforcing relationships are ones in which a change to one element directly causes a change to another element in the same direction. This might force the system toward one or the other extreme. By contrast, in balancing relationships, a change to one element causes a change to another in the opposite direction, forcing the system toward equilibrium.

For example, in the game Jeopardy!, when a player answers a question correctly, she retains control of the board. This presumably gives the leading player an advantage in answering the next question, reinforcing her lead in the game and moving the system toward resolution in their favor. This is a reinforcing relationship, or loop. An example of the same type of relationship, but in the opposite extreme, would be if a Jeopardy! player who answered incorrectly were forced to sit out the next question. This is not a rule in the game, but if it were, it would reinforce the repercussions of answering a question wrong.

Reinforcing loops cause output that either steadily grows or declines. Many games use reinforcing loops to create satisfying risk/reward scenarios for players that drive the game toward an unequal outcome based on player choices. To keep the game from resolving too quickly, however, balancing relationships are also used.

Balancing relationships, on the other hand, try to counteract the effects of change. In a balancing relationship, a change to one element results in a change to another element in the opposite direction. The classic example of a balancing relationship is in football. When one team scores, the ball is turned over to the other team. This gives a boost to the nonscoring team, attempting to balance the effects of the points won. If the advantage were given to the scoring team instead, it would be an example of a reinforcing relationship.

Some balancing relationships are not as easy to distinguish. For example, the board game Settlers of Catan has a procedure that attempts to create balance in the number of resources each player can hold at any one time. In this game, every time a seven is rolled with two six-side dice, any players holding more than seven cards in their hand must give up half of them. This has the effect of keeping prosperous players from becoming too powerful and resolving the game too quickly.

To improve gameplay, a good designer must be able to evaluate how quickly or slowly the game is progressing, understand if there are patterns to growth or contraction in the system caused by reinforcing loops, and know when and how to apply a balancing factor.

INTERACTION LOOPS AND ARCS

by Daniel Cook

Daniel Cook is Chief Creative Officer at Spry Fox. His games include Alphabear, Triple Town, Realm of the Mad God, Tyrian, and many others. In his spare time, he also writes about game design theory and the business of games at Lostgarden.com

All games (and in fact all interactive systems) are composed of common structural elements called *interaction loops*. These describe how a player interacts with a game and how the game in turn responds to the player. Once you learn to spot them in your games, you'll find they provide a powerful analytical tool for debugging both broken systems and confused players.

Interaction loops help you understand:

- Exactly how players go about learning your game
- The skills players acquire and the order in which they acquire them
- Which exact portions of your game are breaking and causing confusion
- How the smallest interactions in a game are tied into the most complex interactions and why players care

Interaction loops

Any interaction within a game involves the following steps:

1. The player starts with a **mental model** that prompts them to...
2. Make a **decision** to...
3. Apply an **action** in order to...
4. Manipulate the game **rules** and in return...
5. Receive **feedback** that...
6. **Updates** their mental model. Or, in other words, they start to learn how the systems of the game work.

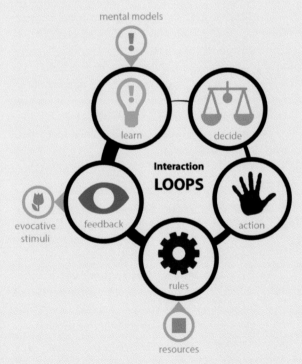

Players then start the interaction loop all over again to gain more practice with a specific **skill**. Or the player decides that what they did wasn't worth it and instead kicks off whole new interaction loop!

Consider Mario from Nintendo's Super Mario Bros learning to jump.

1. You hand a new player the controller. They've never played Mario and have little idea what to do. But they notice that the controller has the **affordance** of buttons and they've got a pretty good pre-existing mental model of how you interact with buttons.

2. They don't have much pre-existing information on evaluating **costs and benefits**, so they throw caution to the wind and randomly choose a button. Even a random sampling of an unknown system will likely teach them something.

3. Then they press the button.

4. The mysterious black box within the game, the game **rules,** begins executing hidden code. Time, an abstract resource, advances. There's anticipation at this moment for the player because they don't know yet what might happen. If this system were completely known, it would not be nearly as interesting to play with.

5. Finally, the computer generates visual **feedback** on the screen that Mario is jumping. This is a form of functional feedback because it tells the player how the black box operates.

6. Aha! After a few more loops through the interactions, the player updates their **mental model** that Pressing the A button *causes* Mario to jump. This realization of repeatable **cause and effect** is a moment of **mastery**, where the player acquires a new mental tool for manipulating the world.

An interaction loop is a **loop** because mastery only arises after repeated passes through each of the steps. Players practice a skill by attempting it again and again. Each time they sample the game, they gain a bit more information about why the system behaves as it does.

Skill chain

Jumping isn't the only interaction loop in a Mario game. Mastering simpler interactions enables players to complete **compound interactions**. For example, to kill a Goomba, the player must first learn how to both jump and move. First they master the simple jump and move. Then they use both those actions together to learn how to kill the Goomba.

Two things are worth keeping in mind when constructing skill chains.

A hierarchical skill chain showing how lower-order interaction loops contribute to a higher-order compound skill (that is also an interaction loop!)

- These loops are arranged in a hierarchical structure where order matters. If a player hasn't learned lower-order skills, they'll be blocked from learning higher-order skills. If a player is failing to learn something about your game, be sure to ask if they've fully mastered precursor skills.

- Each node of the skill tree involves a distinct interaction loop that contains all of the same steps listed above in our breakdown of a generic interaction loop. So if there's a problem with your game, you can zoom in on the exact loop and the exact step that is causing the issue.

Frequency

Interaction loops also occur at different **frequencies**, or time scales, throughout a game. A skill like jumping happens nearly every second, while killing a Goomba might happen only a few times a level. By understanding the interaction loops of a game, you gain a greater appreciation of game pacing.

When to use interaction loops

I think in terms of interaction loops when I'm planning out the skills I want a player to learn in a game. Interaction loops and their associated skill chains are a wonderful structure methodically building up a player's "wisdom," a holistic, intuitive understanding of a complex system. As the player works their way through the game, they create a mental model that contains a thousand branches, successes, failures, and nuances. Game structures rich in interaction loops empower your player to approach unexpected new situations with confidence and a flexible set of proven mental tools.

Interaction arcs

Interaction arcs are another structural element found in games. Unlike loops, which are used to develop skills, arcs are used to deliver evocative content like a story or movie.

Arcs have a similar structure to loops. The player still starts with a mental model; they apply an action to a system of rules and receive feedback. However, in your typical arc, the mental model is updated with a package of predigested practices or evocative stimuli. The general goal of the content author is to convey key ideas as efficiently and effectively as possible.

Consider the ending of Super Mario Bros. You've just beaten the final boss by dropping Bowser into the lava.

1. **Mental model**: You know you've beaten the big enemy, and in the past, that usually leads to a small cutscene with a toad.
2. **Decision**: You don't have a lot of options, so you decide to run to the right. The same thing you've been doing all game long.
3. **Action**: Run to the right.
4. **Rules**: The game shows you some new visual feedback. There's almost no other simulation going on in this screen.
5. **Feedback**: You see the princess! She thanks you and tells you your quest is over.

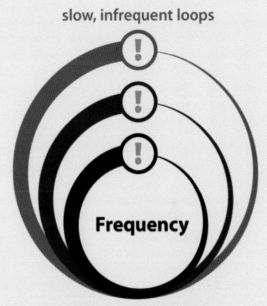

slow, infrequent loops

Frequency

fast, frequent loops

The fastest interaction loops are real time, often looping in less than 200 ms. The slowest in a progression-based MMORPG might take weeks or months.

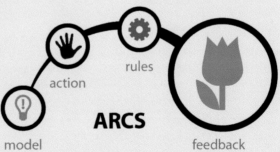

model   action   rules   **ARCS**   feedback

6. This is a rich update of your mental model. The symbol of the 'princess' triggers a cascade of all the stored details your brains know about princesses. The word 'quest' does the same. You mix the two together with your mental sense-making engine. The cutscene content delivery arc is complete.

An arc delivering a narrative payload in Super Mario Bros.

Arcs are built to deliver these carefully authored payloads of preprocessed information. You'll typically find many arcs have the following functionality:

- **Simple modular actions** such as turning a page or watching a movie. Or, in the case of Mario, walking right. These rarely enable player expression because skill isn't a goal. You want players to get to the content as easily and quickly as possible.

- **Simple systems** that display content to player. A page of a book is a simple system that conveys content in the form of text to the player.

- **Evocative feedback** that links together existing mental models in some unique, interesting, or useful manner. For arcs, the feedback is 99% of the payload, and the actions and rules are simply a means to an end. Once this payload is fully delivered, the value of repeated exposure to the arc drops substantially. Note that there is very little of the *functional feedback* we saw in interaction loops because the systems in arcs are kept intentionally simple and obvious.

Where a loop might be executed hundreds or thousands of times, an arc is typically executed once or twice. The game moves on and only very rarely will players return to squeeze out more insights. The movie is watched. The book finished. A handful of players return at a distant later date for nostalgia, comfort, or nuanced insight. But most do not. Within a game session, an arc is a loop you exit almost immediately.

Arcs deliver success stories

Arcs excel at communicating "success stories," a singular ideal **golden path** through a system that someone else previously explored. The best teach a lesson, either informative, positive, or negative. A wise woman might tell you the best way through a level. Or a danger to avoid. This is a brilliant learning shortcut. A story that tells how to build a sturdy bridge or succeed in a difficult relationship might save the novice years of experimentation.

However, the acquired knowledge is often quite different and less robust in the face of change than "wisdom" found in loops. With even a slight shift in context, the learning gained from an arc becomes no longer directly applicable. It is not an accident that we make the distinction between "book learning" and "life experience." Arcs are neither better nor worse than loops. Both are essential tools that serve different design needs.

Sequences of arcs

A common game design issue with arcs is that players **burn out** on them rapidly, rarely desiring to engage with an expensively authored experience more than once. It is possible to give arcs a bit more staying power by stringing them together serially in a **sequence of arcs**. This is a proven technique and is at the base of most commercial attempts to give content arcs longer retention. The pages of a book or the scenes in a movie are a sequence of arcs.

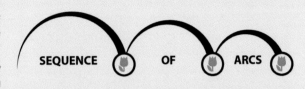

Businesses that rely on a constant sequence of arcs to bring in ongoing revenue often find themselves running along the **content treadmill**. If you stop producing content, the business fails. Game studios that sell expansion packs to stay in business are on a content treadmill.

Expanding loops into arcs

As you analyze your game design, any interaction loop can be superficially described as a series of arcs with one arc written down for each pass you make through the loop. This step-wise or turn-based description is an **expanded loop**. This is useful for recording a single person's **personal experience** of incremental insights. However, the expanded loop tells you little about the broad possibility space described by the loops. Where loops neatly describe a statistical spectrum of outcomes, the expanded arcs laboriously describes only a single sample.

Game architecture: Mixing loops and arcs

Since both loops and arcs can be easily nested and connected to one another, in practice, you end up with chemistry-like mixtures of the two. The structure of loops and arcs is a design's **game architecture**. This can get a bit messy to tease apart. The simplest method of analysis is to ask **"What repeats and what does not?"**

Narrative games are the most common example of mixing loops and arcs. A simple combination might involve intermixing a segment where the player is engaged with loops with a segment of arcs. This is your typical cutscene-gameplay-cutscene sandwich.

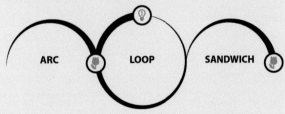

However, the architectural patterns can get far more detailed. For example:

- **Parallel Arcs**: In a typical game, you can treat the emotional payload of game music as an arc that plays in parallel alongside the looping core gameplay.
- **Levels**: The spatial arc of navigating a level provides context for exploring variations on a central gameplay loop. The Golden Path through a level is an authored experiential arc, but players may loop in corners of the level playing with various challenges.
- **Micro Parallel Arcs**: A game like Half Life combines both levels and parallel arcs to deliver snippets of evocative stimuli as you progress through the level.

These structures also exist in traditional media. For example, if you look at a traditionally arc-based form such as a book, you find an odd outlier in the form of the Bible. At one level of analysis, it can be seen as a story arc that you read through and finish. However, it is embedded in a much larger set of interaction loops we casually refer to as a religion. The game-like loops include everything from worship rituals to the mining of the Bible in order to synthesize weekly sermons. The content arc delivers pieces of a rulebook for executing a larger game consisting primarily of loops.

Even in such a complex case, understanding which interactions are a loop and which are an arc helps tease apart the systemic behaviors. Of the two, loops are rarely discussed in any logical fashion. Consumers will note the arcs in a media project and comment on them at length while being quite blind to the loops driving experiential outcomes. Religion is a lovely example of how loop analysis can provide a practical description of a game's ruleset even when the actual players are only vaguely aware of the structures driving their skill and knowledge acquisition. Try applying the same loop-based deconstruction to your games and the communities that surround them.

Untangling loops and arcs in existing game forms

Over time, common game genres become encrusted with a complex mix of arcs and loops. Mature genres often try to woo jaded players by cramming an ever-increasing amount of flashy (and expensive) content arcs into their game. It can be hard to decipher the game's essential structure.

One exercise I've been performing on various games is identifying loops and arcs in a popular genre and then removing the pieces to see if what is left stands on its own.

First, take your favorite genre (such as platform games) and remove all the content payloads:

- Narrative sequences that don't teach skills.
- Big evocative elements like character art or music. Anything that reminds you of a brand or IP should go.
- Small evocative elements like textures, colors, lighting, or other elements that help the player feel, but don't help them learn.

You should be left with a functional, but structurally complete game. This is something that plays mostly the same, but each of those empty moments can now be filled with new content. Most studios organized around servicing a content treadmill create production efficiencies by defining this exact sort of empty template and then filling in the blanks to create a new deliverable.

But we aren't yet done. Next remove the game architecture, those elements that bind loops to arcs.

- Puzzles, missions, or quests
- Levels
- Menus and buttons that take you from one activity to the next
- Any elements of a computer game that you can "beat" or that render the game boring or meaningless upon repeated play

After boiling the game down, what pieces remain? Can you bind them together into a new architecture? Can you flesh out the bones of this new beast with an entirely different set of content? Most of the time you can. And in the process, you'll start learning how to be an inventor of new games instead of a copier of stagnant historical forms.

Now, the point here is not convince you to get rid of arcs or elements like narrative. Instead, it is to help you to understand that loops and arcs are ingredients and the goal is to create a new recipe with a different mix rather than unquestioningly recreating the same meal again and again.

TUNING GAME SYSTEMS

As mentioned earlier, the only way to fully understand a system is to study it as a whole, and that means putting it in motion. Because of this, after a game designer has defined the elements of his system, he needs to playtest and tune that system. The designer does this first by playing the game themselves, possibly with other designers, and then by playing with other players, who are not part of the design process. In Chapters 10 and 11, I will discuss the tuning process in detail and a number of specific issues that your game system can exhibit, but in general, there are several key things that a designer is looking for when balancing a game system.

First, the designer needs to test to make sure that the system is internally complete. This means that the rules address any loopholes that could possibly arise during play. A system that is not internally complete creates situations that either block players from resolving the conflict or allow players to circumvent the intended conflict. This can result in "dead ends" of gameplay and, sometimes, in player conflict over the rules. If players argue over how the rules should deal with a particular situation, it is probably because the system is not internally complete.

When the system is judged to be internally complete, the designer will next test for fairness and balance. A game is fair if it gives all players an equal opportunity to achieve the game goals. If one player has an unfair advantage over another, and that advantage is built into the system, the others will feel cheated and lose interest in the system. In addition, a system can be unbalanced by the availability of dominant strategies or overpowered objects such as those described on pages 342-346. In these cases, the fact that one strategy or object is better than the others effectively reduces the meaningful choices for the player.

When a system is internally complete and fair for all players, the designer must test to make sure the game is fun and challenging to play. This is an elusive goal that means different things to every individual game player. When testing for fun and challenge, it is important to have clear player experience goals in mind and to test the game with its intended audience of players. Generally, this is not the designer or the designer's friends.

For example, when a designer is testing a game for children, she might not be able to accurately judge the difficulty level, making the game too hard for its young audience. Determining the needs and skills of the target players and balancing a system for them requires a clear idea of who the target players are and a process for involving players from that target in the playtesting. Chapter 9, on playtesting, will talk more about how to identify those players and bring them into the design process. Testing for fun and challenge brings up a number of issues regarding player experience and improving the opportunity for meaningful choice that will be addressed in detail in Chapter 11, including the idea of tuning your game for a dramatic conclusion, as discussed in Stone Librande's sidebar on page 392.

CONCLUSION

In this chapter, I have described the basic elements of a game system and shown how the nature of the objects, properties, behaviors, and relationships can create different dynamics of interaction, change, and growth. I have discussed how player interaction with these elements can be affected by the structures of information, control, and feedback.

One of the real challenges in designing and tuning game systems is to isolate what objects or relationships are causing problems in gameplay and to make changes that fix the issue without creating new problems. When the elements are all working together, what emerges is great gameplay. It is the job of the game designer to create that perfect blend of elements that, when set in motion, produce the varieties of gameplay that bring players back time and again.

DESIGNER PERSPECTIVE: MARY FLANAGAN

Mary Flanagan at work in her studio (left) and demonstrating her games at PAX Unplugged (right)

Founder, Resonym

Mary Flanagan is an artist, author, educator, and designer whose work has been exhibited internationally at venues such as The Guggenheim New York, Tate Britain, Museu de Art and collected by The Whitney Museum and ZKM | Zentrum für Kunst und Medien Germany. She is also a prolific board game designer and entrepreneur. Selected board game projects released through her company Resonym include Avant Carde (2024), Glitch Squad (2023), Retrograde (2023), Phantom Ink (2022), Surrealist Dinner Party (2021), Mechanica (2109), Visitor in Blackwood Grove (2017), Monarch (2015), Buffalo (2012), and Awkward Moment (2012).

How did you become a game designer?

In graduate school, I went from experimental filmmaking to making interactive art. When I got out of school, I moved to Austin and joined a game development house called Human Code, founded by a bunch of industrial designers and architects whose ideas were pretty cutting edge at the time. Nicholas Negroponte was one of our advisors and we worked with writers like Bruce Sterling to make digital "infospaces" and invent interactive entertainment. Human Code was a darling of the first dot com wave and I was lucky enough to be a producer/designer on games for The Discovery Channel, Jump Start, and ABC/Creative Wonders.

I've always played board games with my midwestern US family, but I got into crafting board games because I started teaching at a university where there was no available computer lab. I got creative and started teaching rapid paper prototyping, and it stuck. I like cardboard!

On games that have inspired her:

As a kid, I loved playing trick-taking games with my grandmother, and Clue and Dark Tower, and as a designer I would not say they were brilliant games! But they did evoke a strong sense of environment, mood – they had a strong feel. My introduction to 'modern' tabletop games includes Settlers (of Catan), Dominion, and the like, but one that stuck with me was Uwe Rosenberg's Agricola (2009), because while like most of these games, it emphasizes expansion, upgrading and wealth acquisition, it had a meaningful system of sustainability built into it, for example, needing to wait turns in breeding your sheep. Little details like that say something about the larger world and what is important to model. But my favorites don't have to be big games. I also like the elegance of Code Names (2015), because it provides a big play experience with few ingredients. Making games is like crafting poetry, so I'm inspired by games that contain everything they need – and nothing more.

On exciting developments in the industry:

Counter-colonial, pro-environment, and socially aware games are finally being made right now by (mostly) new and emerging game designers who are shifting what's available to play. This means it is an exciting time in board games! The experimentation, the new voices – I hope this trend continues! One of the things games do very well is teach us strategy and ways to solve problems. This kind of thinking is so necessary, for we have really pressing challenges facing the very earth itself. If we make games that offer new perspectives, mechanics and win states, games that don't reproduce colonial tropes, games that make flourishing, sustainable models – we might also invent new solutions outside of games that impact the world. Speculative game design is needed now more than ever.

On design process:

I am inspired about untold stories, and history in general, so I like to design games around a place, time, or social situation that has a particular allure for me. So many experiences just stick with me and turn into artwork and games. A few years ago, I wanted to make a Ouija board game because I had one as a kid and apparently contacted Jack the Ripper, which was terrifying to my young self (what is more disturbing is that my friends wanted to summon him, of all people?). I also wanted to make a game that conjured up seances and the 19th century Spiritualist movement – there was a Spiritualist campground near my grandmother's house and folks still travel from very far places to communicate with loved ones "beyond the veil." I went to a service there and the minister described each spirit guide who was watching over each attendee – down to the details such as height, hairstyle, and even in some cases, names. The game Phantom Ink (2022) evolved from these phenomena. Phantom Ink is a party game for four or more players who play in teams, where one person on each team is a Spirit and the rest are divided into each team's Mediums. The teams compete to guess an object through writing that the Spirits both know but cannot say directly. The game originally was developed using a digital Ouija board that my collaborator Max Seidman at Resonym created in one of the online simulators, and we developed the whole game completely online while located in different parts of the country. And while I really wanted a Ouija board to be the final game board, it was clear in playtesting that it wasn't a graceful solution. The players kept forgetting what the last letters spelled out were, so they had to keep notes... if they were already writing down the letters, why not make that act the central part of the game? In the end, the Ouija board conceit had to go as it just added an extra step in the flow of play, and the game works great as a spooky writing game.

So the process is generally inspiration, prototype, playtest, and then playtest a lot. There are always exceptions. Sometimes my collaborator, Max Seidman, wants to use a particular set of mechanics and I come up with the theme that fits well. Avant Carde (2024) was intended to be an engine-building component of a much larger game, but we decided to separate it and make it a standalone game because it was so engrossing as it was. And of course, at any given moment, a project can be abandoned if something isn't working, or if too much is going into fixing something and it's still broken. Bits and pieces of old ideas will show up in new games. It's part of the flow.

On prototyping:

I absolutely use prototypes to flesh out ideas. When I'm by myself I'll make a choppy paper prototype from my notes in order to test – just playing around with moving parts on a table or for larger projects, mapping out a space with a tape measure helps my brain formulate ideas. In my collaborations with Max, we often use digital simulator tools for prototyping, even communication tools like Zoom, depending on what we are working on. I don't think our process would work for all teams, but because we have worked together a long time, we have developed a lot of shorthand and similar instincts, even though we come at design differently (and I would definitely recommend collaborating with someone who approaches games differently than you!). After play, tweaks are made, and pretty soon the game will be on its way to a playtest group. The fact that some of the playtest groups are online is really helpful, as we can have exponentially more playtesters — we're not located in a city where there are many other designers around. We have a rotating cast of student playtesters and of course we learn from occasional visits to game stores and open play sessions.

On a difficult design problem:

Every game has its own difficult design problem — so each project would hold some kind of example. I'll go back a few years, though, to discuss Monarch (2015), a board game where players play as sisters vying to build the most astute court and inherit the crown. I wanted to have difficult guests in Monarch that sisters could invite to each other's courts. It was a fun idea, based on real guests in my life... Introducing the "Unwanted Guests" suit was a core inspiration for the game. But in practice, if players would send Unwanted Guests to count toward their sister's seven court cards, the court fills up faster, which ends the game. Therefore, a player with a strong court could rush the end prematurely to win. Pulling those guests out of the core court count was a simple fix that stopped that problem. But every game needs to have a trustworthy and fair game close. Endings and things like victory points are tricky to get right on early prototypes. In Avant Carde, players are playing as art collectors trying to win awards for their exhibitions and to earn points for the number of pieces they launch in a show each round. (As a practicing artist I know very well that quantity does not mean quality, but it works in the game!). Players used to have to decide whether to use their funds to improve their deck or invest in trophies, which was originally an okay tension (we see this all the time in modern board games) but in practice was weird — we originally put the trophies in the deck, and therefore getting trophies made your deck less powerful, not more, which is not the feeling you want to achieve in an engine-building game. It's fixed now!

What are you most proud of in your career?

As a woman in the game design space for a long time, it's been an uphill battle to be taken seriously. I'm most proud of sticking to my interests and not giving up to see my dreams realized — the many times I've been mistaken for the office manager, or not published because I've got a female sounding name, or that I made games with female characters, etc. These did not stop me. The game space across the board — from AAA to indie to tabletop — has gotten much better, but it's important to remember that it's only better because a lot of people put up with various derogations and abuses to get us to this place.

Advice to designers:

Games are the universe in which you meet your players. So, while it is an incredible joy to make games, the most amazing part is seeing your game come to life and become something completely new in the hands of a player. Never give up on the awe and wonder of that moment.

DESIGNER PERSPECTIVE: FRANK LANTZ

Director, NYU Game Center

Frank Lantz has worked in the field of game development for the past 20 years. In 2005, he co-founded Area/Code, a New York-based developer of cross-media, location-based, and social network games that was acquired by Zynga in 2011. Before starting Area/Code, Frank was the director of game design at Gamelab, a developer of online and downloadable games. He is known for his work on the hit mobile game Drop7 (2009), as well as experimental games such as Pac-Manhattan (2004) and Chain Factor—Numb3rs ARG (2007).

On getting into the game industry:

I studied theater and painting in school, then did computer graphics for several years at R/GA, a New York digital design studio. I helped to transition that company from a focus on graphics and special effects for film and TV into a focus on designing interactive media, including games. Eventually, I left R/GA to work on games full time, first as a freelance game designer and then as the lead designer at the indie game developer Gamelab.

Five favorite games:

- Go because of the whole simplicity and depth thing, and the whole global and local thing, and the whole black and white thing, and the whole life and death thing.
- Poker because, like Go, it can be approached as a martial art and a spiritual discipline. Not the way I play it, though.
- Shadow of the Colossus because it's so sad and beautiful, and it breaks so many game design rules and still works brilliantly.
- Fungus, a little-known multiplayer Mac game by an unsung genius game designer named Ryan Koopmans. Fungus was probably the first game I played seriously and for a long enough time to start understanding how deep a game can go.
- Wipeout because of the music and the graphics, and then, more importantly, because of the way it encouraged and rewarded a deep, zen-like level of precise skill mastery.
- Half-Life because I can't count. Also Crackdown, Rhythm Tengoku, Starcraft, Nethack, and Bushido Blade for the same reason.

On game influences:

The first one that comes into my head is Magic: The Gathering. It's hard to overstate the degree of influence that game has had on me. First of all, just the idea that you can invent, not just mechanics, but an entirely new genre, a totally new way to think about how games are played and their social context, it's mind-blowing. And then, just the combinatory richness of it. The idea of engines, the way that the game is about players exploring this possibility space constructing these combinatory engines, it's so beautiful!

Also, the board games of Reiner Knizia, and modern German board games in general, are very inspiring because of their constant inventiveness in regards to mechanics and their light touch with themes accompanied by a serious attention to surfaces and materials.

On the design process:

Start with a fun game, put some stuff in it, then take some stuff out.

On prototypes:

I'm a huge believer in the prototype > playtest > redesign loop as the ultimate method for making great games. Sometimes, in reality, you don't have the time and resources you need to really prototype an idea properly, but that's OK. As long as you're continually making games, you can think of each game as a prototype for a better, more finished game that you will make later.

On solving a difficult design problem:

We did a game for A&E about the *Sopranos*, and the main idea was that players had a collection of pieces representing the characters, places, and objects from the show, and these pieces would score points whenever the show was aired, based on what was happening on-screen.

We started with a set of really weird and interesting constraints. First, the game had a prize element, so because of antigambling laws it had to have no randomness, it had to be totally deterministic. At the same time, it had to produce, out of potentially hundreds of thousands of players, a single clear winner; it couldn't result in a tie; it had to have a lot of room at the top, a lot of differentiation between the scores of high-level players. And this was for reruns of season one, a bunch of episodes that were available on DVD. So we could assume that any serious player had complete access to every episode and a complete knowledge of whatever scoring system we were going to use, so no hidden information. Added to this was the idea that the game had to be, you know, actually fun for a broad audience of nongamers, which meant it had to make intuitive sense.

So the game had to be simple and obvious for casual players and "unsolvable" for a very large community of expert players with a lot of time and cash-money motivation to find optimal solutions and complete access to every event that was going to occur during the entire game. In all honesty, however, this isn't as hard as it looks, because this is exactly what games do well!

I'm not a big math guy, but I recognized that what I needed was a game system that was NP-complete. NP-complete is a math term describing a class of problems that become very, very hard as they scale up—the kind of math problems that are used to encrypt billion-dollar bank accounts. Seems complicated, but plenty of games are NP-complete, including Tetris, Minesweeper, and Freecell Solitaire.

Basically, I ended up designing a system in which players scored for groups of touching pieces that lit up at the same time; the larger the group, the more points. Seems pretty obvious in retrospect, it's a system that is totally familiar from puzzle games, but it allowed for an almost infinite variety of arrangements and a lot of different viable strategies.

Advice to designers:

Play a lot. Play deeply. Pay attention. Don't be lazy. Simplificate. Learn how to think like a programmer, and learn how to think like an artist. Be an advocate for the player, but don't treat the player like a child. Fail often. Take something in a game you like and combine it with something new that seems like it might be cool. Don't make games you wouldn't want to play. Persist.

FURTHER READING

Casti, John. *Complexification: Explaining a Paradoxical World through the Science of Surprise.* New York: HarperCollins Publishers, 1995.

Castronova, Edward. *Synthetic Worlds: The Business and Culture of Online Games.* Chicago: The University of Chicago Press, 2005.

Flynt, John. *Beginning Math Concepts for Game Developers.* Boston: Thompson Course Technology, 2007.

Schreiber, Ian and Romero, Brenda. *Game Balance.* Boca Raton: CRC Press, 2021.

Johnson, Steven. *Emergence: The Connected Lives of Ants, Brains, Cities and Software.* New York: Touchstone, 2002.

END NOTES

1. Blizzard website, accessed August 2003. http://www.battle.net/war2/basic/combat.shtml
2. Salen, Katie and Zimmerman, Eric. *Rules of Play: Game Design Fundamentals.* Cambridge: The MIT Press, 2004. p.161.
3. Parker Brothers, Monopoly Deluxe Edition rules sheet, 1995.
4. Yu, Derek. Spelunky–Boss Fight Books Book 11. Boss Fight Books. Kindle Edition, 2016. p. 42.
5. Poundstone, William. *Prisoner's Dilemma.* New York: Doubleday, 1992.
6. Johnson, Steven. "Wild Things." *Wired* issue 10.03.

Part 2
Designing a Game

Now that you are familiar with the basic elements of games, it is time to walk through the process of designing a game of your own. This might seem overwhelming at first, especially if your goal is to create a game like the ones you have played on the major consoles—filled with complex animations and elaborate programming. So before I begin discussing these aspects, let's put aside the ultimate goal for a moment and go through the process of design step-by-step from the beginning.

First, I will discuss ideation—coming up with ideas for your games. This might be easy for you. You might already have an idea of the game you want to make. But what if you cannot get support for your one idea? What will you do then? More importantly, can you create an idea that meets the needs of a team or an employer. Not every situation is about coming up with creative ideas for your own pleasure. Most of the time, you'll need to be thinking of ideas that already have some constraints set up: a particular audience of players, a technology, a genre of play, or the expansion of an existing property. I will show you how you can train yourself to become an "idea person," someone for whom ideas come easily throughout the design process, and whose ideas are part of good solutions to creative questions..

After you have an idea, you will need to execute on it. Many designers jump right to writing

up their design documentation at this point, but I will show you how to prototype your idea and get playtesters involved very early in the process. The playcentric design process that I outlined in Chapter 1 on page 12 is detailed in Chapters 7 (Prototyping), 8 (Digital Prototyping), and 9 (Playtesting). By prototyping and playtesting early, you can grasp which aspects of your system are working well with your experience goals and which are not. It is only after you have seen players interact with your idea that you have enough knowledge to even think about drafting any design documentation.

What will you test for? Chapters 10 and 11 discuss strategies for making sure that your game is complete, that it is fair, that it offers meaningful choices, that it is fun and accessible for your players, and that it meets the experience goals that you have been striving for.

My objective here is to give you an accurate picture of the playcentric design process. If you follow along with the exercises in this section, you will have designed at least one full game of your own. Going through this process yourself will teach you important methods for conceptualizing, building, and examining your work. By the time you are done, you will understand how to design a game, playtest it, and use your knowledge of the formal, dramatic, and dynamic aspects of games to perfect its gameplay.

DOI: 10.1201/9781003460268-7

Chapter 6
Ideation

Coming up with ideas is difficult for many people; coming up with excellent ideas is even more difficult. Coming up with excellent ideas that meet the goals and constraints of a project is one of the most difficult things a creative person can be asked to do. And creative people may be asked to do this on a daily basis! But coming up with an idea is just the beginning of the creative process. Crafting your ideas, fleshing them out, and bringing them to life is all part of the ongoing work of game design that in the end means generating not just one grand idea but rather layers and iterations of ideas that all help to refine, evolve, and realize your original concept. This process will be different for every game designer and for every game on which a

designer works, beginning with different sources of inspiration and yielding a variety of results.

I cannot tell you exactly what your own personal process should be, but I can offer some insight and best practices into the ideation process that will help you learn which methods work best for you and your design team. Not only will you want to try the range of methods I suggest here, but you will also want to come up with methods of your own and vary them from project to project. As prolific board game designer Reiner Knizia says, "I don't have a fixed design process. Quite the contrary, I believe that starting from the same beginning will frequently lead to the same end. Finding new ways of working often leads to innovative designs."[1]

WHERE DO IDEAS COME FROM?

The first thing to understand about ideas is that they do not come out of thin air—even if they seem to at some times. Great ideas come from great input into your mind and senses. Living a full life—full of curiosity, interesting people, places, thoughts, and events—is the starting point to being a person full of ideas. In Chapter 1, I discussed the way in which designers like Will Wright and Shigeru Miyamoto have

been influenced by personal interests and hobbies such as ant farms and exploration. I suggest making sure that you spend a significant part of every day doing something other than playing games: Read a book or a newspaper, watch a film, listen to music, take a photo, exercise, draw or sketch, volunteer at a neighborhood organization, go see a play, study a new language, etc. Whatever it is, do it with passion and curiosity.

DOI: 10.1201/9781003460268-8

Use your interest in something other than games to fill your mind with potential ideas.

Psychologist Mihaly Csikszentmihalyi, whose work on flow we discussed in Chapter 4, has also done a study of creativity, trying to understand how creative people work and how they develop. In his book on the topic, Csikszentmihalyi describes the classic stages of creativity as follows:

- *Preparation*: Preparation is becoming immersed in a topic or domain of interest, a set of problematic issues.
- *Incubation*: Incubation is a period of time in which ideas "churn around" below the threshold of consciousness.
- *Insight*: Insight is sometimes called the "aha!" moment, when the pieces of puzzle, or an idea, fall together.
- *Evaluation*: Evaluation is when the person decides whether the insight is valuable and worth pursuing. Is the idea really original?
- *Elaboration*: Elaboration is the longest part of the creative process; it takes the most time and is the hardest. This is what Edison meant when he said invention is 99% perspiration and 1% inspiration.[2]

He warns, however, that we should not expect creativity to proceed regularly along a path from one stage to another. "The creative process," he says, "is less linear than recursive. How many iterations it goes through, how many loops are involved, how many insights are needed, depends on the depth and breadth of the issues dealt with. Sometimes incubation lasts for years; sometimes it takes a few hours. Sometimes the creative idea includes one deep insight and innumerable small ones."[3]

By encouraging you to become involved and interested in activities outside of games, what I am really saying is that you need to work on the preparation and incubation stages of creativity all the time. No one can say when the aha! moment will come. Perhaps it will be when you sit down to think of ideas, or perhaps it will come when you are taking a shower or driving on the freeway. It is a good habit to always carry a notebook or smartphone in which you can write down your ideas so that they do not fade away after that initial moment of inspiration.

The other stages of creativity—evaluation and elaboration—are just as important as the initial insight, however. Having an idea for a game does not simply mean saying, "I want to make a game about studying Chinese!" As I discussed in Chapter 3, games are formal systems, and an idea for a game usually includes some aspect of that system. Perhaps your study of the Chinese language leads you to an interesting insight about using symbolic characters to represent hidden ideas in a game system. Your game might not have anything to do with Chinese at all. As you work through your idea, elaborating on its unique elements, it might turn out that no one would recognize the influence of your language interests in the final experience, even though you know that is where the initial spark of the idea began. When you train yourself to begin thinking like a game designer, to begin looking below the surface of your daily activities and interests to the intrinsic systems at their core, you will begin to find a wealth of ideas for game systems in their structures.

Exercise 6.1: Below the Surface

Take the subject of the last book or news article you read and think of its systematic aspects. Are there objectives? Rules? Procedures? Resources? Conflict? Skills to be learned? Make a list of the systematic elements of the subject or activity. Do this several times per week with different types of activities or hobbies.

Ideas can also come from analyzing existing games and activities. I talked about developing your critical skills in Chapter 1, Exercise 1.4 when I suggested that you begin a game journal. After you have been keeping your game journal for some time, you will notice that your ability to discuss games critically will improve. Also, you will naturally begin to have ideas related to this criticism of existing game systems. It is important that you use this journal to analyze the games you play in detail, not just to review their features and determine their "coolness." Magazine articles on games often focus on the new, top-level features of a game; don't get caught in this style of writing. Dig deeply into the formal, dramatic, and dynamic elements of the games you play. Also, pay close attention to your emotional responses to gameplay: your cycles of frustration, exhilaration, confidence, uncertainty, pride, tension, curiosity, etc. Record them; they will be difficult to remember later on, and when you are searching for inspiration as you set your player experience goals, you will want to have a record of how a particular game affected you the first time you played it.

In addition to writing your analysis of games in your game journal, another way to improve your critical skills is to present and debate your game analyses with friends or other people who are also studying game design. At the USC School of Cinematic Arts, in the Game Innovation Lab, the students are asked to prepare systems analyses, in which one or more students prepare a formal presentation of their analysis of a selected game. This analysis breaks the game down into its formal, dramatic, and dynamic elements. They present this analysis, along with a detailed walk-through of several game sections to back up their analysis, and lead a discussion about the game. This type of public presentation and analysis helps to critical skills, become more articulate in presenting about systems, and also often generate generate new ideas that arise from the discussion.

Exercise 6.2: Game System Analysis

Take one of the games you have analyzed in your game journal and create a system analysis presentation. Analyze the formal, dramatic, and dynamic elements of the game. If you can, create a PowerPoint presentation from your analysis and organize an opportunity to present this to an appropriate audience. Lead a discussion of your ideas following the presentation.

A very good source of understanding and inspiration for video game designs are the unique and interesting board games that can be found at specialty game and hobby stores or online at sites such as www.boardgames.com. With the current popularity of board games, classics like the following are easy to find at online distributors like Amazon.com as well.

- Settlers of Catan, by Klaus Teuber
- Carcassonne, by Klaus-Jurgen Wrede
- Scotland Yard, by Ravensburger
- El Grande, by Wolfgang Kramer and Richard Ulrich
- Modern Art, by Reiner Knizia
- Illuminati, by Steve Jackson
- Set, by Marcia Falco
- Acquire, by Sid Sackson
- Cosmic Encounter, by Bill Eberle, Jack Kittredge, and Bill Norton
- I'm the Boss, by Sid Sackson

In addition to these classic games, there are many modern board games – too many to list that are a great resource for students of game design, including more and more games by diverse designers like Elizabeth Hargrave, whose game Wingspan is one of the top-ranked board games of recent years. Hargrave also keeps lists of women, non-binary, and Black board game designers on her site at www.elizhargrave.com/women-nonbinary-designers. Designer Mary Flanagan discusses her work in board games in her profile on page 169. One of the reasons that I suggest that aspiring digital game designers play and analyze these games is that they have very innovative and complex mechanics. And, because of the nature of board games, these mechanics are not hidden from you in the code, the way they might be in digital games. They are right on the surface, easy to see, and possible to deconstruct and analyze. You can find interesting discussions about these games and more at sites like www.boardgamegeek.com.

Exercise 6.3: Board Game Analysis

Choose one of the games listed above and play it with a group of friends. Write your analysis of the formal, dramatic, and dynamic elements of the game in your game journal. Now find another group of players who have not played the game before. Have them play the game while you watch and take notes. Do not help them learn the rules. Note the steps of their group learning process as well as their impressions of the game in your analysis.

CONSTRAINTS AND CREATIVITY

Constraints and creativity are often seen as opposing forces. Constraints are seen as limiting our options and creativity as the ability to come up with new and innovative ideas. However, there is a growing body of research that suggests that constraints can actually help to boost creativity. And we know, as game designers, that when we constrain players with just the right amount and types of rules, they are able to exhibit tremendous creativity in their response to game challenges. So, it should be no surprise to us that constraints are a powerful tool in unlocking the creativity of designers as well.

There are a few reasons why constraints can lead to creativity. First, constraints can help to focus our attention and limit the number of options we have to consider. This can free up our cognitive resources so that we can focus on more creative and innovative solutions. Second, constraints can force us to think outside the box and come up with new and unexpected solutions. When we are faced with a focused challenge, we are more likely to come up with creative solutions if we are forced to think in new ways. And finally, constraints can help us overcome the "blank page" problem, where the intimidation of a blank page stops us from being able to begin our creative process.

The great film director Orson Welles is quoted as saying that "The enemy of art is the absence of limitation." And this as true in game design as it is in filmmaking or other arts. The types of constraints that can be useful to game designers, especially in the ideation phase, range from technological (such as platform considerations), to business (such as market considerations), to creative (such as experience goals). When we begin our ideation process it is useful to define constraints that will limit us, and also to define goals that will guide us, often called "pillars" in the design field.

A design pillar is an articulation of values or goals that can help us judge whether ideas are aligned with our core concept. Designer Christina Norman, whose Designer Profile is on page 26, provided Figure 6.1 showing how she envisions the relationship between design constraints and design pillars. In a world where we have all possible solutions to a design problem, only a few will fall within the overlap of all our design constraints. And then within those few, we can use our pillars to guide the team towards the best potential ideas to reach our goals.

Examples of design pillars range from a simple list of systems like:

Concept: Solution Spaces

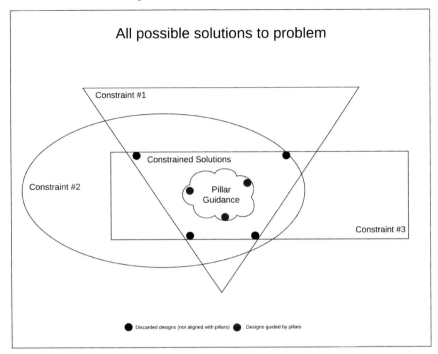

All possible solutions to problem

Constraint #1

Constraint #2

Constrained Solutions

Pillar Guidance

Constraint #3

● Discarded designs (not aligned with pillars)   ● Designs guided by pillars

6.1 Solution Spaces - diagram courtesy of: Christina Norman

- Combat
- Stealth
- Exploration
- Social

Or pillars can sometimes be written as a more specific list of values such as:

- A world players want to be in
- Rewards players care about
- A new experience every day
- Enjoyable by all skill levels

Now, in the playcentric process, I emphasize setting one particular type of design pillar, and that is a "player experience goal." I do this not because these other types of pillars are not important, but because player experience goals are the heart of the game designer's concern

and they must be articulated in a way that can be tested and evaluated against the players' actual experiences in the game. Only then will you know if you are reaching your goals.

The playcentric process is an intentional design process that encourages you to use a controlled approach to reach your goals – not just copy existing experiences or randomly try new things. Think about this when you are setting your player experience goals: what do you want your players to **feel** when they play your games? Can you express that in a way that is:

- simple
- concise
- subjective
- emotional

Here are some examples of experiences goals:

- Players will feel **deep camaraderie** over multiple campaigns with the same team.
- Players will feel **surprise and wonder** at each discovery in the world.
- Players will feel **responsible** for the moral choices they make for their character.
- Players will feel **connected** to the deep backstory of the world and will feel **devastation** when artifacts are stolen or destroyed in battle.

Notice that some of these player experience goals might align with the common design pillars on the earlier lists. Certainly a game that has combat might also be an experience where players would feel deep camaraderie with their fellow players over multiple campaigns. And an exploration game might provide a new experience every day and a feeling of surprise and wonder at each discovery in the world. But way in which the player experience goals are written gives us a clearer constraint to work with in our ideation process and a verifiable set of questions to explore during the playtesting process, which I will talk more about in Chapter 9.

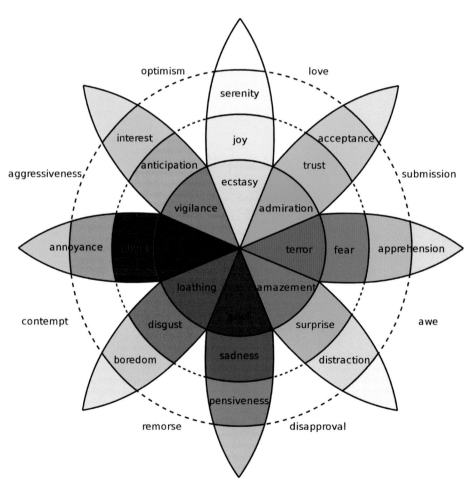

6.2 Wheel of Emotions - diagram by Dr. Robert Plutchick

One of the things you can do, if you are given a set of pillars to work with that are not focused on the player experience is to work with the team to better articulate the experience implied by the pillar. For example, if you are give a pillar that the game will be an "open world," you might ask yourself, how can we better articulate what that will mean to players? Perhaps your open world is build around a dynamically changing society. In that case, you might say that your experience goal is that "players will feel belongingness in a living, evolving culture." Whether or not a game is an "open world" is an easily answered question – one that is basically a check box on a set of technical features. But coming up with ideas for a game that will make players "feel belongingness in a living, evolving culture," is a more interesting problem. It is also a goal that can be tested against when you bring in playtesters to play your game.

In order to set strong player experience goals, you will need to be articulate in the language of emotions. There are a number of resources you can access to help you articulate the emotions you want to elicit in your players. Dr. Robert Plutchick, was a psychologist who proposed a classification system for emotions that he visualized in a wheel shape to show how they were related to one another. Figure 6.2 shows Plutchik's wheel of emotions, organizing the eight basic primary emotions set against their polar opposites and arranged in levels of intensity. So, admiration is the opposite of loathing, and ecstasy is the opposite of grief. Spanning outwards from the center are less intense versions of these emotions, and mixed between them are more generalized emotions like optimism, a mixture of feelings like anticipation and joy; or contempt, a mixture of anger and disgust.

More recently, Dr. Brené Brown has increased our ability to name and understand our emotions with her book "Atlas of the Hear: Mapping Meaningful Connection and the Language of Human Experience." This book should be a must-read for game designers, giving nuanced language and multiple categorizations to 87 specific emotions.

So, when you are defining goals and constraints for your game, know that one of the most important things you can do is to clearly articulate the player experience goals you want to create and to understand the kind of constraints that can help provoke creative solutions to your design challenges.

BRAINSTORMING

What I have focused on so far are setting goals, constraints, and the kind of ongoing training exercises you should do to fill your life and mind with interesting thoughts that might lead to an "aha!" moment, or not. Sometimes, however, it is necessary to solve a specific problem or come up with an idea on demand. Often, when you are working as a creative professional, there is no time to wait for that moment of inspiration to hit; you need a formalized system of idea generation—what is called "brainstorming."

Brainstorming is a powerful skill. And, like any skill, it takes practice to become good at it. There are brainstorming beginners and brainstorming experts, and the difference between their abilities is akin to the difference between an average golfer and Tiger Woods in his prime. Expert brainstormers train themselves in the craft of generating workable ideas and solutions to problems, building on the contributions of their fellow team members. You can brainstorm alone, of course, but ultimately, game development is a collaborative art, and you will want to develop good team brainstorming skills as well. Working with others to generate interesting, innovative ideas is both stimulating and highly productive. Also, it is often a business necessity and a good way to give everyone on the team a sense of authorship in the design process.

The Imagineers at Disney are expert brainstormers; it is a part of their company culture. One of the key skills they have developed is asking the right questions. Bruce Vaughn, executive director of research and development, says, "Whether you're soliciting help from others or tackling the challenge yourself, you must first be able to articulate what the challenge is ... articulating a challenge requires you to let go of all the possible solutions you are considering and pare the challenge back to its core. What is the bare essence of the challenge in front of you?"[4] Articulating a challenge is just one brainstorming rule that can improve your creativity flow, whether you are working alone or with a team. The following is a list of best practices collected from techniques used by the Imagineers, the design consultancy IDEO, and other successful creative thinkers.

Brainstorming Best Practices

State a Challenge

When you sit down to brainstorm, articulate the challenge for the session. Here are some examples:

- Design a game in which players feel strong alliances with other players, but then must betray them.
- Design a game with a special role for parents to play together with their children.
- Come up with a game that makes interesting use of only one button for control.

As you can see, each of these is a very different type of challenge. The first is what I described in the previous section as a player experience goal. The challenge here is to create a specific type of gameplay potential. The second challenge is also audience focused, but it does not address the specific player experience. The third challenge is

completely driven by technology. Each of these can drive a good brainstorming session, but the second two will ultimately need to be refined to specify their player experience goals as described above, so that they can be playtested effectively.

No Criticism

If you are brainstorming alone, do not self-censor or edit your ideas. Write down all of your ideas and worry about their quality later. If you are brainstorming with a team, do not criticize or ignore your colleagues' ideas during the brainstorming process. The process should be about free thinking, about building on each other's thoughts, and if you begin to criticize or edit their ideas before they are fully developed, it will disrupt the flow. Also, certain members of your team, feeling wounded by harsh comments, might limit their contributions, which is the death of creativity. A good trick for this is to practice the "yes, and" rule of brainstorming: Whenever you want to jump into the conversation, start your sentence with the words "yes, and ..." You will find that your contribution will naturally begin to build on that of others, and suddenly you are all part of a single, exhilarating idea-building process. See more about "yes, and" and inclusive brainstorming in the sidebar on page 418.

Vary the Method

Don't rely on just one method for brainstorming. Mix it up. Some structures might work fine for the group leaders but less well for other members. Beginning on page 186, I have created a list of potential structures for generating ideas. If you are a leader, make sure to experiment with structures that you are not comfortable with. Also, ask team members to suggest alternative ways of conducting the brainstorming sessions. You might give them a shot at leading the group. Good leadership doesn't mean being in control of a conversation or a brainstorm. The best teamwork involves trusting and listening to everyone involved.

Playful Environment

Sometimes it is hard to cut loose and be creative in your normal working area, where you are used to sitting at a desk, facing a computer screen. Get up, go someplace else; seek neutral territory, like a conference room, or in the best case scenario, a special brainstorming room. Bring some toys with you to a brainstorming session. Sometimes it helps to just have a Nerf ball to toss around or a stack of blocks to play with while you are thinking. Of course, you do not want to get too caught up in playing, but you would be surprised how having some playful distractions in the brainstorming room can help your team to relax and think creatively.

Put It on the Wall

It is important to get visual with your ideas. A favorite technique is writing on a whiteboard or on large pieces of paper taped to the walls. This can help get people out of their chairs and up on their feet talking and thinking. Writing on a whiteboard lends itself to big ideas, sketches, and side notes. When your ideas are on the wall, they can be seen and absorbed by the whole group. This helps spark even more ideas and facilitates collaboration.

Go for Lots of Ideas

Go for quantity when developing ideas. Try to generate 100 ideas an hour. Be free and do not worry if the ideas are outrageous or if they

6.3 Working at the whiteboard

don't meet your goals right now. A good practice during brainstorming is to number your ideas. It is helpful to be able to refer back and forth between several ideas quickly using shorthand when you are developing a big concept. The numbers allow you to do this without losing your larger train of thought. Aside from that, it is satisfying to generate lots of ideas in a brainstorming session. The numbers will measure your output, serving a function similar to tracking distance when jogging or reps when lifting weights.

Don't Go Too Long

Brainstorming is a high-energy activity. A good session will naturally die down after 60 minutes or so. The mind and body need a break after that much focused time. Do not push yourself beyond what is reasonable. Whatever ideas you have after an hour or so can continue to be worked on in the coming days.

Exercise 6.4: Blue-Sky Brainstorm

In this exercise, use the techniques previously described to do a brainstorm for a "blue-sky" project. By blue sky, I mean that this project could not technically be made today, but we are going to pretend it could. The challenge is to come up with ideas for a "remote control" for a stereotypical character. Choose a character from this list:

- Door-to-door salesman
- Busy mother
- God
- Superhero
- Politician

First, brainstorm about the character: What does the character do? What makes the character interesting? What aspect of the character would it be engaging to control? How does the character react? Does the character have free will? Next, brainstorm features for your imaginary controller. What will it look like? What could each button do? Remember, this is "blue sky," so the buttons can do crazy things. Have fun with this! Come up with as many ideas as you can.

ALTERNATIVE METHODS

Sometimes you need a little help in your brainstorming. Or perhaps you just want to vary your process, as previously suggested. The next sections outline several creativity methods you can experiment with. There is no single best solution. You might find that some methods work better for you than others. I encourage you to try all the methods and vary your approach. The key to productive brainstorming is finding the right balance of stimulation and structure. If you can do this, you will improve both the quantity and quality of your output.

List Creation

One very focused form of brainstorming is making lists. List out everything you can think of on a certain topic. Then create other lists on variations of that topic. You will be amazed at how many great ideas come out in simple lists. The process of writing them down helps you to freely associate and organize at the same time. Lists work great for both group brainstorms and solo efforts. The next time your group needs to focus in on all the possible uses of game features, for example, start by making a list together.

Idea Cards

For more generative brainstorms, a bit of randomness may be just what's needed. Take a deck of index cards and write a single word or idea on each one. Then mix them up in a bowl. Now take out the cards and pair them. For example, "nectar" might appear with "giants." Perhaps, your next game will include "nectar giants," whose bodies are fluid and smell like persimmons. You can concatenate sets of two, three, or four cards. It does not matter. And the more wild ideas you throw into the bowl, the richer the combinations become.

Mind Map

Sometimes you need to build on ideas, layering and connecting thoughts to one another. Mind

6.4   Idea cards

mapping works wonderfully for those kinds of situations. This well-known technique is a way of expressing ideas visually. You start with a core idea in the center and let related ideas radiate outward. You can use lines and different-colored markers to connect ideas. Mind mapping provides a structure for thinking in a nonlinear manner. There are software tools to help generate mind maps, but I find that working on a whiteboard can give the best results when working with a team. One good mind map exercise is to begin with the core concept for your game at the center and then map verbs or actions and the feelings associated with those actions around that central concept. Figure 6.5 shows the results of a 15-minute exercise done at the EA pre-production workshop described in Glenn Entis' sidebar on page 188. This mind map exercise was done by the team that went on to produce the hit game Need for Speed Most Wanted. As Glenn Entis comments, the idea of creating a mind map of game words, "seems basic, but it came after seeing multiple examples where teams did not share simple key vocabulary to describe their game, or where different team members used the same words to mean very different things."

Stream of Consciousness

For more individualized brainstorming, you might try using stream of consciousness as a technique. Sit down at your computer or with a pen and paper and start writing anything that comes to mind when you think of your game. Do not worry about being coherent. Do not think about punctuation or spelling. Just write as quickly as humanly possible. Whatever comes out is fine. After 10 minutes of spewing words on a particular topic, stop and read over what you have done. Sometimes it turns out better than work you have spent days perfecting because you are not self-editing your thoughts.

Electronic Arts Preproduction Workshop

by Glenn Entis

Glenn Entis is currently senior director at Google Research and cofounder and senior advisor of Vanedge Capital, focused on investment in interactive entertainment and digital media. Formerly, he was senior vice president and chief visual and technical officer of Electronic Arts, where he was responsible for leading EA's worldwide community of over 3000 talented artists and engineers. Prior to EA, Glenn was CEO of DreamWorks Interactive and cofounded the pioneering animation studio Pacific Data Images.

The EA Preproduction Workshop was a company-wide program designed to improve our pre-pro skills and create a vocabulary of preproduction that was understood at EA studios around the world.

The workshop was developed in response to a growing awareness that the complexity of games, teams, and platforms had grown faster than our preproduction skills. There was broad consensus about the warning signs—lack of clarity in game design, key roles, and essential processes; a need for more urgency and focus during preproduction; and panic at the end of preproduction as the reality of the remaining schedule sunk in.

We realized that teams did not need or want traditional training. They understood the problem, and in many cases they knew what they should do about it. However, in watching teams struggle to improve their preproduction performance, we realized that teams needed practice in new techniques and enough success in those techniques to form new long-standing preproduction habits. Practice and habits do not come from traditional handouts and lectures; they come from highly engaging, hands-on working sessions that incorporate each studio's local culture and concerns.

The result was the EA Preproduction Workshop, a two-day hands-on workshop delivered to every team in each of our then 12 studios around the world. Each team brought 6 to 10 people—leads from each of the major disciplines on the team (producer, technical director, art director, game designer, various leads, and development director/project manager). At each workshop, we invited 3 to 10 teams—it was important for teams to see other teams at work—that were struggling with the same problems, breaking through barriers, and loosening up to try new things.

Some of the guiding principles that made the workshop effective are discussed in the following sections.

Do Real Work

- *Each team brings its current game:* The team works on real current issues, not classroom exercises.
- *Learn by doing*: Presentations were usually 15 minutes at most; the majority of the workshop time was spent working as a team on a particular technique or phase of preproduction.
- *Keep a fast pace*: Most of the exercises were 15–20 minutes and demanded speed and concentration from the team. This intense time pressure filtered out a lot of mental blocks. Fifteen minutes for a tough task just doesn't give a team enough time to think about all the reasons they couldn't or shouldn't do a task, or shouldn't include, for example, an engineer on a design task. Everyone had to immediately pitch in and work together as one team.
- *Leave with a pre-pro plan:* Over the two days, each team put together (on a whiteboard with Post-it Notes) a pre-pro plan and schedule. It was rough, but that's why Post-it Notes can be moved. For as rough as it was, it was the first time many teams had a detailed pre-pro schedule. More importantly, for many teams, it was the

first time they had developed such a plan as an interdisciplinary group so that multiple points of view could be represented and conflicts and issues identified and handled on the spot.

Above, left - Medal of Honor sandbox: Medal of Honor Frontline and at least two sequels were designed in the sandbox—a cheap, fast, physical way to block out and play test levels. It is as simple as it looks, but when the kids in the sandbox are the lead game designer, producer, art director, and lead environment artist, there is a rapid-fire generation of ideas and on the spot multidisciplinary solutions of problems. And it's fun!

Above, right - Lord of the Rings paper and dice prototype: Paper, card, and dice prototypes are fast, cheap ways to work out the metagame and overall scoring systems. This prototype is from the Lord of the Rings team at EA Redwood Shores.

Left - EA Los Angeles team in 15-minute prototype exercise: The pre-pro workshop asks teams to produce results very quickly. In one exercise, we ask each team to build a physical prototype of a key game feature in 20 minutes. Because game teams rarely build physical prototypes, this exercise often yields surprising results and gives the team a new and more visceral experience of their design ideas.

Matt Birch in flames: In this exercise at one of the EAUK workshops in Chertsey, England, we asked each team to perform one of the key features of their game. Game designer Matt Birch, who was working with the Burnout team at the time, is shown here erupting in flames as he flies through the air, heading for a catastrophic collision with the lorry (a.k.a the black chair) in front of him.

From EA Redwood Shores Maxis pre-pro workshop: Each team works together on preproduction for its own game. In this exercise on physical prototyping, Will Wright is interacting with a creature from Spore.

Burnout team after a brainstorming session: The exercises in the pre-pro workshop are 15–20 minutes each, but they are meant to give the teams practice in new tools that they can adopt and expand outside the workshop. Mindmap-based brainstorming was a new tool for the Burnout team, and after the workshop they continued to develop their skills in this method. This is the aftermath of one such session, roughly one hour of intense brainstorming. Also notable is the interdisciplinary mix of the group; this 10-person brainstorm team includes a producer, game designer, concept artist, art director, sound designer, front-end designer, and lead engineer.

Make It Fun

- People are more creative, more receptive, and more productive when they're having fun.
- Was the fun in the workshop a cause or a symptom of the productivity? Probably both.
- A fast way to create leaders is to ask people to teach. At each studio, we asked local studio leaders to colead the workshop. Those local leaders helped customize the workshop for the games and issues in their studio, they presented, and they committed to follow-up projects as well as additional local workshops. This approach not only made the workshops more locally relevant but also left each studio with local leaders who could passionately drive further progress on preproduction.

Some of the key ideas delivered in the workshop are as follows:

1. Studiowide shared pre-pro concepts and vocabulary
   - Same terms mean the same things—create a common language of pre-pro.
   - Enable communication horizontally (within teams, across teams and studios) and vertically (through layers of management).
2. Rapid, early iteration
   - Make mistakes as quickly and cheaply as possible.
3. Rapid prototyping
   - *Types*: We covered all types of prototypes—paper games (cards and dice), 3D physical models, and simple software prototypes.
   - *Description:* We described the early prototypes as fast, cheap, public, physical, etc.
   - *Fast*: We developed prototypes and iterations quickly.
   - *Cheap:* Cheap prototypes can be thrown or radically changed, and if something is cheap enough, no one has to ask permission to build (it is surprising how often we got questions about "will we be allowed to do this?").
   - *Public*: In this context, "public" means that the team can see and experience the prototype together in some meaningful way. For many design problems, shared play and design are better than sitting isolated in a cube hunched over a big document.
   - *Physical*: Physical prototypes are underrated and underused. Creating opportunities to experience any aspect of the game in an immediate and visceral way is fun, engages every part of the brain, and helps the team to literally feel their way through their blind spots.
4. Preproduction process and discipline
   - The discipline of creative productivity is as important as the discipline of software development. There are few off-the-rack solutions, but by understanding a few general principles and pooling their collective experience in the creative process, each team can develop their own habits and incredibly high standards for creative productivity.

Outcome

The original preproduction workshop was put together for EA Canada by Pauline Moller, Gaivan Chang, and me. I then further developed the workshop and took it global, personally leading the workshop 14 times at EA studios around the world. Scores of other EA members from around the world contributed to the workshop's development and improvement.

The images on this page portray some of the techniques, teams, and collaborative processes found in the workshops.

Shout It Out

This is similar to stream of consciousness, but rather than writing, you shout out whatever comes into your head while a voice recorder is running. After five minutes of auditory gymnastics, go back and transcribe your mad ramblings. There is often a prized nugget hiding in your verbal blitzkrieg.

Cut It Up

Take a newspaper or magazine, open it up to any page, and cut random words and images out of it. It does not matter what they are. Anything that attracts your eye is fine. When you have a pile of pieces, start playing with them, matching them up, and try to come up with a game concept using this random collection. You can do the same with random web page searches or using a dictionary or the phone book.

Surrealist Games

Some of the techniques I have described are variations on techniques used by Surrealist and Dadaist artists to generate unexpected ideas from the collision of chance and the unconscious mind. There are many other games of this type that can be used as brainstorming methods, from the cut-up and stream-of-consciousness methods previously mentioned to more formal games, like the Exquisite Corpse, which can be played either with words or images.

Exercise 6.5: Play Exquisite Corpse

This version of the game is played with words. Everyone writes an article and an adjective on a piece of paper, then folds it to conceal the words and passes it to their neighbor. Now everyone writes a noun on the paper they are holding, folds it again to conceal their word, and passes

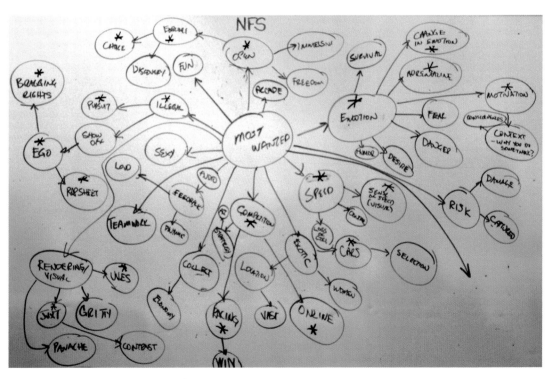

6.5   Mind map of game words

it to their neighbor. Repeat with a verb; repeat with another article and adjective; finally, repeat with a noun. Everyone unfolds their papers and reads the poems they are holding aloud. One of the first poems written this way was: "The exquisite corpse shall drink the new wine," which is how the game gets its name.

Research

Most of the previous techniques try to spark your creativity through a certain amount of randomness. On the other side of the spectrum, you might try doing research into a subject that interests you. Were you always fascinated by giant squid? Find out as much as you can about them. Research how they live and interact with their environment. Is there an idea or concept in this research that you can use in a game?

Research can also mean getting physical experience and understanding of systems you are trying to model in your game. If your game is about fishing, then go! If it is about collecting butterflies, you should try it, or go talk to expert collectors and find out how they go about

it. Doing research means immersing yourself in a subject, and while your game system might not need to be precisely true to life, understanding how the real activity works can help you decide what to focus on and what to leave out for the best possible gameplay. For a game I worked on about scientists searching for microscopic life deep underground, our team visited the research lab of scientists doing this type of work. We took pictures of their work environment, sat in on their meetings, and asked about their process. Many of the details we noticed became part of the core gameplay elements.

If your game is geared to a particular audience, you should do some target player research by watching their interactions with other games and each other. This is not the same as a focus group; it is closer to market research but a bit more fun. For example, if you want to make a game for music lovers, then you should find out what they are already playing and try to watch a group engaged with existing products. Ask them what they are missing, what they wish was there. This might give you some insight that will lead to an idea.

6.6 Cut-up games

Exercise 6.6: Do It

Now it is time to brainstorm your own idea. Get a potential team together—either in class or a group of friends who are interested on working on a game with you. If you cannot get a group together, do it on your own. As you did in Exercise 6.4, in the blue-sky brainstorm, state an interesting challenge for your game, set up a whiteboard or a sheet of butcher paper, and use the techniques previously discussed to generate 100 ideas related to your challenge in 60 minutes. This might sound like a lot, but if you can keep the energy level up, you can do it!

EDITING AND REFINING

What do you do after you have had a successful brainstorming session? Now you have a lot of ideas but no game. Next you will need to edit and refine your pool of ideas. This is the stage of the creative process previously described that Csikszentmihalyi called "evaluation," where you decide whether an idea is valuable and worth pursuing. There are a number of reasons for editing an idea out of your final list. Most of them fall into the following categories.

Aligned with Goals

As described on page 181, when I discussed setting player experience goals, the most important question to ask when you are evaluating ideas is whether or not the idea supports your goals. When we were brainstorming, we didn't cut or dismiss any ideas. Everything was captured, no matter how off-topic it might have seemed. Now is the time to determine which ideas support your goals and which ones do not. It's a good idea to let a bit of time pass — several hours or even a day — before editing your ideas from a brainstorm. This gives participants some distance and it makes it easier and less emotional to do this determination. Of course, sometimes you may disagree on whether an idea will support the goals or not. Try listening to everyone and talking it through. If you can't come to a decision together, it may be that your experience goals are too vague for the team to make strong distinctions between your ideas. This may mean that you need to articulate your goals more clearly.

Technical Feasibility

Sometimes you come up with an idea, like your blue-sky character remote controls from Exercise 6.4, that is just not technically possible yet. You can try to brainstorm ways to make it technically feasible, but sometimes there is just no way. Also, sometimes an idea that would be feasible for a more experienced, or larger, production team has to be cut by a team that has limited resources or expertise. This does not mean it is a bad idea, just that you cannot do it right now. Keep a list of these ideas for later—you never know when a technology advance will make them feasible.

Market Opportunity

Sometimes there is no market opportunity for particular idea. Again, this does not mean it is a bad idea; it just might not be advisable to do it right now. Market trends are affected by world events, by the success (or failure) of other products, by the overall economy, by technology cycles, and any number of other outside influences. It is a good idea as a designer to follow market trends, not so that you can follow the decisions of others, but so that you can make smart creative business decisions regarding your own ideas.

Artistic Considerations

Sometimes you just do not like an idea enough to do it. This is a perfectly valid reason to edit an idea. If you and your team do not feel passionately about the idea when you are beginning the project, think of how you will feel down the line when you have been working on it for months or years. Also, as a game designer, you want to stretch yourself artistically, and if an idea just does not do that, then cut it. Do not rest on the laurels of game genres or ideas that have already been proven. Think about how this idea might break new ground. If you do not think this idea is artistically challenging, then cutting it might be the right decision.

Business/Cost Restrictions

Sometimes an idea is just too expensive, or too ambitious for your team or for the time frame or budget you have available. If the idea cannot be scaled down, then cutting it from your list might be the best answer. As with the other cuts you have made, it is always a good idea to keep a list of these ideas for later, just in case you have an opportunity to do a larger, more ambitious game.

Whether you are working alone or as a team, I recommend that you schedule your editing sessions on different days than your brainstorming meetings. Letting some time go by between the two phases is a good idea. You do not want to blur the line between the two because you might combine editing and brainstorming, which will decrease the productivity of your brainstorming sessions.

Most of the time, people will think about the ideas between the time of the brainstorm and the editing session and will have a list of favorites. The top 5-10 ideas should be thoroughly discussed, going over the merits of each idea. Try to keep the discussion positive. Do not dismiss or attack any ideas. Instead talk about the relative strengths of each idea in terms of the criteria listed above to make sure it meets your goals, is technically feasible, marketable, artistically interesting, and within the scope of your team to produce.

Narrow down the list to three ideas. Then schedule new brainstorming sessions to flesh out these three ideas. In these second-level brainstorming sessions, focus in on features, and clearly define what producers at Electronic Arts often call the "X" of the game. The X is the creative center of the game. It also an alignment tool—aligning the development team, marketing, advertising, and customers so that you can communicate the value of the game to each party in terms they understand.

Electronic Arts' Chief Visual Officer Glenn Entis describes the two parts of an X as "the razor" and "the slogan." The razor cuts—it allows the team to determine which features belong and which do not. The slogan is catchy—it allows marketing and players to determine whether this sounds like something they want to do. For example, the razor for the original Medal of Honor was "GoldenEye set in WWII on a PlayStation." Entis felt this was a great razor because it allowed the team to decide what features the game absolutely needed. It was not a great slogan, however. The slogan that went on the box was, "Prepare for your finest hour." While this was a great slogan, it would not have helped drive the creative process at all.[5]

When you have a clear idea of key features and your X, write your ideas up as short one-page descriptions. Hold an informal feedback group (the process for which will be described in Chapter 9, "Playtesting") and find out how your game concepts appeal to your target players. At this stage, it is very easy to make changes to your concepts. The goal is to keep the process fluid so you do not get locked into a single idea too early or spend too much time perfecting your writing. Your original concept can be refined with early player input, or you might

A Conversation with Will Wright

by Celia Pearce

Will Wright is cofounder of game developer Maxis Inc., now part of Electronic Arts. In 2009, he left EA to run "Stupid Fun Club," an entertainment think tank. He is famous for thinking outside the box with his game creations and is the mind behind SimCity, The Sims, Spore, and many other groundbreaking titles. When Will started work on The Sims, publishers tried to dissuade him from the project on the grounds that no one would play such a game. The Sims is one of the best-selling titles of all time. This is an excerpt of a conversation between Will and game designer/researcher, Celia Pearce. The full discussion appears in the online journal "Game Studies" at http://www.gamestudies.org/0102/pearce/. It is reprinted here with permission.

On Why He Designs Games

Celia Pearce: I wanted to start out by talking about why you design games. What is it about the format of an interactive experience that is so compelling to you? And what do you want to create in that space?

Will Wright: Well, one thing I've always really enjoyed is making things. Out of whatever. It started with modeling as a kid, building models. When computers came along, I started learning programming and realizing the computer was this great tool for making things, making models, dynamic models, and behaviors, not just static models. I think when I started doing games I really wanted to carry that to the next step, to the player, so that you give the player a tool so that they can create things. And then you give them some context for that creation. You know, what is it, what kind of kind of world does it live in, what's its purpose? What are you trying to do with this thing that you're creating? To really put the player in the design role. And the actual world is reactive to their design. So they design something that the little world inside the computer reacts to. And then they have to revisit the design and redesign it, or tear it down and build another one, whatever it is. So I guess what really draws me to interactive entertainment and the thing that I try to keep focused on is enabling the creativity of the player. Giving them a pretty large solution space to solve the problem within the game. So the game represents this problem landscape. Most games have small solution landscapes, so there's one possible solution and one way to solve it. Other games, the games that tend to be more creative, have a much larger solution space, so you can potentially solve this problem in a way that nobody else has. If you're building a solution, how large that solution space is gives the player a much stronger feeling of empathy. If they know that what they've done is unique to them, they tend to care for it a lot more. I think that's the direction I tend to come from.

On the Influences of SimCity

CP: When you were first working on SimCity, what was going on in the game world at that time? Were you responding to games that were out there, were you wanting something different? Were there things that influenced you at all in the game world or were you just totally in a different mindset?

WW: There were things that influenced me—not many, though. There was a very old game called Pinball Construction Set by Bill Budge, which was great. He was kind of playing around with the first pre-Mac Lisa interface, which was icon-based. He actually put this in the game, even though it was an Apple II game. He kind of emulated what would later become the Mac interface. But it was very easy to use, and you would create pinball sets with it, which you could then play with. I thought that was very cool.

Also early modeling things, like the very first flight simulator by Bruce Artwick, which had this little microworld in the computer with its own rules, kind of near reality to some degree, but at a very low resolution. But yet it was this little self-consistent world that you could go fly around in and interact with, in sort of limited ways.

So those are some of the influences. But then mostly, stuff I read. I started getting interested in the idea of simulation. I started reading the early work of people like Jay Forrester, starting with that, going forward. When I did SimCity, the games at the time really were much more about arcade-style action, graphics, very intense kinds of experiences. There were very few games that were laid back, more complex.

CP: *They were more twitch-type games at that time?*

WW: Yeah, the games that were more complex were these detailed war games. I had played those as a kid, these board games. With 40-page rule sets.

CP: *Like what?*

WW: Oh, like Panzer Blitz was a big one, Global War, Sniper.

CP: *Were those ones with the hex-grid boards?*

WW: Yeah, they had a 40-page rule book, and you'd play with your friend. And it ended up being...I mean, I think it would be excellent training for a lawyer. Because you're sitting there, most of the time, arguing over interpretations of these very elaborate rules. And you could actually combine the rules and say, "Well, this was in panic mode so he couldn't go that far." "Well, my indirect fire has a three-hex radius of destruction." So you'd sit there and argue over this little minutia of the rules. And that was kind of half the fun of it—both of you trying to find the legal loopholes for why your guy didn't get killed. So I was familiar with that stuff, but I knew at the same time that most people couldn't relate to that at all. But yet the strategy of those games was actually quite interesting. It was interesting to have a game where you'd sit back and you'd think about it, and the model was far more elaborate than you could really run in your head. So you had to approach it kind of in a different way.

On Experimentation as a Play Mechanic

CP: *I wanted to ask you about this idea of experimentation as a play mechanic. That seems like a big aspect of your games, that play and experimentation are working together.*

WW: The types of games we do are simulation based and so there is this really elaborate simulation of some aspect of reality. As a player, a lot of what you're trying to do is reverse engineer the simulation. You're trying to solve problems within the system, you're trying to solve traffic in SimCity, or get somebody in The Sims to get married or whatever. The more accurately you can model that simulation in your head, the better your strategies are going to be going forward. So what we're trying to do as designers is build up these mental models in the player. The computer is just an incremental step, an intermediate model to the model in the player's head. The player has to be able to bootstrap themselves into understanding that model. You've got this elaborate system with thousands of variables, and you can't just dump it on the user or else they're totally lost. So we usually try to think in terms of, what's a simpler metaphor that somebody can approach this with? What's the simplest mental model that you can walk up to one of these games and start playing it, and at least understand the basics? Now it might be the wrong model, but it still has to bootstrap into your learning process. So for most of our games, there's some overt metaphor that allows you approach the simulation.

CP: *Like?*

WW: Like for SimCity, most people see it as kind of a train set. You look at the box and you say, "Oh, yeah, it's like a train set come to life." Or The Sims, "It's like a dollhouse come to life." But at the same time, when you start playing the game, and the dynamics become more apparent to you, a lot of time there's an underlying metaphor that's not so apparent. Like in SimCity, if you really think about playing the game, it's more like gardening. So you're kind of tilling the soil, and fertilizing it, and then things pop up and they surprise you, and occasionally you have to go in and weed the garden, and then you maybe think about expanding it, and so on. So the actual process of playing SimCity is really closer to gardening. In either case, your mental model of the simulation is constantly evolving. And in fact you can look at somebody's city that they designed at any point and see that it's kind of a snapshot of their current understanding of the model. You can tell by what they've done in the game—"Oh, I see they think this freeway is going to help them because they put it over here." So it gives you some insight into their mental model of the game.

CP: *What's the underlying metaphor of The Sims? The less obvious one, the garden-level one?*

WW: That depends on how you play the game. For a lot of people, the mainstream game is more like juggling, or balancing plates. You start realizing that you basically don't have enough time in the day to do everything that you want to do. And you're rushing from this to that to this, and then you're able to make these time decisions. So it feels very much like juggling and if you drop a ball, then all of a sudden, the whole pile comes crashing down. But other people play it differently. So it's kind of hard. With The Sims I've thought about that, and it's not as clear to me what The Sims is. I think that SimCity has a more monolithic play style, once people get into it, than The Sims does. In The Sims people tend to veer off in a different direction. Some people go off into the storytelling thing. So eventually the metaphor becomes that of a director on a set. You're trying to coerce these actors into doing what you want them to do, but they're busy leading their own lives. And so you get this weird conflict going on between you and The Sims where you're trying to tell a story with the game but they want to go off and eat, and watch TV, and do whatever.

CP: *Like real actors.*

WW: Yes, exactly. Kind of like little actors who just won't do what you want them to do.

On His Favorite Game

CP: *Let's shift gears a little here and talk about your favorite games. And not just limiting it to computer games, but any games you like. What's your favorite game?*

WW: My favorite game by far probably is Go. The board game.

CP: *That's no surprise to me.*

WW: (Laughs.) That game is just so elegant in that it's got two rules really, one of which is almost never used. But yet from those two rules flow this incredible complexity. It's kind of the board game version of John Conway's Game of Life, the cellular automata game. It's not dissimilar.

On the Emergent Properties of Games

CP: *When you were talking about Go, I was thinking that when you create a mental model of the environment as it is now, you're also creating a model of how you want it to be. So in Go the mental models have to do with imagining where the players want the game to go, right?*

WW: Right.

CP: *And then as the game fills itself out, as the emergent properties come forth ...*

WW: ... and of course part of that model is modeling what the other player is likely to do. "Oh, I think they're going to play very aggressively, therefore, my model of them says that this would be the optimum strategy."

CP: *So that's interesting, because there's also this aspect of imagination, which you alluded to earlier.*

And that sort of brings me back to a question about SimCity and The Sims. Each of those games has a different level of abstraction from the other. You can really see the different choices that are made in terms of design. But in terms of this modeling idea, you briefly alluded to the use of The Sims from a directorial standpoint as a storytelling tool, and that in a way, there's a little bit of a dynamic that goes on because the game doesn't want to be, the characters don't want to be used that way necessarily.

So I'm just curious how you grapple with that. I mean you're obviously taking that into account. Are you making a way to use the game as a storyboarding tool, or continuing to play around with the tension that the characters are kind of resisting that kind of control?

WW: It's actually very interesting in The Sims how the pronouns change all the time. I'm sitting there playing the game and I'm talking about, "Oh, first I'm going to get a job, then I'm going to do this, then I'm going to do that." And then you know when the character starts disobeying me, all of a sudden I shift and say "Oh, why won't he do that?" or "What's he doing now?" And so at some point it's me kind of inhabiting this little person, and I'm thinking, "It's me; I'm going to get a job and I'm going to do **x**, **y**, and **z**." But then when he starts rebelling, it's he. And so then I kind of jump out of him, and now it's me versus him. You know what I'm saying?

CP: *Yes, I do. But one of things that interests me about the game is that you have these semiautonomous characters. They're not totally autonomous, and they're not totally avatars either. They're somewhere in between. Do think that's disorienting to the player, or do you think it's what makes the game fun?*

WW: I don't think so. I mean it's interesting. I'm just surprised that people can do it that fluidly, they can so fluidly say, "Oh, I'm this guy, and then I'm going to do **x**, **y**, and **z**." And then they can pop out and, "Now I'm that person. I'm doing this that and the other. What's he doing?" And so now he's a third person to me, even though he was me a moment ago. I think that's something we use a lot in our imaginations when we're modeling things. We'll put ourselves in somebody else's point of view very specifically for a very short period of time. "Well, let's see, if I were that person, I would probably do **x**, **y**, and **z**." And then I kind of jump out of their head and then I'm me, talking to them, relating to them.

At some level I want people to have a deep appreciation for how connected things are at all these different scales, not just through space, but through time. And in doing so I had to build kind of a simple little toy universe and say, here, play with this toy for a while. My expectations when I hand somebody that toy are that they are going to make their own mental model, which isn't exactly what I'm presenting them with. But whatever it is, their mental model of the world around them, and above them and below them, will expand. Hopefully, probably in some unpredictable way, and for me that's fine. And I don't want to stamp the same mental model on every player. I'd rather think of this as a catalyst. You know, it's a catalytic tool for growing your mental model, and I have no idea which direction it's going to grow it, but I think just kind of sparking that change is worthwhile unto itself.

CP: *But you're more interested in setting up the rule space and letting the outcome evolve with the player's experimentation.*

WW: Right, I mean what I really want to do is I want to create just the largest possibility space I can. I don't want to create a specific possibility that everybody's going to experience the same way. I'd much rather have a huge possibility space where every player has as unique an experience as possible.

CP: *One of the things that I think is interesting about what you do as a role model for interactive designers it that you enjoy the unpredictable outcome. When people do things that you didn't plan on, that seems to be something that you embrace.*

WW: To me, that feels like success.

About the Author

Dr. Celia Pearce is a game designer, artist, teacher, and writer. She is the designer of the award-winning virtual reality attraction Virtual Adventures: The Loch Ness Expedition, *and the author* Communities of Play: Emergent Cultures in Multiplayer Games and Virtual Worlds (MIT 2009) *as well as numerous essays on game design and interactivity. She is a professor of game design in the College of Arts, Media, and Design at Northeastern University. She is also the co-founder of the IndieCade Festival of Independent Games.*

discover a better idea by talking with potential players. You can iterate on these ideas, holding more feedback groups, until one clearly stands out as the idea that you and your team should pursue at this time.

Exercise 6.7: Describe Your Game

In one or two paragraphs, describe the essence of your game idea. Try to capture what makes it interesting to you and how the basic gameplay will work. State your "X"—both razor and slogan—as a part of your game description.

TURNING IDEAS INTO A GAME

Now you have a single idea that you like; you have a list of potential features and an "X" that you think will make a great game. But you cannot be certain until you have done some prototyping and playtesting the concept. After all, the only way to know if a game works is to actually play it.

At this point, many game designers try to take a shortcut. They believe that the best way to develop a game concept is to begin with an existing set of mechanics, a "genre" of play. After all, genres produce proven gameplay. That is what publishers want and even what players say they want. That is fine, to a certain extent. Many designers actually do very well by modifying existing mechanics, what we might call "feature innovation." By relying on feature innovation, a designer is sure to attract the core players of the main genre, and they are apt to appeal to their sense of novelty with the new features they have added.

But what if your idea does not fit nicely into an existing genre of gameplay? Should you try to force it to more closely resemble a first-person shooter or a real-time strategy game? Throughout this book, I will encourage you to try to experiment with your game mechanics, to explore new directions of play. This is not because I do not enjoy the existing genres of play. Rather, it is because I see those areas as being "solved problems" of gameplay. What I mean by this is that a lot of designers have spent a number of years working out the specifics of the first-person shooter game as we know it today. They have solved many of the gameplay issues surrounding this genre. Unless you feel that you can ask new questions about this genre (and perhaps you can), I suggest staking out some brand new territory for your gameplay. As I described earlier in this chapter, you should articulate a clear statement of the player experience you would like to create. The formal structure will follow from ideas you have brainstormed around that goal. Perhaps it will have elements of existing games, but overall it will feel like something entirely new.

As you continue to brainstorm, edit, and refine your game idea, ask yourself how you would like your players to act and feel. Come up with a list of game verbs as described in the mind mapping method. What is the role of the player? Does the player have a clearly defined goal? And what are the obstacles in getting to that goal? What kind of resources do they have to accomplish that goal? The game mechanics should stem from the core experience goal. They are an outgrowth of your overall ideation process.

During this process, you will want to refer to the formal and dramatic elements of game design presented in Chapters 2 through 5 of this book. Think about each aspect of your game idea in terms of these elements. If you have forgotten any of them, please go back and review them before proceeding. If you have been playing and analyzing a lot of games in your game journal, you will see that combinations of certain formal elements will begin to emerge, which can elicit the type of player experience you are looking for in your own game. I encourage you not to copy these mechanics but rather to learn from them. As you analyze more and more games, you will train yourself to recognize familiar structures and how they are adding to the gameplay. Your growing experience will eventually help you construct new, groundbreaking systems of your own.

One stumbling block many beginning designers run into is the question of when to focus on the dramatic elements. Story and characters are important for all the reasons I have already discussed, but focusing on them too early in the process can obscure your view of the gameplay. One exception to this is the premise: coming up with a rough dramatic premise can sometimes inspire your search for mechanics. But don't spend time digging into story or lore until you have a good grasp of your formal elements.

Focus on the Formal Elements

The formal elements, as I have discussed, are the underlying system and mechanics of the game. Your initial concept might already include some of the formal elements of your game. As you move forward, you will need to fill in that system more and more. Here are some questions to ask yourself:

- What is the player's role and objective?
- What are the rules and procedures?
- What actions do the players take and when?
- What is the conflict in my game?
- Are there turns? How do they work?

- How many players can play?
- How does the game resolve? How long should it take?

The more questions you ask yourself, the better. And it is okay if you do not know all the answers at this point in the process. In the beginning, you can only guess, and you won't know if you are on the right track until you actually play the game and see how it works. But do not let this stop you from conceptualizing the game. You might feel like you're working blind at first, but soon the game will begin to take form and your design decisions will begin to have more context.

To flesh out the game structure, consider the following:

- Define the player's goal(s).
- What does a player need to do to win?
- Write down the single most important type of player action in the game.
- Describe how this functions.
- Write down the procedures and rules in outline format.
- Only focus on the most critical rules.
- Leave all other rules until later.
- Map out how a typical turn or core loop works. Using a flowchart is the most effective way to visualize this, as I will discuss in Chapter 7 on page 232.
- Define how many players can play.
- How do these players interact with one another?

You might have noticed that this is the very beginning of a prototyping process. I won't go into detail here because Chapters 7 and 8 will take you through of the process of prototyping a game. Suffice it to say that the ideation and discovery process, as it evolves, naturally segues into prototyping and then playtesting.

Whenever you get stuck or feel you can improve upon a particular feature idea, remember to go back and utilize the brainstorming techniques described previously.

Writing a Treatment

One good way to document your game idea at this stage is by writing a short one-page concept document, or, if you are able to begin drafting your idea in more detail, a three- to six-page game treatment. The concept document is just a short description of your idea that can be fairly high level. It does not go into details, but captures the essence of your idea, its premise, possibly the target audience, any mechanics you have ideas for, or experience goals.

If you have begun to get into more detail with your brainstorming exercises, you can also begin developing a treatment, which is a slightly longer document that outlines all of the core concepts you've been defining during your brainstorming sessions. It typically includes the following parts:

- Premise: This is a brief summary of the game's setting, characters, and conflict.
- Goals: This section describes the player's goals in the game. Note that these are not your design goals, but the goals of the player.
- Mechanics: This section explains how the game will be played, including the rules, controls, and feedback system.
- Story: This section provides a more detailed overview of the game's plot, characters, and setting.
- Theme: This section identifies the game's underlying message or message.
- Target audience: This section describes the type of player who would enjoy the game.
- Design Pillars and Experience Goals: As we've already discussed, these are the team's goals for the project and what players will experience as they play.

Writing a concept document or a game treatment at this stage helps to ensure that everyone involved in the project is on the same page about the game's vision. It also serves as a blueprint for the game's development, helping to ensure that the game is created in a consistent and coherent way. Here are some additional parts that may be included in a game treatment, depending on the specific game:

- Level design: This section describes the layout of the game's levels, including the obstacles, enemies, and puzzles that players will encounter.
- Art style: This section describes the game's visual style, including the characters, environments, and objects.
- Audio: This section describes the game's audio, including the music, sound effects, and voice acting.
- Technology: This section describes the game's technical requirements, such as the hardware and software needed to play the game.

The specific parts of a game treatment will vary depending on the type of game being developed. However, the above list provides a good overview of the most common elements. A treatment is not meant to be as comprehensive as a design document or game macro, both of which will be covered in Chapter 14, so try to be brief when writing a treatment. The idea is document and communicate your idea as quickly as possible so you can move on to prototyping and deeper development of your ideas.

Logline

In addition to a treatment, I often ask my students to write a log line for their projects. A longline is a succinct, crystallized version of your idea that is very helpful for talking about to others, sometimes even pitching it to people you meet. When you fully understand your idea, you will be able to distill it into a logline.

Like an X statement, a logline captures the idea quickly, but is not just intended for guiding the team. It is also useful for pitching your game, or simply introducing your idea to an interested colleague or contact. I use a simple fill-in-the-blanks format with my students when they are first formalizing their ideas into loglines. Later, they are able to craft their loglines to better meet the needs of the project. Here is an example format for a first draft logline:

(Project name) is a (genre of play) where you play as (my protagonist—name or description) who must (problem to solve) while also dealing with (challenge). The game is set in a (tone, world) and deals with (theme). Over the course of the game, players will feel (experience goal).

And here are several example loglines from my students' game projects over the years:

The Trials of Snowshoe Thompson is a first person skiing game about immigrant John Thompson on an expedition to deliver mail between remote towns in the Sierra Nevada mountains of 1856. Thompson faces unknown terrain and risks, but also finds his purpose and discovers the beauty of the region. Players will feel the hardships of Thompson's journey, but also the sense of community and skill as they complete his trek.

The Veiled Ones is a 1st person survival/exploration game featuring an unseen Islamic entity: the djinn. You play as a hodja—a Muslim equivalent of an exorcist from Turkey—searching for clues to save your possessed son, while also trying to evade a vengeful djinn. Players will experience terror from a culture that rarely gets the spotlight in horror entertainment.

Charon is a third person action rower where you play as Charon, ferryman of the Underworld, who risks a treacherous journey to help his old friend reach her lost lover in the afterlife. Players get to experience themes of trust and companionship through the bond of Charon and Alexis as they embark on an epic journey.

Key Art

In addition to a treatment and logline, you may want to create a piece of key art for your game concept at this time. If you have art skills, or an artist on your team, you can do something original. But for internal use, you can also use found art on the internet or art generated from an AI tool to create a draft piece of key art. The idea of draft key art is that it can communicate the feel of your game to your team, it can become something that galvanizes your efforts and helps conversation around what matters and what doesn't in the game experience.

Figure 6.7 shows three pieces of student key art—two that were created by student artists, and one that used a piece of found art from the internet to capture the feel of the proposed game. These examples are from the games described in the loglines above. When you read these loglines and see the key art, together they will begin to give you a strong sense of the vision of each of these games.

Practice, Practice, Practice

The first time you go through this process will be the hardest. Each time you do it, however, you will become more capable of generating workable ideas. Every accomplished game designer has developed many more concepts than he or she will ever produce. The key is to be persistent and keep practicing.

Exercise 6.8: Write a Treatment

Take the description you wrote in Exercise 6.7 and expand it into a three- to six-page treatment for your game idea. If you don't have enough details about your idea yet, then start with a one-page concept document instead.

6.7 **Key art from student presentations**

Remember that these initial documents are just drafts. When you go on to the prototyping stage, you will address these questions again in more detail.

Feature Design

Another good way to get practice in coming up with game ideas is to design new features for existing games. Rather than trying to come up with an idea for an entire, original game, you can do a focused brainstorm on improving a specific area of an existing game. This is good practice for designers at any level, and the final concepts make excellent portfolio pieces for potential job interviews. Designing a game from scratch is not something that beginning designers get to do at established game companies until later in their careers. Designing features for existing games, however, is often a task that is assigned to entry-level designers, so it is great practice and a good way to show your skills in a very practical way.

Exercise 6.9: Feature Design Exercise, Part 1

By now you should have a whole list of games you've analyzed in your game journal. Take one one of these games and do a brainstorm on a new feature that you feel would improve its gameplay.

Feature Storyboards

The most powerful way to explain your ideas for new features is to visualize them. You can use Photoshop or any other image editing program you have access to. A good way to begin is to use screenshots from the existing game and edit them to explain what the player sees when they use your new feature ideas.

For example, show how the feature starts (e.g., exactly what the player sees on the screen when the feature is activated) and how the interface changes as the player manipulates the controls to use the feature. Show a series of still images—each with a slightly different on-screen condition—to simulate a player moving through the game using the feature. Storyboards like this can include dozens of still images—each just incrementally different than its predecessor—to show exactly how the feature works. Do not worry if you have poor art skills. The goal is not for the graphics to look perfect but rather to communicate your ideas with simple imagery.

Assemble the storyboard and add some light explanatory text. You can assemble the storyboard using presentation programs such as PowerPoint or Keynote. These programs make it easy for you to put together a long series of images and add light text. Do not put much text on the images because you want your ideas to be communicated visually.

Practice presenting the feature design to others to make sure it flows nicely. Ultimately, this is an exercise in effective communication (i.e., transferring the idea that is in your mind to another person's mind), so treat it accordingly.

Exercise 6.10: Feature Design Exercise, Part 2

Create a visual storyboard stepping through the use of the feature idea you came up with for Exercise 6.9. Assemble the storyboard so that it tells a visual story of a player successfully playing the game. Present your idea to an appropriate group of people for critique, such as classmates or a game design club.

GETTING THE MOST OUT OF FOCUS GROUPS

by Kevin Keeker, Principal Researcher, Sony PlayStation, North America

Kevin Keeker has spent the better part of his career working on game projects as a user researcher. He trained as a social and personality psychologist at the University of Illinois and at the University of Washington before stumbling into usability engineering in 1994. Since then, he has worked on a variety of entertainment- and media-related products at companies such as Microsoft, Zynga, and Sony. Early in his career he managed Microsoft Game Studios' usability group, before shifting focus to game design on Xbox sports titles. He then went to work on social titles such as FarmVille. More recently, he's been at Sony Interactive Entertainment improving the user experience on PlayStation titles such as Horizon Zero Dawn, God of War and The Last of Us Part II. Here, he shares some insight into the psychology of focus groups and how to get the most out of them.

Many people believe that focus groups are a good way to collect feedback on their games. I've learned that they can be if used for the right reasons. Focus groups aren't the best way to gauge the quality or popularity of your ideas. Participants and moderators are prone to influence by a host of biases that are introduced by the social situation.

But focus groups can help you generate ideas for your game. The feedback from a focus group can fuel your own creativity and provide a glimpse into the common points of wisdom and key disagreements in your gaming audience.

They're also a good way to collect feedback on group activities. The same social factors that often introduce misleading bias into individual judgments are the things that make group decision-making different from individual decision-making.

This sidebar describes why focus groups are better for generating ideas, particularly about social activities, than evaluating them. It then provides a few pointers to help you achieve each of those objectives.

First let's examine that bias that can make focus groups poor for evaluating individual preferences. Imagine that you're designing a cooperative sci-fi action game. You know that your primary audience is teens and young adults. You've decided on a good number of maps set in a variety of micro-climates. You'll need various characters, enemies, and vehicle types. You've been tuning the basic play of the game with usability feedback. You've picked some songs for the soundtrack, and you're loving it. But not everyone on the team agrees.

So, you set up a focus group to validate the soundtrack. Your first question is "What are your favorite bands?" You've chosen that because it's a good icebreaker and it gives you a broad sense of player preferences. The front row starts eagerly throwing out names. Others snipe at these suggestions. A third set of participants sinks sullenly back in their seats, and a couple calmly drift off into space.

To reel everyone back in, you remind the group that this is a brainstorm. You start going around the room one-by-one eagerly accepting all suggestions. This generates a pretty sizable list with most of the overlap in tastes centering on well-established bands with some widespread popularity.

Now you move on to some music that you've picked out. You play a song, ask people to give it a thumbs-up or thumbs-down and to please explain their opinions. You notice the participants noticing each other. They look around the room as they make their decision. You probe and encourage people to be open. But, in the end, the bands that are familiar names receive the clearest enthusiasm. At least a few people have heard of them. Most of the songs receive halfhearted enthusiasm. No one likes a few of them. During the wrap-up, you ask for an overall consensus on the musical selection. A few people passionately argue for alternatives. The group as a whole agrees that variety is the key.

You're left with a very uneasy consensus. What do you do now? You could go with your gut. But then the focus group has been a waste of time and a truckload of money. You try to sum thumbs and go with the songs that evoked the least ire. But that skews you toward the bands that you already knew to be the most radio friendly – not necessarily the cutting edge. This scenario points out a fundamental issue in choosing your method. Focus groups are good for generating ideas and poor at validating them.

I don't have to tell you that music preferences are very individual. To engage players with diverse tastes, you'll need a wide variety of music. Focus groups give you a good method to generate ideas on complex and polarizing topics. Adding complication, you're trying to build a great shared experience. You're looking for music that people will enjoy together—even if it's not exactly their style. Focus groups are a good method to explore players' shared experiences in social scenarios.

Why are focus groups better than individual responses for generating ideas, particularly on group activities? Group interaction seeds individual creativity by encouraging us to examine differences between our opinions and those of others. The thoughts of others remind us of the way we feel ourselves. The differences between our ideas and others spur us to distinguish our ideas. They also encourage us to try out alternative perspectives and potentially incorporate elements of those perspectives into our own ideas. Creativity is this process of incorporating new elements into our ideas and putting together disparate ideas to create new ideas.

However, a similar process can lead people to find consensus and avoid stating differences with others. It takes precious mental effort to withstand social pressure, to disagree with others and to generate a plausible reason why you differ from others. Disagreeing becomes significantly harder if you perceive that you're the only person with an opinion. This perception comes quickly in group settings where one person might state an opinion and others might quickly agree. The onus is then on the dissenters to come forward. But the dissenters may take time to reevaluate their positions. Pauses and delays further support the appearance that there is consensus.

On the other hand, some participants will thrive on countering the crowd. This can lead to satisfying discussions. But it's hard to say whether the nonconformists are expressing attitudes about the songs or about the social setting. In psychology literature, the tendency for group discussions to result in more extreme attitudes – both more positive or more negative – is called group polarization (though you might be more amused by the military's term: incestuous amplification). Group polarization can disrupt accurate measurement of the attitudes of your participants.

Group discussion mirrors group activities in social factors and social motives. Group activities require commonality of purpose to progress. When a common vision is shared the group will be more efficient and effective. Take the example of a party-based role playing game. If party members stray or act out of sync, the whole group suffers. This encourages group communication and support of individual members.

Shared experiences lead to shared value, validation, and memory. These are many of the things that make social experiences so enjoyable. Group understandings, attitudes, norms, and memories will be different than individuals' understandings, attitudes, norms and memories. Focus groups are more accurate than individual surveys or interviews at getting at those elements.

What's the right method for your question ? If you want to evaluate ideas, you survey people individually. Give each person a concrete list of alternatives and ask them to choose or rank those alternatives. The clearest answers will come when you present people with suitable thresholds and criteria for their judgments. Does this song fit with this map or this situation? Do you want this song or that song? Make your acceptance criteria explicit. Rather than asking people which songs they like, ask them which songs fit the game that you've shown them.

Use a focus group when you want to generate ideas or obtain group feedback on a group activity. To make these conversations meaningful the question needs to be framed precisely. What style of music would fit this gameplay scenario? Which band do you listen to when playing Game X? Meanwhile, to make answers believable participants need to speak freely and disagree with one another respectfully. Create a temporary culture where it's safe to be the exception. Actively bring dissidents into the conversation ("I'd like to hear from someone who feels differently …"). Paraphrase and clarify ideas ("So, you're saying …"). Encourage healthy consensus ("Some of you seem to be in agreement …"). Draw parallels between ideas ("What if Kelly's chocolate and your peanut butter …"). All of these techniques can simultaneously be used to avoid getting stuck in one area too long and move the conversation forward. In short, set the context properly, encourage people to clearly explain their ideas in a safe and constructive fashion, then encourage group discussion in order to dig into important details and examples.

EXPERIMENTAL GAMEPLAY

by Richard Lemarchand

Richard Lemarchand is an associate professor in the Interactive Media & Games Division of the School of Cinematic Arts at the University of Southern California. He has worked as a game designer in the videogame industry for over twenty years, most recently at Sony-owned studio Naughty Dog, where he led the design of the first three games in the Uncharted series.

What Do We Mean by "Experimental Games"?

The history of game design is full of experimentation and innovation, and most game designers love to explore new territory. However, in the last decade or so, there has been a movement toward the design of games that are deliberately experimental in a focused way, and an international experimental game design scene has grown up around the experimental game makers—many of them indie game designers and game artists—at the forefront of the practice.

Simply put, experimental games are those that have been created in an attempt to do something new with games or to make a game design discovery. They help us to push forward the frontiers of game design by revealing new game mechanics, new patterns of play, and, in the case of particularly successful game design experiments, entirely new game genres. We can also hone our skills as game designers by making experimental games; by doing so, we often expand the range of our artistic "voices."

Experimental social game Johan Sebastian Joust

By making experimental games, we can try out new ideas, playtest new mechanics, and explore what can be done with games as a form, testing our preconceptions and assumptions about what games are and how human beings play. We can explore the porous boundary between games and other artistic forms, and we can discover new things about ourselves as creative people.

Whether you are a game designer in search of exciting new kinds of fun, an artist seeking ways for your audience to become active participants in an unfolding artwork, or an businessperson approaching games in the hope of creating profitable new entertainment experiences, the design of experimental games has a tremendous amount to offer you.

Ultimately, experimental game design is important because it is at the forefront of games as a cultural practice. Culture is to do with our identity, as individuals and as groups, as expressed by the things we do: language, science, technology, art, commerce, education, politics, religion—this list could go on and on. Whether you see culture as a reflecting mirror for the way we live or a battleground on which we test our values and aspirations, the games that we make and play are part of culture and tell us something meaningful.

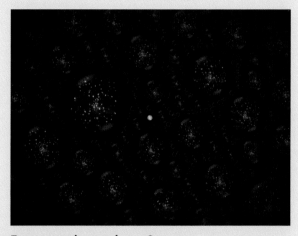

Experimental gameplay in Osmos

What Are Some Good Examples of Experimental Games?

It would be impossible to list every example of great experimental game design here—simply too much great work has been done in the last decade—but here are some of my personal favorites.

Katamari Damacy (2004)—This wildly original, playful, and irreverent, yet strangely thought-provoking game by sculptor-turned-game-designer Keita Takahashi puts the player in the tiny shoes of a cosmic prince who must use a sticky ball to "roll up" everything from thumb tacks to a sports stadium.

Escape from Woomera (2004) — a team of Australian video game industry professionals lead by Katharine Neil joined with an investigative journalist to create a game criticizing the government's treatment of detained asylum seekers in Australia, creating great controversy.

Lapis (2005) — Heather Kelley's groundbreaking game prototype was designed to help teach women about their bodies by interfacing with a cartoon bunny.

World of Goo (2008)—Kyle Gabler of the Carnegie Mellon ETC Experimental Gameplay Project teamed with Ron Carmel to create this innovative and award-winning physics-based puzzle game.

Braid (2008)—Experimental game veteran Jonathan Blow designed this puzzle-platform game that links time, space, and logic together in interesting new ways.

Osmos (2009)—Hemisphere Games' inventive, calming puzzle game brought physics-based gameplay to new levels of nuance and complexity.

Dear Esther (2008 and 2012)—Originally a Half Life 2 mod created for a university research project on game narrative, Dear Esther was entirely rebuilt for a highly successful 2012 commercial release.

Johann Sebastian Joust (2011)—Not all "video games" involve visual representation of moving images—Die Gute Fabrik's indie "digital contact sport" is played to music with PlayStation Move controllers, and draws skill, hilarity, and intense competition out of its players.

Cloud (2005), flOw (2007), Flower (2009), and Journey (2012)—Arguably one of the most successful experimental game groups in the world, thatgamecompany began life in the USC Interactive Media & Games MFA program, and went on to create a trio of groundbreaking games for the Sony PlayStation 3, winning many awards and helping to set a new direction for the console game industry.

What Inspiration Can We Find for Experimental Games in Other Experimental Art Forms?

In the nineteenth and early twentieth centuries, composers like Erik Satie and Igor Stravinsky brought radical new sounds to classical music; both composers' music caused riots at performances of their work. During the same period, the Impressionist painters moved away from a photorealist depiction of the world and instead embraced the role of movement and light in visual perception. Their work drew insults and harsh opposition from the art establishment of their time.

The art movement known as Dada, and its absurdist, highly politicized, and often shocking works, emerged as a reaction against the horrors of the World War I and the appalling bloodshed caused by the mechanization of warfare. Some of the Dadaists went on to help found Surrealism, one of the twentieth century's most famous art movements, whose wildly imaginative and unflinching explorations of the unconscious mind often used games like "Exquisite Corpse" to decipher the symbols embedded in their dreams, hallucinations, and fantasies.

The Beat Generation would embrace some of the same surrealist techniques in the 1950s, with the stream-of-consciousness of Allen Ginsberg, the automatism of Jack Kerouac, and the cut-ups of William S. Burroughs. David Bowie would later adopt Burroughs' cut-up technique, snipping up pages of lyrics with scissors and rearranging them until fresh new images emerged from the chance juxtapositions of words.

The counterculture of the 1960s affected art with new and ever-more-radical ways of thinking. When student riots broke out in France in the late '60s, the Situationist International used language games to subversively transform public space. The group Fluxus, which included the artist Yoko Ono, wanted to drag art off its pedestal in the art gallery and send it into the streets and the homes of ordinary people, using mass-produced "Fluxkits" that could provoke playful creativity and performance. The composer John Cage, who had some connections to Fluxus, experimented with the role of chance in both his composition and performances, effectively playing games in order to create entirely new sounds. These kinds of techniques would later be used to amazing effect by the musician, producer, and artist Brian Eno in his invention of "ambient" music.

The history of pop music is littered with the best kind of radical, populist experimentation. Punk rock angrily reacted to the oppressive political climate of its times by favoring raw energy over musicianship. New Wave refined that energy with the icy cool of newly mass-produced synthesizers. Techno and electro soon followed, incubated in the "Motorik" rhythms of '70s Germany, the suburbs of Detroit, and the boroughs of New York. Two decades later, the affordable software of "laptop" music production studios helped blur the boundaries between different genres and styles, and led to the ongoing musical renaissance that we enjoy today.

All these artistic movements and the struggles that provoked them have the potential to be inspirational in the creation of experimental games, especially if we keep them in mind and turn our gaze to the present day. What is it about the world that makes you angry or sad, joyful or hopeful? What new technologies have come into being that make new kinds of play possible? What has a game never tried to do? The answer to these questions could provide the inspiration for your first experimental game.

How Might You Approach the Challenge of Designing an Experimental Game?

The biggest obstacle to creating an experimental game is the "blank sheet of paper problem"—the challenge of deciding what to make. One of the best ways to overcome this challenge is to choose an almost random subject to base your game on. Perhaps make a list of some things that you're interested in, and then roll dice to determine which one you'll choose. If you're really stuck for subjects, Googling "Wikipedia: Random" will lead you to a random subject from the pages of the world's open-source encyclopedia.

Once you've chosen a subject, stick to it, and explore it thoroughly. Look at your subject in different lights—have you considered it from every angle? Ask friends for their opinions, and brainstorm game mechanics influenced by different aspects of your subject. Don't worry if the game starts to lead you in unusual directions—when you playtest your game, take notice of what is and isn't working, and follow where the game wants to lead. This is excellent advice for making any kind of game, but in making an experimental game, you're particularly free to explore wherever your imagination and your players might wander.

A good approach to experimental game design might be to look at the list of the formal elements of games described in Chapter 3 of this book—choose one, and decide to do something special or unusual with it. The game designer Peter Brinson proposes that an "avant-garde" attitude can often arise when we simply exclude a formal element that is tradition-ally accepted as essential. The art games of Belgian developer Tale of Tales have used this approach to great effect, in games like The Graveyard, which abandoned traditional ideas of "fun."

Finally, make sure to finish your game. Making a commitment to your friends or family members to deliver a finished game can be a great way of providing yourself with the "peer pressure" you need to do this. Making a small game in a very limited amount of time will also help you to finish your project. All these elements form the key to the magic of collaborative, weekend-long game creation events like the Global Game Jam and online game-programming competitions like Ludum Dare. Some of the best experimental games in the world have come out of events like these, where the developers had limited resources and extremely small amounts of development time.

So whatever experiments you choose to conduct in your personal game design practice, I hope that you have fun; that you learn something about yourself, other people, and the world; and that you make a contribution, whether big or small, to the exciting, fascinating, experimental art form that is games.

IDEAS VS. DESIGNS

Articulating new game ideas and features in the manner described above forces you to think through the hard problems of design. There is a big difference between an idea and a design. An idea is a loose concept that you present verbally or via a short written description. A design, on the other hand, is a detailed plan for an idea. Translating ideas into designs is an invaluable skill for a professional game designer. We will talk about how ideas become designs through prototyping (in Chapters 7 and 8) and documentation (in Chapter 14).

CONCLUSION

Most beginning game designers simply borrow elements from successful games and adapt them to their own purposes. This is fine, and many experienced game designers make a career out of doing the same. My goal, however, is to enable you to go beyond borrowing and begin innovating.

The game designers we all admire are the ones who break conventions and go where other designers dare not tread. The advantage of computers is that improvements in technology often allow us to do things that were previously impossible. This gives the designer a unique chance to experiment with novel types of gameplay.

But do not rely solely on technical advancements to open up new avenues of design. Many of the greatest designs come about through tireless experimentation. For example, take board games. Technically, they have not advanced much in the past 200 years—they still use cardboard, dice, and tokens—but conceptually, they keep advancing all the time. The top designers come up with games that break all the old rules or push the envelope in terms of creativity and gameplay. Play the games suggested in Exercise 6.3 for inspiration.

The same is true in the digital world. You will find that some of the most inventive games were designed on so-called "primitive" systems. Sometimes limiting yourself to the basics helps you focus your ideas more clearly. With that in mind, it is time to see if the ideas you have generated actually work. This is called prototyping and playtesting—the subjects of the next three chapters.

DESIGNER PERSPECTIVE:
JOSH HOLMES

Cofounder, Octopus Panic Games

Josh Holmes is an experienced creative leader and gaming entrepreneur whose credits include NBA Street (2001), Def Jam: Fight for NY (2004), Turok (2008), Halo 4 (2012), Halo 5 (2015), and Scavengers (2021). Before co-founding Midwinter Entertainment, and more recently, Octopus Panic Games, he was the franchise creative director and studio head for Halo at 343 Industries.

On getting into the game industry:

Designing games has been my passion since childhood. I started by remixing family board games and creating paper RPGs for my friends. I also dabbled in level and mod creation using map editors, despite my limited programming skills at the time. At the time, accessible game engines and scripting tools were not readily available.

My professional break came as a tester at Electronic Arts. I was determined to make it into the industry using any opportunity I could find and I worked my ass off to transition into production and later into design roles at EA. My first opportunity to lead the design of a new game was NBA Street, which became a surprise hit and opened a lot of doors for me.

My journey into the industry has been fueled by a lifelong passion for games, a relentless drive to succeed, and many opportunities that I've had the great fortune to receive. Each step has been a learning experience, and I'm grateful for the doors that have opened, allowing me to pursue my dream career.

On games that have inspired him:

There are so many games that have inspired me as a designer, both big and small. Here are some that have made a lasting mark on me:

- **Sid Meier's Pirates!:** This game, with its nonlinearity in narrative and cohesive blend of different gameplay experiences, left a profound impact on me. It showcased the power of open-ended gameplay and player agency.
- **Doom:** A true revelation, Doom realized my dream of an immersive first-person action experience. It pioneered competitive multiplayer in FPS games and empowered players to create their own levels and mods.
- **Halo:** Halo took the immersive qualities of first-person shooters to new heights with its deep sandbox gameplay, responsive AI, and realistic physics system. Playing Halo for the first time inspired me and fueled my aspiration to work on similar games.

- **ICO and Journey:** These emotionally impactful games with abstract yet moving narratives showcased the expressive potential of the medium. ICO, in particular, was the first game that brought tears to my eyes, demonstrating the power of games as a form of expression.
- **GTA and Skyrim:** These sweeping epics captivated me with their incredible sense of player agency within rich narrative-driven universes. They demonstrated how a well-defined world and player freedom can combine to create immersive and unforgettable experiences.

What is the most exciting development in the recent game industry?

The most exciting development in the game industry is the "democratization" of game development and the rise of indie developers. Now, more than ever, individuals with a vision can bring their game ideas to life, share them with the world, and potentially forge a rewarding career. It's an era of unprecedented opportunity, and we're merely scratching the surface of what lies ahead.

The accessibility and user-friendliness of modern game development tools have made game creation more approachable than ever before, while allowing diverse voices and innovative ideas to find an audience. Now more than ever, anyone with a vision can bring that game to life, share it with the world, and potentially make a great living.

On his design process:

In my design process, I embrace the belief that great ideas can come from anyone, at any time. I'm not seeking to dictate every aspect of the games I work on. When collaborating with a talented team, ideas naturally arise from various sources. As a creative director, my role is more like an editor. I shape the overall experience by combining ideas that align with the core vision for the game, synthesizing them into a cohesive whole. This process involves plenty of experimentation and iteration, guided by valuable player feedback.

Typically, I begin by formulating a guiding vision for the game. I strive to articulate this vision through a focused statement of intent and a small number of key pillars or principles that will drive the overall experience. Working closely with the team, we explore visual inspirations and references from diverse sources. Whenever an idea emerges that harmonizes well with the vision and pillars, we swiftly prototype and communicate it to gather hands-on feedback before giving it the green light for production.

Once in production, constant iteration becomes paramount. We extensively test the game by inviting groups of new players to experience it for the first time. By carefully studying their feedback and reactions, we gain crucial insights that inform our polishing efforts. This stage of development plays a vital role in ensuring that the experience realizes its full potential.

Throughout the design process, collaboration and a willingness to embrace ideas from all team members remain central. By fostering an environment where creativity flourishes, we cultivate a collective effort that brings the best ideas to the forefront and enhances the overall game experience.

On prototyping:

Prototyping is an essential aspect of effective game design. While theory-crafting has its merits, it can only take you so far, especially when you're venturing into new territory. The sooner you can demonstrate an idea and let people interact with it, the faster you'll learn what works and what doesn't. The prototyping process can vary depending on the concept being explored, but the key is to find the most efficient and straightforward way to showcase and test the core idea.

In some cases, pre-visualization may suffice, particularly if the intended mechanic is well understood, and the focus is more on aesthetic presentation. Other times, a rough playable prototype using primitive models and minimal animation might be necessary to test a specific mechanic. If the mechanic needs to integrate with established gameplay systems, it's crucial to prototype within that context. On the other hand, demonstrating the idea in an isolated testbed can be sufficient for certain scenarios. Ultimately, the approach to prototyping depends on the specific needs of each idea and its intended execution.

For instance, imagine you're designing a unique puzzle mechanic for a platformer game. You might create a simplified prototype that allows players to interact with the core puzzle elements, testing the viability and appeal of the mechanic. On the other hand, if you're exploring a complex combat system, it would be crucial to prototype within the context of the larger gameplay framework, ensuring that it integrates seamlessly with other gameplay mechanics.

The goal of prototyping is to iterate quickly, learn from the results, and refine the design accordingly. By embracing prototyping as an integral part of the creative process, you can identify potential issues, uncover new possibilities, and ultimately shape a more polished and engaging gameplay experience.

What are you most proud of in your career?

One accomplishment that I am particularly proud of in my career is the success we achieved with Halo 4. Taking over a beloved franchise from a celebrated developer, we formed a new studio and embarked on the challenge of creating a game with enormous expectations as our inaugural project. Throughout the three years of development, we encountered skepticism and doubts from many who believed we would fail. However, as a team, we poured our hearts and souls into Halo 4, and the end result filled us with immense pride.

In addition to Halo 4, my career has been defined by a passion for underdog stories and a drive to accomplish what others deem impossible. For instance, while at EA, I helped create two successful new IPs at a time when the Company was prioritizing sequels to its established franchises. I've also had the opportunity to build new studios from the ground up, including Propaganda Games, 343 Industries, Midwinter Entertainment, and currently, Octopus Panic.

Each of these ventures involved taking risks and overcoming obstacles, and each one represents an important part of my personal journey.

All in all, Halo 4 remains a standout moment for me. It's a testament to what can be achieved when a passionate team comes together, defies expectations, and pours their hearts into a project. It's a milestone that will forever hold a special place in my career journey.

What words of advice would you give to an aspiring designer today?

My advice to aspiring designers today is simple: dive into game design and start building games immediately! Whether you're interested in creating smaller, "indie-style" games or aiming for the grandeur of "epic-scale" projects, here's what you should keep in mind:

- **Get started now:** Don't wait for the perfect moment. Powerful tools are readily available for aspiring designers to bring their visions to life. Take the leap and begin your journey today.
- **Embrace learning:** Seize every opportunity to learn and grow. Focus on developing technical skills to support your creative ambitions. A solid technical foundation will not only help you effectively demonstrate your ideas but also earn the respect of more technically-oriented team members.
- **Teamwork matters:** If you're aiming for "epic-scale" games, teamwork becomes crucial. You'll be working with a larger team consisting of specialists with diverse personalities. Learn to work well with others, champion your ideas effectively, and communicate across the team.
- **Cultivate empathy:** Empathy is a critical skill for any designer. It allows you to understand the perspectives of others and create experiences that resonate with players. Put ego aside, foster empathy, and embrace the collaborative nature of game development.

Remember, great games are born out of passion, drive, and the willingness to overcome obstacles. With hard work, there's no limit to what you can achieve as a game designer.

FURTHER READING

Brotchie, Alastair and Gooding, Mel. *A Book of Surrealist Games*. Boston: Shambhala, 1995.

Csikszentmihalyi, Mihaly. *Creativity: Flow and the Psychology of Discovery and Invention*. New York: HarperCollins, 1996.

Edwards, Betty. *The New Drawing on the Right Side of the Brain: A Course in Enhancing Creativity and Artistic Confidence*. New York: Putnam, 1999.

Gladwell, Malcolm. *Blink: The Power of Thinking Without Thinking*. New York: Little, Brown and Company, 2005.

Michalko, Michael. *Thinkpak: A Brainstorming Card Deck*. Berkeley: Ten Speed Press, 2006.

END NOTES

1. Salen, Katie and Zimmerman, Eric. *Rules of Play: Game Design Fundamentals*. Cambridge: The MIT Press, 2004, p. 22.
2. Csikszentmihalyi, Mihaly. *Creativity: Flow and the Psychology of Discovery and Invention*. New York: Harper Perennial, 1996, pp. 79-80.
3. Ibid, pp. 80-81.
4. The Imagineers. *The Imagineering Way*. New York: Disney Editions, 2003, p. 53.
5. Glenn Entis at EA@USC Lecture Series, January 2005.

Chapter 7
Prototyping

Prototyping lies at the heart of good game design. Prototyping is the creation of a working model of your idea that allows you to test its feasibility and make improvements to it. Game prototypes, while playable, usually include only a rough approximation of the artwork, sound, and features. They are very much like sketches whose purpose is to allow you to focus in on a small set of the game's mechanics or features and see how they function.

Many first-time designers would rather jump in and start making the "real" game rather than starting with a prototype. But if you invest the time, you will discover that there is nothing more valuable for improving gameplay than a well-thought-out prototyping process. When you are making a prototype, you do not need to be concerned with perfecting how it looks or whether the technology is optimized. All you need to worry about are the fundamental mechanics, and if these mechanics can sustain the interest of playtesters, then you know that your design is solid.

METHODS OF PROTOTYPING

There are many types of prototypes, including physical prototypes, visual prototypes, video prototypes, software prototypes, etc. A single project might require a number of different prototypes, each addressing a unique question or feature. The important thing to remember when prototyping is that you are not creating the final design, you are simply trying to formalize your ideas or isolate issues so that you can discover what works best for meeting your pillars and experience goals before going on to create the final design. This chapter will deal mainly with physical prototypes, those made using pen and paper, cards, dice, etc. to test the core game mechanics. Such paper designs are one of the most powerful tools a designer has to work with, but they are only one method of prototyping. Chapter 8 will discuss digital prototyping and how to successfully use software prototypes in your design process.

DOI: 10.1201/9781003460268-9

Physical Prototypes

Physical prototypes are the easiest type of prototype for most game designers to construct on their own. These are typically created using slips of paper, cardboard, and household objects with hand-drawn markings. You are free to use anything you like, from lead figures to plastic toys to pieces borrowed from other games. Whatever you can cobble together is fine.

The benefits of physical prototyping are many. First, it allows you to focus on gameplay rather than technology. Over the years, in the many game design classes and workshops I have taught, I have found that when a team starts programming, they become very attached to their code. Making changes to the gameplay becomes a challenge right away. But if the design is on paper, iterations do not seem as difficult. Don't like the way a turn structure works? Just change it and try it again. Games can go through more iterations in a shorter period of time and with little wasted effort. Another benefit of physical prototyping is that you can respond in real time to player feedback. If players come up with an issue or idea, you can incorporate it on the fly and see how it works.

Physical prototyping also allows for nontechnical team members to participate at a very high level in the design process. No one needs

specialized knowledge or expertise in a programming language to give their input, which will allow for a wider variety of perspectives in the design process. And finally, physical prototyping allows for a broader and deeper experimentation process simply because it can be done without major cost or use of resources.

In early drafts of your physical prototype, I recommend that you pay very little attention to the quality of the artwork. Stick-figure drawings are the norm. The goal is to rough out system components so that you can see how the game operates on a mechanical level. Spending time on the artwork only slows down the process. Also, if you invest too much time crafting the look and feel of the prototype, you might become attached to your work and be reluctant to make changes. Because the prototyping process is all about iteration and change, this becomes counterproductive.

Battleship Prototype

I am going to walk through the process of developing several physical prototypes so that you can get a sense of how they are made and used. I will start with a classic board game with a simple system you have probably played before. If you are not familiar with Battleship, it is a two-player board game in which the object is to be the first player to sink your opponent's fleet.

One of the interesting things for us in terms of creating a prototype of this game, which has many of the formal elements of a classic strategy game (two-player, turn-based, capture or destroy objective on territory of a spatial grid) is that it uses a hidden information structure, which I discussed in Chapter 5 on page 156. This kind of hidden information is more typically found in modern strategy games, where chance has been introduced into the system to create suspense and variance of play. Here, hidden information replaces the open information structure found in classic strategy games so that guessing can be used as the core mechanic. As we will see, this

7.1   Prototyping materials

makes the game more appropriate for younger players.

Let's construct a physical prototype of Battleship. When starting to create a prototype, it is best to identify the key elements of a game and then handcraft each element. In this case, take four sheets of paper and draw a 10 × 10 grid on each. Label the rows on each grid with the letters A through J. Label the columns on each grid 1 through 10. Put the following titles on the four grids: Player 1 Ocean Grid, Player 1 Target Grid, Player 2 Ocean Grid, and Player 2 Target Grid. The final set will look like Figure 7.2.

Next find two players and give each an Ocean Grid, a Target Grid, and some colored markers, such as small beads. Players should shield their grids from their opponent's view. You can do this however you like, but one simple way is to have the players play back to back. They will be able to speak to one another, but they won't be able to see each other's grids. In the commercial game, the players' grids are hidden by the lifted lids of their playing cases – each player has a plastic case that contains their grid, their ships, marker pegs, and a lid that, when opened, conceals their grid from the other player. Since we want to create a paper version of the game, we need to creative about how to conceal the board information from each player.

Each player distributes the following five ships by drawing on his Ocean Grid. If you don't want them to draw on the grids, so that you can use them again, you can also make slips of paper that are right size to cover the number of cells listed below. The numbers in parentheses are the ships' sizes on the grid:

- Carrier (1 × 5 cells)
- Battleship (1 × 4 cells)
- Destroyer (1 × 3 cells)
- Submarine (1 × 3 cells)
- Patrol Boat (1 × 2 cells)

All segments of the ships should be drawn or placed on the playing grid. Ships may not be placed diagonally. Figure 7.3 shows an example of ships placed on the using dark slips of cardboard.

Now that you have the prototype assembled, it is time to play. On a player's turn, that player calls out grid coordinates, such as "B5." If the opponent has a ship on that cell, then he answers "hit." If not, he answers "miss." When all segments of a ship have been hit, the opponent says, "You sank my battleship!" Simple enough?

Players track hits and misses on their target grids. If B5 is a hit, the player marks a hit on her target grid. In my prototype, I've used different-color beads to mark the difference between hits

7.2   Battleship grids

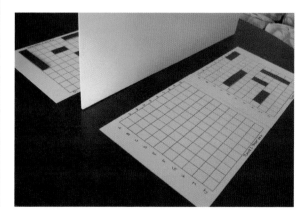

7.3   Battleship grids with ships

7.4 Battleship grids during play

and misses. Players take turns calling coordinates like this until one player sinks all five of the opposing ships. Figure 7.4 shows an example of what grids will look like during play.

Play this game prototype with a friend. Think about it in terms of how it functions as a prototype. Does it accurately represent the game mechanics? Although the artwork is crude and the rules are rough, do they provide enough of an experience for someone to grasp the game and give feedback? If this is the case, then the prototype is a success.

As you can see, making a playable game prototype does not require programming skills or art skills. The experience generated by the paper version of Battleship is almost identical to the experience generated by the fully produced Milton Bradley version.

The advantage of prototyping is that as you assemble the game, you gain a tactile sense for how the mechanics fit together. Abstract rules suddenly become concrete. You can look at the grid and ask yourself, "What if I made this ship bigger? How would that affect the gameplay?" Changing the board is simple; it is just a matter of getting out a piece of graph paper and drawing a different size grid box. Then you can replay the game and see if the experience is better or worse.

As you manipulate elements of the game structure, it will invariably spark more ideas, and it is not uncommon for entirely new systems to materialize during this process. You can then spin some of these systems off into their own games. After you become experienced at prototyping, you will find that this is probably the most effective way to create gameplay because it takes you right down into the mechanics and permits you to experiment in a way no other process can.

More Examples
Physical prototypes are critical for designing both board games and sophisticated electronic games. Many famous electronic games are based on paper games. The system for digital role-playing games such as Diablo III, Baldur's Gate, EverQuest, Asheron's Call, and World of Warcraft are derived from the paper-based system of Dungeons & Dragons. Likewise, the system for the famous computer game Civilization is based on a Civilization board game published by Avalon Hill.

The designers and programmers of these games used the paper-based originals to figure out what would work electronically. Also, many video game designers started out as board game designers, including Warren Spector, whose Designer Perspective you can find on page 29. Building and revising paper prototypes instills a deep understanding of formal elements of games, and it does so in a setting that is not bogged down by the complexities of software development.

One good way to train yourself in the design of game mechanics is to challenge yourself with controlled design exercises in which you take an existing game system, set a new player experience goal, and make changes to the system to meet that goal. While not as difficult as designing a game from scratch, this is good practice in thinking through design problems and designing to meet a goal.

We are going to do just that with my next example, which will use another simple system, a children's game by the company Ravensberger called Up the River. You might not have played this game, because it is out of print now, but it is a system I have used for many years with my students and in design workshops all over the world. I have see hundreds of variations on this game using this exercise, all extremely different, and it is a remarkably flexible simple system. First, I will walk through the original rules and the creation of an initial prototype in the same way I did with Battleship.

7.5   Up the River

Up the River Prototype

Up the River has an unusual board design. The board is made up of 10 equally sized pieces, as can be seen in Figure 7.5. These pieces are lined up to form the river. To make your own board pieces, just cut up regular white paper as shown in Figure 7.6. When the game begins, the piece at the bottom of the river is the sand bar, and the fifth piece from the bottom is the high tide. These are special terrain that will be explained later; be sure to mark them on your prototype board pieces. At the top of the river sits the harbor or goal card, which you will need to create as well. This card has 12 numbered docks, or spaces,

7.6   Up the River prototype

across its top. In addition to the board, you will need some player pieces and a six-sided die. You can use beads or buttons of four different colors for the player pieces, or boats, and you will need three of each color. To begin, players line all their pieces up on the fourth piece from the bottom of the board, as seen in Figure 7.5.

The objective of the game is to move all three of your boats to the harbor card and earn the most points. Your score is the total of all docks your boats are placed at, and the player with the most points wins.

The procedures of the game are simple: The youngest player goes first. On their turn, a player rolls the die and chooses one of their boats to move forward that many spaces. A player can only move one boat per turn. If a boat lands on the sandbar, it must stop there until the player's next turn, even if the roll was higher. If a boat lands on the high tide card with a direct throw, it advances three extra spaces, even if this means it advances into the harbor. A player does not need an exact throw to enter the harbor.

So far the game seems fairly mundane—a dice race that will be resolve entirely by chance. But there are two special rules that give the system just enough of a twist to make it interesting. The first is called the waterfall. After each player has had a turn, the bottom piece of the board is moved to the top. This simulates the current of the river pushing the boats back downstream. Any boats that are on that bottom piece are lost and taken out of the game. Suddenly our simple dice race has a more dramatic twist! Each time you choose a boat to move, you must consider the placement of your other boats as well. Are they at risk? Will they be at risk the next time the waterfall occurs? As I have discussed, this simple dilemma adds conflict to the system.

The next special rule is called good wind/ill wind. This occurs when a player rolls a six. Instead of moving six spaces, the player must now make a choice: whether to move any one of their boats *up* to join their next boat farther up the river—good wind—or whether to move one of their opponent's boats *down* to join the nearest boat of the same color—ill wind. When choosing good wind, if a boat moves past the sandbank, it must stop there. When choosing ill wind, if a boat moves past the sandbank, it need not stop. If the player who rolled the six has only one boat, or if all their boats are on the same card, the good wind option is not available. If their opponents have only one boat or all their boats are on the same card, the ill wind option is not available. If neither option is available, the player who rolled loses their turn, and the turn moves to the next player. The good wind option may not be used to move into the harbor.

The good wind/ill wind option adds an interesting choice to this simple system. Players can, in effect, choose to act for themselves or against their opponents. This moment of choice is an example of player-to-player interaction that creates an interesting moment of gameplay. When players move their boats into the harbor, they place them on the next available dock and score the number of points on that dock. The game ends when all the boats have either gone over the waterfall or entered the harbor. All the points are added up, and the player with the highest score wins.

Play your Up the River prototype and analyze how each element in this simple system adds to the game. Ask yourself these questions about the formal system:

- What is the relationship between the size of the board and the number of points on the die? What happens if you change the size of the board?

- What is the relationship between the number of boats each player has and the starting position? What happens if you change the starting location?

- Why is the starting position of the sandbar important? What about the high tide card?

- What skills are necessary to play this game? Is the game ultimately decided more by skill or by chance?

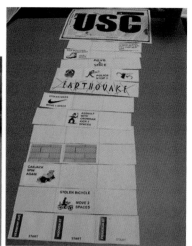
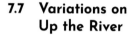

7.7 Variations on Up the River

- What does the good wind/ill wind option add to the game?
- Why does play begin with the youngest player?
- Who is the market for this game?

Thinking about these and other questions should lead you to see some potential changes you might make in the game system, but change for the sake of change is not the goal here. Before you begin modifying this system, brainstorm several possible player experience goals for your new version of the game. Here are some examples:

- Players will feel loyal to their team members as they trek up a dangerous mountain – and may even have to sacrifice themselves to save others.
- Players will feel the desperation of angry drivers trying to vie for the last parking spot at USC.
- Players will feel a sense of community with their fellow players as they work to save drowning friends.

As part of your new player experience goal, you will want to come up with a dramatic metaphor for your new game that works with the goal. Figure 7.7 shows several variations on Up the River based on the goals listed above. These include a mountain climbing game that required teamwork, a sea rescue game where players collaboratively worked to save swimmers from drowning, and a parking game that enhanced the formal structure by breaking each row into three columns.

Exercise 7.2: Up the River Variation

Create your own variation of Up the River. Set a player experience goal first and brainstorm ideas to change the system to meet that goal. Then modify your Up the River prototype, or build a new one, to reflect your changes to the system. Play your variation with friends and see if you have met your experience goal.

You can create your own controlled design exercises and continue practicing your design process. Just start with an existing game system and analyze it to clearly understand its formal, dramatic, and dynamic elements. Then come up with a new player experience goal and make changes to the system to meet your design goal. I advise starting with very simple games. And remember, even small changes to a tightly balanced system can have a great impact on the gameplay. By practicing this process, you will become a stronger designer and gain a deeper understanding of many different types of mechanics.

Prototyping a First-Person Shooter

It's one thing to prototype a simple board game, but you are probably wondering if it is possible to create a physical prototype of an action-packed video game. The answer is yes. While a paper prototype of a digital system has limitations, it is still quite valuable to the design process. For example, you can create a paper prototype of a game in the first-person shooter (FPS) genre. Classic examples of first-person shooters include Quake, Castle Wolfenstein, Battlefield 1942, Half-Life, Unreal Tournament, and Call of Duty. The core game mechanics of these games involve player units running around shooting other units. That is simple to understand, but how do you model one of these games on paper, and, more importantly, what can that do to inform our design process?

A physical prototype of a first-person shooter can help you understand the larger tactical and strategic issues of weapon balance, territorial control, etc., but it won't help you to understand the fluid process of running, aiming, and shooting in a 3D environment. In this way, it is possible, in fact probable, that an accurate paper prototype of a first-person shooter will fail to capture the essence of the game's player experience while still providing a valuable design process. But if your FPS has story elements, or an innovative experience goal, a paper prototype

may be able to help you determine how these elements should be incorporated into the project. As I will discuss in the following chapter on digital prototyping, one game can have many different prototypes, each addressing different questions about the design. A paper prototype is well suited to some questions about the design of a first-person shooter, for example, those regarding level design and weapon balance, while not being suited to others. The distinction should become clear to you as we construct our physical prototype for a first-person shooter.

Arena Map

Take a large sheet of hexagonal graph paper. Hexagons are nice for prototypes because they allow units to move diagonally. You can purchase this graph paper at most board game stores or print it out using one of several freeware and shareware programs available online, such as Hexographer. The grid will serve as the arena for your game.

Cut out a small paper chit and color it red to mark spawning points. A spawning point is the cell on the grid where units materialize after they are killed.

Put lines on the grid to represent walls. Units cannot move or shoot through walls. It is helpful to make walls out of objects that can be repositioned on the grid. Matchsticks are perfect for this. Having moveable walls makes it easier to tweak the system.

You probably already have questions like: How many hexes should be on the grid? How big should each hex be? How many spawning points do I need? and Do I need lots of walls or only a few? The answer to all of these questions is: Take your best guess. There is no way to know what will work until you play the game. No matter what you decide, you will probably wind up changing it later on. Pick whatever parameters you deem reasonable and proceed with the process.

CATASTROPHIC PROTOTYPING AND OTHER STORIES

by Chaim Gingold

*Chaim Gingold is a game designer and theorist with 20 years of research and design experience in both industry and aca-
demia. He is most well known for designing the Spore Creature Creator and creating Earth: A Primer, and his design expertise
and research interests include authoring tools, simulation, and play. He has been a researcher at Y Combinator Research (YCR)
/ Human Advancement Research Community (HARC) and an independent developer, designing projects such as the award-
winning Earth: A Primer.*

My hard drive was full of failures. Twelve years after learning to program, I looked back on all my software: Almost none
of it was finished, and what was wasn't ambitious enough. The projects that started out ambitiously always seemed to fall
back to earth, like failed rockets lacking the power to propel their own weight into orbit. Sure, there were interesting ideas
in there, lots of wacky toys, and I had even attempted a few large projects, but none of them ever came together like the
cool games and software I had always admired.

Sure, I had become a pretty good programmer and learned to make cool stuff, but clearly none of it would ever
amount to anything. I just didn't have what it took.

I went to graduate school at Georgia Tech and read some Chris Crawford. I learned that he had the same problem. But he
didn't think of it as failure. For him, this was an organic part of the development process. The failures filling his head were actually
prototypes that helped him decide which ideas were worth pursuing. For each good idea, there were a large number of stupid
ones that didn't work out. Failing, for this successful designer, was a way to find the good ideas. The revelation hit me like a ton of
bricks. Maybe I had a chance after all.

Ken Perlin came to Georgia Tech and gave a talk on his work with emotional software actors. His work blew my mind.
He had an infinite series of cool little toys, which he considered to be sketches or studies. Master artists like Escher or van
Gogh don't just sit down and crank out a finished piece. Artists create numerous sketches and studies before they under-
take finished paintings, let alone masterpieces. Ken's larger demos clearly built on top of what he had learned in previous
ones. It all formed one long line of inquiry and research. In Ken's world, my failures, which I was now calling *prototypes*, are
like an artist's studies, a necessary part of any major undertaking.

All of my software failures, which I was now thinking about as prototypes, sketches, and studies, had taught me a thing or
two about design and programming. If you want to learn to draw, you have to make a ton of bad drawings first. The difference
between practice and failure is simply a matter of attitude. One thing led to another, and my experience, plus being in the right
place at the right time, led to an internship with Will Wright. He was working on a new game at the time, code named Spore,
and had a small team working on prototypes.

I went to Walnut Creek for the summer, joined the impossibly small Spore team, and it all finally started to click into
place. Maxis was in the thick of The Sims Online, and the other intern and I were placed in the hallway outside of Will's
office, next to the Elvis shrine, on folding tables. Under my "desk" was one of Will's old Macs, a fancy machine from the
mid-1990s, which, to my delight, we hooked up. Spending the summer at Maxis was like going to Santa's workshop at
the North Pole and finding out how the elves made the toys.

The old Mac was like a treasure cave, a historical archive of blueprints, prototypes, projects, and concepts. I could
study the source code to some of my favorite games, like SimAnt, SimCity, and SimCity 2000. But that wasn't even the
best part. I found an ambitious Maxis project about tribal civilization from the early 1990s that was never completed. It was
like a murder mystery. Why had this project died? The hard drive was full of prototypes for a secret project, which turned
out to be The Sims. Apparently, Maxis had been working on the game for a long time, and many aspects of it had been

prototyped in isolation, including a 2.5d character animation system and editor, the motive- and decision-making AI, and a house editor. The code to the last prototype was clearly a hacked version of the SimCity 2000 engine. I found a program that used genetic algorithms to procedurally generate SimCity-style buildings with a blind watchmaker-style interface. That program had clearly been written as efficiently as possible, not from a runtime point of view, but from an implementation standpoint. It was using the SimCity 2000 code base

Prototypes from Spore

as a host organism for some rapid experimentation. Will's imagination had clearly been running faster than proper software engineering practice allowed. All of this, plus the awesome array of prototypes the Spore concept team had been cranking out, made a big impression on me. I joined in and contributed some of my own wacky prototypes to Spore.

What was going on here? What did all of this mean? Thinking back, I realized I had made two classic mistakes. First, my eyes were bigger than my stomach. The ambitious projects I had undertaken in the past "failed" because I made the mistake of not proving out the core ideas in prototypes. You can't send a rocket to the moon if you haven't first experimented with launching simple toy rockets. My sense is that the tribal civilization game died for similar reasons: Its author had launched into an ambitious finished project without doing the proper research, sketches, and prototypes.

Secondly, my success/failure evaluation function had been wrong. While the code to the The Sims prototypes wasn't in the final game, they had clearly informed the final product. All of my small "failures" were actually a series of small successes that had improved my design skills, and they were in fact studies I could incorporate into larger projects. I had it backward the whole time. My "successful," but incomplete, large projects were the real failures. I had invested too much energy into large projects that would fail because I hadn't done my homework. It's a hard lesson to take and one that most people probably have to learn the hard way.

So I dusted off my ACM programming competition skills, which taught me to make tightly focused programs in minimal time and with minimal frills. I became a better designer, really fast. I gained tons of design experience points by slaying so many gremlins.

I finished at Georgia Tech and joined Spore. My vast collection of tiny student projects, bite-sized personal projects, and work prototypes I had made added up to a huge amount of experience and intuition. Compared to my peers, I had a tremendous amount of design experience, simply from writing, evaluating, and throwing away so many ideas. I witnessed good prototypes move mountains. I like to think of good prototypers as powerful ninjas who can drop into hard design challenges, or tedious design debates, and cut them to shreds with one swift movement of their prototyping blade.

Here are a few prototyping rules of thumb. Even with years of experience, I often find a prototype going nowhere and can usually trace the problem to not following one of these rules:

- *Always Ask a Question*. Always ask a question, which will give you purpose, and have a hypothesis, which is a specific idea you are testing out. For example, you might be thinking about mouse-based control schemes for a school of fish. Your question is: How do I control these fish with a mouse? A hypothesis might be: Flocking will make the fish move together, and every mouse click will drop an invisible "bomb" that will act as a repulser upon every fish's steering AI, and it will take a few seconds to complete exploding. A good way to make sure you aren't going to waste time implementing ideas you don't actually have, which happens to me more often than I'd like, is to diagram the idea on paper first and work out as many details with a pen as possible. This also speeds up writing the prototype.

- *Stay Falsifiable.* Just like good science, you must validate the results of your experiment. Did your hypothesis work? Does your fish flock control scheme feel good to you? Do your friends find that it feels good? Does it work in the context of your game idea? You can never user test and playtest an idea too early. I have seen many cool ideas go down in flames because their owners were overprotective, didn't think it was ready, didn't believe the feedback they were getting, explained away people's responses, or thought that only their opinion mattered. Eventually users will play with your work, and by then it will be much harder to fix the design. Incorporate the user into the design process as early as possible. Be honest with yourself and your players, and you will be richly rewarded. This one is easy for me because, as a designer, my main intent is to entertain and transform other people, so I'm always interested in what effect my work has on others. Watching people use what you make will also make you a smarter designer.

- *Persuade and Inspire.* We're making entertainment and art—your prototype should be cool and fun and should excite people. If you and your peers are compelled, your players will be, too. On the flip side, if something isn't resonating with other people, perhaps your idea or approach should be reconsidered. Prototypes can be powerful persuasive devices. Keita Takahashi, the designer of Katamari Damacy, couldn't convince anyone that rolling around a giant sticky ball would be fun. Until they played the prototype.

- *Work Fast.* Try to minimize time to your first "failure" (rejecting a hypothesis), and don't be afraid to push the eject button. A classic error is to spend months working on an engine, architecture, or something else that has nothing to do with proving out your core design idea. Prototypes don't need engines. Prototypes are slipshod machines held together by bubble gum and leftover bits of wire that test and prove simple ideas as quickly as possible. If you find yourself weeks or months into a project with only an engine, you've failed. Perhaps you need to articulate a specific gameplay idea to validate. For me, the ideal window of time to start and finish a prototype (including design, implementation, testing, and iteration) is two days to two weeks. Anything longer than that sets off alarm bells.

- *Work Economically.* You're making something small and beautiful, so invest development effort wisely. To work fast, you must stay small: Don't do too much at once or you'll never make progress. Be realistic. Here are some questions to ask yourself when you are considering how much effort to spend on proper engineering, art, interface design, or any aspect of your prototype. What's the purpose of this prototype? Who will use it? What's important? Look? Kinesthetics? Load time? Run time? Usability? Persuading your peers? Be a cheap, lazy, slothful programming bum. Just make it work so you can test your idea. Don't go above and beyond the call of duty in programming, art, or any other aspect of your prototype.

- *Carefully decompose problems.* Don't bite off more than you have to at once. If you prototype all systems simultaneously, you will fail because you can't work fast or reach any kind of conclusion. To build it all at once is to build the actual game, which is hard. The prototype designer's job, like a good Go player, is to cut and separate the enemy stones (your design problem) into small, weak groups that can be killed or manipulated at will. Wisely divide your problem into manageable pieces. You must be careful because problems are sometimes connected in nonobvious ways and bite you later. Through practice, your designer's intuition and experience will help you see the connected nature of the problem you are trying to subdivide and make the most judicious cuts.

Units

Units are your characters in this game. You can represent them with coins or plastic army men or other household objects. Whatever you use should fit within one cell on the grid. In addition, a unit should clearly show which direction it is aiming. For example, if you use coins as units, draw an arrow on them to indicate their direction.

This prototype is designed so multiple units can play at the same time. To determine starting cells for the different unit on the grid, roll a die. The player with the lowest number places their unit on the grid first. Go in clockwise order from there and have each player choose a starting cell. An example of what your prototype might look like is presented in Figure 7.8.

7.8 FPS prototype example

Exercise 7.3: Movement and Shooting

If you want a challenge, stop reading now and come up with your own movement and shooting rules. Explain your reasoning behind this set of rules.

Movement and Shooting Rules

Here is one possible solution for movement and shooting. There are endless other creative possibilities, and I encourage you to experiment with them.

Each player gets the following nine cards:

- Move 1 space (1)
- Move 2 spaces (1)
- Move 3 spaces (1)
- Move 4 spaces (1)
- Turn any direction (2)
- Shoot (3)

Play is executed in rounds.

1. *Build stack:* Each player chooses three cards and places them face down on the table in a stack.
2. *Reveal:* Each player turns over his top card.
3. *Resolve shoot cards:* Players with a shoot card fire in the direction their unit is pointed. They follow an imaginary line across the grid. If this line intersects with a cell containing another unit, the shot hits. If this line comes to a wall or otherwise does not intersect with a unit, it misses. Shots happen simultaneously so that two or more players can hit at the same time.
4. *Resolve turn cards:* Players with turn cards turn their unit to whatever direction they please. If two or more players have turn cards, roll a die to determine who turns first.
5. *Resolve move cards:* Players with move cards move their units the number of spaces specified on the card. If two or more players have move cards, roll a die to determine who moves first. Players cannot occupy the same cell.

6. Repeat steps 2-5 for the second card in the stack.
7. Repeat steps 2-5 for the third card in the stack.

If a unit is shot, it is removed from the grid, and the player chooses one of the spawning points on the grid and reappears there at the beginning of the next round.

Exercise 7.4: Build It Yourself

Build the physical prototype described just previously and test it out. Describe any problems that you encounter. Also, list out any questions you have while building it.

This process of prototyping an action-based game might at first seem to be complex, but if you think about what I have described, it is pretty amazing. In just a few pages, I have completely detailed how to build a prototype of a first-person shooter using only pen and paper. When you play with this model, you will see that it is both flexible and simple to use.

Now, so far in this discussion of building our shooter prototype, I haven't mentioned our experience goal. The core mechanics of our experience, to be honest, are quite bland because of this.

Can you think of a good experience goal for this prototype that might guide us in more interesting directions?

Exercise 7.5 Define an Experience Goal

Brainstorm an experience goal for this shooter prototype. Some examples might include the following:

- Players will feel like an elite team of specialists, each with their own role.
- Players will learn more about their opponents' history as they explore, until they feel unsure about which side they are on.

- Players will have many options other than shooting to make their way through the level, so they will feel less aggressive and more strategic.

These are just examples. Articulate your own goal before moving on to the next section.

Features

Here are some suggested feature to your first-person shooter prototype Would any of these features guide your prototype toward fulfilling your experience goal? If not, brainstorm some other potential features.

- *Add a scoring system*: Make players track the number of kills they get. The first player to get 10 kills wins the game.
- *Include a hit percentage*: Suppose the chance that a shot hits is 100% when two units are standing on adjacent hexes on the grid. This percentage decreases by 10% for each hex of distance added. Calculate hits and misses using a 10-sided die.
- *Provide hit points*: Have each unit start with five hit points. One shot suffered removes one hit point.
- *Drop in first aid*: If a unit stands on a first-aid hex on the board for a full round, then his hit points return to their original amount.
- *Add in ammo*: Units start with 10 rounds each. Every time they shoot, one bullet is removed. If a unit stands on an ammo hex for a full round, he will reload his clip.
- *Introduce other weapons*: New weapons can be placed on the grid. If a unit stands on the weapon, he can use it in the next round. Enhancements to weapons include more damage per shot, higher accuracy, more bullets, etc.
- *Introduce alternative objectives*: What if this game were not focused entirely on direct combat but had alternative objectives for the players, such as rescuing nonplayer characters or finding narrative objects within a constrained time limit?

Exercise 7.6: Features

Incorporate some of the features mentioned previously or ones that you've brainstormed yourself to meet your experience goals into the physical prototype. Play your prototype and take notes on how they affect your gameplay.

New rules and features can continue to be added, altered, and removed as you strive to meet your goals. You can use the basic prototype we've created here to create capture-the-flag games, cooperative play missions, and other interesting twists. You can continue adding, testing, and tweaking until you come up with the right combination for your specific goals. Each time you add a rule or feature, it might spark new ideas and lead you down a path you did not expect to go. This is the heart of the creative process, and you should encourage yourself to try things that might seem ridiculous or absurd and just see what happens when you play the game. Completing these exercises will give you insight into how many first-person shooters and 3D adventure games are designed and the potential for changing their features to create new types of gameplay experiences.

7.9   FPS prototype example with additions; clockwise from top left: hit percentage, hit points, and first aid

Exercise 7.7: Working Backward

Now let's apply what you have learned to a different type of game.

1. Take two different real-time strategy (RTS) games, such as StarCraft II and Age of Empires IV, and work backward. Strip away the external feature set and show what both games have in common. These are the core game mechanics.
2. Translate the core game mechanics for one of the RTS games to paper in a playable format.

Remember, all we care about are the rules that correlate between the two games. These rules represent the core gaming system and will form the basis for your RTS physical prototype.

Perspective on Physical Prototyping

People who are not used to physical prototyping might argue that this method does not accurately represent the player experience on a computer. They might think a pen and paper prototype might work for a turn-based game, but not for an action-based shooter because gameplay is integrally tied to the 3D environment and the ability of the players to act in real time. I am not arguing that physical prototyping replaces those things. What I am saying is your overall design process can benefit tremendously in its early stages by building a physical prototype and experimenting with various ways of meeting your experience goals.

Physically prototyping allows you to build a structure for the game, think through how the various elements interact, and formulate a systemic approach to how the game will function. The sensory experience created by a digital game—for example, the feeling of moving through a 3D space—is only one component of an engaging game experience. Although it is a critical component, it can be isolated and focused on later in the process. At a minimum, physical prototyping forces you to think through the design elements and define them. You can always change them down the road, but this gives you a framework to build upon, and that in itself can provide better focus when it comes to working and communicating with a production team.

Imagine starting a project with a new group of artists and programmers who know nothing about the concept, and imagine trying to describe to them the game you have in your head. It is not easy. If you want to create gameplay that people have never seen before, it might be impossible. A physical prototype that they can sit down and play ensures that they will be able to grasp your vision of the game. It gives you all a starting point for concrete discussions about how the game will function. A written treatment or design specification is part of the process, of course, but when it comes to communicating a complex system, these documents are best supported by a prototype, or set of prototypes, that the team can actually play and discuss.

PROTOTYPING YOUR ORIGINAL GAME IDEA

Now that you have some experience creating and modifying prototypes, it is time to take one of your game concepts and create your own original prototype. The first step is to pick one of the ideas that you brainstormed in Chapter 6, "Ideation." When your idea and concept document or treatment are done, you will be ready to make your first prototype. But before I dive into the mechanics of constructing the prototype, make sure you have clearly articulated the core gameplay that will be created.

Visualizing Core Gameplay

If you try to design the entire game at once, you might become confused and overwhelmed. There are so many elements in a typical game that it is difficult to know where and how to start. What I recommend is that you isolate the core gameplay loop and build out from there.

The core gameplay loop, or "core mechanic," can be defined as the procedures that a player repeats most often while striving to achieve the game's overall goal. Games are repetitive by nature. While the meaning and consequences of what a player does can change over the course of game, the core procedures tend to remain in place and are built on as gameplay progresses. See Dan Cook's discussion of gameplay loops on page 161 for more about understanding these core game mechanics.

Figure 7.10 shows a visualization of the core loops for each of the paper prototypes we have built in this chapter. As you can see, these loops are quite simple. Even if we were to expand our first person shooter prototype into a digital version, as shown in the lower right corner of the diagram, the gameplay loop remains very simple to understand. Were we to add new features, as suggested in Exercise 7.6, the core loop might become more complex and include more diverse risks and rewards for the player to consider.

Figure 7.11 is a visualized analysis comparing the core actions of Spider-Man 2 with True Crime that was done by Jeff Chen, game analyst, and Carl Schnurr, senior director of game design, both at Activision. As you can see, player actions in these diagrams are interrelated with meters and rewards. In the case of Spider-Man 2, challenges, exploration, and rewards all translate into points, which can be spent in the Spidey Store to buy upgrades, combos, health, etc. This is a very clear reward system that will motivate players to look out for opportunities to gain points. If you look at the diagram for True Crime, you can see it is a much more complex design. The player activities pay off in multiple forms of rewards, and these rewards and meters in turn have an effect on the overall world system. It should be noted that more complex designs do not always make for a better player experience.

As I discussed in Chapter 5, sometimes you will find your mechanics are creating a positive or negative feedback loop that throws the play out of balance. By diagramming your core game loop, you are likely to spot such a problem early on. Your visualization does not have to be done in a formal presentation style like the examples

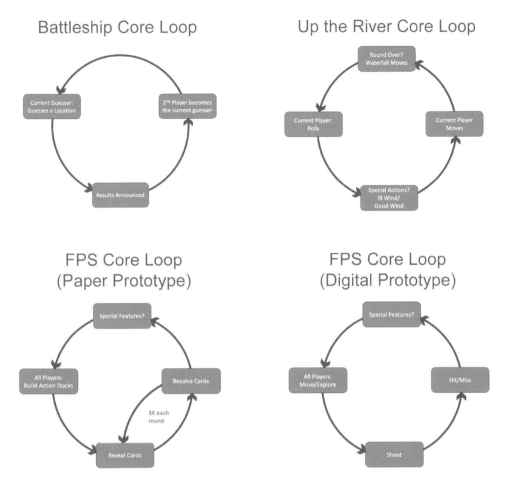

7.10   Core Loops for Battleship, Up the River, and First Person Shooter Prototypes

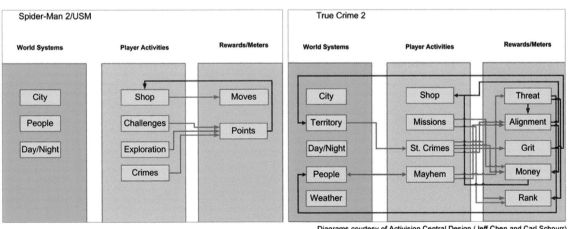

Diagrams courtesy of Activision Central Design (Jeff Chen and Carl Schnurr)

7.11   Visualization of gameplay mechanics for Spider-Man 2 and True Crime 2

from Activision. You can just sketch it on a piece of paper or on a whiteboard as in Figure 7.12, which is a very rough visualization of the core

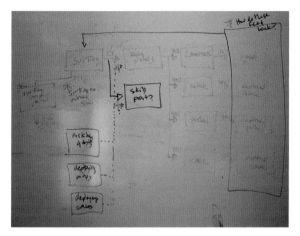

7.12   Rough visualization of core gameplay

loop for a student game prototype. Even a rough sketch such as this can expose features that are not integrated into the main mechanics and allow you to go back and redesign to better integrate these features.

Here are some examples of popular games and brief descriptions of their core gameplay mechanisms:

- *WarCraft III*: Players build and move units on a map in real time with the intent of engaging opposing units in combat and destroying them.
- *Monopoly*: Players buy and improve properties with the goal of charging rent to other players who land on them in the course of play.
- *Diablo III*: Players battle monsters, seek treasure, and explore dungeons in an attempt to amass wealth and become more powerful.
- *Super Mario Bros.*: A player controls Mario (or Luigi), making him walk, run, and jump,

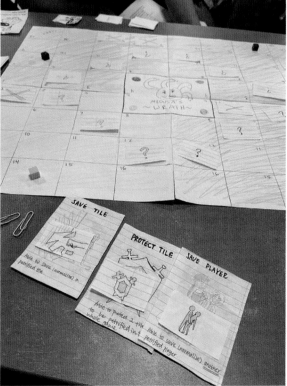

7.13   Physical prototype examples

while avoiding traps, overcoming obstacles, and gathering power-ups.

- *Atomic Bomberman:* Players move their Bombermen around a maze and drop bombs next to their opponents in an attempt to blow them up.

Exercise 7.8: Diagramming Core Gameplay

If you are familiar with these games, you can probably sketch out a visualization of their core gameplay mechanisms fairly quickly. If you are not familiar with them, choose two or three games that you know, write a short description of their core gameplay, and then sketch a visualization of it like the ones previously shown.

Exercise 7.9: Diagramming Core Gameplay 2

Now try diagramming the core gameplay of your own game idea. Your treatment from Exercise 6.8 on page 204 should give you a head start with this. If you find you do not know how some of the activities should interrelate, just take your best guess. The answers are going to evolve as you prototype and revise your game, so do not let them slow you down here at the beginning.

Building the Physical Prototype

Now that you have practiced by making and changing prototypes of existing games, you are ready to begin prototyping your original game concept. Here are four steps that will help you build a physical prototype efficiently.

1. Foundation

Build a representation of your game environment and core loop. Get some arts and crafts materials, such as cardboard, construction paper, glue, pens, and scissors. Draw a board layout or rough map if has concepts like terrain, and cut pieces out of the cardboard and paper.

As you do this, questions will come to your mind. How many squares should a player be allowed to move? How will the players interact with one another? How is the conflict resolved? Do not try to answer all these questions at once. In fact, place the questions on the back burner and focus on the core gameplay.

Designing the basic game objects (physical setting, units, resources, etc.) and the key procedures for the game (those repetitive action cycles that keep the game in motion) are the heart of the foundation stage.

Try playing your core gameplay on your own—it might not be much of a game, but you will be able to see if the basic concept is worth pursuing. After you have your foundation in place, questions that you will want to answer become evident. But watch out. Try to test the game without expanding the rules at this point. If you have to add a rule to make the prototype playable, then add it, but only do this if it is absolutely necessary. Your goal should be to keep the core game loop down to as few rules as possible.

In the FPS prototype, the first element that I fleshed out was simultaneous movement because this is the core mechanic of these types of games. The idea that all players should reveal an action card at the same time to simulate real-time movement was conceived. This was a foothold to build upon. From there, the next logical question was: What are the options on the action cards? The answer was: move, turn, or shoot. Other ideas for action cards popped up as well, such as stand, crouch, go prone, etc. However, I decided to keep the options as simple as possible at first. These options lead us to the next stage of our prototype: structure.

2. Structure

After the foundation is in place and seems to function, it is time to move on to structure. The best technique for doing this is to prioritize what is most essential to the player experience you are striving for. In my FPS prototype, some structural elements I added were the three action options: (1) number of spaces a unit could move,

THE DESIGN EVOLUTION OF MAGIC: THE GATHERING

Magic: The Gathering is one of the most important and influential games of our time. It was an instant hit when it first appeared at the Gen Con game convention in 1993 and has grown steadily in popularity since. This is a special two-part look at the creation and development of the game as written by the designer, Richard Garfield. Richard wrote the first part, "The Creation of Magic: The Gathering," over 30 years ago when the game was first released. In it, he muses about the design challenges of a collectable trading card game, and recounts the game's fascinating playtest history.

The second part, "Magic Design: A Decade Later," is a retrospective on the original design notes. In it, Richard provides insight about how and why the game evolved the way it did, including thoughts on the Magic Pro Tour, Magic Online, and the following 10 years for the game.

The Creation of Magic: The Gathering

by Richard Garfield (written in 1993)

The Ancestry of Magic

Games evolve. New ones take the most loved features of earlier games and add original characteristics. The creation of Magic: The Gathering is a case in point.

Though there are about a dozen games that have influenced Magic in one way or another, the game's most influential ancestor is a game for which I have no end of respect: Cosmic Encounter, originally published by Eon Products and rereleased by Mayfair Games. In this game, participants play alien races striving to conquer a piece of the universe. Players can attempt their conquest alone or forge alliances with other aliens. There are nearly 50 alien races that can be played, each of which has a unique ability: The Amoeba, for example, has the power to Ooze, giving it unlimited token movement; the Sniveler has the power to Whine, allowing it to automatically catch up when behind. The best thing about Cosmic Encounter is precisely this limitless variety. I have played hundreds of times and still can be surprised at the interactions different combinations of aliens produce. Cosmic Encounter remains enjoyable because it is constantly new.

Cosmic Encounter proved to be an interesting complement to my own design ideas. I had been mulling over a long-time idea of mine: a game that used a deck of cards whose composition changed between rounds. During the course of the game, the players would add cards to and remove cards from the deck so that when you played a new game it would have an entirely different card mix. I remembered playing marbles in elementary school, where each player had his own collection from which they would trade and compete. I was also curious about Strat-o-matic Baseball, in which participants draft, field, and compete their own teams of baseball players whose abilities are based on real players' previous year statistics. Intrigued by the structure of the game, I was irritated that the subject was one for which I had no patience.

These thoughts were the essence of what eventually became Magic. My experiences with Cosmic Encounter and other games inspired me to create a card game in 1982 called Five Magics. Five Magics was an attempt to distill the modularity of Cosmic Encounter down to just a card game. The nature of Cosmic Encounter seemed entirely appropriate for a magical card game—wild and not entirely predictable, but not completely unknown, like a set of forces you almost, but don't quite, understand. Over the next few years, Five Magics went on to inspire entirely new magical card games among my friends.

Ten years later, I was still designing games, and Mike Davis and I had come up with a board game called RoboRally. Mike was acting as our agent, and among the companies he approached was a brand new gaming company called Wizards of the Coast. Things seemed to be going well, so that August, Mike and I made our way to Portland, Oregon, to meet over a pizza with Peter Adkison and James Hays of Wizards of the Coast.

Both Peter and James were very receptive to RoboRally, but they informed me that they weren't really in a position to come out with a board game right away. This wasn't what I had come out to hear, of course, but I didn't want the trip to be a total waste. I asked Peter what he would be interested in. Peter replied that he really saw a need for a game that could be played quickly with minimal equipment, a game that would go over well at conventions. Could I do it?

Within a few days, the initial concept for a trading card game was born, based on another card game I had developed in 1985 called Safecracker. It hadn't been one of my best games. But then I remembered Five Magics.

The First Designs

I went back to graduate school at the University of Pennsylvania and worked on the card game in whatever spare time I had. It wasn't easy; there were three months of false starts on the project, there are so many aspects of card game design that have to be reconsidered when designing trading card games. First of all, you can't have any bad cards—people wouldn't play with them. In fact, you want to prevent too much range in the utility of cards because players will only play with the best—why make cards people won't play with? Besides, homogeneity of card power is the only way to combat the "rich kid syndrome" that threatened the game concept from the start. What was to keep someone from going out and getting ten decks and becoming unbeatable?

It was a major design concern. I had numerous theories on how to prevent purchasing power from unbalancing the game, none of which were entirely valid but all of which had a grain of truth. The most compelling counter to this "buy out the store" strategy was the ante. If we were playing for ante, the argument ran, and your deck was the distilled fruit of ten decks, when I did win, I would win a more valuable card. Also, if the game had enough skill, then the player purchasing their power would surely be easy prey for the players dueling and trading their way to a good deck. And of course there was the sentiment that buying a lot of poker chips doesn't make you a winner. In the end, however, the "rich kid syndrome" became less of a concern. Magic is a fun game, and it doesn't really matter how you get your deck. Playtesting showed that a deck that is too powerful defeats itself. On the one hand, people stopped playing against it for ante unless a handicap was invoked; on the other, it inspired them to assemble more effective decks in response.

The first Magic release was affectionately named Alpha. It consisted of 120 cards split randomly between two players. The two players would ante a card, fight a duel over the ante, and repeat until they got bored. They often took a long time to get bored; even then, Magic was a surprisingly addictive game. About 10 o'clock one evening, Barry "Bit" Reich and I started a game in the University of Pennsylvania Astronomy lounge, a windowless, air-conditioned room. We played continuously until about 3:00 A.M.—at least that's what we thought until we left the building and found that the sun had risen.

I knew then that I had a game structure that could support the concept of individually owned and tailored decks. The game was quick, and while it had bluffing and strategy, it didn't seem to get bogged down with too much calculation. The various combinations that came up were enjoyable and often surprising. At the same time, the variety of card combinations didn't unbalance the game: When a person started to win, it didn't turn into a landslide.

From Alpha to Gamma

Except for the card mix, little has changed about Magic since alpha. In alpha, walls could attack, and losing all your lands of a particular color destroyed the associated spells in play, but otherwise, the rules are much the same now as they were in the early stages of playtesting.

Moving from alpha to the beta version was like releasing a wild animal. The enjoyable game that was alpha now burst the confines of the duel to invade the lives of the participants. Players were free to trade cards between games and hunt down weaker players to challenge them to duels while gamely facing or cravenly avoiding those who were more powerful. Reputations were forged—reputations built on anything from consistently strong play to a few lucky wins to good bluffing. The players didn't know the card mix, so they learned to stay on their toes during duels. Even the most alert players would occasionally meet with nasty surprises. This constant discovery of unknown realms in an uncharted world gave the game a feeling of infinite size and possibility.

For the gamma version, new cards were added and many of the creature costs were increased. We also doubled the pool of playtesters, adding in a group with Strat-o-matic Baseball experience. We were particularly anxious to find out if Magic could be adapted for league play. Gamma was also the first version that was fully illustrated. Skaff Elias was my art director: He and others spent days poring over old graphic magazines, comic books, and game books searching for art for the cards. These playtest decks were pretty attractive for crummy black-and-white cardstock photocopies. For the most part, the cards were illustrated with serious pictures, but there were a lot of humorous ones as well. Heal was illustrated by Skaff's foot. Power Sink showed Calvin (of *Calvin and Hobbes*) in a toilet; after all, what is a toilet but a power sink? Berserk was John Travolta dancing in *Saturday Night Fever*. Righteousness pictured Captain Kirk, and Blessing showed Spock doing his "live long and prosper" gesture. An old comic book provided a Charles Atlas picture for Holy Strength, and a 98-pound weakling getting sand kicked in his face for Weakness. Instill Energy was Richard Simmons. The infamous Glasses of Urza were some X-ray glasses we found in a catalog. Ruthy Kantorovitz constructed a darling flame- belching baby for Firebreathing. I myself had the honor of being the Goblins. The pictures and additional players greatly added to the game atmosphere. It became clear that while the duels were for two players, the more players playing, the better the game was. In some sense, the individual duels were a part of a single, larger game.

Striking the Balance

Each playtest set saw the expulsion of certain cards. One type of card that was common in alpha and beta was rare in gamma and is now nonexistent: the type that made one of your rival's cards yours. Yes, Control Magic used to permanently steal a creature from your opponent. Similarly, Steal Artifact really took an artifact. Copper Tablet no longer even remotely resembles its original purpose, which was to swap two creatures in play. ("Yes, I'll swap my Merfolk for your Dragon. On second thought, make that my Goblins—they're uglier.") There was a spell, Planeshift, that stole a land, and Ecoshift, which collected all the lands, shuffled them and redealt them—really nice for the user of four or five colors of magic. Pixies used to be a real pain—if they hit you, you swapped a random card from your hand with your opponent. These cards added something to the game, often in the form of players trying to destroy their own creatures before their opponents took them for good or even trying to take their own lives to preserve the last shreds of their decks. However, in the end it was pretty clear that the nastiness this added to the game environment wasn't worth the trouble, and no card should ever be at risk unless players choose to play for ante.

It was around this time that I began to realize that almost any decision made about the game would be opposed, often vehemently, by some players. The huge amount of dissent about what should and should not be part of the card mix has led players to make their own versions for playtesting—a significant task that involves designing, constructing, shuffling, and distributing about 4000 cards. Each of these games had its merits, and the playtesters enjoyed discovering the quirks and secrets of each new environment. The results of these efforts would form the basis of future Deckmaster games that use the structure of The Gathering while containing mostly new cards.

To Build a Better Deck

Playtesting a Deckmaster game is difficult. Probably the only games harder to playtest are elaborate, multiplayer computer games. After developing a basic framework for Magic that seemed fairly robust, we had to decide which of the huge selection of cards to include, and with what relative frequencies. Common cards had to be simple, but not necessarily less powerful, than rare cards—if only rare cards were powerful, players would either have to be rich or lucky to get a decent deck. Sometimes a card was made rare because it was too powerful or imbalancing in large quantities, but more often, rare cards were cards that were intricate or specialized—spells you wouldn't want many of anyway. But these design guidelines only got us so far. The whole game's flavor could change if a handful of seemingly innocent cards were eliminated or even made less or more common. When it came down to actually deciding what to include and what to do without, I began to feel like a chef obliged to cook a dish for 10,000 people using 300 ingredients.

One thing I knew I wanted to see in the game was players using multicolor decks. It was clear that a player could avoid a lot of problems by stripping down to a single color. For this reason, many spells were included that paralyzed entire colors, like Karma, Elemental Blast, and the Circles of Protection. The original plan was to include cards that thwarted every obvious simple strategy, and, in time, to add new cards that would defeat the most current ploys and keep the strategic environment dynamic. For example, it was obvious that relying on too many big creatures made a player particularly vulnerable to the Meekstone, and a deck laden with Fireballs and requiring lots of mana could be brought down with Manabarbs. Unfortunately, this strategy and counter-strategy design led to players developing narrow decks and refusing to play people who used cards that could defeat them flat out. If players weren't compelled to play a variety of players and could choose their opponent every time, a narrow deck was pretty powerful.

Therefore, another, less heavy-handed way to encourage variety was developed. We made it more difficult to get all the features a player needs in a deck by playing a single color. Gamma, for example, suffered from the fact that blue magic could stand alone. It was easily the most powerful magic, having two extremely insidious common spells (Ancestral Memory and Time Walk), both of which have been made rare. It had awesome counterspell capabilities. It had amazing creatures, two of the best of which are now uncommon.

Blue magic now retains its counterspell capability, but it is very creature poor and lacks a good way to do direct damage. Red magic has little defense, particularly in the air, but it has amazing direct damage and destruction capability. Green magic has an abundance of creatures and mana but not much more. Black is the master of anticreature magic and has some flexibility, but it is poorly suited to stopping noncreature threats. White magic is the magic of protection, and it is the only magic with common banding, but it has little damage-dealing capability.

Sometimes seemingly innocuous cards would combine into something truly frightening. A good part of playtest effort was devoted to routing out the cards that contributed to so-called "degenerate" decks—the narrow, powerful decks that are difficult to beat and often boring to play with or against. Without a doubt, the most striking was Tom Fontaine's "Deck of Sooner-Than-Instant Death," which was renowned for being able to field upward of eight large creatures on the second or third turn. In the first Magic tournament, Dave "Hurricane" Pettey walked to victory with his "Land Destruction Deck." (Dave also designed a deck of Spectres, Mindtwists, and Disrupting Sceptres that was so gruesome I don't think anyone was ever really willing to play it.) Skaff's deck, "The Great White Death," could outlive just about anything put up against it. Charlie Catin's "Weenie Madness" was fairly effective at swamping the opponent with little creatures. Though this deck was probably not in the high-win bracket of the previous decks, it was recognized that, playing for ante, Charlie could hardly lose. Even winning only one in four of his games—and he could usually do better than that—the card he won could be traded back for the island and the two Merfolk he lost, with something extra thrown in.

In the end I decided that the degenerate decks were actually part of the fun. People would assemble them, play with them until they got bored or their regular opponents refused to play against them, and then retire the deck or trade off its components for something new—a Magic version of putting the champion out to stud. Most players ended up treating their degenerate decks much like role players treat their most successful characters: They were relegated to the background to be occasionally dusted off for a new encounter.

After the pursuit of sheer power died down, another type of deck developed: the Weird Theme deck. These decks were usually made to be as formidable as possible within the constraints of their theme. When Bit grew bored of his "Serpent Deck" (he had a predilection for flopping a rubber snake on the playing surface and going "SsssSssSs" whenever he summoned a Serpent), he developed his "Artifact Deck," which consisted of artifacts only—no land. It was fun to see the "Artifact Deck" go up against someone who used Nevinyrral's Disk. But the king of weird decks was, without a doubt, Charlie Catin. In one league, he put together a deck that I call "The Infinite Recursion Deck." The idea was to set up a situation where his opponent couldn't attack him until Charlie could play Swords to Plowshares on a creature. Then he would play Timetwister, causing the cards in play to be shuffled with the graveyard, hand, and library to form a fresh library. Swords to Plowshares actually removes a creature from the game, so his rival has one less creature. Repeat. After enough iterations, his rival was bloated with life given by the Swords to Plowshares, having maybe 60 life points, but there were no creatures left in his deck. So Charlie's Elves started in—59 life, 58 life, 57 life—and the curtain closes on this sad game. I still can't think about this deck without moist emotional snorts. The coup de grace is that this league required players to compete their decks 10 times. And, because his games often lasted over an hour and a half, he received at least one concession.

Words, Words, Words

It was not just determining the right card mix that players and designers found challenging. This becomes increasingly clear to me as I participate in the never-ending process of editing the rules and the cards. As my earliest playtesters have pointed out (in their more malicious moods), the original concept for Magic was the simplest game in the world because you had all the rules on the cards. That notion is long gone.

To those who didn't have to endure it, our struggle for precision was actually rather amusing. My own rules discussions about card wordings were mostly with Jim Lin, who is the closest thing you will ever encounter to a combination rules lawyer and fire hose. A typical rule-problem session would go:

Jim: Hmm—there seems to be a problem with this card. Here is my seven-page rules addition to solve the problem.

Richard: I would sooner recall all the cards than use that. Let's try this solution instead.

Jim: Hmm—we have another problem.

[Repeat until...]

Richard: This is silly—only incredibly stupid and terminally anal people could possibly misinterpret this card.

Jim: Yes, maybe we have been thinking about this too long. If you're playing with that kind of person, you should find some new friends.

A specific example of something we actually worried about is whether Consecrate Land would really protect your land from Stone Rain. After all, the first says it prevents land from being destroyed and the second says it destroys the land. Isn't that a contradiction? It still hurts my head getting into a frame of mind where that is confusing. It is perhaps a little like wondering why anyone would give you anything for money, which is, after all, just paper.

But, then again, I could never tell what was going to confuse people. One of the playtesters, Mikhail Chkhenkeli, approached me and said, "I like my deck. I have the most powerful card in the game. When I play it, I win on the next turn." I tried to figure out what this could be; I couldn't think of anything that would win the game with any assurance the turn after casting. I asked him about it, and he showed me a card that would make his opponent skip a turn. I was confused until I read exactly what was written: "Opponent loses next turn." It was my first real lesson in how difficult it was going to be to word the cards so that no two people would interpret the same card in a different way.

The Magic Marketplace

Another thing I realized in the second year of playtesting really surprised me. Magic turned out to be one of the best economic simulations I had ever seen. We had a free-market economy and all of the ingredients for interesting dynamics. People valued different cards in different ways—sometimes because they simply weren't evaluating accurately but much more often because the cards really have different value to different players. For example, the value of a powerful green spell was lower for a person who specializes in black and red magic than for one who was building a deck that was primarily green. This gives a lot of opportunity for arbitrage. I would frequently find cards that one group of players weren't using but another group were treating like chunks of gold. If I was fast enough, I could altruistically benefit both parties and only have to suffer a little profit in the process.

Sometimes the value of a card would fluctuate based on a new use (or even a suspected new use). For example, when Charlie was collecting all the available spells that produced black mana, we began to get concerned—those cards were demanding higher and higher prices, and people began to fear what he could need all that black mana for. And, prior to Dave's "Land Destruction Deck," land destruction spells like Stone Rain and Ice Storm were not high-demand spells. This of course allowed him to assemble the deck cheaply, and after winning the first Magic tournament, sell off the pieces for a mint.

Trade embargoes appeared. At one point a powerful faction of players would not trade with Skaff, or anyone who traded with Skaff. I actually heard conversations such as:

Player 1 to Player 2: I'll trade you card A for card B.

Skaff, watching: That's a moronic trade. I'll give you card B and cards C, D, E, and F for card A.

Players 1 and 2 together: We are not trading with you, Skaff.

Needless to say, Skaff was perhaps a bit too successful in his early duels and trades.

Another interesting economic event would occur when people would snatch up cards they had no intention of using. They would take them to remove them from the card pool, either because the card annoyed them (Chaos Orb, e.g.,) or because it was too deadly against their particular decks.

I think my favorite profit was turned during an encounter with Ethan Lewis and Bit. Ethan had just received a pack of cards and Bit was interested in trading with Ethan. Bit noticed that Ethan had the Jayemdae Tome, began to drool, and made an offer for it. I looked at the offer and thought it was far too low, so I put the same thing on the table.

Bit looked at me and said, "You can't offer that! If you want the Tome you have to bid higher than my bid."

I said, "This isn't an offer for the Tome. This is a gift for Ethan deigning to even discuss trading the Tome with me."

Bit looked at me in disbelief and then took me aside. He whispered, "Look, I'll give you this wad of cards if you just leave the room for 10 minutes." I took his bribe, and he bought the Tome. It was just as well—he had a lot more buying power than I did. In retrospect, it was probably a dangerous ploy to use against Bit—after all, he was the person who was responsible for gluing poor Charlie's deck together once, washing a different deck of Charlie's in soap and water, and putting more cards of Charlie's in the blender and hitting frappé.

Probably the most constant card-evaluation difference I had with anyone was over Lord of the Pit. I received it in just about every playtest release we had, and it was certainly hard to use. I didn't agree with Skaff, though, that the only value of the card was that you might get your opponent to play with it. He maintained that blank cards would be better to play with because blank cards probably wouldn't hurt you. I argued that if you knew what you were doing, you could profit from it.

Skaff asked me to cite a single case where it had saved me. I thought a bit and recalled the most flamboyant victory I had with it. My opponent knew he had me where he wanted me—he had something doing damage to me, and a Clone in hand, so even if I cast something to turn the tide, he would be able to match me. Well, of course, the next cast spell was a Lord of the Pit; he could Clone it or die from it, so he Cloned it. Then each time he attacked, I would heal both of the Lords, or cast Fog and nullify the assault, and refuse to attack. Eventually, he ran out of creatures to keep his Lord of the Pit sated and died a horrible death.

Skaff was highly amused by this story. He said, "So, when asked about a time the Lord of the Pit saved you, you can only think of a case where you were playing somebody stupid enough to clone it!"

Dominia and the Role of Role Playing

Selecting a card mix that accommodated different evaluations of the cards wasn't enough; we also had to develop an environment in which the cards could reasonably interact. Establishing the right setting for Magic proved to be a central design challenge. In fact, many of our design problems stemmed from an attempt to define the physics of a magical world in which duels take place and from building the cards around that, rather than letting the game define the physics. I was worried about the cards' relationship to each other—I wanted them to seem part of a unified setting, but I didn't want to restrict the creativity of the designers or to create all the cards myself. Everyone trying to jointly build a single fantasy world seemed difficult because it would inevitably lack cohesion. I preferred the idea of a multiverse, a system of worlds that was incredibly large and permitted strange interactions between the universes in it. In this way, we could capture the otherworldly aspects of fantasy that add such flavor to the game while preserving a coherent, playable game structure. Almost any card or concept would fit into a multiverse. Also, it would not be difficult to accommodate an ever-growing and diverse card pool—expansion sets with very different flavors could be used in the same game, for they could be seen as a creative mingling of elements from different universes. So I developed the idea of Dominia, an infinite system of planes through which wizards travel in search of resources to fuel their magic.

In its structured flexibility, this game environment is much like a role-playing world. I don't mean to suggest that this setting makes Magic a role-playing game—far from it—but Magic is closer to role playing than any other card or board game I know of. I have always been singularly unimpressed by games that presumed to call themselves a cross between the two because role playing has too many characteristics that can't be captured in a different format. In fact, in its restricted forms—as a tournament game or league game, for example—Magic has little in common with role playing. In those cases, it is a game in the traditional sense, with each player striving to achieve victory according to some finite set of rules. However, the more free-form game dueling with friends using decks constructed at whim embodies some interesting elements of role playing.

Each player's deck is like a character. It has its own personality and quirks. These decks often even get their own names: "The Bruise," "The Reanimator," "Weenie Madness," "Sooner-Than-Instant Death," "Walk Into This Deck," "The Great White Leftovers," "Backyard Barbeque," and "Gilligan's Island," to name a few. In one deck I maintained, each of the creatures had a name—one small advantage to crummy photocopied cardstock is the ease of writing on cards. The deck was called "Snow White and the Seven Dwarves," containing a Wurm named Snow White and seven Mammoths: Doc, Grumpy, Sneezy, Dopey, Happy, Bashful, and Sleepy. After a while I got a few additional Mammoths, which I named Cheesy and Hungry. There was even a Prince Charming: my Veteran Bodyguard.

As in role playing, the object of the game in the unstructured mode of play is determined largely by the players. The object of the duel is usually to win, but the means to that end can vary tremendously. Most players find that the duel itself quickly becomes a fairly minor part of the game compared to trading and assembling decks.

Another characteristic of Magic that is reminiscent of role playing is the way players are exploring a world rather than knowing all the details to start. I view Magic as a vast game played among all the people who buy decks, rather than just a series of little duels. It is a game for tens of thousands in which the designer acts as a gamemaster. The gamemaster decides what the environment will be, and the players explore that environment. This is why there are no marketed lists of cards when the cards are first sold: Discovering the cards and what they do is an integral part of the game.

And, like a role-playing game, the players contribute as much to an exciting adventure as the gamemaster. To all the supporters of Magic, and especially to my playtesters, I am extraordinarily grateful. Without them, if this product existed at all, it would certainly be inferior. Every one of them left a mark, if not on the game itself, then in the game's lore. Any players today who have even a tenth of the fun I had playing the test versions with them will be amply pleased with Magic.

Magic Design: A Decade Later

by Richard Garfield (written in 2003)

Magic and the trading card game industry have undergone a lot of changes since the time I wrote those design notes. In the meantime, Magic has grown stronger with each successive year—as the game itself is improved and as more people are brought into trading card games from products such as Pokémon and Yu-Gi-Oh!

It is difficult for people these days to appreciate how little we knew about the game design space we were entering in the early nineties. My design notes failed to mention what, in my mind, is the strongest sign of that—after describing the concept of a trading card game to Peter Adkison, I concluded with the cautious statement, "Of course, such a game may not be possible to design." It is hard for me to imagine that state of mind today, in a world where trading card games have reached every corner and are a part of almost every major entertainment property. This is a world where trading card games have left their mark on all areas of game design, from computer games to board games, and where trading card games have directly inspired games ranging from trading miniature games to trading tops games. This is a world where Jason Fox, from the comic strip *Foxtrot*, complained that a deck of cards coming with only four aces was some sort of ploy to get people to buy expansion kits.

That could be left as the end of the story; Magic was designed—as the design notes of a decade ago portray—and 10 years later, it was still going strong. But this leaves out a large part of the story because Magic has been anything but a static game since then. The changes and improvements to Magic warrant design notes of their own.

First and Foremost—A Game

One thing that might look arcane in my notes to people who know something about the game market is my reference to the form of game that Magic launched as a "trading card game," rather than a "collectable card game." I still use TCG rather than CCG, which became the industry standard despite my efforts from its earliest days. I prefer "trading" rather than "collectable" because I feel it emphasizes the playing aspect rather than the speculation aspect of the game. The mindset of making collectables runs against that of making games—if you succeed in the collectable department then there is a tendency to keep new players out and to drive old ones away because of escalating prices. One of the major battles that Magic fought was to make it perceived principally as a game and secondarily as a collectable. Good games last forever—collectables come and go.

This was not merely theoretical speculation—Magic's immense success as a collectable was severely threatening the entire game. Booster packs intended to be sold at a few bucks were marked up to 20 dollars in some places as soon as they hit the shelves. While many people view this time as the golden age of Magic, the designers knew that it was the death of the game in the long run. Who is going to get into the game when it was immediately inflated in price so much? How many people would play the game if doing so was wearing holes in some of their most valuable assets? We might be able to keep a speculation bubble going for a while, but the only way Magic was going to be a long-term success—a classic game—was for it to stand on its game play merits, not on its worthiness as an investment.

During "Fallen Empires," the fifth Magic expansion, we finally produced enough cards that the speculative market collapsed. The long-term value of Magic could perhaps thrive, but it wouldn't immediately price itself out of the reach of new players before they got a chance to try it. There was an inevitable negative patina that Magic got for a while, and Fallen Empires still has, but from this point on, Magic was sinking or swimming on its game merits. Fortunately, Magic turned out to be a strong swimmer.

Binding the Unbounded

The part of my notes that, I believe, reveals my biggest change in thinking over the last decade is the statement that in the future we would publish other games with mechanics similar to Magic. What I was referring to is what became Ice Age and Mirage, two expansions for Magic. Why did I think these would be entirely new games, rather than what they ended up being—expansions for the main game?

We all realized from the start that we couldn't just keep adding cards to Magic and expect it to stay popular. One reason for that is that each successive set of cards were a smaller and smaller percentage of the entire pool of cards, and so they would necessarily have less and less impact on the whole of the game. This was illustrated vividly by players of Ice Age talking about how the entire set introduced two relevant cards to the game. One can imagine how the designers felt—working for years to make Ice Age a compelling game to have it boil down to a mere two cards. Another, perhaps more important reason, is that new players wouldn't want to enter a game where they were thousands of cards behind, so our audience would inevitably erode.

Initially we saw two solutions to this problem:

1. Make cards ever more powerful. This is a route many trading card game makers followed, and one I greatly dislike. It feels like strong-arming the players to buy more and more rather than really providing them more game value. But it would bring new players in because they wouldn't need the obsolete old cards.

2. Eventually conclude Magic: The Gathering and start a new game—Magic: Ice Age, for example. I advocated this approach because I believed we could make exciting new game environments indefinitely. When one set was finished, players wouldn't be forced to buy into the new game to keep competitive, they could move on if they wanted a change, and new players could begin on equal footing.

When it actually came time to do Ice Age, it was absolutely clear that players would not stand for a new version of Magic, so we had to think of something else. Additionally, we were also worried that fragmenting the player audience was a bad idea; if we made a lot of different games, people would have a harder and harder time finding players.

The solution we found was to promote different formats of game play, many of which involved only more recent sets of cards. Today there are popular formats of play that involve only the most recently published cards, cards published in the last two years, and cards published in the last five years, in addition to many others. While this does fragment the player base—because you might not be able to find players who play your format—it is less draconian than different games because you can apply your cards to many different formats over time. This was a far more flexible approach than the first because it didn't command players to start fresh; it allowed them to, and it allowed new players to join the game without being overwhelmed.

Trading Card Games Are Not Board Games

I used to believe that trading card games were far more like board games than they are. This is not surprising because I had no trading card games before Magic to draw examples from, and so I was forced to use the existing world of games to guide my thinking on TCGs. A lot of my design attitudes grew from this misconception. For example, my second trading card game was designed to be best with four or more people, and it took several hours to play. These are not bad parameters for a board game, but trading card games really want to be much shorter because so much of the game is about replaying with a modified, or entirely new, deck.

In a similar vein, I used what I saw board game standards to be when it came to rules clarifications. It was common in board games to find that a different group played a slightly different way or had house rules to suit their tastes. With board games, different interpretations of the rules and ways of play were not a major problem because players tended to play with fairly isolated groups. This led me to be quite antiauthoritarian when it came to the "correct" way to play. It turned out that a universal standard for a trading card game was far more necessary than a board game because the nature of the game form made the interconnectivity of the game audience far greater.

This meant that we had to take more and more responsibility for defining the rules and standards of play. In some ways, this is analogous to being forced to construct the tournament rules for a game. The rules to bridge are not that complex, but when you write out the official tournament rules—really try to cross the Ts and dot the Is—you have a compendium.

I had also hoped that players could moderate their own deck restrictions. We knew that certain card combinations were fun to discover and surprise someone with, but they were not fun to play with on an ongoing basis. So we figured players would make house rules to cover those decks and the responsible cards. The highly interconnected nature of Magic made it unreasonable to expect that, however, because every playgroup came up with a vast number of restrictions and rules, and they all played with each other. This meant we had to take more responsibility in designing the cards and, when necessary, banning cards that were making the game worse.

The Pro Tour

All this precision invested in the design of the rules and cards made Magic a surprisingly good game to play seriously. We began to entertain ideas of really supporting a tournament structure with big money behind it—big enough that players could, if good enough, make a living off of playing Magic. This was a controversial subject at Wizards of the Coast for a while, the worry being that making the game too serious would make it less fun. I subscribed fully to the concept of a Pro Tour, thinking of how the NBA helped make basketball popular and didn't keep the game from being played casually as well.

The Pro Tour had an almost immediate effect. Our players rapidly became much better as the top-level ones devoted time to really analyzing the game and as that game tech filtered down through the ranks. Before the Pro Tour, I am confident that I was one of the best players in the world, now I am mediocre at best.

Now there are thousands of tournaments each week, and many players have earned a lot of money playing Magic, some in the hundreds of thousands of dollars. At the last World Championship, there were 56 countries competing. There is a never-ending buzz of Magic analysis and play as players attempt to master the ever-changing strategic ground of Magic. I believe this is a major part of Magic's ongoing popularity—if even a small group of people take a good game very seriously, there can be far-reaching effects.

Magic Online

Online Magic didn't come into its own until last year. For a long time, I have wanted to see an online version of Magic that duplicated real-life Magic as closely as possible. That is, the online game would connect people, run the games and the tournaments, and adjudicate rules, but little else. At first, we tried to form partnerships with computer game companies to do this, but our partners always had other ideas about how to do computer Magic. Eventually we hired a programming studio to do it our way, and now we have Magic Online.

One of the striking things about Magic Online is that we use the same revenue model as in real life. Despite exhortations to use a subscription model, we chose to sell virtual cards, which you could trade with other players online. This allows players to buy some cards and then play them indefinitely with no further fee—as in real life.

It was important to us that we not make it a better deal playing online than off—we wanted it to be the same. That is because we feel the paper game contributes a lot to Magic's ongoing popularity, and it could be threatened if many of its players go to the online game.

For this reason, one of the prime targets for the online game was going to be lapsed players. Many studies had been done on how long people play Magic and why they leave the game, and for the most part, they didn't leave because they were bored with the game; they left because they had life changes that made it more difficult to play, for example, getting jobs or having kids. These players would potentially rejoin the game if they could play from their own home on their own hours.

Magic Online is still a bit too young to be sure about, but it appears to have acquired a dedicated sizeable audience of players without hurting the paper game. Many of the players are formerly lapsed players, as we had hoped.

The Future of Magic

Who knows what the next decades will bring? Ten years ago, I had no clue at all; it was an exciting time, and we were riding a roller coaster. Now I am more confident. I believe that Magic is fairly stable and that there is every reason to believe that it will be around and as strong in another 10 years. At this point, it is clear that Magic is not a fad, and as many new players are coming in each year as are leaving the game.

Certainly Magic has stayed fresh for me. I get into the game every few months—joining a league, constructing a deck, or perhaps preparing for and participating in a tournament. Every time I return I find the game fresh and exciting, with enough different from the previous time to keep me on my toes but enough the same that I can still exploit my modest skills at the game. I look forward to the future of the game.

(2) procedures for turning, and (3) hit and miss rules for shooting. Our army men were moved and turned on the table as mock units using the rules.

These experiments solidified some ideas about moving and shooting and caused other ideas to be dismissed, which resulted in a very crude system for simultaneous movement and the basics of shooting. I also considered adding rules about movement and starting points, as well as assigning a turn order to the players. If I had adopted the experience goal about making players feel like an elite team, I might have taken this moment to define several player types. Perhaps a scout, a sharpshooter, and a medic. Depending on your experience goal, you might have made different choices for your prototype at this point.

Think of it this way: Once you have built the foundation, you then need to build a framework for your game that will support the specific experience you want for your players. Every experience goal will lead you towards different choices at this point. It is not a matter of what you think is coolest or most saleable; it is about constructing a skeletal structure that can support the rich and varied feature set that you think are best for meeting your experience goal. What you need to do first is decide which rules are essential and which are features that those structural elements have to support. Your gameplay visualization and your experience goal statement should help you make these decisions.

At this point in the construction of the FPS prototype, the movement and shooting foundation begged for the structure of a scoring system and unit hit points. As I added these elements, my crude movement and shooting system was retested with them in place. The tests illuminated problems that could only be seen with the system in motion. The whole system was revised to address the problems. At this point, the system was still messy and ill defined. Nothing had been written down. There were open questions everywhere. However, the system was basically functional.

When working through this, keep in mind the distinction between what are features and what are rules. Features are attributes that make a game richer, like adding more weapons or new vehicles or a nifty way to navigate the space. Rules are modifications to the game mechanics that change how the game functions, such as winning conditions, conflict resolution, turn order, etc.

You can add rules without adding features, but you can never add a feature without changing or adding rules. For example, if you added a new type of laser gun to your game, the rules would dictate how this gun could be used, what damage it would do, and how it would relate to all aspects of the game. One new feature might introduce 10 or more new rules to support it. As you modify your game, you will be constantly tweaking the rules to enhance gameplay and accommodate a growing feature set.

Your best strategy for adding structure is to focus on rules first and features later. Rules, by their very nature, tend to be inextricably linked to the core gameplay, while features tend to be peripheral. That is a generalization, but if you keep it in mind, it will help you to structure the development of your game.

3. *Formal details*

The next step is to add the necessary rules and procedures to the system to make it into a fully functional game. Focus on what you know about formal elements to decide what your game needs. Is the objective interesting and achievable? Is the player interaction structure the best choice? Most importantly, do I get a sense that I'm getting close to my player experience goals? Are there rules or procedures that you wanted to add, but they were not part of the core mechanic or that detract from your experience goal? The trick is to find an appropriate level of detail to add. Beginning game designers typically add too much. The art of game design often involves paring a bunch of feature ideas down to a small, important set of features that all contribute to meeting your experience goal for the game.

At this point in the development of the FPS prototype, I added the hit percentage, health, and scoring. Many other ideas were considered, including mines, shields, vehicles, mechanisms for hiding, and more. However, I scrapped all of them and focused on rules affecting the central gameplay, rather than a set of new features that I believed would create the most interesting game. How did I decide on some elements and not others? It was a creative judgment backed by input from my playtesters.

One way to add formal details efficiently is to isolate each new rule and test it individually. If you feel the game cannot function without this rule, then leave it in the game and add another rule. But do not overuse this privilege. Not every rule is critical, and the less you add, the cleaner your skeleton. A lot of what you consider rules are probably features. Try to draw a clear distinction, and keep your core rule set as clean as possible.

Test each rule, then remove it, and add another rule, and test it. It will be clear that some of the rules are optional and others must be included in the game if you are to continue to expand the

gameplay. This is a litmus test. If you can continue to build out the game without a specific rule, no matter how amazing that rule seems, you should leave it out. You can always add it later, but it should not be included at this early stage.

4. *Refinement*

At this point in the process, the prototype is a playable system, although it might still be somewhat rough. By experimenting and tweaking, the play system will become more refined. The play experience created by the game will flow. Instead of questioning the fundamentals of the game (and possibly thinking it will never work), you will switch to questioning the smaller details, and, of course, the big questions: Is your game compelling? Is it meeting your goals? If not, what will make it so? This process of refinement can continue for a number of iterations.

During refinement is also the time to add all those great ideas for features that have come up while testing but were not really essential. I went back to those ideas about mines and teleport pads and specialist roles for my FPS at this point. Again, be careful not to get ahead of yourself. It is tempting to add five new features, create a bunch of rules to support those features, and then start playing, but this blurs

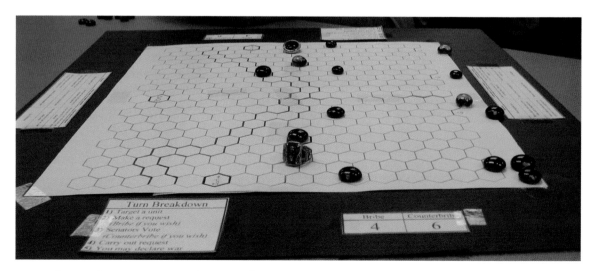

7.14 Physical prototype with procedures outlined

your view of the game. It becomes difficult to tell which features are making the game more fun to play and which are causing problems.

To avoid this, rank your features in terms of necessity, how they contribute to your experience goal. Then introduce and test each one. Test how it affects overall gameplay, and then remove it. This might seem cumbersome, but it will keep your game structure from getting convoluted. If you add too many features too early, you will find yourself losing your grasp on what the game is about. I have seen this happen over and over again with beginning designers, and this is why I caution you to postpone the pleasure of creating the ideal game from the outset, and instead recommend that you focus on what is needed step by step.

As you do this, you will discover that some rules and features that seemed like great ideas actually diminish the playability, while others that appeared dull add a whole new dimension to the player experience. You can only know this by testing each one in a controlled environment without the interference of other features. After testing each new twist, write down an analysis. Be sure to use your playtesters, and incorporate their feedback into your analysis. They are your eyes and ears. You might love a rule or feature so much that you are blind to its flaws. Trust your testers.

Exercise 7.10: Prototype Your Own Game

Use what you have learned to create a paper prototype of the game idea you described in Exercise 6.8 on page 204. This is a hard task. Break it down into the iterative steps described on pages 235 and 247-249 (i.e., foundation, structure, formal details, refinement). If you get stuck on a step, just take your best guess and move on. With prototyping, you always have room to iterate.

7.15   More physical prototype examples

Refining Your Visualization

As you prototype, you will probably wind up changing the relationships of the various activities in your game. I recommend refining your gameplay visualization as you go along so that you can see how your changes affect the overall flow of the system. As you analyze and refine the structure, you will be able to see if there are activities that have little or no payoff for the player or other activities that are overvalued. You will want to make sure that the core procedures have significant impact for the player and that each is there for an appropriate reason. I will talk more about balance and tuning of your game in Chapters 10 and 11.

MAKING THE PHYSICAL PROTOTYPE BETTER

The prototype you have created may or may not be very playable. Parts might be out of balance, and rules might conflict. Your game might also feel slow or disjointed. Some beginning designers become discouraged at this point and walk away. They feel that their game is hopeless, and the only solution is to start from scratch with a new game idea.

This might be true, but before you take such drastic measures, it is good to go back to your core game mechanics and your player experience goal. Think about why your prototype isn't reaching your goal – or whether or not your goal is clear enough to be interesting. You may need to re-state your goal more clearly to make better progress. You may also need to re-think some of the procedures or features of your prototype. Strip away all the additional rules and then reintroduce them one by one in an attempt to isolate the problem. In doing this, you will come to understand how each rule and feature actually fits into the system. Some features and rules might seem innocuous at first, but as you add and remove them, it will become apparent how they can throw the whole system out of balance.

Your game is a complex system, and specific elements might interact with others to produce a result that is unexpected. Your job is to systematically determine the problems and experiment with solutions until you solve them. Sometimes this can be a painstaking process, as you rip apart rules and rebuild them over and over again, but it is the only way to truly figure out what part of your game is actually broken.

When you get to the point where you are absolutely certain that your prototype is both playable and fun, and that it is meeting or even partially meeting your experience goal, then you are ready to start all over again. Yes, that's right. Just because your game is good does not mean it is finished. Before you move on to the next stage, you will want a great prototype. And even if it is great, there might be a way to make it better.

BEYOND THE PHYSICAL PROTOTYPE

Now that you have experimented with physical prototyping and iterated several designs, you are probably beginning to get a good sense of what it means to be a game designer. The physical prototype of your original game concept is working, though perhaps not perfectly. At this point you will want to do some playtesting of your prototype, as discussed in Chapter 9.

But physical prototyping is only the first in a long set of steps to completing a functional digital game. You and your team can use the physical prototype as the blueprint for a software prototype. Because you have spent a lot of time thinking through the core mechanics and most important features of your game by building a physical prototype, articulating those mechanics will be much simpler.

Obviously, taking your physical prototype from a physical to a digital design will change the nature of how players access the game, but the core mechanics of the system are still valid. For example, in the FPS prototype, I could lay out the arena, spawning points, ammo, first aid, etc., in the software prototype exactly as I had them in the physical prototype. The programmers would implement a real-time system for movement and shooting, making my card system obsolete, but the basic gameplay would remain intact, and the map I created would provide a good design guide. I would also be able to articulate what player roles we needed to make available in order to meet the experience goal. There would be no hand-waving, arguing, or uncertainty: we would have the start of a solid plan of development.

Some core challenges you will find in translating your physical prototype to a digital design are in the controls and interface for the target system. Rather than players moving their army men on the grid, now you have to provide a control map for a keyboard and mouse, a proprietary controller, or whatever other input device for which you are designing. Also, you have to design a visual display of the game environment that is compatible with the platform you are targeting. Chapter 8 goes into more detail on this process.

CONCLUSION

Creating a physical prototype is a critical step in the design of your original game concept. It will save your team tremendous amounts of time because everyone will have a clear understanding of the game you are making. In addition, a physical prototype will enable you to focus your creative energy on the game mechanics, without becoming distracted by the production and programming process. And most importantly, making a prototype gives you the freedom to experiment as you try to meet new types of experience goals—and through experimentation comes innovation.

DESIGNER PERSPECTIVE: JAMES ERNEST

President, Cheapass Games

James Ernest is a prolific designer of tabletop games, including Kill Doctor Lucky, Lords of Vegas, Button Men, Diceland, Give Me the Brain, Lord of the Fries, Falling, Brawl, and Fightball. He has also done freelance design work for several major game companies, including Hasbro and Microsoft.

On getting into the game industry:

I met some of the people at Wizards of the Coast in 1993, shortly before they released Magic: The Gathering. I worked with Wizards on support material for that game, and I designed new games to submit to them for publication, with limited success. Eventually, with a backlog of unpublished designs, I started my own game company in 1996.

On favorite games:

I like simple games, whether they have deep strategy or not. For example, I'm a sucker for casino games of all types. Judging by the time I spend playing them, my five favorite games would have to be poker (by a wide margin), Diceland, blackjack, Dungeons & Dragons, and my family's unique version of cutthroat pitch. I also play plenty of computer games, mostly of the casual, puzzle, and arcade variety. Poker tops the list because of several factors: I can make money at it, so I'm pretty fascinated by that. The rules are incredibly simple, but the strategy is deep. Hands are only a couple of minutes long, so in a sense you're always getting a fresh start. And it has strong components of both mathematical and psychological strategy, so I can focus on whichever one I'm most interested in at the time.

On game influences:

Magic: The Gathering inspired me both to imitate the things it did right and to learn from its mistakes. Before Magic came out, I'd given very little thought to formal game design (though I'd written a few games, including a chess variant). Being closely associated with Magic in its early stages, I became aware that games were something you could design for a living. One of the most inspiring things about Magic was its original format: To imitate that success, I continue to experiment with new formats. I haven't made a hit yet, but at least I deserve a little credit for trying. I'm also a fan of popular European games like Settlers of Catan and Puerto Rico, which I like for their structure and balance, and traditional and casino games, which prove that it doesn't take many rules to create a compelling game.

On design process:

Many designers seem to invent game mechanics first, then theme, or at least they give preferential treatment to mechanics. In my experience, if a game is going to have a theme or a story, you need to settle on that part first because it's so much harder to do it last. I have been in too many design meetings (for my own games and others) where we have a perfectly functional game but now need to come up with a name or theme. Those sessions are awful, and it's often impossible to come up with the right answer. Conversely, if I know the theme of a game, I have absolutely no trouble coming up with mechanics that deliver on it. In fact, a good theme usually suggests new mechanics that I would otherwise never have considered.

On prototypes:

Even when designing computer games, I try to build a paper prototype if it's at all possible. I need to put the game in front of real players for several rounds of quick, iterative testing, and paper prototypes are much quicker to modify. On the paper side, I try to prototype every meaningful element of the game as soon as I can. For example, when creating Pirates of the Spanish Main, a miniatures game for Wizkids, I built modular, miniature pirate ships exactly the size of the final models, using Lego bricks. The result gave us a very good idea of what would and wouldn't work. Having real models, rather than generic pieces, made testing and refining the game much easier.

On balancing Diceland:

Diceland is one of the most challenging games I've ever designed, and it took about six years between the original concept and the final product. It's basically a miniatures game that uses paper dice, and it deals with damage, range, and distance in very abstract ways. Each character is an eight-sided die, and each face of the die represents the character in a different state, such as wounded, healthy, blinded, in command, etc. A core design challenge was to balance light, nimble fighters against large, bulky ones in a way that made sense. The solution involved mapping the surface of the die, controlling the damage path, and understanding all the relationships between sides. When a character moves, he tips from one side to an adjacent side. A similar thing happens when he takes damage, though not always in the same direction. Understanding and mapping the "recovery" moves, that is, those that move a character from a weaker to a stronger face, gave me the control necessary to give smaller fighters a real sense of agility.

Advice to designers:

When you're new to a discipline, everything will feel like a lot of work, and something that was a lot of work can be hard to let go. Don't get so attached to your work that you can't be honest about it. Change everything if it needs changing, even down to the roots. Also, become addicted to simplicity. It's always tempting to fix a game by adding rules, but it's better (and much harder) to take bad rules away.

A lot of game designers will tell you to borrow liberally from existing games, and you can, but only when you understand what you're doing. Don't decide that your game uses seven cards just because your favorite game also uses seven cards. Decide because seven cards is the right number for your game.

It's easy to copy what you see in the market, but it's more productive to look for what isn't there. You can try to write a game for a player you don't know, but your best target will always be yourself. That's why the sign in my office says, "Write the game you want to play."

DESIGNER PERSPECTIVE: KATIE SALEN

Professor, Department of Informatics, UC Irvine and Co-Founder and Chief Designer, Connected Camps

Katie Salen is Professor in the Department of Informatics at UC Irvine, a member of the Connected Learning Lab, as well as Chief Designer and co-founder of Connected Camps, an online learning platform powered by youth gaming experts. She is founding Executive Director of Institute of Play and led the design of Quest to Learn, an innovative New York City public school. Katie is co-author

of Rules of Play, The Game Design Reader, Quest to Learn: Growing a School for Digital Kids, and Affinity Online: How Connection and Shared Interest Fuel Learning.

On getting into the game industry:

I fell into working with games via a project I ran with some students on the Texas Lottery. At the time, I was interested in thinking about how lottery tickets effectively functioned as formal, social, and cultural interfaces and quickly realized that games were an incredible platform for creating compelling, interactive experiences. I started making games as part of this work, met a bunch of interesting game designers in Austin and New York, and starting digging into a myriad of gaming subcultures, including machinima. My career as a game designer and writer on games grew from there.

On favorite games:

This is always a challenging question to answer because there are so many games I love. But if I were to name the games that have most influenced my thinking and work, Rez, Mafia, Guitar Hero, four square, and DDR would top that list. Each of these games totally transformed the way I think about designing play to transform how a player relates to their social and physical surroundings, and each has a particular interactive aesthetic to which I am drawn. I also am deeply affected by the cultures of production that have emerged around some of the games on the list and the way each of these games create performative spaces as part of their play.

On inspiration:

I tend to find design inspiration in particular moments of a game, rather than in a game as a whole. Sometimes the inspiration comes from a particular moment of play of a game that was unexpected but traceable to the game's design or from an especially elegant core mechanic. The exquisite feeling of the handholding mechanic in Ico, for example, or the egalitarian structure of a race game like the New York Marathon gets me thinking about the kinds of experiences games can provide. Katamari Damacy inspired me on the level of a core mechanic that led to the invention of strange stories and worlds. SuperMario for the DS inspired me on the value of game balancing and the pure pleasure of failure. Because I was a high-level athlete into my postcollege years (volleyball), I find that I also look for inspiration in that experience, which was intensely competitive and wholly collaborative. As a player, I learned to respect what the game demanded from me; as a designer, I work to translate this feeling of respect into a kind of social contract binding player to player and player to game. I really feel like it is this state of mutual respect that makes game design so interesting.

On the design process:

I see game design as requiring a balance between a systematic analysis of constraints, understanding of precedent, and sheer imagination. Most often I begin by trying to define exactly what it is I want a player to experience—how I want them to feel, what physical movements or actions I want them to enact, in what ways they might interact with other players or contexts. I also think a lot about what kinds of meanings I want the game to express and where and by whom the game will be played. I explore core mechanics that fit with answers to these questions, doing physical or paper prototyping to gauge the effects of the mechanics, and then work with a team to embed those mechanics into a larger design system. Game ideas also sometimes start with an image—the Big Urban Game, for example, started with the image of giant bowling pins wandering through a city; the slow game Skew with an image of players running through stores scanning game pieces. I also rely heavily on brainstorming ideas with other designers and making lists and lists of kinds of experiences I'd like to create.

On prototypes:

Prototyping is a key part of my design process because it is the very best way to understand what your player will experience and to begin to see the kind of possibility space the game provides. I use many different prototyping methods: paper prototyping, physical prototyping, scenario writing, interactive prototyping, etc. Prototypes become the basis for playtesting, which I use throughout the entire design process. Sometimes the prototypes are incredibly simple—a few chits and cards used to model a core mechanic or balancing scheme; later in the process, especially with digital games, the prototypes can become quite complex and require a number of people to produce. In all cases, I use prototyping and playtesting to help me see what is and isn't working about the game, to explore unexpected outcomes, and to constantly assess the quality of experience the player is having.

On solving a difficult design problem:

I remember with the Big Urban Game, Frank Lantz and Nick Fortugno and I were struggling with the overall balance of the game. As a race game that took place between three teams over the course of five days, we needed to figure out how to make sure that the race felt dramatic throughout and that each team, each day, would have a chance to win, even if one of the teams took an early lead. We chose to add a "power-up" feature where anyone could show up to one of the race checkpoints and roll a pair of giant dice to help power up their team's game piece. Formally, this feature did what we needed it to do—a team could come from behind if they received enough dice rolls, but the feature also did something else: It invited a whole other kind of player into the game. These were the super-casual players whose entire engagement with the game was a single role of the dice. Surprisingly, because the mechanic of the dice roll was embedded in a social context (the checkpoint where lots of players were hanging out), those players felt as much a part of the game as the hardcore players did. Designing a game where a single move was felt to be equally valid as days of play by players was pretty incredible, and it was an experience that continues to inform my work. If we were to redesign the game, we would have built on this feature even more.

Advice to designers:

Be open to the possibilities of history, diversity, and ideas that you feel matter. Prototype ideas rather than talking about them. Practice. Practice. Practice.

FURTHER READING

Buxton, Bill. *Sketching User Experiences: Getting the Design Right and the Right Design.* San Francisco: Morgan Kaufmann, 2007.

Henderson, John. "The Paper Chase: Saving Money via Paper Prototyping," Gamasutra.com, May 8, 2006. https://www.gamasutra.com/view/feature/131099/the_paper_chase_saving_money_via_.php

McElroy, Kathryn. *Prototyping for Designers: Developing the Best Digital and Physical Products.* Sebastopol: O'Reilly Media, Inc., 2017.

Nielsen Norman Group. *Paper Prototyping: A How-to Training Video.* DVD available at ⟨https://www.nngroup.com/reports/paper-prototyping-training-video/⟩

Sigman, Tyler. "The Siren Song of the Paper Cutter: Tips and Tricks from the Trenches of Paper Prototyping," Gamasutra.com, September 13, 2005. https://www.gamasutra.com/view/feature/130814/the_siren_song_of_the_paper_.php

Snyder, Carolyn. *Paper Prototyping: The Fast and Easy Way to Design and Refine User Interfaces.* San Francisco: Morgan Kaufmann, 2003.

Chapter 8
Digital Prototyping

Now that you have some experience creating physical prototypes, you can see their usefulness in thinking through your design and getting early feedback from players. However, physical prototypes have their limitations; if your final game will be released on a digital platform, at some point in the development process, you will need to create a digital prototype of your concept. This does not mean starting from scratch—your physical prototype helped you to formalize and test the foundation of your game mechanics. The digital prototype extends that design work into a digital form and allows you to test the essence of your game in its intended format. The understanding of your formal system gained from the physical prototyping experience will breathe life into the designs for your digital game. It will inform the decisions you make and give you ideas you would otherwise have never thought of.

As part of your digital prototyping process, you will want to build models of core systems that you have questions about: game logic, special physics, environments, levels, etc. Additionally, two of the core tasks of digital prototyping will be envisioning your gameplay using the input and output devices of your digital platform. This means prototyping your control systems, such as keyboards, mice, multitouch, gesture, proprietary controllers, etc. It also means visualizing your gameplay in the form of an intuitive, responsive digital interface.

An important thing to keep in mind when you are doing digital prototyping is to consider your reasons for each prototype that you make. Are you trying to answer game design or technical questions? Are you trying to establish an effective production pipeline? Or are you trying to communicate your vision to your team or to a publisher? The following section will help you to craft your digital prototype for these very different situations.

TYPES OF DIGITAL PROTOTYPES

Like physical prototypes, digital prototypes are made using only the elements needed to make them functional. They are not finished games, and if you spend too much time making them like finished games, you will defeat the purpose of prototyping at all. Generally, digital

DOI: 10.1201/9781003460268-10

Game Mechanics   Kinesthetics -- "feel"

Technology   Aesthetics -- "look, sound"

8.1   Four areas of investigation for digital prototyping

prototypes are made with minimal art or sound; even their gameplay is incomplete, focusing only on unanswered questions and parts of the design that need clarity. Eleanor Todd, who was development director for Spore, divides the prototyping process into four distinct areas of investigation, which can be seen in Figure 8.1.[1] These are: game mechanics, aesthetics, kinesthetics, and technology.

Prototyping Game Mechanics

Game mechanics are, as I have already discussed, discrete features of the formal aspects of the game. If you have already created a physical prototype, you have a head start in this area of your design. Sometimes, however, a gameplay question you pose to yourself is not easily modeled in a physical prototype. In this case, you can actually begin with a digital gameplay prototype. The important thing to remember when you do this is to make it simple and focused on a particular question—do not try to integrate all of your questions about the game into a single prototype, at least not at first. Later you can prototype the integration of features, but when you are first starting out, you will want to start with your core mechanic, just like I did when I built the FPS prototype.

An example of using digital prototyping for gameplay questions can be seen in the work of independent game designer Jonathan

Blow, who was one of the original organizers of the Experimental Gameplay Workshop at the Game Developers Conference. Blow spoke at the conference about his work on experimental gameplay related to time. His game Braid is an innovative action platformer that allows the player to "rewind" time in unusual ways, making that feature an integral part of the gameplay. Before deciding on the final mechanic, Blow actually prototyped a number of other potential mechanics related to time. One question that resulted in an interesting prototype was something he called Oracle Billiards. Blow asked himself how the game of billiards would change if the player could see the future. In addition to seeing the balls on the table, the game showed the final positions of the balls after being struck. When he tested the prototype, he realized that it was not fun, but it was informative. "It didn't do what I wanted," he says, "but I got a feeling out of it that I never got out of any game I ever played before."[2] The learning from this prototype and others eventually led to the design of Braid.

Another example comes from the Spore prototyping process described by Eleanor Todd in her Game Developers Conference presentation on the topic. One big question for the design team revolved around the creature editing portion of the gameplay. The question was how to make it simple and intuitive to use but still complex enough to give a wide variety of results so that players without any 3D design experience could make truly unique creatures. Team member Chaim Gingold, who designed the Spore Creator suite, (and whose sidebar on prototyping can be found on page 226), had an idea for the feature, but when he tried to explain it to the rest of the team, they did not understand how it would work. So, to prove his point, Gingold put together a rough 2D prototype (Figure 8.3, top left) to demo his idea. This prototype helped the rest of the team understand exactly what he was talking about. The successful communication of the

8.2   Oracle Billiards and Braid

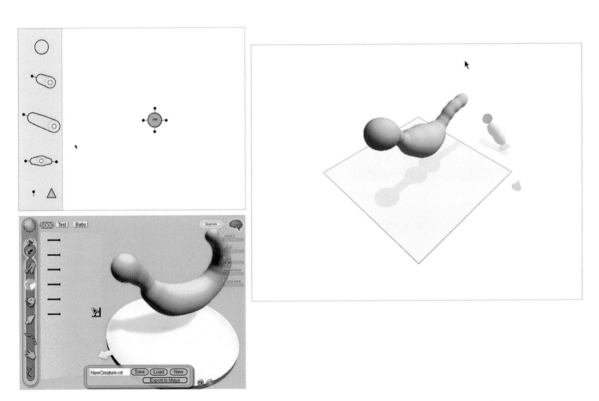

8.3   2D and 3D creature editor prototypes for Spore (Top left and right prototypes by Chaim Gingold; Bottom left by Spore team.)

8.4   Student research game Cloud

rough idea made Gingold decide to go further (Figure 8.3, top right), before it was elaborated into an integrated prototype with other Spore team members (Figure 8.3, bottom left). Such prototypes helped define a large portion of the gameplay.

This type of digital gameplay prototype is not just something done by professional developers; it is also extremely useful and practical for students and beginning designers. During the development of the student research game Cloud, at the USC Game Innovation Lab, a number of prototypes were created to answer the team's many questions about how to use the gameplay mechanics to evoke a feeling of relaxation and freedom in the player. You can read more about the prototyping process for Cloud in the sidebar on page 268.

Gameplay prototypes need not be stand-alone programs. Often, the questions you will have about your mechanics will involve the kind of number crunching that can be tested using a customized Excel spreadsheet or Google spreadsheets. These tools allow for embedding fairly complex game logic into a spreadsheet that allows you to test permutations of your game mechanics in a stripped-down fashion. See Nikita Mikros' sidebar "Using Software Prototypes in

Game Design" on page 264 for an example of this approach to gameplay prototyping.

Prototyping Aesthetics

Aesthetics are the visual and aural dramatic elements of your game, which I have told you repeatedly not to worry about for your physical prototype. The same holds true for most of the digital prototyping work you will do. However, sometimes you will want to break this rule. Adding just a little bit of visual design and sound to a prototype can often help articulate the game mechanics. The trick is to know when you are adding just enough and when you are wasting valuable time.

Additionally, sometimes you have questions about aesthetic issues in your game that you need to test early on. For example, how will the character animation work with the combat system? Or how will a new interface solution work with the environments? Some simple ways to do this are with storyboards, concept art, animatics, interface prototypes, and audio sketches.

- Storyboards are a series of drawings that show a rough sketch of a visual sequence. These are often used in filmmaking to determine how scenes will be shot, but they are also useful for cut scenes in games and mapping out potential play within a level.

- Concept art consists of paintings or sketches of characters and environments, exploring potential looks, palettes, and styles for the visual aesthetics.
- An animatic is an animated mock-up of the game in action. An animatic does not use the real game technology, and it does not give a sense of the kinesthetics, but it can help communicate both the aesthetics of the game and some portions of the gameplay.
- An interface prototype is a mock-up of the visual interface. This can be done in a static board or using an animatic. This can even be done first as a paper prototype and playtested before moving on to a digital format.
- Audio sketches are early drafts of the music and sound effects that can really help to set the tone of the game and are useful for bringing life to animatics and other prototypes.

The team at Insomniac Games described their animation prototyping process for Ratchet & Clank as saving time not only for the animators but for the design and programming staff as well. "As a rule," says animation technical director John Lally, "our prototypes emphasized function over style.... For the animators, this meant that prototype

characters needed to jump to their correct heights, attack to their design specifications, and run at their proper speeds." The "protocharacters" were constructed with primitive objects and only roughly resembled their future incarnations, as can be seen in Figure 8.5. These animation prototypes allowed the artists to test attributes such as timing, measurement, and interaction with other characters, all of which have a direct impact on gameplay.[3]

Similarly, the team at Naughty Dog, creators of the Jak series of games, when faced with the complicated challenge of designing a customization interface for Jak X: Combat Racing, used a number of aesthetic prototypes to prove out their design ideas. Game director Richard Lemarchand says,

The interface system for Jak X: Combat Racing was more complicated than the interface for any game that Naughty Dog had created before, since the player had to be able to customize their cars and select online multiplayer missions, as well as move through a single-player game. We designed the interface first in a flowchart accompanied by rough pencil sketches of the screens and then prototyped it in Macromedia Flash to quickly give us a sense of how the flow between the different components would feel and whether or not some of the interface gimmicks we had in mind would come off. When we implemented the final interface, we were able

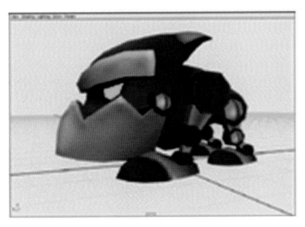
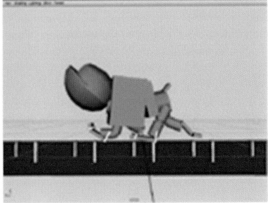

8.5   Animation prototypes for Ratchet & Clank

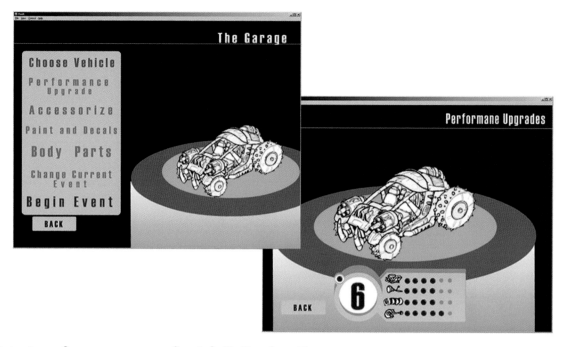

8.6   Interface prototypes for Jak X: Combat Racing

to save a lot of time because of the discoveries we'd made by working out problems with the original design in the Flash prototype.

Figure 8.6 shows two stages of the prototype in progress.

Prototyping Kinesthetics

The kinesthetics are the "feel" of the game, how the controls feel, how responsive the interface is, etc. Unlike gameplay and aesthetics, each of which can be tested using physical or analog methods before moving to a digital prototype, kinesthetics for a digital game are something that must be prototyped digitally. As I will discuss in the controls section on page 271, the feel of a digital game has a great deal to do with the type controls you have available to use. A game designed for a keyboard and mouse will have a very different feel from a game designed for a multitouch screen. It is important, when you are conceiving your gameplay, to

keep in mind the controls that will be available on the final platform so that you can design with them in mind.

An example of the usefulness of a kinesthetic prototype is in the story behind the development of Katamari Damacy. Keita Takahashi, the game designer of Katamari, had an idea about a game in which you could roll a sticky ball around and pick things up with it. He was a student at a Namco-sponsored university at the time, and the prototype for Katamari was made as an exercise for his thesis. The game, explained verbally or even with storyboards, sounds strange and does not fit into any particular genre of gameplay. Nevertheless, when the executives at Namco played the prototype, they, like all the players since, were convinced by the simplicity and charm of the game, which uses only the two analog sticks on the PS2 controller for its simple, compelling control scheme.[4]

Another example of a successful kinesthetic prototype was actually an animatic with a clever setup. Game designer Keiichi Yano was inspired to create the beat-matching game Osu! Tatakae! Ouendan (remade for Western audiences as Elite Beat Agents) when he first saw a demo of the (then) new Nintendo DS. The core mechanic of the game involves tapping the DS screen in time with the music and visual markers to "cheer on" the game characters. According to Yano, the development team put together a Flash pitch for the new idea that mimicked the feel of the interface and controls. "When we presented this to Nintendo, I played it on my notebook. I had them use a regular pen. They were touching my PC screen to get an idea for how the game would play. ...I got a lot of scratches."[5] The gameplay of this animatic/kinesthetic prototype looked and felt fairly close to the final version, and it sold the executives at Nintendo on the concept quickly.

Prototyping controls can sometimes lead to the genesis of an entire game idea. For example, the interactive music title PixelJunk 4AM began as an investigation of the Sony Move SDK. As lead designer Rowan Paker describes, "With a skeleton team of two programmers and one designer, we prototyped at least 12 different control methods for 4AM, all utilizing the Move to control music in space. Some of the control schemes varied from casting musical 'spells' in the air to replicating an eight-way arcade stick and inputting Street Fighter commands in the air. Regardless of how ludicrous each idea seemed, though, the only test that mattered was whether we could ask, 'Can I make music, and is it fun?' " Without that experimental control prototyping, Parker says, he might never have pushed the Move enough to find the innovative control scheme that the game is based on. "It would have been a hell of a lot easier to just implement a menu and pointers, but it wouldn't have been 4AM!"[6]

Prototyping Technology

Technology prototypes are just what they sound like: models of all of the software that it will take to make the game work technically. This could

8.7   Elite Beat Agents

include prototypes of the graphics capabilities for the game, the AI systems, the physics, or any number of problems specific to your game. It can also include a prototype of the production pipeline. Prototyping in this area is about testing and debugging the tools and the workflow for getting content into the game.

Prototyping is not about software engineering, however. It is an opportunity to try out ideas in a quick and dirty fashion. It is not the "real" code. In their Game Developers Conference presentation on the topic,[7] Developers Chris Hecker and Chaim Gingold advise "stealing it, faking it, or rehashing it" when you are building your prototype. After you have learned what you have to

USING SOFTWARE PROTOTYPES IN GAME DESIGN

by Nikita Mikros, CEO and game designer at BumbleBear Games

Nikita Mikros is the co-creator of the award-winning Killer Queen Arcade Game - the world's only 10-player arcade strategy game. In addition to Killer Queen, he has worked on various titles including ZOMBEEZ, Black Emperor and Pixel Prison Blues. Prior to forming BumbleBear Games, he was creative director and owner of Tiny Mantis Entertainment where he worked on roughly 60 games for clients including Nickelodeon, Cartoon Network, MTV and Adult Swim. Other credits include Propaganda Lander (2010), a fast paced, lander game inspired by Gravitar and Lunar Lander; Supremacy: Four Paths to Power (2005); the award-winning GameBoy Advance title I-Spy Challenger (2002); and The Egg Files (2002). Mikros is a recipient of the Bernie DeKoven Big Fun Award and a three time IGF finalist. He has taught programming and game design at the School of Visual Arts since 1995..

In a successful game, the rules of the game interact with each other and give rise to interesting but controlled emergent subsystems and compelling play patterns. Having a solid understanding of how one system interacts with another is essential in writing a comprehensive design document, answering questions from the team about the project, resolving unforeseen problems, and ultimately creating a compelling, balanced game. As games become increasingly complex, it becomes more and more difficult for the game designer to keep a complete image of all the elements or systems of gameplay in his or her mind.

Scientists use simulations and visualizations to gain understanding of complex data. Similarly, game designers can employ their own set of tools to gain insight into their own creations. These tools include daily logs, design documents, paper prototypes, and software prototypes. Software prototypes should be one of many tools at the game designer's disposal, and although they can be extremely useful, without clear goals, they can easily escalate into monsters more complex to build than the problem the designer is trying to solve. The goal in building a software prototype should always be to create a tool to help in your game design efforts, not to show off fancy graphics or elegant software architecture.

When Do You Need Software Prototypes?

Many games lend themselves very easily to paper prototypes, and even if the whole game cannot be modeled this way, isolated parts can often be playtested and designed using this process. However, there are times where one cannot really get a feel for a game without a software prototype. Additionally, some game prototypes are just simpler to implement with software. A simple example would be the game of Tetris. Tetris was inspired by pentominoes, a puzzle/toy based on building shapes out of pieces that are constructed from five basic blocks. In Tetris, the pieces are simplified from five to four blocks (tetrominoes) and are dropped at a constant rate, allowing the player to spin and move the pieces trying to construct solid horizontal rows on the bottom of the board. When a horizontal row is created, that row of building blocks is eliminated from the game. The pieces stack up, and eventually the game is lost when the player can no longer fit pieces onto the board. Although they share many similarities, constructing shapes with tetrominoes is very different from playing Tetris. How would one model the game of Tetris in a physical/paper prototype? Although the game has its origins in a physical puzzle, it is very tightly bound to a type of interaction that can only be modeled on the computer. In this case, a physical/paper prototype would be more difficult to construct than a software prototype.

Supremacy: Four Paths to Power

The creation of any software prototyping tools should be carefully considered due to the costly and time-consuming nature of writing software. The questions that the designer should ask before diving into such a project are as follows:

1. Is the tool/prototype really needed?
2. What are the requirements of the tool/prototype?
3. What is the quickest way to build the tool?
4. Will the tool be flexible enough?

In the following section, I will address how I attempted to resolve these questions for a particular problem in a project we completed a few years ago.

Supremacy: Four Paths To Power is an open-ended strategy war game that is waged on two fronts: the metagame, which is a battle in space, and the ground battles that determine the individual capture of planets. Each type of planet has different natural resources that the player can exploit to build unique military units and ultimately try to defeat his or her enemies. Overzealous players can destroy their own planets due to overproduction. Supremacy went on to be a finalist in the 2005 Independent Games Festival.

Is the Tool/Prototype Really Needed?

My first task was to build a paper/physical prototype and test my ideas by getting feedback from the rest of our team, whom I volunteered to be playtesters. Two separate paper prototypes were created: one simulating battles on the ground and one simulating the larger battles in space. The ground battle prototype worked fine; the math was straightforward, and keeping track of all the stats was relatively simple. Excited by the first prototype, we set out to play the space battle prototype, and disaster struck. After much groaning and moaning, we somehow slogged through seven or eight turns in what seemed like as many hours before calling it quits. The accounting of resources that was required was daunting. We were so caught up doing math that we could not see the forest for the trees. When one of the playtesters declared, "This game is hurting my head," I decided it was time to create a software prototype.

What Are the Requirements of the Tool/Prototype?

My first impulse was to build a full visual prototype, but upon further consideration I decided to ignore the "programmer within" and opted for a simpler solution. What I decided upon was a nonvisual representation of the game in software and the old paper prototype for visual representation. It was easy for us mere mortals to move pieces, count squares, calculate line of sight, and do all the things that take many person-hours to express in code. Alternatively, it was very easy to program the software to do all the accounting calculations as well as some other tedious tasks like keeping track of turns. The "prototype" looked nothing like a game; it looked like an ugly Excel spreadsheet with lots and lots of buttons. It took me about a day and a half to write it.

What Is the Quickest Way to Build the Tool/Prototype?

My first attempt was to build the tool in a spreadsheet program, but I quickly realized that it was not feasible due to the nature of some of the calculations. I decided to build it using Java and the Metrowerks RAD (rapid application development) toolset. This was a good option because I could quickly and easily lay out my tables, buttons, and other widgets and doodads. I was already familiar with the language and the development environment, so it was a natural choice. For me, writing this type of software is somewhat liberating because the end product is more or less a throwaway. I am far less

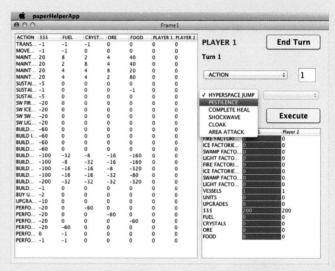

Game prototype with data

concerned with software design, architecture, optimization, coding standards, and all the other things that go into building solid software. Remember, the goal is to create a tool to help your game design efforts, not to create elegant, airtight software. Ultimately, I believe that you should write your prototypes in whatever language or authoring system you feel comfortable in and that allows you to experiment and change things quickly and easily. If you are not a programmer or are unfamiliar with any type of authoring software, then you must rely on your programming team. This can be difficult because ultimately programmers want to write good code, and their first impulse is always to build well-engineered reusable code that they can then use in the final product. This is not a bad idea when you have a clear idea of all the elements of your game, but this approach to rapid game design prototyping is like building a tractor to make a sand castle. It is overkill, and it prematurely locks you into something that you might not be trying to build.

Will the Tool Be Flexible Enough?

Ultimately, you want to be able to change rules and values easily and have the ability to experiment as quickly as you would be able to in a paper prototype. Although this is somewhat of a holy grail, there are things you can do to make your software prototyping tool more flexible. Here are some simple suggestions:

1. Everything is a variable.
2. Try to avoid using any literal constants in your code; in other words, a code snippet that looks like this:

```
totalOutput = 15 × 2
```

should look like this:

```
totalOutput = rateOfProduction × numFactories
```

3. Expose as many variables in the interface as possible.

4. Litter your prototyping tool with editable text fields; any value that has a remote possibility of changing should be editable through these fields. Your tool will be as ugly to look at as your high school yearbook picture, but you'll be happy when you don't need to recompile or go rifling through your code looking for a variable in the middle of a play testing session.

5. Don't even think of reusing this code. When I was an undergrad studying fine art, I had a drawing professor by the name of Marvin Bileck, and everybody called him Buddy. One day Buddy made us all go buy some sheets of very expensive drawing paper. We all came to class the next week with our beautiful drawing paper, ready to draw. At this point Buddy instructed us to throw the paper on the ground and stomp on it. If we weren't doing a good enough job he came over and joined in on the destruction of our precious paper. At the end of this exercise he declared that we were ready to start drawing. The point of the exercise was clear to me: If you want to be creative, don't hold on to anything too tightly, don't make anything so precious that you can't see beyond it. This is the way you should think about your prototyping code. In the end you may wind up reusing parts of the code, but this should not be a goal as you create it. You should be fully prepared to throw it away.

Conclusion

Software prototyping is a tool that can be used to understand and ultimately control the elements of your game. You gain nothing by writing software that prototypes a part of your game that you already thoroughly understand or that you can playtest via cheaper methods like paper prototypes. Every game is different, with its own special characteristics and requirements. If we had been working on a first-person shooter, or a fighting game, a totally different type of prototype would have been needed. I believe in this particular case that the software prototype was successful. It allowed me to visualize emergent behaviors in the game that I would not have been able to see with just a paper prototype. This prototype worked because it addressed the specific problems I was trying to solve and because I could build it quickly and easily.

PROTOTYPING CLOUD

by Tracy Fullerton

Cloud was a student research project from the USC Game Innovation Lab with an unusual experience goal for its time: Create a tranquil, relaxing, and joyful emotional experience similar to the archetypal childhood daydream of flying in the sky and creating shapes in the clouds. As faculty advisor for the project, Tracy Fullerton worked with the team at each stage of the process to define and iterate the design. This award-winning game was been downloaded more than 1.5 million times from www.thatcloud-game.com and launched the careers of award-winning game designers Jenova Chen (Designer Perspective, page 443) and Kellee Santiago (Sidebar on page 453).

When we began working on Cloud, we had only an innovative experience goal: to somehow evoke the feeling of relaxation and joy that you get when you lie back on the grass on a clear summer day and look up at the clouds wandering across the sky. Everyone does this. And at some time or another, we've dreamed of flying up in the clouds and moving them, shaping them into funny creatures or smiley faces or lollipops, or whatever comes to mind. It seemed like entirely new territory for a game. It seemed risky and interesting. So we decided to give it a try.

But how to do it? The first step was to create a series of prototypes based on the core mechanic of flying and gathering clouds. These prototypes were implemented using the Processing development environment and were iterated over several generations, starting in 2D and moving into crude 3D to test control, camera, and gameplay integration.

This core gameplay was tested by the team and a number of playtesters, and several conclusions were reached. The first was that the 2D perspective, while simple and practical, was not emotional enough. Although the final project had always been planned as a 3D game, there had been an open question of how to achieve a usable player viewpoint, and whether it made sense to use a 3D environment, but to lock the play within that environment to a two-dimensional plane within the 3D world.

At this point, the team began to sense that there was a conflict between the desired clarity for gameplay (which called for a 2D playing field) and the equal desire for an emotional sense of freedom in flight

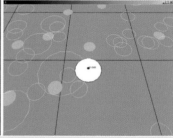

Figure 1   2D gathering clouds prototype for Cloud, left, and control, camera, and rudimentary gameplay prototype, right

Figure 2   Camera simulation prototype; left shows camera zoomed out for view of entire sky, right shows camera zoomed in to fly close to the character

(which called for freedom of movement within a 3D space). So we created a camera prototype in Maya that simply tested the idea of allowing the player to zoom the camera in and out at will. For example, we knew we wanted the player to be able to zoom far out to see what they had written in the sky, but we also wanted to be able to fly close up with the character, to feel the emotion of flight. As it turned out, this concept, especially when combined with another feature—"free flight" within the 3D space—solved both the practical interface issue and the emotional issue of flying close-up with the child.

In addition to experimenting with the core mechanic and viewpoint, at this point, the team began to envision a game without the traditional goals and conflict that drives most games. It would be a simple game that would encourage creativity and playfulness. To achieve this, we began designing the features that would allow players to draw and erase clouds in the sky as easily as chalk. Also, we began to realize that every aspect of the game needed to reinforce these positive emotions. The game needed to be relaxing and refreshing in its play as well as in its look and feel. So to eliminate all the psychic stress, there is no time pressure in the game, and failure is almost impossible. There are no elements that will trap players, and they can pick up and leave at any time with no repercussions.

While our gameplay prototyping was going on, focused on mechanics and camera controls, the programming team had several other hurdles they knew they had to face. The most important, obviously, was the simulation of believable, malleable, and computationally practical clouds. The team came up with an interesting solution: the use of a Lennard-Jones particle simulation underlying the clouds that would give them a dynamic underlying structure that would feel like playing with globs of mercury.

The first implementation of this concept was most useful in the fact that it proved we could create "clouds" out of clumps of dynamic particles—and that we would be able to support a lot of them. The preceding image of the particle simulation prototype shows the result of several thousand particles in a prototype environment that are (thankfully) not overtaxing the machine. These particles can be grabbed and shaped, much as the team had envisioned the cloud drawing feature.

The next stage of prototypes focused on making that underlying particle simulation feel more puffy. The previous figure shows such a test. In this version, tests revolved around using the clumps of clouds to draw faces and pictures, and an overall excitement about how the clouds would ultimately feel to play with started to permeate the team.

In addition to creating this underlying simulation, the team also implemented a billboarding method for rendering the cloud art onto the simulation. The following cloud simulation layer screenshots show images from the final game with rendering turned on and off to demonstrate how the method mapped to the final simulation.

Throughout the prototyping process and into production, extensive playtesting, both by the team and by outside players, led to a number of changes and decisions. In the end, a number of technical features were cut to concentrate on the cloud simulation and

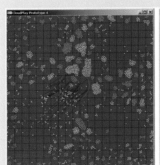

Figure 3   Particle simulation prototypes

the free flight controls. Concepts like wind, a day and night cycle, terrain features linked to cloud state, etc., were all prioritized under the response from playtesters for the need for a satisfyingly dynamic sky and intuitive flight controls.

These decisions are examples of the importance of playcentric design on the design and development process. While a traditional design team might have tried to implement all the features, but with less depth in each, the iterative testing and reevaluation of the design based on overall experience made it clear that players were focused on the feel of the clouds and flight, not necessarily interactive terrain, day and night cycles, wind, or other missing elements.

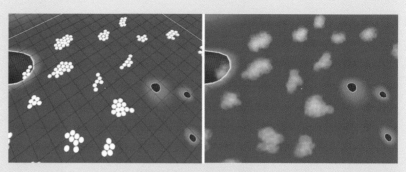

Figure 4   Cloud simulation layer (left) and with rendered clouds overlying simulation (right)

In the end, Cloud proves that even a student research project can provide a strong model for gameplay innovation. Overall, though the design process had fits and starts throughout, and though we were not always certain of success, the methodology of playcentric design, and a clear goal of finding new areas of emotional experience for games, brought this project safely to conclusion. So while risk was high, we had confidence in both the type of innovation we were exploring and the method by which we were doing our exploration.

learn, you can go back later and write the real code much cleaner and faster. The key here is to actually do so—not to take the prototype code and try to make it into the final game code. The takeaways from a prototype should be abstract ideas, like algorithms or gameplay concepts.

One good way to keep yourself from the trap of turning your prototype into the final product is to prototype in another coding language or engine. This way, won't be able to use the prototype code directly. However, there are exceptions to this technique. Many smaller game productions actually do evolve their prototypes directly into their final game code. While not optimal, it is a practical production process for a small team.

Up until now, we have concentrated on a single prototype for your game—the physical prototype. But digital prototyping is often more effective when it is done in small, fast throwaway projects. This is called "rapid prototyping," and it means that you pose a question about some aspect of

your gameplay, come up with a potential solution, and then build a quick and dirty model of that solution so that you can see if your idea will work. As Hecker and Gingold point out, prototypes do not generate ideas; they simply validate good ideas or refute bad ideas. A good rapid prototype makes a testable claim and provides actionable learning about that claim. See Chaim Gingold's sidebar on page 226 for more on his prototyping techniques.

Exercise 8.1: What Do You Need to Prototype?

What concerns do you have about the gameplay, aesthetics, kinesthetics, or technology in your original concept? Of these concerns, which is the highest priority? Which will kill the game if they do not work? Depending on your answer, decide where to focus your efforts for your first digital prototype.

DESIGNING CONTROL SCHEMES

One of the key tasks in designing any digital game is developing good, intuitive controls. Designers often say that three of the most important things you need to determine for a digital game are the three "C's": character, camera, and control. Not all games have characters, but we will discuss both camera and controls here.

When video games were first invented, they were limited in terms of controls. Steve Russell and several other students at MIT programmed Spacewar in 1962, which is often credited as the first digital game, and in doing so, they found the toggle switches built into the front of their DEC PDP-1 to be too cumbersome, so they built their own special controller to go along with the game. Spacewar had only four controls: rotate left, rotate right, thrust, and fire.

8.8   Spacewar on the DEC PDP-1 and custom controller

Controls have come a long way since the 1960s. Today's controls include the keyboard, mouse, joystick, steering wheels, plastic guns, guitars, bongo drums, multitouch screens, motion sensors, data gloves, virtual reality headsets, voice recognition, and more. Recently there has been a great deal of development in alternate controllers, including motion-trackable VR controllers and gesture and voice recognition. Mobile phones and tablets have made multitouch a ubiquitous interface that crosses multiple market segments for games and beyond. These advances in control technology are able to attract new audiences to games, such as players who are interested in the active immersive play of the Oculus, Vive, or Sony PlayStation VR or the simple, intuitive play available on their phones and mobile devices.

As a designer, you need to make sure that you understand the capabilities of the controller for the platform you are designing to. This means creating a kinesthetic prototype and testing the controls until they are perfectly integrated with your gameplay. The sidebar "The Core Mechanic" by designer Eric Zimmerman, available on gamedesignworkshop.com, describes how his team's desire to create an interesting new control idea scheme led to the idea for their game Loop. In this case, they created a digital prototype of the core mechanic—the "looping" control—and tested that thoroughly to make sure it was intuitive and fun before progressing further with the idea.

After you understand the input device, you need to think about how your game can best utilize it. You need to decide this in conjunction with your interface design, which I discuss on page 281. A good way to begin is to look at the list of procedures for your physical prototype. These procedures need to be translated into a set of digital controls. For example, in my first-person shooter prototype, I had procedures for moving forward, backward, turning left, turning right, etc. I also had procedures for firing weapons, changing weapons, etc. Each of these will need to be mapped to a control. If you have a highly detailed set of controls, you will probably wind up grouping them under a menu system or other visual device that can be accessed using a single control or set of controls.

When you have decided how the controls will work, create a control table to make sure you have thought of everything. In one column, list the controls, and in next column, list the game procedure taken when that control is activated. If your game is complex, you might have to make several tables, each representing a specific game state. For the purposes of controls, a new game state exists each time the controls change.

For example, if it is a game where you can drive a car, fly a plane, or ride a bike, there will be three game states. In this case, the designer should try to keep the controls as similar as possible between the three states to avoid confusing the player.

Exercise 8.2: Original Game Controls

Define a control scheme for your original game. For example, if your game is intended for a game console, such as the Xbox, make sure to label every button on the controller. If a button has no function, then label it as non-functional. If the control involves the motion sensors, describe the controller movement for each game action in the button column.

Designing controls, like designing gameplay, is an iterative process. Your first attempt might not be as intuitive as you believed. The only way you will truly know if the controls work is to test them.

Your goal should be to make the controls as effortless as possible. Players do not want to think about the controls when they are immersed in a game. They want the controls to feel intuitive. In this case, less is more. You will find that

8.9   VR and multitouch experiences

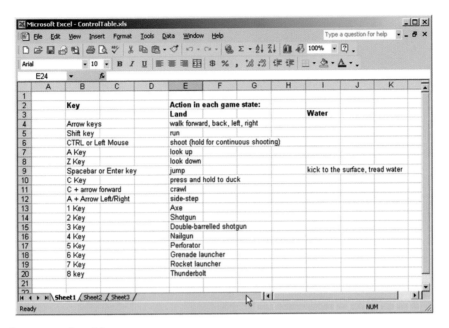

The table in the image contains the following control mapping:

Key	Action in each game state:		
	Land		**Water**
Arrow keys	walk forward, back, left, right		
Shift key	run		
CTRL or Left Mouse	shoot (hold for continuous shooting)		
A Key	look up		
Z Key	look down		
Spacebar or Enter key	jump		kick to the surface, tread water
C Key	press and hold to duck		
C + arrow forward	crawl		
A + Arrow Left/Right	side-step		
1 Key	Axe		
2 Key	Shotgun		
3 Key	Double-barrelled shotgun		
4 Key	Nailgun		
5 Key	Perforator		
6 Key	Grenade launcher		
7 Key	Rocket launcher		
8 key	Thunderbolt		

8.10   Simple control table

adding too many control options frustrates the average user. For expert players, these detailed controls might be desirable, as will custom control schemes, but you will need to do a lot of playtesting to make sure you do not alienate less experienced players.

SELECTING VIEWPOINTS

The interface for a digital game is a combination of the camera viewpoint of the game environment and the visual display of the game status and controls that allow the user to interact with the system. The controls, camera, and interface all work together symbiotically to create the game experience and allow the player to understand and have agency within the system.

As with control systems, the viewpoints for the first video games were limited, and they were mainly comprised of text descriptions of the environment. This does not mean that they were ineffective—just the opposite—anyone who remembers playing an Infocom text adventure probably also remembers the sense of immersion that can come from a well-written story line. Text-based games have experienced a reemergence of interest in in the independent space with the availability of tools like Twine, an open-source tool for creating interactive stories.

However, the majority of digital games today utilize graphical worlds and interfaces, which, while they have evolved in complexity as technology has advanced, remain essentially the same today as they were the first time we looked down on the classic Pong tennis court.

Overhead View

Looking directly down at an object is a somewhat unnatural angle, but affords a clear view of terrain and so can be useful for some types of games, for example, those in the tower

PROTOTYPING FOR GAME FEEL

by Steve Swink

Steve Swink is an independent game designer and author currently working on Scale, an experimental puzzle game. Previously, he worked as lead designer on the Atlantis Remixed project at the Center for Games and Impact at Arizona State University, a series of curriculum replacement games for high school kids. Before that, he was a game and sound designer at Flashbang Studios, working on the Blurst series of games. He got his start as a game designer at Neversoft Entertainment working on Tony Hawk's Underground. Steve wrote "Game Feel: A Game Designer's Guide to Virtual Sensation," published by Morgan Kaufmann.

What is good game feel? Among other things, it might mean that the feel of controlling the game is intrinsically pleasurable. The feel of Super Mario 64 fills me with thoughtless joy, enhancing every aspect of the game. From the first few seconds, I'm hooked, sold, ready to spend endless hours discovering the endless challenges and permutations implied by this tantalizing motion. Every interaction I have with the game will have this base, tactile, kinesthetic pleasure. How was this sensation designed? What's behind the curtain? Wherein does the "magic" of game feel lie?

The problems of game feel quickly become intertwined with the problems of the design as a whole, but it is possible to separate out the relevant components of game feel to make them a bit more manageable:

- *Input*: How the player can express their intent to the system
- *Response*: How the system processes, modifies, and responds to player input in real time
- *Context*: How constraints give spatial meaning to motion
- *Polish*: The impression of physicality created by layering of reactive motion, proactive motion, sounds, and effects, and the synergy between those layers
- *Metaphor*: The ingredient that lends emotional meaning to motion and that provides familiarity to mitigate learning frustration
- *Rules*: Application and tweaking of arbitrary variables that give additional challenge and higher-level meaning to constrained motions

Note: In the interest of brevity, the following discussion focuses on input, response, and context. The concepts of polish, metaphor, and rules are equally important.

Input

Input is the player's organ of expression in the game world, and the potential for expression is deeply affected by the physical properties of the input device. Consider the difference between a button and a computer mouse. A typical button has two states: on or off. It can be in one of two positions, which is about the minimum you can get sensitivity-wise. A mouse, on the other hand, has complete freedom of movement along two axes. It is unbounded; you can move it as far as the surface underneath allows. So an input device can have an inherent amount of sensitivity, what I call "input sensitivity."

An input device can also provide opportunities for natural mappings. That is, what kinds of motion are implied by the constraints, motions, and sensitivity of the input device? My favorite example is Geometry Wars for Xbox 360. Look at Geometry Wars, and then look at the Xbox 360 controller. Notice the way that the joystick is formed and how that transposes almost exactly to the motion in Geometry Wars. It's almost one for one: The joystick sits in a circular plastic housing that constrains its motion in a circular way. That means that pushing the control stick against the edge of the plastic rim that contains it and rolling it back and forth creates these little circles, which is almost exactly the motion that gets produced on-screen by Geometry Wars. This is what Donald Norman would refer to as a "natural mapping." There's no explanation or instruction needed because the position and motion of the input device correlates exactly to the position and motion of the thing being controlled in the game.

The controls of Mario 64 have this property; the rotation of the thumbstick correlates very closely to the rotation of Mario as he turns, twists, and abruptly changes direction.

The overall implication for game feel prototyping is to consider the overall sensitivity of your system and add or remove sensitivity to get a feel that is sufficiently, but not overly, expressive. The sweet spot is difficult to pin down, but it can be achieved with a high- or low-sensitivity input device, depending on how the system responds to a given input.

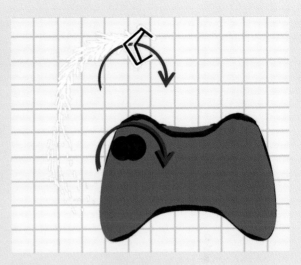

Figure 1   Natural mapping

Response

A very simple input device with very little sensitivity can, by virtue of a nuanced reaction from the game, be part of a very sensitive control system. I call this "reaction sensitivity": sensitivity created by mapping user input to game reaction.

The NES controller was just a collection of buttons, but Mario had great sensitivity across time, across combinations of buttons, and across states. Across time, Mario sped up gradually from rest to his maximum speed and slowed gradually back down again, more commonly known as dampening. In addition, holding down the jump button longer meant a higher jump, another kind of sensitivity across time. Holding down the jump and left directional pad buttons simultaneously resulted in a jump that flowed to the left, providing greater sensitivity by allowing combinations of buttons to have different meanings from pressing those buttons individually. Finally, Mario had different states. That is, pressing left while "on the ground" has a different meaning than pressing left while "in the air." These are contrived distinctions that are designed into the game but that lend greater sensitivity to the system as a whole so long as the player can correctly interpret when the state switch has occurred and respond accordingly.

The result of all these kinds of nuanced reactions to input was a highly fluid motion, especially as compared to a game such as Donkey Kong, in which there was no such sensitivity.

This comparison, between Super Mario Bros. and Donkey Kong, shows very clearly just how much more expressive and fluid Mario's controls are. The interesting thing to note is that Donkey Kong used a joystick, a much more sensitive input than the NES controller. No matter how simple the input, the reaction from a system can always be highly sensitive.

Context

Returning to Mario 64, imagine Mario standing in a field of blank whiteness, with no objects around him. With nothing but a field of blankness, does it matter that Mario can do a long jump, a triple jump, or a wall kick?

If Mario has nothing to interact with, the fact that he has these acrobatic abilities is meaningless. Without a wall, there can be no wall kick. At the most pragmatic level, the placement of objects in the world is just another set of variables against which to balance movement speed, jump height, and the other parameters that define motion. In game feel terms, constraints define sensation. If objects are packed in, spaced tightly relative to the avatar's motion, the game will feel clumsy and oppressive, causing anxiety and

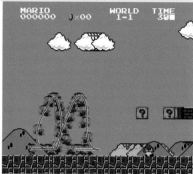

Figure 2   Comparison of character motion in Donkey Kong and Super Mario Bros

frustration. As objects get spaced farther apart, the feel becomes increasingly trivialized, making tuning unimportant and numbing thoughtless joy into thoughtless boredom.

Concurrently to the implementation of your system, you should be developing some kind of spatial context for your motion. You should put in some kind of platforms or enemies, some kind of topology that will give the motion meaning. If Mario is running along with an endless field of blank whiteness beneath him, it will be very difficult to judge how high he should be able to jump. So you need to start putting platforms in there to get a sense of what it will be like to traverse a populated level.

Constraint is also the mother of skill and challenge. Think of a football field: There are these arbitrary constraints around the sides of the football field that limit it to a certain size. If those constraints weren't there, the game of football would have a very different skill set and would arguably be a lot less interesting because you could run as far as you want in one direction before bringing the football back. The skills of football are defined by the constraints that bound it.

Conclusion

There is an aesthetic beauty possible with game feel. That is, something beautiful is created at the intersection of player and game. The act of play can create something aesthetically beautiful, aurally, visually, and/or tactilely.

Before you dive in and start coding, consider the overall sensitivity of the system, the affordances of the input device, and the sensitivity of the response from the game. Concurrently, develop some kind of spatial context for your motion. The idea is to create a "possibility space" that will, through tweaking the variables you've exposed, give rise to the game feel you want, the thoughtless joy that will hook them, engage them, and keep them playing.

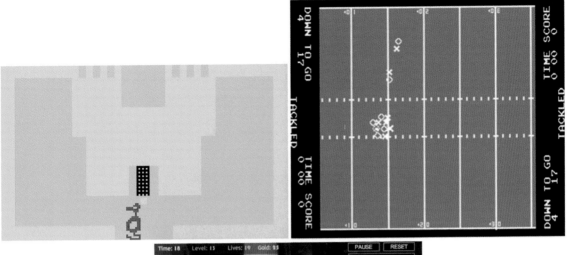

8.11 Overhead views: Atari Adventure and Football, Desktop Tower Defense

defense genre. Early digital games used this viewpoint quite a bit, in everything from sports and adventure games to action puzzles like Pac-Man.

Side View

The side view is popular with arcade and puzzle games like Donkey Kong, Tetris, and Angry Birds, but it probably has had the most influence in the form of the side-scroller or platformer genre. The fact that the player only has to control units in one plane leaves a significant amount of cognitive effort for solving complex puzzles and other forms of play. Indie hit Bit.Trip Runner created a

twist on this by making the player's movement automatic and focusing gameplay on rhythm and response time to obstacles.

Isometric View

Popular in strategy games, construction simulations, and role-playing games, this viewpoint is a 3D space with no linear perspective. It is very good at allowing a "god's eye" view. The distinctive feature of this point of view is the amount of information the player can easily have access to. Games like Myth and WarCraft III use the isometric view in a fully 3D environment, allowing players to move their perspective closer

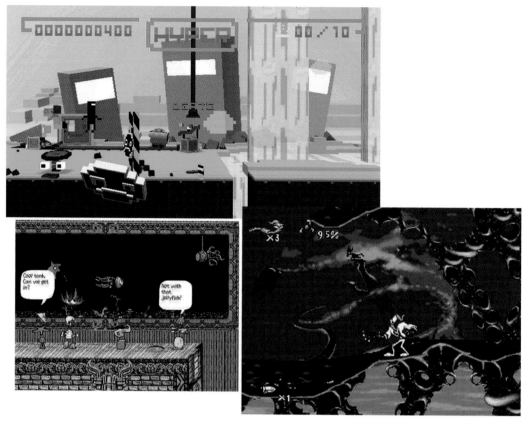

8.12   Side views: Bit.Trip Runner, Castle Infinity and Earthworm Jim

or further away from the action. Many social games, like FarmVille 2, use an isometric view.

First-Person View

This is a perennial favorite among players and developers and is supported by a deep technological infrastructure of game engines and tools that are widely available to all levels of game developers. From a creative standpoint, the first-person view creates immediacy and connection with the main character, literally putting the player in the character's shoes. This view also limits the player's overall knowledge, allowing for dramatic moments of tension and surprise as enemies might lurk around any corner or even approach from the rear.

Third-Person View

Directly related to the side view but in three dimensions, the third-person view generally follows a character closely, but it does not put the player directly inside the character's view. Adventure games, sports games, and other games that depend on a more detailed control of character actions tend to use this viewpoint. Games that use the third person allow for a sense of empathy to develop with our player character that may be greater than that developed through other viewpoints.

These views have become so ingrained in how we think of games that often a designer will choose without stopping to consider several important questions that lie behind all interface

8.13   Isometric views: Myth and Dungeon Siege Dungeon Siege trademark Microsoft Corporation

8.14   First person view: Unreal 2

8.15   Third-person view: Last of Us and Ratchet & Clank

design: What is the purpose of the interface? What is the state of the game, and how much information should the player know about it? These are essential questions that you will want to ask during your digital prototyping process. You may want to consider creating prototypes from alternative viewpoints, and with alternative interface designs, to see how they change the experience of play. In Chapter 5, I discussed the information structure of games—how much and what type of information about the game state was given to each player. The viewpoints I have just described provide degrees of access to the state of the world, as well as placing the player in a varying relationship to the character or other game objects that they must deal with. This makes the choice of interface view both a formal and a dramatic design element.

Should the player feel extremely close to the game character, sharing their sense of movement in addition to their lack of knowledge at times? Or should the player remain close, but somewhat outside of the character, and be able to see more of the environment, perhaps pick up on clues or tools that might not be in the character's direct vision? Perhaps there is no character in your game, or maybe there is no world; in this case, what is the view of the game state that makes the most sense for your design?

Exercise 8.3: Viewpoint

What viewpoint is the best choice for your original game? Why? Describe how this choice affects both the formal and dramatic elements of your game.

EFFECTIVE INTERFACE DESIGN

In addition to the game's viewpoint, you will also want to prototype how information about the game state and options will be communicated to players. This might include points or progress in the game, status of other units, communication with other players, choices that are always open to them, or special opportunities to take action. How will you incorporate this information in or around your main view? The interface to the game, as mentioned previously, works together with the controls and viewpoint to create the game experience, and it needs to be extremely understandable.

Just as with designing controls, your goal should be to make the interface as easy to understand as possible. The ideal interface is fresh and innovative, but it feels like something you have used a thousand times before—a very difficult design problem indeed. The following design techniques are ways of approaching your process that can help your game reflect both original thinking and sensitivity to user expectations.

Form Follows Function

You might have heard the phrase "form follows function." Louis Henri Sullivan, the architect who introduced this phrase to popular culture, was making the statement that the design of an object must come from its purpose. If you are going to build a building, ask yourself about the purpose of the building before you design the doors. If you are going to build a game, ask yourself what the formal elements of the game are before you design its interface or controls. If you do not, you wind up with a game that looks and acts like every other game.

Today many designers simply revert to saying things like, "My game is Call of Duty, but it is set in a maximum security prison, where you have to escape." In most cases, the designer will borrow the interface and control scheme from Call of Duty and then design the content to fit within these parameters, with perhaps a new feature or two thrown in. That is fine, and it might be a fun game, but it is never going to be innovative. The key to avoiding producing nothing but clones of existing games is to go back to your original concept and ask yourself, "What is special about this idea?"

In the prison example, the concept was to escape from prison. The conflict is clear: The prisoner must outsmart the security. Now how can you do this in a new way? What does a prisoner need to do to break out of prison? What types of tools and weapons and obstacles are there? As designer, you should play with how to represent the tension of this particular situation and the excitement of it in both the controls and the interface. Experiment with new ways of visualizing these elements, assign them properties, and allow them to interact with one another. As you can see, the interface is coming from the gameplay, not vice versa.

The best approach is never to design the interface first, but let it evolve from the necessities mandated by the function of the game. In other words, form follows function.

Metaphors

Visual interfaces are, at their roots, metaphorical. They are graphical symbols that help us to navigate the arcane universe that is the computer. You are probably most familiar with the desktop metaphor that both the Microsoft Windows and the Macintosh operating systems share. File folders, documents, in-boxes, and trash cans are all metaphors for various system features and objects. This metaphor has been successful because it helps users contextualize the experience of working with various objects on the computer in a way that is familiar.

When you design your game interface, you need to consider its basic metaphor. What visual metaphor would best communicate all the possible procedures, rules, boundaries, etc., that your game contains? Many games use physical metaphors linked to their overall themes. So, for example, the objects a character can carry in a role-playing game are placed in a backpack. Just like in my discussion of premise in Chapter 4 on page 109, interface metaphors take the dry, statistical facts linked in the computer's memory and display them in a way that fits with the experience of the game.

When creating a metaphor, it is important to keep in mind the "mental model" that players will bring with them to the game. This mental model can either help players to understand your game, or it can cause them to misunderstand it. Mental models include all of the range of ideas and concepts that we associate with a particular context. For example, if I were to make of list of concepts that come to mind when I think about a circus, I might come up with something like this: the ringmaster, the rings, clowns, high wire, barkers, sideshows, animals, popcorn, cotton candy, master of ceremonies, etc.

If I were making a game that used the metaphor of a circus for its interface, I might decide to have the ringmaster be the host or help system. The rings might be different game areas or types, and popcorn and candy might be power-ups. Using this metaphor helps to visualize this information in an entertaining way.

However, if you are not careful, your metaphor can also obscure navigation. Each of the concepts I listed has its own range of associations as well, and sometimes the mental models we bring to a metaphor can cause more confusion than clarity.

Exercise 8.4: Metaphors

Generate a list of potential metaphors for your original game interface. They can be anything: a farm, a road map, a shopping mall, a railroad—you choose. Now free associate on each metaphor for five minutes. List any concepts that come to mind.

Visualization

In the midst of a game, players often need to process many types of quantitative information very quickly. A good way to help them do this is to visualize the information so that a glance will suffice to let them know their general status. We are all familiar with visualization techniques: the gas gauge in your car sweeps in an arc from full to empty, the thermometer bar rises as the temperature goes up. These examples both use cultural expectations to cue us as to what they mean—the arc sweeping left or down means the amount of gas is declining; a rising bar means that something is going up. This is called "natural mapping," and game interfaces can make good use of them.

The Quake interface is actually a classic example of using natural mapping to visualize an aspect of the game state. The face in the center represents my health—when I start the game, the face is angry and snarling but healthy. As my character takes hits, the face becomes bruised and bloody, letting me know my status in a glance.

The avatar interface for a game such as Dance Central 3 is another good example of natural mapping. Many Kinect games, this one included, mirror the player's body movement as part of the interface. In Dance Central 3,

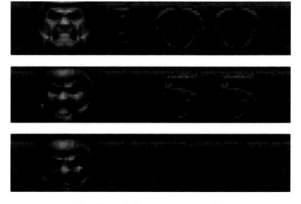

8.16   Quake health meter in three states

the movement is enhanced by animations that make the players feel empowered in their dance abilities.

Exercise 8.5: Natural Mapping

Are there any opportunities to use natural mapping in your original game interface? If so, sketch out these ideas to clarify how the designs might function. You can use these ideas later when you lay out your full interface designs.

Grouping Features

When you organize your desk, you probably sort things into similar groups—all the bills go together, all the business cards together, all the pens and pencils together, etc. Designing an interface requires the same kind of thinking. It is often best to group similar features together visually so that the player always knows where look for them.

If you have several types of health meters, for example, do not put them in different corners of the screen—group them together. If you have several combat features, you can make them more convenient to access by putting them on a single control panel. Or if you have communication features in your game, it will make sense to group these as well.

Exercise 8.6: Grouping

Take a stack of index cards and list one control from your interface on each card. Sort the cards into groups that make sense to you. Try the same exercise with three or four other people. Notice the similarities and differences between each person's decisions. Does this exercise give you any ideas on how best to group your game's controls?

Consistency

Do not move your features from one area to another when changing screens or areas of the game. As Noah Falstein counters in his *Game Developer* magazine column "Better By Design," consistency might be the hobgoblin of small minds, but it is also important in establishing a usable interface.[8] Have you ever played a game in which the exit button moved from the upper right on one screen to the lower right on another? If so, you have experienced the frustration of inconsistency.

Feedback

Letting the player know, through visual or aural feedback, that their action has been accepted is critical. A good designer always provides some sort of feedback for each action the player makes. Feedback systems are something that you will want to incorporate into your digital prototype early to test whether it is actually communicating effectively to players.

Aural feedback is very good for letting the player know that input has been received or that something new is about to happen. Audio designer Michael Sweet discusses aural feedback in his sidebar on page 402. Aural feedback, while very useful for creating a responsive interface, is not usually effective for giving precise data like the exact status of a player's resources or letting the player know where their units are. In this case, you will likely need to come up with a method of visual feedback.

Exercise 8.7: Feedback in Your Game

Determine what types of feedback your game needs to communicate effectively to the player. Decide how best to present this feedback: aurally, visually, tactilely, etc.

PROTOTYPING TOOLS

You might have noticed that this is the first chapter of this book to deal directly with programming your game. That is because I feel that games should be approached first in terms of their experience design, and their technology should provide solutions for that overall experience, rather than driving the design process. It is beyond the scope of this book to teach you how to program, but I highly encourage you to learn at least one programming language—even if you do not plan to be a programmer. Game designers need to be literate in programming concepts so that they can create feasible designs and also so that they can communicate effectively with their technical team members. (Programmers should also be literate in the design process for the same reasons.) Being literate in programming concepts is what is called "procedural literacy." In this context, it means having a good grasp on how computers work, how code is structured, and the general principles behind game programming.

Programming Languages

If you do not have programming skills, I recommend that you take a class in beginning programming; you can usually find classes like this at local community colleges, universities, or even at many high schools You can also find very good classes online at Udemy.com, Coursera.org, or at sites associated with game engines such as learn.Unity.com. If you cannot find a class, there are also many books on the subject. Make sure you use a book that is exercise driven—the best way to learn to code is to do it. Which programming language you learn is up to you. The standard languages for today's PC and console games are C++ and C#. Mobile games range from Objective-C for the iPhone to J2ME to Java or C++/C#. One of the benefits of both C++ and C# is that they are object-oriented languages, which means sections of code

can be reused. This leads to efficiencies during production and is good for creating large-scale applications where dozens of programmers are working on the same project.

However, before you jump into C++ or C#, you may want to get started with something simpler. A good tool for beginners, and especially visual and creative thinkers, is Processing. This open-source programming language is very easy for creative designers to pick up, even if you have no programming background. And, best of all, it is completely free. You can download it at processing.org. There are also great resources for learning how to program in Processing available at that site. I recommend Daniel Shiffman's *Learning Processing* if you are brand new to programming.

Game Engines

Using a game engine to prototype can save you a lot of time and resources. However, it can also push you into design decisions based on what the engine can do, so using a game engine is a trade-off. Some game engines are open source, meaning that if you have the ability, you can go into the engine code and modify it to support your original gameplay ideas. Others only allow you to script game action using the existing features of the engine.

Unity 3D and Unreal Engine offer the most popular game engines for prototyping and also for indie development. These editors allow even beginning developers to create a range of sophisticated gameplay, from 2D to 3D, and to deploy it on varied platforms, including Mac, PC, online, iOS, Android, consoles, and VR systems. They both have free option for students and indies so that you can get started on your game without a big budget for purchasing tools. Once you start making money, you can upgrade to the higher-level subscriptions. If you look carefully at the screenshot of the editor for the Unreal Engine in Figure 8.17, you will notice that it includes the same formal elements found in my first-person shooter prototype – a map grid, rooms, units, objects, etc. In fact, spending time using an editor such as this is a good way to get a feel for a specific genre of game.

Other easy-to-learn game engines include Godot, GameMaker Studio 2, Construct 2, Buidbox, Gamesalad, and RPG Maker. Each of these has its limitations, but they can offer the beginning game designer/programmer a chance to prototype ideas quickly and effectively. Development tools that are not full game engines but are nevertheless very useful for prototyping are Twine and, as I've already mentioned, Processing. And for younger game designers, there are tools and modifiable games like Scratch from MIT, Microsoft's Kodu, Gamestar Mechanic, Minecraft, and Roblox, all of which are game-like or game-based game creation tools for player/designers as young as 9 or 10.

Popular Creation Tools

One good way to learn about digital game making, even if you do not have a background in computer science, is to experiment with creation tools. Creation tools like those associate with Minecraft and Roblox have vibrant communities associated with them, and it is easy and fun to get started making projects with them. Working with tools like these will expose you to the working systems of games and help you understand how to prototype your own ideas. Most creation tools are free, and some even are set up so that you can make money from your published projects.

Figure 8.18 shows a third-party editor for Minecraft. This editor allows you to edit blocks, mods, and players to create new content for the game. The Minecraft community has created hundreds of such tools to support its desire to develop content within the

8.17   Unreal Engine editor (game type: first-person view)

8.18   Minecraft editor

8.19   Roblox Studio: Creator Dashboard

game. And Figure 8.19 shows the Roblox Studio Creator Dashboard, where you can design and publish your own games to the Roblox community. Designing with creation tools like these is a great way to get your feet wet in digital development. Unreal has recently released its editor for Fortnite, making it even easier to get started learning its tools.

Exercise 8.8: Creating a Digital Prototype

Take the question or concern about your original game concept that you generated in Exercise 8.1 and come up with a potential solution for that concern. I advise starting simply, with a question about your controls or interface, for example. Then develop a digital prototype of your solution. Test your idea using the playtesting techniques described in Chapter 9.

CONCLUSION

Now you have worked through your game concept as both a physical prototype and started working through your digital prototyping process. As you continue, you are sure to discover more questions about your design that will lead to new and different ideas that will need prototyping. Playtesting and iterating these concepts is an exciting and creative process. The next several chapters deal with how you take your initial ideas and, through a rigorous playtesting process, develop them into working gameplay that is ready for production.

Designer Perspective: David Perry

CEO, GetCarro.com

David Perry is a game designer, producer, author, and entrepreneur whose long list of credits includes Teenage Mutant Ninja Turtles (1990), The Terminator (1992), Cool Spot (1993), Global Gladiators (1993), Disney's Aladdin (1993), Earthworm Jim (1994), Earthworm Jim 2 (1995), MDK (1997), Sacrifice (2000), Enter the Matrix (2003), and The Matrix: Path of Neo (2005). In 2012, Sony bought Gaikai, a cloud gaming company he co-founded, for $380M, and in 2017, he became the CEO of GetCarro.com to enter the $1+ Trillion eCommerce industry.

On getting into the game industry:

I started getting paid to make games before you could buy games in local stores. Back then, you purchased video game magazines or books filled with games written in a programming language called "BASIC." The reader would have to type the entire game that they wanted to play into their computer by hand. Sometimes it would take them hours, then when they tried to play the game, if they had made one single typo, the game would likely break, and they could spend another hour just looking for their mistake. Interestingly, by seeing the code, you quickly learn how it works. So that's what I did; I wrote tons of games to be printed in magazines and, finally, books. When games were sold in stores, I was offered a job to start making a "real" professional game (in a box), so I left school at 17 (without a degree) and never looked back.

On favorite games:

I like the Battlefield series (multiplayer) and Grand Theft Auto because you feel you can do anything. The world is your oyster. You can choose to play the way the game wants you to, or choose to just have fun and entertain yourself. I think that's a great option for gamers because some want to be entertained *right now*, and some are very creative and quite happy to entertain themselves. I like The Last of Us and Max Payne for their action sequences as you feel immersed in their world and can really get into the action. I like real-time strategy games (starting with Command & Conquer) because I love the chaos of managing lots of things at once. For sports, I like FIFA, as it keeps improving, and for simulation, you can't beat Microsoft Flight Simulator. Flight Simulator. Do I play mobile games? Yes, I've spent thousands of dollars on them.

On inspiration:

I like designers who think big, so I'm always interested to see what people like Rob Pardo, Peter Molyneux, or Hideo Kojima do. They think big right out of the box. You can take it to the bank that whatever they do next will be interesting and challenging.

On the design process:

I tend to find that I get most of my ideas in my car when driving. It usually starts with a hook, meaning something I want to experience in the game I've not seen or experienced before. Some programmers love this, some hate it, because you can be sure I won't propose anything that's easy.

On prototyping:

The "feel" of a game is critical, so fast-path whatever you are doing so you can see how it "feels". Don't continue until it feels great.

On solving a difficult design problem:

I get pitched a lot of games, and the biggest design problem I see is not to be cliché; don't be like everything else out there. I made a book called *David Perry on Game Design* as I found some ways to help people generate completely new game ideas. One area I wish there was more focus is "humor," as even a tiny bit goes a long way. Just imagine Angry Birds with zero humor; it would be "The Catapult Game," with the exact same physics, tossing rocks and knocking things down. That's WAY less interesting than funny bird sounds and feathers flying. I think one of the key things that helped Earthworm Jim was that it supplied some humor when so many competitors didn't.

On taking risks:

Over the last 30 years, I have taken a lot of risks, and luckily, enough of them have paid off. As a result, I've had my share of number-one hits, but I've also had games that, well, cough cough, kinda sucked! Making games is all about learning, and I can assure you that all these years later, I'm still learning new things every single day. I think I am most proud of the fact that I ran a development studio for 12 years and some of that was through pretty difficult times. We had a lot of fun, paid millions in royalties to the teams, and many team members had pretty fantastic career boosts. On the development side, the last game I personally programmed was Earthworm Jim, and I still remember that time very fondly. (Someday I'll get back to programming!)

Advice to designers:

Overall? Passion is key! If you feel interested in getting into the industry, that's not enough. You need to be willing to put everything else aside (including sleep) if you plan to compete in this industry. Play every hit game, even if you don't like it and step outside your body and watch yourself playing. Why are you having fun? Why are you frustrated? Great knowledge to have! Those with the passion will go far; those without will end up frustrated and tired. Is it worth it? Heck yes!

How do you know if you're a designer? Can you SEE the world & situations in your mind and describe them in detail? If yes, then you seem to have the DNA. Good luck!

DESIGNER PERSPECTIVE: ELAN LEE

Creator of Exploding Kittens and Bears vs. Babies

Elan Lee is a game designer and creative entrepreneur whose credits include the groundbreaking alternate reality games The Beast (2001), I Love Bees (2004), and Nine Inch Nails–Year Zero (2007), as well as the breakout hit card game Exploding Kittens. He began his career at Industrial Light and Magic, and co-founded several innovative game companies, including 42 Entertainment and Fourth Wall Studios. Before starting Exploding Kittens, he was chief design officer at Xbox Entertainment Studios.

How did you become a game designer?

Years of hard work and determination, and never losing sight of...kidding! Games were just the thing I did while I should have been studying in school. Wrote tons of mods, designed my own levels, and quickly became obsessed with the kinds of stories a game could tell (and luckily for me, were not currently being told).

I started a series of companies, largely by begging and stealing money from friends to remedy the situation.

On games that have inspired him:

The first game I can remember blowing my mind was Captain Kangaroo's "Picture Pages" when I was around five years old. Don't judge!

The basic notion was to encourage kids to pester their parents into buying a weekly book called "Picture Pages" which was loaded with awesome puzzles, drawings, and stories. Then, on the weekly TV show "Captain Kangaroo," The Captain (I can call him that because we go way back) would draw pictures and solve puzzles in his magical book and it was the SAME BOOK YOU WERE HOLDING IN YOUR HANDS!

It was pure wizardry for me. My parents constantly told me that the people in the TV couldn't actually see me, but here was burning proof in my two little mitts that I knew something they didn't.

Today, when I design games, they always include:

- Breaking the fourth wall
- Empowering the audience to take action
- Instilling a sense of discovery
- Making the real world feel a bit more magical
- Including the audience in the storytelling process

In looking back at those ideas, it seems pretty clear when the seeds were planted.

What exciting developments do you see in the industry?

This would be such an easy question if I only had a name for the thing I want to talk about. Okay so there have been a few big advances in the art of storytelling. Things like the campfire, the western theater, the printing press, the motion picture camera and now...this new thing. What should we call it? The Internet? Social networks? The Globally Connected Temporal Cross-Platform Meta Infrastructure? Yup, that sounds like a winner. Let's go with that. We can call it the GCTC-PMI for short.

Whatever you call it, the fact that we can use it to build games that take us out into the real world, games that move from one screen to another, games that we can play as a team of humans, and games that generally make us all feel like superheroes for doing the things that we're already badasses at, makes me pretty excited to get to wake up in the morning and wear the title "designer."

On a difficult design problem:

One of my majors in college was psychology (the other was computer science, which it turns out is a special combination that upon graduation gets you a call from the nice folks at the CIA asking if you'd be interested in exploring employment opportunities) and one of my most favoritest topics in psych was "reinforcement." Reinforcement is the process of rewarding good behavior or punishing bad behavior and breaks down into a few basic categories:

- Positive Reinforcement—Give the rat a treat every time he pushes the button (makes for very well-trained, but eventually too-fat-to-move rats).
- Negative Reinforcement—Give the rat a giant electric shock every time he doesn't push the button (makes for EXTREMELY well trained rats that spend most of their day cowering in the corner hoping for the sweet release of oblivion).
- Random Schedule Reinforcement—Randomly determine whether or not to give the rat a treat every time he pushes the button (makes for extremely determined rats that are thrilled to spend their days repeatedly pushing the button because they're sure they'll get a treat if they push that button JUST ONE MORE TIME!!)

So that third one really left a mark on me. It's the notion that drives pretty much all of Las Vegas, and if one were to use his/her power for good instead of evil, it could make for some pretty awesome gameplay.

So when I was designing I Love Bees for Halo 2 the pitch basically went, "Okay, we're going to take Chapter 1 of a radio drama, cut it up into little parts and broadcast them out to the audience over ringing payphones! It'll be amazing!"

They bought it, and the first week went pretty well. We posted a massive list of GPS coordinates and hundreds of thousands of players around the world dutifully went out to answer phones and reconstruct the story. They were excited. We were excited. There was much merriment in the world. Then came week number 2.

The plan for week 2 was to do the exact same thing. More GPS, more payphones, and more story goodness. So it turns out that when faced with another wall of GPS coordinates and the daunting task of doing the exact same thing as the previous week, players started grumbling. By the third week of payphones, players started posting things like "Bees Raped my Childhood." Thousands of players signed a petition called "For the love of god, no more payphones!!!" It was at about that time that I could most easily be found curled up in a ball under my desk weeping silently.

But then I remembered the rats from college. The next week, instead of just making pre-recorded phone calls, we put a live actor on one of the phones at random—barking orders, giving challenges, and recording the entire interaction so that the lucky player who answered the randomly assigned payphone would literally get written into the story of Halo. Good old Random Schedule Reinforcement.

The effect was glorious. Answering payphones was transformed overnight from a mundane chore to a coveted community event. Players started dressing up in costumes to answer payphones. They started taking their friends with them to answer payphones. They even started hosting parties around the randomly ringing payphones in their cities.

I Love Bees is commonly referred to as the largest Alternate Reality Game in history, and I have those poor tortured rats to thank. It was a magical moment for me, and one of the most important game design lessons I've ever learned.

Next time, I'll try the electric shock method just to make sure it wasn't a fluke...

FURTHER READING

Arnowitz, Jonathan, Arent, Michael and Berger, Nevin. *Effective Prototyping for Software Makers.* San Francisco: Morgan Kaufmann, 2006.

Dawson, Michael. *Beginning C++ Game Programming.* Boston: Thompson Course Technology, 2004.

Gazaway, Dax. *Introduction to Game Systems Design.* Hoboken: Pearson Education, Inc., 2021.

Gibson Bond, Jeremy. *Introduction to Game Design, Prototyping, and Development: From Concept to Playable Game with Unity™ and C#* (3rd Edition). Hoboken: Pearson Education, Inc., 2021.

Norman, Donald. *Design of Everyday Things.* New York: Doubleday, 1990.

Nystrom, Robert. *Game Programming Patterns.* gameprogrammingpatterns.com, 2014.

Shiffman, Daniel. *Learning Processing.* Burlington Elsevier, 2008.

Tufte, Edward. *Envisioning Information.* Cheshire: Graphics Press, 1990.

END NOTES

1. Todd, Eleanor. "Spore Preproduction through Prototyping" presentation at Game Developers Conference, March 23, 2006.
2. Carless, Simon. "GDC: Prototyping for Indie Developers," Gamasutra.com, March 6, 2007.
3. Lally, John. "Giving Life to Ratchet & Clank: Enabling Complex Character Animations by Streamlining Processes," Gamasutra.com, February 11, 2003.
4. Takahashi, Keita. "The Singular Design of Katamari Damacy." *Game Developer.* December 2004.
5. Stern, Zach. "Creating Osu! Tatakae! Ouendan and Its Recreation As Elite Beat Agents," Joystiq.com, March 8, 2007.
6. Parker, Rowan. "Postmortem: Q-Games' PixelJunk 4AM," Gamasutra.com, April 3, 2013.
7. Hecker, Chris and Gingold, Chaim. "Advanced Prototyping" presentation at Game Developers Conference, March 23, 2006.
8. Falstein, Noah. "Better By Design: The Hobgoblin of Small Minds." *Game Developer.* June 2003.

Chapter 9

Playtesting

Playtesting is the single most important activity a designer engages in, and ironically, it is often the one that designers typically understand the least about. The common misconception is that playtesting is simple—just play the game and gather feedback. In reality, playing the game is only one part of a process that involves selection, recruiting, preparation, controls, and analysis.

Another reason that designers often fail to playtest properly is that there is confusion over its role within the game development process. Playtesting is not when the designer and her team play the game and talk about the features. That is called an internal design review. And playtesting is not having the quality assurance team go through and rigorously test each element of the software for flaws. That is quality assurance testing. And it is not when you have marketing execs sitting behind a two-way mirror watching a representative sample group play and discuss the game while a moderator asks them how much they would pay for this product. That is focus group testing. And it is not when you systematically analyze how users interact with your software by recording their mouse movements, eye movements, navigation patterns, etc. That is instrumented usabilty testing.

So what is playtesting? Playtesting is something that the designer performs throughout the entire design process to gain an insight into how players experience the game. There are numerous ways you can conduct playtesting, some of which are informal and qualitative, and others that tend to be more structured and quantitative. Many development teams combine methods of testing, creating hybrid techniques to help answer questions about how their game is working for players. For Halo 3, for example, Microsoft Game Studios conducted over 3000 hours of playtesting with more than 600 players in one of the most sophisticated playtesting facilities in the world.[1]

User research pioneer Dennis Wixon, whose sidebar on "Metrics in Game Design" is on Page 320, uses the term "quantitative playtest" to refer to a specialized type of testing done at Microsoft in such an instance. In these tests, groups of up to 30 testers played a game for an hour and then filled in a long questionnaire including both quantitative and qualitative questions. This technique was applied to both Microsoft published game and competitive games published by other companies. The tests were generally run within a week of the game's launch. Wixon says, "The intent was to quantify the first hour of experience which we though was

DOI: 10.1201/9781003460268-11

important to understand. It proved very useful to studios who usually had an understanding of who their competitors were. In effect, we could show them data about their competitors strengths and weakness. It was also quite use if a studio was planning multiple releases. We could say, 'here are the strengths and weakness of your previous version'."[2]

Most professional games go through some level of playtesting, if not this extensive, either at their publisher's facilities or with an external testing group. Your game might have 10 or 20 playtesters, possibly playing in your garage. All of these are valuable and important tests that are performed at the level of facility available. But the one thing all of these forms of playtesting have in common is the end goal: gaining useful feedback from players to improve the overall experience of the game.

As you develop the game, other groups will perform other types of tests. The marketing people will try to determine who is going to buy the game and how many units can be sold. The engineering team will utilize the QA department to test for bugs and compatibility problems. The interface designers will employ a variety of tests to see if people can operate the game in the most efficient and user friendly way. If your game is launched online, the distribution team may even test after it is launched to see how it performs and ask for changes based on that testing. But as a designer, your foremost goal while you are developing the game is to make sure it is functioning the way you intended,

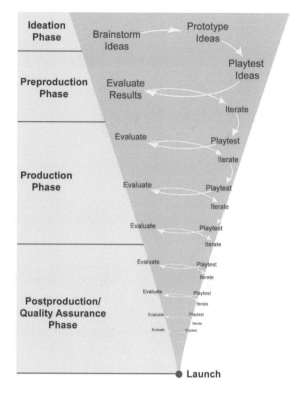

9.1   Model for playcentric game design: prototype, playtest, evaluate, and iterate

which includes meeting your experience goals, and making sure that it is internally complete, balanced, and fun to play. And this is where playtesting comes in.

PLAYTESTING AND ITERATIVE DESIGN

Recall that I said the primary role of the designer is as an advocate for the player. This does not just mean in the early stages of design; the game designer must keep that relationship with the players' needs and perspective throughout the design and production process. Often, as teams work at a project long days and nights for months at a time, they forget the player in their own quest to make the game live up to their vision.

A continual iterative process of playtesting, evaluating, and revising is the way to keep the game from straying during that long arduous process of development. Of course, you cannot keep changing the basic game design—after all, the goal is to release a product eventually. Figure 9.1 shows how the testing cycle gets tighter and tighter as production moves forward, signifying smaller and smaller design issues to solve and changes to make, so that you are not making fundamental or dramatic changes to the game as the process draws to a close. This method of continually testing your assumptions with players will keep your game on track throughout the production.

You might be thinking: But testing is an expensive process, isn't it? Wouldn't it be better to wait until we have a fully working game—say, about the time we have a beta product—and test it then? That way, players will get the best experience. I cannot argue against this way of thinking strongly enough. By that time in the process, it is really too late to make any fundamental changes to your game. If the core gameplay is not fun or interesting at this point, you are stuck with it. You might be able to change some top-level features, but that is it.

I advise playtesting and iterating your design from the very moment you begin. And I can show you how to do it without much expense—just your own time and some volunteers. The expense you will save is the cost of changing your game at the very end of production or releasing a game that does not live up to its full potential.

RECRUITING PLAYTESTERS

Before you can playtest, you must have playtesters. But how do you begin and who should you trust? In the early stages, when you are creating your first prototype, the single best tester you have is yourself.

Self-Testing

As you build a working version of your game, you will naturally try it out repeatedly to understand how it functions. If you are collaborating with other designers on the prototype, you will self-test both as a group and as individuals. Self-testing is most valuable in the foundation stage of a prototype when you are experimenting with fundamental concepts. It is a large part of the process that enables you to design the core mechanics for the system. It is also where you create solutions to glaring problems with the play experience. Your goal at this stage is to make the game work, even if it is only a rough approximation of the final product. You will continue to self-test throughout the life of the project; however, as you progress and your game evolves, you will have to rely more and more on outside testers to gain an accurate understanding of what it is you have created.

One good skill to learn that will make your self-tests more valuable is to try playing with a "beginner's mind." By this I mean clearing your mind, as much as possible, of what you know of the game and playing naively. The term beginner's mind comes from Zen Buddhism, and it means trying to come to each situation you're placed in as if it is the first time you are experiencing it. This may seem difficult at first, but it is something that you can learn to do, and it will serve you well as you self-test your prototypes over many iterations.

Exercise 9.1: Test It Yourself

Take either the digital game prototype that you developed in Exercise 8.8 or the physical prototype you created in Exercise 7.9 and playtest it yourself. Describe in detail what goes through your head as you play the game. Start a playtesting notebook in which you record all of the feedback you get from yourself and other testers.

Playtesting with Confidants

When you move past the foundation stage and the prototype is playable, test it with people you know well, such as friends and colleagues not on the design team. These people will bring fresh eyes to the project and will uncover things you have not considered. You might need to be present to explain the game to them when you begin. This is because the prototype will likely be incomplete in the structure stage. The goal is to get to a version that people can play without much intervention from you. You should be able to give playtesters the prototype, and they should have enough information to begin playing. With a physical prototype, this will require that you write a full set of rules. With a software prototype, the user interface will need to be in place, or you might need to provide some written rules.

When your game is playable and you have a clearly defined set of rules, you must wean yourself from your confidants. Testing with friends and family might feel like it works,

and it does in the early stages, but it won't suffice when the game matures. The reason is that your friends and family have a personal relationship with you, and this obscures their objectivity. You will find that most of them are either too harsh or too forgiving. It all depends on how they are used to interacting with you. Even if you believe that your confidants are providing balanced feedback, it is best not to rely too heavily on a small group of individuals. They will never give you the objective, broad criticism that you require to take your design to the next level.

Exercise 9.2: Test with Confidants

Now take your original prototype and give it to some confidants. Have them test it. Write down your observations as they play. Do your best to determine what they are thinking as they play the game without asking them any leading questions.

9.2   Friends and family playtest for a prototype of Flower at thatgamecompany. Game designer Jenova Chen explains minimal information to get the game started

Playtesting with People You Do Not Know

It is often hard to show your incomplete game to strangers. It means taking criticism from people you have just met. But it is only through the process of inviting total strangers to play your game and criticize it that you will gain the fresh perspective and insight you require to improve your design. This is because outsiders have nothing to lose or gain by telling you honestly how they feel. They are also untainted by any knowledge of the game or personal ties. If you choose them carefully and provide the right environment, you will see that they can be as articulate and dedicated as your coworkers and confidants. There is no substitute for finding good playtesters. Make them an extension of your design process, and the results will become apparent immediately.

Finding the Ideal Playtesters

So how do you find these perfect playtesters who have never heard of you or your game? The solution is to tap into your community. You can recruit playtesters from your local high school, college, sports clubs, social organizations, churches, and computer user groups. The possibilities are endless. You can also find a broad demographic of recruits by posting online or putting an ad in a local paper. The more sources you try, the better your candidate pool will become. It is as simple as putting up a notice on an online server, such as a Discord server, in a, college dorm, library, or recreation center. You will find that people want to be part of the process of creating a game, and if your invitation sounds attractive, you should not have trouble lining up testers.

The next step in recruiting is actually screening out and turning down applicants. You can only do this after you get enough applicants. What you should be looking for is a group of testers who are articulate enough to convey their opinions to you. If they cannot hold a decent conversation in an email or video chat, they probably won't be of much use. I do not expect you to be an expert in demographics or sampling, but it does not hurt to ask a few questions to help sort out which applicants are going to be useful and which are a waste of time. Questions can include: What are your hobbies? Why did you respond to my post? How often do you buy this type of game? If the tester is not a consumer of the type of game you are making, their feedback will be less useful.

Playtesting with Your Target Audience

The ideal playtester is someone who represents your target audience. You want testers who actually go out and spend their hard-earned money to buy games like yours. These people will give you far more relevant feedback than someone who would not be attracted to your game in the first place. They will also be able to compare your game to others they have played and provide you with additional market research. And, most importantly, they know what they like and what they dislike, and they will be able to tell you this in excessive detail. When you tap into your audience, you will uncover a wealth of information and gain an insight into your game that no one else can provide.

Exercise 9.3: Recruiting Playtesters

Now it is time for you to recruit several total strangers to playtest your game prototype. Make sure that they are in your target audience. Set up a time with these playtesters to conduct the test. Exercise 9.4 will help you prepare to get the most from the session.

The more diverse a group you can recruit, the better. By diverse, I mean a broad range of people within your target audience. You want to tap people who play your games, but you do not want to focus on too narrow a section of your total audience. Your pool of testers should represent the entire spectrum of consumers of your product. Posting notices on discussion board for similar games is a great way to recruit testers.

If you are worried about people stealing your ideas, have them sign a nondisclosure agreement (NDA). This is a simple agreement where a person promises not to tell anyone about your product until it is released. In game companies, playtesters are typically paid in cash or free games. With independent games and personal projects, the testers are typically not paid, but they gain the satisfaction of contributing their thoughts.

The level of caution you take is up to you, but remember this: Do not be paranoid. The fact is that 99.99% of the people out there have no intention of stealing your ideas, and even if they did, the vast majority would not know what to do with your game after they stole it. The benefits of using playtesters far outweigh the perils. In fact, the risk of using testers is negligible when compared to what else can go wrong during a production.

For most tests, you will need to recruit new playtesters so that you get fresh input, but later in the design process, you might want to bring some of your most articulate testers back in to gauge how they feel the game has progressed. You might even find that features that you removed or changed do not work as well, and these testers will be able to point that out. Figure 9.3 shows the various stages of prototyping and the types of playtesters you should involve at each stage.

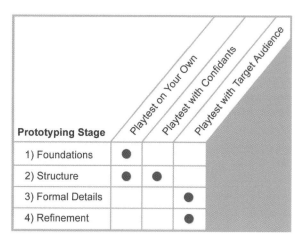

Prototyping Stage	Playtest on Your Own	Playtest with Confidants	Playtest with Target Audience
1) Foundations	●		
2) Structure	●	●	
3) Formal Details			●
4) Refinement			●

9.3   Types of playtesters appropriate for each stage of prototyping

CONDUCTING A PLAYTESTING SESSION

So now that you have all these strangers in your office, living room, or in an online video room, what do you do with them? At this point, many game designers make a common mistake—they begin to tell players about their game, how it works, their plans for future developments, their hopes and dreams for the game. But this defeats much of the purpose of getting a fresh perspective on the game. Once you have told a playtester how the game is supposed to work, you can never go back and see their natural first impression. I tell my game design students to always keep in mind that "you don't come in the box," meaning that when the game goes out to the public, you won't be there to explain it to each and every player.

Your role at this point is not that of the game designer but that of an investigator and observer who must give these playtesters access to the game, lead them through a useful playtest, record what they say and do, and, later, analyze their responses. Rather than telling players what to think about your game or explaining how it works, let them play it with no or minimal explanation. Allow them to make mistakes. See how each person approaches the game. Maybe your rules are confusing. Provide answers if they get really stuck, but for the most part, let your testers figure it out. You will learn much more from the mistakes players make than you will if they play the game flawlessly based on your explanations.

The best way to run a playtest is to have an objective person run the test while you watch from behind a one-way glass or on a video feed. These days, many playtests are held online using tools like Zoom or Discord to share screens and video of the player's reactions. A great way to use tools like these is to shut off your own video during the test so that you can watch, but not influence the player's experience. If you are doing a test by yourself, you might not have the option of having an objective person run the session. The next-best solution to help control your impulse to talk too much is to create a test script. This script will keep you on track and remind you of your role as an observer. Your script should include at least the following sections and

WHY WE PLAY GAMES

by Nicole Lazzaro, President, XEOPlay, Inc.

Nicole Lazzaro is an award-winning interface designer and the leading authority on emotion and the fun of games. Her 17 years of research defined the mechanisms of emotion that drive play and reshaped the fun of over 40 million player experiences including, Myst, the Sims, Diner Dash, and smart pens. She has helped clients such as EA, DICE, Ubisoft, Monolith, Sony, PlayFirst, and Maxis explore new game mechanics and audiences. A frequent speaker, she enjoys sharing her research on why people play. Prior to founding XEODesign in 1992, Nicole earned a degree in cognitive psychology from Stanford University and worked in film.

To take games to the next level of emotional engagement, we at XEODesign wanted to know more about the role that emotions play in games. Since opening our labs in 1992, we have seen gamers get excited, angry, amazed, and even cry. We were curious as to what could be said of all computer games. How many emotions come from gameplay? Are emotions what makes games fun? To find out, we conducted research by watching people's faces as they play.

People play games in four ways. They enjoy the opportunity to master a challenge and to fire their imaginations. Games also offer a ticket to relaxation and an excuse to hang out with friends. Based on our research, each of these playstyles offers the player a distinct set of emotions that come from different ways of interacting with a game. Best-selling games such as Bejeweled, World of Warcraft (WOW), Halo, and Diner Dash tend to offer three out of the four types of fun, and players tend to rotate between these playstyles during a single play session.

We call these playstyles the "4 Fun Keys" (Hard Fun, Easy Fun, Serious Fun, and People Fun) because each is a collection of game mechanics that unlocks a different set of player emotions. Game designers cannot create the experience of play directly; instead they design rules that create the emotional response in the player. Like tasting chocolate or wine, each game has a unique emotion profile. The character of a fine wine comes from the way its flavor profile creates a variety of sensations over time, such as a nose, a head, and a nice long finish. Games are similar, only the emotion profile of games has more dimensions than beverages because the game offers opportunities for a distinct array of emotions based on player choice. In XEODesign's research, players do not want next-generation graphics. What creates next-generation player experiences (PX) is a range of emotions coming from four types of play.

"Games are a series of interesting choices." Sid Meier.

Game designers forget that emotions are more than the prize at the end of a stimulus–response–reward loop. Emotions involve goals and things that people care about and that happen before, during, and after choices. Emotions are not just for entertainment. Emotions around decisions shape the player experience before, during, and after a move in a game.

Emotions play five roles in games. Players **enjoy the sensations** that emotions create. Emotions **focus attention**; a boiling lava pit gets players' attention more than a city sidewalk. They **aid in decision making**; without the aid of emotional systems, people can logically compare the consequences of two options but cannot make the choice itself. For example, in Splinter Cell, the choice between certain death and escape via a narrow window ledge is easier to make than selecting a door in an empty office corridor. Emotions **affect performance**. The negative emotions in Battlefield 2 facilitate the type of repetitive behavior the game rewards: shoot the sniper and move on. The positive emotions from Katamari Damacy inspire creativity and problem solving, helping the player figure out how to roll their little sticky ball from the floor to up on a table. Finally, emotions **reward and motivate learning** because all games teach.

To learn about the most important emotions from play experiences, we observed the emotions that appeared on players' faces as they played their favorite games. Based on the work of psychologist Paul Ekman and others, there are seven emotions you can measure in the face: anger, fear, disgust, happiness, sadness, surprise, and curiosity. There is a reason why games feature boiling lava monsters, dark hallways, spewing blood, and narrow paths along cliffs. Fighting and survival horror games use these techniques to create the first three emotions. The other three facial emotions, including the 30 we have identified that come from gameplay, involve player decisions from other aspects of gameplay.

"I always know how my husband feels about a game. If he screams 'I hate it! I hate it! I hate it!' then I know two things. A) He's going to finish it. B) He's going to buy version two. If he doesn't say these things he will put it down after a couple of hours."

Games provide players with the opportunity for challenge and mastery. One of the most important emotions from games is fiero, an Italian word for the feeling of personal triumph over adversity. Overcoming obstacles, puzzles, levels, and boss monsters helps players feel like they won the Grand Prix. It is a big emotion and ironically requires the player to feel frustrated first. To feel fiero, games get the player so frustrated that they are almost ready to quit and then they succeed. Then there is a huge phase shift in the body. The players go from feeling very frustrated to feeling very good. Unlike films, games provide fiero directly from choices that players make themselves. A film will never hand the audience a Jet Ski to save the world from nuclear doom, but a game has to because in games, player choice matters. For a game to continue to offer fiero from Hard Fun, the difficulty must increase to match player skill. The best games offer options for new strategies rather than simply adding more obstacles in less time. For example, in Diner Dash, the trophy from winning level 4, such as a coffeemaker, changes the strategy for level 5.

"In real life if a cop pulled me over I'd stop and hand over my driver's license. Here I can run away and see what happens."

Beyond challenge, players also enjoy games for exploration, fooling around, and the sheer joy of interaction. Great games engage the imagination as well as the desire to achieve a goal from Hard Fun. Easy Fun is the bubble wrap of game design. Curiosity drives players to drive the track backward in Gotham Racing, put their Sims in the pool and pull out the ladders, and role play. Like improv theater, games offer players opportunities for emotions. In basketball, in addition to the score and making baskets, players enjoy dribbling or doing tricks like a Harlem Globetrotter. In Grand Theft Auto 3, players can drive any car they want, and the game offers other things such as plate glass store windows. The game leaves it to the player to see how the two interact. Games that respond to player choices off the path to a high score offer Easy Fun. For example, in Halo, when the Hard Fun is finished and all the aliens are gone, players enjoy the novelty of running around blowing things up or exploring a surrealistic ring world where the horizon curves up overhead. Players move between the Hard Fun and the Easy Fun of the game to prevent themselves from becoming too frustrated. The designers of Myst believe that the journey is the reward.

"I play after work to blow off frustration at my boss."

In Serious Fun, players play with a purpose. They use the fun of games to change how they think, feel, and behave or to accomplish real work. Through gameplay, players express or create value. People play Dance Dance Revolution to lose weight and Brain Age to make themselves smarter or ward off Alzheimer's. Players blow off workplace frustration, relieve boredom standing in line, and laugh themselves silly. Some choose to play games such as Wii Sports over violent games because it reflects their values. The repetition and collection mechanics in games like Bejeweled create emotions and increase engagement in a visceral way. If, instead of rubies and diamonds, the player matched dirty broken glass and animal droppings, the game would feel very different to play. With Serious Fun, players feel good about the value that the game creates before, during, and after play.

"People are addictive, not the game."

Games offer an excuse for social interaction and forming social bonds. Games that provide opportunities for players to cooperate, compete, and communicate offer People Fun with emotions that come from relationships such as amusement, schadenfreude, and naches (Yiddish for the pride and pleasure experienced when someone you helped succeeds). Massively multiplayer online games (MMOs) such as WOW connect people to compete, cooperate, and share. People playing in the same room express more emotions than those playing in separate rooms. In collocated group play, the game shrinks to the corner, and the whole room becomes the stage for play. Emotions feed off each other as players jostle each other, add content to the game, and outdo each other with witty put-downs. The most common emotion when people play together is amusement. Players laugh even at negative events. The most important emotion between people is love or the feeling of closeness and friendship between players. These social emotions also relate to computer characters, such as virtual pets in Nintendogs and WOW. Diner Dash combines Hard Fun and People Fun because to win, the player must keep restaurant customers happy. Emotions from playing with others are so strong that people play games they don't like, or they play games when they don't like playing games just for the opportunity to spend time with their friends. In subscription MMOs, as with all games strong in People Fun, players come for the content, but they stay for the connection they feel with other players.

To innovate and create more emotion, we must first develop both the language and the tools to design specific emotions around gameplay. A game's core value proposition involves player choice, and choices are impossible without emotion. This makes the design of emotion central to game design. Without emotion, players lack the motivation to play. By planning an emotion profile at the start of game design, a game designer can target specific emotions with different game mechanics. Prototyping and testing these mechanics with players can gauge the success of these decisions. Offering emotions from all four types of fun broadens the opportunity for player emotion in the game, not just in response to a game event; it is equally important to design the flow of emotions before, during, and after play. Games create emotions. By intentionally crafting and heightening emotions in player experiences in the future, games will evoke more emotions than movies.

perhaps several others, depending on the type of test you are doing.

Introduction (2-3 Minutes)

First, welcome the playtesters and thank them for participating. Introduce yourself—your name, occupation, a bit about what you are doing. Then give a brief explanation of the playtesting process and explain how this will help you improve your game. If you are audio- or videotaping the session, let the players know and ask if they have any problems with this. Assure them that this is for your reference only and won't be shown outside the design team. Also, if you are using a special usability room (i.e., with one-way glass), let them know if there are other people watching the test from behind the glass.

Warm-Up Discussion (5 Minutes)

Develop several questions to find out about the games they play that are similar to your game, what they like about them, what their favorites are, etc. Some suggested questions are as follows:

- Tell me about some of the games you play.
- What do you like most about these games?
- Where do you go to play/find out about new games? Why there?
- What was the last game you purchased?

Play Session (15–20 Minutes)

Explain to the playtesters that they will be trying out a game that is still in development. The purpose of the session is to get their feedback on the experience. Make sure they understand that you are testing the game, not their skill. There are no wrong answers, and any difficulties they have in playing the game will help you improve your design.

There are two ways to proceed at this point. One is to leave the playtesters alone with the game and watch them play from behind a one-way glass or on a video feed if you are playing online. The other is to stay in the room and watch quietly from behind the playtesters. In either case, it is important to ask the playtesters to "think out loud" when they are playing. By this, I mean that you want to hear what choices they are making and what uncertainties they have when playing. For example, "I think this is the inventory button, so I'll click it. Oh, I guess it's not. Well then this one must be … hmmmm. Where is it?" You can see that by having a running monologue of what the player is thinking, you will learn a lot more about their expectations than if they were simply sitting quietly and clicking on buttons. If playtesters forget to think out loud—and they often do—you can gently remind them by asking them a question about what they are thinking.

You should let your playtesters play for at least 15–20 minutes while you observe them. If they play longer than this, they tend to get tired. If the testers have a tremendous amount of difficulty, you can give them help to move the session forward, but be sure to put in your notes where and why the problem occurred.

Discussion of Game Experience (15–20 Minutes)

After about 20 minutes, hopefully at the end of one or more levels, you will want to wrap up the play session and have a one-on-one discussion with the testers. You will want to develop a set of questions for this discussion that probe for overall appeal, interest level, and challenge level, and that check for understanding of game features. Some example questions are as follows:

- Overall, what were your thoughts about the game?
- What were your thoughts about the game mechanics?
- How did you feel about learning to play the game?
- What is the objective of the game?
- How would you describe this game to someone who has never played it before?
- Now that you have had a chance to play the game, is there any information that would have been useful to you before starting?
- Is there anything that you did not like about the game? If so, what?
- Was anything confusing? Please take me through what you found to be confusing.
- Would you recommend this game to others? Why or why not?

As your design process goes on, you will have more specific questions in this section regarding difficulty, progression of levels, look and feel, sound effects, music, tone, characters, etc. This discussion should focus on the most important design questions you have at this point in the process.

Wrap-Up

Thank the playtesters for coming in. Make sure you keep their contact information so you can let them know when the game is finished. If you have a token gift, like a T-shirt for your game, you can give it to them now.

Exercise 9.4: Writing a Playtest Script

Write a script for the playtest session you set up in Exercise 9.3. Be sure to address areas of your game design that you have questions about. Do not lead or suggest ideas to the playtesters.

The most difficult part about this process will be learning to listen to the playtesters' feedback without responding to every point. You, as the designer, invariably feel a strong attachment to whatever it is you have created. You have spent a lot of time and effort on your game and it is only natural to become defensive. I advise you to try to ignore your ego. If you are going to gain anything from a playtesting session, you have to learn to take feedback without emotional response. Do not answer criticisms, just write them down. Learn to listen carefully to what players are saying. Keep in mind that your goal is not to have these people tell you that they love the game but to discover what they do not like about it or do not understand. Far too many designers fail to learn to listen to criticism. They try to either answer any negative comments or make excuses for their game because taking the criticism is too painful.

If you refuse to take feedback, or if you lead your testers into saying what you want to hear, you will find that they will gladly fall in line. You invited them to play your game, and they do not want to upset you. They want to please you. And if you let them, they will tell you whatever it is that you want to hear. If you are determined to hear only good news, then that is what you will

9.4   Leading a playtest session, view from behind one-way glass

9.5   Playtesting sessions for physical prototypes: designers Matt Kassan and Richard Wyckoff give student designers feedback on their designs

get. It might make you feel like a genius, but it won't make your game any better. Instead, try to embrace the criticism you receive from your playtesters. Even if you feel awful remind yourself that you need to hear the problems because you cannot fix them if you do not know what they are. And it is better to hear the bad news now than later from a game critic. Do not let this chance slip past.

There are times when the criticism can get a bit heavy. If you are testing in a group, one tester might be particularly vocal and begin to sway the others. Many professional usability facilities isolate playtesters for this very reason. However, you might not have that luxury. It helps to make it clear at the beginning of the session that you are open to feedback and want everyone to be honest, but at the same time, there is a certain etiquette you would like the

testers to follow. Everyone should respect each other's opinions and allow each other a chance to speak. There is no right or wrong answer, and no tester should ever criticize another tester's ideas. If you lay down some good rules for the discussion at the outset, you should avoid most problems.

Most people want to be helpful, after all: that's why they volunteered. Before you take offense at the comments of a playtester, be sure to look in yourself for the answer. Are you being too sensitive? Is the criticism truly harmful, or is this person unaccustomed to giving feedback? How are the other testers reacting to this person? It's true that one bad seed can skew results, casting a negative spin on everything, but do not jump to conclusions. Your ultimate goal is to take what you are given and learn from it, not silence anyone who says something that you do not like.

9.6   Playtesting sessions for digital prototypes

You will make mistakes at first, but leading an effective playtest is a skill you should practice over and over. Becoming a good listener and maintaining objectivity when taking criticism is something that will help you throughout your career. The same skills can be applied to your production environment. In addition to playtesters, you need your team's input and constructive criticism, and the best way to elicit this is to make your entire production a safe environment where everyone is encouraged to speak their mind while being careful not to personally criticize each other. If you apply the same rules described earlier to all of your group meetings, you will wind up with a far more productive and motivated team that feels invested in the product you are creating together.

Exercise 9.5: Playtesting Your Prototype

Conduct the playtesting you set up in Exercise 9.3. Use the playtesting script you wrote in Exercise 9.4 to keep the session on track. Take notes in your playtesting notebook from Exercise 9.1 recording feedback and problems.

METHODS OF PLAYTESTING

Most professional play testing takes place individually. It is a generally accepted rule that group dynamics are good for generating ideas but very bad for evaluating ideas. On the other hand, you might have no choice, depending on the nature of your prototype and environment, so do not feel like you cannot playtest just because you do not have the perfect setup.

Here are a number of different ways you can structure your tests, each with their own positives and negatives, but one or more should work for the environment you have available.

How Feedback from Typical Gamers Can Help Avoid Disappointing Outcomes

by Bill Fulton, Director of Online Services, Insomniac Games (a Sony Interactive Entertainment studio)

Bill Fulton is one of the pioneers of User Research in the games industry. He founded the User Research Group at Microsoft Game Studios in 1997 and led it until 2004 when he moved into game design. In 2008, he founded a game UX consultancy (RoninUX) that spread Games User Research throughout the games industry (his clients included Sony, EA, Disney, Wargaming, and Insomniac Games, among others). He also co-founded the Games User Research Special Interest Group of the IGDA, which now hosts yearly conferences for its 3500+ members. To learn more about games user research, see: https://grux.org.

The Problem

Compared to the giddy expectations of the developers at the kick-off of a project, most games are disappointing: commercially, critically, or both. After all, few people set out to spend that much time and money to produce a game resulting in ambivalent reviews and low sales. Solving this problem is one of the holy grails of game development because it would remove substantial risk from making games.

The Traditional Analysis of This Problem and the Solution

Why does this disappointment happen? The traditional analysis of the problem is that teams are too close to their game to see it objectively, much the way that many parents seem to believe their child is above average. Because of this analysis, myriad ways to get feedback from fellow game development professionals (coworkers, publishers, journalists, playtest teams, etc.) have sprung up. While the traditional analysis has some merit, and the solution to combat the problem is quite useful, it doesn't seem to explain (or fix) the whole problem. Most games still fail to find critical or commercial success.

An Alternative Analysis and Solution

An alternative analysis for why games don't live up to the expectations of the developer is that professional game developers aren't like the people for whom they are designing the game: typical gamers. Game developers are so knowledgeable about games and game development that they have a hard time designing for the typical gamer who knows comparatively little about games (see Figure 1 for an illustration).

This situation of game developers being very unlike typical gamers suggests that when the game is fun for the developers, it might not (yet) be fun for typical gamers, who might find it too hard or might not find the fun that is in the game. This is similar to the way that modern art is often unappreciated by anyone without a degree in art history. But to make games for the masses, it is the responsibility of the game developer to show typical gamers how to have fun with the game.

Many publishers and developers have come to see the problem this way, and they have engaged marketing research firms to do focus tests on the game to combat this problem. But often the goal of the focus test is to learn how to sell the game, not how to make the game more fun and accessible for more players. Furthermore, focus tests are often done too late in development to make many changes to the game. Because of the constraint of schedule and emphasis on selling as opposed to improving the game and time, many game developers are mixed about focus testing.

User Testing from an HCI Perspective

Getting feedback from consumers for the purpose of improving products is a major goal of the field of usability, a subset

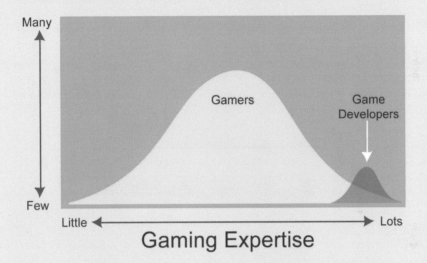

Figure 1

Gaming expertise: a comparison of hypothetical distributions of gaming expertise for typical gamers and typical game developers. This figure illustrates how all game developers know more about games than all but the most dedicated gamers. The point of this figure is to show how game developers can't simply make games that are only accessible to people like themselves if they want to make a game that the majority of gamers can understand and enjoy.

of the human–computer interaction (HCI) field. Most major software companies have usability departments staffed with HCI professionals. The games industry has been slow to adopt this practice.

This is changing; the use of HCI professionals in game development is gaining greater acceptance. One major game publisher has been doing some form of usability work on games since 1998, but other game publishers and developers are beginning to employ usability professionals as a way to make their games more fun. As more game developers and publishers do usability testing on their games in development, the typical quality of games from those developers and publishers will only get better.

An Example of User Testing from Age of Empires 2: Age of Kings

Age of Empires 2 (AoE2) is an excellent example of how user testing from an HCI perspective can improve games. The first AoE game was both a critical and commercial hit. In fact, it sold so well that the only way the sequel (AoE2) could sell any better would be if it expanded beyond the kinds of gamers who played the first AoE.

The developers and publisher decided to aim for the stars and make the game accessible to nongamers. AoE2 would be a game that someone who had never played a computer game would be able to pick up and play. This was a lofty goal because AoE2 is a complicated game, and nongamers lack the background to learn the game on their own. We also knew from testing that the first AoE was a difficult game to learn for some experienced gamers.

To achieve this level of accessibility, it would be necessary to provide a robust tutorial and do a great deal of user testing. The details of the testing are better described in a different article, but the following anecdote from the final test of the tutorial gives a bit of flavor.

The final test of the tutorial was done on a Saturday at 10 a.m. At 9 a.m., I noticed an elderly lady (maybe in her 70s or 80s) waiting outside the building. I thought she was lost or looking for someone, but it turned out that she had been scheduled for the test. I was surprised, but she technically fit the kind of people we were looking for (never played a retail computer game, could operate a computer, was older than 40), so I let her in. I apologized for her being given the wrong time for the test, but she told me that she was told 10 a.m. was the time, "but always showed up an hour early for appointments."

I was a little concerned that she might be put off by the nature of the game (build a nation, raise an army, destroy your neighbors), and offered that she could leave if she wanted to. But she thought the idea of testing a game was "interesting" because her grandkids played them, and she wanted to be helpful. So we let her go through the test like all the other middle-aged folks. It was a bizarre sight to see dozens of parent and grandparent types playing Age of Empires 2 in the lab.

After they had completed the tutorial, they were instructed to play a random map game against the computer. Toward the end of the test, I went by the elderly lady and saw that she had the semblance of a nation going—she had several villagers collecting all four resources, and she had many of the right buildings built (barracks, granary, mining, etc.). When the Mongol hordes came over the hill and invaded her nation, she did several things right—she hid her villagers and started to build a (woefully inadequate) army. Unfortunately, she was too slow and got overrun; Age of Empires 2 had just crushed grandmother's nation. When I escorted her from the lab, I asked her what she thought. She said she could see how her grandkids would like it, but the game wasn't her "cup of tea."

While the grandmother didn't enjoy the game, after completing the tutorial she was able to understand the basics of the game and responded reasonably to being attacked. This was a dramatic improvement over the original AoE, where sometimes even experienced gamers got stuck and couldn't figure out the game without going to the manual. The reliance on testing AoE2's tutorial with real people, not just paid game industry professionals, resulted in a game that almost anyone can pick up and play.

In the end, AoE2 sold dramatically more units than did the first version, in large part due to improvements to the game that stemmed from doing user testing throughout the development of the game.

9.7 More playtesting sessions for physical prototypes: Steve Ackrich, head of production at Activision and gaming analyst Neal Robison give student designers feedback on their designs

- *One-on-one testing:* As described in the previous test script, you sit down with individuals and watch over their shoulders, from behind a one-way glass, or online using a screen-sharing tool like Zoom or Discord, as they play the game. You take notes and ask them questions both before and after the session.

- *Group testing:* You get a group of people and allow them to play your game together. This works best for physical prototypes, but it is also useful for digital prototypes if you have access to a lab with several computers. You observe the group and ask questions as they play.

- *Feedback forms:* You give each person who tests your game a standard list of questions to answer after playing and then compare the results. This is a very good method for getting quantitative feedback. Professional testing facilities, like Microsoft Game Studios,

use digital forms that feed into a database of user responses and allow them to generate reports for analyzing the data. You can do this too, if you like, using online tools such as SurveyMonkey.com, Qualtrics, or even a Google survey.

- *Interview:* You sit down face to face with the playtesters and give them an in-depth oral interview after the playtesting session. This is not a discussion; it is more of a verbal quiz.

- *Open discussion:* You conduct either a one-on-one discussion or a group discussion after a round of playtesting and take notes. You can either promote a freeform discussion or have a more structured approach where you guide the conversation and introduce specific questions.

- *Metrics:* As playtesting becomes integrated into the design process as well as the post-launch process of online games, new tools and techniques are being developed for gathering information about how players engage with games. At Zynga, for example, metrics are collected on all game sessions. This data is then analyzed to show what features players are using and those they are not. This information is then used to tune games and add and subtract features. Dealing with metrics might be beyond your level of expertise, but it is good to know about such techniques because they will undoubtedly be an important part of your experience as you become a professional game designer.

You can combine the previous approaches to fit your game and your space. For example, you can have players play a game together and have a group discussion afterward, but before the discussion ask each person to fill out a feedback form individually. You will be surprised how differently people respond between the individual form and the group dynamic.

Over time, you will find out which methods work best for you at each stage of testing. My goal is to encourage you to test no matter what

A Primer for Playtesting: Don't Follow These Rules!

by Nathalie Pozzi and Eric Zimmerman

Nathalie Pozzi is an architect, whose projects cross the boundaries of architecture, installation, and art, exploring the critical intersection of space, light, material, and culture. Eric Zimmerman is a game designer and a 20-year veteran of the game industry. He co-founded Gamelab, an award-winning NYC-based studio and is the co-author with Katie Salen of Rules of Play. Currently, he is a professor at NYU Game Center. Nathalie and Eric's game collaborations have produced playable installations that have appeared in Paris, Berlin, Dublin, Moscow, Los Angeles, and at the Museum of Modern Art in New York City.

During our 2012 residency at the University of the Arts Berlin, we spent the summer with Graduate Fellows playtesting projects from theater, architecture, sound installation, games, philosophy, and more. This essay outlines the playtesting methodology we used by suggesting possible "rules" for structuring your own playtests.

What is Playtesting?

Playtesting is a methodology borrowed from game design where unfinished projects are tested on an audience. A playtest happens when people come together to try out a work in progress. The next steps for changing the project are based on the results of the playtest.

Playtesting is also an attitude towards the creative process, an approach that emphasizes problem-solving through iteration and collaboration with members of your audience.

When is Playtesting Useful?

Playtesting can help develop any kind of work that involves interaction between a created experience and a participatory audience. Although many of the ideas of playtesting come from game design, they can be applied in any field.

What Does Playtesting Look Like?

Playtesting can look like any number of things. At the University of the Arts, we met as a group on a regular basis and shared works in progress. We would spend about 30–60 minutes interacting with and discussing one project—perhaps in a studio space, perhaps outdoors in a park or on the street—and then move on to the next.

Isn't Playtesting the Same as User Testing/Editing/Rehearsal/Critique?

Yes and no. Playtesting is not discipline-specific and versions of it can be found in many practices. The style of playtesting we outline here comes from game design and is particularly relevant for projects that involve direct audience interaction.

THE "RULES"

.....before you playtest

A. Playtest before You Think You Are Ready

You always playtest a work in progress, not a finished design. That means you should playtest as early as you possibly can—usually much earlier than you think you should. It is much much better to playtest your ugly prototype than to wait and playtest a more polished project. A playtest is not a presentation. If you feel ready and comfortable to present and playtest your design, you have waited too long—it is probably too late to make substantial changes. Train yourself to overcome your discomfort and playtest as early in the process as you possibly can.

Is it too early for you to playtest? If the answer is yes, then playtest anyway.

B. Strategize for Early Playtesting

Figure out how to create a working prototype far in advance of any final deadline. This is often a question of tactical implementation. Can you make a paper prototype of a digital project? Can you scale down a work meant for 100 participants to something you can playtest with a dozen? Rather than plan your entire project in advance, focus instead on what is needed to enable the next playtest.

Simplify your project so that you can playtest today.

C. Know Why You Are Playtesting

Enter into every playtest with a concrete idea about what you want to learn and what questions you hope the playtest will answer. Narrowing what you want the playtest to investigate can help you simplify your project and playtest sooner. Generating research questions in advance will also help you structure the playtest itself. If you are doing things right, your playtest will raise issues and questions that you did not anticipate. However, you should still go into every playtest with a clear agenda.

What is the one key question that you want your playtest to answer?

D. Prepare Variations

Go into a playtest with different versions of your project to try out. This allows you to make the most out of the playtest session, and it also helps you to improvise and try out new ideas during the playtest. Variations might mean different sets of game rules to play, software settings to cycle through, or contexts for a performance. Variations give you options if something breaks down, and they let you do comparisons to see which variation works best. One tip: change as little as possible each time (only one element) so that you can understand better the exact effects of your change.

What can you change to try out different variations of your project?

E. Be Grateful to Your Playtesters

Whoever is playtesting your project is doing you a big favor. They are donating their time and attention for the sole purpose of helping you with your unfinished project. Playtesting is hard. But no matter how much stress and uncertainty you might have about the project, try to maintain a feeling of gratitude toward your playtesters. Be happy they are there and be sure to let them know how thankful you are for their time.

Take a deep breath and say thanks.

F.   Design the Learning Experience

Remember to design the way that people will learn about your project. If you are creating a complicated interactive system, the experience of learning how to understand and interact with the system is an important part of the overall design problem.

Does your playtest address the learning process?

G.   Blame Yourself, Not Your Playtesters

Remember to warn your playtesters that they will be interacting with an unfinished, rough version of what will at some later point be a smoother experience. Be sure to tell them that if they are frustrated or confused, it is not their fault—it is your fault for not designing a better experience for them. It's okay for them to be confused—after all, the most valuable part of the playtest is not what they do understand, but what they don't.

Never make your playtesters feel foolish.

H.   Know Your Testers

What do you need to know about your playtesters before the playtest begins? If you are meeting them for the first time or don't know them very well, talk with each person and take notes that will help put their reaction to your project in context. Playtesters come in many varieties. For example, the learning curve of a hardcore gamer is very different than someone without deep experience in a particular game genre.

Do you know who your playtesters are?

I.   Don't Explain

Put the project ahead of the theory. Resist the temptation to explain the ideas and intentions behind your project to your playtesters. Instead, let them interact with the LEAST possible explanation from you in advance. By explaining your ideas beforehand, you are ruining the chance to see the authentic reactions that your project provokes. It is hard to hold back and not explain. But by forcing your project to carry your ideas (rather than your explanation), you are challenging your work to be better.

Is it possible not to say anything before the playtest starts?

J.   Take Notes

In game design, we often prepare a sheet of paper for each playtester, with questions written out and room to take notes. The notes page is structured to facilitate what you need to know BEFORE, DURING, and AFTER each playtest. During a discussion, taking notes will help to elicit better feedback—if your testers see you taking notes, they will be more likely to give you detailed and thoughtful answers.

Prepare a notes sheet and use it. It is worth the extra effort.

....during a playtest

K.   Be Selfish

The purpose of your playtest is not for your playtesters to have fun. It is for you to learn what does and does not work about your project. If you try too hard to give playtesters a good time, you will lose the opportunity to get the hard truth from them. Don't be afraid to show your playtesters something broken and half-finished. That is, in fact, the entire premise of the playtest.

Don't worry about being entertaining.

L.   Encourage Your Playtesters to Talk Aloud

If it is possible for your project, ask your playtesters to talk out loud about their thoughts and feelings as they interact with your work. A "think-aloud" playtester can give you valuable insight into how they are perceiving and interpreting the details of your project. Let your playtesters tell you why they are doing what they are doing and what they think is happening as a result. This may require that you periodically remind them to vocalize.

Don't be shy about reminding your playtesters to think aloud.

M.   Notice Everything

Prepare on your notes sheet the categories of the main things you want to observe, such as when players seemed frustrated, what makes them laugh, or how many times they tried and failed before they gave up. Keep track of how long it took to run the playtest, which variations your testers preferred, and any other important information. Try to take notes on everything that you can—otherwise, you will be at the mercy of your selective memory, which will cast everything in the best possible light.

Are you noticing everything—or just what you want to see?

N.   Shut Up

While you are observing the playtest, say as little as possible. You will feel an overwhelming urge to help out your playtesters, to tell them what to do and what they are doing wrong. But you must do everything you can not to interfere. Their mistakes and misunderstandings are extremely useful: You must let them explore the project on their own. If they are completely confused, step in and assist them, but in general, you should do everything you can to shut up. If you tell them what to do, you lose the main purpose of the playtest, which is to see how OTHER people react to your project. Learning to shut up during a playtest requires discipline.

Can you shut up—not a just little, but really, completely, shut up?

O.   See the Big Picture

As your playtesters interact with your project, remember not just to focus on the workings of your designed system. Try to see the human element at play. What are the emotional responses of your playtesters, what is their body language, how are they interacting with each other? Seeing the bigger picture can help you understand when your audience is engaged and when they are bored. It is easy to focus too much on what you designed, rather than on the effect it is having.

Stay focused on the impact of the project, not just the project itself.

P.   Don't Be Afraid of Data

One way to get objective about your playtest is to record data and put it in a spreadsheet. Every project has data to collect: At what moments did everyone fall silent? How many steps did each participant take as they walked through the space? If you are working in software, the program can record important user input, such as time spent in different areas of the experience. Otherwise, just remember to record the data in your notes. Too much data can be overwhelming to interpret, but tracking the right data can be incredibly valuable.

What is the data that will answer your key questions?

Q.   Answer a Question with a Question

When playtesters ask you how something works, or what something means, it is probably because they are confused. Rather than explain it to them, you can answer their inquiry with a question of your own. Don't tell them what the blue button does—instead, ask them what they think it does, or even better, what they think it SHOULD do. It's more important to get them to speculate about your project than for you to explain it to them. Their opinions are more valuable than yours.

Every time a playtester asks you something, ask them something back.

R.   Hunger for Failure

One of the attitudes that helps with playtesting is to yearn for your project to fail. Of course, we all want successful results, but unsuccessful moments are much more useful. If you are only looking for the successes, you will remember the smiles and laughter and think that your project is in perfect shape (we call this the "happy face syndrome"). But you need to cultivate a desperate hunger to focus on what is not working properly. Otherwise, your project will never get better.

Are you enjoying the successful moments too much and ignoring the failures?

....after a playtest

S.   Discuss What Happened

After the playtest, talk about the experience with your playtesters. Use your notes sheet to structure the conversation. Begin with very specific questions, such as what was most difficult for them to understand about the project, or why they reacted to a particular aspect of the design. Finish with more general questions, such as what they liked best about the experience or what they would change to make it better.

The more concrete your questions, the more useful answers you will get.

T.   Put Feedback into Context

It can be useful to distinguish between expert and nonexpert testers. Experts are familiar with what it means to make a project like yours. Nonexperts aren't. When getting critical feedback from nonexperts, remember that they are the patient and you are the doctor—you can take their suggestions as symptoms of what is and isn't working in the project, rather than as directions for the next steps in your design. If someone tells you to tear down a room and make it bigger, they are really telling you that it feels small. Rather than take their advice, perhaps just rearrange the furniture. Don't expect your players to understand all of the ramifications of every suggestion they make.

Ask for feedback, but don't take suggestions literally.

U.   Collaborate with Your Playtesters

One of the most thrilling moments of playtesting is collaborating with your playtesters—brainstorming with them, trying out their ideas, and seeing how the changes affect your project. Plan your playtest session so that you have time to experiment with new ideas as they emerge through the playtesting itself. They are seeing the project with fresh eyes and so their ideas are often better than yours.

Embrace shared authorship with your playtesters.

V. The Cruelly Honest Playtest

Playtests represent moments of truth—when your brilliant ideas may all come crashing down. Playtests are truthful because they are a safe place to simulate your final context. When your project is completed, you probably won't be there to explain away all of the problems and defend your intentions. In a playtest, you get to cruelly see whether your ideas actually work in practice. Part of the playtest attitude is building up your pain tolerance and coming to enjoy the hard truth of the playtest.

Face the truth of your playtest, even if it hurts.

W. Embrace the Unexpected

Never forget that play is half of playtest. Being playful means being open to unexpected, happy accidents. Let go of the way you want your work to be used or interpreted. Be open to the strange new things people do with your project. Accidents are for those who are ready to take advantage of them.

If things don't go as planned, you may be on to something better.

X. The Playtest's the Thing

The playtesting process is as important as the actual project you are making. If you can manage to get the process right, then you will find that the problems in your project begin to solve themselves.

Forget what you are making. Focus on how you make it.

Y and Z. Break These Rules

There is no single magic solution that will solve every problem you encounter. So you need to create the process that works for you. Don't follow these "rules." They are not meant to be followed—they are meant to be twisted, modified, broken, and refashioned into something new. The best playtest is the one you invent yourself.

your limitations are. If none of the structures on my list work for you, then think creatively and come up with your own methods. Try some of these different processes if you can. You will see how each method produces different results, and you will broaden your testing techniques and experience.

THE PLAY MATRIX

One valuable playtesting tool you can use is the play matrix. I developed the play matrix to help playtesters and students give context to their discussions about game systems.

The horizontal axis of the play matrix is a continuum between skill and chance. The vertical axis is a continuum between mental calculation and physical dexterity. I chose these two continua because they are core aspects of interactive experiences, and all games can be plotted along them. Think about the game of chess. It is a game of pure strategy, a type of skill. There is absolutely no chance involved. So on the skill versus chance continuum, it would be plotted to the far left. It is also a game of pure mental calculation. There is no physical dexterity required to play the game. So on the mental calculation versus physical dexterity continuum, it is plotted at the very top. When chess is plotted on both of these dimensions at the same time, it appears in the top left corner.

Now let's think about the game of blackjack. It involves chance, but the outcome is not determined purely by chance. It therefore falls somewhere to the right of center on the continuum. No dexterity is required to play, so it plots at the top of the mental calculation versus physical dexterity line.

Exercise 9.6: The Play Matrix

Now it is your turn to use the play matrix. Plot a popular type of video game, such as The Last of Us, Call of Duty, or Ridiculous Fishing, on the play matrix. Compare this to a game like Twister or Pin the Tail on the Donkey. Now try plotting a board game like Monopoly, Risk, or Clue. Describe the differences and similarities between the three types of games. What does the play matrix show you?

The play matrix is not an absolute system that produces the same results every time. Different people might have different opinions on where games plot, which is okay. Everyone's opinion has value. It is best to use the play matrix as a tool for stimulating discussion and analyzing gameplay. The goal is to get your playtesters to think about the game and verbalize their feelings.

Figure 9.9 shows the play matrix with several games plotted in each quadrant. Can you see patterns in the types of games that fall in different quadrants? Many popular video games fall in the lower left (physical + skill). Many popular board games and turn-based video games fall in the upper left (mental + skill), many gambling games fall in the upper right (mental + chance), and many games for very young children fall in the lower right (physical + chance).

Exercise 9.7: Plotting Your Favorite Games

Take five of your favorite games and plot them on the play matrix. Describe what pattern you see. What does this tell you about yourself?

When conducting a playtesting session, it is sometimes helpful to ask your testers to plot your game on the matrix. Then follow by asking them these questions: (1) Is the outcome of the game determined more by chance or by the skills of the players? (2) Is the outcome determined more by mental skill or physical dexterity? Ask playtesters if they would move the game more toward one quadrant or another; what would they prefer? Different audiences often gravitate toward one quadrant of gameplay even if they enjoy different genres. For example, players who enjoy strategy games from the upper left corner might also gravitate toward other mental + skill-based play, such as trivia or puzzles. Young children often gravitate toward games in the lower right, focusing on physical + chance, but as they get older, they choose games requiring mental + chance.

If players are dissatisfied with your game, they might be able to verbalize it by placing games they do enjoy in other quadrants. Ask yourself what game variables you could change to move the play experience toward a quadrant

9.8   The play matrix

9.9   The play matrix including games

with games your target audience enjoys. For example, you might want to move from the upper right (mental + chance) to upper left (mental + skill).

The solution might be to change a variable determined by chance into a variable determined by player choice. In a physical prototype, this might be accomplished by removing dice from the system and replacing them with cards that a player can choose to play. In an electronic game, this might be accomplished by giving the player a choice of where to start or what weapons to use instead of randomly generating them.

TAKING NOTES

As mentioned, it is imperative to keep notes of your playtests. You think you will remember all of the comments later on, but what you will really remember is those comments you expected to hear or wanted to hear. If you do not keep notes, you will lose all the really important details of the playtesters' reactions. These notes should be filed chronologically in a notebook or folder or entered into a database. Each time you conduct a test, write down the date of the test, all feedback gathered from your testers, and any of your own observations.

Figure 9.10 is a form you can use to capture observations and playtester comments. It is broken into three parts: (1) in-game observations, which are thoughts that you write down while the testers are playing the game; (2) postgame questions, which are questions that are designed to help elicit opinions about the key aspects of a game system; and (3) revision ideas, which is a space for you to articulate ideas for making the game better.

This form is not intended to be used instead of a test script but rather in addition to it. The script keeps the session on track; the form is a place to take notes. If you like, you can merge these two lists so that your script has room to take notes and a list of all your questions.

You might be asking yourself right now, "What should I be testing for?" Don't worry—that is the subject of the next two chapters. For now, these are just example questions you might ask of your playtesters. After you have gone through Chapters 10 and 11, you can create your own

9.10   Observations and Playtester Comments

In-Game Observations

[Your thoughts as you watch the testers play.]

In-Game Questions

[Questions you ask the testers as they play.]

1. What did you feel as your turn ended?
2. Does the navigation seem confusing?
3. Why did you move to that location?
4. Why are you pausing there?

Postgame Questions

[Questions you ask the testers after they have played.]

General questions

1. What was your first impression?
2. How did that impression change as you played?
3. Was there anything you found frustrating?
4. Did the game drag at any point?
5. Were there particular aspects that you found satisfying?
6. What was the most exciting thing about the game?
7. Did the game feel too long, too short, or just about right?

Formal elements

1. Describe the objective of the game.
2. Was the objective clear at all times?
3. What types of choices did you make during the game?
4. What was the most important decision you made?
5. What was your strategy for winning?
6. Did you find any loopholes in the system?
7. How would you describe the conflict?
8. In what way did you interact with other players?
9. Do you prefer to play alone or with human opponents?
10. What elements do you think could be improved?

Dramatic elements

1. Was the game's premise exciting?
2. Did the story enhance or detract from the game?
3. As you played, did the story evolve with the game?
4. Is this game appropriate for the target audience?
5. On a piece of paper, graph your emotional involvement over the course of the game.
6. Did you feel a sense of dramatic climax as the game progressed?
7. How would you make the story and game work better as a whole?

Procedures, rules, interface, and controls

1. Were the procedures and rules easy to understand?
2. How did the controls feel? Did they make sense?
3. Could you find the information you needed on the interface?
4. Was there anything about the interface you would change?
5. Did anything feel clunky or awkward?
6. Are there any controls or interface features you would like to see added?

End of session

1. Overall, how would you describe this game's appeal?
2. Would you purchase this game?
3. What elements of the game attracted you?
4. What was missing from the game?
5. If you could change just one thing, what would it be?
6. Who do you think is the target audience for this game?
7. If you were to give this game as a gift, who would you give it to?

Revision Ideas

[Ideas you have for improving the game.]

questions that are specifically geared for your own game.

You will find that sometimes not all of the questions on the form will be relevant. For example, if you are testing for interface flaws, then data about the overall play experience might be less important to capture. I encourage you to tailor this form to your specific needs. Many of the questions will be unique to a game, so it is important for you not to rely on my questions but to create your own. Questions designed to get at issues that you have with your particular game will be the most valuable to you.

A good way to begin is to identify key areas of your game you need input on and create questions geared to get feedback on those areas. Write down more questions than you plan to use and then rank them in order of importance. Then group the top questions by type as I did in Figure 9.10. You can develop your own categories of questions and structure. It really comes down to the type of information you wish to gather and how your playtesting sessions are structured.

One thing to avoid is getting carried away and overwhelming your playtesters. If you ask someone 20 or more questions in a row, they will become exhausted and might stop answering accurately. Remember, it is not the number of questions you ask but the quality of the responses.

BASIC USABILITY TECHNIQUES

Asking questions is a vital part of conducting a playtesting session, but there are other methods for eliciting good responses. Some of these include techniques commonly employed in usability labs. Usability research involves real people using products and giving their feedback before those products are marketed to the public. In the next sections I have listed three techniques that you can apply to game testing.

Do Not Lead

You will learn the most from your testers by quietly observing them play. If playtesters ask a question, respond by asking them to describe what they think they should do. If they reach an impasse while playing, then you have identified something important that needs to be fixed.

Remind Testers to Think Out Loud

As previously discussed, you should ask your testers to explain to you what they are thinking as they play. Their commentaries will provide a window into their expectations and choices as they play your game. Most people are not used to thinking out loud, so you might have to help them get started and remind them throughout the test.

Quantitative Data

In addition to taking notes on what players like and do not like, on what they pick up quickly and have difficulty grasping, use feedback forms to generate data that shows trends. After a playtest session, you can use this quantitative data to prioritize the severity of issues.

Some game companies work with professional usability experts who might employ more sophisticated methods and use special facilities for playtesting. If you have the budget, this can be extremely beneficial. Not only do professional labs tend to produce superior results, but you can learn from the process and apply some of their methodology to your in-house playtesting sessions.

Metrics in Game Design

by Dennis Wixon

Dennis Wixon recently retired from an associate professor position in the Interactive Media and Games Division of the School of Cinematic Arts at USC. Previously he managed Games User Research at Microsoft. Jerome Hagan is a user research lead at Microsoft Studios User Research. He conducted the user research described the Crackdown example. Ramon Romero is an experience director at NetEase games. He presented the work described here at GDC in 2008. Currently, Dennis is an independent consultant, specializing in user research and management.

Metrics can be very useful in helping game design teams realize their vision. Most game design teams share a passionate commitment to user experience. Metrics can help them understand that experience and assess if players are experiencing the game as the team envisions it. One of the riskiest assumptions that a design team can make is that users will respond to the game as they do. While it's useful for team members to play a game and provide feedback, that feedback cannot fully substitute for testing with the intended audience of the game.

One way to look at designing a game is that it is a process that makes a vision real. A team often begins with a vision of their game. That vision has many parts and may be expressed in many ways. One way in which it can be expressed is stating the intent for the user experience. For example, we may say we want users to feel excitement, accomplishment, fear, enjoyment, or some more complex experience like transcendence. It's critically important that team have a shared way of understanding how well their game is creating that experience among users. Metrics provide one way of doing that.

For example, if a team wants to know how difficult a puzzle is for the intended audience, the best approach is to collect metrics from users. The team may be very experienced in designing puzzles of given levels of difficulty. But the only way to be sure that a puzzle is as difficult as you expect it to be is to test it. There are two classes of metrics that can be used. The first is behavioral: measuring things that people do. The second is attitudinal: measuring things that people report. Either kind of metric can be simple or complex.

Measuring What People Do

An example of a commonly used simple behavioral metric is what proportion of people succeeded at a task. It could be our puzzle, or any task in the game. This metric is relatively straightforward to collect; just give a set of people a task or puzzle and ask them to complete it. That set can be small (as few as 5 people) or large (thousands of players). The test situation can be carefully controlled, (in a lab, with no distractions) or can be ecological (a beta version played at home). Beyond the overall test condition, various other decisions need to be made. Can users play as long as they want? Or do we stop them after a predefined period of time or a certain number of attempts? If we plan to intervene, when will that intervention occur? What will that intervention be? It could be a direct prompt or a subtle hint. In the lab, an observer could initiate help after a period of time or a number of trials or could wait until the user asks. In a field test, the system could intervene automatically to provide a hint.

Each of these characteristics of the test reflects an opportunity to collect data. If the user initiates a request for a prompt, we could note both the time the user tried to complete the task and the simple fact that they asked for a prompt. In that case, we have two metrics: time to hint and the fact that a hint was given or not. These are both behavioral metrics. They are based on things the user does and they could be used to measure the challenge of the puzzle.

If no users could figure out the puzzle without asking for a prompt and they worked for on average an hour to try to solve the puzzle before asking—then we know something about how difficult this puzzle is for users. The implications of that knowledge depend on what the design team intended. If the design team thought most users would solve the problem within 10 minutes without a prompt, then expectations were clearly not met. In other words, the puzzle was more difficult than intended. It may be time to redesign the puzzle.

This example illustrates a characteristic of metrics. They make explicit both what the team intended and how the players were performing with respect to that intention. Scientists call this "operationalizing a concept," which really means specifying exactly what we mean by the concept by defining how it is measured. In this case, the difficulty of the puzzle is operationalized by the time it took to solve it and the proportion of people who asked for help. If we all agree on how to "operationalize" puzzle difficulty, then we can decide on how difficult we want a puzzle to be and measure the difficulty with intended users.

Measuring What People Report

A second class of metrics is attitudinal metrics. These measure player reaction to or opinion about a game. Collecting this type of metric requires that the design devise a method for asking the users for their reactions to a game. Unlike behavioral metrics, they are not automatic or unobtrusive. They require that the players be asked a clear question.

Taking the example of our puzzle, we could ask players to judge how difficult they found the puzzle. The effectiveness of this type of question depends on several factors. Obviously, the question should be posed in an unbiased way. Players should be able to rate the puzzle as either easy or difficult. Second, it should be clear to the players that they are rating their own experience of the puzzle—how difficult did *you* find the puzzle? Third, it's very useful to know what led the players to rate the puzzle as easy or difficult. Asking this question provides valuable information to help the team address any problem in the puzzle.

This kind of question is called an "open-ended" question. An example would be "What about the puzzle made it easy or difficult for you?" In this case, the metric and the rating of difficulty by players let the team know if the puzzle has the effect on the players that the team intends; for example, it was moderately difficult for these players. The open-ended question helps the team make an informed guess about why players are rating the puzzle as easy or difficult. The team can also construct a set of questions that ask the user to rate factors that make the puzzles easy or difficult. These could include factors like the clarity of any hints, the time allotted to solve the puzzle, the similarity between this puzzle and other puzzles in the game or others.

Like any attitudinal measure, the "score" reflects the user perception of these factors. Those perceptions may or may not be "accurate," but if the questions are well constructed and the test participants are appropriately selected, then the answers do reflect how players see these factors.

Attitudinal metrics are most effective when they are part of a standardized program of data collection. A standardized program of data collection will allow the team to compare scores on various games and assess more sophisticated intentions. For example, if we have data from other games or from previous versions of this game, then we can test a more complex or sophisticated intent, for example, "we would like people to rate our puzzles as more challenging than competitor A or more challenging than the last version of this game."

These two types of measures, behavioral and attitudinal, work very well when used together. In general, the success of a game depends on how users play it and how they feel about playing it. The following example illustrates how both behavioral and attitudinal metrics can help improve a game.

Case Study: Crackdown

Crackdown is a popular game on the Xbox platform. It is offered both as a retail game and a downloadable game. It was developed by Real Time Worlds and published by Microsoft. In the game, the hero fights to bring law and order to a fictional Pacific City, which is controlled by three crime bosses. The game is a sandbox game in which the player can choose her own path through the quests. It has sold over 1.5 million copies and been positively reviewed. It was extensively tested by the Games User Research team at Microsoft, and those tests contributed greatly to its success.

The tests included Microsoft's "standard" playtest. In these tests, players play the game for a limited period of time and then complete an extensive questionnaire. The questionnaire collects user reaction to the game with both quantitative and open-ended questions. One of the questions asks users to rate the game in terms of how much fun it was to play.

In initial playtesting, Crackdown scored 3.8 on a five-point scale, which is about average for a game of this type. However, in response to a qualitative question about what made the game fun, several users mentioned a type of power-up: the "agility orb." In other words, many users noted that increasing the capabilities of the protagonist was what made the game fun. These comments led the research team to wonder if players who earned more agility orbs found the game more fun. The research team had also collected data on the final state of each user's avatar so they could determine how many agility orbs each test participant had collected. They compared the fun rating with the number of agility orbs.

This is a relatively straightforward analysis method called cross-tabs. The result was that we found that people who had given the game a high fun score also had many power-ups. This result provides empirical support for the users' answers to the open-ended question "What made this game fun?" That is, those users who earned more power-ups found the game more fun.

As a result of this finding, the research team made several recommendations: the first was that more agility orbs be added in the early stages of the game, the second that more and clearer cues be provided to the user so that they would notice the orbs, and the third that more accessible tall buildings be added in the early stages of the game so that the user could experience the fun of jumping with increased agility.

The final standard playtest ended up scoring a 4.2 fun rating, which was in the top third of games and a significant improvement from the early score. For the downloadable demo version of the game, the team wanted to help players experience the fun of the game even earlier than in the full game. To do so, the team looked closely at questionnaire and behavioral data they had collected and found the following: players started having the most fun about three hours into the game. So, the team accelerated protagonist skill advancement so players reached the same level in 30 minutes rather than 3 hours.

For the playable demo, the changes led to a fun score of 4.5, which was one of the highest ever achieved by any game (among literally hundreds of games in the data set). Crackdown was released to positive reviews and went on to become one of Microsoft's more successful downloadable games.

Conclusion

Several important lessons about metrics can be derived from the Crackdown example. First, any metric becomes much more useful if can be compared to a set of metrics. In this case, Microsoft had an extensive set of results from previous tests of similar games. That informed the team that the initial scores were about average and led them to look for improvements.

The second lesson is that qualitative and quantitative metrics can be used together to help produce insights. In this case, looking at the qualitative results showed that people were explaining what made the game fun for them was power-ups.

Third, collecting behavioral data from each user, that is, how many agility orbs they had collected, allowed for the comparison of this performance measure (behavior) with a fun rating (evaluation). This comparison (cross-tabs) confirmed the expected association and led to the recommendations with respect to the agility orbs. Finally, the fact that the game was commercially and critically successful is an excellent case study of how research and design can work together to make a successful game.

The use of metrics in game design is likely to increase in the foreseeable future. There are many reasons for this, including examples such as the Crackdown study, which shows the value of metrics in the design process. Also, metrics are increasingly simple to collect, especially for online games, and there is tremendous interest regarding data metrics for these games. And, as games move beyond entertainment into areas like education and healthcare, research data will be needed not only to build effective games but to assess and demonstrate that effectiveness. Overall, we can expect to see much greater use of metrics in the future, and can look forward to a time when the use of these metrics is as critical to the development process as quality assurance.

DATA GATHERING

So far, I have mostly discussed how to obtain qualitative feedback, but you might also want to go after detailed quantitative feedback, such as recording the time it takes someone to read the rules, counting the number of clicks its takes to perform a certain function, or tracking the speed at which a player advances in level. You might also ask testers to rate the ease of use of the game as a whole or of certain features. Or, you might ask them to rank order several options to see which ones are most preferred.

If you use a rating system, be sure to limit the range of the scale to five choices, and provide positive and negative anchor points at the ends and a neutral center point. So, from our end of session questions on page 318, you might ask about the game's appeal by stating: "Overall, the game is appealing to me," and then providing a positive anchor of "strongly agree" at "5," a negative anchor of "strongly disagree" at "1" and a neutral center point at "3."

This kind of scale is called a "Likert scale" and it can be used to measure player attitudes about many subjective aspects of your game. The important things to remember about creating Likert scale questions are to make sure you format them as a value statement, and provide a balanced and symmetrical set of choices for the user to evaluate. Five choices is the optimum,

with one strongly postive choice, one postive choice, one neutral choice, one negative choice and one strongly negative choice.

The type of data you gather depends upon the problems you wish to solve. If the game feels clunky and people are taking too long to get started, then measuring the time they spend on each procedure to determine where the trouble spot might be is a good approach. However, if the problem is that the game does not feel dramatic enough, a series of qualitative questions might produce superior results. In addition, quantitative and qualitative questions can be used in a single questionnaire.

Exercise 9.8: Gathering Data

Go back to your original prototype and think of three pieces of quantitative data you can measure that will answer three clearly defined questions you have about the gameplay.

If you are successful at gathering quantitative data, you might suddenly find yourself buried in numbers. It is nice to have data on every conceivable aspect of your game, but if you do not know how to interpret the numbers, they are not much use. I recommend that you conduct your data gathering with clearly defined objectives in mind. Before you set out to measure something, write down your assumptions and purpose. What is most important to know? Then structure your test to answer that question. For example, you might feel that a certain feature in the game is causing a problem, so you design an experiment that measures the time it takes people to reach a specific point in the game with and without that feature. You might also combine this with a qualitative approach where you ask the testers how they feel about the new feature. The combination of the qualitative and quantitative should give you the answers you need.

As I mentioned above, the use of game metrics is becoming more and more integrated into the design and distribution of games. Companies like Zynga have created in-house tools to track player activity, but there are also third-party analytic tools, like those built into the Unity game engine, that offer data collection for games, which allows developers to track how many people use a game, how actively they use it, whether they invite others to play, and other custom data points that allow the developers to improve the game over time. As games become more like services, this kind of ongoing use of metrics after launch to track player engagement can make the game more fun as well as more profitable.

In terms of metrics used during the development period, however, it is important to understand their strength and weaknesses. Dennis Wixon discusses this in his sidebar bar on page 320. Wixon was the founding manager of the user research group at Microsoft Game Studios, where his group created custom software tools to record game data during playtesting sessions. The developers then use specialized tools and visualization software to help analyze this data and determine the effectiveness of different game elements and features. One type of visualization is called a heat map and visualizes data in the form colors. So, for example, the number of player deaths can be easily seen on the area of a level. The ability to visualize such information is very important for level designers. If a particular area is a death-trap for players, there may be a systemic reason. Heat maps may be customized to visualize many different types of data, for example, where players have explored in the map, quests activated or completed, resources picked up, and so forth. This information can be used to adjust the design of the map for better play outcomes.

In addition to visualization of data culled from gameplay, other types of data that can be collected during the design process include information from eye-tracking devices, galvanic skin response, heart rate, blood pressure, and other physical markers. These can measure changes in physical excitement, tension, and other physiological changes in players while engaging with the game. However, they do not measure the quality of those physiological changes. In other words, they can tell you that the players are excited but not whether that "excitement" is positive (joy) or negative (frustration).

Although analysis of data from emerging techniques like this is a powerful tool, it is not a replacement for the designer's creative judgment on how to tweak game variables. This is because data can be misleading. If playtesters are new to the game, they might not be playing as efficiently as they could because they have not learned the subtleties of the system yet. Or, at the other end of the spectrum, if the testers are experienced with the game, they might have set opinions about how to proceed and not see an innovative way of playing. And physiological data is subject to very different interpretations by those observing. The bottom line with all game metrics is that they are a good tool that should be used in combination with other playtesting methods to have the best overall results.

TEST CONTROL SITUATIONS

A tool for improving the efficiency of your playtesting sessions is to utilize controlled game situations. A controlled game situation is when you lay down parameters that force players to test a specific portion of the game mechanics, such as:

- The end of the game
- A random event that rarely takes place
- A special situation within a game
- A particular level of a game
- New features

You can set up to test different aspects of your game independently of one another during different prototyping stages. In the foundation stage, you can test basic functionality without worrying about balancing or fairness. In later stages, you might want to test for loopholes and dead ends. Or you can focus sessions on the accessibility of the interface or navigation system.

This type of controlled test situation is vital because it allows your testers to repeatedly experience an event under a variety of conditions. For example, let's say you were designing Monopoly, and you wanted to test the "going to jail" feature. Instead of waiting for it to happen by chance, you could force this event to occur and see the results under various conditions. How does going to jail affect a player who owns very little property versus another player who owns a vast amount of property? You might choose to start the game in the middle with the player already in jail, then play for 30 minutes and observe what takes place. Then repeat the experiment with a change in the player's financial position.

Exercise 9.9: Test Control Situations

Create three test control situations for the original prototype that you created. Describe the purpose of each control and how it functions. Then try it out and make note of your observations.

RAPID ITERATIVE TESTING AND EVALUATION

How often you should test your prototype and the number of players you should test with are questions you may be asking as you think about playtesting your game prototype. A method called Rapid Iterative Testing and Evaluation, or RITE, can offer some useful insights. The RITE method, proposed by researchers including Dennis Wixon, suggests that testing with 4-5 participants will uncover about 80 percent of the problems that have a high likelihood of being discovered.[3] You may be surprised that this number is so small, but it is because the issues are highly discoverable. Issues that are less discoverable (for whatever reason) will require more testers to find. But testing your game with small groups regularly, tracking issues clearly, and getting those issues to the team in time for them to implement solutions, will allow you to solve issues that many of your players will encounter.

Figure 9.11 shows two diagrams from student playtesting teams at USC Games under the mentorship of Dennis Wixon. The left image shows the testing progress for one student game project over a semester. The red bars are problems detected each week, the blue bars are solutions implemented each week. As can be seen, this project team worked hard to implement solutions on pace with their testing schedule, so that each week a new iteration of the project could be tested.

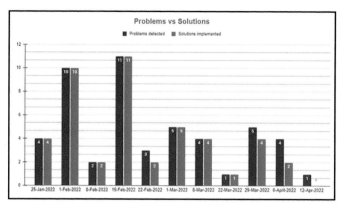

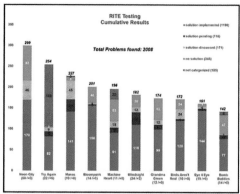

9.11   RITE Testing Charts

On the right is an image of cumulative testing results from a cohort of projects at USC Games. Each project is represented by a column showing the total number of issues discovered over a semester, the solutions implemented (in blue), solutions discussed (in yellow), pending (in red), not categorized (in orange), and no solution (in green). Issues that have "no solution" may be issues that didn't require a solution, such as problems with the test itself, the script, or other issues that the team has decided not to implement a solution for. In this diagram, having more issues is not a good or a bad thing, but what is important is the relationship between issues found and issues solved or pending. So, while the Neon City team has discovered the most issues, they also have a significant number of solved or non-issues. The Blindsight team has discovered fewer issues, and has solved a significant number of them, but also has quite a few pending.

Tracking your team's progress on discovering and solving issues can allow you to objectively see how testing has affected your design and give the team a sense of momentum. It can also keep you on pace solving and re-testing the design of your game. Keep in mind that every solution you implement and re-test has the possibility of fixing the issue, but it also may cause new issues in the design, which is why you need to continue to do rapid iterative tests and evaluations throughout the process.

You do not have to have your testers start from the beginning and play the game all the way through. You can start at any point: beginning, middle, or end. You can make one of your players grossly more powerful than the others and see what happens. This type of testing is not about being fair to your testers or making sure that they enjoy the game. It is about seeing what happens under various conditions. Many of these are rare cases and need to be forced so that they materialize at key moments in the game. This way you can see how it affects the gameplay. Does it ruin the experience? Or is it a nice surprise?

Also, when testing, your time is limited, and some games take hours to play. If you do not have the time, you will find yourself relying on test control situations almost every session. One of the most common control situations is starting a game near the end. To do this, you set up the prototype to simulate where players would be in the final conflict. You define the parameters to create the type of ending that you want to test, and then you start the session from this control point and study how the end game plays out. Because it is a controlled situation, you might be able to test the end game four times in one hour.

This is one of the reasons that cheat codes exist for electronic games. They are tools that the game developers use so that the team can test controlled situations. For example, the designers of a real-time strategy game might find it helpful to have a cheat code for turning off the fog of war. This would allow them to better monitor the AI for the computer-controlled units, while a cheat code for infinite resources would allow them to test how the game plays with the maximum number of units. It has become a tradition among game developers to leave some of the cheat codes in the final releases of game titles. One reason is so that players can have fun experimenting with different game situations that would otherwise be impossible.

PLAYTESTING PRACTICE

I have found that it is easier for designers to learn the process of playtesting by using a game that they have no emotional connection with—it is easier to be objective when your design skills are not on the line. So, for the next few exercises, I will take a simple, familiar game and use it to demonstrate the essence of playtesting. As I do this, much of what I discussed earlier will become apparent, and some new concepts will be introduced.

Connect Four

For this exercise, we're going to use a children's strategy game called Connect Four. There is an image of the game in Figure 3.21 on page 78 for reference if you're not familiar with it. In this simple game, two players take turns dropping red and black checkers into a vertical grid. The first player to get four of their units in a row (horizontally, vertically, or diagonally) wins the game.

1. Create the prototype

First, you need to create a simple prototype for Connect Four. To do this with pen and paper, draw a grid, seven squares wide by six squares tall, on a piece of paper. One player will use a black pen to represent black units on the grid and a second player will use a red pen to represent red units. Make sure to have a stopwatch handy to time your playtest sessions. Next, decide who goes first. Each player, on his turn, chooses a column in which to place a unit. He then draws units at the bottom of the chosen column as if gravity dropped them from the top. Units stack on top of one another when they "land" in the grid.

2. Prepare your questions and script

Write down the questions you plan to ask in advance and prepare a script for the session.

3. Recruit testers

Go out and find two playtesters.

4. Playtesting

Introduce your testers to the game and let them begin playtesting.

5. Alternate the grid size

Play according to the previous description a few times. Use your stopwatch and mark how long each game takes to resolve next to the game grid. Next, draw the game grid at 9×8 instead of 7×6. Play this a few times using the same rules. What happens to the play experience in the 9×8 version? What happens to the time it takes to resolve? Which version is more interesting? Why? Does changing the grid size give you ideas for changing other variables?

6. Alternate the objective

Go back to a 7×6 grid, and this time change the objective, so that winning requires connecting five in a row. Play this a few times. What happens? Does changing the objective give you ideas for changing other variables as well? For example, you might find that a 7×6 grid is too small. If so, try the "connect five" version on the 10×8 grid.

7. Alternate turn procedure

Now go back to the original rules (that is, Connect Four on a 7 × 6 grid). This time change the turn procedure. Players can now place two units on each turn; the second unit must be placed in a different column than the first unit. Play the new version of the game. What happens? How does this change affect the players' strategies? Is the game still balanced?

8. Alternate number of players

Go back to the original rules (that is, Connect Four on a 7 × 6 grid). This time, change the number of players to three—you can act as the third player yourself if you do not have another playtester. Use a third color for the new player. Take turns as usual and play the new version of the game. What happens? How does this change affect the players' strategies? How does it affect the social dynamics of the game?

Final Analysis

Clearly, changing system variables has a direct effect on the play experience, and the only way to determine this effect is through playtesting. How do these alternate versions compare with the original? How did each change affect the player experience?

Compile your notes and analyze your results. What changes would you make to the game of Connect Four as a result of this playtesting session? Do your notes point to any conclusions?

The previous exercise exposes you to the basics of playtesting and iterating on the fly. This works great if you are testing a physical prototype like the Connect Four game we created. However, the same process can also take place over a series of tests as you change and iterate your digital prototype. I used the Connect Four example so that you could quickly and easily see the change in the game experience over several iterations. Understanding and practicing this iterative process of playtesting and revising over and over is fundamental to the creation of good games. In the exercises for the next two chapters, you will test your own original game in the same way—though it might take longer than the Connect Four example—as you iterate and improve your design over a number of playtests.

CONCLUSION

As you can see, playtesting is an involved task, but it is a critical part of game design that cannot be rushed through or sidelined. Your job as a designer is to make sure playtesting remains at the heart of the game design and development process. As soon as you let it slip into the background, then you give up your chance to see your game as the players will see it when they play for the first time.

Playtesters are your eyes and your ears. They allow you, as the designer, to keep your finger on the pulse of the game, even after you have played it hundreds of times. If you learn to listen to your playtesters and analyze what they are saying, you will be able to see the game mechanics for what they are, not what you want them to be or imagine they should be. And that is the key to good design. It is understanding what it is you have created and being able make it even better, not in one flash of brilliance, but step-by-step over months and even years. If you can master this process, then you have mastered one of the key skills to being a great game designer.

FURTHER READING

Drachen, Anders, Mirza-Babaei, Pejman, and Nacke, Lennart. *Games User Research.* Oxford: Oxford University Press, 2018.

Dumas, Joseph and Redish, Janice. *A Practical Guide to Usability Testing.* Bristol: Intellect Books, 1999.

Hodent, Celia. *The Gamer's Brain: How Neuroscience and UX can Impact Video Game Design.* Boca Raton: CRC Press, 2018.

Kuniavsky, Mike. *Observing the User Experience: A Practitioner's Guide to User Research.* San Francisco: Morgan Kaufmann, 2003.

Nielsen, Jakob. *Usability Engineering.* San Francisco: Morgan Kaufmann, 2004.

Rubin, Jeffrey. *Handbook of Usability Testing: How to Plan, Design, and Conduct Effective Tests.* New York: John Wiley & Sons, 1994.

END NOTES

1. Thompson, Clive. "The Science of Play." *Wired.* September 2007.
2. Personal email with Dennis Wixon
3. Medlock MC, Wixon D, Terrano M, Romero R, Fulton B (July 2002). Using the RITE method to improve products: A definition and a case study. Usability Professionals Association. Vol. 51. Orlando Florida. pp. 1963813932–562338474.

Chapter 10

Functionality, Completeness, and Balance

Now that you have tried your hand at the playtesting process, you are probably wondering what to do with all the comments your testers are giving you. How can you prioritize all these ideas and comments into a helpful list of changes to your game? You need a way to focus your thinking about the next steps and take your game step-by-step from a mock-up of the core gameplay to a fully functioning model of your game concept. This chapter provides some tangible steps you can take to make sure your gameplay is functional, complete, and balanced.

The process I suggest here is based on years of watching student and professional game designers work through this very problem. What I have found in this experience is that it is important to break the playtesting process down into several discrete phases, with each phase focusing on specific aspects of the design, perfecting these aspects, and only then moving on to the next phase.

Of course, as I have discussed, games are dynamic, interrelated systems. A change to one part of the system can completely change the player's perception of another. I realize this, and the process I am about to walk through is a vast simplification of what you will actually experience when you try this yourself. What is important to take away from this process is the need to focus your mind on the distinct goals of each phase, not to try to fix everything in your game all at once. I want you to feel in control of this process, and giving you these goal-based phases and a method to move your game through them is a good way to do that.

WHAT ARE YOU TESTING FOR?

When you built your original prototype, I discussed the four basic steps of design: foundations, structure, formal details, and refinement. These four steps allowed you to visualize first the core gameplay or foundation, then carefully add structure to the system, one rule or procedure at a time. Only then did you go on to the formal details and refinement.

DOI: 10.1201/9781003460268-12

When I talked briefly about these steps in Chapter 7 on pages 235 and 247-249, I spoke mostly in terms of prototyping—getting your ideas into physical form. I did not talk much about playtesting, revision, or your goals at each of these stages. At that point, I just wanted you to get some experience building out a design of a game from scratch. Now that you have a handle on the art of prototyping and playtesting, I can go back to these basic steps and discuss the design goals you should keep in mind as you work your way through each of these phases of development, using the iterative process and playtesting at each step along the way.

Foundation

During this stage, your main concern is that the basic idea for your game is fun, engaging, and has potential to reach your experience goals. Your prototype might only consist of a main core mechanic with which to engage, and there might not be much else. You might have infinite loopholes, dead ends, etc., but do not worry about all of that right now. At this point, you just need to get a sense of the core of the system you have thought of, so that you can judge whether it is a compelling base for a game. As I mentioned in Chapter 9, at this stage, you will probably be playtesting the system on your own. The game is really only valid as an exercise in confirming your intuition that the idea makes a good foundation for the game you want to build.

Structure

When you have a solid foundation, your next goal is to add enough structure to make the prototype functional for playtesters other than yourself—probably your close friends or coworkers, but still, someone other than yourself. I will discuss the essence of "functionality" in detail, but intuitively, you already know what it means:

Your prototype works at a basic, albeit clunky, level. You need to build out the rules and procedures to the extent that the system can be played by people who don't have a full vision of the end experience in mind.

What you want to know when you get to this stage is: Was your intuition right? Does the foundation hold up under the rigors of a real playtest with real players? Your focus here is on both functionality and fun. Are the formal elements working together even in this basic state? Is your experience goal starting to take shape? Is there a beginning, middle, and end to the experience? Can the players reach the objective? Are they engaging in the conflict you have designed? Are they enjoying that challenge? Is there a spark to your game? Should you even continue with this idea, or is it time to head back to the drawing board?

Formal Details

Let's say the spark is there—you are onto something. Now you've got the problem of having to build out a fully functional version of the game system you envisioned. What should you do first? You know there are problems—they have already come up in the first few playtests—but where to start? The answer to that question is the basis of this chapter. During the formal details stage, your focus should be on making sure the game is (1) functional, (2) internally complete, and (3) balanced.

These three tasks might seem deceptively simple at first, but they require skills that you can only learn through practicing the craft of game design. Every game is intrinsically different, so the answers you found during one playtesting process are not the right answers next time. Experience will help you judge what decisions to make, what choices will make your game a clean, well-balanced system. But this process is really an art. A game can sink or swim during the formal details stage.

What about fun, you say? Why don't we test for fun during this stage? Of course, you are always keeping your eye out to make sure your game stays fun as it develops, but remember, I am trying to keep you focused here, to break down the process so that you do not have to worry about everything all at once. Making sure your game is functional, complete, and balanced is a huge undertaking. And fun is a very difficult metric to track when playtesting early prototypes. Often, you'll need to look for responses in your playtesters that show the promise that the game will be fun once it has all its elements. If players are engaged with the core mechanic, if they feel like they are making meaningful choices, if they are asking questions about future features and iterations, you can take these as positive signs that the game will eventually be fun when you've finished your work.

Refinement

During the refinement stage, I am going to assume your game is functional, complete, and balanced. You tested primarily for fun and engagement in the first two stages of design, by yourself and with confidants, and if your core gameplay was engaging players to begin with, completing and balancing the game should not have detracted from that; on the contrary, it probably added to it. But perhaps something of that original spark got lost in the process. Now is the time to focus all your energy on making sure the experience you envisioned from the start is there in spades.

You probably noticed that I've started using the word "engagement" here, rather than simply "fun." This is because fun is such a broad term that it is almost impossible to define what it is and how you make sure your game has it—especially at the earliest stages of prototyping and playtesting. And yet, if you ask a player

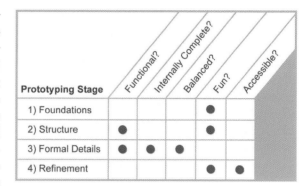

Prototyping Stage	Functional?	Internally Complete?	Balanced?	Fun?	Accessible?
1) Foundations				●	
2) Structure	●			●	
3) Formal Details	●	●	●		
4) Refinement				●	●

10.1   What are you testing for?

what they want in a game, 9 times out of 10 they say it should be fun. We all know when we are having fun, even if we cannot define it. Chapter 11 will get into how you can make your game more fun for players, with strategies and ideas for adding that elusive emotional pull to a game system that keeps players coming back for more.

Last, but not least, during the refinement stage, you will be testing for accessibility. Remember, your game has to stand on its own without you there to explain it. You might have the most functional, complete, balanced, fun game in the world, but if it is not accessible, players won't ever know this. And so this final aspect is as critical as any of the others that come before.

When you feel overwhelmed by the process of playtesting and revision, review Figure 10.1 to remind yourself of the stage of design you are in and where your design focus should be. If you do not try to solve every issue in your game at once, your tasks will suddenly become simpler, and your next steps much clearer. With these steps in mind, let's look at functionality, completeness, and balance in detail.

IS YOUR GAME FUNCTIONAL?

Before you can even think about completeness, you must have a functional game. By functional I mean that the system is established to the point where someone who knows nothing about the game can sit down and play it. It does not mean the tester won't run into trouble or that the experience will be thoroughly satisfying, but it does mean that they can interact with the game unaided by you. In a paper prototype, this means the players can play the game—following the rules and procedures properly—and not reach an impasse. In software prototypes, it means players can use the controls and the core loop and make progress in the game. How much progress will depend on the focus of your prototype, the question you are trying to answer about the game at this point. In both types of prototypes, it means that the components of the system interact properly and a resolution can be achieved.

Beyond this, deciding your game is "functional" is really a matter of judgment and what you are trying to achieve during each successive playtest. If you are testing a particular version of a feature, then being able to use it meaningfully in gameplay should be part of your definition of functional. You will need to determine what your goals are at each stage of design and use those goals to focus your development process. In terms of prototyping, let's say that if your players can use the game features you are testing without help from the designer, we'll call the game functional. Once you have moved beyond prototyping into actual production, more and more of your game will be functional and ready to test.

Exercise 10.1: Testing for Functionality

Take the physical game prototype you developed in Exercise 7.10 or a digital gameplay prototype and test it for functionality. Give the game to a group of people who have not played the game before with no verbal instructions—only the challenge to "play the game." See if they can play your game from start to finish without any input or assistance from you. If they can, your game is functional. If they cannot, figure out what was missing, and revise the game to make it functional.

IS YOUR GAME INTERNALLY COMPLETE?

As you playtest, you will invariably notice places where your game is functional but incomplete. For example, early in the first-person shooter prototyping process, I established movement and shooting rules so the system could function, but I had no rules about hit percentages or winning conditions, so it was still incomplete. Some of these missing elements are obvious, but others are much more difficult to discern. Only by testing every possible permutation under all conditions can you be certain that there are no sections of the game that are left unfinished. Your job as the game designer is to identify and resolve these issues.

This sounds simple, but it is not. Most games are quite complex systems that can act in unexpected ways under different conditions. The more you test, the more you will discover how malleable your game is. Players will do things that you could have never anticipated. There might be gaps in the rules that made sense on paper, but when they are actually implemented in the game, they lead to irresolvable situations or gray areas. In board games, this often leads to disagreements between players, with each side interpreting the rules in their own way. In software, it leads to a loophole that players can exploit, a dead end in the player experience, or a complete breakdown of the system. You might hear your testers making comments like, "The rules don't say either way," "I'm completely stuck," or "You can't do that!" These types of reactions are red flags that something within the game is not complete and needs attention.

After identifying an incomplete portion of your game, the first thing to do is go back to the design plan. Whether you are working on a digital game or a board game, you should have a design document or a rule sheet that clearly describes how your game is to be played. See the discussion in Chapter 14 on page 469 about communicating your designs in documentation. What you will discover is that what you thought was a clear set of rules actually has holes in it. You now have to plug the hole (or complete the rules) so that it makes sense. Doing this can often affect other parts of your game, so it is a delicate task and might require several testing sessions and revisions before you get it right.

Exercise 10.2: Testing for Completeness

Take the physical or digital game prototype you have been working with and test it for completeness. This time, look specifically for moments in which players reach an impasse, question the rules, or have to make a judgment call about what happens next. If players argue about the rules or reach a dead end, your game is not complete. Revise your game to deal with the issues you find and test again.

You will find that sometimes playtesters uncover problems in a system despite the fact that the rules are unambiguous. For an example, let's go back to the first-person shooter prototype from Chapter 7 on page 225. Is it internally complete?

Here is a potential problem that plagues many first-person shooters, including our prototype: When more than two people play this game, it is possible for players to camp near both of the spawning points on the arena map. When a

recently killed opponent appears at either spawning point, the campers can promptly shoot the opponent. Players stuck in the position of being shot are furious at this seemingly unfair tactic.

The problem is that the rules are comprehensive, and the players are behaving within the bounds of the rules, but certain players have figured out a way to gain an advantage that the designer did not expect. Thinking as the designer, how would you alleviate this spawn camping problem? For a challenge, stop reading now and think through your own solution. Then compare yours with the following four possible solutions.

Solution #1

The number of spawning points on a map should be equal to the number of players in the game.

- *Pros*: Players will always have at least one safe point on which to spawn.
- *Cons*: You have to design arena maps specific to the number of players that will play on it. Maps cannot facilitate the fluctuating number of players that most online FPS games allow.

Solution #2

A force field shield surrounds each spawning point hex. A spawning player can fire and move outward through the force field. However, no one can shoot or move back in. The force field incinerates a spawning player if he remains on the spawning point hex for more than one turn.

- *Pros*: Players are safe when they first spawn, and they can fire upon a single camper.
- *Cons*: Multiple campers can still wait nearby, making the turn after spawning difficult for players.

Solution #3

Players who fire at a newly spawned enemy within three hexes of the spawn point are punished by losing a portion of their own health for every shot taken.

- *Pros*: This solution reduces player interest in camping by spawning points by making the newly spawned players a "poison pill."
- *Cons*: This solution adds an element of over-policing the system that some players will object to.

Solution #4

Do not fix this because it is a feature, not a problem.

- *Pros*: Some players think spawn camping is just part of the game. Leaving the system as is will force players to fight for choice camping spots, which will create a game in itself.
- *Cons*: Other players are extremely frustrated by spawn camping and feel it is bad sportsmanship.

Discussion

The options listed illustrate that there are many potential ways to tweak this system during the process of making a game internally complete. As I noted, the spawn camping problem is not unique to my first-person shooter prototype. If you do an Internet search on the phrase "spawn camping," you will see dozens of websites discussing the pros and cons. You will also notice that many fans have created numerous work-around mods to alleviate the spawn camping problem. Some of the mod solutions are similar to the options I listed previously. Some are different. One solution makes a player invisible for two to three seconds after spawning. This lets a player run around and shoot without being seen, giving them a fighting chance.

Exercise 10.3: Spawn Camping

Write down three original solutions not mentioned previously to the spawn camping problem. Describe why you feel these solutions are inferior or superior to the ones mentioned.

Loopholes

Finding loopholes is an essential part of testing for completeness. A loophole can be defined as a flaw in the system that users can exploit to gain an unfair or unintended advantage. There are always some ways in which players can gain advantage in a system—otherwise, no one would win—but a true loophole allows for a type of play that ruins the experience for all players. As long as unintended loopholes exist, your game cannot be considered complete. Your goal as a designer is to eliminate loopholes without closing down all potential for emergent play.

This is no simple task, especially with digital games. The very nature of a computer program makes it easy for loopholes to go undetected. In most digital games, there are so many possibilities that no designer can test them all, and some gamers actually make a point of ferreting them out. To these gamers, the challenge of finding loopholes is irresistible. They love to tout their discoveries and use them to their full advantage when competing against other players. Finding loopholes has become a form of play in itself for these players, who make a sport out of finding flaws in game systems and posting them for others to find.

Consider a classic example from the PC game Deus Ex. Deus Ex, released in 2000, was a pioneering piece of work due to its genre-mixing design and its open and flexible game environment. One of the weapons available in the game is called a "LAM." LAMs can be attached to walls and used like proximity mines, meaning that they explode a few seconds after someone stands in close proximity to them. They are great for blowing up doors and for killing unsuspecting opponents. Apparently, however, they were also good for something the designers never anticipated.

Creative players learned that they could attach multiple LAMs to a wall and then quickly run up them like a ladder before they detonated. Doing this allowed players to climb into places on game maps in ways that the designers had not anticipated. This meant that some levels were less challenging than originally planned. If this can happen to world-class game designers, it can happen to you. Players are much more creative and resourceful than you would ever imagine.

Another example comes from the classic Atari game, Asteroids. This game was a smash hit in the arcades when it was released in 1979. In this game, you control a spaceship and must blast your way out of a field of floating asteroids, and you also gun down flying saucers that come on screen to shoot you.

Engineers at Atari played the game incessantly for six months before it was released and had recorded a company high score of 90,000 points. No one believed that a normal player—someone not familiar with how the game was programmed—could ever achieve a score like that. However, shortly after the game's release, Atari began receiving reports that players all over the country were scoring three and four times that many points. In fact, the players were beating the machine because the Asteroids scoreboard maxed out at 99,990 points and, when surpassed, the score started over at 0.

The engineers at Atari were stunned. They drove out to an arcade to investigate firsthand. Eugene Lipkin, then president of Atari's coin-operated game division, was quoted in *Esquire* magazine in 1981 as saying, "What had happened, was that a player had been smart enough to understand the movement and the programming on the product and had then come up with an idea of how to work around it. It took about three months for that to happen. Then, all of a sudden, we began hearing the same thing from all over. People had figured out that there was a safe place on the screen."[1]

The safe place on the screen occurred because the player's bullets can "wrap around" the screen—meaning that when bullets are fired off the right side of the screen, they reappear from the left on the same trajectory, whereas the flying saucer bullets cannot wrap around.

Players learned that if they destroyed all but one asteroid floating on the screen they could lurk near an edge and pick off the flying saucers as they appeared.

The small flying saucer is normally very formidable and is worth 1000 points. With the lurking strategy, however, a player could shoot a flying saucer with wraparound bullets and get it from behind, or if the saucer appeared on the same side of the screen as the player, they could quickly blast it before it could get off a shot. It still takes a lot of skill to do it effectively, but when mastered, this lurking practice allows players to rack up huge scores. Asteroids purists regarded the practice derisively. However, this did not keep players from exploiting it to the fullest. Atari had to wait until the next version of the game, Asteroids Deluxe, to fully fix the problem.

Loopholes versus Features

Sometimes it is debatable whether a system issue enables a loophole or is actually a benefit to the game. You will see heated arguments online, where players take both sides of the issue. The first-person shooter spawn camping loophole discussed on page 334 is one example of this. When you identify one of these subjective issues, you must make a creative choice on how to handle it. Sometimes it is possible to make variants on the game to satisfy different types of players.

As an example, let's look at how massively multiplayer online role-playing games (MMORPGs or MMO's for short) have dealt with one specific type of loophole. Ever since MMO's were introduced, players have debated the pros and cons of being able to kill other players. MMO are persistent online worlds where players role play and interact as virtual characters. Most people dislike players who maliciously kill other players. These people are called "player killers." The remaining players would prefer that the game designers, for a given MMO tweak the system to prevent player

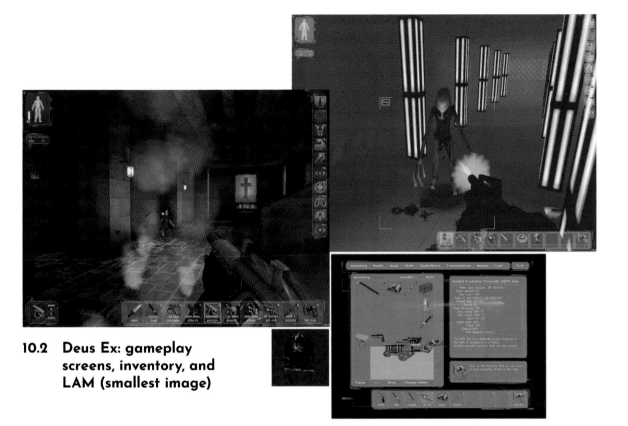

10.2   Deus Ex: gameplay
        screens, inventory, and
        LAM (smallest image)

killing from happening. However, some people think that player killing adds to the richness of the game because evil characters are free to play evil roles, and it creates a more intriguing and challenging environment.

Which side is correct? Does the presence of player killing mean that an MMO has a loophole and that the game is not internally complete? The solution that MMO designers developed over time—through playtesting with real players—was to provide spaces for both types of players. In essence, many MMOs have two variants: one where players cannot hurt one another and another where they can. Each variant is internally complete in its own way. The following are examples of how several well-known MMOs have evolved through play and revision to deal with player killing.

Ultima Online was one of the first MMOs. Early in the game's history, new players complained about being bullied and killed for no reason by more powerful players. Newbies had no protection. The problem was spoiling the fun for many players and deterring others from joining. People generally loved the game but hated the player killers—whom they called cowards. They filled online message boards with complaints. Articles appeared in magazines about the problem. The designers at Ultima Online needed to tweak their game system to alleviate the tension.

In response, Ultima Online's designers created a reputation system for characters in the game. Players who murdered other players were given red name banners and designated as "dishonorable." When law-abiding characters saw a red character, they would likely not trust or cooperate with them. This made it harder and less fun to be a player killer. In addition, and perhaps more dissuasive, was the fact that experienced law-abiding characters would band together to hunt down red characters. This created a system of vigilante law in the game, which greatly alleviated the tension, but it also developed its own set of problems.

Over time, the game designers continued to tweak their system to make it less and less appealing to be a player killer. For example, they placed invincible computer-controlled guards at the entrances to all but one city in the game world. The guards killed red characters on sight. This meant that the cities were safe for law-abiding characters, and player killers were relegated to an outlaw's existence, either out in the wilderness or in the one town that accepted them—a dangerous place called Buccaneer's Den. This solution accommodates both law-abiding players and player killers. It also meant that player killers could camp outside of towns, ready to pounce on any hapless players who might wander outside the city limits.

Since its release, Ultima, as well as the many other MMOs that have followed since the release of Ultima, has addressed the problem of player killing in many different ways. One solution was to divide the game into two separate types of servers: one in which player killers run free and one in which player killing is disabled by the system. Other solutions have included creating reputations for player killers and other forms of marking players within the system.

Asheron's Call, another early MMO that had to deal with the same problem, came up with its own unique solution. In the first version of Asheron's Call, the designers created an allegiance and fellowship system. When a new player came into the world, he had the option of swearing allegiance to another player character. In return, the new player might receive protection or even money and weapons from the experienced player, who was designated as his "leader." From that point onward, a share of the new player's experience points would go to his leader. Likewise, a share of the leader's experience points would go on to that character's follower (if she had one) and so on. This created a mutually beneficial pyramid structure that helped protect players.

10.3   Ultima Online: EvilIndeed makes a kill

In addition, Asheron's Call players had the option of joining fellowships. Fellowships were temporary agreements with other players, usually formed to go on a quest or pursue a goal. Experience points generated while the players were a fellowship were distributed across the group. Individuals in the group received a share of the points based on their experience level. For example, a third-level character received a bigger share of the points generated by the fellowship than a second-level character, etc. The designers at Turbine Entertainment developed these systems as an elegant way of rewarding players for working together. They made it more fun to cooperate and less fun to be a spoiler.

Even with these systems in place, law-abiding players of Asheron's Call still complained about player killers. Turbine responded by tweaking the game so that, by default, players could not be attacked by other players. The story of the game was tweaked to say that the powerful magic of the world of Dereth protected them from one another. This made all players completely safe from one another, but it was disappointing to players that wanted the thrill of battling other live players. In response, Turbine created a way for players to voluntarily convert to player killer status. The interested player had to find a special altar in the game world to do it. After conversion, the player could kill and be killed by other player killers. In this approach, all players could inhabit the same game space, but only players designated as player killers could battle one another.

EverQuest, released after Ultima and Asheron's Call, learned from their solutions. The developers at Sony Online Entertainment created a system in which players who chose to convert to player killer status could kill or be killed by other players. To further appease player killers, EverQuest offered player killer-only game servers. On these servers, all players were susceptible to attack from one another. These types of servers are popular with hard-core players. By responding

to player feedback—a form of playtesting—the Sony designers succeeded in closing a disruptive problem and made their game internally complete in regard to the player killer issue.

In most cases, you will never find all the loopholes before the release date, and this is why many game developers opt for a public beta test. Especially with massively multiplayer online games, it is a valuable tool for finding and solving loopholes before final delivery.

Whether you initiate a public beta or not, it is your responsibility to make sure that there are no loopholes that will ruin the player experience. Whenever a loophole is discovered, your job is to tweak the system and perform another playtest to see if the disruptive technique works. Eventually, you will find a solution that eradicates the loophole. It is an iterative process, and each loophole can take days or even weeks to solve. By the time a game is released, most designers manage to do a pretty good job at eliminating the obvious flaws, but even with the most sophisticated testing schemes, some loopholes seem to find their way into the final products. This is because the number of people who play a released title is so much larger than the number of dedicated testers any company could manage to recruit, and all it takes is one player to uncover the flaw that everyone else missed. Here are some tips for finding and weeding out loopholes:

- Use control situations, as described in Chapter 9 on page 325, to test aspects of the system in isolation. This will force testers into situations they might otherwise avoid, exposing flaws that otherwise would not be apparent.

- Do a series of playtests where you instruct testers to attempt to disrupt the system. Challenge them to see who can come up with the most creative way to get ahead.

- If possible, find testers who enjoy figuring out alternative or subversive solutions. Hard-core gamers are good at finding loopholes in games.

10.4 EverQuest

Exercise 10.4: Loopholes

A loophole is an unintended system flaw that a player can exploit to her advantage; take the game prototype you have been developing and test it for loopholes. In this exercise, use seasoned playtesters who know your game inside and out. As advised previously, instruct testers to disrupt the system. Challenge them to see who can come up with the most creative way to subvert the rules.

Dead Ends

A dead end is another type of common flaw that disrupts the gameplay experience. Dead ends are not loopholes, in that they do not allow a player to exploit a game, but like loopholes, they must be fixed before a game can be considered internally complete.

A dead end occurs when a player gets stranded in the game and cannot continue toward the game objective no matter what they do. Adventure games, where players have to collect objects in the world and then use these objects later to solve the puzzle, are susceptible to this. If the player cannot solve the puzzle because they are missing a piece, they have reached a dead end.

Dead ends can also occur in other types of games. For example, in a strategy game, a dead end can be a situation where the players cannot resolve the conflict because their forces wind up without resources. In exploration game, a dead end can be a virtual space that a player stumbles into and cannot get out of. Most titles have ironed out dead ends before they are released, but now and then, one slips through the playtesting cracks.

Wrapping Up Completeness

The idea of completeness can be summed up by the following statement: An internally complete game is one in which the players can operate the game without reaching any point at which either the gameplay or the functionality is compromised.

This is both an objective and subjective decision. You can say your game is complete at almost any point, and that will hold true until someone uncovers a flaw. In reality, no game is ever complete. There is always room for improvement, and in most cases, there are unknown or irresolvable issues lurking within the game system.

Schedule and budget constraints often preclude designers from ever fully completing this stage of the process. But your job as designer, and specifically your focus during the formal details stage of design, is to enforce a high enough standard and to lay out rigorous enough tests so that you can be certain beyond a reasonable doubt that there are no critical deficiencies lurking within your game. Only when you have accomplished this can your game be considered internally complete.

Is Your Game Balanced?

As with fun, the concept of balance is often used to describe the process of making a game better. I offer a specific definition of balance here. Your game might require specific balancing techniques not addressed in this definition. But hopefully this will help you get started and help you focus your thoughts as you step through this sophisticated process.

Balancing a game is the process of making sure the game meets the goals you have set for the player experience: that the system is of the scope and complexity you envisioned and that the elements of that system are working together without undesired results. In multiplayer games, it means that the starting positions and play are fair (i.e., no player has an inherent advantage), and no single strategy dominates all others. In single-player games, it means that the skill level is properly adjusted to the target audience. For short, I call these four balancing areas variables, dynamics, starting conditions, and skill.

Resolving issues of balance is one of the most difficult parts of designing a game. This is because the notion of balance encompasses so many different elements, all of which are dependent on one another. Many of the concepts involved in balancing also involve complex mathematics and statistics, which you may or may not be skilled at computing. Do not let that deter you from the process, however. Balancing is as much about gut instinct as it is about numbers; with enough experience, you will be able to tweak the variables in your physical prototype, or give detailed feedback to the programmers for your digital game, without a degree in advanced mathematics.

Balancing Variables

The variables of your system are a set of numbers that define the properties of your game objects, whatever those might be. These variables can define how many players the game is designed for, how large the playing area is, how many resources are available, the properties of those resources, etc. In the game Connect Four, used in the playtesting example from Chapter 9 on page 327, the properties included two players, a 7 × 6 game grid, 21 red units, and 21 black units. Indirectly, these variables also determine important aspects of how your game will work when it is set in action.

For example, in Connect Four, when you changed the grid size from 7 × 6 to 9 × 8, you would have had to increase the number of units from 21 of each color to 24 of each color. If you didn't, your players might have run out of units before the game was over. This is because you need enough units to fill every cell on the grid: $9 \times 8 = 48$, $48 \div 2 = 24$. Hence, the change in one game variable necessitated a change in another.

Changing the grid size changed some other aspects of Connect Four, which you undoubtedly discovered during your playtest as well: (1) the playing time was increased and (2) the game became less exciting. The reason for the first discovery is somewhat obvious. With more area to fill, players had more options to explore and less contention for the space.

The second discovery is an interesting and perhaps unexpected one. With nine columns, rather than seven, the game is less exciting. Why is this? In the game with seven columns, the center column is flanked by three columns on each side. This means any horizontal or diagonal row of four units must include a unit in the center column. This places great importance on that center column. The battle for control of it draws the players into conflict with each other quickly and makes the overall experience more exciting.

Thus, the original size of the grid is more successful than the 8 × 6 grid. You can only learn what scope will be most effective for a system through repeated testing with alterations in the game variables.

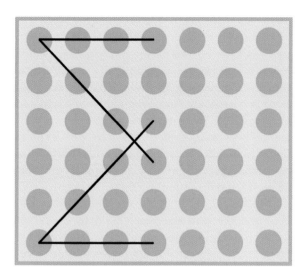

10.5   Connect Four: the center column is flanked by three columns on either side

Digital games operate under the same principles. In Super Mario Bros., you start with three lives. If you started with 1 life, the game would be too hard. If you started with 10 lives, the game would be too easy. Changing the number of lives changes how the game plays. Playtesters act differently when they have 10 lives versus 1, so the experience and balance of the game shifts.

Many variables in video games are hidden in the computer code. This makes them more difficult for you to analyze, but you can conceptualize them. I have already looked at several examples of game variables: the number of properties in the game of Set (page 139), as well as the unit properties in Diablo 2 (Figure 5.1 on page 136). Although it is not as easy to visualize, the number of resources available at any given time in the world of World of Warcraft, as well as the running speed and jumping height of a game character like Mario, are also variables that can be adjusted to control the experience of the game.

Can you imagine playing Mario if he moved like a slug? It would be boring. Likewise, can you imagine if Mario moved really, really fast? It might be frustrating because he would be too

hard to control. Game designers at Nintendo tweaked the numbers for these variables up and down to arrive at a comfortable speed that would appeal to the majority of players.

The purpose of manipulating variables all comes back to your basic goals for the game: the player experience you are trying to create. You can only effectively judge the viability of your system variables if you have a clear picture of that experience.

Exercise 10.5: Game Variables

List out the game variables in the game prototype you have been working on. Make a change in one variable and observe how it affects other variables. This is an opportunity to test how your system plays under different conditions. Can you make easy, medium, and hard levels simply by tweaking the variables?

Balancing the Dynamics

When I talk about balancing the dynamics, I mean the forces at work when your game is in action. As I discussed in Chapter 5, when systems are set in motion, sometimes there are unexpected results. Sometimes a combination of rules creates an imbalance. Sometimes it is a combination of objects, or even a "super" object that unbalances play. Other times it can be a combination of actions that provide an optimal strategy for players who know the trick. Whatever it is, these types of imbalances can ruin gameplay. You will need to identify them and either fix the rules that create the problem, change the values of the objects, or create new rules that mitigate the optimal strategies.

Reinforcing Relationships

As I described in Chapter 5 on pages 159–160, a reinforcing relationship occurs when a change in one part of a system causes a change in the same direction to another part of the system. For example, if a player earns a point, she would be rewarded with an extra turn, thereby strengthening her advantage. This starts a cycle that rewards the stronger player over and over until the game concludes, probably prematurely, with that player the winner.

This type of problem might be solved by changing the reinforcing relationship you have set up into one that balances the power more fairly; for example, when a player earns a point, the turn is passed to the other player, thereby balancing the effect of the point advantage.

Basically, you want to keep the strong player from accumulating too much power from a single success. Instead they might receive a small, temporary bonus, but nothing that throws the game out of balance. In games with rounds, designers may make the winner pay a price for taking a strategically important position. This tends to balance out the gains, ratchet up the tension, and provide the loser with a chance to come back.

Other techniques include adding an element of randomness, which can come into play and alter the balance of power. This can take the form of external events, like shifting alliances, natural disasters, and unfortunate circumstances. You might also want to enable the weaker players to group together to battle the dominant one or have a third party intervene.

The goal is to keep the scales balanced without causing the game to stagnate. After all, this is a competition and someone has to be able to win eventually. Naturally, in the last stages of a game, the scales will tip, and when this happens, let the scales tip dramatically. There is nothing as satisfying as a sweeping victory. This makes the winner feel good and provides for a swift, merciful defeat for the loser. You never want to drag out the ending. Think of your game in terms of its dramatic arc; when you have passed the climax, wrap it up fast. Stone Librande talks about tuning for this kind of dramatic finish in his sidebar on page 392.

A game that dealt creatively with this type of problem is the strategic multiplayer shooter, Battlefield 1942, released in 2002. In assault matches of Battlefield 1942, one team starts with a single spawning point and the other team controls every other spawning point and area of the map. The attacking team must fight to take ground. An example of a map that works like this is Omaha Beach, which simulates the D-Day invasion. The Allies start on board a ship and must take spawning points on land from the Germans. Battlefield 1942 incorporates a tickets system. Each side begins with a certain number of tickets that are reduced whenever a player is killed in action and subsequently respawns. When the number hits zero, the game is over. However, fulfilling certain victory conditions will cause the opposing team's tickets to slowly deplete until they manage to reverse the situation by reclaiming a required control point. This gives teams a chance to come back from the brink of disaster, or at least it gives players the resolve to stay in a losing game and manage a minor, rather than a total, defeat based on the percentage of tickets by which they lost.

Exercise 10.6: Reinforcing Relationships

Analyze your original game prototype for reinforcing relationships. Is it common for the player who gets an early lead to win the game? If so, you might have a reinforcing relationship that is creating an imbalance in the system. Identify the issue and change the relationship to balance the play.

Dominant Objects

A good rule of thumb is to keep similar game objects within a game proportional in terms of strength. For example, in a fighting game, no single unit should be significantly more powerful than the others. "Super units," as they are sometimes called, ruin the gameplay by becoming

	Rock	Paper	Scissors
Rock	0	+1	-1
Paper	-1	0	+1
Scissors	+1	-1	0

10.6 "Rock, paper, scissors" payoff matrix: rotational symmetry

so valuable that none of the other units matter. One of the best ways to keep every element in proportion but still provide a range of choices is to think in terms of strengths and weaknesses. Every unit can be balanced by giving it a special advantage and a corresponding drawback.

Think of the classic rock, paper, scissors game. This game works because each element has a clearly defined power and failing. In this game, two players simultaneously choose one of three items: rock, paper, or scissors. Each item wins, loses, or ties depending on what is played by the opponent. Rock beats scissors, scissors beats

paper, and paper beats rock. When illustrated in a payoff matrix, it looks like Figure 10.6.

On the matrix, 0 equals a tie, +1 equals a win, and −1 equals a loss. It shows that the three options balance each other out. This concept, sometimes called "rotational symmetry," is often used to balance digital games as well. For example, as Ernest Adams points out in his article "A Symmetry Lesson" on Gamasutra.com, The Ancient Art of War by Brøderbund was designed so that knights had an advantage over barbarians, barbarians had an advantage over archers, and archers had an advantage over knights.[2]

Many games use this technique in one form or another. In fighting games, each unit or character has his killer moves and Achilles' heel. In racing games, some cars are good at going up hills but handle poorly on corners. In economic simulations, some products are more durable but cost more, while others have a limited shelf life but higher profit margins. Assigning strengths and weaknesses is one of the fundamental aspects of game design and should be kept in mind whenever balancing gameplay.

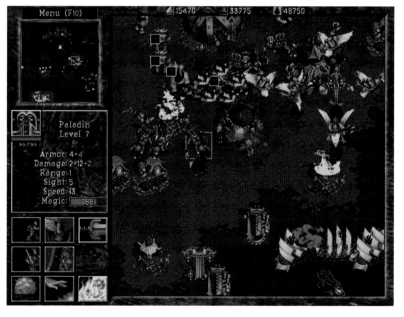

10.7   WarCraft II–bloodlusted orcs attack a human stronghold

Let's take WarCraft II, in which players can play a human or an orc civilization. The two sides are symmetrical in many respects but have minor differences. Both civilizations have the same types of units and buildings, which yield the same types of abilities. For example, the humans have a peasant unit that has the exact same hit points, cost, build time, and abilities as the orc's peon unit. The name and the artwork associated with human peasants and orc peons are different, but from a formal perspective, they are identical.

An example of a difference is the orcs' bloodlust ability versus the humans' reciprocal healing ability. Taken only at face value, bloodlust is more powerful than healing. It enables orcs to deal triple damage in battle. A gang of bloodlusted orcs can easily slay a same-sized gang of humans in direct combat. To balance out this discrepancy, the designers at Blizzard gave the humans other abilities and strengths. However, the player must choose an appropriate strategy to benefit from them. Healing is not very useful in direct combat with orcs, but it can be effective when utilized as part of a hit-and-run strategy. To do this, the humans must attack the orcs, then retreat quickly, heal their units, and attack again. This works particularly well as a strategy for gryphons because they can fly away.

Humans also have slightly more powerful magic spells than the orcs. However, they require both skill and strategy to employ. The human mage unit can make other units invisible so they can sneak into an orc camp for a surprise attack. Or the mage can cast a polymorph spell that will change an orc unit into a harmless sheep. Both of these spells are expensive in terms of mana and require the player to execute complex maneuvers, but the payoff is there. Overall, the orcs are more powerful in direct ground combat, but humans can compete through crafty choices and acquired skills. The point is that there are discrepancies between orc and human units, but overall, the game does a good job of balancing the strengths and the weaknesses, which is no easy task.

Dominant Strategies

Sometimes players can discover one or two strategies in a game that effectively dominate all others. This has the effect of narrowing the number of overall choices in the game because no one will choose the weaker strategies when the dominant ones are known.

For example, if one way of attacking is far superior, the players will gravitate toward this method. Even a minor imbalance in this regard can have a significant effect upon a game's playability. When balancing a game, make sure there is ample choice in all areas and that as the game progresses, nothing limits the players' options. When players focus on only a limited set of options in pursuit of a win, games often become dull.

Can you imagine trying to play a game in which your opponent has already calculated the dominant strategy and simply executed it? The game would be frustrating for you and boring for them. If you both knew the dominant strategy, it would be a rote entry of choices on each of your parts, resulting in an experience that you could have predicted from the outset. Tic-tac-toe is a game in which there is a dominant way of playing, and thus it is not an exciting game.

What makes games interesting and challenging is the fact that their systems do not offer a dominant strategy—at least, not at first glance, or even upon repeated play. As a designer, you should always be on the lookout for dominant strategies. When you see one, find a way to make it less attractive to players so that they do not simply latch onto that method at the expense of everything else perhaps it has a higher cost, or risk associated with it.

One word of caution: A dominant strategy is not the same as a favorite strategy. If hard-core players discover a way of playing your game that they like to employ over and over, but it is not always effective, this is not a dominant strategy. If the game is balanced properly, then other players might have ample choice of opposing strategies to counter with.

Exercise 10.7: Dominant Strategy

In your original game, can you identify a dominant strategy that limits player choice? If you cannot find one, list out some strategies that do work. What are the opposing strategies that players can utilize?

Balancing Positions

In balancing the starting positions for your game, the goal is to make the system fair so that all players have an equal opportunity to win. This does not always mean giving each player the exact same resources and setup. Although many games are symmetrical in this way, just as many others are not. As I showed in my discussion of player interaction patterns in Chapter 3 on page 63, there are various and interesting ways to design the competition in your game—a symmetrical competition is only one.

Additionally, the challenge of balancing multiplayer games is different from that of single-player games. This is because single-player games often involve a computer "player" or AI that competes against the human player. To understand how this affects balancing, let's look at two basic models for multiplayer games: symmetrical and asymmetrical.

Symmetrical Games

If you give each player the exact same starting conditions and access to the same resources and information, your system will be symmetrical. In chess, black has the same 16 units as white, opponents start in a mirror image configuration of each other on the board, and opponents have the same amount of space on the board to maneuver. Connect Four, Battleship, Othello,

checkers, Go, and backgammon are likewise symmetrical systems.

In turn-based games like the ones just mentioned, there is one asymmetrical aspect that must be dealt with. It is the issue of who moves first. This issue could throw off the fairness of the game if not balanced correctly. In his article on symmetry mentioned previously, game designer Ernest Adams points out that you can reduce the effects of one player going first by establishing a system where the first move provides little strategic advantage.[3] Chess is set up so that only the pawn or the knight can move at the opening. These are two of the weakest pieces in the game. Additionally, four rows separate the opponents at the opening, which means neither side can threaten the other with the first move. The game of Go has the komi system, which compensates the player who moves second with a predetermined number of points. (This number varies depending on what part of the world you are playing in, under which rule set, and the comparative ranks of the players.) The game of Hex, a connection game invented separately by mathematicians Piet Hein and John Nash, uses the "pie rule" (or swap rule) in which player 1 moves, then player 2 chooses whether to switch positions (or colors) with the first player, thereby negating the advantage of the first move.

Another option is to balance the system so that a game takes many moves to resolve. This renders the first move of little strategic significance. Chess is a fairly long game, so going first has little effect over the course of a whole game. Contrast chess with a very short game such as tic-tac-toe. In tic-tac-toe, moving first is an enormous advantage, so much so that it enables a rational player to always win or tie.

Adams also points out that you could incorporate chance elements to reduce the effect of one player going first. Symmetrical board games like Monopoly and backgammon require players to throw dice to move. The dice are chance elements. Because the first player could have a bad roll and the second player could have a good roll, the first mover advantage is mitigated.

Asymmetrical Games

If you give opponents different abilities, resources, rules, or objectives, your game will invariably be asymmetrical. An asymmetrical game, however, must still be fair. As a designer, your goal is to tweak the variables so that the system balances out. If played properly, each opponent will have roughly the same chance of winning, regardless of the other factors.

This type of asymmetry is powerful in games because it can be used to model conflicts and competitions from the real world. Historical events, nature, sports, and other aspects of life are full of situations where opponents compete with differing positions, resources, strengths, and weaknesses. Imagine trying to recreate a World War II battle where the players had to begin with the same units on a symmetrical board. It wouldn't make sense. For this reason, the vast majority of digital games tend to be asymmetrical. Let's look at a few examples and see how they deal with the issues of asymmetrical abilities and resources.

In the fighting game Soul Calibur II, there are 12 different characters, each with its own set of ability statistics. A typical character has about a hundred fighting moves and a distinct fighting style. As in many fighters, a move can inflict a variable amount of damage—from none all the way up to a kill—depending on the counter move played by the opponent. Each time one character attacks another, a damage payoff is determined for one or the other or both of the characters. Mastering the game requires an understanding of how and when to play fighting moves in different situations against different characters. In this

10.8   Command & Conquer: Generals

example of asymmetry, designers at Namco balanced a system where opponents have the same objective and basic movement resources but different abilities.

In the RTS game Command & Conquer: Generals, players choose one of three different armies: America, China, or an underground terror organization called the Global Liberation Army. Players adopt a playing style that matches the strength of their chosen army. The Americans utilize high-tech weaponry, the Chinese swarm opponents with sheer numbers, and the Global Liberation Army relies on cunning and sneakiness. The key to this game is that the armies have different resources that are balanced so that, if played skillfully, any one of them has ample choices to beat the other two.

Another game with asymmetrical resources is NetRunner, a collectible card game designed by Magic: The Gathering creator Richard Garfield. In this game, one player plays a corporation using one deck of cards, and another player plays a runner (kind of like a cyber hacker) using another deck of cards. The cards in the two decks are completely different. The corporation uses cards to build and protect data forts, with the ultimate goal of completing corporate agendas. The runner uses cards to hack corporate security and steal agendas before the corporation can complete them. The competing sides in this asymmetrical game utilize completely different resources and abilities, but they share the same overall objective: to score seven agenda points.

10.9   NetRunner–corporation cards versus runner cards

and intrigue to a game. You can offer asymmetrical victory conditions when opponents are otherwise equal, or you can combine asymmetrical objectives with asymmetrical starting positions for a real balancing challenge. In this case, your motive might be to add variety or evoke a real-life situation. Following are several models for offering asymmetrical objectives. Notice that in each case, the differing objectives are still balanced against each other to keep the game fair.

Ticking Clock

Many digital games allow maps to be set up where a weak defender must fend off a strong attacker. The defender's objective is to hold out for a set amount of time. The attacker's objective

---

Exercise 10.8: Symmetrical versus Asymmetrical Games

Is your original game prototype symmetrical or asymmetrical? Describe how and why.

Asymmetrical Objectives

Another type of asymmetry involves offering each player different objectives. This can add variety

is to kill all defenders before time runs out. The second mission in the original StarCraft tutorial works this way. In it you must build a small human base and hold out for 30 minutes before being overrun by a horde of attacking Zerg.

The ticking clock is a staple in mission-based games, including Homeworld, WarCraft, and Command & Conquer. The model is also used in turn-based military board games such as Panzer General. Here, the ticking clock victory condition is measured in a set number of turns versus a set amount of time. The weaker defender must hold out for 30 turns.

The multiplayer mode in the RTS game Age of Empires lets players choose to start the ticking clock as a victory condition on their own. They start it if they choose to build an expensive building called a "wonder of the world." When one player builds a wonder, all opponents see the ticking clock start on their screen. The player must now defend his wonder from being destroyed by all other players. If he can hold out until time runs out, then he wins the game. In this case, the ticking clock is a victory condition chosen strategically by a player. It is balanced into the game to enable richer methods of play.

Protection

This is a variant on the ticking clock, and it can be equally dramatic. In this model, one side tries to protect something (such as a princess, magic orb, secret document, etc.) and the other side tries to capture it. If the defenders protect or sneak the thing to safety, they win. If the attackers capture the thing, they win. Many games include missions that work like this. One example is the beach invasion map in the World War II-based game Return to Castle Wolfenstein. On this map, the Allies' objective is to storm a beach held by the Axis. Then they must penetrate a seawall, infiltrate the base, and steal several top-secret documents. The Axis objective is to protect these things and keep the Allies from completing their goals.

Combination

It is also possible to combine ticking clock and protection devices. Take, for example, multiplayer assault maps in the FPS game Unreal Tournament. These maps have a ticking clock (usually 4 to 7 minutes long), as well as objectives that need to be protected. The attackers' goal is to reach the headquarters, steal the code, or blow up the bridge. They try to do this as quickly as possible, while the defenders protect the objectives for as long as possible, or until the ticking clock runs out. When the goal has been met, the time to beat is displayed. The two teams then switch roles. They play the same map, but the team who was just attacking is now defending. The new attackers try to beat the time set by their opponents in the previous round. This type of game can be extremely exciting because of its clear objectives and dramatic use of time.

Exercise 10.9: Asymmetrical Objectives

Take the original game prototype you have developed and create a variant with asymmetrical objectives. If your game is a single-player game, add a choice of objectives. Describe what happens to the gameplay when you test the game with these changes.

Individual Objectives

In the classic board game Illuminati, designer Steve Jackson uses asymmetrical objectives in a novel way. It is a game of politics, diplomacy, and sabotage in which opponents vie for control of societal groups such as the Mafia, the CIA, the "Boy Sprouts," Trekkies, and convenience stores. Each player can play for a shared objective: to control a specific number of groups, between 8 and 13 depending on the number of players in the game. Or players can go for their own individual objective. For example, the individual

10.10 Illuminati Deluxe

objective for the "Servants of Cthulhu" is to destroy any eight groups. The individual objective for "Discordian Society" is to control five "weird" groups. Players must watch to ensure that no one gets the shared objective while also battling and negotiating to ensure that other players cannot achieve their individual objectives. The differing objectives create an environment of shaky alliances and mutual distrust. The game is balanced so that, to win, players must cooperate with one another in some instances and betray one another in others.

The previous models are only a few ways to think about asymmetrical objectives in games. Like many concepts in game design, there are other ways to go about it, some of which can be found in existing games and some of which have yet to be invented.

Complete Asymmetry

Scotland Yard is a popular board game in which just about everything is asymmetrical. In this game, one player takes on a group of opposing players who work as a team. This player is the fugitive, Mr. X, and the other players are a team of Scotland Yard detectives trying to track him down. To make this contest fair, the designers at Ravensburger balanced the system so that Mr.

X has the ability to hide. He also has unlimited subway, bus, and taxi tickets (i.e., resources) from which to choose. Mr. X moves around London invisibly but must surface every four or five turns according to a turn schedule. The detectives use information about where Mr. X was last sighted and work in coordination to try to surround him and cut off potential lines of escape. The detectives have a set number of movement tickets. If one of them runs out of a type of ticket, he cannot use that mode of transportation anymore. Mr. X's objective is to evade capture for 24 turns. The detectives' objective is simply to catch Mr. X at any time. Essentially, the following are balanced against one another: Mr. X with unlimited resources and the ability to hide versus four or more detectives with limited resources and the ability to work in coordination. The game variables are tuned so that over the course of a whole game, each side has an equal chance of winning.

In the symmetrical and asymmetrical multiplayer models I have just described, the most important balance to work out is between the various players. Because most models of multiplayer interaction employ other players as the basis of the game conflict, the question of balance often comes down to a question of how resources and powers are distributed to each party at the start of the game.

In single-player games, however, conflict is usually provided by the game system, either in the form of obstacles, puzzles, or AI opponents, which I discuss on page 353. As with multiplayer models, single-player games can also employ symmetrical or asymmetrical forms of play.

Balancing for Skill

Balancing for skill involves matching the level of challenge provided by the game system to the skill level of the user. The challenge with this is that every user has a different skill level.

For some games, it is practical to simply offer multiple skill levels. For example, the original

Feature	Chieftan	Warlord	Prince	King	Emperor
Endgame Year	2100 AD	2080 AD	2060 AD	2040 AD	2020 AD
Starting Cash	50	0	0	0	0
Content Citizens Number of Citizens per city born content.	6	5	4	3	2
CP Rows of Food Number of Rows in Computer Player's food storage box.	16	14	12	10	8
CP Resource Cost Multiplier Computer Players have cost to build units and improvements multiplied by this amount.	1.6	1.4	1.2	1.0	.8
CP Lightbulb Increment per Advance Each time an advance is discovered, the cost of the next advances by this amount.	14	13	12	11	10
Human Player Lightbulb Increment per Advance Each time an advance is discovered, the cost of the next advances by this amount.	6	8	10	12	14
Barbarian Unit Attack Strength Multiplier Barbarian's attack strengths are multiplied by this number.	.25	.50	.75	1.00	1.25
Parley Coin Demand Multiplier Peace payment demands are multiplied by this number.	.25	.50	.75	1.00	1.25
Civilization Score Multiplier Used to convert final score to percent for High Score ranking.	.02%	.04%	.06%	.08%	.10%

10.11 Civilization difficulty levels

Civilization offers five skill levels: chieftain, warlord, prince, king, and emperor. Each of these levels is progressively more challenging to play. The difference between the skill levels in this system is simply a different balance of numbers in the system variables.

When you play Civilization at the easy level, chieftain, you start with cash reserves of 50, and when you play at the emperor level, you start with cash reserves of 0. At chieftain, the computer opponents attack at 0.25 strength,

whereas at emperor, their strength is multiplied by 1.25. Figure 10.11 shows a chart of the system variables for each Civilization skill level.

Exercise 10.10: Skill Levels

Does your game have a design that incorporates skill levels? If so, describe how they work and the method you used to balance them. If not, why not? Can you add skill levels, and how would they affect the gameplay?

10.12   Balancing for the median skill level

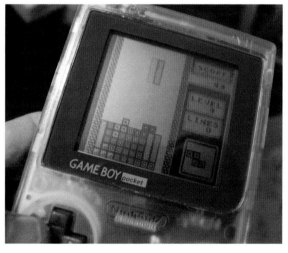

10.13   Tetris for Game Boy

What if it is not practical to offer multiple skill levels for your game? Perhaps your design is not as dependent on starting variables as the Civilization example. In this case, your best bet is to balance the system variables against the median skill level of your target players.

Balancing for the Median Skill Level

Balancing for the median skill level requires extensive playtesting with players from your target audience across the range of ability levels—from novice to hard-core gamers. Designer Tim Ryan suggests a good way to find the proper ability levels in his article on Gamasutra.com.[4] First, set the high-water mark of difficulty by testing with hard-core gamers. Next, set the low-water mark by testing with novices and progressively adjusting the difficulty level downward.

When you have these boundaries established, you can balance the system variables to be in the median between these two marks. In games that are structured in progressive levels of play, which is most single-player video games, you can incrementally increase the difficulty level for the player as you move from level to level in the game. Of course, each level will have to be balanced individually.

Balancing Dynamically

In some types of games, it is possible to program the system to adjust to the ability level of the players as they play. Take Tetris, for example. In this famous game, different-shaped blocks fall downward from the top of the screen. The player rotates the blocks and moves them left or right as they fall to attempt to fit them together at the bottom. If the player fits pieces together to fill a row completely across, that row disappears and points are scored. When the game starts, the blocks fall slowly, so it is fairly easy for the player to fit them together at the bottom. But as the score increases, so does the speed at which the blocks fall. The system is balanced so that the difficulty increases automatically as the player's ability increases. In this case,

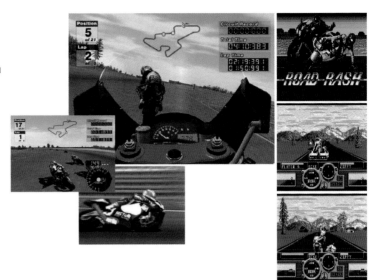

10.14 MotoGP and Road Rash

MotoGP © 1998 2000 Namco Ltd., All Rights Reserved. Courtesy of Namco Holding Corp.

difficulty is directly related to the variable of speed.

Single-player racing games such as MotoGP, Road Rash, Gran Turismo 3, Project Gotham Racing, and Mario Kart 64 have a self-balancing mechanism. In these games, when a race starts, the computer opponents (i.e., the other cars) accelerate up to their maximum speed. This speed is slightly slower than the maximum speed achievable by a human player if he drives perfectly. The computer opponents remain at maximum speed as long as the human is close or leading the race, meaning the pack will be tight. When the human crashes his car, the rules for the computer opponents change. They slow down to a reduced speed so that the human can catch up.

When the human player closes in on the computer opponents, they accelerate back to their maximum speed. The human players can be unaware that this is going on. The ideal is for the human players to feel that they are successful because of their own abilities, but at the same time keep the game balanced so that novice players are not shut out from the possibility of winning.

Balancing Computer-Controlled Characters

A problem with designing computer characters is that they must seem to be human and make mistakes. Otherwise a computer-controlled racecar could whiz through a track at maximum speed without crashing; a computer-controlled rifleman could hit an opponent between the eyes with every shot. This would clearly be no fun for a human player. Designers solve this problem by designing a character to act within a range of possibilities. Here's how the flying saucers work in Asteroids, as explained by the programmer, Ed Logg:

> Sluggo [the big saucer] fires at random. Mr. Bill [the little saucer] aims. Mr. Bill knows where you are, and he knows what direction you're moving in. He takes this information and picks a window bounded a few degrees on each side of you, and then shoots randomly inside of that. For this reason, you should never move straight at him. It makes you bigger relative to him. [Also] the higher your score the more accurate Mr. Bill becomes. When your score reaches 35,000, he narrows down his firing window and increases his chances of hitting you.[5]

In this example, the saucer aims randomly within a few degrees of the player. This provides a variable that can be tuned to balance the game. If the number of degrees is increased, then the saucer is more likely to miss, and the game is easier. If the number is decreased, then the saucer is less likely to miss, and the game is harder. The result is a balanced, challenging, but not impossible, computer opponent.

Programmers have created many clever ways of coding their computer-controlled characters. In fact, there are many books just about programming game AI. What is important for you as a designer is not how the characters are coded but that they can be tuned to provide a balanced and satisfying experience.

TECHNIQUES FOR BALANCING YOUR GAME

As you work through these aspects of balancing your game, you might be tempted to dive right in and change everything at once. The playtesters say they want more of X and less of Y, they want to change procedure A and make a new rule B. Before you know it, you have a real mess on your hands—your balancing process is out of control.

On the following pages are some techniques for keeping a calm head and making changes that truly improve your game. Obviously, these apply at all stages of revision, but right about now is probably when you need them most. If you master these techniques, you will be able to take a game that works marginally well and fine-tune it without making changes that lose your previous work.

make alterations because one change can throw off the balance of seemingly unrelated parts of the game.

The key to dealing with this problem is to isolate the subsystems and abstract them from one another. This type of functional independence is a critical part of large-scale game design. It is similar to object-oriented programming, where each object is clearly defined with a set of input and output parameters, so you when make a change somewhere else in the code, you can track how it affects every other object. The same holds true for game design. If you keep your subsystems modular, when you tweak one element of your game, you know exactly what impact it will have on the other parts.

Think Modular

Most games are not comprised of a single system but a set of interrelated subsystems. A good way to simplify a game is to think in terms of modularity. Breaking your game up into discrete functional units allows you to see how the mechanics of each unit interrelate. If you think of a game like WarCraft, it has a combat subsystem, a magic subsystem, and a resource management subsystem. Each of these subsystems is a part of the greater game system. The more interconnected the various pieces, the harder it can be to

Purity of Purpose

Along the same lines, try to design your game with a purity of purpose, meaning every component of your game has a single, clearly defined mission. Nothing is fuzzy, nothing exists without a reason, and nothing has more than one function. To accomplish this, break your game mechanics down into building blocks using a flowchart and define precisely what the purpose is of each block. This will help you to avoid creating a morass of rules and subsystems, which will grow increasingly convoluted

A Conversation with Rob Pardo

Rob Pardo was formerly the chief creative officer at Blizzard Entertainment in Irvine, California. In 2014, following his 17-year career at Blizzard, he departed for new adventures. By 2016, his passion for game development led him to founding Bonfire Studios. While at Blizzard, he worked on some of the most respected and best-selling games in the industry including, the WarCraft, Diablo, and StarCraft series, among other games. In this conversation, Rob shares some details about the game-balancing process he developed with the team at Blizzard and also some of his views on being a professional game designer today.

GDW: One of the things we're interested in for this conversation is the process that goes into balancing a game such as the ones that Blizzard makes. Is a lot of what you do involved with game balancing?

RP: Balance is a very important component of any Blizzard game. The first game that I did balance on was the original StarCraft, where for the first time we had three totally asymmetrical races. With StarCraft I learned how important it is to be an expert player yourself so that you understand what elements cause a unit, spell, or race to become under- or overpowered. Many designers will try to balance entirely from the spreadsheet that has the various unit abilities and stats, but often there are so many elements that change the balance of a unit that don't appear in a spreadsheet. For example, in StarCraft we made a radical change to the early game where we drastically slowed the speed of the Zerg Overlords. This change was made due to the huge reconnaissance advantage it gave to Zerg players.

On WarCraft III, as lead designer, I had broader responsibilities. It went to unit design; it involved working with Chris Metzen, our storywriter; it went to working with our level designers and determining the gimmicks and play features for each level and how they all fit together. It went to, you know, "how does the mini-map work?" spec'ing out the design documentation and giving it to programmers and artists where appropriate. It's basically all areas of the game that the player sees and interacts with.

Game balance is just one small, but important, part of what we do.

On the process of designing WarCraft III:

GDW: Can you tell us about the process of designing WarCraft III?

RP: WarCraft III was interesting because it went in a couple of different directions. First of all, it was our first 3D game. So that presented some challenges. Also, we wanted to do something different from StarCraft. We had just rolled off StarCraft and we felt that we'd nailed that form of gameplay—you know: macromanagement, action, RTS—whatever you want to call it. When we rolled onto WarCraft III, we thought about the fantasy elements of the game, and we wanted to take a new tack. So we decided to add a lot of RPG elements.

With 3D, we decided to bring the camera down quite a bit and try out some things. The problem was with the camera pulled all the way down, it became a pseudo-third-person experience. It was disorienting when you went around the map, and it was difficult to select units in battle because your camera frustum was pointed in one direction so you didn't have a good view of the battlefield. It was a challenge because we still wanted a fun strategy game. Eventually we pulled the camera into a more traditional isometric view, and that's when we really started making progress.

GDW: *What were the first things that you built for WarCraft III? Did you make a prototype?*

RP: Yes. Since it was our first 3D game, it was really important to get the 3D engine up and running. And we had to get the art path ready so the artists could start testing art files with the new engine. Something we did for the first time on WarCraft III (and now we've been doing on all our projects) is we committed to making a build that ran every day. So when we finally got the engine running, we could immediately put art in it. From that point forward, every day the team could come in and boot up the newest version of WarCraft III and it would work. Obviously, not every day did the new build work—there would be bugs sometimes—but that was a commitment and it really helped us see where we were. On StarCraft, it wasn't until right before beta that we started getting stable builds on a regular basis. So that was a big step for us. So we spent a lot of time prototyping the look of the world and what we wanted to do with the camera and what elements we wanted to go with.

GDW: *It sounds like figuring out where to put the camera was a part of the prototyping process.*

RP: Yes, for sure. Something we believe in strongly here at Blizzard is iterative design. You know, prototype can mean a lot of different things. We didn't really have a prototype that was made of blocks that we could test gameplay on like are often made at other companies. In this case, we did more of a technology and art prototype rather than a gameplay prototype. So once we had the art and the actual 3D engine in there, that's when we actually started messing with the camera, messing with the units, trying to figure out exactly what kind of game we wanted to make for WarCraft III.

On developing the WarCraft III races and units:

GDW: *Can you tell us about the process for developing the races and units?*

RP: We knew we didn't want to do StarCraft. We knew we wanted to add role-playing elements to the game, and we knew we were going the 3D route. Some people on the team wanted a lot of units. Some people wanted to do a few units. That was a contentious topic in the early days.

One of the first things we came up was the concept of "heroes." In the old days, we called them "legends." We actually referred to the game itself as "Legends." We didn't want to refer to it as WarCraft III because we felt we might end up making just a sequel to WarCraft II. So we referred to the game entirely as "Legends" with the thought that we might release it with that name.

Early on, we designed a lot of legend/hero units. We designed many heroes, including the Archmage and Warlord. We built them in prototype form and started playing around with different spell kits and tried to figure out how they should work. We asked: "Should they work like Diablo heroes?" We tried to figure out what a hero was; what that meant in a strategy game versus a pure role-playing game. We experimented with stuff like "Well maybe you can only have units when they are following their heroes."

Those concepts formed a lot of the core gameplay early on. But it was a baseless sort of gameplay at that point. Then, on the art side, we were trying to figure out what we could do with 3D: what was possible, what wasn't. At the same time we were also experimenting with different network models and technological concepts that were going to dictate certain gameplay elements. So there was interlinking between gameplay, art, and technology.

GDW: *So the idea of hero units was an early concept that you built on. What about the four races in the game? How were they developed?*

RP: Early on we had lots of discussions about races. We talked about different cool abilities and play styles they might have and quickly decided that Undead should be a race. It was interesting: In the early days, we sketched ideas for nine totally different races. That was never really reasonable, though—it was more like nine core concepts from which we could draw the coolest ideas. Nine races went down to six and then that later went down to five. We really thought we were going to release with five for a long time. So in the beginning we had lots of races and units designed on paper.

We started implementing Humans and Orcs first and then the Undead. The fourth race, the Night Elves, was next. They were a compromise between early race concepts we had for Dark Elves and High Elves. We wanted to get elves in the game in a way that hadn't been done before. The fifth race was Demons. We didn't cut them until probably right before alpha. The problem was: We wanted Demons to be the ultimate bad guys in the story line, but we also wanted to be able to balance them into multiplayer play. We were having a lot of kit issues with how they should work and how they should interact with the other races. Ultimately we decided to keep them as bad guys in the story but drop them as a full-blown playable race.

GDW: *Interesting. You said you had "kit" issues?*

RP: Yes. When we look at a race, we think: "What's this race about? Is it a sneaky race? Is it a micromanagement race? Is it a heavy ground race? Is this race supposed to be really versatile? Is it magic?" When we looked at Demons, we said, you know: "Really powerful. Good at Fire Magic. Lots of incredibly tough units." It seemed weird to come up with, say, a Peon or Footman unit for the Demons. They just didn't lend themselves to that. We decided we'd make Demons less cool by filling out all the roles that races need to fight each other on Battle.net.

On "concentrating the coolness":

GDW: *Game balancing always seems to involve tuning system variables numbers up and down. Sounds like with WarCraft III you guys thought really big early in the project and then tuned some numbers downward as you went along.*

RP: That's right. Early on, we brainstormed tons of cool ideas. We have lots of sharp, creative people here, so we come up with way more ideas than we could ever put in a game. Then the designer's job over the next year or two years (however long the dev cycle is before the beta) is to hone all those ideas. Some we have to get rid of, some we have to modify, and some become a cornerstone of the gameplay.

One of our mantras—we have lots of mantras around here—is "concentrating the coolness." With WarCraft III, for example, we could've blown out to 20 or 30 units per race if we wanted to, but we wanted each unit to be meaningful. And we wanted to make sure each race had a unique feel. So even though every race has flying units, and worker units they still all do things in different ways.

We wanted that idea to carry through to heroes, too. Each race should have a little set of heroes that made it unique. When we started detailing out the heroes' spell kits, we originally had four heroes per race. But the spell kits were muddled with overlap, so we cut down to three heroes. That decision created a big controversy with our fan base because it led to us cutting the Human's Ranger hero. The Ranger ended up on the cutting room floor and there were petitions and all kinds of stuff like that online. So it was quite a contentious cut.

GDW: *Wow. Talk about a rabid fan base. They were petitioning the loss of a character before they'd even played the game.*

RP: Yeah. Crazy, isn't it (laughs)? We like to have a big fan community going even before we go beta. It's great to have fans that are really into it. The downside is you can't just blackbox a game and bring it to market. Lots of people are watching.

The day the Ranger was cut was big. People knew about her because we'd shown her on our website. When she disappeared one day, it caused quite a ruckus. Again, it was that kit argument I was talking about. Humans already had a ranged magic hero with the Archmage, and they had a cool tanklike hero with the Mountain King, and they had the Paladin hero as well. I was a little heartbroken to see the Ranger go, too. But I looked at the Night Elves and they had lots of archer units. Even looks-wise the Ranger looked like an Elven archer. We had to differentiate the races, so she got cut. It was still really tough.

On the effect of balancing heroes in WarCraft III:

GDW: *That's interesting. The heroes have really affected the gameplay dramatically. One thing I notice in WarCraft III is that I end up playing with smallish parties of units and not the huge armies that I play with in StarCraft.*

RP: That's right. When we started developing WarCraft III, a lot people wanted another game with StarCraft-style gameplay. You know, macromanagement and that. But we wanted to branch out a bit. We wanted a game with units that were tougher and more meaningful. In StarCraft, you can just throw lots of units into the battlefield and not care whether they live or die. You can get an army of 50 to 100 units going and it's no big deal.

For WarCraft III, we wanted to get rid of what we call the "fodder" unit. We want you to care about every grunt and every footman. Part of the reasoning for that was the increased focus on heroes. We wanted a hero to be a dominant force in the battlefield because, well, that's what you think of as a hero. So if we know there's going to be 50 units on the battlefield, then we'd have to make the hero ridiculously powerful for him to have a meaningful impact. If you have a battlefield with, say, 10 or 20 units, then the hero could be more realistically balanced. For WarCraft III to work the way we'd envisioned, the hero had to be balanced proportionally to the number of units that could be in a battle. Right? If the game was designed for 50-unit battles and then a hero gets into a fight with, say, only 10 units around, then he'd just mop them up. In WarCraft III, it's normal to see people running around with maybe 12 to 15 units. That's like an army in WarCraft III. Twenty-four units is almost the max.

Trying to enforce that mechanic, though, was a challenge. It was like, "How do we do that?" We had the mechanic in the game, "food," which kind of limited the number of units you have. We also had gold and lumber intakes for resources. But what was happening early on was that with just those mechanics in place players would build up to the cap in the game and just play there. Then if they lost their units they'd have this big gold and lumber surplus that they'd just spend to rebuild their army and max out again. It just didn't play very fun.

GDW: *This sounds like how you came up with the system for "upkeep."*

RP: Right, that's where upkeep came from. Upkeep was a concept that was pretty controversial and we tried a bunch of different ideas beforehand. But that's what we eventually settled on.

The concept of upkeep is: The bigger your army is, the more it saps your gold income. If you build up a big army, then upkeep siphons off your excess gold income so you can't get these huge gold surpluses. The idea was to encourage you to fight more when you have fewer units.

Originally, we tried to encourage small armies just through tweaking unit numbers and costs. But as we watched people play around here—with giant armies—we realized we'd have to go back to the drawing board. We sat down and said "We want a game that plays with fewer units where heroes feel important. How do we make that happen?"

Everyone brainstormed up a bunch of ideas and we talked through each one. We just kept picking at it and testing ideas for a couple of weeks until we had a system that worked. Actually, lots of people hated upkeep at first, so getting it implemented was controversial. Part of the problem was we originally called it "Tax." I guess it gave people, I don't know, like April 15 flashbacks or something (laughs). They couldn't accept the game dynamic just because of the name. Once we came up with the name "upkeep," though, the last people opposing it said, "Okay, let's try it."

Upkeep was a game mechanic that got developed to encourage the hero-based gameplay we had set as a goal. As a game designer, figuring stuff like that out is series of big conversations to little ones to minibattles to see which elements work, which don't, which need to be changed, and which need to be yanked. You know, it's an ongoing process every day.

On iterative design and balancing a game after it has been released:

GDW: *So it sounds like iterative design is a key component for how this gets done.*

RP: Absolutely. We hone system variables over and over as we play and test a game. We're not afraid to pull a unit, pull a major design system, or put in a new one all the way up until beta. In fact, with WarCraft III, we actually introduced a couple of spells post beta. We had designed them ahead of time knowing we might need them. I figured we should go into beta with about 90% of the racial units and spells in the game. I'd learned from previous betas that, no matter how great we think the units play, once pro gamer-types—who're going to play much more than we'll ever play and at a much higher skill level—get a hold of it that, we're going to have to change things. So I went ahead and left some holes in each race so we could fill them with different things if we needed to. And, sure enough, we did that.

GDW: *Interesting, so you were still balancing things after beta?*

RP: Yep. We did patches to the StarCraft balance for two years after we released it. It definitely evolves. You could probably do a sociology class on the evolution of a game community.

There are two things that I see that happen once a game's been released. First of all, imbalances are discovered that just were never discovered before. This is because a million people playing a game is a lot different than a thousand people playing from the beta. Somebody out there will come up with a creative play technique that no one else has thought of. Then once he starts using it on Battle.net, every person he plays sees the imbalance and it spreads across the community like a virus. That forces our hand into doing something.

The other thing that happens is just evolution of gameplay. Sometimes I see things that I want to patch slowly. Like, suddenly one race might be winning a larger proportion of games on Battle.net for a couple of weeks and it seems like a dominant strategy has emerged. And we could certainly go in and "fix" it. But usually what's happening is just an evolution of how people play. You see spikes and valleys. What happens is—let's say the Humans become dominant for a couple of weeks. Well, you've got to give the community a chance to see the new strategy and develop a counter strategy. You see the same thing happen in professional sports sometimes. You know, in NFL football, the 3–4 defense dominated for a few years. It wasn't an imbalance that they had to go to the rules committee and say, "We need to outlaw the 3–4 defense because it's too badass." The offensive coordinators just had to scheme and develop their playbooks to attack it. I see the same thing sometimes in our game community. It can be really challenging sometimes post release to decide what to patch and what not to patch. So it's a process.

GDW: *Tell me about the software tools you use to do this. You can track what players are doing pretty closely via Battle.net?*

RP: Yes. For WarCraft III, we hired a web programmer to make a system that could track all kinds of data. We found someone who had created a really amazing fan site that tracked statistics from our other games and gave him a job. Like we'll say, "We want to see how races play against each other on a map-by-map basis." And he can make a report of that. We do that pretty often. So there'll be times when my game balance designer wants to make an adjustment to the Orcs or something. And I'll say, "Okay, that sounds reasonable, but let's look at the stats too." And we'll look at the stats and we'll go "Hey, actually Orcs aren't really having that problem, so let's hold off for a while."

GDW: *So you use the data to determine whether the imbalances are perceived or real.*

RP: Yeah. We're not slaves to it, though. It's just one of many tools we use. You have to have an intuitive sense of it also. Luckily, the game balance guy on WarCraft III is a really good player.

We also have a group of top-level players that send us feedback directly. Like, if we see something like the Undead hammering the Humans in a peculiar way, then we might gather replays from top-level players and look at exactly what they're doing.

GDW: *Sounds like there's a symbiotic thing going on between the fan community and the development team. For example, you hired the web programmer from the fan base.*

RP: Yes, our webmaster had one of the top WarCraft II websites back in the day. He got hired as a QA tester and then moved himself up on the web side. Even if you're the best programmer in the world, we're not going to hire you unless you're a game enthusiast. If someone's a fan of our games and they have development skills too, then that's perfect.

GDW: *It must be a dream job for them.*

RP: Yeah. They tend to be pretty happy employees (laughs).

On playtesting at Blizzard:

GDW: *Okay, this is a good segue to the next point: I'm curious about your process for playtesting early versions internally.*

RP: Before we go beta we're—as a development team—playing on a fairly regular basis. We don't have structured play sessions like where we say "Friday is playtest day" or something because, like I said, we're all a bunch of gamers. Everyone here loves to play these games. So once the game gets playable, everyone on the team is playing it. There'll be lunchtime sessions where all the artists play together. They work in a bullpen so they're really close. And the designers will be playing together and the programmers will be mixing and matching. One way we know when a game is fun is when we have to say to some people, "Hey you're playing too much of the game. Start working some more." (laughs)

On being a game designer:

GDW: *Tell us something you've learned about the craft of being a game designer.*

RP: One thing I've learned from starting young to where I am now is: Yes, you need to have all the game design skills, and you need to know about different development disciplines so you can design smart. A designer needs to wear a lot of different hats. But the other side of it that I don't see talked about much is the skill of working with your team.

The game designer, at least here, is not the primary idea generation guy. He's the primary vision holder for the game. I struggled early on when I used to really fight for my ideas versus other people's ideas. What I learned was, "Hey, I'm in a position where I can put in a lot of the game design elements, and it's really important for me to be a conduit for everyone else's ideas." When I made that mental shift, it was a pretty big day.

Now I look at my job and see that it's really important to listen to everyone else on the team and try to get their ideas in when they are good for the game. Sometimes a team member will have great idea but not know how to package it within the overall framework of the game. So that's where I come in. I might work with them and try to get it into the game in a way that works from a game system perspective. Once you do that, then your job becomes a lot easier. Everyone trusts you more. And it's just this domino process: You're not fighting your ideas versus their ideas; you're not explaining to them why their ideas suck. You're working with them, and you're their tool for getting good ideas into the game. Then everything just flows better.

as your game evolves. When this principle is adhered to, tweaking an element only changes one aspect of the gameplay, rather than several aspects, and the job of balancing your game will become methodical, rather than a haphazard guessing game.

Exercise 10.11: Purity of Purpose

Think about your original game prototype. Are there any extraneous elements—elements that have no purpose? Remove the least important element of your game and test the system without it. Does the game still function? Is it complete? Balanced? Remove another element. Continue stripping elements from your game and retesting until you reach a point where your game no longer functions. Now again answer the question: Are there any extraneous elements in your design?

One Change at a Time

Train yourself to make only one change at a time. Limiting yourself to just a single change often feels cumbersome because after each change,

you have to test the entire system again and gauge the affects. However, if you change two or more variables at once, it becomes difficult to tell what effect each of those changes has on the overall system.

Spreadsheets

When balancing a game, nothing is more valuable than a good set of spreadsheets. As you design, you should track of all your data in a spreadsheet program like Excel or Google Sheets. This will make the job of balancing your game much smoother.

If possible, your spreadsheets should mirror your game's structure. This will allow you to better communicate with your programmers. I strongly recommend sitting down with your technical team and laying out the spreadsheets together. Each subsystem within your game, whether it is combat, economic, or social, should have its own set of interconnecting tables. Apply the same principles of purity of purpose and modularity to your spreadsheets. Look at the spreadsheets as both your starting point—a great tool for laying out the game design—and your ending point—a tool used in refining and perfecting the gameplay. If you can, create a tool that will allow you to export and import these spreadsheets easily. This way, you can create variations for testing purposes and switch them out on the fly during a session. This will allow you to see how changes affect the overall gameplay.

Exercise 10.12: Spreadsheets

Take the game variables you listed in Exercise 10.5 and put them into a spreadsheet program like Excel or Google Sheets. Make sure that the structure of the spreadsheet parallels that of the game system. Now you can use this tool in balancing your game.

CONCLUSION

Congratulations, by now your original game should be functional, internally complete, and balanced. That means you are ready to begin refining your game, the final stage of the design process. But before I move on, one word about how you "know" your game is really balanced. I have filled you up with rules, tools, and methods, but when it comes to balancing a game, much of what you do will depend on your gut.

I mentioned this briefly early on. There is no way to teach you how to use your instincts in a book. Intuition is both a gift and a learned skill. The more you design, the finer your gut instincts will become. You will know when a game is out of balance without a tester raising an eyebrow, and you will be able to spot a loophole or dead end immediately and implement the proper fix. My goal in this chapter has been to give you a head start, and hopefully, when you combine this with your natural sense for game design, you will be able to master the process quickly and see your game reach its full potential.

DESIGNER PERSPECTIVE: SHAWN ALEXANDER ALLEN

President/Design Director, NuChallenger

Shawn Alexander Allen is an artist, writer, game designer, and the founder of games and culture company NuChallenger. He has over 13 years of experience making & marketing games, from AAA titles including GTA IV, GTA V, Red Dead Redemption, Max Payne 3, and LA Noire to independent award-winning games including Corporate Vandals (2014), Treachery in Beatdown City (2020), and Treachery in Beatdown City: Ultra Remix (2023). The LA Times called Beatdown City "The most relevant, antiracist game of 2020".

How did you become a game designer?

While in high school I wanted to design games but didn't know how to. I had a few ideas for games, but the tools to make them really weren't there yet. I'm not a programmer, and in the 90s, you only really had games like RPG Maker to make other games.

My initial attempts at making game-like things actually came from making some Pokémon joke cartoons using the Gameboy sprites and hooking up some rudimentary buttons in Flash. You could make your way through a heavily scripted fight that had an ending.

Beyond that, I just had this itch for turning my comics into games, which stayed with me through my days in computer art and graphic design in college.

Because the path toward making games seemed so... difficult and vague, and because I felt the discussion around the merits of games was pretty bad from the magazines of the time, I started to write my own criticism, which comprised mostly of breakdowns of games and why I liked/disliked them.

Eventually I started going to NYU Game Center talks and festivals, and found that I was able to hold a game design conversation, even though I wasn't an official "game designer" myself.

All of this, combined with seeing the indie games movement of the time blowing up, and the proliferation of tools such as Game Maker, made it much easier to grasp the idea of actually making my own games, so I decided to do it.

I found early on that I had a knack for ideas, and the ability to communicate those ideas through writing up documentation that expressed the how/why and what of game mechanics, story, etc. and I was working with someone who let me experiment with ideas. The rest is history.

On games that have inspired him:

I'm a fairly aesthetics and feel driven designer — if I don't like the way a game looks, I usually won't play it. That's mostly to preface that many of these choices will echo this preference.

Double Dragon (NES): Double Dragon on the NES was one of the first games I played. And as a kid, it felt like reality — like 80s New York. The vibrant, yet dark palette, the ominous music, the re-skins of enemies to be all sorts of skin shades... they felt like growing up. This game's vibe has stuck with me forever.

Also, the enemies were built with fairly sophisticated surrounding behavior, which I studied a lot.

Street Fighter II: The original fighting game love of my life. They made such a huge leap in graphics, the game felt unreal at the time. And the way they did so much, with so little. The emphasis on strong key frames, and various game feel adjustments, like slowdowns when you win, some screen-shake when enemies fall, etc. as well as the iconic cast has made Street Fighter a cultural phenomenon.

Final Fantasy IV/VI: These games taught me to love games storytelling. I was an avid reader as a kid, but these games brought such vivid worlds to life, with complex characters that floored me, and are still so memorable to this day. This is definitely where I started to think game stories could be bigger.

Chrono Trigger: Chrono Trigger solidified my love of Akira Toriyama's art, while showing that games could be both bigger, and smaller at the same time. RPGs were massive, and Chrono Trigger felt a lot smaller, but still very complete. The time mechanic really allowed them to play with the world in a way that I had never seen before, which meant everything felt more cohesive. One of the first video games I dreamed up at the age of 15 was supposed to surpass Chrono trigger in content and gameplay, but the concept of multiple endings, time travel, and multi-phase enemy fights were things I wanted to iterate on from Chrono Trigger. That game idea has been left in a binder, but I always think about returning to it one day.

Ogre Battle: This is like the MF Doom of RPGs, if that makes any sense. It is SO driven by choices that it can feel overwhelming. In fact, the game starts with some very *deep* questions to decide your alignment, many of which were way too mature for me as a teenager, but I appreciated the way it treated me.

There's one choice in the game where you have to save the life of an unpopular nobleman, taking a reputation hit in the process, in order to get the best ending, which just really said something to me at the time.

Fire Pro Wrestling D: The Fire Pro Wrestling series is something of a miracle — a fairly old series with a complex behavior system that allows you to put on your own "sim" wrestling matches. At a very low point in my life, I found FPW:D and a community of folks working on wrestler "edits", all with the goal to make their favorite wrestlers be able to function as CPU characters in the way that a real person would. I was so interested in the behavior system that we had to rebuild elements of it for *Treachery in Beatdown City*.

Killer 7: Can I say that I was obsessed with this game? An on rails adventure game mashed up with light gun mechanics? All to deliver a tension that almost makes it a horror game? With a beautiful cel shaded aesthetic and a penchant for mixed media? Killer 7 has inspired me for a long time to just do something different. There's also some really cool in game moments where the game is telling you a story, and you're still in control, which makes you feel like you can avoid what's coming next, but really, you're being made to suffer through the events as a participant, not as a voyeur.

On exciting developments in the industry:

This may seem a bit trite, but the most exciting development in the recent game industry for me is seeing more Black folks making games. I'm happy to see folks of all backgrounds making games, of course, but as a Black creator, who has seen the amount of work it's taken to get Black artists and film makers on the map, I get a lot of joy seeing that there are more folks than ever working on games. There are only a few notable Black game designers from the old industry, and we just need to see more Black folks being given the ability to make games, do it their way, and succeed or fail based on their own skills.

I'm not sure why, but people often conflate my interest in seeing more Black folks making games with Black folks making games... for other Black folks, which is pretty racist, and in tune with how people see other media. For some reason a show with a majority white cast is for everyone, but a show with a majority Black cast is for Black people. Same with games. Japanese team? "for everyone" White team? "for everyone" Black team? "for Black folks only."

But that's not what we (the collective of Black developers) are doing. We're just making games our way, from our perspectives. And what we're seeing is many subsections of cultures (because Black folks are not a monolith) who have been in love with games and other art for many years, who are now finding their way into the industry, and we're seeing some VERY cool things coming out of it.

The next thing I'd like to see, is the industry REALLY going to bat and supporting Black game dev's games... because that still is a big struggle for even the best games to pull in a good audience.

On design process:

You know, ideation is interesting. I'm a very visual designer, very much about themes, aesthetics. I always have been. I've been a writer since I was a kid – I made some children's books when I was in elementary school. I LOVE to tell stories, with words and pictures and so I think of stories, or ... settings that would be interesting for a game, and then I think about what type of mechanics would fit in there, because I obviously want to make a cool game that supports those ideas, and one of my favorite aspects of game design is when play creates and/or supports a narrative in a game. Like hip hop, where going all city, i.e. seeing your tag on a train in each borough, was a goal for taggers that required a lot of extra steps to set up, like obtaining paint, climbing buildings, sneaking into tunnels; risking your life, basically. But I've also sometimes built a game off of a single game mechanic and let the aesthetics come through afterwards.

Treachery in Beatdown City was actually a compromise of a BIGGER beat 'em up game idea. I spent a while coming up with characters and themes for a beat 'em up. I watched movies, wrote a story, played beat 'em ups, wrote down my mechanical goals. When I started designing, I didn't even realize what we were doing was more akin to a shmup style brawler, but because of design issues and technical constraints, I had to rethink everything.

A literal shower moment kicked off the rest of the development. I went to work researching even more games, more games in how they handled turns, enemy behavior, animation, and the works. And then, I wrote a good amount of it down, on a lot of index cards, and then typed it up, because we needed solid documentation. This all drove the rest of development.

One thing that hindered progress is that I was a bit all over the place then, as I didn't really know how to prioritize the project's needs, so I obsessed over things like animation issues, rather than focusing on the greater whole. Eventually getting a producer job helped me understand scope, prioritizing tasks, and how to hone and polish what works, and leave what doesn't on the floor.

Do you use prototypes?

I do, in a sense, but mostly to just prove what we're doing is good, ha-ha. I've had to recently realize that prototyping is a lot smaller than the big prototype you pitch with. You prototype individual ideas that build a bigger prototype of a game, so it's important to realize any idea should just go in quickly to see how it works, and what needs reworking. I like to think of it more of just getting the idea out there so that you can see if the basic implementation can lead to more things.

I like the idea of fail fast, but mostly for discarding elements of a game that don't work, not for invalidating an entire game concept.

One good example of how I've had to do it in a weird direction is UX design. I worked with a team that made the final designs for a free-to-play game I was working on. I would do thumbnails for the images based on a document I wrote. These thumbnails were created to show what I thought the implementation should look like, and the UX team would take it and develop it into more finished art which we would implement. However, sometimes we would stumble onto some issues if something wasn't thought all the way through ahead of time. So, we'd take the implementation, hack up the art and make new concepts, or rework the order of things appropriately. We couldn't abandon the concept, so we had to finesse it.

I also worked on a paper prototype to see what would happen if you added the ability to cross out other player's pieces in tic tac toe, that the game would be more interesting. I was playing with this concept for Corporate Vandals, our sticker-based turf warfare game. Even though it was intended to be multiplayer, I actually paper prototyped by myself. I started playing rapid games of tic tac to by alone, not trying to think too hard, just impulsively going over each player's X or O. I found the process to be fun, and I kept building out the grid to make it even more interesting. After some rounds alone, I printed out some rudimentary stickers, cut them up, and played a few games with a small group of friends. After a few games with them, I bought $2000 worth of stickers.

Then, when we showed the game at No Quarter, I kept adapting and changing the rules because the game is focused on the unpredictable nature of graffiti/sticker bombing, and it went really well; we tagged up the rules, even. It was a great live playtest of a prototype sent out for experimental purposes.

On a difficult design problem:

I think the easiest one to talk about is making Treachery in Beatdown City work, since the combat we were trying to build just wasn't hitting, no pun intended. Up until this point I think I had explored every conventional beat 'em up I could, but with the turn-based aspect, I had to then go and replay a bunch of titles, record, them, and write up my findings, and then, turn that into something that could be made into a game that felt like a cohesive whole.

I didn't know the term "design pillars" at the time, but that's how we kept the game relatively on track. If it supported the goals of making the game we wanted, we kept it. Anything else we jettisoned.

To "solve" our problem, I just had to do a lot of writing and rewriting. Some small sketches of what the game could look like, some in game mockups. I just had to do a lot of iteration, and sometimes just gut instincts for what would fix a certain issue.

What are you most proud of in your career?

Honestly, it was launching Treachery in Beatdown City. Despite launching huge hundred million- and billion-dollar games at Rockstar, or other projects at other companies, this game was mine.

One of the problems with game design is that even if you have a hot idea, it takes time to really bring everything together. And that often requires money, or a lot of free time, which can keep the goals of a project scattered, which can threaten a project's success.

But we managed to ship a game after working on it off and on for about a decade, and it was better than we could have expected it to be.

Advice for designers:

I always recommend thinking outside of games for games inspiration. Don't harp on genre, as that's less important than what you want your game to do, to inspire, to allow players to feel. Trying to make a platformer for making a platformer's sake, and then tacking on some stuff won't cut it. But making a game that requires jumping because it evokes some sort of feeling, or allows you to create a certain puzzle that only platforming will allow, is a much better way of looking at design.

Nobody listens to Kendrick Lamar just because he's a "rapper." They listen to his records because they are these multifaceted creations that speak to something bigger, or they listen because his tracks are bangers, and folks just miss the point entirely. You can't control your audience, and how they react. You can only do the best you can, think your project through as best you can, and put it out there.

DESIGNER PERSPECTIVE: HEATHER KELLEY

Founder, Kokoromi experimental game collective

Heather Kelley is a game designer whose credits include Thief: Deadly Shadows (2004), Tom Clancy's Splinter Cell: Chaos Theory (2005), Star Wars: Lethal Alliance (2006), and SUPERHYPERCUBE VR (2016). Experimental projects include Lapis (2005), Trente pas entre terre et ciel (2012) and Grow Still (2023). She was a curator for the groundbreaking exhibition Joue le Jeu at Paris's Gaîté Lyrique in 2012. In 2013, she was awarded the Microsoft's Women in Gaming "Innovator" Award, and was named one of the five most influential women in gaming by Inc. Magazine. She is currently a professor at the Entertainment Technology Center at Carnegie Mellon University and Sensory Director at LIKELIKE playful arts gallery (Pittsburgh, PA).

On getting into the game industry:

I was in grad school in Austin, studying gender and technology. A company called Girl Games opened in Austin with the goal to make games for preteen girls. I got on board as a researcher for their first game, Let's Talk About Me! and then became the producer and content manager of the website, which included games, entertainment, and community features. Over the next ten years at various companies, I learned to apply my skills to design smart toys, PC, console, handheld and VR games. Basically, like many creatives, I was at the right place at the right time, with just enough skills and experience!

On game influences:

I generally like games that present a complete aesthetic package and that exist outside the mainstream.

- *Raaka-Tu for TRS-80*: Probably the first computer game I ever played—a text adventure. I never finished it! In retrospect, the design was not too great (extremely arbitrary), but I was captivated by the exotic locale and mysterious events.
- *Dragon's Lair in the arcade*: This one showed me that games could captivate the imagination in a completely different way. The gameplay was of course terribly unforgiving, and the traditional cel animation style was unlike anything else in the arcade at that time of 8-bit graphics. It was like night and day in both visual treatment and gameplay concept.
- *Vib Ribbon for PS1*: An early beat-matching game from famed music game designer Masaya Matsuura. What inspires me is the completely unique vector graphics, the warm but creepy soundtrack, the zen-out rhythm combo gameplay, and especially the ability to use your own CDs to generate levels. The game allowed you to take the game out (with the entire game running in memory on a PS1), put your own CDs in, and let the game generate the game level from the songs from your own collection. This was user-generated content way ahead of the curve, and it was a big inspiration for Kokoromi's event GAMMA 01: Audio Feed.

- *Seaman for Dreamcast*: This game amazes me on a couple of levels—the absolutely bizarre underlying concept (a talking pet fish with a human face that you grow in a virtual tank, and which eventually starts to psychoanalyze you), the well-honed vocal recognition system (it shipped with a microphone, and the software's ability to understand relevant conversational keywords was just eerie at the time), and of course the voice-over intros by Leonard Nimoy.

On the design process:

In professional contexts I'm often given constraints to work within, and my process for those might differ from situations in which I'm starting from scratch. For my own personal work, I usually have an idea or emotion I want to convey and then think about what interaction and goals could put the player in a position to experience those feelings or ideas firsthand.

On the prototypes:

I use them as much as I can. I'm not a coder, so if it's a gameplay system concept that can't be worked out in a paper prototype, I usually work with a programmer to get them done. First I'll have a very "high-level" design document on paper—maybe just one or two pages long. Then I will meet with the programmer and we'll talk about the idea, sketch it out more, and decide if anything specific needs to be documented. Then, from these documents and the conversations, the programmer creates a piece of interaction. We review that and talk about it some more, and continue the process like that. Of course that sometimes means throwing out stuff that you thought was a good idea on paper but which turns out not to work when you get it in your hands. That's what prototyping is all about!

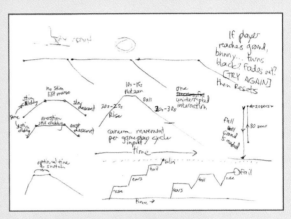

Game design sketch by Heather Kelley

Advice to designers:

Keep your communication lean by picking the best medium for each bit of information. Draw sketches, make a flow chart, pull reference images and videos from the net, or heck, perform it live if you need to! And whenever you can, build things with interactivity to represent your concepts. Make a low fidelity paper prototype like a board game, or use one of the many software tools out there — even ones that are not game engines. I once made a quick and dirty game prototype in slide presentation software!. Hone all these communication skills now so you can use them flexibly throughout your career.

FURTHER READING

Conway, John. *On Numbers and Games.* Natick: A K Peters, 2001.

Knizia, Reiner. *Dice Games Properly Explained.* Surrey: Elliot Right Way Books, 2000.

Lecky-Thompson, Guy W. *Infinite Game Universe: Mathematical Techniques.* Boston: Charles River, 2001.

Nowakowski, Richard J., ed. *Games of No Chance.* Cambridge: Cambridge University Press, 1998.

Schreiber, Ian, Romero, Brenda, *Game Balance.* Boca Raton: CRC Press, 2021.

Tweet, Jonathan, Williams, Skip and Cook, Monty. *Dungeons & Dragons Core Rulebook Set.* Renton: Wizards of the Coast, 2003.

Weinberg, Gerald M. *An Introduction to General Systems Thinking*, Silver Anniversary Edition. New York: Dorset House Publishing, 2001.

END NOTES

1. Owen, David. Invasion of the Asteroids. *Esquire.* February 1981.

2. Adams, Ernest. "A Symmetry Lesson," Gamasutra.com, October 16, 1998.

3. Ibid.

4. Ryan, Tim. "Beginning Level Design Part 2: Rules to Design by and Parting Advice," Gamasutra.com, April 13, 1999.

5. Owen, Invasion of the Asteroids.

Chapter 11
Fun and Accessibility

Remember when you first started testing your core idea, when you had just built out the foundations and structure of your game? All you were worried about at that point was making sure the idea was fun, that it seemed like it had the potential to meet your experience goals, and that it was a good idea for a game. Now that you have gone on and created a functional, complete, and balanced game, it is time to go back and really make sure the essence of what you thought was fun and appealing is still there, and that that game really is meeting those experience goals. Of course, you have been paying attention to whether your game was fun and engaging throughout the process, but now is the time to make fun, engagement, and accessibility your primary focus.

Before you can test for fun, let's think about what is really meant when we use the word "fun." Unfortunately, fun is one of the most elusive concepts you will ever try to pin down. As with many aspects of art and entertainment, fun is subjective, contextual, and entirely up to personal taste. You might think washing dishes is fun (I do not), or you might think shooting bad guys is fun. Your favorite game might be entirely based on strategy, while a friend's game requires physical skill and dexterity. Early in your process, you have set specific experience goals that better define the type of emotional appeal you have been trying to reach with your game. These are related to the "fun" of your particular game.

To best meet those goals, you want your game's definition of fun to be specific, so that it provides the right kind of emotional appeal for your players. Games are voluntary activities; they require player participation—a high level of participation. Unlike movies or television, the show does not go on if players cease to play. So if your game has no emotional appeal, players are apt to stop playing or never pick it up in the first place. There are many different types of emotions that make a game engaging—not all of them are what we usually call "fun," but for simplicity, we use that overriding term because it's such a universal theme in what players are looking for in a game. All of the emotional and dramatic elements that drive a player to pick up your game, to try it out, and to continue to play it are usually what players cite when asked about what makes a game fun. Nicole Lazzaro discusses four very different types of fun in her sidebar, "Why We Play Games," on page 299. They are Easy Fun, Hard Fun, Serious Fun, and

DOI: 10.1201/9781003460268-13

People Fun. Qualities such as these, as well as your own specific experience goals for player engagement, are what you will be looking for when testing your game during this next stage.

Is Your Game Fun?

How can you tell if your game is fun? By this time, you know the answer: Ask the playtesters. But playtesters are not often able to articulate exactly where the fun is lacking, so you will need some tools to help you identify the fun factor yourself.

When I discussed the dramatic elements of games, I talked about the fact that these elements are what engage players with the formal system—what gets them and keeps them emotionally involved in the game. Challenge, play, and story can all provide emotional hooks that captivate players and invest them in the outcome so that they will keep playing.

Challenge

In Chapter 4 on page 102, I talked in detail about some of the elements of challenge, including the state of "flow" that players can reach when the challenge the game offers is perfectly tuned to the participants' skill levels. The following list of thoughts and questions addresses several of the most import aspects of challenge to consider when testing your game for fun. Ask yourself and your testers these questions to measure where the challenges in your game are working and where they can be improved.

Reaching and Exceeding Goals

The desire to achieve goals is a fundamental part of being human. How can your games tap into this desire? Does your game have one goal at the end, or are there subgoals along the way? Reaching subgoals can charge your players up emotionally and get them ready for the long haul to the end of the game.

Are your goals too hard to reach? Too easy? Are they clearly defined? Or are they hidden from view? Ask your playtesters to talk out loud about their goals as they play the game; this will help give you a sense if they are engaged in the goals you have planned or if they are moving off on tangents.

Competing against Opponents

Many of us are competitive by nature, and competition provides a natural challenge in a game, whether it is directly multiplayer or indirect in the form of rankings or other criteria. We like to see how we compare to others, whether it is in terms of skill, intelligence, strength, or just dumb luck.

Are you missing a chance to create competition in your game? Listen to your players talk to each other if your test is face-to-face. If your testers are in different places, make sure they have a way to communicate with each other. Trash talking, ribbing, and the kind of chest thumping that happens naturally during playtests can give you a great idea for what is driving the competition in your game, however be sure that you are thinking about how to kept this kind of behavior in the realm of good sportsmanship!

Stretching Personal Limits

The goals we set for ourselves often carry a power that the goals set by others do not. We know our own limits better than any game designer can. When we set our own goals and surpass those personal limits, there is a sense of accomplishment beyond any in-game payoff system.

Some of the most popular games of all time allow players to set their own goals—challenge themselves, so to speak. Of course, not all players enjoy this type of system; they find it too open ended. Can your game incorporate this phenomenon? You need to know your potential audience and judge whether you should strive to offer this type of freedom.

Ask your playtesters to talk out loud about their personal goals in the game as they play. Are they setting their own goals? Would they like to be able to set goals for themselves? You will be surprised to find out how often players create their own subgoals within a system, especially if they know they cannot win, but they want to feel a sense of accomplishment anyway.

Exercising Difficult Skills

Learning a skill is hard, but the process has its rewards when you finally master it—even more so when you get to show it off. Presenting your players with the opportunity to learn difficult skills is a challenge, but it is a hollow one unless you provide ample opportunity for them to master and display that skill. And remember, people do not master skills after five minutes of a tutorial. Learning a new skill often takes time and trials. Rewarding the player for sticking with it will make the process enjoyable.

Making Interesting Choices

Game designer Sid Meier once said, "Games are a series of interesting choices." These choices can range from where to place your blocks in Tetris to how many peons to produce in WarCraft III. If the choices have consequences, then they are interesting. If not, they are merely a distraction. Is

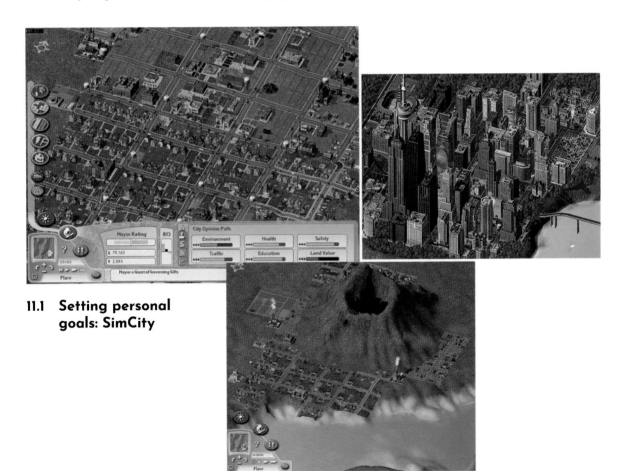

11.1   Setting personal goals: SimCity

your game providing choices with consequences? Or are your players simply micromanaging? Are players aware of the consequences as they make those choices? Creating dilemmas, where players must weigh their choices carefully, is a powerful way to challenge your players.

Ask your playtesters to explain what they think the consequences of their choices will be as they play. What factors are weighing into their decisions? Are they correct? Or are they making arbitrary decisions? Arbitrary decisions can kill a player's sense of responsibility for an action. How can you improve the choices, macro and micro, that players are making in your game?

Play

Along with presenting challenges, games are an arena for play. As I discussed in Chapter 4, there are as many different types of play as there are players. What forms of play does your game employ? Are you making the most of that opportunity? Can you offer other areas of play for different types of players, or do you want to deepen the play for a single type of player? Think about your game in terms of these natural types of play.

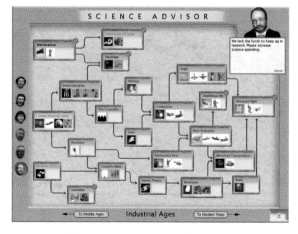

11.2   Making interesting choices: Civilization III

Living out Fantasies

The desires for pleasure, romance, freedom, and adventure are all powerful forces. Most people dream of being something they are not—an astronaut, snowboarder, general, rap star, etc. Let your players live their fantasies, even for a moment, and you will have a captive audience. Role-playing games have their basis in this kind of fantasy play, but all games can gain from tapping into people's dreams for themselves. What aspirations does your game put within reach for its players? What fantasies does it fulfill?

This concept can be extended to imaginative play scenarios that are not necessarily fantasies that a player wants to fulfill but rather scenarios that are intriguing to explore even though they go against a player's personal ethics. Grand Theft Auto V, for example, fits this description. Players may be compelled by the game even though they don't fantasize about robbing and killing.

Social Interaction

People love interacting with one another. Games offer an amazing forum for social interaction, one that is equally about the game and the relationships people bring to the game. Adding this element to your game creates an unpredictable, emergent layer that is often enough for many players to stay hooked on a game long after its release. Some online games with strong social interaction have such loyal players that they have found ways to keep playing even after the official servers and support for the game have ended. Is your game making the most of any potential social interaction? Have you provided time and opportunity for people to get to know one another?

Exploration and Discovery

Nothing is so thrilling as venturing into uncharted waters and seeing what you find. If your game makes this promise to the player and then fulfills it, you will create an enchanting experience.

11.3   Living out fantasies: Star Wars Galaxies

Most great adventure, role-playing, and walking simulator games include an element of exploration. The act of discovering something is magical. But creating that sense of trepidation when turning a new corner, anticipation when you think you might have found something, fear of getting lost, and exhilaration of discovery is a difficult task. Are you telegraphing the right direction to the secret treasure? You want to help your players, but you do not want the process of exploration to become rote. Try going on an adventure yourself. Go for a hike on a new trail, or take a walk through a part of town you do not know. Think about the emotions you feel as you make your way—how can you recreate these feelings in your players?

Collection

Some remnant of our hunter-gatherer ancestors must drive this need, but there is nothing like letting players create collections for engaging them in a game. Whether it is a collection that only lasts a single hand of a card game or a collection of Magic: The Gathering or Yu-Gi-Oh trading cards that spans years of play and hundreds, perhaps thousands, of dollars of spending, collection is fun for many different types of players.

Stimulation

A game that stimulates the senses and imagination is a treat. Whether it is immersive 3D graphics, surround sound, or a gestural control system that gets you up on your feet acting out the part of an adventurer or a tennis player, sensory stimulation adds to the fun factor. Designers have more opportunity than ever to design innovative new gameplay using today's new control systems that include VR headsets, motion sensors, cameras, footpads, guitars, bongos, biofeedback devices, and other inventive attachments.

Self-Expression and Performance

As human beings, we have a desire to express ourselves, whether it is in the form of artwork, poetry, or building a character in a game world. Giving people the chance to show off who they are and be creative makes for an engaging experience and will add a new dimension to your game.

Construction/Destruction

Construction is a great tool for making players feel invested in a game. Whether it is constructing cities, armies, space colonies, or characters, building things is fun. On the other hand, as much as we humans enjoy construction, we also like tearing things down. Anyone who has built a sand castle only to stomp it down again can tell you that. Giving players the opportunities to both build and destroy provides different types of fun, both of which can make your game successful.

Story

Story can be a powerful mechanism for engaging people's emotions. As one of the earliest forms of entertainment as well as communication, we have a natural urge to tell and listen to tales about one another. By incorporating dramatic elements into your game, you can tap into this fascination with narrative and storytelling.

As I discussed in Chapter 4, however, drama in a game has a different source than that in a traditional story. In a movie or novel, drama comes from our investment in characters who struggle to overcome obstacles, both internal and external; it is what we call empathy. In games, drama can arise from our own struggle to overcome those obstacles ourselves, as in agency, or when we are so involved in the anticipation and interpretation of the story that we experience a deep empathy with the characters and situations. The difference between creating drama using agency and empathy presents a very difficult problem to the game designer. Ask yourself some questions about the drama in your game, such as:

- Do you have a compelling, imaginative premise that the players care about?
- Do you have unique characters who are faced with compelling challenges?
- Does your story line drive the gameplay or emerge from it?

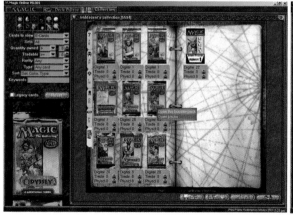

11.4 Magic: The Gathering Online: card collection screens

Illustrations used with permission of Wizards of the Coast, Inc.

11.5   Destruction: The Hulk

Hulk: TM & © 2003 Marvel Characters, Inc. Used with Permission.
Image courtesy of Universal Interactive, Inc. and is used under license.

- Are your players playing your game because of its story or in spite of it?
- What is it about the story, the characters, etc. that is working or not working for them?

Read Bruce Straley's discussion on page 129 of how he and the team from The Last of Us considered every aspect of the narrative beats in the game and integrated the gameplay with them to get players invested in the characters, their story, and the dramatic situation. Make sure you're thinking about the narrative beats of your game story at this level of detail.

Analyzing Appeal

The preceding list encompasses some of the elements that can, if executed well, improve your game's appeal and help to meet your experience goals. Do not try to cram all of them into your game design, though. It is more important to analyze the core pleasures of your game concept and

make sure they are complementary and clearly apparent to players. Let's take a look at a couple of popular games and see how they have incorporated these elements.

World of Warcraft

- Overarching goal of growing your character combined with the smaller goals inherent in quests, adventures, and tasks
- Competition among players to become more powerful, popular, and/or famous than others
- Fantasy of being in a world of magic and adventure
- Social interaction with other players online
- Exploration of huge, unusual fantasy world
- Stimulation of beautiful 3D graphics and sound
- Self-expression through role playing
- Huge back story and legends of the world and characters

- Construction of character, building wealth, accumulating possessions, etc. and destruction of monsters and other players (if you choose)
- Collection of inventory items

Monopoly

- Goal of owning all the property on the board
- Competition among players
- Fantasy of being a real estate tycoon
- Social interaction with other players, trading properties, etc.
- Construction/destruction of houses, hotels, and monopolies
- Collection of property sets

Tetris

- Goal of clearing all your lines of blocks
- Stimulation of catchy music, colorful blocks
- Collection of all the blocks in a single row
- Construction/destruction of rows of blocks

As you can see, I identified 10 distinct types of pleasure, all elements of challenge and play discussed above, in World of Warcraft, just six in Monopoly, and four in Tetris. And yet each of these games has been wildly successful in its own way. Clearly, there is no relationship between the number of elements and the amount of fun a player can derive from a game. Tetris might be one of the most universally addictive games ever, and it is quite simple. Making games fun is not about including every possible type of challenge or play but in finding the right combination. If you can do that, you will delight your players and keep them interested in your game.

Exercise 11.1: Challenge and Play

As I did with World of Warcraft, Monopoly, and Tetris, analyze the opportunities for challenge and play that are present in your original game prototype. List the types of challenges that players must face and the ways they can express themselves through fantasy or play. Describe how these elements work in your design to make your game fun or meet your experience goals. Or, identify how they might be improved in your design.

IMPROVING PLAYER CHOICES

Because it is simply one of the most powerful aspects of fun in gameplay, we need to look more closely at choice as an aspect of fun. What makes a choice interesting versus uninteresting? How can you design choices that are more interesting than not?

One of the most important aspects of choice is consequence. For a game to engage a player's mind, each choice must alter the course of the game, or at least our perception of it. This means the decision has to have both a potential upside and a downside; the upside being that it might advance the player one step closer to victory, and the downside being that it might hurt the player's chances of winning. This concept is often called "risk versus reward," and it is something we face every day in our own lives, not just in games. When Sid Meier says "interesting choices," what he means is that the game must present a stream of decisions that directly or indirectly impact the player's ability to win. This is because, in addition to story elements, drama and suspense in games can arise naturally from asking players to make decisions that have weight and consequence.

As a designer, this is what you must strive for. But how do you make sure that the choices in your game have significance? To start with, let's step back and analyze your game. Look at the gameplay diagram you created in Exercise 7.8. What types of decisions are your players making? Are those decisions truly meaningful or are they tangential to the main objective? To help analyze this, I use a concept I call the decision scale, which is shown in Figure 11.6.

If there are too many decisions in your game that seem inconsequential or minor, you may have a problem. Go back and rethink the choices you are giving your players. Is there a way to make those choices matter—if not systemically, then dramatically? And if a choice does not matter systemically or dramatically, those choices may need to be reconsidered if they are not adding anything to the game. Now take a look at the decisions higher up on the diagram. Is there a way to make some of your players' decisions fall into these categories? These are the types of decisions your players want to make.

The decisions you ask your players to make should not all be life and death, however. Nonstop action can get boring, too; it is in the breather between waves of enemies that we can appreciate our accomplishments, anticipate the next wave, and steel ourselves for the battle ahead.

To create a truly engaging game, you want some peaks and valleys. Let the decisions rise and fall, and as the game progresses, ratchet up the tension by making the decisions gradually more important until, by the climax of the game,

everything hangs in the balance. This structure mirrors the same dramatic arc that I discussed in Chapter 4 on page 123.

Types of Decisions

It is easy to say that games should have interesting choices, but why is one choice more interesting than another? The answer lies in the type of decision you ask to the player to make. If the player has to choose between two weapons, and one weapon is only slightly superior to the other, even though the player might be faced with a life-and-death encounter, the decision itself does not reflect this. To make this decision interesting, each weapon must have a dramatically different impact on the player's chance of winning.

But if the decision itself is too easy, then it is not a decision at all. If it is obvious that the player should use the golden arrow to slay the dragon, there is no real choice. Why would the player risk using anything else? This decision, although it appears to be life and death, is meaningless. The player will invariably choose the golden arrow unless he does not know about its powers, and in that case, it is an arbitrary choice, not a decision.

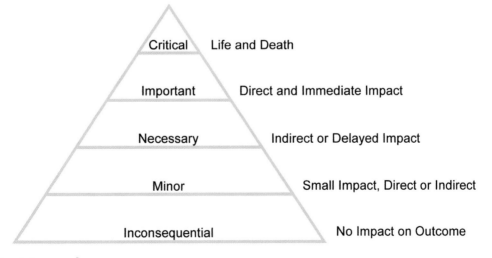

11.6   Decision scale

The key to making this decision interesting is for the player to know that the golden arrow is the right choice but also to know that if he uses the golden arrow now, he won't be able to use it later when he has to fight the evil mage. To make this decision truly dramatic, the player must be put in a position where both paths have consequences. If the player does not use the arrow now, his faithful companion, who is not immune to dragon fire, might die during the battle. However, if the player uses the arrow, it will be much harder to destroy the evil mage later on. Suddenly the decision has become more complex, with consequences on both sides of the equation.

Some decision types are as follows:

- Hollow decision: no real consequences
- Obvious decision: no real decision
- Uninformed decision: an arbitrary choice
- Informed decision: where the player has ample information
- Dramatic decision: taps into a player's emotional state
- Weighted decision: a balanced decision with consequences on both sides
- Immediate decision: has an immediate impact
- Long-term decision: whose impact will be felt down the road

In the example of the golden arrow, the decision is a combination of the previous decision types. It is an informed decision because the player knows a lot about situation he is in, it is a dramatic decision because the player has an emotional attachment to his faithful companion, it is a weighted decision because there are consequences balanced on both sides, it is an immediate decision because it impacts the battle that is taking place with the dragon, and it is a long-term decision because it impacts the future battle with the evil mage. All of these combine to make the decision of whether to use

the golden arrow a critical choice in the game, and this makes the game interesting.

Exercise 11.2: Decision Types

Take your original game and categorize the types of decisions you ask your players to make. Are there any hollow, obvious, or uninformed decisions? If so, try to redesign these choices.

Not all decisions in a game need to be as complex as the one with the golden arrow. Simple decisions are fine, just so long as they are not hollow, obvious, or uninformed. As a rule, you do not want to waste the player's time with nondecisions, though there is often a place in games for decisions or situations that are purely creative, expressive, dramatic, or exploratory. Finding a balance between the types of decisions that players find interesting and engaging throughout the flow of your game is more important than relying on one type of decision-making.

Dilemmas

Dilemmas are the situations where players must weigh the consequences of their choices carefully, and in many cases, where there is no optimal answer. No matter what the player chooses, something will be gained and something will be lost. Dilemmas are often paradoxical or recursive. A well-placed dilemma and trade-off can resonate emotionally with a player when encountered during the struggle to win your game.

Mathematician John von Neumann used dilemmas as a framework for studying how players in gamelike situations make choices and how conflicts are resolved in both game-based and real-world dilemmas. The branch of mathematics and economics that he co-created was called "game theory," and though the games that this discipline studies are not the type of games that I am discussing here, you might find parts of this methodology useful to study player choices in your own and other designers' games.

To understand dilemmas, von Neumann broke them down into very simple structures called moves. Each move was diagrammed on a matrix, showing the potential outcomes of each strategy as they pertain to each player. To understand this concept more clearly, let's look at a classic scenario with a simple move structure and payoff matrix.

Cake-Cutting Scenario

A mother wants to divide a piece of cake between her two children. To avoid arguments about how large a piece each child should get, she makes one child the "cutter" and one child the "chooser." The cutter gets to cut the cake, and the chooser gets to choose which piece. If we assume that each child wants the bigger piece (i.e., wants to "win" the game), we can diagram this conflict to show the potential strategies for each player, the dilemma they face, and the payoffs for each potential outcome.

As we can see, each child has two possible strategies. We know that it is impossible to cut the cake exactly in half—there will always be one crumb more or less on either side—but the cutter can choose to cut the cake as evenly as possible, or she can choose to cut one piece bigger than the other in an attempt to get the larger slice. Since we have determined that one piece will always be larger than the other, even if just by a crumb, the chooser also has two strategies. He can choose the smaller piece or the larger piece.

By looking at the payoff matrix created by combining these two possible strategies for each player, we can see that in this simple scenario, there is an optimal strategy for each player. Because we have said that each child will try to get the bigger piece, the chooser's optimal strategy is obvious: He will choose the larger piece. Because the cutter is also trying to get the largest piece possible, she will try to cut the pieces as evenly as possible. The optimal strategies for each player meet in payoff #1: The chooser gets a slightly bigger piece.

Chooser's Strategies:

	Choose Bigger Piece	Choose Smaller Piece
Cut as Evenly as Possible	**Chooser gets a *slightly* bigger piece.**	Chooser gets a *slightly* smaller piece.
Cut One Piece Bigger	Chooser gets a bigger piece.	Chooser gets a smaller piece.

Cutter's Strategies:

11.7   Cake-cutting scenario payoff matrix

The cake-cutting scenario is an example of a zero-sum game. By this I mean that the total amount won at the end of the game is exactly equal to the amount lost. In this case, the chooser gains the crumb lost by the cutter. Because of the nature of zero-sum games, the interests of the players are diametrically opposed. What one player loses is gained by the other.

What von Neumann discovered in his study is that there is an optimal strategy for each player in games of this nature that will produce the best possible results in a given situation. He called this concept "minimax theory."

Minimax theory states that there is a rational way for players to make choices in a game, if we are talking about a two-player, zero-sum game. The optimal strategy for all players is to "maximize their minimum potential result." In the case of the cake-cutting example, while the cutter cannot win the game, her optimal strategy will still maximize the amount of cake she gets to eat.

Games that fall easily into optimal strategies might be interesting for mathematicians, but for game designers, they are something to be avoided. If you present your players with a game as simple as the cake-cutting scenario, they will always make the optimal choice, and the game will play out the same way every time. How can we create scenarios that are more complex, where the players must weigh the potential outcomes of each move in terms of risks and rewards—scenarios that truly are dilemmas?

A scenario that has a more complex payoff structure was created by two RAND scientists in the 1950s. Called the "Prisoner's Dilemma," it is a simple, baffling game that shows how games that are not zero-sum can create situations where the optimal strategy for each player can result in suboptimal results for both.

The Prisoner's Dilemma

Two criminals commit a crime together and are caught by the police. For the purposes of my example, I will call the two unlucky criminals Mario and Luigi. Mario and Luigi are held in separate cells with no means of communication.

Mario's Strategies:

	Rat on Luigi	Don't Rat
Rat on Mario	Mario = 3 years Luigi = 3 years	Mario = 5 years Luigi = 0 years
Don't Rat	Mario = 0 years Luigi = 5 years	Mario = 1 year Luigi = 1 year

Luigi's Strategies:

11.8   Prisoner's dilemma payoff matrix

The DA offers each of them a deal and discloses that the same deal was made to his partner in crime. The deal works like this: If you rat on your partner, and he denies it, you can go free and he gets five years. If neither of you rat on each other, the DA has enough circumstantial evidence to put you both away for one year. If you both rat, you will each get three years. Figure 11.8 shows the payoff matrix for each potential strategy.

Using the same process we used to determine the optimal strategy for the cake-cutting dilemma, we can see that the optimal strategy for Mario is to rat on Luigi. If he rats, he gets either three or zero years. If he does not rat, he gets one or five years. The optimal strategy for Luigi is also to rat on Mario for the same reasons. This is completely rational decision-making; there is no question that the optimal strategy for both of these prisoners is to rat out their partner. Simple, right? But wait: If both players choose the optimal strategy, they will both serve three years! More years total will be served in jail than in any other resolution, and in fact they will both do much worse overall than if they had used a more naïve, intuitive strategy of keeping their mouths shut.

To be clear, the hierarchy of payoffs in the Prisoner's Dilemma is as follows:

- Temptation for defection: zero years
- Reward for mutual cooperation: one year each
- Punishment for mutual defection: three years each
- Sucker's payoff for unreciprocated cooperation: five years

The actual numbers in this hierarchy are not important. What is important is that they ascend in this order: Temptation > Reward > Punishment > Sucker. If this hierarchy exists, the optimal strategy for each player will always result in a payoff that is less than if they had acted cooperatively. As opposed to the cake-cutting scenario, the question put before these two prisoners does not have an obvious or optimal solution. If the prisoners use rational thinking to make their decision, they will be punished more than if they rely on mutual trust. But trust is a risky business. Now we are talking about a true dilemma. What will Mario and Luigi do?

Exercise 11.3: Dilemmas

Does your original game contain any dilemmas? If so, describe these choices and how they function.

In a presentation at the Game Developers Conference, designer Steve Bocska of Radical Entertainment applied the hierarchy of payoffs in the Prisoner's Dilemma to a hypothetical game design to show the usefulness of game theory concepts to designing compelling dilemmas.[1] Bocska imagines an online game in which two players are building and customizing spacecraft with a budget of $10,000. The game requires bartering and trading of raw materials, but at a high transaction cost: $8000 of "shipping and handling" in a typical game round. A technology can be purchased that allows materials to be "transported" with no transaction cost, but for it to work, both players must purchase it. The cost of the technology is $5000. Bocska asks:

Under these conditions, what is a player likely to do? If both players purchase the transporter equipment, they will reduce their transaction costs for the game from the usual $8000 to a one-time cost of $5000 for the transporter—a savings of $3000. If, on the other hand, neither player purchases a transporter, the transaction costs throughout the game for each player will amount to the usual $8000. What if only one player purchases the machine? With nobody else to connect the transporter to, their machine becomes effectively useless, resulting in them receiving the "sucker's payoff"—the cost of the equipment plus the added cost of continuing to barter using the traditional costly method ($5000 + $8000 = $13,000).

The payoff matrix in Figure 11.9 shows the results of the potential strategies.

Unlike the Prisoner's Dilemma, Bocska envisions a game in which the players can communicate, negotiating with each other when and if to purchase the technology. This complex payoff structure creates a dilemma for the players that can make for compelling strategic moments and potentially deceitful or cooperative decisions play after play.

This is exactly the type of situation you should strive to create in your games. If possible, give the players dilemmas as part of the core gameplay. Make sure to tie the dilemma into the overall objective of the game. If you can accomplish this, it will make the choices much more interesting.

Puzzles

Another format for structuring interesting choices in your games is by incorporating puzzles. As puzzle designer Scott Kim describes in his sidebar, "What Is a Puzzle?" on page 43, puzzles are defined by the fact that they have a right answer. While there are many variations of form and genre that a puzzle can take (abstract, word, action, story, simulation, etc.), the underlying similarity is that they are solvable or have a right answer, as Kim suggests.

Puzzles are also a key element in creating conflict in almost all single-player games. There is an innate tension in solving a puzzle. They can contextualize the choices that players make by valuing them as moving toward or away from the solution. Suddenly, the act of rifling through a treasure chest takes on new meaning if you are searching for the key to open the door to a maze rather than just looting the castle.

If you tie this into a system of rewards for solving the puzzle and punishments for failure, the puzzle transforms into a dramatic element. For example, take Myst, one of the best selling adventure games of all time. This game is essentially comprised of puzzles. It incorporates story and exploration as well, but at its core, the mechanics of the game are a collection of

Player 1's Strategies:

		Buy a Transporter	Keep the Status Quo
Player 2's Strategies:	**Buy a Transporter**	Player 1 = $5,000 Player 2 = $5,000	Player 1 = $0 Player 2 = $13,000 (Player 2 goes Bankrupt)
	Keep the Status Quo	Player 1 = $13,000 Player 2 = $0 (Player 1 goes Bankrupt)	Player 1 = $8,000 Player 2 = $8,000

11.9 Transporter game payoff matrix

interlocking puzzles integrated into the environment. Similarly, Ico, another adventure game, also incorporates puzzles into its environments, balancing its action mechanics with puzzle solving.

The popular genre of first-person shooters also often uses puzzles, especially in single-player mode. Take Medal of Honor. You have to plant bombs, unlock doors, find medical kits in a labyrinth of rooms, and figure out how to use weapons and explosives in just the right way. As with Ico, the action elements of the game are enhanced and balanced by the puzzle-solving elements. The same holds true for many other single-player games.

You will notice that I keep using the qualification "single-player." This is because in multiplayer mode, you do not necessarily need puzzles to provide conflict. The conflict can come from the competition with other players, whether they are human or computer controlled. But in single-player mode, especially when you are sent on a quest or mission, puzzles play an increasingly important role. That is why every game designer should also consider herself a puzzle designer. The better your puzzle design skills, the better your game will be.

An example of a multiplayer game that does include puzzle elements, however, is Puzzle Pirates. In this online multiplayer game, players must play single-player "duty" puzzle games such as "bilging" and "carpentry" onboard virtual pirate ships. However, they must also play multiplayer puzzle games such as "drinking," "brawling," or "swordfighting." Puzzle Pirates combines puzzle games with role-playing elements such as a persistent world to create its unique, and successful, play experience.

Another example of a multiplayer game that uses puzzles is Sky: Children of the Light from thatgamecompany. This game has no player-to-player conflict, instead inviting players to work together to solve environmental puzzles to access new areas of its world. Getting players to respect and befriend each other through cooperative play is a core experience goal for this game.

One consideration when designing puzzles in your games is to make sure that the elements of the puzzle are woven into the fabric of the game. By this I mean that it advances the player toward his overall goal. If a puzzle does not enable progress, it is a mere distraction and should be redone or removed. A puzzle can also advance the story line. You can use the puzzle to tell the player something about the unfolding plot. If you can integrate your puzzles into the gameplay and the story, they won't feel at all

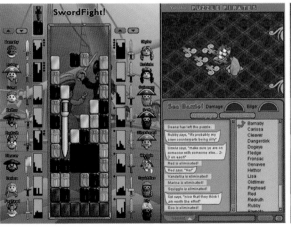
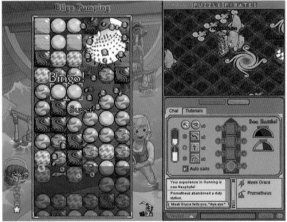

11.10   Puzzle Pirates

like puzzles but rather like integral, interesting choices a player must make to progress in the game as a whole.

Rewards and Punishments

The most direct consequences for player choices are rewards and punishments. Obviously, players enjoy being rewarded and dread punishments. Nothing is more natural. So when designing a game, a designer often emphasizes the rewards while limiting the punishments. This makes sense; players are not playing games to suffer the hardships of life. And in reality, you do not want to punish players so much that they stop playing your game. But often, the threat of punishment, if not the actual punishment itself, carries a dramatic tension that can add layers of meaning to even the most trivial choices a player makes.

Think of a game that forces the player to be stealthy, like Thief or Deus Ex. The tension, when you are trying to accomplish a task without being caught, is tremendous. Getting caught and attacked—and let's face it: killed—is not fun. But that moment when you oh, so quietly pick a lock and sneak past the security bots

without incurring any harm is made much more effective by the threat that the anvil of punishment was hanging over your head all the time.

Coming up with a balanced system of rewards and punishments is a way of making the choices in your games much more interesting for players. The type of rewards you offer can vary, but the best rewards are those that have utility or value in the game. When you develop your rewards system, use the following guidelines:

1. Rewards that are useful in obtaining victory carry greater weight.
2. Rewards that have a romantic association, like magic weapons or gold, appear to be more valuable.
3. Rewards that are tied into the story line of the game have an added impact.

Make each reward count, and if it can both push the player closer to victory and advance the story line, that's even better.

The timing and quantity of rewards is also critical. If you give a steady stream of small rewards, it can become meaningless. Players know the rewards are coming, no matter what they do, and they stop caring.

11.11 Being stealthy: Thief

Psychologist Nick Yee has studied the reward/punishment structure of an extremely addictive game system, EverQuest, and he believes its addictive power lies in a behavior theory advanced by B.F. Skinner called "operant conditioning." Operant conditioning claims that the frequency of performing a given behavior is directly linked to whether it is rewarded or punished. If a behavior is rewarded, it is more likely to be repeated. If it is punished, it becomes suppressed. It is usually explained by using the example of a Skinner Box, a glass cage equipped with levers, food pellets, and drinking tubes. Rats are placed in the cage and rewarded with a food pellet for pressing the lever, using reinforcement to shape their behavior.

Yee writes:

> There are several schedules of reinforcement that can be used in Operant Conditioning. The most basic is a fixed interval schedule, and the rat in the Skinner Box is rewarded every five minutes regardless of whether it presses the lever. Unsurprisingly, this method is not particularly effective. Another kind of reinforcement schedule is the fixed ratio schedule, and the rat is rewarded every time it presses the lever five times. This schedule is more effective than the fixed interval schedule. The most effective method is a random ratio schedule, and the rat is rewarded after it presses the lever a random number of times. Because the rat cannot predict precisely when it will be rewarded even though it knows it has to press the lever to get food, the rat presses the lever more consistently than in the other schedules. A random ratio is also the one that EverQuest uses.[2]

While this might seem surprising, if you relate it to your own actions in games and in the real world, it begins to make more sense. Have you ever sat down to play five minutes at a slot machine and looked up to realize you had been there, determinedly pulling that lever, for several hours? In many ways, Las Vegas is simply a giant Skinner Box. We might all be just rats in a cage, but there is one type of reward that is very powerful and that cannot be delivered like a pellet, and that is peer recognition. We crave acknowledgment for our achievements, especially in multiplayer games. If there is a way for you to make the players, even the ones who are not winning, feel recognized for their efforts when they do achieve a goal, then you will have a much stronger game.

Many games do this through the Internet, tracking scores or providing tournaments and ladders. There are more immediate ways to provide recognition in the moment as well. One is to track and broadcast the players' achievements during the game, highlighting and dramatizing each success for everyone to see. If it is an online strategy game where one team is pitted against another, make it clear when a player pulls off a brilliant maneuver. Let his comrades know exactly what happened and how it impacts the victory conditions. If it is an online role-playing game, allow the players to show off their conquests to the world, either in the form of legends, artifacts, or admirers who follow them about.

Exercise 11.4: Rewards

Analyze the rewards system in your original game prototype. Look at each reward and determine if it is useful, romantic, and/or tied to the story line. How are rewards timed? Does the timing reinforce the player's desire to continue playing?

Anticipation

The Skinner Box example works well for game mechanics that are repetitive and apt to become rote. For larger, more complex choices, however, the more clearly you allow players to see, and anticipate, the consequences of their actions, the more meaningful their choices will be.

In chess, and other games with open information structures, the entire state of the game is visible to both players for evaluation. Nothing is hidden. If players are experienced, they can calculate out moves dozens of turns in advance and see exactly what will and will not happen. The anticipation that players feel in a situation like this is heightened by the knowledge of when they will be able to capture a piece or get in a particular position.

Can games with closed or mixed information structures create anticipation? Definitely. Real-time strategy games often use limited visibility to offer the player a glimpse of the opposition, but only while her units are posted in enemy territory. Because the game state is always changing, the view quickly becomes outdated, and the player winds up making decisions based on only partially accurate information (see Figure 11.12).

In this example, players accept the lack of information as one of the conditions of the game and understand that their job is to maximize their position given the limited information they have available. In fact, the lack of visibility can increase a player's sense of tension. With the knowledge that the game state is in flux, players feel compelled to act swiftly to counter anticipated enemy moves. In this case, the hiding of knowledge has added a new dramatic twist that is lacking in the completely open strategy games.

Surprise

Surprise is one of the most electrifying tools at a designer's disposal. People love to be surprised, especially when they feel they should have anticipated the event. Too many surprises will alienate players, however, so how do you know when to use surprise and when to telegraph an event?

A surprise outcome to a player's choice can reinvest them in the game; perhaps they thought they were going to find 20 gold pieces behind door number three, but it turns out to be a trusted friend ready to join their journey instead—a much greater reward.

Surprises might feel random to players, but in a good way. The trick is to find the right balance between the randomness of surprise and the importance of making player choices meaningful. Take the example of a real-time strategy game, where you might send a simple foot soldier up against an ogre because he is all you've got. The foot soldier has strength of 1-5, while the ogre

11.12   Warcraft III: fog of war turned off (left) and on (right)

has strength of 1–20. Odds are that the ogre will win. But there's always that chance, no matter how small, that the foot soldier will prevail.

Randomness, and surprise, in this case add a level of drama—the tension of not knowing exactly how a highly probable event will play out. Will this be a David and Goliath story or just another dead foot soldier? In most well-designed games, the element of choice remains dominant. If every choice a player makes results in random effects, they will feel like their choices have no meaning. But keep surprise in mind; used judiciously, it can create a wealth of fun and excitement.

Exercise 11.5: Surprise

Are there any surprises in your game? Try taking one type of choice and adding an element of surprise to the outcome. How does this affect the gameplay?

Progress

Nothing is quite as satisfying as seeing the choices you make result in progress. It is part of human nature to derive joy from the act of advancing toward a goal. The small payoffs along the way are often sweeter than the final victory. The same is true in a game. Allowing players to feel that they are moving forward is the best way to draw someone into a game and keep them engaged.

One approach for structuring progress is to design milestones for the players. These are small goals along the way to the grand goal of winning. Advertise these milestones to the players so that they know what they are striving for, and reward them after each accomplishment.

Many games do this well. In games like Medal of Honor, the milestones come in the form of missions. They give you a map and let you see where you are headed and what you have to achieve to get there. This helps the player feel like they are

11.13 Mission: Medal of Honor: Mission 2-4 "What Comes Around"

making progress throughout a long campaign. The same is true for games that use story to block out their single-player levels, preparing the player at each step and setting out clear and obtainable objectives, and then rewarding the player at the end of each sequence with graphics, praise, and another chapter of the narrative.

No matter what the game, whether it is an arcade shooter or a simulation, providing a path for the player to follow gives a sense of achievement. Be creative in finding new ways to represent progress for your players. Do not limit yourself to just one system. There is no reason you cannot measure progress in several ways at once.

When you consider the pacing of progress that players can make in the game, you might also consider the typical amount of time a player spends with a game. Veteran game designer Rich Hilleman, formerly Chief Creative Officer at Electronic Arts, says that their designers plan "mini-arcs" of about one hour into the overall game progress. This is because they have found that this is the length of time an average gamer plays in a single sitting.

At the end of each mini-arc, the designers try to make sure the player encounters a "memorable moment" of gameplay, which makes sure they will return for another play session. These mini-arcs, when aggregated, form the overall dramatic arc of the game.

Exercise 11.6: Progress

Take your original game prototype. Is the ultimate goal clear? Is the player always moving toward this goal? Make sure that you have milestones established along the way. Does your system help motivate the player to reach the final goal? Describe how.

The End

By "the end," I am not talking about when a player dies; I am talking about the moment when the play completely resolves. After investing hours, days, weeks, or even months, this is the instant when your most loyal players deserve a reward for all their effort.

Multiplayer games have their own reward built in: the satisfaction of beating the other players, or, if you have created a cooperative, unilateral, or team interaction structure, the satisfaction of having worked together to beat the game or the other side.

But what of your single-player game? After all the conflict, struggle, and time invested, make sure to give the player a satisfying reward. Too often, the end of all that work is just a beautiful cutscene, where the hero is showered with praise and adulation. If you are going for an ending like this, why not build the reward into the story? Make that animation a moving moment in your hero's quest for whatever he lacks.

Exercise 11.7: Endings

Is the ending or resolution of your original game prototype satisfying? If not, how could you make it even better?

FUN KILLERS

For all your efforts, you may have implemented some features that killed the fun in your original concept. Here are just a few I have seen come up in first-time games over and over.

Micromanagement

Micromanagement is a common problem with games that give players a lot of control over minute details. For hard-core strategy gamers, like those addicted to games like Starcraft II, this control is critical. They want to tweak everything and dissect each element of the game. But there is a fine line between granting your hardcore players control and burdening your average players with unwanted chores.

As a designer, how do you know when you have given players enough control and not too much? Start with the basics. Is the task necessary? Make sure the decision the players are given is not obvious, hollow, or uninformed. If it passes these tests, it still might fall into the micromanagement trap. Micromanagement takes place when a task becomes repetitive or tedious to a player. The best way to know this for certain is to bring in fresh playtesters. If they complain that certain mechanics are too much work or too tiresome, this is a red flag.

One solution to this issue is to simplify your game system. Micromanagement usually comes from breaking up a task into too many small pieces. The overall impact of the combined decisions might be important on a strategic level, but each individual decision is too burdensome to be worth the effort. You might look at combining the microdecisions into one macrodecision. For example, if deploying an army requires choosing what weapons each unit will use, what supplies they are going to carry, what form of transportation they will utilize, and what route they will travel, you might be asking too much of your players. You can solve this by making some of these choices for them. Set default values that make sense and leave only the most important decisions, like what route to travel, up the players.

In addition to eliminating lesser decisions, you can give the players the choice of automating certain tasks, like resource management, troop deployment, and logistics. Allowing this choice provides hard-core players with the degree of control they desire and lets other players avoid dealing with the details. Micromanagement in itself is not an issue; it is only a problem when it affects the player experience. You will often find that different people want different experiences from your game, and the more flexible a system you can provide while still keeping the game relatively simple, the better.

Exercise 11.8: Micromanagement

Are there any elements of micromanagement in your game? If so, how can you streamline the choices players make so that they are not bogged down by unimportant details?

Stagnation

Some games fall into a pit of stagnation, where nothing new seems to be happening for a long period of time and choices stay at the same level of importance and impact.

A common source of stagnation is repetition, where players are caught doing the same task over and over. For example, if the players are forced to fight the same type of battle repeatedly, the game can feel like it is at a standstill. The players might actually be advancing in levels or moving closer to their ultimate goal, but the actions they are performing are so repetitive that they mask any progress being made. In this case, the solution is twofold. First, you should vary the type of action being performed. Next, you need to communicate how each action is bringing the player closer to victory.

Another type of stagnation is a balance of power. For example, you have three players competing to conquer the world, and whenever one player gets ahead, the others gang up and smash the leader down, thus creating an endless cycle where no one is able to achieve victory. The solution here is to create a condition that tips the balance of power so far in favor of the winner that she can defeat the combined strength of the opposition.

TUNING AND BALANCE: US VS. IT

by Stone Librande

Stone Librande is a lead designer at Riot Games. Prior to Riot, he was creative director at EA/Maxis and the lead designer on both SimCity (2013) and Spore's Cell Game. In addition to his full-time job at Riot, he has also been teaching game design classes at Carnegie Mellon University since 2014.

The word "balance" comes up often when talking about game design. It is a wide-ranging subject that encompasses nearly every facet of a game. It can be applied to the starting conditions (is there an advantage to going first?), the obstacles (are they too easy or too hard?), the choices (are some options always better than others?), and even the players themselves (who has more experience?).

Typically, when people talk about game balance, they are referring to the concept of fairness. In other words, do all players have an equal chance to achieve the game's goal? Fortunately, from a game designer's viewpoint, this is relatively easy problem to solve: simply make all the players play by the same rules.

The designer's job gets much trickier (and a lot more interesting) when a game allows players to compete against each other with completely different rules. A simple form of this concept can be seen in arcade fighting games, where each player chooses one of several different characters, each with a unique set of combat actions. It can also be seen in games that allow for handicapping the stronger player. For instance, a chess master might give himself only 15 minutes of game time, while his novice opponent can take as much time as needed. The more differences that there are between the rule sets, the harder the designer's balancing task becomes.

Balancing an asymmetrical game is a highly iterative task. Although there are mathematical methods for determining if two different rule sets are balanced, there is no substitute for playing the game, recording the results, making changes, and playing it again. Each time you loop through the game sequence, you gain more information that will help you determine which rules need changing and which ones are fine as is.

The *Us vs. It* exercise will give you the opportunity to try this process out for yourself. It is a cooperative game that teaches asymmetric balance through iterative tuning. The following conditions apply:

1. Each side has a different starting condition.
2. Each side has a unique set of rules.
3. Each side has a different goal.

The game is played in two stages. First, a group of players work together as "scientists" to build the ultimate battle robot. As often happens, the robot breaks out of the lab and goes rampaging toward a nearby town. At this point, the players take on a new role as "soldiers." Their job is to attack the robot with a battalion of tanks in an attempt to stop it from reaching the town. During the soldier phase of the game, the players cannot directly control the robot; it must mechanically follow the program written for it by the scientists in the previous phase.

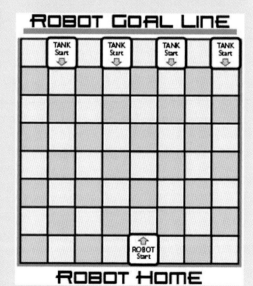

Figure 1:   Starting positions.

Set Up

For this exercise, you will need a standard 8 × 8 checkerboard, four "tanks," and one "robot." If you cannot find suitable plastic toys, then you can use pennies for the tanks and a quarter for the robot (the presidents' noses will point to the "front" to determine facing). Make a copy of the programming chart on 394. The four tanks will start on one side of the board and the robot will start on the other, as shown in Figure 1.

The game works the best with four players in a group, but you can use any number. You can even try it as a solo exercise if you wish.

Goal

The players must try to design a robot that is strong enough to get all the way across the board, but not so strong that it can cross the goal line.

Of course, it is trivial for the scientists to create a speedy robot that races past the tanks and crosses into the town on the first turn. Or they could construct a heavily armed robot that destroys every tank on the battlefield with one volley of guided missiles. Conversely, a passive group of scientists could create an unarmored robot that explodes the first time it is hit by a tank. But since this is an exercise about balance, none of those results are interesting.

Instead, you must attempt to tune the robot in such a way that it explodes at the most dramatic moment possible. Most of the tanks should be destroyed, the robot should be one step away from exiting the board, and ... on the final turn ... the last remaining tank should launch the shell that blows the robot to bits. Think "Hollywood ending."

Programming the Robot

In the first stage of the game, your group acts as scientists in charge of building a top-secret military robot. Fill in the actions that the robot will perform each turn. You have 10 slots, but you do not need to use them all.

The actions are listed on the right side of the programming sheet: Laser, Crush, Move and Face [Goal/Left/Right/Home/Tank]. You can use the same action multiple times and ignore actions that you don't need. For instance, the action list may have the following 8 commands: Move, Face Right, Laser, Move, Face Left, Crush, Move, Face Goal.

If the action causes damage, then fill in the damage squares with a number from 1 to 4. (Higher numbers are not necessary since 4 damage points is enough to destroy a tank.)

Finally, if you want your robot to self-destruct when it reaches 0 hit points, then fill in the damage and range squares in the Body section.

The Robot's Actions

Laser: The robot's long-range weapon. The laser attacks the closest tank in a straight line out from the robot's front. It does damage equal to the number in the damage grid.

Crush: The robot's close-range weapon. Similar to the laser, but it can attack all tanks in the five adjacent squares (the 3 in front and 1 on each side) simultaneously.

Face: When choosing this action, select a facing direction: either Goal, Left, Right, Home, or Tank. When this action triggers, the robot will turn its front to face the given direction. (Note that "Left" and "Right" are relative to the goal line, not to the robot's current facing.) If you choose "Tank," then the robot "scans" for a target by turning clockwise

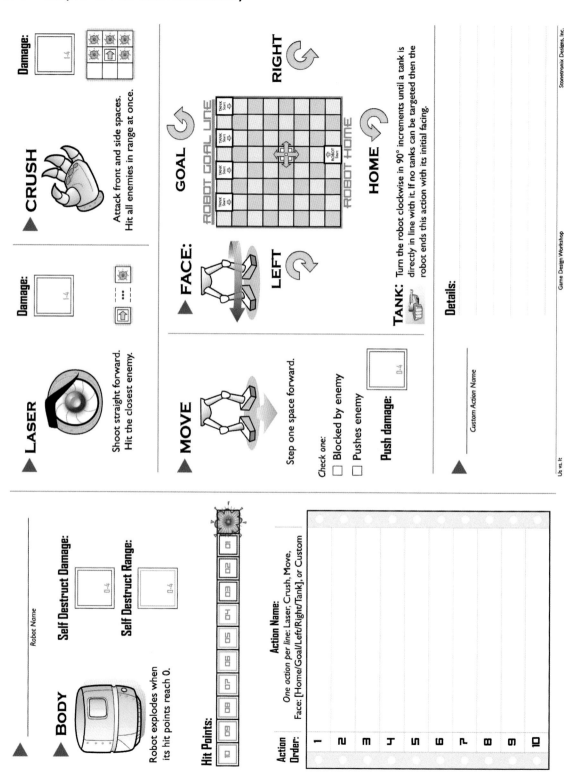

CRUSH

Attack front and side spaces.
Hit all enemies in range at once.

Damage:　1-4

LASER

Shoot straight forward.
Hit the closest enemy.

Damage:　1-4

FACE:

GOAL

LEFT

RIGHT

HOME

ROBOT GOAL LINE

TANK Start

ROBOT Start

ROBOT HOME

MOVE

Step one space forward.

Check one:

☐ Blocked by enemy

☐ Pushes enemy

Push damage:　0-4

TANK: Turn the robot clockwise in 90° increments until a tank is directly in line with it. If no tanks can be targeted then the robot ends this action with its initial facing.

Details:

Custom Action Name

BODY

Robot Name

Self Destruct Damage:　0-4

Self Destruct Range:　0-4

Robot explodes when its hit points reach 0.

Hit Points:

| 10 | 09 | 08 | 07 | 06 | 05 | 04 | 03 | 02 | 01 |

Action Name:
One action per line: Laser, Crush, Move, Face: [Home/Goal/Left/Right/Tank], or Custom

Action Order:	
1	
2	
3	
4	
5	
6	
7	
8	
9	
10	

in 90° increments until a tank is directly in line with it. If the robot cannot find a valid target, then it ends this action with the same facing it had when it started.

Move: The robot moves forward one space. The robot cannot move into a space off the side or back of the board. If an action would cause this to happen, then ignore it. If you want your robot to move more than one space per turn, then you will need to specify multiple Move commands in the action list. Decide whether your robot will be blocked by tanks or whether it will push them. If so, does this push cause damage? If a tank is pushed off the board, then it is out of the game. If a tank is pushed into another tank, then it creates a chain reaction; all the affected tanks will move in the same direction and take the same amount of push damage.

Battling the Robot

In the second stage of the game, the robot token is placed in the robot start square and the tank tokens are placed in the four tank start squares along the opposite edge of the board (see illustration). The robot moves first.

Look at the first action in the robot's list and resolve any attack, movement, or facing actions. If the robot hits a tank with a Laser or Crush action, then the tank takes damage equal to the number in the "damage" box. (Use beads or paper and pencil to keep track of each tank's damage.) A tank that takes four points of damage during the course of the game is destroyed and removed from the board.

Continue down the robot's action list in order, executing each action in sequence. The robot's turn ends when you get to the bottom of the action list.

Now it is the tanks' turn. Each tank gets to choose 3 of the actions from the list below. A single action can only be performed up to two times per turn. For instance, a tank could move twice and shoot in the same turn, but it cannot shoot three times in the same turn.

TANK ACTIONS:

A. **Shoot** straight forward for 1 damage. Your shots go over the top of the other tanks.

B. **Move** forward 1 space. You may not move into the same space as another tank or the robot.

C. **Rotate 90°** clockwise or counterclockwise.

Every time a tank hits the robot, then the robot will lose 1 hit point. When the robot takes its tenth hit, it explodes and does self-destruct damage (if applicable). Tanks caught in this final blast take damage and may be destroyed.

Ending the Game

The game ends in one of three ways:

1. The robot exits the board and enters the town.
2. The robot destroys all the tanks.
3. The robot takes ten hits of damage and explodes.

Back to the Drawing Board

When the game ends the players should check for "drama." Preferably, the robot should explode while on the last row of the board and all of the tanks but one should be damaged or destroyed. It is likely that it will take you several iterations before this outcome happens. If the robot died too soon, then the players should reprogram the robot to make it stronger.

If the robot escaped off the board, then the players should weaken the robot. If not enough tanks were destroyed, then try giving the robot more attack actions or increase its laser, crush, or push damage.

Note that although you are not allowed to tune the tanks, you and your teammates may find yourselves becoming better at strategizing and maneuvering. Avoid the temptation of making suboptimal moves with the tanks in order to make the robot more effective. If the robot needs some extra help, then that is a job for the scientists, not the soldiers!

Keep tuning the robot's program and battling against it with the tanks until you find a combination of robot actions that provides just the right amount of power to create a climatic Hollywood ending.

Custom Action

After you get a feel for the basics of the game, try adding in a super power at the bottom of the sheet. This can be anything you want, from transforming into an airplane, to laying mines, to hacking into a tank's computer. Think back to all of the giant robots you have seen in movies and comic books. What made them special?

Anything goes here, as long as the primary design goal is met: The robot should be tuned so that it dies on the last row of the battlefield, and the majority of the tanks should be damaged or destroyed.

Robot vs. Robot Battles

When all the groups have fine-tuned their robots, then it is time for the ultimate showdown! (When I teach this exercise, I keep this finale a secret from the players until the end. If you are teaching *Us vs. It*, then consider keeping it a secret, too.)

Form larger groups by getting multiple teams together. (Four robots per group is recommended.) Each team is in charge of controlling their own robot as it fights against the robots from the other teams. There are no tanks in this mode. Each robot starts along a different edge of the board. You do not win by crossing the goal line; the winner is the last robot standing.

A team may need to modify their robot's program slightly in the following ways:

1. Replace all references to "tanks" with "enemy robots."
2. The "Goal Line" is now the opposite side of the board from where the robot started. This means that each robot will have facing directions that are relative to the side it started on.
3. If a robot steps over its own goal line, then it does not win. Instead, immediately teleport it back to its starting square.

Pick one robot to go first and execute its first action. Go around the table clockwise executing each other robot's first action in turn. Then go around the table again and execute each robot's second action. Continue doing this until every robot has done their ten actions. After that, start the process all over again with the first action. If a robot has fewer than ten actions in its program, then it "rests" while the other robots finish all of their actions.

Despite the wildly different custom powers, you should notice that the battles tend to be very close. This is because all the robots have been tuned to be approximately the same strength as the four tanks.

Final Thoughts

Maximizing your game's dramatic tension is an excellent way to ensure that your players will want to play your game again and again. Try to align the end goal with the moment of peak excitement and avoid rules and systems that force long drawn-out anticlimactic endings. (You may have noticed that the end games of *Monopoly* and *Risk* frequently have this failing.) Ultimately, your goal as a designer is to entertain your players. Crafting rules that generate emotional experiences is a key way to achieve this. Making your game end shortly after the peak emotional moment is even better. There is a reason that most Hollywood movies and best-selling books tend to end shortly after the climax. Strive to achieve the same drama in your games.

A third type of stagnation is a reinforcing or balancing loop, as discussed in Chapter 5 on page 160. This type of stagnation occurs when a game device traps the players in a cycle that balances rewards with penalties. For example, in a business simulation game, a player might get caught in a trap where all his profits are being eaten up by debt payments. No matter how long he plays, he cannot get over this hump. One solution is to shake things up with an unexpected event, like a windfall or natural disaster, that will either push the player over the hump or knock him into bankruptcy. Of course, you could also tweak the game so that players never get stuck in this type of situation. Give the player debt relief or jack up interest rates—whatever it takes to move the game in one direction or the other.

The last type of stagnation is where it feels like nothing is happening because nothing is actually happening. In other words, no progress is being made, either because the game is poorly designed or because there is no clear goal. An example of this might be an adventure game with a poorly defined objective. The players roam around but have no idea where they are supposed to go or what they are supposed to do. In this case, the solution is to go back and design the game so the objective is clear.

Exercise 11.9: Stagnation

Is there any point in your original prototype at which the game play stagnates? If so, determine what is causing this problem. Do you have a balancing loop? A balance of power? How can you break the cycle and improve the progression of the gameplay?

Insurmountable Obstacles

Another problem area to avoid when designing a game is an insurmountable obstacle. Despite the name, these might not actually be impossible situations, they just seem that way to a certain percentage of players.

Whether this occurs because of a dearth of information, a missed opportunity, or lack of experience or intuition, the result is always the same: Your players wind up banging their heads against the same obstacle over and over and over. Look at your watch—how long is it before they shut the game off in frustration, never to return again?

Most of us have been trapped by an insurmountable obstacle at one time or another and wound up going in circles looking for that hidden doorway or secret panel. As a designer, make sure that the game has some way of recognizing when a player is stuck, and provide her with just enough assistance to make it past the obstacle without diluting its challenge completely. Of course, this is easier said than done. Nintendo adventure games, such as those in the Zelda series, are typically good at providing information when players are stuck. Game characters are placed in strategic spots to provide clues and other information that will help you overcome the obstacles. As with other variables, clues have to be balanced to provide an appropriate level of difficulty for the players.

Building this kind of intelligence into the game is costly and time consuming. Sometimes it does not need to be that sophisticated. In a presentation at the Game Developers Conference on making games more fun through user testing, Microsoft User-Testing Manager Bill Fulton (see his sidebar on user testing in Chapter 9 on page 306) used an example from the opening moments of the original Halo to illustrate how a task that seems obvious to the designer might seem like an insurmountable obstacle to the player.

Immediately after the introductory tutorial of this first-person shooter game, your character is asked to follow a guide character to the bridge of the spaceship you are on. Of course, you do, but seconds later, the guide character is killed in an explosion right before your eyes, leaving you trapped behind a partially open doorway with no guide and no clue how to open the door.

As part of his presentation, Fulton showed a videotape of just one of many user tests in which a playtester stumbled around the corridor, pressing every button on the controller, trying everything he could think of to open the door, all the while talking out loud about how he did not know what to do. This went on for several minutes until it became clear from his tone of voice that if this player were at home, he would have given up only five minutes into the game. As Fulton pointed out humorously, "I hope you all recognize this as "not fun.""[3]

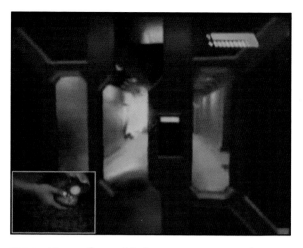

11.14   Tape from Halo user test: stuck at a broken doorway—note video insert of player's hands trying different control combinations, lower left

The goal of the Halo designers, in leaving you guideless and trapped behind the door, was to create a sense of confusion and vulnerability that lasted only a few seconds for dramatic purposes. They assumed the player would immediately realize the door was not going to open, see the alternative exit to the corridor they had planned, and be on their way. User testing proved that most players needed a little help past this obstacle.

In the final product, a second explosion, timed a few seconds later, drives the player instinctively away from the half-opened door that will, in fact, never open. A text prompt pops up showing the player how to jump over objects, and a carefully designed floor mat points toward another opening in the corridor. The opening is blocked by a set of pipes, but if you know how to jump, that is no problem at all. With just a few modifications, the opening moments of the game were changed from an exercise in frustration to an exciting scene filled with drama and tension.

Arbitrary Events

As much as random events can be used to good effect in certain circumstances, like fortuitous surprises and unforeseen dangers, badly designed randomness can be the downfall of a game. Many games involve some form of randomness. I have described how randomness can affect combat algorithms in real-time strategy games and how it can stop movement mechanics from becoming predictable in board games. These types of randomness add to gameplay.

But there is a big difference between utilizing randomness to change up gameplay and allowing for totally arbitrary events to disrupt the player experience. For example, if you have spent weeks building a sophisticated character in a role-playing game, and then suddenly a plague, for which there is no cure, kills your character, it is hard not to feel cheated because you had no chance to defend yourself and all your hard work has gone down the drain. We all know that life is full of unexpected events, some of which are devastating. So why shouldn't games include them?

The problem is that, as in life, good surprises are welcomed by players, but bad surprises are not. So how can you include random events that are negative in nature without alienating the player? Whether it is a meteor storm that levels a city, an economic fluctuation that bankrupts a company, or a surprise attack that wipes out an army, you have to make sure it fits into the players' expectations of the game. Prepare your players in advance for the possibility of such an event and give them options to mitigate the damage. Just do not tell them when it is coming or how bad it is going to be.

If we take the example with the plague, you should warn the player about the possibility of diseases and allow them to purchase an antidote in advance. If they choose to ignore the warning signs and take no action, then when the event does come, it is their fault, and they will know it.

A good rule of thumb is to caution your players at least three times before hitting them with anything catastrophic. Random events that have a lesser impact require smaller warnings or even no warning at all. It is fine for a player to learn through experience to expect events of smaller consequence. But the bigger the impact, the more of a heads-up you should provide. If you follow this rule, the events won't appear to be arbitrary, and your players will feel like they are in control of their destiny.

Predictable Paths

Games with only one path to victory can become predictable. As I discussed in Chapter 5, linear or simple branching structures often lead to this type of predictability. If you want to add a greater sense of possibility to your design, consider treating the structure in a more object-oriented approach. Giving each type of object in the world a simple set of behaviors and rules for interaction, rather than scripting each encounter separately, often leads to creative and unusual results.

An example of this type of thinking is Grand Theft Auto V, which has a level structure and story line that the player can follow, or she is free to wander the world, stealing cars, committing crimes, or running a taxi service if that is what she wants to do. While wandering the world does not advance the player very far in terms of the overall game objectives, it does give the sense that the world of the game is responsive and unpredictable. At any moment, she might attract the attention of the police and wind up in an unscripted high-speed chase. Simulation games are other examples of this type of design. Games like the SimCity series can evolve in many directions, all based on the choices of the players.

Another way to keep game paths from becoming predictable is to allow players to choose from several objectives. For example, in Civilization III, the player can choose between six paths to victory: conquest, space travel, cultural advance, diplomacy, domination, and overall score. Each choice takes careful planning and will cause the player to weigh each choice anew, making the game not only interesting the first time around but also extremely replayable. Simply choose another path to victory and the game takes on an entirely new twist.

Not every game has to have the scope of a Civilization or a Grand Theft Auto, but when finding the balance between too much possibility and too much predictability, it is usually best to err on the side of greater possibility.

BEYOND FUN

As games develop into a more mature medium, they are finding other venues beyond entertainment. For example, games are now being used in education, civic engagement, journalism, and for health and wellness. There are games that are more experiential than competitive, and there are those that might be considered fine art rather than popular culture. For these, and other new forms that games might take, fun might not be the most useful measuring stick for the appeal they have to players. As a part of the playcentric process of design, however, you will have to set other, more appropriate goals for your gameplay. In this case, these are the goals you need to be testing for. Game designer Jane McGonigal talks about setting goals for real-world positive impact in her

Designer Perspective on page 54. It is one of the most exciting trends in today's game industry that games are now being thought of as a agents of societal change, but such change doesn't have to lack fun. As Adrian Hon and Matt Wieteska describe in their sidebar on mobile game design on page 502, the game Zombies, Run! has helped hundreds of thousands of players get on and stick to an exercise plan—all through a clever and fun game design. The real possibilities for games such as this are just being discovered today; it is a wide-open field for designers and I have suggested some further reading at the end of this chapter for those of you who want to take your gameplay beyond the realm of fun.

IS YOUR GAME ACCESSIBLE?

The final aspect to refining your game is making sure that it is accessible for the intended players and also for players who may have different usability needs—differently sighted players, those with alternative cognitive, hearing, or control needs. All of these things will need to be considered in your final designs. Can players of all abilities, pick up your game, understand it, and access it without any help from you, and realistically, without much help from the directions?

Accessibility is a strange paradox for the designer because the better you understand your own game, the less able you are to anticipate problems that players might have in encountering it for the first time. Testing for accessibility is related to testing for usability; however, the full range of accessibility testing is much deeper issue given the range of possible player needs. Usability tests are generally done by usability experts in usability labs. I highly encourage you to utilize such a group if you or your publisher has access to them. For advanced accesibility guidelines, I suggest consulting the website gameaccessibilityguidelines.com.

Usability engineers are generally trained psychologists or researchers whose focus is on testing and evaluating how users interact with various products. The general software industry has incorporated usability testing into its product cycle for years and the game industry has recently followed suit, with many large publishers establishing internal groups dedicated to usability testing for their games.

Professional usability labs are often set up with sophisticated recording equipment, allowing the researchers to insert a close-up view of the participant's hands on the controls—keyboard and mouse or console controller—within a shot of the main interface. Sometimes another camera shows the participant's facial responses, and her voice is recorded over the sound of the product as she talks out loud about what she is thinking. The researchers usually sit behind one-way glass with the designers and producers of the product and communicate with the participant via intercom.

The researchers prepare a test script for the session—similar to but more detailed than the one you created in Exercise 9.4—that asks the participant to walk through a number of areas in the product or complete a set of tasks. Data on how successful participants are in completing these tasks and an evaluation of how critically any findings will impact the product are compiled in a report.

When I ask you to test basic accessibility in your game, I am basically asking you to do a layman's usability test. By now, you have probably playtested your game with quite a few different people. Unfortunately, these people are now

11.15   Microsoft playtesting lab

Multiple participants are playing games, each at their own station. Stations have partitions between them and headphones to minimize distractions. This is done so that one participant's experience does not affect another's. Each participant's opinions and preferences are collected via a web-based questionnaire on the monitors at each station. (Photo by Kyle Drexel.)

11.16   Microsoft usability lab

A participant (background, on the right) is playing a game. In the foreground, a user-testing specialist is observing the participant play the game in an adjacent room, separated by one-way glass. The one-way glass allows the user-testing specialist and development team members to discuss the game and participant behaviors without being overheard by the participant. (Photo by Kyle Drexel.)

Using Audio as a Game Feedback Device

by Michael Sweet

Michael is an accomplished audio composer and has been the audio director for more than 100 award-winning video games over the past three decades. From 2008-2019, Michael Sweet led the development of the video game scoring curriculum at Berklee College of Music in Boston. His work can be heard on the Xbox 360 logo and on many award-winning games from Niantic, Lego, Cartoon Network, Sesame Workshop, PlayFirst, Microsoft, and MTV, among others. In addition, Michael's sound sculptures have traveled around the world, including the Millennium Dome in London and galleries in New York, Los Angeles, Florence, Berlin, Hong Kong, and Amsterdam.

Sound can have a profound impact on the game by intensifying the level of engagement by the player and extending the creative style of the game. Since music and sound work on a subconscious level, it can help dictate emotional context to the player. Whether you're struggling to make it to the end of a level or waiting for the next monster to appear from around the corner, the sonic landscape can make the player's heart race or stomach drop. In this article, we'll be exploring two titles that I composed the music and sound design for and how we utilized audio to solve design challenges and give a rich aural experience to the player.

Walden, a game

One recent title that takes a unique approach to audio is *Walden, a game* from the USC Game Innovation Lab. The game, on which I collaborated with the author of this book, won the 2017 Game of the Year award at the Games for Change Festival. In this 3D first-person experience, the player walks in the footsteps of the American author Henry David Thoreau during the time he spent at Walden Pond in Massachusetts from 1845-1847.

Sunset in Walden, a game, high inspiration

Our three primary goals with sound design and music in Walden were immersing the player in the environment, offering audio feedback to the player, and supporting the storytelling.

We began the environmental sound effects by recording almost all of the sound effects, including birds, insects, frogs, footsteps, and weather, near or at Walden Pond. Sound effects were recorded with a portable recorder along with a shotgun microphone. In addition, we consulted with local experts about the migration of birds, and took great care to include only birds that Henry would have heard during his time at Walden. For instance, birds like cardinals may be quite common today near Walden Pond, but their migration northward occurred as a result of rising temperatures after Henry's time at Walden Pond.

These environment effects were then implemented into Unity, our game development engine. Since immersion of the player was one of the primary audio goals, we took care to create a surround environment for all the sound effects. With the birds, it meant localizing them in individual trees throughout the map, and keying their songs to times of the day and season. Birds sing more often at dawn and in the spring than as we approach fall and winter. When the birds are placed individually in trees as opposed to having a single audio ambience, the player will perceive their location as they turn and move about the space.

Similarly we wanted the wind, weather, and insects to be spatialized as well. For these, it was impractical to create all the individual sources in the 3D world, so we chose instead to place a fixed, virtual quad speaker array around the player avatar in the world. Therefore, as the player rotated, the cardinal positions of the virtual quad system would stay static, having localizing each source appropriately.

When combined together, all of these dynamically controlled environmental effects combined to create a procedural soundscape that immersed the player in the changing landscape of Walden Woods.

Another important aspect of the sound was to leave audio clues around the world where the player could make discoveries. These audio clues were attached to arrowheads in the world, which, when picked up, would give you insight into Henry's life at the pond. This sound effect was spatialized so that it would pan dynamically as the player moved in the world to help them find the clue. Scattered through the game world, these sounds, and the glittering arrowheads they are attached to, attract the player's attention and act as subtle lures to encourage exploration.

Music in the game is used primarily to support the emotional arc of the experience, and to tell the story of Henry's time in the woods. Music themes were written for each season of the year, and, since Thoreau felt that four seasons were too few to describe the drastic seasonal changes throughout the year, our seasonal system, including the music, represents eight seasons. In addition, we created themes for various locations and characters within the game, and a special theme for reflective points in the game, called "solitude cairns."

The soundtrack also provides an important feedback mechanism to inform the player how "well" they are doing in the game. Each of the season themes is split into four separate musical layers. These layers fade in and out based on how much inspiration the player has. This inspiration parameter grows for players who spend time seeking out the small wonders and beauties of the woods—seeking solitude, interacting with animals, reading books that they find, and listening to sounds in the distance.

The creative direction behind the music drew upon Thoreau's own philosophy of transcendentalism and further inspired by the minimalist rhythmic landscape of the world that surrounded him. We created a hybrid-score, which combined virtual instruments, along with real musicians to make the music come alive. The music was sequenced in Digital Performer, then recorded and mixed in Pro Tools.

The main takeaway from Walden is: Enhance your game by immersing your player with music and sound. Embrace uniqueness when approaching your sonic palette to give your game a unique vision and style. The music should help the storytelling in your game on an emotional level by representing the themes, characters, and plot of your game.

BLiX

Another title that takes a completely different approach to sound is an innovative puzzle game called BLiX. The game won the IGF Award for Best Audio in 2000. The object of BLiX is incredibly simple: Get the balls into the cup. The game itself was designed to be played by all ages; the interface was iconic, the scoring system didn't use numbers, there was also no real language in the game design itself.

This title takes a completely different approach to music. When designing the sound, I wanted the player to create the music through gameplay without actually realizing they were participating in it. All the sound effects are musical phrases that get added to an underlying loop of ambient background techno music. In addition, the game space is divided into a grid of nine spaces that have rollovers, so as the player moves around the screen placing bumpers and playing the game, these musical rollovers trigger simple drum hits and synth notes. In essence, the score is self-generated by the user.

At the time, with limited toolsets, we introduced some fairly unique concepts to an Internet puzzle game: the creation of music centered around gameplay. Today there are many newer technologies that allow the composer to really shape narrative in real time through seamless branching of the musical score and dynamic created sound effects. At the time BLiX was done, we had to be creative about the use of the limited technology, trying to break the rules of the system.

There were a total of about 30 different sound assets for the game, including 14 background music loops and many sound effects. The sounds themselves were created using software packages Rebirth, Reason, and Pro Tools. I wanted to integrate lots of delays and effects into the individual sounds. I wanted to also recognize a retro arcade feel to the game, taking beeps and blips to a whole new level. The other developers were all old arcade heads and we wanted to recognize our heritage, so to speak.

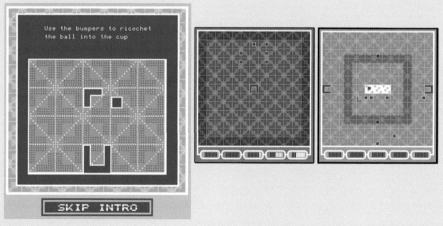

BLiX

Adding delays to the sounds added file size to the game. The co-designers of the game let me collaborate on file size, which really allowed me to be creative first, instead of being led by the technology or inherent difficulties of the limitations of an Internet game. Although we took out assets to maintain file size when Shockwave.com acquired BLiX, it really allowed me to open up creatively and experiment in ways I really hadn't before. It's important to work with a team that values audio and is willing let you experiment and try new things.

Audio feedback is incredibly important. When I talk to people who play BLiX, they always mention the *game over* sound and how they hate hearing it. I was in the process of taking it out during the creation of the game because I felt it was too harsh, when the other designers (Peter Lee and Eric Zimmerman) told me how much they liked it. Players of BLiX hate getting to the game over sound, and they immediately start a new game as a result.

The one sound in the game I didn't create was the timer running out sound. Peter Lee found this sound and we ended up not changing it because it's another sound that jolts you back to reality. After playing the game for a while, you get that sort of numb Tetris-like feeling where the game is a machine and you're part of it. All of a sudden the timer is running out, and it jolts you back to the reality that the game is about to end.

It was really important to me that the audio feedback during the game be a single audio-rich experience. The sound effects in BLiX needed to be tightly integrated into the music. Even though we didn't have the ability to sync sounds to the beats, the sounds are so well designed (ultimately to my initial disbelief) and synergistic with the background loops that everyone just considers it music instead of two separate elements.

Something frequently overlooked is that audio feedback can also establish the rhythm of interaction for the player. Digital gameplay has a player interaction that has a specific speed of movement, mouse clicks, and keystrokes. These interactions have rhythm all on their own that the music and sound effects can support or detract from. Dynamic rhythm has been used in many retro arcade games, including Space Invaders. The use of cascading rhythm can really involve your player, intensifying the gameplay experience.

Similar to film, the game sound designer can use motifs and themes to create metaphors for characters, help transitions, and give direct or indirect feedback to the user about how they're doing in the game. The power of sound design can also create emotions that are hard to achieve strictly by the visual representation of the game; things like empathy, hatred, and love can all be represented through music and sound.

Each game designer should recognize the power that audio has to increase every aspect of his or her game. Studies have shown that higher-quality audio often gives the game player a perceived increase in the overall visual look of the game and heightened awareness during game play.

disqualified for your accessibility testing. The right people to test for basic accessibility are:

- Part of your target market
- Objective (not friends or relatives)
- Have never played your game
- Players with a range of accessibility require ments

You will need a fair-sized group: Three to five people in each segment of your market (if there is more than one) are sufficient.

To make things go smoothly and to get the most out of the session, you need to identify the most critical areas of your game. Your list will probably include starting a game and some of the more critical choices or features. Now create a script you can use to get the participants to these critical areas and present them with tasks that will give you insight as to how they are working. The script does not have to be elaborate; its purpose is to help you keep the session on track with as little fumbling and forgetting as possible. You want the participants to concentrate on your game, not on you.

Unless your game demands a multiplayer environment, it is best to do this type of testing one on one. You want to see where people are stumbling or guessing, and people sometimes try to hide that, or they copy from a neighbor in a group. If you have to have participants in the same room during a test, explain to them that they should not help each other with the tasks. You can also do this kind of test online, using a screen sharing tool like Zoom or Discord.

You might want to have a friend help you out, if you cannot record the session, by taking notes while you walk through the script with the participant. Have the note-taker sit out of the participant's peripheral view to lessen, or turn off your video feed if you are doing an online test. When you have run several tests, you will undoubtedly begin to see a pattern. You might be surprised to learn that your game is not as accessible as you believed. The example of the first few minutes of Halo shows how easy it is for game designers to miss potential areas of confusion simply because they are so familiar with the game. Just remember that participants in a test like this are never wrong. As tempting as it might be to believe that a feature is obvious, your opinions do not count in this type of testing. If your players cannot play, there is no game.

Identify the areas that are causing problems, make revisions, and do another series of tests. Continue this process until you are satisfied that a majority of your target players can access the most critical areas of your game. In a perfect world, you could test every aspect of your game for usability and accessibility, but you probably won't have the time or resources to do it. What you can do is make the game easy to get into, easy to understand, and accessible to play.

Exercise 11.10: Usability Testing

Conduct a set of usability tests for your original game prototype as described previously.

1. Write a script for a usability test in which you focus on critical tasks like starting a game, understanding objectives, making key choices, etc.

2. Recruit a group of new testers who have not played your game before.

3. Conduct the tests and analyze the results. Come up with three ideas to improve your game's usability.

CONCLUSION

You now should have a game that is functional, complete, balanced, fun, and accessible. That is a major accomplishment. Whether you have gone through this process alone, working with a paper prototype, or whether you have managed to get a team together and create a digital prototype of your game, the fact that you have gone through all the phases of design and testing means that you had an idea that was worth the effort. This certainty will be what you need to carry you through the full production and release of this game.

Before moving on, take a look back at the process you have just been through:

- You not only came up with an idea for an original game, you learned skills and techniques that will make you a valuable member of any design team.

- You have translated your ideas into a physical prototype and possibly a digital prototype of a working game.

- You have playtested your prototypes and revised them until your gameplay delighted your testers and achieved your gameplay experience goals.

At this point, you should feel empowered by your control of the playcentric design process. No longer a mystery, the process of game design is one you should feel confident practicing on your own, with friends, or as a member of a professional design team. You can use your skills to create games on your own, or you can try to get a job with an established developer or publisher. Whatever you decide to do, you will have the experience and the critical skills to approach the task of game design as both a personal art and a social, collaborative dialogue between the designers and the players of games.

DESIGNER PERSPECTIVE: WREN BRIER

Creative Director, Witch Beam

Wren Brier is the Creative Director of the award-winning indie game Unpacking (2021). She's worked in the games industry for 9 years, starting at Halfbrick and later working as a freelance artist before partnering with Witch Beam Games to bring Unpacking to life. Wren is a member of the GDC Independent Games Summit Advisory Board and runs Women in Games Brisbane.

How did you become a game designer?

I never expected to become a game designer, honestly. When I was growing up, I always wanted to be a film animator. Due to some complicated circumstances, I ended up studying animation at a games-focused course, which led me to become a generalist games artist. While I was at Halfbrick Studios there was something they called "Halfbrick Fridays" where anyone could pitch a game and if you could get a small team together you could make a prototype over the course of five Fridays. I got an idea the day before we were due to present, so with some encouragement from a couple of coworkers I stayed back late to work on my pitch and presented it the next day. Enough people liked it that I got to make my prototype! I consider that my very first design role. I continued to dabble in design on various projects I worked on as a freelancer—I was an artist, but I often ended up influencing the design if the folks I was working with were open to it. Officially, though, Unpacking is the first project I worked on as a designer.

On games that have inspired her:

I think a little something from every game I play lodges itself into my brain, but Animal Crossing has definitely been a major influence. I've played three games in the series, and it's been interesting to see what changed from game to game—how certain elements that were more punishing were removed: In earlier games your villagers could leave without any notice and your flowers could wilt if you didn't water them, while in the latest game villagers don't leave without explicit permission and watering flowers is rewarded with cross-breeding, without penalty for *not* watering. Both options are valid design directions, but they lead to a pretty different kind of experience for the player. It made me think a lot about how small decisions like this can affect the tone of a game and influenced my design decisions in Unpacking.

Another game that's inspired me a lot is Don't Starve—I think it does an incredible job of creating what feels like a real ecosystem with how its various creatures and plants all interact. Most recently, Tunic inspired me with its brilliant ability to hide layers upon layers of secrets, often in plain sight. I'd like to hide more secrets in my future games.

On exciting developments in the industry:

I am excited by the rise of "wholesome games"—slow-paced games that favor coziness and nurturing over fast-paced hardcore action and conflict. I say this as someone who loves both The Binding of Isaac and Animal Crossing. I think there is plenty of room in our industry for all types of games to thrive; escapism comes in many flavors. These days especially, while we're all facing world-wide catastrophes like a pandemic and global warming and everything feels so uncertain, a fantasy where your life is simple and normal and happy is actually powerful. It gives players a sense of control and order and peace in a small corner of their life. I'm happy to see more and more of these games, and I'm sure I'll make another game in this space myself.

On design process:

I usually get ideas when I'm doing things unrelated to games. Unpacking came from a real-life house move, when my partner (and co-creator) Tim moved in with me. The idea I'm currently playing around with was inspired by a certain activity I did while on holiday in Japan. After coming up with the initial idea I talk to someone else about it to brainstorm and further flesh it out. I daydream about the idea and jot down notes. It's important to me from early on to have a very clear hook that I can communicate in a one or two sentence pitch, something that makes the game sound distinct. I draw some sketches to visualize what the game might look like, which helps me with figuring out how it might play, too.

On prototypes:

Yes, prototyping is essential to my process. With Unpacking, the first thing we prototyped was the central mechanic of taking things out of boxes and placing them around a room. I specifically chose a kitchen as the room for the prototype as it's a room that by its very nature is full of dozens of items regardless of who the person living in the apartment might be. That way we could forget about the story initially and focus on making the physical act of unpacking things feel great. If the core mechanic didn't feel good, there was no point in dressing it up in a story, even in a game as story centric as ours.

On a difficult design problem:

Translating Unpacking's mouse controls into touch controls for the Nintendo Switch and for phones and tablets was a lot trickier than Tim and I expected. The two input methods seemed like they would be similar, but there were some crucial differences: Touch controls don't have the concept of *hovering*, and there is no right click. We had to completely reimagine and reengineer the controls.

Hovering: In the mouse version, the player simply clicks on an item to pick it up, moves the mouse around to hover the item over different surfaces, and clicks again where they want to put the item down. In touch, items can similarly be picked up with a tap and dropped with a tap, but that's hard to do precisely with a finger on such a small screen. So, we made dragging and dropping also work. The two options can even be used in combination: pick up an item with a tap, then touch and drag in the location where you want to put the item to get it into just the right spot.

Right-clicking: In the mouse and keyboard version, you can rotate a held item by right-clicking it. In the touch version, we added a small on-screen rotate button that appears right next to the item while it is held. That solved the rotation issue, but the other use case for right clicking in Unpacking is secret interactions the player can discover by right-clicking on an item they are not currently holding. For example, the player can turn on a CD player by right clicking it or set the time on the microwave with a series of right clicks. So now, we needed to give the player the ability to right click an item they are *not* holding, too. And only in a few specific cases! We wanted to allow these interactions without giving the player an obvious indication that they were there, because they were intended as secrets to be discovered.

After a lot of thinking, we ended up giving those few special items a special state: if they are tapped, they are selected without being picked up. In that state, they get a special *interact* button next to the usual *rotate* button. The player can still click elsewhere on the screen or drag the item to move and place it. If the item is rotated, it's treated like it's been picked up. In both of those cases the interact button disappears. But if the interact button is pressed, the item is deselected and completes its special interaction (e.g., turning the music player on) without being lifted.

The touch controls we ended up with feel intuitive to play with, but they sure weren't intuitive to design!

What are you most proud of in your career?

It's not directly tied to game development, but the thing I am most proud of in my career is the talks I have given. I used to have a debilitating fear of public speaking. Even giving a five-minute talk in front of my class at university left me shaking for half an hour. But it felt like an important skill for my career, so over the past eight years I've slowly pushed myself to get over my fear and spoken at many games events. I started by participating in fairly casual panels at PAX Australia, then giving my first talk in front of an audience of mostly students at a small local event. I gave the same talk at a bigger venue in front of Australian industry peers later that same year. After that, I did a few panels and a talk every year, until the year after Unpacking came out. That year I gave five different talks, including two opening keynotes. I still get nervous, and there is definitely room for improvement in my public speaking, but I feel like I've achieved my goal.

Advice for designers:

I would advise to look for inspiration outside of games. Looking only at other games for inspiration is an easy trap to fall into, which is why we end up with the meme "it's the Dark Souls of..." and unexciting pitches of "it's like [Game X] meets [Game Y]". Games are such a powerful medium and the possibilities are endless, but so often we keep on trying to replicate something we have already seen done. It's hard to come up with something fresh that way. I am not saying you need to make something the likes of which no one has ever seen before, or that looking at other games isn't useful; I certainly drew on existing concepts from games when designing Unpacking and I can name specific games that helped inspire it— Gone Home, Florence, and The Sims. But it was also inspired by a real-life activity, and the story for it was inspired in part by a song—"The Bed Song" by Amanda Palmer. Mixing in influences from other mediums and one's real-life experiences together with familiar game concepts can help your game feel unique and stand out in a crowded market.

FURTHER READING

Bogost, Ian. *Persuasive Games: The Expressive Power of Videogames*. Cambridge: MIT Press, 2007.

Cooper, Alan and Reimann, Robert. *About Face 2.0: The Essentials of Interaction Design*. Indianapolis: Wiley Publishing, 2003.

Gee, James Paul. *Good Video Games and Good Learning: Collected Essays on Video Games, Learning and Literacy*. Bern: Peter Lang Publishing, 2007.

Hiwiller, Zack. *Players Making Decisions: Game Design Essentials and the Art of Understanding Your Players*. New York: New Riders, 2016.

Koster, Raph. *A Theory of Fun for Game Design*. Scottsdale: Paraglyph Press, 2004.

Maeda, John. *The Laws of Simplicity: Design, Technology, Business, Life*. Cambridge: MIT Press, 2006.

McGonigal, Jane. *Reality is Broken: Why Games Make Us Better and How They Can Change the World*. New York: The Penguin Press, 2011.

Norman, Donald. *Emotional Design: Why We Love (Or Hate) Everyday Things*. New York: Basic Books, 2004.

END NOTES

1. Bocska, Steve. "Temptation and Consequences: Dilemmas in Video Games," Game Developers Conference, 2003.

2. Yee, Nick. "EQ: The Virtual Skinner Box." http://www.nickyee.com/hub/home.html

3. Fulton, Bill. "Making Games More Fun: Tips for Playtesting Games," Game Developers Conference, 2003.

Part 3
Working as a Game Designer

The first two sections of this book were designed to help you become literate in the structural elements of games and to learn the art of prototyping and playtesting your own game concepts. In this third section I will turn to focus on practical information that will help you to become a working game designer. To succeed as a game designer, you will need to be able to work effectively on a team, communicate with diverse types of people, and understand how the changing structure of the game industry can affect your project.

I start out this section with a discussion of how development teams are structured in the industry. I provide insight about the types of people who work on game projects, from the executives at the publishing company to the QA testers who assure that the game is ready to release. Then I look the various stages of development that digital games go through from ideation to completion.

In addition to having a clear grasp of team structure and the stages of development, you will need to be able to communicate game concepts effectively with the entire team. In recent years, this process has changed a lot. Many teams have gone from using a single design document to the use of smaller, more flexible communications. These are often created using collaborative tools such as Google docs or a wiki making them easier to access and change by the entire group. No matter what collaborative tools you decide on, I will show you how to think through and describe your design so that it reflects the gameplay you have designed, prototyped, and playtested. I will also discuss how to make your design documentation a useful tool for team communication.

The final two chapters are a brief discussion of today's rapidly changing game industry and how to get a job, distribute an independent project, or fund an original idea. In Chapter 15, I explain the various parties that make up the game business, the platforms and genres that have driven the industry along with new platforms that will likely emerge as leaders in the next several years, and the nature of publishing deals on these various platforms. The final chapter discusses practical strategies you can follow for getting a job in the industry, pitching your own original game ideas or starting a company and distributing your games independently.

DOI: 10.1201/9781003460268-14

Chapter 12

Team Structures

When digital games were first commercialized in the 1970s, one person, with a decent knowledge of programming, could create the entire product. That person would act as game designer, producer, programmer, and even graphic artist and sound designer. A finished game averaged only eight kilobytes or less in size; on-screen characters were represented by blocks of pixels, and sound effects consisted of generic "beeps" or "bonks" generated from the sound card. To give you a sense of the state of the art, the arcade classic Space Invaders, from 1978, was four kilobytes in size, including all art and sound. Asteroids, released in 1979, was eight kilobytes in total, and Pac-Man, released in 1982, was 28 kilobytes.

As PCs, game consoles, and mobile technologies have become more powerful, the size and complexity of the games on these platforms have grown exponentially. The amount of art and audio that can be incorporated into games has surpassed and now dwarfs the computer code. Today's console titles can require downloads of 100 gigabytes or more. And their overall production values rival those of of television and movies. Elaborate visual effects, sound effects, music, voice acting, and animation are all standard fare in today's games. Some, such as Until Dawn

(Rami Malek) or Grand Theft Auto: San Andreas (Samuel L. Jackson), rely on the voices and 3D models of well-known television and film actors to give life to game characters, while others, like Medal of Honor, set their epic cinematic game scenes with music performed by live orchestras. Along with this rise in production values has come the need for much larger teams composed of people from many different backgrounds. From database programmers to interface designers and 3D graphic artists, console game teams are becoming increasingly composed of a wide range of specialized talent. This increased emphasis on media production is even greater for immersive VR experiences.

On the other hand, there is also a rise in small games made for mobile devices. These games may be made by teams of just a few members and are often limited in the scope of media assets they can include. For many beginning and indie developers, the fact that you can develop a game of such a small scope, but that can be distributed to the very large audience of smartphone users, makes this an exciting emerging market. Even if you have a small team, however, you will want to run it as professionally as possible. So, understanding the various roles that will need to be played is

DOI: 10.1201/9781003460268-15

important. You may find yourself taking on several roles at once, but you should know what the responsibilities of each are and be aware of the complexities that arise when you do double duty. In this chapter, I will look at the roles of each of these types of individuals and how the game designer fits into the team structure.

TEAM STRUCTURE

Figure 12.1 illustrates the basic job categories that make up most development and publishing teams in the game industry today. Note that this diagram only shows the types of individuals who are involved in the production at some level. I purposely did not include human resources, accounting, public relations, sales, and support because they do not typically become involved in the actual production and are outside the scope of this discussion.

Publisher versus Developer

To understand team structure, let's first examine the relationship between the publisher and the developer. As any game developer can tell you, this relationship is critical. It determines how everything else will be structured. The types of relationships vary. Sometimes the developer will do almost everything but sell and market the game. Other times the publishers will pick up much of the development and internalize it, utilizing the developer only for specific tasks. But in a classic relationship, the arrangement will break down according to the chart in Figure 12.2.

Typically, the publisher gives the developer an advance against royalties, and the developer uses this money to pay the team members, cover overhead, and subcontract certain portions of the work. The developer's main task is to deliver the product, while the publisher's is to finance and distribute it.

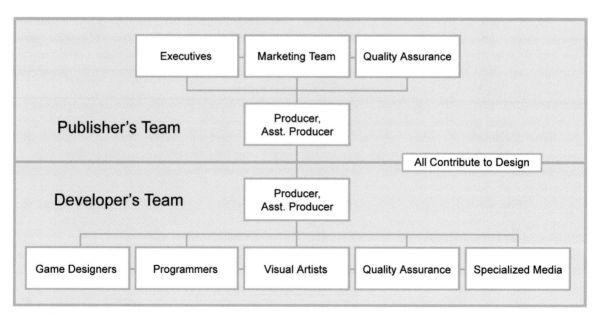

12.1   Team structure

Publisher	Developer
- Chooses which titles to produce - Finances titles - Provides QA testing - Markets titles - Distributes titles	- Pitches creative ideas and demos to publishers - Uses money from publishers to produce titles, including game design, programming, art, audio, etc.

12.2 Publisher/developer responsibilities

One confusing aspect of the developer/publisher relatinoship is that many game publishers also develop games internally. Electronic Arts is one example of a publisher that develops a number of its titles in-house. Additionally, some game developers are owned by publishers. For example, Media Molecule and Naughty Dog are both developers that are owned by Sony.

Even in these cases, however, there is a basic publisher/developer relationship between the internal development group and the rest of the company. In many respects, in-house development teams, as they are called, act like small companies that are responsible for their own cash flow, profit and loss, schedules, and staffing. This helps the publisher to gauge the success of each developer and analyze whether it is more cost effective to work with internal or external groups.

For independent game developers, the line may be even further blurred, as a small company, or even an individual, may take on all roles: creating the game and then working to distribute it, usually without much or any marketing support. It's a difficult thing to do successfully, especially when there are so many other indie developers out there trying to get their games noticed. On page 463, Sam Roberts, Festival Director of IndieCade, discusses opportunities for indies and how festivals can serve as a place for small teams to get their work noticed.

I will look at the typical individuals involved in a game production from the publisher's side on page 427, but first, let's focus on the production team from the developer's perspective.

DEVELOPER'S TEAM

Game development companies often begin life as small groups of people, usually friends, who enjoy working together. Many times, especially in the beginning of a company's existence, the exact job descriptions might not be clear. "Everybody does everything" is a common comment at small start-up game companies. But as the team grows larger, budgets grow bigger, and projects grow more and more complex, even the best of friends have to determine who is responsible for what—and when.

Most established game developers clearly delineate job descriptions for every member of their team. This does not mean that individuals do not work together closely, they just sometimes ignore the exact lines of their formal job descriptions. It does mean that each individual has a specific focus, however, and a set of skills that makes he or she the best person to be ultimately responsible for certain aspects of the project.

Let's look at each of these types of individuals closely, beginning with the game designer, because our primary goal is to understand how the game designer fits into the structure of the team and interacts with all of these other individuals.

Game Designer

As I have already discussed, the game designer is responsible for the play experience. From conception through to completion, it is the designer's job to ensure that the gameplay works at all levels. Because gameplay is so intricately linked with how that play is programmed, visualized, and supported by music, voice-over, etc., the game designer must collaborate closely with just about every other team member.

Because you have had experience designing your own games by now, you know the designer's primary responsibilities. To review, they are as follows:

- Brainstorms concepts
- Creates prototypes
- Playtests and revises prototypes
- Creates concept and design documents and updates throughout production
- Communicates vision for the game to the team
- Creates levels for the game (or works with level designers; see page 426)
- Acts as advocate for the player

Not all companies have dedicated game designers. This role is sometimes undertaken by programmers, artists, executives, or producers. Depending on the scope of the project and the skill of the individual taking on multiple roles, this practice can sometimes have a detrimental effect on the design process.

For example, a game designer who is also the programmer of a game might not be objective about the success of a crucial feature of gameplay simply because the feature took them several weeks, or even months, to code. If the roles are divided, the game designer can approach playtests and feedback with a more objective mindset.

This conflict of interest is true of game designers who also play the part of producers, artists, or executives. It is seen most clearly when

the role of game designer is combined with that of the producer. Because the producer is ultimately responsible for the schedule and budget of the project, there is a natural conflict with the designer's role. How can a single person advocate expenditures of time and money to ensure the best gameplay possible, while on the other hand making sure the team sticks to a strict bottom line?

As a solution to this problem, at some companies, like Electronic Arts Canada, the producer does act as the game designer, but many of the producer's traditional responsibilities are handled by another individual who is called the development director.

In the end, exact titles are not as important as job descriptions. What matters most is that on every game there is someone who is able to focus specifically on the workings of the gameplay without the distraction of too many other responsibilities. We call this person the game designer.

To take on this responsibility, especially on games as complex or innovative as those being made today, is a full-time job, and the industry has moved to a system where dedicated game designers can concentrate on the gameplay and the player experience without being burdened by budgeting, scheduling, resource allocation, and other production duties.

Additionally, on some titles, this role is so important, and has grown beyond a focus on gameplay to include visioning and directing the emotional and dramatic arc of the game, that some designers are taking on the title "game director." Games such as The Last of Us and Journey are examples of games that have a game director as well as game designers.

Producer

The simplest definition of a producer for the developer's team is that she is the project leader. The producer is the person who is responsible for the delivery of the game to the publisher as promised. To make this delivery, the producer must create a plan for that delivery, including a schedule, budget, and resource allocation.

In most productions, there is a producer on the publisher's team as well as one on the developer's team. These two producers, in a good working structure, serve collectively as the single point of contact for important decisions regarding the production that have to pass between the publisher and developer. By making this single point of contact the main conduit of information between the two teams, the producers can work together to make sure that both teams are acting on the same assumptions and that important decisions are communicated to the right people on each team as they are made.

In brief, the responsibilities of the producer for the developer are as follows:

- Team leader for developer's team
- Main communication link between developer and publisher
- Responsible for schedule and budget for the production from the developer side
- Responsible for tracking and allocating resources as well as forecasting
- Manage developer team to make sure deliverables are completed on time
- Motivate team and solve production related problems

Meeting the delivery schedule usually involves making some tough decisions during the course of the production; some of the producer's many responsibilities might include hiring or firing employees as well as saying no to excessive resource or spending requests. Ultimately, being a producer can be an extremely rewarding role. Producers interact with the contacts on the publisher's team more than the other team members. They might also be asked to represent the team in public, at conferences, or in the press. The office of the producer often serves as a "United Nations" for the production team—the place where everyone comes to air their grievances and concerns and, hopefully, to resolve them.

There might also be an executive producer on each team whose job it is to oversee multiple productions or sometimes an entire development group. Additionally, there might be assistant producers and associate producers on each team whose job it is to support the producers. Most producers start out as assistant producers and associate producers then work their way up the ladder to producer, senior producer, and eventually executive producer.

As a game designer, you must work hand in hand with the producer. This means sitting down together at the start of any production and going over the design in detail. It is your job to make certain that the producer crafts a realistic schedule and budget, and the producer cannot do this without a clear understanding of the game you plan to make. If you do not clearly communicate the entire scope and vision of the project, the producer will wind up using canned numbers or rough estimates, and both the schedule and budget for your game will be inaccurate, potentially insufficient, and the cause of a lot of unnecessary anxiety.

This means that to be a really efficient game designer, you need to understand the ins and outs of scheduling and budgeting almost as well as the producer. You do not have to create these documents or be responsible for tracking them, but you should review them carefully and understand each line item. Make sure they match your vision of the project, and articulate any issues you see as early as possible in the process.

Programmers

I use the term "programmers" as a catchall to refer to everyone involved in technically implementing the game. This includes high- and low-level coders, network and systems engineers, database programmers, computer hardware

BUILDING INCLUSIVE DESIGN TEAMS

by Tracy Fullerton

One important issue in today's game industry is diversity and the creation of inclusive teams for game design and development. We know that the game-playing public has become more diverse over time, with women now making up a larger percentage of players than men, and the average age of gamers rising to 35 years. Development teams are also becoming more diverse, with team members from very different experiences and backgrounds working together on a variety of new platforms and with innovative new experience goals for the games they are creating.

And diversity doesn't always just mean people of different genders, ages, races, or backgrounds. It can also mean people who have different ways of communicating, such as extroverts versus introverts, or people who have different preferences in gameplay, such as casual versus hardcore. When you are working on a team, you may assume that everyone has the same background and sensibilities that you do, and in doing so, you may wind up missing the ways they are trying to communicate with you. Or, you may inadvertently dismiss ideas that don't appeal to you because they are outside your realm of experience. But these ideas are valuable, just like yours, and need to be fully considered in your process. Otherwise, you're missing the opportunity to bring these new ideas into your projects.

That's why it's so important to build skills for inclusive design processes as a part of your preparation for becoming a game designer. The culture of design in which a game is created has a great effect on its eventual outcome, and one of the most important things you can do for your game is to build it in a community where ideas can come from all areas of the team, in an inclusive and respectful environment.

In my game design classes, I use many different exercises that help build skills for this kind of inclusive design. The two that I've included here are techniques you can try yourself, either in class, if you're studying game design, or with your team, if you're working on your own.

Skill Sharing

The first exercise is one I call "skill sharing." This exercise came out of something I noticed early on: that students tended to group themselves with others that shared the same skills they already had. So programmers tended to group up with programmers, artists with artists, etc. But as I've already pointed out, games are inherently multidisciplinary and the best games are made by teams that work well together across these disciplines. It's best that everyone know some programming, everyone know some art, etc. To do this, I needed to help students bridge their natural tendency to group with like minds.

Skill sharing is a great exercise for large groups, like classrooms, but can also work on a team as small as three people. The purpose of the exercise is to encourage groups to share knowledge and working methods and to break down barriers between disciplines. In my classes, we start this exercise on day one as an ice breaker and work on it for the entire semester. At the end of the semester, we have a day where we share the outcome of the exercise with each other.

To begin, we have a discussion about skills and passions. What skills does everyone in the room have? What are they passionate about—both in the discipline of game design and beyond, in life? What are skills they would like to have that they don't? Once we've warmed up to the topic, everyone writes three skills they feel they could teach to someone else on sticky notes of one color and pastes them to their shirts. Then, on another color sticky note, everyone writes three skills they'd love to learn and also pastes them to their shirts. They become walking "billboards" for their skills and interests.

Student skill sharing exercise at USC

I should note that participants are allowed to pick anything they like for these skills—of course, some skills are more marketable than others, but there are no constraints. We've had a lot of programmers teaching C++, and artists teaching Maya, but we also have had people teaching budgeting, or dancing, fencing, or even surfing. The idea isn't to determine which skills are valuable and which skills are not, but to begin to build an understanding that all skills have their own kinds of value, and that the more varied the community is in its skills, the more each of them has the opportunity to learn.

Then, the group mingles and meets each other, discussing the skills on each other's sticky notes. As they mingle, their goal is to each find one person who will teach them a new skill and one person to whom they will teach a new skill. The only rule is that these can't be the same person and each person can only have one teacher and one student. Sometimes partners need to do a bit of negotiation to agree on what part of a skill the student is really interested in learning. But eventually, they shake on it and once everyone has one student and one teacher, we seal the contract in a matrix detailing everything the class will be teaching and learning from each other over the course of the exercise. I should mention that this is all in addition to the standard course material. Students meet outside of class to share and to learn at their own discretion. When we show off what has been learned at the end of the semester, there is always an amazing array of new skills to demonstrate.

Now, in my classes, every entering group of students does this exercise every year, so what has happened is that the exercise has become a kind of ritual. Everyone wants to know what your skill was, what you taught, what you learned, and what this means is that the entire maker community beyond the class is poised to know a bit about each student as they fold into group projects. And some skills are in such demand that ongoing study groups form around them, encouraging students to look beyond the prescribed curriculum and to think of themselves as lifelong and self-driven learners, and as part of a community of people willing to help them with their learning goals.

So how does this translate into teamwork and interdisciplinary projects? Well, as I've already stressed, game teams are made up of many different kinds of people: engineers, artists, designers, musicians, producers, writers, and user researchers all working together to produce interactive experiences. Skill sharing builds understanding, respect, and personal ties between these team members, who learn to value the input of every member of the team, to learn from their different skills, and to take that sense of difference as a good value into their future work in the industry.

Yes, and

One of the key places where inclusivity is often challenged is in brainstorming meetings, which can sometimes be dominated by some team members. This usually isn't intentional, but rather that people get excited when generating ideas, and stop listening as carefully to others. Because this is such a critical part of the design process and also one of the areas where diverse thinking is the most needed, I've developed an exercise called "Yes, and" to help people from different disciplines learn good techniques and a common language for working together.

"Yes, and" is an adaptation of a common theater technique that you may already be familiar with. Here, I've adapted it to focus specifically on brainstorming in groups. At its root, "Yes, and" is an exercise in building on the ideas of others rather than focusing on getting your own ideas accepted. By making brainstorm participants conscious of the language they use when working creatively with others, we can start to help them be more collaborative and more inclusive in that collaboration.

"Yes, and" card game

For my version of "Yes, and," I've made a simple card game. In this card game, there are two kinds of cards: goal cards and "yes, and" cards. Goal cards are the ideas we're going to brainstorm about—they are intentionally a bit weird and blue sky to spark everyone's imagination. Here are some examples of goal cards:

- A game that takes 30 years to play
- A game to learn a language
- A game that you can only play in one place
- A game to play across generations

- A game that makes you mellow
- A game about the future.

Each group chooses one goal card to start. Then, the "yes, and" cards are shuffled and dealt out. As can be seen in the image at left, "yes and" cards each have a phrase on them that must be used when a player wants to add to the conversation. So, obviously, one of these phrases is "yes, and." But there are also many other "building" phrases a student might use to add their idea to the common brainstorm.

These include phrases like:

- I love that idea!
- I like the way you're thinking
- Exactly, so
- How about...
- What if we combine...
- Let's dig into that...
- That makes me think...

I might play my "I'm glad you brought that up" card before adding my idea to yours. Or "exactly, so" "definitely!" "also, we could," and so on. Each of these is a positive reinforcement of the last speaker's idea before the addition of your own. Not all of the cards are as clear an affirmation, however. If I play "this is out of left field, but" it acknowledges that I'm changing the subject away from your idea, but in a way that at least does not negate what you've just said.

The cards are color coded to show their level of positive building impact. So we might see neutral cards, like "so, to summarize" or, getting less neutral, "in my opinion" or "no, but," all the way to "shut down" cards like "I don't see it" or "that won't work." Since the cards were shuffled and dealt, players will have a range of cards to choose from in their hand. Anyone can speak at anytime in the brainstorm and as many times as they like, as long as they play a card and begin their contribution with the language on their card.

The brainstorm continues until each player has contributed at least once and, at the end, we share out their results—not only the creative idea they came up with, but also how they felt the brainstorm went and the impact of specific language on the process. I can tell you it's very illuminating and helps participants build their own vocabulary bank of good brainstorming terms.

If you'd like to try the "Yes, and" cards with your team, they are available on theGameCrafter.com: https://www.the-gamecrafter.com/games/yes-and...1

Conclusion

These are just two of the kinds of exercises I use to help build our game design community into an inclusive and welcoming environment for all kinds of creative voices. Building intentionally inclusive interdisciplinary communities is key to the future of the industry. How can you challenge yourself and your team in this regard? Take a look at your team and how you communicate; are there ways that you can create better dialogues between team members? Is everyone being heard at your meetings? Use these methods to break down barriers and help engage everyone at a higher level.

support, etc. Programmers are also referred to as engineers and software developers at some companies. Advanced positions in this track are senior programmer, lead programmer, and technical director, all the way up to CTO. Some companies break down the titles according to specific areas of specialization, such as tools programmer, engine programmer, graphics programmer, database programmer, etc.

In general, the programming team's responsibilities include the following:

- Drafting technical specifications
- Technical implementation of the game, including:
  ◇ Software prototypes
  ◇ Software tools
  ◇ Game modules and engines
  ◇ Structuring data
  ◇ Managing communications
- Documenting code
- Coordinating with QA engineers to fix or resolve bugs

As a game designer, if you do not have a technical background, you might find it difficult to communicate your ideas to the programming team. While you do not need to become an expert programmer, if you are going to design digital games, you do have to learn the basic concepts of programming to have a common language with which to speak to the engineers. There is no right way to do this. If you learn best by reading, then buy a book on programming for beginners. If you need a structured environment in which to learn, then take a class. If you have a good relationship with a programmer, then ask them questions about their work. Everyone likes to talk about things they are good at. If you express genuine interest, most programmers will talk your ear off about how games are programmed.

After you have a strong understanding of how games are implemented technically, you can use this knowledge to write better design specifications and to describe your game concepts more clearly to the technical team. This, in turn, will make programmers more open and accessible to talk to about tweaks and changes to the gameplay as they are required.

Throughout the production cycle, you will find that almost every change you need to make to the gameplay requires alterations in the code. If you have designed your game modularly, as I discussed in Chapter 10 on page 354, this won't mean drastic repercussions to the entire system, but it will still mean additional work for the programming team. To achieve the kind of relationship with the programming team that will allow you to suggest these changes without an uproar, you will need to use all your communication skills and your knowledge of programming.

Whether your team is large or small, there is likely a hierarchy you will need to respect to get things done. No matter how much you would like to circumvent the technical director, for example, and go straight to the database engineer to ask for a quick change, try to avoid such an action. This undercuts the technical director's authority, and there is no better way to create an adversary out of this person.

You need to partner with the technical director, lead programmer, or whoever is in charge of your programming team. It is this person's job to communicate your ideas to the other team members, and you want to establish a relationship where they will respect your ideas in the same way that you respect their expertise and contribution.

The goal is to have your programming team become active participants in the iterative improvement of the game. They will soon look for validation of their work by asking you when the next playtest session is, and you will have a solid partnership with one of the most important groups who will work on your game.

Visual Artists

As with the term "programmers," I use the term "visual artist" as a catchall to refer to those team members who are tasked with designing all of the visual aspects of the game. This includes the character designers, illustrators, animators, interface designers, and 3D artists. Advanced positions in this track include art director, senior art director, and lead animator. In some companies there are even positions like creative director and chief creative officer, whose responsibilities include making sure there is a consistent look and feel across a company's entire product line.

Visual artists come from many different backgrounds. The best artists may or may not have a degree in the field. Some artists have always worked digitally; others might have come to digital media after gaining a background in traditional art tools. Before hiring your artists, you need to think about what skills your team will need. Will the game require predominantly 3D art? Will you need someone who can animate? Does your interface need to appeal to a specific market segment?

As you look at various portfolios, you will find that some artists are brilliant at creating intricate cityscapes and imagining 3D worlds, but when it comes to animating a character, they simply cannot do it. For this reason, teams tend to be structured around the key tasks required in the production, and artists will be hired for specialized tasks like 3D modeling, animation, rigging, texture mapping, interface design, etc.

Overall, the responsibilities of the visual artists are to design and produce all visuals for the game, including the following:

- Characters
- Environments and objects
- Interfaces
- Animations
- Cut scenes

Game designers and artists can also have trouble communicating even if there is no technical barrier of understanding, as with the programming team. It is the job of the artists to make the game as visually appealing as possible. Sometimes the needs of the game design can get in the way of a beautiful screen. You might find yourself in a situation where the wireframes you created, showing each important feature and detail of the design, have been only loosely followed. Artists might take it upon themselves to condense features to make the layout look better.

In a situation like this, your first reaction might be to insist that your designs be followed to the letter. This is one way to get things done. Another way might be to evaluate the work of the artists more objectively. After all, if they thought your design was convoluted, perhaps players will as well. You might be able to compromise and find that your designs become better and more intuitive as they are rethought by someone with a skilled artistic eye. Of course, you need to make sure that features are not hidden or lost for the sake of beautiful artwork. Remember, it is your job to think about how a player will respond to these screens. They won't care about the beauty if they cannot find the feature they need to continue on in the game.

Another issue that might come up between artists and game designers is in the overall style of the game. As you work with different artists, you will find that they all have their own unique styles and techniques. While most artists are trained to work outside their personal style, they will always respond more enthusiastically to a project that mirrors their own interests more closely. To use an analogy, if you were starting a rock-and-roll band, you might think twice about hiring a percussionist from a philharmonic orchestra to play drums for you. In the same way, try to assemble an art team that is passionate about the look and feel you are striving for.

It might not be possible to choose the specific artists who will work on your project. If you are at a larger company, you might be simply assigned a team of artists. In this case, you will have to make a decision: Either change your vision to utilize the skills of the people you have, or find a way to communicate your ideas clearly enough so that the team can implement them.

Artists are visual people, and a great way to communicate with them is through visual reference material. Most art departments have a great deal of reference material—other games, magazines, art books, etc. For example, game artist Steve Theodore uses video to capture reference, as well as textbooks on human and animal motion to create visuals.[1] If needed, bring in your own reference material to get the conversation going. When I was working on a game for Microsoft that had a retro space-age style, my art team and I collected samples of brightly designed 1950s fabrics from flea markets and scanned their patterns and colors to create the visual palette for the game.

As with the programming team, you will get the best results if you partner with the lead artist or art director in the process of design. Explain your vision, but listen to their responses. Chances are, your artists have seen and studied far more visual references than you have, and they might have some fantastic ideas that take your initial concepts much further than you could have yourself. Look at these references together, and be specific about what you like and do not like about them.

When you have decided on an approach, the artists will begin creating concept art, and you will need to start giving criticism. Keep in mind that the purpose of criticism is to move the project forward. Even if a sketch or design is not exactly what you want, there might still be some elements in it that are useful. Search for those elements before you start speaking. Try to see what the artist was going for. And when you do start speaking, it is always nice to begin on a positive note.

Giving and taking feedback is probably one of the hardest things to do in life. As you saw when players were critiquing your gameplay, it is often a complete surprise to find that people do not respond to a part of the design that is very close to your heart. Your most important ally in the process of giving feedback to the artists is the art director. You must work together with this individual to set the tone of the project. Listen carefully to your art director and try to come up with solutions that appeal to both of you. Remember, there is more than one answer to each design problem, and by creating an open dialogue, you might find another approach that neither of you has considered.

Ultimately, unless you have the skills to create the art yourself, you need to allow the artists some freedom to move beyond your initial concepts and bring their own ideas and passion to the project. If you have created a good working relationship with the art director, chances are that you will feel a strong sense of authorship in the final artwork, even if it is not what you initially imagined, just as the rest of the team will feel that they have contributed to the overall game design.

QA Engineers

QA (quality assurance) engineers are also referred to as testers or bug testers. Many game professionals start their careers as QA engineers, and then they move to other tracks, such as producer, programmer, or designer. Advanced positions on this track are QA lead and QA manager. As noted on the team structure diagram, there are QA engineers on both the publisher side and the developer side. Publishers typically QA projects themselves before they accept delivery of the code.

The responsibilities of the QA team are as follows:

- Create a test plan for the project based on the design and technical specifications
- Execute the test plan
- Record all unexpected or undesirable behavior
- Categorize, prioritize, and report all issues found during testing
- Retest and resolve issues after they have been fixed

As the designer, you should take it upon yourself to make sure the QA staff has everything they need to create a comprehensive test plan. Do not assume that they have a complete understanding of the game just because you have distributed a design document or build of the game. Offer any assistance they might need to create the best test plan possible. But do not be surprised if they want to experience the game first without your input; as with playtesters, it is often best if QA testers have some objectivity about the game when they begin the testing process.

QA testers can be the designer's best friends. Other than your playtesters, they are the last line of defense you have before your game ships out to the masses. Do not be upset if some of your design features come back listed as bugs. This is not a criticism of your design—this is QA's way of helping you make sure your design is working properly. Their job is to make sure your game is functioning both technically and aesthetically. If you get a bug back that says the font you have chosen for the character screen is illegible under certain circumstances, do not bristle defensively. Be grateful that you have the chance to fix it before the game goes to the players.

It might help for you to sit down with the QA team and observe their process. You can learn a lot by consulting with your QA engineers and going through the game element by element. Because they are seasoned testers, they might be able to provide you with insights no one else can.

Another consideration is to let your QA manager review your designs early in the process. They might find problems with the flow of the game or interface layout before you even start to implement it. Starting the QA process early and making the QA team part of the design process will mean they are more invested in your game. This means that in crunch time, they will make your game a priority and put in the extra hours it takes to find every last glitch.

Specialized Media

As I have mentioned, games have grown to include many specialized types of media—too many to address each possible role on all game productions. Your game might require the skills of writers, sound designers, musicians, or even motion capture operators, karate instructors, and dialogue coaches. I include these in a group as "specialized media" because they are too numerous to list. These types of individuals are usually hired for a short period of time on a contract basis, rather than coming on as full-time employees.

One of the most important things that you can do as a designer is to define what you need from these professionals as clearly as possible before they start working. When people are hired as contractors, they often charge by the hour or day. If you bring in contractors and waste time trying to figure out what to do with them, you can wind up also wasting a lot of money that would be better spent elsewhere in the production.

Some of the most typical contractors that you will work with include writers and sound designers. In the case of a writer, the responsibilities can range from creating bits of dialogue where needed to scripting the entire story. How much writing you will need depends on what skills you have as a designer. If your strength is writing, you might not need a writer at all. If you are not a strong writer, you can bring a writer in very early and work with her throughout production. For games that involve a rich narrative, you may find that having a writer involved from the ideation stage onward is the best way to get that narrative integrated into all the other aspects of the design.

In the case of a sound designer, the task might be limited to creating special effects and music for the game when it is almost completed. Or, if you are striving for a more integrated sound design, it might encompass laying out a plan for the entire audio design for the project up front and working with you to make sure the audio supports the gameplay effectively. Sound and music affect players at a very emotional level; if you involve a sound designer more deeply in the project, you might be surprised at the improvement it can make to the player experience.

As productions continue to grow more complex, they will invariably require more media professionals in a diverse range of fields. As the designer, you will have to interact with many of these media professionals and give them direction and support. As you deal with people who might not work exclusively on games, it is important to communicate with them in terms they are familiar with. Many of these media professionals will not be hard-core gamers, and they might get lost if you use shorthand or game jargon. To bring out the best of their talents, you will have to learn as much as you can about their specialty, and act as their guide when it comes to game production.

Level Designer

Games that are organized into levels will need someone to actually design and implement each level. If your project is very small, you might design all the levels yourself. On a larger project, however, the game designer often leads a team of level designers who implement their concepts for the various game levels and sometimes come up with ideas for levels themselves.

Level designers use a toolkit or "level editor" to develop new missions, scenarios, or quests for the player. They lay out the components that appear on the level or map and work closely with the game designer to make these fit into the overall theme of the game.

Responsibilities of level designers include the following:

- Implementing level designs
- Coming up with level concepts
- Testing levels and working with the designer to improve overall gameplay

Level design is an art, and it is a great way to enter the industry. Good level designers often go on to become game designers; an example is American McGee, who won notoriety for several of the levels he designed while working at id Software. Other level designers might move on to become producers.

As a game designer, you will want to develop a close working relationship with your level designers. Levels are the structure within which the players will experience the gameplay you have designed. They might include story or character elements that are crucial to the development of the game. Because levels are so critical, sometimes game designers can become somewhat controlling of how they are implemented.

As with artists, however, you can usually achieve better results by fostering creativity in your level designers rather than making them toe a strict line. If you have created an amazing system of gameplay, it will inspire your designers to come up with combinations and situations that you might not have even thought of in your initial pass at the game levels. Try not to micromanage your level design team, and you will find that they will work harder and come up with better results than if they had implemented your designs to the letter.

The fact is that you are the designer of the game, and their hard work and innovations will only make you look better. So tuck any insecurity away and treat your level designers as partners with whom to experiment and take the game to places that even you did not think was possible.

Exercise 12.1: Recruit a Team

Now that you know a little bit about the roles of team members in a game production, think about enlisting some friends or recruiting some talent to work on the original game idea you prototyped in Part II. Decide which of these positions you cannot fill yourself, and go out and try to fill them. Post notices on local or online bulletin boards or websites. You are sure to get a response because many people out there are eager to work on game projects.

PUBLISHER'S TEAM

Publishing companies are often huge corporations, with offices in many cities and sometimes countries. They employ thousands of people who you might never meet but who might work indirectly or directly on your game in the process of getting it to the shelves. Here I have focused on those you are most likely to interact with while working on your game.

Producer

As with the producer on the developer's team, the producer for the publisher is also a project leader. Unlike the producer on the development team, however, the producer for the publisher will spend less time interacting with the production team and more time marshalling the forces of the marketing team and making sure that the executives at the company continue to stay behind the game concept throughout development.

The responsibilities of the producer for the publisher are as follows:

- Team leader for the publisher's team
- Main communication link between the publisher and developer
- Responsible for schedule and budget for the production from the publisher's side
- Responsible for tracking and allocating resources as well as forecasting
- Approve work accomplished by the developer so milestone payments can be made
- Coordinate with internal executive management, marketing, and QA personnel

The producer for the publisher is one step removed from the actual production, although they are usually more involved than any other person from the publisher's team. This position means that the producer has a vested interest in the success of the game when it goes to market, but is also somewhat removed from the day-to-day struggle of production and is sometimes able to see the game and its potential more objectively than the game designer and the rest of the production team.

There is a sense in many creative industries—the game industry is no exception—that executives and producers who are removed from the process do not understand the plight of creative teams. The suggestions and direction of these people are often met with resistance and scorn. While it is true that no one understands your game design the way that you do, it is also true that these individuals are skilled at publishing and marketing successful games, and they very likely have some good points to make if you remain open to their feedback.

No one gets into the game industry because they want to make bad games. The producer and executives on the publisher's team are no exception. They want to make great games, games that they feel a sense of authorship in just like everyone else on the team. And if you can find ways to incorporate their suggestions into your game in ways that improve the gameplay, rather than dragging your heels, you will find when it comes time to sell the game that the publisher is more likely to be behind it all the way.

Marketing Team

The goal of the marketing team is to find ways to sell your game to the buyers. In some cases, they might have direct involvement during the production process, giving feedback on game concepts and holding focus groups for various character designs. In other cases, you might never meet them until the game is almost ready to ship. The marketing team can be an incredible asset to the open-minded game designer. This is because they are the strongest link to the demands and desires of buyers. It is their job to know the market, and if you can interpret the data they have creatively, you can address the trends and features that people are interested in without sacrificing your core gameplay.

One important factor that the marketing team has a strong influence on is the target hardware platform titles. Marketing professionals study things like the projected penetration of different operating systems, processors, available RAM, average screen sizes, etc.

If it is important to you as a designer to have a best-selling product, it is smart to bring the marketing team in early. Tap them for information, invest them in the project, and give them credit for their insight. Sometimes having a clear concept of what those key bullet-point features will be for your game can help you stay on track

with your designs when ideas are flying in from all directions. The marketing team can help you with this, and you will have a powerful ally when it comes to publicizing your game or getting a new project off the ground. Nothing speaks louder than sales, and the marketers often represent the voice of the buyers.

Exercise 12.2: Marketing

Design an online advertisement for your original game idea. Come up with a slogan or tag line that will capture buyer interest. Write call outs for the top three or four features in your game. Really try to sell your game through your ad design. Think about what aspects of the game will illustrate these points. Will your ad show screenshots, character designs, or original artwork? Show your ad design to some of your playtesters and do an informal focus group on your design. This process will help you develop a good sales pitch for your idea, which I address in Chapter 16.

Executives

Executive management can include the CEO, president, CFO, COO, assorted VPs, and directors of the publishing company. It is beyond the scope of this discussion to detail all the responsibilities of all these individuals. Suffice to say that it is the job of the executive management to run the publishing company. This means providing leadership and direction, overseeing every department, and ultimately publishing great games.

Of course, there might be upper management on the game developer's team as well, if the company is large enough. In many cases, executives at game development companies are the founders of the company, or they have risen up from the core design team to take on more responsibilities.

At publishing companies, people in upper management can come from all types of backgrounds. Some might have business or marketing degrees or experience in other industries. Others might have extensive experience in game production but otherwise no business background. The nature of the game industry is that it grew out of a hobbyist culture, so there are many people who are very skilled in the development and publishing of games, though their academic or other credentials would not tell you so.

The best-case scenario for a game designer is when an executive has considerable experience with game development and a deep understanding of the market, and is willing to take a hands-on approach. Unfortunately, most game designers do not see it this way. As a rule, designers tend to resent upper management's involvement in the production process. They want management to put out the money for the game and then leave them alone to create their masterpiece.

As I said before, no one wants to make bad games, executives included. You might want to take the time to find out what games or products the executive you are dealing with has worked on, and what their expertise was before they moved up the ladder, before disregarding their input or pushing back on their suggestions.

If you do this and still find that you just cannot get along with an executive, try to learn from their mistakes. What are they doing that you do not like? Is it the way they present their ideas or the ideas themselves? Is it their attitude or the content of their suggestions? Use this interaction as an opportunity to improve your own management skills. Write down what it is that they are doing that is ineffective, annoying, or counterproductive, and then make sure that you are not doing the same thing when it comes to your own team.

If all else fails, at a certain point, you might find that the decisions coming down to you from the executives are "ruining" the game. You might be fed up and ready to walk. But before you blow a gasket, consider this: It is part of your job to communicate the vision for the game to the upper management, and you might be partly to blame if they are on the wrong track. Design documents may be abstract, elaborate, or detailed, and they might not have read yours. Development code is clunky and unstable, and they might not have had time to install and play with your latest build. All in all, they might not have a clear idea of the finished product from either of these sources.

Take a step back from the situation and try to educate them. Perhaps you can have a brainstorm on the area under question with the entire team and invite the executives to participate. This will allow them to give advice in an open forum and to see some of the issues you are up against in implementing their suggestions.

In most cases, everyone will walk away from such a discussion feeling that their ideas have been taken seriously, and they will be invested in the decisions that were made. No one wants to be told what to do—not you, and not the executive team. Everyone wants his or her opinion to be heard and respected. An open discussion for the purpose of solving design issues accomplishes both of these objectives. In the end, you might wind up having to make the changes anyway, but perhaps you will have formed a new channel of communication for the next project.

QA Engineers

The QA team for the publisher's team functions in much the same manner as that of the developer's team. The two exceptions are that they probably are not as familiar with the game, because they do not work side by side with the production team, and their overall goal is to determine whether to accept the build as a deliverable. This acceptance may trigger a payment to the developer, so it is important that the build pass muster with the publisher's QA team and their typically strict technical requirements.

Usability Specialists

Some game companies use the services of usability specialists as part of the development process. As I discussed in Chapter 11, usability specialists can be an important part of making sure your game is intuitive and accessible to your target market. They evaluate a user's abilities to perform important tasks in the game and understand key concepts. Usability testing generally happens at a point in development when the core gameplay is already established, which distinguishes it from playtesting.

Usability specialists can be third-party companies that are hired by the publisher or the developer for a specific series of tests at a point fairly late in the development cycle. Some larger publishers these days, however, have in-house usability labs, and they have integrated usability into the development process from start to finish.

This is the ideal situation if it is available to you. Usability testing can make an incredible difference in the player experience of your game. Like playtesting, it brings the player to the forefront of your design process and allows you to respond to playtesters' input before your game ships and it is too late to make changes.

Responsibilities of the usability specialists are as follows:

- Heuristic evaluation of interfaces (this is an application of general interface principles and reporting of potential issues)
- Creation of user scenarios
- Identify and recruit test subjects from the target market
- Conduct usability sessions
- Record and analyze data from sessions (this might be visual, in the form of video and audio, or quantitative, in the form of task success/failure reporting or questionnaire data)
- Report findings and recommendations

A common mistake game designers make is to push off usability testing until the end of development. Some designers associate it with focus testing and marketing. In general, usability testing has not been as widely accepted in the game industry as it has been in the rest of the software industry. This is changing as the industry reaches out to markets beyond core gamers and there is a need to make sure that games play with audiences that are not represented by the development team. For many game designers, however, there is still a resistance to outside input on the game that makes them fear and dislike the testing process.

Unfortunately, these designers are missing out on a great opportunity to improve their game and learn more about how players interact with games. Every usability session can teach a designer something new about the craft of game design. Interacting with usability engineers can also teach designers how to break down issues with play, navigation, control, etc., to test these issues and solve them.

It seems obvious that learning how to solve issues with gameplay will make you a better designer. A smart and successful game designer will bring usability engineers into the process as early as possible and try to learn as much as possible from them during their work on the project.

Exercise 12.3: Usability Experience

Contact a third-party usability lab and find out if you can either watch one of their test sessions or participate as a user. What types of tasks were you or the subjects asked to complete? Were you able to use the software being tested successfully? Why or why not? How do you think the input from the usability tests helped the designer of the software that was tested?

User Research and Metrics

Related to, but not the same as, the usability specialists are user researchers who develop and analyze metrics related to gameplay. As more and more games have online play, or are distributed and updated online, there is an opportunity for the publishers (and by extension the developers) to have an ongoing sense of how the game is being used by players. This is tracked through metrics that can be analyzed and used to improve both player engagement and the profitability of the game.

A company that has made a great investment in this type of user research is Zynga, which is now owned by Take-Two Interactive. Zynga tracks the uptake of new games, and features within each game, extensively. In their offices, they have huge monitors tracking game metrics in real time. These metrics are not only related to the daily and monthly active users (though these are certainly two of the most important metrics in the online social space), but also to which game features players are using, which ones they are not, which items are being purchased in relation to features, and which are not, etc. This is critical information once you start thinking of games as a service, rather than simply a single-purchase product.

As a designer in an industry that is becoming more and more of a service industry, you will want to understand how metrics can be used to improve player engagement for your game. And, if you develop such an understanding, you will be able to communicate well with the user researchers who may be important contributors to the ongoing success of your game.

TEAM PROFILE

As I touched on at the top of this chapter, the number of people involved in typical game production has grown steadily since the beginnings of the industry. Additionally, both budgets and timelines for production have increased. Today's console teams may have 200 people working on them for three years—sometimes even longer. For example, Grand Theft Auto V took more than five years to develop. This is a major increase from even the prior generation of consoles, which averaged about 40 people and two years of development time. On the other hand, we also see smaller indie and mobile teams working today, with relatively small budgets and timeframes. An indie team might have five people working for eighteen months or so on a project. A mid-sized team working a project that doesn't require the highest-resolution graphics might have 40 people working for twenty-four months. Each of these cases results in a very different cost and eventual product. This divergence in team sizes, project timelines, and scope is part of the rapid diversification we are seeing across the game industry.

You might be wondering how many people from each job category work on a typical title. The fact is that larger teams are incredibly specialized, so that some developers will only work on narrowly defined aspects of the game. On the other hand, small teams remain generalized, with everyone pitching in to get the project done. In general, the art and programming teams will be the largest percentage of any size team, with the need for specialized talent emerging fairly quickly as a project grows in complexity.

For large teams with long production schedules and huge technical challenges, the stress of productions, professionally and personally, may be extreme. Small teams may also have the stress of limited resources and large ambitions. The following sections are designed to help you understand what factors can make a team come together, how to build a team, and how to keep that team communicating during the entire production, no matter its scope.

ALL CONTRIBUTE TO THE DESIGN

Notice the phrase "all contribute to design" on the team structure diagram in Figure 12.1 on page 414. This does not mean that everyone will literally participate in the design process, but it does mean that in a well-run project, each and every member of the team is able to contribute their special talents to the articulation and execution of the design at whatever level they might be involved.

In some cases, this might just mean that every suggestion is always received with respect and consideration. In other cases, it might mean that the designer actively solicits input from the team when making decisions about the design. In the Agile methodology discussed in Chapter 13, it means that each feature team is responsible for the design of their aspect of the game, though they will work in concert with a lead designer. Every designer and every team will have their own process. But the end result should be that everyone who works on the game should have a sense of authorship in the final product and be able to say with pride about some aspect of the experience, "I worked on that."

As the designer, and also as a producer, fostering this sense of authorship is a vital part of the job. You should take the time to establish good channels of communication with each of the team members we have discussed in this chapter and to structure your interaction with the team so that everyone's input is heard. There is no single way to orchestrate something like this, but there are some tips I can give you that will help.

- Set up weekly lead meetings where the heads of each group gather to discuss the current status of the project.
- Start a suggestion list—an open list of ideas that may or may not be used.
- Take time for one-on-one creative talks with key members of the team.
- Have open brainstorming sessions during the design phase for anyone who wants to attend. This includes everyone from the production assistants to the QA team. Shutting people out of the design process fosters cliquishness and might deprive you of hearing some great ideas.
- If you get stuck on a design issue, ask your coworkers to help solve it. Present the issue as a creative challenge.
- Share authorship. When you speak, make sure to use "we," not "I." This is a subtle but effective way to let everyone share in the ownership of the ideas.

TEAM BUILDING

In addition to having a great idea, the next most critical thing you can do to make sure you produce a great game is to build a team that can bring that idea to life. This does not just mean hiring a group of talented people, throwing them together, and expecting miracles. The structure you define for your team and the working environment you create will determine their ability to succeed.

Talent is always a key ingredient to team building, and, of course, you want the most talented individuals you can find. Microsoft is an example of a company with a corporate philosophy of hiring the smartest, most talented individuals who are available. But talent only goes so far. Finding the right mix of talent and personality is even more crucial. Some people are brilliant at what they do individually, but, when put on a team, they are unable to interact productively with their teammates and cause more trouble than their contribution is worth.

When assembling your team, you have to look at each person as an individual and as a potential team member. Examine their track record and make sure to talk with people who have worked with them before. Ask about both their individual performance and how they interact in a team.

In today's entertainment industry, it is critical to make sure that the people on your team are able to act professionally and respectfully in a creative environment. This means checking references thoroughly. Make sure that you're inviting someone onto your team who treats others badly or is otherwise unable to work well with a wide range of team members. If you find that your team has developed an issue with respecting each other, it is best to speak up immediately. Don't assume that bad behavior will fix itself, or it is likely to become a larger problem. The game industry has a far way to go in this respect and all game companies today are responsible for improving the work environment for their employees.

TEAM COMMUNICATION

Notice on the team structure diagram that in addition to the vertical lines of hierarchy, there are also horizontal lines of communication connecting the different groups. This is to illustrate that all of the groups interact with each other laterally as well as reporting to the producer. In fact, they may interact more with their colleagues on their feature team than with others in their discipline. This does not mean that the production has no hierarchy; it is the job of the producer and the leads from each group to make decisions about the big-picture vision for the project and the day-to-day tasks each group should be working on.

There is also one communication line on the diagram between the producer's lines for the developer and the publisher. This line is important because it signifies that one person from each team is responsible for communication between these two groups. Veteran developers know that it is important to have a single person on the publisher side who is empowered to approve their work and authorize payments. It would be problematic if team members from each side were making decisions without having the producers involved to maintain consistency.

The same goes for communication within the development team. As I mentioned, if you need to work with the database programmer or make changes to part of the interface, you might need to go to the technical director or the art director to make your request, not to the person directly responsible for that change. If you are working in Agile feature teams, this kind of communication will take place more naturally; however, there is still the issue of coordinating communication between all of the feature teams, which requires a well-organized production.

Conducting Meetings

Meetings are the best way of getting your team members to communicate. But conducting effective meetings is not as simple as gathering your coworkers together in a conference room and beginning a conversation. You need to structure the meeting so that it produces the desired results.

If you are calling the meeting, you will need to set the agenda. The best meetings are ones for which there is a definite goal, everyone knows the goal ahead of time so that they can come prepared, and by the resolution of the meeting the goal has been accomplished. If you do not have a clear agenda in mind, you are likely to waste everyone's time and accomplish very little in your meeting.

If you are asked to participate in a meeting, you will need to come prepared. Find out the agenda and goal and make sure you have all the material you will need to contribute. This might mean doing some research for a brainstorming meeting or evaluating your workload for a status meeting. If you do not come prepared to a meeting, you will also be wasting other team members' time and have very little to contribute.

At the meeting, the person who called it will most likely function as the discussion leader. This person might designate other individuals to run certain parts of the meeting, but it is still up to the discussion leader to keep the meeting on track and moving toward the goal.

As in the rules for brainstorming, many of the rules of meetings involve personal and social skills. No one should be left out of the conversation intentionally, and those who speak should be able to do so without being criticized. No personal attacks should be permitted. If people make personal remarks, they should be warned, and if it continues, they should be asked to leave the meeting. Make it clear that differences of opinion are helpful in sorting out the problem, and allow people to approach the same topic from multiple angles. See the discussion of inclusive team building on page 418 for more on this topic.

As the meeting draws to a close, you should make sure to review the decisions that have been made and any action items that have been assigned to the team. If the discussion requires a follow-up meeting, determine when it will be and make sure that everyone will have time to prepare for that follow up. And last, if you have called the meeting, you should always send out notes and reminders of the decisions and assignments to the participants and to any key team members who were unable to attend.

Agile Development

Agile development represents state-of-the-art thinking for software development. It is a modular framework that strives to make the development process more adaptive and people-centric. A popular variant used by forward-thinking game developers is called "Scrum." Scrum organizes teams into small cross-functional teams. These teams prioritize their work each day and embrace iteration—especially short-turnaround iterations. Short iteration and review forces strong communication and builds bonds with team members. Scrum development is especially good for game environments because the ability to change fluidly is important for solving hard game design problems. Big game productions organize Scrum teams around game features. This allows a large number of creative people to work effectively on a project without the burdens of too much top-down management. I will discuss Agile methods and Scrum in more detail in Chapter 13, when I talk about the stages and process of development.

UNIONS IN THE GAME INDUSTRY

At the time of this writing, several game unions have been formed to represent team members. Workers at Raven Software, Blizzard Albany, ZeniMax, Tender Claws, and Sega of America had formed unions to address some of the ongoing issues that team members face across the industry.

One of the most important issues is "crunch" and burnout. Crunch happens when games are produced in an environment that lacks checks and balances on the creative process. As I've discussed many times in this book, your process needs to take into account the real resources you have and the be mindful of how much time each of the features and designs you are planning for will actually take. Evaluating your progress, and getting a sense for your team's real working speed is the only way to balance your designs against your real capabilities. Many development teams just keep pushing harder when they get behind. And in environments where people fear to speak up, or fear for their jobs, team members can push themselves until they make themselves ill, until they lose their sense of perspective, and sometimes until they lose their relationships or families. Crunch is a terrible price to pay to create something you love and anyone who dreams of being a game developer should take these issues seriously. Unions hope

to help employees negotiate for better working situations that can combat crunch.

Additionally, unions can negotiate for fair wages, better benefits, and protection against discrimination and harassment. The game industry, unfortunately, has a history of sexism, racism, and a lack of equity for lower levels of workers. As the industry grows and matures, it is important for these issues to be dealt with. As other entertainment forms, like film, television, radio, and theater, have found, unions can provide protection and collective bargaining for the individuals doing a great deal of the work in creative industries. It is likely, by the time you are reading this, that more unions will have formed, spanning multiple disciplines and departments.

CONCLUSION

Understanding your role in a team and having the interpersonal skills to work within a team structure are as important as any of the design skills I have discussed to this point. Game development is a collaborative art, and game teams, large or small, are involved in complex and innovative work that requires every bit of social skill you can muster. I urge you to take the time to practice your team-building abilities before you are thrown into the maelstrom of production.

Take the time to understand the roles of the other team members and to learn to communicate with them. Make sure they know who you are and what your role is on the production. Participate at the highest level possible in team discussions. Always come prepared, and focus your input toward achieving the goals of

the meeting. Whether you are starting at the bottom or you are leading the team, be the best team member you possibly can, and your contribution will act as an inspiration to others.

Just as there is no one way to design a game, there is no one way to go about structuring and building the best team. The concepts I have introduced here are just a starting point. You will need to find the right way to set up your specific project and the individuals who work on it. Feel free to experiment; take the rules I have given you as a starting point and expand from there. But remember, your objective is to create an environment where all individuals are able to contribute to the very best of their abilities. Succeed at this, and your game will reflect excellence in every aspect of its development.

DESIGNER PERSPECTIVE: NAHIL SHARKASI

Executive Producer, Cliffhanger Games, Electronic Arts

Nahil Sharkasi is the Executive Producer at Cliffhanger Games working on an original Black Panther game in collaboration with Marvel Games. Her released games and other products include Kinect Fun Labs (2011), Kinect Star Wars (2012), Halo 5: Guardians (2015), Halo 5: Forge (2016), the Windows Mixed Reality Home Experience (2018), the Microsoft Mesh App (2021) as well as HoloLens and HoloLens 2.

How did you become a game designer?

I never imagined that I would end up in this career path, but now I can't imagine doing anything else. I got hooked in graduate school at the University of Southern California volunteering in the Game Innovation Lab for a research project for the Corporation for Public Broadcasting, who were looking to create a game that can be used to teach American constitutional history to high school students. As a former journalist and documentary filmmaker, I was excited by the opportunity to use new tools and technologies to tell this story. We weren't simply communicating a narrative to an audience, but creating a tool set and a space for the audience to discover the story themselves through their experience. I found this incredibly powerful and absolutely fell in love with the collaborative and creative process of making games.

On games that have inspired her:

I love games that blur the lines between the real and the virtual. Sharkrunners is a game where players take on the role of researchers and chart courses for their boats in the ocean hoping to encounter a shark. The boats on the screen are virtual but the sharks are driven by real live sharks in the ocean with GPS units attached to their fins. The thrill of catching a shark in this game knowing that there really is a shark out in the ocean that crossed paths with your boat is incredible. With augmented and virtual reality, I'm inspired by the possibilities for adding game elements to the physical world in order to create new meaning, better understanding or magical experiences.

On exciting developments in the industry:

I love the new emphasis and understanding of inclusive representation in games and in the industry. I remember feeling like one of the only women in the whole building. Not only do I not feel that way anymore, but there is so much more space to be different and bring your whole self into game teams than ever before. If I'm playing a game with an avatar system I can expect to be able to represent myself without compromising who I am or how I want to show up. I love that this is the new standard, and it's hard to believe that it wasn't that long ago that we were forced to choose between limited selections of skin tone, body shape, or "girl hair." There's so much work still to do, but I'm optimistic about the progress I've seen.

I'm also excited about virtual and augmented reality opening up so much opportunity for innovation. I've always loved exploration mechanics, and these experiences are even more compelling with AR and VR technology. I'm really excited about the transformative potential of being immersed in another world that you can achieve in VR. The challenge is the ability to interact with virtual content more like you would in the real world with devices that can track your movement and gestures. We're on the verge of a new era in computing which will certainly have an impact on games, as well as all kinds of entertainment and work we do in the digital world.

On design process:

The creative process needs fuel. It's important to be a ravenous consumer of all kinds of media, and to explore genres and art forms outside of your taste preference. When my team is brainstorming, I encourage them to take creative field trips, to get out into the world and experience new things, develop your sensitivity to different kinds of emotional experiences so that you can recreate these feelings for your players. When it comes to brainstorming, I like to try different approaches as a kind of interval training for your brain. You have to shock your brain with different stimuli, feed it with lots of good art, and good ideas will happen. Once we have a good idea we want to pursue, we like to work "lo-fi to high-fi," meaning implement the idea in the quickest and cheapest way possible to try it out. Get feedback, and iterate from there. If the feedback is good, take it up a level in fidelity, maybe add some art or tune your mechanics for a better experience. The important thing is not to be precious; a great idea can be disastrous once you try it out in a prototype, and a-not-so exciting idea might be really fun once you try it.

On prototyping:

Prototyping is an essential part of development, especially when working with new technologies, like Kinect or Hololens. As a producer, I am constantly trying to balance the ambiguities that come with working in incubation with the need to produce and deliver real experiences to consumers. My teams have used a rapid prototyping approach where we give ourselves a set amount of time to hit on a magical experience. We start with our most promising ideas and work down a prioritized list. Each idea should only take a day or two to prototype (work as quickly and as cheaply as possible). If you hit magic, keep going: take it to the next level of fidelity. If you don't hit magic, move to the next idea on the list.

On a difficult design problem:

On Kinect Star Wars, we encountered a challenge awarding Xbox Achievements in multiplayer scenarios. It was really important for that game to encourage families and groups of friends to easily be able to jump in and share an experience together. However, the technical certification guidelines required that we correctly identify the player and that they be signed in to the game to receive the achievement. We definitely didn't want to interrupt gameplay for a long sign-in process that would have been counter to the goals of the project. We instead negotiated with the certification team and rewrote some of the achievements to allow us to proceed with awarding achievements to all signed-in players without interrupting game play. The lesson here was to recognize that the rules were written before Kinect, and hadn't been tested for all the scenarios this technology unlocked. It's important to question whether rules apply, and give yourself permission to change the rules to achieve the goals you want.

What are you most proud of in your career?

In 2016, my team at 343 Industries brought Halo to Windows 10 with Halo 5: Forge. This game gave Halo's Forge Mode as well as multiplayer custom games to fans for free, and it was my first time leading a project this big. Halo fans are passionate; the pressure was on to make sure the action and combat of Halo felt as good on PC with mouse and keyboard as it does on Xbox with a controller. We worked really hard with the studio and fans through so many iterations to make sure we got it right. When we first debuted the game at an exclusive event for fans at 343 Industries, I was blown away by the gratitude we got from the community, and even more impressed by the creativity of the maps they created in Forge. This was a proud moment for the whole team because we had created something that the fans loved and got new fans engaged in trying Halo out for the first time. As the production lead, I'm also really proud of the team culture and partnerships we formed. When you invest in strong relationships across the team, the tough times become easier and the gift you have after you ship is a group of people you would want to work with again.

Advice to designers:

Make. There are so many platforms and options open to you, there's no excuse for keeping your ideas in your brain and to yourself. Share your ideas and your perspective and be confident that your voice matters. Find a team, learn your tools, and share your ideas with the world. Make something you love and odds are that other people will love it too.

DESIGNER PERSPECTIVE: ELIZABETH LAPENSÉE

Narrative Director, Twin Suns Corp.

Elizabeth LaPensée, Ph.D. is an award-winning designer writer, and artist of games who was named a Guggenheim Fellow in 2018 and inducted into the Global Women in Games Hall of Fame in 2020. She is Irish, Anishinaabe, and Métis and her Indigenous heritage is often reflected in her works, which include Honour Water (2016), Thunderbird Strike (2017), and When Rivers Were Trails (2019), an adventure game about land allotment in the 1890s which won the Adaptation Award at IndieCade in 2019.

How did you become a game designer?

I was drawn to delving into pixels and mechanics. I started off messing around with 8-bit mods as a way to deconstruct and understand game design. Before then, my first gig was working for America Online as a community manager of a collaborative writing community, i.e. text role-players who wrote in paragraphs with punctuation. Very fancy. In that role, I learned to recognize being a designer as being a *facilitator*. I designed the spaces we played in by gathering feedback from our community. Where there weren't enough characters to fill out a story, I jumped in with support characters, often writing for multiple characters at a time in an environment where most wrote for one character. My aim was to support players' experiences and their ability to express themselves. Today, I apply this lesson by being responsive to players and making design decisions that in turn give players opportunities to make their *own* decisions.

On games that have inspired her:

Ultima Online still hits the nostalgia sweet spot for me, because the design supported player self-expression in a server-based MMORPG (Massively Multiplayer Online Role-Playing Game). There was just something so tangible about being able to remove items from your backpack and create with whatever you had, such as coins for artwork and logs for structures. Even though anything placed in the environment was temporary and disappeared when the server reset, players were driven by creating in the moment (and sharing screenshots). As I think through design possibilities now, player choice is always a key factor for me. Even in games without that capacity for expressing creativity, there are ways that providing choice can enable a player to co-create their gameplay.

Beyond that, I'm still unraveling what has inspired me. For example, I recently came across Star Wars: The Empire Strikes Back (1982 video game) displayed at an event. Although I wouldn't have been able to recall it by name, the moment I saw the gameplay, memories of playing flooded back to me. Similarities in design choices I've made before hit me. In Thunderbird Strike, you play as a thunderbird and, just like this '80s throwback, you're able to fly in all directions in a left-to-right side-scroller. Ha! I'm sure there are many more games that I played during my childhood that I've been influenced by. I draw from some experiences knowingly, while others are embedded. It's an adventure finding out the answers!

On exciting developments in the industry:

I'm excited for current and forthcoming games from the next generations of game developers who have grown up with so much more access to tools, communities, and resources. My mind is still blown by the game engines out there, the open-source software, the wide range of tutorials, the variety of funding sources, the robustness of festivals and venues to share work, and the growth of communities. I'm especially encouraged by seeing indie games like Umurangi Generation and Button City make it to console distribution. Accessibility encourages diversity, and through that, the game industry will be all the better.

On design process:

Ideas come from connecting closely with what a game is focused on, ongoing discussions with collaborators, and then letting possibilities form on their own. Those ideas are then always prototyped in one way or another. I often prototype in paper first, surrounded by anything that reflects a game's tone, even if it's not directly used within a game. I consider these inspiration nodes; they could include anything from raw materials to photos to instruments and more. They may not even be within the paper prototype, but they certainly influence where it goes. Once I have a solid paper prototype, I may choose to share that or, more typically, take those lessons and apply them to a digital prototype. From there, the development process shifts into iteration based on input from players and, in some cases, collaborators as well.

   If I'm working directly with hands-on collaborators, I knock things together just enough to provide the framework for them to contribute content, such as art or writing, depending. If it's not me doing that myself, then it's a small team who adapt to this approach. It can mean that portions of the game are treated more as templates to understand the parameters and then be able to share those with collaborators. For example, writers for When Rivers Were Trails were provided guidelines, shown examples of interactive text that were made for the game, and then given space to break those parameters as needed to express themselves. In this process, a game forms based on who is involved and the designer purely upholds those voices.

On prototyping:

Prototypes are my lifeline! The prototyping process varies according to what the goal is: scope, mechanics, or tone. I often experiment with paper prototypes. Although they don't answer all questions at once when I'm working on what will ultimately be a digital game, they do help me focus and make design decisions to bring over and balance with the various components of a game.

   With a scope prototype, I'm looking for the answer to the question: Is there anything here at all? For Thunderbird Strike, this meant drawing and then copying multiple silhouettes of possible targets and environment assets on printer paper. I then taped up levels all along the living room wall and moved around paper as needed to get a sense of the structure and focus of the gameplay. This was an important step that could have also been done in a game engine with shapes or even scans of what I had drawn, but for me at this stage, I was trying to literally feel out the game. Did it even feel like something? And oh yes, it did.

   With a mechanics prototype, I'll hone in on one specific question and do my best to just focus on that. In When Rivers Were Trails, I needed to know if players could navigate their journey via a map interface and how that might inform the design of levels. This paper prototype took the form of printing out maps and setting them up on the floor. I then drew paths by hand and measured the dimensions of a 1920 x 1080 screen to determine how many levels there would need to be in relation to the land of Indigenous communities highlighted in the game and how the player might travel through them.

For a tone prototype, my hope is to understand how a game feels and what work needs to happen. Honour Water was a unique experience, because I had been asked to make the game by White Earth elder Mary Renville and worked with contributors who I had existing connections with. In order to better understand and convey Honour Water, I gathered together materials such as copper, photos of water, and birch bark, and my knowledge of Anishinaabe songs that weren't going to be in the game, but which echoed the tone. I started with sketches with the intention of showing the nuts and bolts of how the game function, but instead ended up with an art print that represented the concept. However, through this art print, I was able to convey the purpose of the game, which was informed by Mary Renville. This sparked discussions with Bois Forte Band elder Sharon Day, Fond du Lac musician Lyz Jaakola, and the Oshkii Giizhik Singers— all Anishinaabe women who sing together. Before game design could move forward, it was essential to establish protocol for how songs would be determined and depicted in a mobile game. As a result, in Honour Water, players can listen to or sing Anishinaabe water songs which were specifically made to be shared with all people and were therefore approved to be adapted into gameplay. Although a tone prototype doesn't dig into mechanics, it can help with communicating concepts and moving forward to the next phase of development.

Clockwise from top left: "The Women, They Hold the Ground," Concept Art by Elizabeth LaPensée, Honour Water, 2015; When Rivers Were Trails, Art by Weshoyot Alvitre, Indian Land Tenure Foundation, 2019; Thunderbird Strike, Art by Elizabeth LaPensée, 2017

On a difficult design problem:

Working with several writers creating content simultaneously that needs to fit together has been a fun challenge. For When Rivers Were Trails, one of the aims was the self-determination of Indigenous collaborators. Since the game traverses from Minnesota to California, that meant involving around 30 writers. And, since we were on a deadline to meet the goals of the Indian Land Tenure Foundation, they needed to work on their contributions at the same time, very often without knowing what other writers were up to. This meant that the player journey and how they moved from level to level via the map interface was designed in relation to what writers contributed, ranging from locations on the map to possible gains and losses. The team found that where the player can travel and what options they have to contribute to or threaten their survival were getting imbalanced by this approach. For me, telling writers what to do was off the table, so I suggested another approach. Instead, we integrated new random interactions where the player comes across opportunities to gather foods and medicines. Decisions like this contribute to how When Rivers Were Trails manages to have variety with different types of interactions, yet it feels cohesive.

What are you most proud of in your career?

Throughout my career, I've woven back and forth between academia and industry. Often, I've done both at once. As a freelancer, I balanced multiple contracts simultaneously just to make it by. As an academic, I could afford to choose what I wanted to work on. Despite the stability academia provides and the level of job security that I earned when I was approved for tenure, I made the leap back to the game industry full-time. It's the biggest risk I've ever taken in my career and one that I'm proud of myself for. Wherever it leads, I'm glad I went for the opportunity. I'm gaining invaluable experience working with a standout team of developers. I hope to continue sharing lessons from my work with whoever is interested and who could gain something from it. In the meantime, I will continue learning.

Advice to designers:

Create and collaborate. The sooner you apply yourself—no matter if it's through a customizable level, a mod, a paper prototype, or any other form—the more opportunities you'll have to gain skills and approaches for working with a team. Understanding how to listen to your team and your players is just as important as communicating your design ideas. Game design is an inspiring space to be in, with all sorts of opportunities for collaboration and self-expression as game development continues to expand with a myriad of possibilities.

DESIGNER PERSPECTIVE: JENOVA CHEN

Cofounder and Creative Director, thatgamecompany

Jenova Chen is a game designer and entrepreneur who has designed several critically acclaimed experimental games including Journey (2012), Flower (2009), flOw (2007) and Sky: Children of the Light (2019), winner of the iPhone Game of the Year and an Apple Design Award. Journey was honored with multiple game of the year awards in 2013 as well as a Peabody Legacy Award. Jenova's other credits include the student research game Cloud (2006) and the online version of flOw (2006).

On getting into the game industry:

When I was still a sophomore in college, my dad happened to know people from Ubisoft Shanghai. Because of him, I was hired as the only intern for the summer. For the most part, however, it just gave me a taste of what a video game company is like. My first opportunity to enter the game industry happened when I graduated from undergrad in China. Because of the student games we made during college, my team got lots of publicity. In a country without any systematic video game education, it was very easy for us to get special attention from the game industry. Nearly the entire team got offers from Shanda Network, biggest Chinese online game publisher and developer at the time. However, during the interview, I got a sense that the games I wanted to make and play would not be born in Shanda or even China for a long time. The only shortcut I knew at that time was to go abroad and pursue more education.

So in August 2003, I started my graduate studies focusing on interactive media in the School of Cinematic Arts at the University of Southern California. I was surprised that video game education was also new to America. The program I was in was merely one year old at that time. Though my language skills were pretty weak, my game-making experiences from undergrad got me my first job as a teaching assistant in video game modeling and animation. I then worked on various video game-related jobs across campus. In 2004, Electronic Arts made a major endowment to our school, and I was informed that there were student internships available, which eventually became my first step into the commercial video game industry. Meanwhile, I worked on multiple popular student video game projects such as Dyadin, Cloud, and flOw, which helped me to step further into this field.

On learning on the job:

Designing video games is exciting and challenging. But making video games is also exhausting. It is a constant process of compromising and self-correcting. One interesting thing that occurs is when you read reviews about your own games. Knowing that your work has inspired, encouraged, or moved other people is the most rewarding thing in your life. At the same time, when you find out that others did not understand your game, you might want to laugh and cry at the same time.

On getting a degree in game design:

Though many brilliant designers did not graduate from college, I was lucky to learn about game design from my graduate education at USC. Though game design is still a new field, and its education system is still young, I was able to read and speak about game design in an academic way. This design vocabulary is going to replace "fun" and "cool," allowing you to see deeper into video games. Video games are so new that the theories and rules applied in this field usually come from elsewhere. I learned theories from film, screenwriting, and psychology, and I came up with my own rules out of them. If I hadn't gone to grad school, I probably would have never touched those areas.

On the design process:

I've found that nearly everybody I talk to in the video game industry has good ideas. Not only the people from the industry, but young gamers also have great ideas. However, I often find that people mix up the concept of a good idea with a good game design. In my opinion, everybody has good ideas. However, very few can keep refining their ideas for years and eventually realize it as something practical.

My design process is very much about refining a simple idea that has not been done before. For example, Cloud was based on the idea, "Can we make a game about the beautiful clouds in the sky?" After we digested the idea for a while, it evolved into, "Can we make a game that evokes the exciting but peaceful feeling when you look at the blue sky and white clouds?" As we started developing the game, more details were needed to guide the direction of the gameplay. We solidified this feeling and bound it with the idea of childhood daydreaming, which helped us to further shape the avatar character, the story, and the world of Cloud.

In terms of how I come up with game ideas, I see video games as entertainment rather than an interactive software product. When you design products, you care a lot about features. This seemed to be a common video game industry trend in the early 2000s. When you come up with ideas for entertainment, you start from a feeling, a sense of emotion. From there, unique game ideas are within inches. Today, more and more video games win critical acclaim not because of their technology but because of their story and emotional impact.

On prototypes:

If you consider video games as an art form such as painting, then prototypes are the sketches of video games. Prototypes help you to shape the final gameplay experience in your mind, to give the designer a holistic view of the feature, and sometimes the entire game. Literally, prototyping is a collection of all your previsualizations: art, sound, and gameplay. Video games are still a young media, and the gameplay aspects are least understood when you are working on something original. Therefore, prototypes tied to gameplay previsualization are the best tool you can have to iterate on your designs.

We make prototypes to solve difficult game design problems, namely games that the team and I haven't seen in the past. We like to spread the net wide and prototype as many of our alternatives as possible before we dive in deep into details without knowing whether it is the best direction. Like painting, after you deal with one prototype for too long, you will become too used to it to tell the hidden problems. When that happens, we won't hesitate to abandon it and start a new one.

On solving a difficult design problem:

I focus on creating new emotional gaming experiences. Nearly all the projects I have designed were difficult because of the lack of similar game designs. Cloud, for example, was focused on the emotion of relaxing. During the design process, I often was distracted by thinking of fun and challenging mechanics from the classic games I have played. I knew those mechanics worked, and they worked well. It would be very easy to assume those mechanics would also make the game I'm making better. However, "challenging" and "relaxing" are contradictory goals. The only way to solve the problem is to constantly remind and question myself: What am I making? What kind of feeling do I want the game to evoke? Will this type of gameplay help to communicate that emotion? Because of that, Cloud ended up becoming a very unique game experience.

On the future:

I hope I can prove what I believe about where video games should be going. I wish to be one of those who will make that change; literally, use the games we create to move and inspire the new generations of video game makers and accelerate the video game's evolution toward a mature entertainment media for everyone.

After the release of Journey:

I travelled to many places and met with many video game students and independent game developers who are passionate to push the boundary of what video games can communicate to the players, how strong a video game can make you feel. However, many of them have trouble finding a studio or publisher that allows them to pursue their visions. I realized that while quite a lot of games have proven that video games can be art to many players and developers, there is still no good financial incentive for investors and publishers to support more development in this field. In the next five years, I would like to see artistic video games created with hearts and souls played by a mass audience, becoming a commercial success that will enable more studios to go towards that direction.

Advice to designers:

There is no so-called "natural born talent." There is a person's passion toward something he loves to do. If he loves what he is doing, he is likely to spend more time and effort on doing it, thinking about it, and dreaming about it. As time and effort accumulate, others who spent less time are likely to call this person "talented."

Like in a video game, you need to have very clear goals to start your own "hero's journey." Like in a video game, you need to be aware of your intermediate goals and the progress and rewards they bring to you. Like in a video game, you need to adjust your challenges to match with your current abilities so that you are in the flow of achieving goals instead of giving up on them because of boredom or anxiety.

A man's true potential comes when his various talents and knowledge are fully utilized to create value for others. A company's true value comes when the entire team uses their talent to create the maximum value for the society.

FURTHER READING

Bennis, Warren G. and Biederman, Patricia Ward. *Organizing Genius: The Secrets of Creative Collaboration*. New York: Perseus Books, 1997.

Brooks, Frederick P. *The Mythical Man-Month: Essays on Software Engineering*. Boston: Addison-Wesley, 1995.

Catmull, Edwin. *Creativity, Inc.: Overcoming the Unseen Forces That Stand in the Way of True Inspiration*. New York: Random House, 2014.

DeMarco, Tom and Lister, Timothy. *Peopleware: Productive Projects and Teams*. New York: Dorset House Publishing, 1999.

Schwaber, Ken and Beedle, Mike. *Agile Software Development with Scrum*. Upper Saddle River: Prentice Hall, 2002.

END NOTE

1. Theodore, Steve. "Artist's View: And a Partridge in a Poly Tree." *Game Developer*. November 2003.

Chapter 13

Stages and Methods of Development

Producing digital games is a complex and expensive process. A developer's goal is to produce the highest quality game within the limits of its resources and budget. The publisher's goal is to produce the best-selling game while limiting its risk by keeping costs low. There is a common interest in producing a successful product between these two parties, and there is also a conflict of interest in how much money and time that product should require.

In order to communicate expectations between publishers and developers, the industry has evolved standard stages of development that can be used to define contracts and milestones for a game project. Typically, a developer is paid a specified amount for each milestone it reaches as agreed upon in the contract. Even if you do not plan to be a game producer, as a game designer, you will need to work with a producer and understand these stages of development clearly.

Additionally, best practices for producing games are evolving to recognize the need for flexibility and iteration as part of the game development process. Most developers now use a mix of Agile development methods, including "Scrum" or variations on Scrum, and traditional software production methods to produce their games. The core difference between Agile development methods and more traditional software methods is a focus on creating working software versus documentation and managing the team so that it can respond to discoveries in the process, rather than following a predetermined plan.

In this chapter, I will walk through each of the high-level stages of development and talk about the goals of each of these stages. I will also discuss the basics of Agile methodology and Scrum and how these can help you manage your development process throughout these stages.

DOI: 10.1201/9781003460268-16

STAGES DEFINED

Figure 13.1 is a graphical representation of the stages of development. Notice that the five stages are drawn in a "V" shape. This is to represent that in the beginning of a project, the creative possibilities are broad, open, and changeable. Early on, changes can be made with little financial consequence. If you want to alter your idea from an ant simulator to a submarine combat game, for example, the ideation phase is the time to do it. Any later than that and you are taking a major risk with your project plan. As the process moves along, ideas must become more focused, and smaller and smaller changes can be made to the design without disrupting the production.

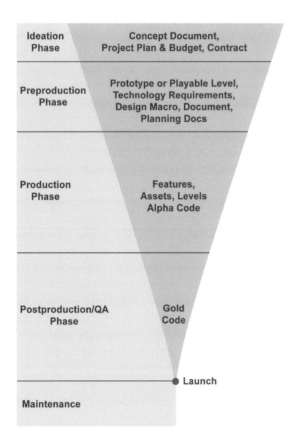

Ideation Phase	Concept Document, Project Plan & Budget, Contract
Preproduction Phase	Prototype or Playable Level, Technology Requirements, Design Macro, Document, Planning Docs
Production Phase	Features, Assets, Levels Alpha Code
Postproduction/QA Phase	Gold Code
	● Launch
Maintenance	

13.1 Stages of development

By the time you reach the middle of a production, it is virtually impossible to alter the broad vision of a game, but you can still improve and refine features or concepts within it. For example, during the production stage, you might find yourself discussing the way in which the dive controls would work on your submarine game. This will change your gameplay implementation but probably won't require significant restructuring of the application or starting over in terms of the existing art and animation. During later stages of production, it becomes increasingly difficult and more expensive to make major modifications to the game design.

As you approach the postproduction/quality assurance stage, only the completion of details is an open area of discussion. Any major or even moderate changes are usually out of the question. At this point, you might discuss things like whether the texture for a German U-577 submarine is displaying correctly, but you would never suggest adding another model of a new submarine.

Within these stages, there is a large degree of flexibility for teams to define and manage their implementation process. This is where Agile methodology comes in. Rather than a traditional software process—in which a detailed design would be created up front and then executed directly—the Agile process focuses on creating working software from the outset, evaluating and iterating on that software in short daily group meetings, called Scrum meetings, to determine next steps and goals. As you can see, this kind of flexible, iterative process fits very well with the kind of early and regular playtesting I've been recommending for your game. It doesn't mean that you won't be making decisions during each stage, and that those decisions won't be getting smaller and smaller as the process continues, it simply means that your team will be working closely together in cross-disciplinary groups, executing and iterating on ideas from the beginning, and that playtesting will be a big part of how you evaluate the progress of your production.

Naturally, the time frame of each of these stages will be different depending on the platform and scope of the game, as well as for teams with different levels of experience. If you are an independent developer, funding your own game, you may not even have a contract phase.

From Concept to Contract

Selling a game is one of the hardest tasks for a developer. Unless you are an experienced developer with at least one hit under your belt, getting a publisher to even consider funding your idea can be a challenge. There are options these days for indie developers, however, which include self-publishing online, in the various mobile app stores, or even as an indie console developer for Xbox, PlayStation, or Nintendo, all of which have some support for small developers. You may find it difficult to market your game on these platforms as an indie, but you can, at the very least, make it available. If you do work directly with a publisher, your goal at this stage is to get them to commit to funding at least the first milestone.

I will talk about how you can get in the door with a publisher in Chapter 16, but for now, let's assume that you're going the route of working with a publisher, have found the right contacts, and are getting ready to make your pitch. In this case, the publisher will base its decision on three things: the team, the project plan (which includes a schedule and budget), and the idea.

The Team

Above all, a publisher wants to see an experienced development team. This is because game production is expensive, complex, and risky, and the publisher can reduce its risk considerably by going with a proven group of individuals.

When listening to a game pitch, the publisher is going to weigh its merits against the strength of the team. In the publisher's mind, ideas are

important, but it is implementation that is critical. Can you deliver a groundbreaking game on budget and on time? The best gauge of this is a proven track record, and publishers tend to fund the teams who have already published games. Sometimes, however, a first-time developer gets lucky, and the kind of ideas coming from first-time and indie developers these days have shown that the industry needs these creative voices. To learn about thatgamecompany's experience in developing its first title for the PlayStation as a young development team, see Kellee Santiago's sidebar on page 453.

What makes up a winning team? First, it is important that the group has worked together in the past. As I discussed in the last chapter, teamwork is critical. If you have talent from all across the industry, but they have never worked together, the risk is higher than a less talented team that has demonstrated they can deliver a product. The publisher will look closely at your team's history and try to predict how well you can execute. Are there clear leaders in each area of production? Who performs what functions within the company? What obstacles have you overcome and how have you dealt with them? Is there a good history with previous publishers?

Second, the publisher will want to know if your team can deliver the type of product that you are proposing. If your team is known for producing simulation games, but what you are proposing is a first-person shooter, there is obviously more risk involved. The publisher will wonder if your group can really deliver a compelling game in a different genre. Do you have a handle on the technology, which is quite different from that of a simulation? What about the gameplay elements? A good first-person shooter and a good simulation game are two entirely different play patterns. Because of this, publishers often pigeonhole developers, expecting them to produce the same type of games that they are known for.

Lastly, the publisher will want to know if you can deliver on the platform of choice. This varies, depending on the publisher's internal objectives. Some publishers only focus on console games, while others cover PC and mobile games as well. If it is a console game, then a developer who has produced hundreds of PC games might be deemed more of a risk than another developer who has produced one hit console game—the point being that platform matters. Publishers want a team that is experienced in exactly what has to be delivered. This is because both the schedules and budgets are so tight that there is little room for error.

If your team meets all those qualifications, then at least you are in the running. I am not saying this to discourage you. What I want is for you to focus your efforts on the areas that maximize your chances of success. The bottom line is that if you are starting out, you will likely have to work your way up by joining a established developer or publisher and developing a track record of success before you can take on projects of your own.

The Project Plan

Next in importance is the project plan, which includes a budget and schedule. The project plan shows the publisher that you have thought through the needs of the production and understand what it will take to implement it. The project plan should articulate the goals and priorities of the project, a schedule of how long it will take your team to complete these goals, and a budget for the people and resources that will be needed.

You might be thinking: How can I think through every element of the production if I don't know what they will be? A flexible Agile process seems somewhat incompatible with a detailed project plan, and in truth, it is difficult to schedule such a complex process accurately. But you can estimate how long it will take you to develop the core features for each component of the game. And you know that there will need to be some time in your schedule for iterating and improving on those features. So, you can create

a schedule that includes time for both implementation and iteration. As you work, the details of your plan will change, but if you've estimated fairly well, you will be able to meet the major milestones in your contract.

Even if you aren't working with a contract from a publisher, a project plan is arguably the most important document in the production because it sets expectations on all sides. As an indie developer, you may be managing very few resources and asking people to contribute their time for free or in exchange for future compensation. When this is the case, you need to be extremely sensitive to the demands you put on your team. Ballooning your schedule without warning can cause bad feelings, crunch, and eventually team attrition. If you are working with a publisher, the project plan is typically an addendum to the signed contract. This means that after the publisher approves it, you are legally obligated to adhere to it. My advice is to take your time thinking through the project plan, evaluate it with each group lead, and make sure that everyone is on board to execute the plan.

The Idea

In many ways, the idea is the least important thing to the publisher. This is not to say that publishers are not interested in great ideas. But the criteria by which a publisher judges an idea are very different than that of a developer. Throughout this book, I have taken the perspective of a designer and developer. I have encouraged you to seek the essence of great gameplay and to pursue it, no matter the genre or precedent. This is the way to develop great game ideas, but, unfortunately, it is not necessarily the way to sell great game ideas. And publishers want to find and fund games that they can sell.

Publishers rely on market data to determine what types of games the audience wants buy. Because of this, if your game does not fit into a top-selling genre, a publisher will be hesitant to fund it. While publishers do like to see innovation, they like to see it implemented on top of a proven genre of game. For example, Deus Ex was a truly innovative game. But its gameplay has a solid basis in two proven genres: the first-person shooter and the role-playing game. While Deus Ex actually has more innovation than most publishers would feel comfortable supporting, it also had an amazing team behind it, including the game designer and project director, Warren Spector, whose years of experience in the industry balanced the risk involved in such an innovative project (see Warren's Designer Perspective on page 29).

When you present your idea to the publisher, it is called a "pitch." Pitching is an art, and I will go into more detail on this art in Chapter 16 on page 529. Briefly, your pitch materials need to communicate the strength of all three things I have talked about: the team, the plan, and the idea.

It might take a long time to get there, but at the end of the ideation stage, a developer who is planning to work with a publisher should have a signed agreement. This agreement will spell out the terms of the association, including rights, deliverables, and the payment milestones. The first milestone is signing the contract and approving the project plan. Subsequent milestones occur during each stage of development, as described next. If you are not planning on working with a publisher, you should still have established a strong project plan that can help you keep on track with your independent project.

Preproduction

During preproduction, you'll want to have a small team working on the project to verify the feasibility of the idea. This team will typically work to create one playable level or environment of the game, focusing on proving out differentiating features and risky technology. As Steve Ackrich, head of production at Activision, explains, this is the most critical period in development. If a game looks like a dog after six months of preproduction, he will kill it.

The team at this point will be small because a small team is inexpensive. Until the publisher is certain that the game concept and technology are going to work, they won't fund a full team. The job of the small team is to further refine the idea, and to develop a working proof of concept for the design, technology, and implementation of the game. For a great breakdown of preproduction methods, see the sidebar by Glenn Entis of Electronic Arts on page 188.

If a software prototype was not created in the ideation phase now is the time to make it and playtest it. This is also when you will start working with the Agile development methodology, which I will describe in more detail on page 456. As part of the milestones for this stage, the team will explore visual design ideas, develop story ideas (if appropriate), and build gameplay prototypes. These design ideas can all be captured in collaborative design documents, which should be considered living documents, rather than specifications for implementation. In Chapter 14, I will discuss some ways in which design documents have evolved recently to respond to more Agile environments.

In addition to refining the game design, preproduction is the time to build prototypes of the risky technology elements and prove the feasibility of your approach. This helps to reduce the potential risk for both developer and publisher. It would be foolhardy to begin a technically ambitious project without a clear sense of the viability of the ideas or the time to complete implementation. At this point, the technology does not need to be 100% complete, but the publisher needs to see that the game is technically achievable before funding the next stage of development.

At the end of preproduction, the publisher will evaluate the prototype or completed level, the progress on the technology, the visual designs and storyboards, and the updated project plan to make a decision to finance the production or kill the project. Smart publishers will not hesitate to kill projects that they think are too risky or do not seem marketable. At this point, their overall investment is fairly low, and the loss is negligible compared to the cost of releasing a product that does not sell.

If the publisher does kill the project at this point, it will pay the developer the milestone payment for the preproduction and cancel the rest of the development. Then, depending on the rights negotiated in the contract, the developer can either go to another publisher with their work or start over on a new idea. Problems can crop up if the developer has spent more money than planned during the ideation and preproduction stage while counting on the next milestone payment to make up the difference. More than one developer has gone out of business at this stage.

Production

Production is the longest and most expensive stage of development. The goal in this stage is to execute on the functional vision established during preproduction. Because you are now expanding the scope of the implementation, there will be more resources working on all of the various features. In the process of iterating and improving each of these features, changes will inevitably be necessary that may affect the entire production. In many cases, sweeping creative changes to the concept will not be possible if you want to meet deadlines and stay within budget; however, you want to remain open to the discovery that Agile methods make possible. So, while the scope of changes that can be made to the concept begins to be constrained, the Agile method of implementation continues.

During this stage, the programmers write the code that makes the game function. The artists build all the art files and animation. The sound designers create sound effects and music. Writers write dialogue and other in-game text. QA engineers familiarize themselves with all aspects of the project and do some light testing of early builds. Keeping all of these groups in sync and working together closely is often a challenge. In Agile productions, smaller interdisciplinary teams of programmers, artists and designers are created around specific feature sets, in effect making that part of the game a project within a project. The producers will work with all of these groups to make sure communication remains ongoing, that the vision remains consistent, and that the schedule and resources are within scope.

There are many tools available for managing the production process, including Trello, Asana, Jira, and ClickUp. Additionally, your team may benefit from using communications apps such as Slack, Basecamp, Google Hangouts, or Skype. Most of these have varying levels of cost and service, including free levels for very small teams.

As the production gains momentum, levels and environments are fleshed out, art and sound files are integrated into the working builds of the code, and the game begins to take shape. One recommendation that Steve Ackrich, head of production at Activision-Blizzard, makes to his teams is to build the first levels last. This is because the team will have worked out kinks in their production process and tools and will know the limitations of the game system, and because of this, the levels built last will likely be the best-designed ones in the game. You want users to have an amazing experience with the first levels because that is what will get them hooked on the game.

The goal of the production stage is to get to "alpha". This means that all features are complete and no more features will be added.

On my teams, it also means that we are "experience complete." By this I mean that the full experience of the game can be played through, even if there are missing assets throughout. I emphasize experience complete versus feature complete because a game is not just a set of features—it is an experience. And by alpha, you should be able to play that experience. Sometimes the team has to cut ambitious features to meet the alpha milestone and stay on schedule. For example, let's say the original concept called for a feature that allows users to import names from their e-mail

From Classroom to Console: Producing flOw for the PlayStation 3

by Kellee Santiago, video game producer, designer, and investor

Kellee Santiago co-founded thatgamecompany in 2006 with Jenova Chen and developed flOw, Flower and Journey. She has since championed innovative and inclusive game development through her work at OUYA, Google Play, Google Daydream, and Niantic.

What was it like to ship our first commercial title? It was totally insane. We were a small group of recent grads and friends from game festivals, and we had all the makings of great new developers: We were naive, optimistic, naive, energetic, and naive. None of us had ever shipped a commercial title before and we were ready to change the world...

Jenova Chen and I founded thatgamecompany in May of 2006, just as we were graduating from the USC School of Cinematic Arts. We saw an opportunity in digital distribution to make the kinds of games we loved and earn a living doing it. Because of the surge in digital distribution, big publishers were willing to take creative chances on small games and even smaller teams because distributing games through the digital channel greatly reduced financial risk.

We knew we wanted to complete our first game relatively quickly—definitely under a year. There was a lot to learn about developing a commercial title with a publisher, from start through shipping, so we needed the project to be simple enough to allow for our inevitable mistakes. Therefore, developing Jenova's thesis project, *flOw*, for the not-yet-announced PlayStation Network, emerged as a good choice for our first game. We felt that a lot of the heavy lifting on the design had been done while creating the Flash version of game, and most of the difficult challenges had already been tackled. Also, the game itself is about simplicity—a perfect match!

We pitched a PS3 version of flOw to Sony. Additions included more creatures to play, each in their own unique world, and it would be in 3D. Nooooooo problem.

We realized a couple of months into development that these additions presented three major challenges:

1. Designing controls for one player character is hard, and we were about to tackle five.
2. Developing a game on a platform that is also in development (next-gen or not) is *always* difficult.
3. Changing the game from a completely 2D game into a game that plays in 2D but lives in a 3D environment actually creates a significant change in design.

In short, we realized we were in just a bit over our heads. These challenges culminated only two months after we had begun development when we decided to submit a demo of the game to the Tokyo Game Show. It was during that time that we realized a huge difference between academic and professional development: a deadline. You make it, or you die. The game had to be completely self-contained, and it could not crash. Oh yeah, *and* it had to stand alongside the other Sony games in development at that time. Yikes! While this was one of the most horrendously stressful periods of production, we learned an important lesson about what it takes to make a game shippable. We learned that on top of the challenges previously listed, there was also going to be this period of optimization and bug fixing that would take a long time and eat into our production schedule quite a bit. And we learned the limits of ourselves as mortals. Passion for your work takes you a long way, but there are definite limits that you have as a human being.

So, what could we do to fix this situation? We simplified. However, because our initial approach to the game was based on what we wanted the game to *feel* like, and what we wanted the player to *feel*, it was possible to simplify the game without losing any of its essence.

In flOw, the player is one of five aquatic organisms, eating, growing, and evolving their way through a surreal abyss. The Flash game was a demonstration of the application of Flow Theory (the theory of how and why humans have fun) into games. Therefore, there is a constant underlying zenlike, relaxing, zone experience. Each creature lives in their own abyss, and each one is meant to evoke a different emotion, all under the umbrella of this relaxing feeling. I think of it as an adventure down a river—the scenery might change and the water might move in different ways or at a different pace, but you are always traveling along the same river.

To address designing five unique player creatures, there was not too much we could do to change the situation we were in, other than just focus on making eating, growing, and evolving through a unique environment as fun as possible. We cut anything that didn't have to do with enhancing these core actions because if your core game isn't fun, you just don't have a game at all.

flOw

Developing the game alongside the development of the PS3 was an extremely difficult situation to be in. We didn't know much about programming for the PS3, and while we wanted to tap into the technology, we were so unfamiliar with the platform that we didn't have much time to delve into it. From the start of the project, we should have designed a game that didn't need the features of the PS3, so we wouldn't have been dependent as much on the platform.

The changes that occurred when we moved the player character from 2D to 3D were very unexpected, although looking back, they probably shouldn't have been. The possibilities for movement and camera angles of course increase greatly, so you can create these completely different experiences just by changing a couple of variables. However, we knew we had to remain true to the simplicity and the feeling of flowing through the game from the Flash version, so this acted as our guide through the design. If it wasn't simple, it wasn't flOw. Although a word of warning: a simple, elegant design solution is often the most complicated to implement.

I am still, to this day (no matter when you are reading this!), glad we chose flOw as our first title. While we had more design challenges than we initially suspected, we were right that developing the Flash game first helped a lot. The Flash game really helped to solidify the core concept and feeling of the game, which then acted as our guide throughout the development of the PS3 game. It taught me how important it is to know the core of your game from the very beginning. What do you want the player to feel? What is the fun in your game? If you have the answers to the questions, you will be much better equipped to handle all of the difficult design and production challenges of developing a video game.

address book into the game. Then, during gameplay, those names would appear on units as they come into the game. That would be fun, and it is actually a feature in the game Black & White. However, if the team is running out of time and this feature is not complete, the idea might be classified as low priority and cut. Alternatively, the team may have discovered new features during their iterative process that are clearly more important to playtesters. In this case, the team might make them a higher priority than other planned features.

As the team members work on the code, they will continually assemble versions of the project, which are called "builds." In an Agile schedule, these builds are created after each short feature Sprint. Each build is given an incremental number so that any issues or bugs can be referenced as to what build they were found in. When the developer reaches alpha, they send a build to the publisher's QA team. If approved, the publisher pays the developer for reaching the milestone, and the team moves on to the postproduction and quality assurance stage.

Postproduction and Quality Assurance

In the last few months of development, the focus shifts from producing new code and features to making certain that what has already been built functions as expected and that the levels and artwork are complete and polished.

During this stage, the developer takes the alpha build and transforms it into the final product that players will experience. The user experience grows tighter and more complete. Levels are fine tuned. Game designers, programmers, and QA engineers work together to iron out timing issues, bugs, and annoying interface and control problems. As Steve Ackrich points out, 70% of the quality of a game comes during this last 10% of development. He cautions developers to leave enough time in their production schedules to truly refine the game.

It is in this last stage that the developer has a chance to truly see its game for what it is and to make sure it offers the best possible experience for the player. The difference between a game rushed off to market and one that has had the luxury of a good polishing can be enormous. It is the subtle tuning of gameplay and tweaks to timing and controls that can create an unforgettable player experience, and this is the level of quality that makes break-out hits.

As I have mentioned before, QA testing is an art, and it is something that should not be taken for granted. In brief, the QA team creates a test plan, a document that describes all the areas and features of the product, and the various conditions under which each will be tested. The QA engineers then run the tests against the current build and note when the game does not behave according to spec. This is called a "bug."

Bugs are entered into a database with a description of the exact steps to be taken to recreate the problem, the severity of the issue, and the name of the tester who discovered it. There are dozens of bug databases available; some are expensive and some are free. For student or independent developers, I recommend using a free or open-source system such as BugNET (available on GitHub), Mantis or Bugzilla.

To keep track of what has been fixed, by whom, and in what build, bugs are assigned to specific individuals. For example, a bug related to a game's database will be assigned to the database programmer. When the programmer has fixed the bug, she sends it back to the QA team for retesting. When the QA team is satisfied that the bus is fixed, they mark that issue "resolved" in the database.

When the development team gets together to assess the current state of the code and prioritize and resolve bugs, it is called a "triage" meeting. A typical console title will have several thousand bugs in the database. The programmers work through the database systematically, eliminating the highest priority bugs first. Bugs can be found in all areas of the game. There might be bugs that require the attention of the visual designers, the programmers, and even legal staff if there are outstanding questions on things like disclaimers or registration. When all of the features are complete and there are no more "priority 1" bugs in the database, the project is considered to be at beta.

The final goal of this stage is to reach what's called "gold code." This means that all bugs have been resolved. Interestingly, nearly every game ships with some minor bugs in the code. At the very end of the project, the producer resolves remaining minor bugs as "deferred." This means that time has run out and the producer has determined that the remaining bugs are so unobtrusive that they can ship with the game. An example would be something like a slightly wrong font size on an alert message. It might be annoying to the art director, but it does not impact gameplay, so it is left in.

Maintenance and Updates

Today, many games require ongoing updates—whether to live software or via "patches" distributed online. This means the team monitors user feedback when the game is shipped and continues to fix bugs and sometimes add features even though the product has already launched. As games become more and more service oriented, ongoing maintenance and updates becomes a larger part of their development budget. Many online games have ongoing production teams for years after launch, with designers who refresh content and features, programmers who keep the technology current, and user researchers who analyze player activity and make recommendations to improve usage as well as profitability.

USING AGILE DEVELOPMENT

As I mentioned in Chapter 12 when I introduced the concept of Agile development, this methodology strives to make the software development process more adaptive and people-centric. By this I mean that rather than having the team follow a detailed specification that is created up front, developers will address the priority features to set short-term goals and work together closely to implement those goals in short periods called "Sprints." They meet daily or weekly to evaluate their progress, set new goals, and determine if there are gating issues to progress.

The core of the Agile methodology focuses on small interdisciplinary teamwork, communication and input from stakeholders, and ongoing implementation and iteration. There are a number of important techniques you can learn to lead effective Agile teams, but these three are critical to the methodology:

- Working in Sprints: Sprints are fixed-length goals for working iterations of the game. The goals of a Sprint should be clear and doable and result in a playable build that can be evaluated by the team and playtested by users and by the publisher or client. A Sprint should be measured in days or weeks—if your Sprint is more than this you need to break down your goals into smaller tasks.

- Holding Scrum meetings: Scrum meetings are short daily meetings where the team members show what they have accomplished, set goals for the following day's work, and discuss any obstacles keeping them from accomplishing their goals. These meetings are led by a "Scrum Master."

- Prioritizing and working on features based on input from potential players and other "clients," including management and the publisher. The producer or product manager owns this list of features and makes decisions with the team about how these features are prioritized.

Here is an example of a small team working in an Agile methodology. The team consists of a game designer, a programmer, an artist, and a producer. They are working on a mobile puzzle game that combines two types of puzzle mechanics: set making and word making. Both mechanics are controlled by touching letters on a screen grid, and the player can perform the two activities simultaneously. The game will need to be able to recognize the difference between a set of letters (a sequence or group of the same) and a word in order to score the player properly.

The team is currently involved in a two-week Sprint to implement their core mechanic. In this case, the goal of the Sprint is to create a build in which a player can touch letters on a screen that are evaluated by the two planned game mechanics. Today's meeting is occurring at the end of the first week, and during today's meeting, the Scrum Master (who leads the meeting) asks the programmer what she has accomplished since yesterday. The programmer shows the working letter grid and explains that you can now touch letters and they will disappear. Tomorrow she will begin working on storing the letters that were touched in an array so that they can be evaluated and scored. She will need a complete list of letter sets and conditions as well as a searchable dictionary very soon, which the game designer will need to provide. This becomes an action item for the game designer. On seeing the build, the visual designer realizes that the letters should not be disappearing, but rather should have a selected state until the move is evaluated and scored or rejected. He shows the work that he has been doing on the scoring animations, but states that he will work on the selection state right away, so that this feature can be implemented more clearly. The team remains standing during this meeting, and it is short and decisive, taking no more than

10-15 minutes. The follow week, when the Sprint is over, the Sprint review will consist of a live demonstration of the working core mechanic of the game.

This is a very simplistic example of Agile methodology, which can be used on small games like our mobile game example, or very large complex projects. When Agile methods are used on larger project, there will be multiple interdisciplinary teams, each working on their own aspect of the game. Because each team is small, communication can be quick and efficient, and the dependencies are quickly uncovered, as in the example of our visual designer and the select state.

There are more detailed management techniques involved in Agile methodology and Scrum that you may be interested in learning. If so, there are courses and books that can help you refine your abilities. I've included some references in the further reading list and encourage you to look into them. However, if you are just starting out, you can still practice Agile methodology by simply structuring your project plan around Sprints, holding daily Scrum meetings, and practicing ongoing team-based planning, as discussed in the following section.

AGILE PROJECT PLANNING

As mentioned, the project plan is one of most important documents that the developer creates. This set of documents is a road map for producing the game, albeit a road map that is destined to change. It includes an estimated schedule and the budget, which are generally attached to the contract for the production. You may wonder how you can create a schedule and a budget for your project if you don't know all of the details of what will be produced yet. The most important thing to know is that your schedule should be task based, and that the people doing the work need to be actively involved in creating the schedule.

As I've already discussed, Agile development focuses on an iterative process, with feature teams working to build and improve their part of the game concept. Figure 13.2 shows how each separate team, working in Sprints, iterates on its area of the production, coordinated with the other feature teams, and the larger project emerges. It is the producer's role to coordinate this effort as a whole and to make sure that these teams are all adding to the vision of the game as a whole. If you are working on a very small game, you may only have one team, but you can still plan your project around Sprints and iterative releases.

Goals

First, articulate all the goals of the project. Include gameplay goals, such as mechanics and levels, and technical goals, like enabling multiple players over the Internet. Also include the target platform and proposed launch date. An example might be to launch on iOS and Android for summer.

Exercise 13.1: Goals

Working with the team you have recruited, write down the goals for turning your original game idea into a finished product. Make sure to include both gameplay goals and technical goals.

Priorities

Now organize your goals by priority. Some of your goals will clearly be of high priority—for example, your core mechanic will be of the highest priority. Others, like a leaderboard, will be important, but fall below your core mechanic. Sometimes you may have a great idea for a feature, but you know that you could launch without it. That would be a stretch goal, and it would have a lower priority.

Exercise 13.2: Prioritize

Organize the goals you just stated by priority. Consider the importance of each goal to your current idea of the game. This may change as the production goes on, but do your best based on your current knowledge. Work with your team members to make your priorities as accurate as possible.

Schedule

An Agile schedule is made up of time-bounded iterations, usually of 2-4 weeks. Each of these will focus on implementing prioritized features into a working build. The overall schedule is an estimate of how long it will take your team to

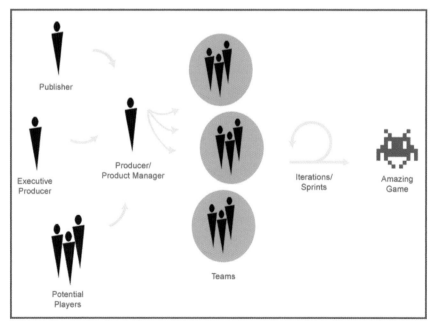

13.2 Agile team process

Task Name	Start Date	End Date	Duration	
⊟ Sprint 1 - core gameplay	09/09/13	09/17/13	7	
Core flying mechanic	09/09/13	09/13/13	5	
Temp terrain	09/16/13	09/16/13	1	
Temp resources	09/17/13	09/17/13	1	
⊟ Sprint 2 - collection mechanics	09/18/13	09/27/13	8	
Flight controls	09/18/13	09/19/13	2	
Inventory UI	09/20/13	09/23/13	2	
pick up items	09/24/13	09/25/13	2	
drop items	09/26/13	09/27/13	2	
⊟ Sprint 3 - test level	09/30/13	10/09/13	8	
TBD	09/30/13	10/09/13	8	
Sprint 4 - playtest revisions	10/10/13	10/21/13	8	

13.3   Sample sprint schedule in Gantt chart format

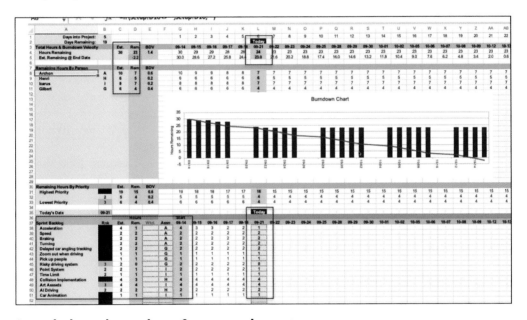

13.4   Sample burndown chart for a simple project

implement all of the features that you have for your game. The features will each be broken down into tasks, prioritized, and worked on in Sprints per that prioritization.

Because the team owns an Agile schedule, the best way to develop it is to work with your team to create your feature goals and priorities, break them down into tasks, and estimate how long each Sprint for these goals will require. Once you have an estimate for each

of the Sprints, you can figure out the length of the full schedule. As we know from experience, it is easier to plan for tasks that we are closer to, because we have a stronger grasp on the extent of what needs to be done. So, the later Sprints on your schedule will likely be less detailed, as seen in Figure 13.3. Also, your estimates will all be relative to the experience and size of your team and will clearly change as the project moves forward. At first, your team may have some difficulty estimating the time it will take for each task, but as they begin to work together, they'll have a better idea of both their own capabilities and the work to be done. Because of this, the schedule will become a living document. Ongoing planning and scoping of the project is a core part of the Agile process.

A great internal tool for agile teams that will help track progress against priories, and also to measure true team working pace is called a burndown chart. A burndown chart such as the one shown in Figure 13.4 shows the amount of work that has been completed and the total work remaining. It does this by tracking each team member's actual progress on assigned tasks against the projected number of hours on remaining tasks. In Figure 13.4, for example, Team member Archon was tasked with 10 estimated hours of work on some of the highest priority tasks. Even though they've been working for several weeks, they still estimate that they have 7 hours left on these tasks. The rest of the team is also working quite slowly. At the rate they are going, they are not going to make it through their backlog of tasks by their deadline, so they'll need to get going or re-scope!

The burndown chart can be used to predict your team's likelihood of completing the project in the time available, so that you can make re-scoping decisions quickly, before too much creep gets your schedule way off track. For his book "A Playful Production Process," designer Richard Lemarchand created a burndown chart template you can access to use for your own teams. You can find that and other templates here: https://www.playfulproductionprocess.com/templates/

A burndown chart is a great internal tool, but if you are working with a publisher, you will most likely also need to have an overall milestone schedule with deliverables and dates on which they are due. This means that your original estimate will need to have some accuracy. If you promise an alpha by March, but when March arrives you have only implemented the core mechanic, you will likely lose the faith of the publisher and they will hold your milestone payment until you deliver an alpha. On top of this, reaching this alpha becomes problematic if you can't pay your team.

All of this is to say that the schedule, while flexible, also needs to be a tool to keep the production scoped properly and on schedule. By scoping, I mean the process of evaluating how much work you can do with the team you have. If you have a very small team, but a very long list of goals, you will either need to scope your list of goals down to a reasonable size, or you will need to lengthen the time that you work on the game.

To begin making your schedule, take all of your goals and estimated Sprint lengths and assign dates to them. If you have multiple feature teams, then some of these goals can be addressed in parallel. If not, you'll need to do them linearly. Some may be dependent on each other, so be sure that if they are, they are in sequence. You can use a spreadsheet like Excel or even a paper calendar to plan the first draft of your schedule, or you can use one of the project management tools I mentioned earlier. Asana, for example, integrates with a tool called Instagantt, which allows you to view and manage your project tasks in a Gantt chart format, adding start dates, time estimates, and dependencies. When you are done, you will have an overview of your production time line, which is what you can use to produce your budget.

One of the realizations that you will have very quickly is that the farther out you look in a development process, the harder it becomes to forecast accurately. It is reasonable to ask a team to plan in detail for the next 2-4 weeks, but it becomes harder to be accurate beyond that. For this reason, an Agile schedule has multiple levels of detail. You can put your high-level milestones on this schedule, along with the feature goals that will bring you to those milestones, but the outcome of each Sprint will likely cause you to re-evaluate these goals as you progress.

It is possible that this could cause issues with your publisher; however, if you are using an Agile process, you should always have a working build to be able to show them, which can help tremendously with the communication process. It means that if you are somewhat off schedule, but your team has done some amazing work on a particular feature, you will be able to communicate that change in plan clearly by sharing the build.

Overall, you should use your schedule as a way to keep the team focused on the implementation vision of the project. Used as a communication tool between individuals and feature teams, the schedule provides a way for everyone to get a sense of where the game is and where it is going.

Exercise 13.3: Schedule

Using either scheduling software or a paper calendar, create a schedule of Sprints for the development of your original game. Work with your team to do this so that they can help estimate time frames for each feature goal.

Budget

The budget is a direct function of the schedule. If you know how many people you will need and for how long, it is not hard to calculate the production costs for your game, as salaries make up the majority of a game budget. Other direct costs include things like software licensing, specialized services, hardware, and travel.

The sample budget in Figure 13.4 was created using Microsoft Excel and shows several important elements of a budget. The cover page on the left shows total costs for various types of production labor: project management, game design, graphic design, digital video, 2D/3D animation, and software development. It also shows the direct costs for testing, production supplies, media, licensing, and administrative costs. The right-hand callouts show examples of how several of the totals on the front page are calculated from a breakdown of line items.

Overhead expenses refer to all nonlabor expenses that are required to operate the business. For game developers, it generally includes rent, utilities, supplies, insurance, and other such costs. A true overhead percentage can be calculated by an accountant as a function of the developer's real labor and nonlabor costs. This percentage is extremely important because many developers do not calculate it correctly and wind up shortchanging themselves.

After the benefits and overhead are calculated for a specific line item, it is included in the total for the group of resources and carried over to the front page. All the various costs are added in a subtotal. Then several important percentages are calculated. The first is "production insurance." If you have taken any insurance out to back up your company's ability to complete the job, you will need to add that cost here. In this case, the developer has not done so.

The second percentage to be calculated is "markup." This is a percentage that the developer charges above their costs. Thus, it might be possible for a developer to actually make some money on a production if they manage it closely and meet their expectations. This is important in the case of developers who do work for hire—that is work that they do not own or have a royalty interest in.

Exercise 13.4: Budget

Now it is time to create the budget for your original game. Use the sample budget in Figure 13.5 as a starting point. It is okay to put down your best guess for the various costs because you will revise your estimates later.

13.5   Sample budget

Scoping and Revising

After you have gone through the first four steps, do not be surprised if you wind up with a gigantic budget number that far exceeds what you know the publisher will advance to you. Your next step is to go back to the beginning: Look at your goals and cut or revise them. After you revise your goals, you will need to revise your priorities and Sprint schedule. Then, you can reflect those changes in your budget.

The biggest mistake that beginning developers make during the budgeting process is to not change their goals and schedule but instead fiddle with the budget numbers until they come out looking "reasonable." Always start with your goals and work down through the priorities and schedule. If you overpromise and underbudget, you will run the risk of losing money, overworking your team, and being unable to complete the project as promised.

Exercise 13.5: Revise

Now assume the publisher has asked you to cut 20% out of your budget. Starting with your goals and working your way through the priorities, schedule, and finally the budget, revise your plan to reduce costs.

Milestones and Approvals

Each time a stage of development has been completed and approved by the publisher, the developer receives a milestone payment. It is important that the developer keep a written record of all approvals and decisions from the publisher. Quite often the publisher will ask for changes to the design in the middle of production, which will increase the cost of production. If the producer for the developer has been

OPPORTUNITIES FOR INDIE GAMEMAKERS

by Sam Roberts

Sam Roberts works as a creative director, designer, and entrepreneur in digital and live entertainment and events, including the recent mobile game FREEQ, the big game P.O.S.E., and a well-received interactive livestreamed show called The Maze on Planet 7. He is a co-founder of the IndieCade Festival of Independent Games and also serves as the Assistant Director of the Interactive Media & Games Division at USC, where he continues to work to promote the medium of games and the next generation of talented gamemakers.

Humanoid Asteroids at IndieCade's Night Games

We are making the future of games everyday–every design experiment, every new idea, every technological discovery, each innovative interface crafts the future of this amazing field. How do you bring attention and acclaim to your interactive art object, small game about your passions, or experience that no one is really sure whether it is a game or not? The making and engaging in the practice of design can be its own reward, but these projects deserve exposure at one of a growing number of outlets for experimental, artistic, and independent play. IndieCade, the international festival of independent games, is your first and most important destination for the magical experiences you craft.

IndieCade, supports independent game development and organizes a series of international events showcasing independent, artistic, and experimental games. It publicizes and cultivates innovation and artistry in interactive media, helping to create a public perception of games as rich, diverse, artistic, and culturally significant. IndieCade offers an unparalleled opportunity to share your work with an amazing community of designers working toward parallel goals and whose ideas, insights, and passion match your own. Through its events, IndieCade provides a forum for game developers to promote their work to media and the public, and a forum where a diverse audience will play your work, where you can gather feedback on actual player experience and hear dozens of different opinions about what you have made. IndieCade gives you the chance to make your game a star.

IndieCade is the home of Night Games, the magical afterhours event of beautiful large-scale play, and the IndieCade Conference, where the independent design community share their ideas, experiments, and successes. IndieCade is the home of brilliant designers working to reinvent and reimagine the field. IndieCade was the first festival to show Train by Brenda Bathwaite, a designer working to highlight the expressive power of games with her Medium is the Message series, the first to show The Night Journey, an experimental videogame from artist Bill Viola and designer Tracy Fullerton. IndieCade award winner Fez took the games space by storm. IndieCade was the festival showing roguelike games before they were revived in the mainstream, and was an early screening home for many indie game successes like Braid, Unfinished Swan, Everyday Shooter, and Flower.

IndieCade's events and related production and publication programs are designed to bring visibility to and facilitate the production of new works within the emerging independent game movement. Like the independent videogame developer community itself, IndieCade's focus is global and includes producers in Asia, Latin America, Europe, Australia, and anywhere else independent games are made and played. As a part of a growing movement, IndieCade is only one of many opportunities for designers and developers to find exposure for their work, introduction to the larger community, and like-minded peers to form bonds with and to discuss the future of play.

Alongside IndieCade sits the Independent Game Festival (IGF), a more industry-focused competition that helps bring independent games to the attention of publishers and media. Beyond IndieCade and the IGF are a growing number of competitions and events, including Games for Change, a conference focused on serious, persuasive, and educational games; Come Out & Play, a festival for big games; IFComp, a competition for interactive fiction; the Experimental Gameplay Workshop, a panel highlighting experimental design; Game Devs of Color, an event celebrating the work of diverse game developers, and many smaller independent game competitions. We also live in the age of the Game Jam, starting with the Global Game Jam, and including everything from a small local jam hosted by your school to large international jams organized around new platforms or technology. Participating in the Global Game Jam, one of IndieCade's Jams, or the 7-day Roguelike Jam is a fantastic way for a young designer to practice their chops, get involved in a game-making community, and experiment with small but innovative ideas. Look for competitions and jams focused on your area of interest, or with support and developers working in your area of the world, and get involved right away.

IndieCade and other festivals create a conversation and community around design, design methodology, and play. The conferences at IndieCade, Games4Change, the Game Developer's Conference and more provide opportunities to hear many of the most thoughtful, insightful, and inventive designers of our time talk about their ideas, their methodologies, and their projects. The community of working designers who attend IndieCade, play the finalist games, and spend the weekend together creates a space where new ideas are discussed, shared, and actively thought about. This discussion is a major contribution to the games industry, as inspiration from new ideas drives designers to try new things, to improve their own design practice, and to steal and share one another's ideas. This community drives new design practice and industry experiments that become important products, genres, and ideas for the future of games and interactive play. IndieCade nominee Outer Wilds has gone on to win many prestigious Game of the Year Awards, and Her Story, an IndieCade winner of the past has led to a new genre of video based gameplay.

IndieCade provides a valuable opportunity to network, to meet other game and interactive designers, and to make career connections and develop future work opportunities. The open, collaborative spirit leads to new teams forming and new ideas being explored—the Copenhagen Game Collective and later Die Gute Fabrik formed out of a collaboration that began at the first IndieCade festival, where Nils Deneken showed Ruckblende, a narrative and artistic exploration of memory, and Doug Wilson, Lau Korsgaard, and Dajana Dimovska from Copenhagen ITU brought Dark Room Sex Game, an audio-only two-player game exploring the idea of rhythm in intimacy.

IndieCade's breadth has led to many success stories and great games that premiered at IndieCade and used it as a stepping stone to publishing contracts, console release, and wide acclaim. This includes games such as Johann Sebastian Joust, a large-scale game played in real space using PlayStation Move controllers, where players try to knock other players' controllers violently enough to register while protecting their own; The Misadventures of P.B. Winterbottom, a student game from USC's Interactive Media & Games program with a unique art style and time clone puzzle-solving gameplay; Antichamber, Alexander Bruce's 3D philosophical puzzle game built on non-Euclidean geometry; Skulls of the Shogun, a multiplayer online tactical title designed to be inviting and playable to a large, non-hardcore audience; and Quantum, an inventive board game from Eric Zimmerman and John Sharp that uses dice as changing player pieces and has a modifiable game board. These games showed at IndieCade first, and you can see the growing trends of digitally assisted real-space games, single-screen multiplayer, procedural generation, and more showing up at the IndieCade festival before they start to permeate the mainstream. IndieCade is the first step to taking your brilliant idea to the masses.

IndieCade shows digital and non-digital games, games meant to be played in large groups or alone, games meant for display in museums or to be played for 60 seconds on a mobile phone while waiting at a bus stop—the unifying thread is games that innovate, that do something new, different, or exciting. In 2020, IndieCade showed I Was A Teenage Exocolonist, a brilliant narrative choice game exploring high level systemic storytelling; Thousand Year Old Vampire, a physical book containing a beautiful roll and write solo play game exploring your history as a vampire; Mutazione a procedural audio adventure and platformer with innovative gardening mechanics; Terrarium, an alternate reality game used to on board new students at the University of Chicago into an imaginative exploration of climate science; and Sin Sol, and augmented reality universe dealing with issues of depression and environment. Another 50 games were shown in the IndieCade Selections. IndieCade continues to diversify its content and show games from every imaginable style of play—table, board, big, role-playing, serious, experimental, artistic, casual, and beyond. IndieCade provides a showcase for developers practicing their craft in dozens of different ways.

IndieCade's focus on excellence and innovation leads the way into the future of games, play, and interactive experience. As a developer interested in IndieCade, you should think about that focus. Design what makes you passionate, explore your wildest ideas, and you will be creating games that appeal to IndieCade. This remains true for any festival, with some games having a more specific focus—when making a submission for Come Out & Play, you should still design the game that you are passionate about, the one that is a wild and crazy idea, but you should make sure it is a game meant to be played physically in space by one or more people. Festivals like IndieCade are looking for passion work by developers and exist as venues for innovative and inventive explorations and sharing truly excellent, passionate work. You can never go wrong following your heart for the game you want to design.

For game design students, IndieCade has a new offering: IndieCade Horizons, a conference focused on game design students and providing hands on conference sessions and advice to beginning your career and starting to shape the community of thought that drives innovative gameplay among your peer group.

Different festivals reach different audiences, and applying to many of them with your games will give you a chance to reach diverse audiences. The important audiences for a designer looking for opportunities for their work are the industry audience, whose attention can bring you new work; the public audience, whose attention brings you new fans to download your products; the media audience, whose attention becomes press stories and reviews of your game that can serve to drive a public audience or promote you inside the industry; and the designer audience, whose attention brings you concentrated feedback and notoriety inside game design circles, often centered around a specific genre or type of play. IndieCade, by looking at large bodies of submissions and selecting chosen pieces to share, serves as a unique venue for helping designers making new, innovative, and superb work reach all of those audiences at once.

IndieCade serves as a showcase for your experimental and artistic work, a community to develop game design ideas, and a launch pad for games and genres to enter the mainstream. As a working game designer, game festivals, competitions, and showcases provide an amazing opportunity for you to bring attention to your work, get audience feedback, and join a community of thinkers around games.

thorough about getting approval on the stages of development, she will be in a good position to discuss an increased budget for additional feature requests.

These details that seem so formal and unnatural in the rather casual environment of game production can mean the all difference in the development process. As I have said already, a lot of good producing comes down to maintaining clear lines of communication and documenting all decisions and requests for changes.

CONCLUSION

Games tend to be some of the most technically advanced software in the world, and the challenge in creating them keeps growing as technologies advance and player expectations increase. Knowing how to put a good process in place and understanding what to expect at each stage of development are ways that you can ensure the success of your design ideas. Although designers are not typically responsible for creating the project plan or managing it, the more you know about the process of development, the more you can contribute to your team's plan, and the better designer and team member you will become.

DESIGNER PERSPECTIVE:
MICHAEL JOHN

Associate Teaching Professor and Vice Chair, UC Santa Cruz Games and Playable Media Professional MS program

Michael John has designed video games for over twenty years. His design credits include the original Spyro the Dragon games (1997-1999) on the Sony PlayStation and the PSP classic Daxter (2008). Currently, he is Associate Teaching Professor and Vice Chair at the UC Santa Cruz Games and Playable Media Professional MS program in Silicon Valley. Before coming to UC Santa Cruz, he was game director at GlassLab, where he developed innovative learning games.

How did you become a game designer?

It's so different to how people become designers today. I kind of drifted into the field, first with a QA job, and then eventually working into design. I had a very lucky break when I was hired by Universal Studios to work closely with Mark Cerny, and ultimately Insomniac Games. "Designer" was not a common title at the time so it was kind of, help out where I can during the development process. I can't do art or code very well, so that ended up being a lot of level design, things like that. I'm not sure exactly when, but at some point I realized I had a career (and job title).

Being in education I know that the paths are really different now, often (though by no means always) going through specialized education. And there's the whole independent development path which is much more accessible than even just a few years ago. I'm thrilled that people can begin calling themselves "game designer" so early in their careers.

On games that have inspired him:

The game that I played that just changed everything was Mario64. I had grown up on 2D games, like other kids my age. But Mario64 said no, there is a whole world here—quite literally a whole horizon—that is ready to be explored. Tomb Raider hinted at it, but Tomb Raider had walls. Mario64 had a horizon. The horizon changed everything... it was an inviting detailed world that nonetheless felt infinite: infinite and intimate at the same time. While there had been plenty of 3D rendered games before Mario64, I think an awful lot of the action games we see today owe a huge debt to Mario64.

Also, that game inspired me because of its creator. I had assumed that the transition to 3D was going to chew up Shigeru Miyamoto and he wouldn't be dominating that design space like he had the 2D platformers. I could not have been more wrong, and it's so inspiring to see someone who adapted so thoroughly and elegantly, even well into his career, to new technology and new ways of doing things.

On design process:

I have processes that I believe in, and that I teach, but the most important thing is simple: just commit to a process. You don't have to commit early to a design, but you do want to commit to a process. A lot of the material in this book (and also in Richard Lemarchand's excellent *A Playful Production Process*) are great resources. I think it's especially easy for people working in smaller groups or on their own to neglect process, and this is something I frequently see with students. Encouraging them to have a process, and to honor its value, is at the end of the day probably the most important thing I teach.

I'm most proud of ...

I have to preface this answer with acknowledgment of the tremendous good fortune that defines the early part of my career. I'm not smarter or more creative than most of the people reading this – I was in the right place, at the right time, and was blessed with working with marvelous people. So that being said, now 20 years on, I am really gratified seeing how the *Spyro* games mean so much to a lot of people, sometimes citing specific things that I worked on. YouTube and Twitch have been great ways to observe how they feel. I never in my wildest dreams imagined the games would be that meaningful to people, but it's hard not to feel proud that they were.

Advice to designers:

Don't listen too much to people like me. We know a lot of useful things about design and production processes, but one of the wonderful things about the video games medium is that it is constantly opening up new vistas (sometimes literally) for new ideas and creators. Ultimately we don't know any more than you do. Get in there and learn, and go for it.

FURTHER READING

Chandler, Heather M. *Game Production Handbook*. Burlington: Jones & Bartlett Learning, 2014.

Hight, John and Novak, Jeannie. *Game Project Management*. Boston: Thompson Learning, 2007.

Irish, Dan. *The Game Producer's Handbook*. Boston: Thompson Course Technology, 2005.

Keith, Clinton. *Agile Game Development with Scrum*. Hoboken: Pearson Education, Inc., 2020.

Lemarchand, Richard. *A Playful Production Process: For Game Designers (and Everyone)*. Cambridge: The MIT Press, 2021.

McCarthy, Jim. *Dynamics of Software Development*. Redmond: Microsoft Press, 2006.

Chapter 14
Communicating Your Designs

I have said throughout this book that digital game development is an inherently collaborative medium. In the last two chapters I have talked about all the various types of people who make up that collaborative environment, as well as the stages of the production process. One of the most important parts of managing this process is sharing the overall vision of the game between all of the team members. If your team is very small, or if you are working alone, this might not be a problem. But most games are complex enough, and most teams are large enough, that the most effective way to ensure communication is some form of documentation.

There are no industry standards for this documentation, though there are several trends that have taken hold over the evolution of the industry. The first trend was a large, single document created by the game designer. This "design document" described all of the elements of the game in as detailed a manner as possible, including mechanics, user interface, art, sound, story, and levels. Design wikis were an evolution of the design document that allowed for online collaboration between team members. Many teams now use simple online collaboration tools such as Google Docs to document and share ideas. And some teams use only minimal documentation, such as "design macros" relying on strong communication, rapid prototyping, and execution skills. Most teams require some level of documentation, however, in order to align their vision and work effectively.

No matter what format, tools, or level of detail are used, the goal of design documentation is the same: to communicate ideas and decisions that have been made about the game among all of the members of the team. Designs change as the team works, so you can't think of this documentation as something that is ever set in stone. Rather, think of it as capturing the results of a Sprint, a design review, or a brainstorm. These results are ephemeral. You think you will remember what the scrawled diagram on your whiteboard means later on, but unless you clarify and document, that information will fade away quickly. In this chapter I will describe some good techniques for balancing the need for design documentation with the evolution of a game project. Not all of these techniques will be applicable to your current game or team, but you may find them useful in future situations.

DOI: 10.1201/9781003460268-17

VISUALIZATION

One of the most effective ways to communicate complex information is visually. Think about how much information can be shown in something like the blueprint of a building. The size of rooms; the layout of the space; the placement of doors and windows, stairs, and electrical outlets. Imagine reading a block of text describing your house versus seeing a layout of the same information. Like a building, a game is a complex combination of spatial, temporal, and tactile designs. Communicating these designs is sometimes best done by abstracting and visualizing key components.

Riot Games' Lead Designer Stone Librande advocates what he calls "one page designs,"[1] a visualization that gets to the core of a design quickly and simply. Librande came up with this idea when he noticed that the programmers on his team would tack up his UI flow diagrams above their desks for easy reference, while ignoring the larger design document. He quickly realized that these visualizations were communicating just the right level of information in a way that was easy for them to access.

Some of the elements of games that are best visualized in this way include the spatial layout of levels, the UI, the relationship between unit types, character evolutions, and more. Examples of Librande's one page design from Electronic Arts'

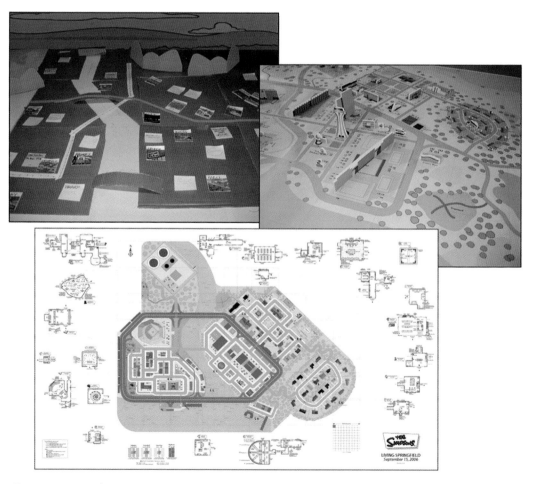

14.1   Design visualizations

The Simpsons Game can be seen in Figure 14.1. This shows the evolution of the game map from a paper prototype to a digital map, to the fully detailed design with callouts for each game area.

Sometimes the aspect of a design you're trying to communicate is more abstract than a map. Perhaps you need to communicate a change in tone over time. If you think back to the diagrams created by Jenova Chen to describe the emotional arc of the game Journey on page 126, you can see that his visualization of that arc was a key part of communicating his design concept.

FLOWCHARTS

If you are trying to communicate a hierarchy or a process, using a flowchart to visualize this idea might be the best solution. A flowchart like the one in Figure 14.2 is a great way to think through all the possible paths that a player might take through your game.

Often, you can combine a basic flowchart with rudimentary UI designs to give a full sense of what will be on each screen. These rough UI designs are called wireframes, and they are an excellent communication tool between the designer, the artists, and the UI programmers.

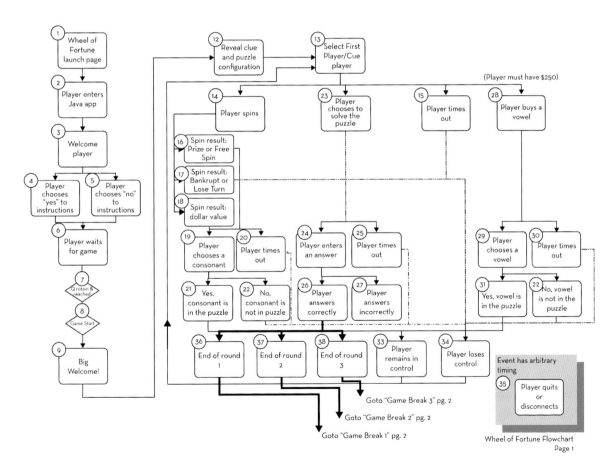

14.2   Wheel of Fortune flowchart

As can be seen in Figure 14.3, the initial UI wireframes don't address look and feel or final layout, but rather block out all of the elements in a simple manner that can be referenced as visual concepts and technology are developed. Later in the process, the QA team will likely refer to them as well when creating a test plan.

In addition to wireframes, flowcharts can also be used to visualize relationships between various game objects, like unit types or characters. So, you can show how a unit might be upgraded, or how a character's abilities might change as the game progresses. You can make flowcharts using a tool like Lucidchart, Microsoft Visio, Drawio.net, or

14.3 Wheel of Fortune wireframes and interface designs

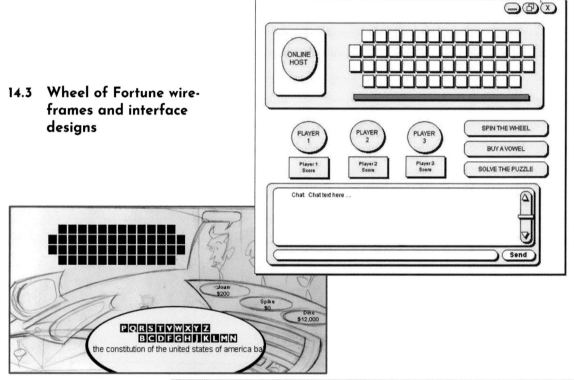

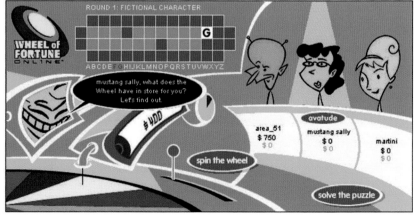

Cacoo. Many flowcharting options are also build into digital whiteboarding tools such as Miro.com, Lucidspark, Gliffy, and many more. Most of these have free entry-level options or options for student accounts. Since so many people are now working remotely, there has been a boom in available tools for digital collaboration and design. For UI mock-ups and wireframes, there are also extremely efficient design tools such as Figma, Balsamiq, and Adobe XD, which are great for sketching and testing ideas. Some of these tools allow you to create simple click-through prototypes of your UI designs for simple prototyping, animatics, demos, and testing.

Exercise 14.1: Flowchart and Wireframes

Either on paper or using one of the tools mentioned earlier, create a full flowchart for your original game design. Next, create a complete set of wireframes for every interface state in the game. Last, annotate your wireframes with callouts describing how each feature works.

TABLES AND SPREADSHEETS

In addition to territory, processes, and hierarchies, you may also need to visualize data using a table or spreadsheet. One of the most valuable skills you can learn as designer is how to work with spreadsheets. For example, imagine your game has many different unit types, all of which cost varying amounts of money to purchase and have different strengths and weaknesses. Visualizing all of this data in a spreadsheet cannot only help communicate this information to your teammates, but it is also the best way to test and tune these variables. If you are able to save out a data file from your spreadsheet to test in a game build, you'll be able to try many variations quickly and efficiently. In this example, the design documentation functions as a prototyping tool as well as a communication tool, which is the best of both worlds.

Tables can also be used to communicate relationships between game objects or actions. For example, if you think back to the Prisoner's Dilemma matrix shown on page 382, each strategy represents a potential player action and the matrix describes the outcomes of those actions in combination.

CONCEPT ART

One of the most common types of visualization that is used in planning a game is concept art. On the one hand, this is extremely useful in giving an emotional sense of how the game will feel in play—the environments, the characters, the action, the tone. On the other hand, concept art rarely gives details that can be acted on by the programmers or even, sometimes, the artists. Concept art is most useful early in the process, when you are trying to find the feel of the game. As discussed in the sidebar on "AI & the Creative Process" on page 475, many small game teams are turning to AI tools to help generate concept art in their early stages. This has both a plus and a minus — if you don't have an artist available at all, it could be helpful to round out your pitch. However, the concept art created by AI is not something your team will be particularly invested in, and will not

	A	B	C	D	E	F
1	Unit name	Cost	Speed	Damage	Armor	Range
2	Redshirt	10	50	30	70	5
3	Blueshirt	10	25	50	50	5
4	Command	20	10	30	20	20
5	Scout	30	75	10	20	80
6	Medic	30	30	10	50	10
7	Security	5	40	90	90	10
8	Comms	40	90	0	0	90

14.4 Spreadsheet of unit data

14.5 Character sketches from Jak & Daxter and Ghost

likely be usable for the game itself. due to copyright issues It may be helpful to articulate your idea to a certain extent, but keep in mind that

you want your game to feel original in its final form. Later, once the team knows what it is going for, more detailed forms of visualization become important, such as breakdowns of the character animations, level maps like those in Figure 14.1, or UI mock-ups.

For complicated sequences, storyboards are often a useful way to visualize the flow of an experience. You might use these for a cut scene, or even for an intricate level design. In addition to storyboards, a good visualization tool in the early design process is the creation of an animatic. This can be interactive or just an animation that shows how it will look when someone plays the game. As discussed on page 260, storyboards, concept art, and animatics are all techniques of aesthetic prototyping that help with the visualization and design process.

Exercise 14.2: Concept Art

Create some concept art for your original game idea, either for the environments or characters or both. You can make your own sketches, or you might use this occasion to recruit an artist for your team. If you can't find an artist, try experimenting with an AI tool like Midjourney - or a newer tool as they are evolving every day.

DESCRIPTION

While descriptive text may not be the optimal way of communicating your game design, it can be effective if it is all you are able to provide. When writing about your game, there are several levels of description to keep in mind.

The first is the kind of persuasive, creative writing that helps paint the top-level picture. This is what you'll need when you write your concept document or a top-level summary of your game idea. Think of it as a more eloquent elevator pitch, one that communicates the gameplay and the sensibility of the project very quickly.

Here's an example from a sample concept document: "Alphaville is an fast paced word-making game in which hundreds of players cooperate to form words and score the highest points. Each player represents a single letter of the alphabet and their goal is to join up with other player-letters within the game space and to form high scoring words. Once a word is formed, players are re-spawned as a new letter."

Note that this high-level description doesn't give any info about how the game is going to be made, the look and feel, technology, etc. It is just

ARTIFICIAL INTELLIGENCE & THE CREATIVE PROCESS

By Steven S. Hoffman

Steven Hoffman (Captain Hoff) is the CEO of Founders Space, a startup accelerator. He began as a game designer at SEGA, then cofounded LavaMind, creating the indie classics Gazillionaire and Zapitalism. Next, he cofounded Spiderdance, which pioneered interactive TV games, and then headed Infospace's US Game Studios, which developed mobile versions of Tetris, Wheel of Fortune, Hitman, Tomb Raider, X Files, and more. Throughout Hoffman's career, he has produced, published, and/or designed over 100 game titles and wrote four books, including Surviving a Startup, Make Elephants Fly, and The Five Forces. He was also the co-author of Game Design Workshop, 1st Edition.

Artificial Intelligence (AI) has opened Pandora's box and game design will never be the same. But don't worry, AI is not going to replace human creativity just yet—let alone take over the world. What it will do is change the tools and development process, allowing designers to iterate faster and become more creative. There are literally hundreds of new AI tools for writing text, generating images, composing music, and much more. There are so many tools, and more becoming available every day, that it's impossible to cover them all in this sidebar. Instead, I'm going to talk about how designers can use AI to accelerate and enhance the creative process.

Let me start by sharing my own journey with AI. As a creative person, I've spent a lot of time experimenting with the various AI tools for my projects. First, I tried using ChatGPT to write poems and short stories, and it dazzled me. I couldn't believe how simple it was to enter a prompt and get poetry and prose. But the more I used it, the more its limitations became apparent, especially when it comes to writing fiction. It's almost impossible at this point to get AI to write a substantial fictional story. It simply can't or won't do it. You can have it expand upon an existing story, but at a certain point, it just breaks down, and the result is a wandering narrative with no real focus or cohesion.

Also, all the stories all start to sound the same. The AI tries hard to make tidy narratives, which means it simplifies everything, relying far too much on tropes and clichés. The result is that the stories feel repetitive and generic, even when they're about different subjects. I tried having AI write dialogue in the style of celebs, like Howard Stern and Britney Spears. On the surface, it does an amazing job, but if you write enough, it winds up sounding like a parody, reusing the same signature expressions over and over. The more lines of dialogue the AI generates, the less impressive it becomes. These are just a few of AI's limitations.

What generative AI is good at is giving you starting points for ideas. It's the perfect brainstorming tool. For instance, you may ask it to generate ideas for ghost stories, and even if ninety percent of those ideas are rehashed versions of what you already know, a couple may stand out, sending your mind off in a new direction and stimulating the creative process. AI is equally good at working as a writer's assistant. For example, if you ask it to describe a haunted Victorian hotel lobby, it will describe the scene and may include some details you'd never have thought of. These details are where the value lies. AI isn't good at creating truly compelling fictional narratives or even fully formed scenes, but it is good in filling in the gaps and illuminating the path forward when you get stuck.

AI can also help write design docs, business plans, and go-to-market strategies. In fact, it can guide you through the game design process. It's good at making lists of the next steps you need to take, and the resources required. It's also a fantastic tool for answering questions you may have, from how to create a compelling storyboard to how to conduct focus group testing.

When it comes to AI visual tools, I find them fascinating. I've spent a great deal of time with Midjourney, and I have to say, some of the art it produces is truly jaw dropping. I couldn't believe the level of detail and creativity. People say computers can't be creative, but what they forget is that a good deal of creativity is combinatorial play. Given enough data, AI is particularly good at this. It can create works of art that not only mimic the greatest artists in history but can rival them. Even art critics have a hard time discerning which digital images are created by AI or humans.

That said, generative art tools, like Midjourney and Dall-E, also have their limitations. Yes, they create remarkable visuals, but as a designer, it's difficult to get exactly what I need. The images are always off in some way. Even after extensive prompt engineering, I find it nearly impossible to get the image in my head to appear on screen. What comes out might surprise and delight me, but it's seldom what I want for the project.

Even when I do manage to generate a suitable image, it isn't in a form that's manipulable in graphics tools like Adobe Photoshop. This is because generative art lacks layers to keep elements in a composition separate, so there's no way to move, edit, and delete one element without affecting everything else. This is fine if you're just playing around or generating concept art, but if you want to create usable game assets, it's a real problem.

Collaborating with the right artist, on the other hand, is a totally different experience. Often, through a series of iterations, it's possible to achieve a shared vision with an artist—the designer and artist's thoughts align, but each bring their own unique ideas. When working with a human artist, they can produce not only individual images but an entire world rich in detail and unified in design. This is something that AI just can't do right now.

This brings me to another limitation of the current generation of AI graphics tools. They have a very hard time being consistent. Let's say you generate a character using Midjourney. Try getting the AI to generate that same character from other angles or in other settings in a visually consistent manner. It's a Sisyphean struggle. This isn't to say these problems won't be solved. I'm sure these limitations won't exist in the future, but we'll have to wait for that to happen.

If you're an AI enthusiast, you might be thinking that these are just temporary issues, and next generations of AI will solve them. But even when AI can generate suitable text, images, or music for the final production of a game, there are legal risks you need to be aware of. According to US copyright law, intellectual property can be copyrighted only if it is the product of human creativity. When creative works are made entirely by a machine, they cannot be copyrighted. But there's a caveat: if a human substantially alters the content, in essence creating something new, then the resulting intellectual property can be copyrighted.

What does this mean for game designers? It means you have to be careful. No one wants to release a game and be denied the copyright for the main characters or story. In addition, at this writing, there are lawsuits pending over AI using data that contains previously copyrighted material. For example, if you ask AI to generate an image in the style of Andy Warhol, and the AI accesses Warhol's previous works, what rights should the copyright holders have? Just because you can't copyright a design or style, doesn't mean the copyright holders don't have any claim over the AI generated work. What about the rights of the actors who performed the initial motion capture that AI animations are based on? Or the audio samples that are the basis of AI generated voices? As a side note, the legal issues around AI-generated art are so unsettled and open up so much liablity that the images I created to illustrate this essay could not be included due to the publisher's restrictions on using AI art!

These legal issues will likely be resolved in the coming years. But until they do, it's good to error on the side of caution, which means not using materials generated by AI that were trained on copyrighted datasets. Right now, this includes most of the major platforms, like ChatGPT, Google Bard, and Midjourney.

There are companies, like Adobe, who are offering generative AI tools where they own the rights to the underlying data, eliminating third-party copyright issues. Because the AI has been trained on Adobe's stock images, openly licensed content, and public domain material, the visuals it generates should be safe from lawsuits. Roblox is doing something similar, allowing its community to use generative AI tools trained on their own assets. It's a contained system that doesn't rely on outside data. We're going to see a lot more of this moving forward.

Even with systems trained on copyrighted datasets, there's one area where generative AI shines. AI is the perfect tool for rapidly creating concept, reference, and placeholder art. When developing my projects, I don't hesitate to use generative AI in the early stages. The beauty of AI is that with very little skill, a designer can create passable images, sound effects, and music and insert them into a prototype to test whether the concept works or not. And if it doesn't work, the designer can toss them out, quickly generate new assets at almost no cost, and try again. This acceleration of the iterative process is the superpower of AI, and it's one of the aspects makes it such an indispensable tool for the concept and prototyping stages of development.

There's no doubt AI will transform the game design process, in the same way that earlier tool revolutions have done. We're only seeing the tip of the iceberg right now. But what we often forget is that AI wouldn't be able to do any of this without human creativity. These machines are not operating independently of us. They are literally feeding off human creativity. ChatGPT and Midjourney wouldn't be able to produce a thing without data, and that data comes from people uploading billions of creative works, thoughts, and ideas to the internet.

In the end, AI is simply an extension of human creativity. Whether we work directly with it or not, it's shaping our society. Like all technologies, it has its pros and cons, but when used correctly, it has the potential to greatly enhance humanity and enable us to express ourselves in ways that were previously unimaginable. Just like radio, film, and TV transformed our world, AI is on the cusp of completely altering the way in which we live, work, create, and communicate.

There are already AI platforms that can dynamically generate video from text prompts. The video isn't professional quality yet, but it's a start. There are also apps that can create virtual spaces and worlds on the fly. And there are platforms for creating AI characters that we can interact with and even emotionally connect with. Eventually, we'll have AI that can write complete screenplays and novels. And yes, at some point, we will have AI that can design and develop fully functional games.

But the best games and works of art will always come from the interplay between human consciousness and AI. The emotions, intelligence, and relevance cannot be separated from the human experience, and if we remove human designers from the loop, we will lose that connection. When AI feeds off its own data, without any human editing or guidance, it tends to degrade and produce stale, uninteresting results. Closed AI systems, without human input stop being relevant.

The future of AI isn't a world where algorithms replace us—but a world where our machines empower us, making us more creative and productive. This human-AI symbiosis is the next frontier for AI developers. And as game designers, it's up to us to leverage AI and use it appropriately to produce meaningful and socially responsible content. We are the custodians of this new, incredibly powerful technology, and it's our job to determine what role it plays in the creative process and how it affects the final product.

VIRTUAL REALITY AND BEYOND

by Laird Malamed

Laird Malamed is the director of strategy and operations for Reality Labs Research, a division of Meta Platforms where he works on long term technology research in virtual/augmented/mixed reality. He also holds an adjunct professor position at USC's School of Cinematic Arts. Malamed was the founding COO and CFO of Oculus VR which was acquired by Facebook (now Meta) in 2014 just prior to the first consumer VR device, The Oculus Rift, releasing. Before Oculus, Malamed was senior vice president and head of development at Activision Blizzard overseeing software, hardware, and manufacturing for products such as Guitar Hero, Call of Duty, and Skylanders. Malamed held a variety of roles at Activision during his 16+ year tenure, including key positions in Activision's internal studios, marketing, and European studios. Prior to joining Activision, Malamed worked as a sound editor at Sony Pictures and at Lucasfilm. Malamed holds a bachelors degree from MIT and a masters of arts from USC's School of Cinematic Arts.

The early beginnings

Virtual reality (commonly called "VR") sprang out of ideas created in the 1950s by Douglas Engelbart (who would go on to build Xerox PARC, investors of the common GUI interface among other daily used innovations). Facing a decade of McCarthyism, scientists, and others dreamed of controlling reality and began to contemplate how computers, then room-sized behemoths, could offer an escape even if the world did not change. Others did not receive well Englebart's ideas about computers moving beyond large adding machines. Still, the idea remained popular with a handful of enthusiasts through the 1960s and 1970s, so work and research in the area continued. In the 1980s, VR became a popular idea again as exemplified by TV's Star Trek: The Next Generation (the Holodeck) and cinema's The Matrix (and later movies such as Inception and to some extent Marvel's Dr. Strange continuing that fascination).

Encyclopedia Britannica broadly defines virtual reality as "the use of computer modeling and simulation that enables a person to interact with an artificial three-dimensional (3-D) visual or other sensory environment."

Put more elegantly, the promise of virtual reality is to allow the user to be transported to another reality with a true sense of "presence"—a feeling of actually being there. This can be a "real" reality such as visiting Paris while sitting in Auckland. One would look around and see the Eiffel Tower, smell the fresh croissants and coffee, and hear native Parisian French spoken against a background of car horns while a light wind ripples across leafy gardens. (Gershwin's An American in Paris music is an optional add-on.) Or it can be an imagined reality like the canyon of some Earth-like planet orbiting a distant binary sun. Or even still, a past reality—Paris again, but this time the Eiffel Tower is being built, and the car horns do not yet exist but horse-drawn buggies stampede by in a rush. This vision has been fueled by a passion to see and experience new and exciting moments but with a power akin to actually perceiving through our natural senses. No more boundaries on shimmering screens or surround sound created from just five speakers.

The implication for gaming was evident early in VR's existence, and in the 1990s, perhaps tied to its rising public awareness, several failed attempts at VR systems for gaming fizzled in the market. As the definitions above state, VR presents an artificial world. Yet for consumer-level prices, the 1990s did not offer enough processing power and visual fidelity to sway buyers. Additionally, the field of view (how wide an image the user saw) did not pass above 40 degrees, far less than the 130+ degrees humans typically see. Thus, the experience was neither very virtual nor very real. VR failed.

While VR research never abated over the subsequent 20 years, particularly in military and medical research, VR for the masses remained elusive. Work by Professor Mark Bolas at the University of Southern California and others pushed the size of VR units down in size and weight. Computers and graphic cards improved in raw output. Could VR be finally ready?

Enter 18-year-old Palmer Luckey, who had spent much of his high school years tinkering and repairing cell phones. He also was a keen collector of old VR prototypes, amassing more than 40. A lifelong gamer, Palmer wondered if the lightweight, high-density cellular displays and some inexpensive optics and sensors could be cobbled together to form an affordable VR device. A series of events led him to connect with 3D-gaming godfather John Carmack, and ultimately his company Oculus VR was formed in mid-2012. A series of other companies such as Valve, HTC, Sony, Microsoft, and Samsung launched their own devices shortly thereafter.

The original Oculus Rift developer kit and headset

Virtual reality devices, such as original Rift or current devices such as Meta Quest 3, contain a headset resembling ski goggles within which are mounted small screens. These include integrated audio and plenty of adjustment points to make the experience comfortable for all users. Two optical magnifiers help create a 100°+ degree stereoscopic image. Exterior-facing sensors and pass-through cameras allow the device to track location in real space as well as track hand gestures and movement, to ensure the wearer's head and body movements are reflected in the rendered world while avoiding real world obstacles. When worn, the Quest displays virtual images completely filling the wearer's vision; the outside world is blocked (unless the user wants to show the real world—that is where the terms augmented and mixed reality take hold). With all-in-one units, the device is calculating the head and body position approximately 100x per second to ensure the proper rendering of content to the player. When the software is optimized and design thoughtfully implemented, VR can be a complete immersion with fantastic comfort and experiences. Units can be tethered to computers for even more powerful simulations.

But what about content? Ultimately, VR platforms are canvases for designers and artists to paint. At the launch, The Rift received numerous accolades for its ease of use and integration software. Any game may be modified in a few days to display images on the Rift. However, making that experience fun and being careful not to create simulation sickness experiences (where the brain's physical sensory inputs are mismatched from the visual and auditory ones) is crucial. Today, all modern game engines, such as Unity or Unreal, have plug-ins to assist publishing to the VR ecosystem fairly quickly and easily. With the availability of these engines to students and independent developers, this means that virtually anyone can develop for virtual reality. However, there are a number of challenges inherent in the format.

Like any platform, the device does many things well but has a number of limitations. Some of these are obvious – the user cannot see the real world for true VR immersion; some become obvious when programming for the device – reading text in VR can be difficult – and some are subtle and challenging to solve – user interfaces require thoughtful design with a strong sense of the player experience in mind. Even the most basic of choices – will the software use controllers of hand gestures for input must be prototyped and designed for each experience. Voice recognition continues to evolve as another form of input. While Mixed Reality devices such as Quest 3 (with virtual passthrough), dedicated AR devices such as Hololens and the Apple Vision Pro all have attempts to navigate these challenges, the designer still has to make crucial decisions early in prototyping about addressing the limitations.

Designing for VR

What VR does well is encompass the player in a whole new world of the designer's choosing. Screen edges do not matter. The sense of scale is extraordinary. In fact, VR is most powerful when the player is encouraged and rewarded for looking around. Gamers have become accustomed to controlling a game world by using hands and fingers to manipulate mice, keyboards, and gamepads. However, the head and neck are excellent at looking by moving around. The most powerful experiences to date have focused on this direct control mechanism.

For instance, CCP, the Icelandic developer/publisher of EVE Online, received praise for their early VR-only game EVE Valkyrie. Players sit in a spaceship cockpit and engage in space dogfights. Ship control is accomplished by joypad (simulating what a pilot might manipulate in a cockpit), but aiming at enemies is done entirely by looking and tracking the targets with head movement. The view is first person, and one can even see one's body when glancing down.

Valve Software added a VR mode to the popular Half-Life 2. First-person action games present some unique challenges because the user is controlling the movement of a virtual character. The first-person view perfectly matches VR's direct view. Yet turning and moving can confuse the senses (a phenomena less likely to happen in cockpit-based games such as EVE-V and Hawken because the brain understands it is control-ling a vehicle in which the player is sitting). Valve's Michael Abrash has reported that when playing VR games in short sessions over a week, people develop their "VR-legs." What makes HL2 remarkable, though, is the experience of NPCs speaking directly to the player as they speak. Alex, a female ally, is eerily real and engaging in a way not felt in the non-VR mode. She seems to make real eye contact. This power to engage the player directly provides an interface for developing experiences beyond any to date.

Beat Saber continues to be one of the most popular VR experiences across a range of platforms. A rhythm game mechanic where players use their glowing "sabers" to slice geometric objects in harmony with a pulsating music track, the concept is easy to understand. Yet what makes the title so popular is its strong adherence to good VR principals such as a generally fixed player position (although kneeling and turning are helpful at times), an interaction model that is physical and fun (slashing and swiping) with either controllers or hands, and an endless ability to extend the fun with music packs (which is not even specific to VR). In fact, Beat Saber provides some amount of a healthy workout so much so that schools allowed it for pandemic PE credit. I have placed people into Beat Saber who have zero gaming experience (let alone VR) and they are smiling and having fun in seconds. Now that is good game design.

Known brands have also taken steps into VR which adds an exciting mix of existing universes to those developed for VR. An early example is Star Trek Bridge Commander from Ubisoft which allowed for a single or multiplayer experience commanding a starship. VR Kobayashi Maru!

Taking this idea a step further into virtual storytelling has been the team at ILM Immersion. Their slogan of taking storytelling to "storyliving"—making you the VR participant the center of new and exciting narratives within the Star Wars universe. Vader Immortal finds the player descending into Vader's mysterious and dangerous castle where an ultimate confrontation with the Dark Lord awaits. With the visuals, sounds and music firmly linked to the 45+ year franchise creates immediate familiarity and motivation. The story's reaction to the player's actions that unfold within the 360 degree experience transcend watching the films (even on the best and largest IMAX screen) into being in them. All within your living room.

Extending the VR Dream

Location based entertainment, where visitors participate in a thirty-minute experience complete with props, a pre-show setting the tone and mood and often with friends has populated across malls and theme parks. The VOID was an early leader in this space with Star Wars and other stories available. As of this writing, three companies active in the space are Dreamscape VR, Divr Labs and Zero Latency VR. The latter features an experience based on the long standing and popular video game franchise, Far Cry.

As displays improve, VR will find applications in a whole range of experiences beyond games. Medical interests include remote surgeries and training. Military applications range from war games to cultural simu-lations. Generals may view battlefields differently if able to fly over them in VR. As written above, Apple is focusing on productivity and a truly virtual, infinite office space.

Education will be improved as students learn via VR. Because experiences may and should extend beyond replicating real-world realities, students may also float inside a cell and watch DNA replication as researchers at MIT created with Cellverse and then piloted in Boston Public Schools. On the Morning You Wake (to the End of the World) is a three-part virtual reality documentary overseen by Games4Change that captures the voices of the people in Hawai'i who experi-enced the real and imminent threat of nuclear weapons through a ballistic missile notification. Mission: ISS: Quest is an Emmy-nominated simulation game where participants journey to the International Space Station to experience what it is like to be an astronaut. Real-life NASA astronauts lead a tour through the ISS by using informative videos and images.

More than likely, these non-game solutions will drive mixed reality (MR or xR) forward including wearable consumer glasses in the Augmented Reality (AR) space. Fortunately, all of these techs are ripe for innovation in gaming as well.

And projects like Henry or The People's House, narrated by former President Barack Obama, have already won Emmy's and BAFTAs for their exceptional VR experiences.

An ever changing landscape — and opportunity

2015-2020 saw the true launch of consumer Virtual Reality (VR) in affordable, comfortable packages with a myriad of content options. At the impetus of innovators such as Palmer Luckey and Brendan Iribe at Oculus and work done at Valve Software in partnership with HTC, the first units shipped in the 1000s to eager early adopters. Initially clunky cabled-PC accessories or mobile phone shells, the true glimpse of 60+ years of research was visible. As the calendar rolled over into the 2020's, the success of Oculus Quest (now Meta Quest) with developers able to build and sell software for profits ensured VR had a place particularly in gaming, entertainment consumption and fitness. However, promises of the "metaverse" remain in the future, and clarity on technology (AR/VR/xR/MR) is anything but clear, and true "killer" applications are few. VR is still a niche platform. Yet, with Meta continuing to invest billions of dollars each year, Sony supporting VR on its consoles, Apple participating with a device that will unlock "spatial computing" focused on productivity, and publishers and developers creating more and more content, this frontier of technology and interac-tion paradigms is a fast paced and fun space in which to work.

How will you drive VR forward?

the bare bones of the concept, teasing the very basics of the gameplay.

This kind of text is useful for early design communication, but very quickly, you'll need to get into specifics. When you do, be precise and clear. Often it is useful to write in lists or bullet points rather than full paragraphs. Figure 14.6 shows a partial interface mock-up for the Alphaville game, which might be accompanied in your document by this bulleted list of features.

- **Time Remaining**: Displays the time left in the game.
- **Letter Value**: Shows the values of the letters by color.
- **You Are**: Lists the player's current letter, point value, and current score.
- **Map**: Clicking on this button brings up the Map.

- **Activities**: This section has the controls that allow a player to make a word, join to the left, join to the right, and separate from joined letters.
- **Navigation**: Buttons for moving the player's letter.
- **Message**: If the user types in letters on the keyboard, they will appear in the Message area. On hitting Enter, the Message will appear for the rest of the players in the room to see.

Always keep in mind that you are not creating the design document for its own sake—your objective is communication, so do whatever it takes to accomplish that goal. The text does not need to be lengthy or eloquent to get the job done.

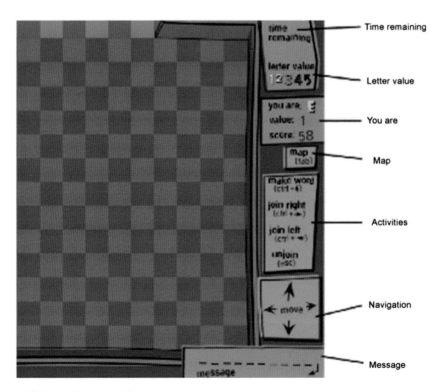

Figure 14.6   Alphaville interface

FORMATS FOR DESIGN DOCUMENTS

When design documents were first introduced, they helped teams organize their ideas because now all of the information was in one place. Also, by writing the document, the game designer had to get into detail with her designs. The act of writing forced the designer to think though all of the elements of the game. Unfortunately, design documents were also long, tedious, and mostly text based. So inevitably, many of the team members did not read them or read them thoroughly. Also, as the game elements changed and evolved over the course of production, it became difficult to keep the design document current. Some designers still use stand-alone design documents, but as online collaboration tools have become available, most designers have moved to more collaborative tools such as a wiki or Google Doc.

Design wikis are an evolution of the design document that solves some of the problems of a single document. A wiki allows for multiple authors to easily work on different sections. It is easier to access the most current version of the design, because it is always available online. It can be configured modularly, in small chunks of information, making it much easier to read and for team members to find the aspect of the design they are interested in. A wiki is decentralized, meaning that all of the team members can easily contribute, and since wikis offer tracking features, it is easy to see who made changes and when. By design, however, wikis lack central management features, so if many people are working on them, their organization can become sprawling and difficult to understand very quickly. One simple-to-use wiki tool is Notion.so, which allows for collaborative and very simple-to-use workspace creation that is great for a shared design process.

For small teams, collaborative tools like Google Docs can serve some of the same purposes as a wiki and/or design document with less overhead. Teams can group edit documents, spreadsheets, and presentations and save in shared folders. Like a wiki, this solution allows for collaborative work on the design in small chunks.

Whether you use a wiki or a stand-alone design document, the goals are the same: to communicate the overall concept of the game, the gameplay mechanics, interfaces, controls, characters, story, levels, etc. In short, everything the team needs to know about the design of the game. This design will change as the team works, so don't think of it as something that is set in stone. As the feature teams review their working builds, they may find ways to simplify and merge features, or the artist may streamline the flow of the UI. These are great outcomes of a team that is working well together. Team communication is the overall goal of whatever methods you use to describe your design.

CONTENTS

The game industry has no standard organization for documenting designs. It would be nice if there were a set formula or style to follow, like the standards for screenplays or architectural blueprints, but this simply does not exist. Everyone does agree that a good design document needs to contain all the details required to create a game; however, what those details are will be affected by the specifics of the game itself.

In general, the contents of a design document can be broken up into the following areas:

- Overview and vision statement
- Audience, platform, and marketing
- Gameplay

- Characters (if applicable)
- Story (if applicable)
- World (if applicable)
- Media list

The design document can also include technical details, or these can be articulated in a separate technical design document. The technical design document or the technical sections of the design document are generally prepared by the technical director or lead engineer.

Exercise 14.3: Research Collaboration Tools

To get a feeling for the collaboration tools that you might use for your game documentation, research some of the examples above. What are their strengths and weaknesses? Talk with your team about their preferences. Decide on a tool for your team to use together.

When you approach the writing of a design document, it is easy to get distracted by the scope of the document and forget the ultimate goal: to communicate your game design to the production team, the publisher, the marketing team, and anyone else with a vested interest in the game. This is one reason I advise you not to write your design documentation until you have built and playtested a working prototype of your idea. Having this type of concrete experience with your proposed gameplay can make all the difference in your ability to articulate that gameplay in what you write about your game.

You should also keep in mind that your design document is a living document. You will likely have to make a dozen passes on each feature or section during the development process. In fact, if you use the visualization techniques described above, your goal would be to have team members mark these up with changes as new ideas arise. Images like these make great conversation

starters, and an excellent design meeting might be entirely focused on marking up a diagram or a flowchart that you've just made. So don't be too concerned with the sections listed below—be concerned with visualization and communication and adopt these sections only if they are useful to you.

Also, try to organize your document modularly so that it will be easier to update and manage as the information accumulates. This will make it easier for each group to find and update the sections that affect their work. Using a wiki to create your design document will naturally enforce this idea of modularity. You will want to create separate pages for the various areas or features and subpages for areas that require deeper descriptions, images, charts, or other materials.

The following outline is an example of how you might organize your design document. It is overly detailed in order to cover many possible types of information that you might need to include. I have noted under each section the types of information it should contain. Keep in mind that my goal here is not to give you a standard format that will work for every game, but rather to provide you with ideas for the types of sections you might want to include. Your game and its design should dictate the format you use for your own document, not this outline, and I don't recommend creating a document containing all of these sections or levels of detail.

1. **Design History**

   A design document is a continuously changing reference tool. Most of your teammates won't have time to read the whole document over and over again every time that a new version is released, so it is good to alert them to any significant modifications or updates that you have made. As you can see, each version will have its own section where you list the major changes made in that iteration. If you use a wiki, this section will be replaced by the editing history feature of the software. This makes it simple and effortless to track changes to the document and to backtrack changes if it becomes necessary. For example, the following version list shows how the document is evolving as team members add and edit content:

1.1   Version 1.0—Concept and top-level game play

1.2   Version 2.0 Added platform info and control chart

    1.2.1   Version 2.1—Updated control chart to include PS4 controls

    1.2.2   Version 2.2—Updated platforms to include Nintendo Switch

1.3   Version 3.0—Levels 1-5 added

Exercise 14.4: Loglines

As described on page 203, I give my students a fill-in-the-blank format to generate their loglines when they are first starting out. As they develop their ideas more clearly, they move away from this format, but it's a good starting point. Try filling in these blanks for your game concept now:

(Project name) is a (genre of play) where you play as (my protagonist — name or description) who must (problem to solve) while also dealing with (challenge). The game is set in a (tone, world) and deals with (theme). Over the course of the game, players will feel (experience goal).

2. Vision Statement

This is where you state your vision for the game. It is typically about 500 words long. Try to capture the essence of your game and convey this to the reader in as compelling and accurate a way as possible.

2.1   Game logline

In a couple of sentences, describe your game.

2.2   Gameplay synopsis

Describe how your game plays and what the user experiences. Try to

keep it concise—no more than a couple of pages. You might want to reference some or all of the following topics:

- *Uniqueness*: What makes your game unique?
- *Mechanics*: How does the game function? What is the core play mechanic?
- *Pillars and experience goals*: Be sure to include your design pillars and experience goals in your top level synopsis!
- *Setting*: What is the setting for your game: the Wild West, the moon, medieval times?
- *Look and feel*: Give a summary of the look and feel of the game.

3. Audience, Platform, and Marketing

3.1   Target audience

Who will buy your game? Describe the demographic you are targeting, including age, gender, and geographic locations.

3.2   Platform

What platform or platforms will your game run on? Why did you choose these platforms?

3.3   System requirements

System requirements might limit your audience, especially on the PC or mobile devices where the hardware varies widely. Describe what is required to play the game and why those choices were made.

3.4   Top performers

List other top-selling games in the same market. Provide sales figures, release dates, and information on sequels and platforms, as well as brief descriptions of each title.

3.5 Feature comparison

Compare your game to the competition. Why would a consumer purchase your game over the others?

3.6 Sales expectations

Provide an estimate of sales over the first year broken down by quarter. How many units will be sold globally, as well as within key markets, like the United States, England, Japan, etc.?

4. Legal Analysis

Describe all legal and financial obligations regarding copyrights, trademarks, contracts, and licensing agreements.

5. Gameplay

5.1 Overview

This is where you describe the core gameplay. This should tie directly into your physical or software prototype. Use your prototype as the model, and give an overview of how it functions.

5.2 Gameplay description

Provide a detailed description of how the game functions.

5.3 Controls

Map out the game procedures and controls. Use visualizations like control tables and flowcharts, along with descriptions.

5.3.1 Interfaces

Create wireframes, as described on page 472, for every interface the artists will need to create. Each wireframe should include a description of how each interface feature functions. Make sure you detail out the various states for each interface.

5.3.2 Rules

If you have created a prototype, describing the rules of your game will be much easier. You will need

to define all the game objects, concepts, their behaviors, and how they relate to one another in this section.

5.3.3 Scoring/winning conditions

Describe the scoring system and win conditions. These might be different for single-player versus multiplayer or if you have several modes of competition.

5.4 Modes and other features

If your game has different modes of play, such as single- and multiplayer modes, or other features that will affect the implementation of the gameplay, you will need to describe them here.

5.5 Levels

The designs for each level should be laid out here. The more detailed, the better.

5.6 Flowchart

Create a flowchart showing all the areas and screens that will need to be created.

5.7 Editor

If your game will require the creation of a proprietary level editor, describe the necessary features of the editor and any details on its functionality.

5.7.1 Features

5.7.2 Details

6. Game Characters

6.1 Character design

This is where you describe any game characters and their attributes.

6.2 Types

6.2.1 PCs (player characters)

6.2.2 NPCs (nonplayer characters): If your game involves character types, you will need to treat each one as an object, defining its properties and functionality.

6.2.2.1   Behavior

6.2.2.2   AI

7. Story

7.1   Synopsis

If your game includes a story, summarize it here. Keep it down to one or two paragraphs.

7.2   Complete story

This is your chance to outline the entire story. Do so in a way that mirrors the gameplay. Do not just tell your story, but structure it so that it unfolds as the game progresses.

7.3   Backstory

Describe any important elements of your story that do not tie directly into the gameplay. Much of this might not actually make it into the game, but it might be good to have it for reference.

7.4   Narrative devices

Describe the various ways in which you plan to reveal the story. What are the devices you plan to use to tell the story?

7.5   Subplots

Because games are not linear like books and movies, there might be numerous smaller stories interwoven into the main story. Describe each of these subplots and explain how they tie into the gameplay and the master plot.

7.5.1   Subplot #1

7.5.2   Subplot #2

8. The Game World

If your game involves the creation of a world, you may want to go into detail on all aspects of that world.

8.1   Overview

8.2   Key locations

8.3   Travel

8.4   Mapping

8.5   Scale

8.6   Physical objects

8.7   Weather conditions

8.8   Day and night

8.9   Time

8.10   Physics

8.11   Society/culture

9. Media List

9.1   Art direction

9.2   Interface assets

9.3   Environments

9.4   Characters

9.5   Animation

9.6   Music and sound effects

List all of the media that will need to be produced. The specifics of your game will dictate what categories you need to include. Be detailed with this list, and create a file naming convention up front. This can avoid a lot of confusion later on.

10. Technical Spec

As mentioned, the technical spec is not always included in the design document. Often it is a separate document prepared in conjunction with the design document. This spec is prepared by the technical lead on the project.

10.1   Technical analysis

10.1.1   New technology

Is there any new technology that you plan on developing for this game? If so, describe it in detail.

10.1.2   Major software development tasks

Do you need to do a lot of software development for the game to work? Or are you simply going to license someone else's engine or use a preexisting engine that you have created?

10.1.3 Risks

What are the risks inherent in your strategy?

10.1.4 Alternatives

Are there any alternatives that can lower the risks and the cost?

10.1.5 Estimated resources required

Describe the resources you would need to develop the new technology and software needed for the game.

10.2 Development platform and tools

Describe the development platform, as well as any software tools and hardware that are required to produce the game.

10.2.1 Software

10.2.2 Hardware

10.3 Delivery

How do you plan to deliver this game? Over the Internet? Via an app service? At a brick-and-mortar location? What is required to accomplish this?

10.3.1 Required hardware and software

10.3.2 Required materials

10.4 Game engine

10.4.1 Technical specs

What are the specs of your game engine?

10.4.2 Design

Describe the design of your game engine.

10.4.2.1 Features

10.4.2.2 Details

10.4.3 Special considerations

If your game includes special technical considerations what are they?

10.4.3.1 Features

10.4.3.2 Details

10.5 Interface technical specs

This is where you describe how your interface is designed from a technical perspective. What tools do you plan to use, and how will it function?

10.5.1 Features

10.5.2 Details

10.6 Controls' technical specs

This is where you describe how your controls work from a technical perspective. Are you planning on supporting any unusual input devices that would require specialized programming?

10.6.1 Features

10.6.2 Details

10.7 Lighting models

Lighting can be a substantial part of a game. Describe how it works and the features that you require.

10.7.1 Modes

10.7.1.1 Features

10.7.1.2 Details

10.7.2 Models

10.7.3 Light sources

10.8 Rendering system

10.8.1 Technical specs

10.8.2 2D/3D rendering

10.8.3 Camera

10.8.3.1 Operation

10.8.3.2 Features

10.8.3.3 Details

10.9 Internet/network spec

If your game requires an Internet connection, you should make that clear in the specs.

10.10   System parameters

I won't go into detail on all the possible system parameters, but suffice to say that the design document should list them all and describe their functionality.

10.10.1   Max players

10.10.2   Servers

10.10.3   Customization

10.10.4   Connectivity

10.10.5   Web sites

10.10.6   Persistence

10.10.7   Saving games

10.10.8   Loading games

10.11   Other

This section is for any other technical specifications that should be included, such as help menus, manuals, setup and installation routines, etc.

10.11.1   Help

10.11.2   Manual

10.11.3   Setup

I want to emphasize again that the previous outline is merely a list of suggested topics that might need to be addressed to communicate your design. Every game will have its own specific needs, and the organization of your design document and process should reflect these needs.

Exercise 14.5: Table of Contents

Outline the table of contents for your original design document. Consider all the features of your prototype, flowchart, and wireframes when you are deciding how to describe your game. Draw from the example documents you downloaded from the web and the generic template found in this chapter.

DESIGN MACROS

The list of potential types of information I've just presented you with is clearly too much for most games and for most teams to deal with in a realistic way. However, at each point in the development, certain types of information will be necessary. You'll want to focus on creating documentation that is just enough. You need to discus and listen carefully to your team members to find out exactly what they need from you and when.

One way to organize a useful high-level view of the game is by using what developer Naughty Dog calls a "design macro."[2] This is a spreadsheet of all the story beats, character goals, and gameplay moments that they plan to create. This information is worked out in meetings with the team and is synopsized in the macro. Because it is so concise, it can be easily moved around in the spreadsheet as the design changes and progresses. It is more compact and abstract than a design document and gives an excellent overview of the intended game experience. Of course, you may have more detailed information and visualizations for each section of the game that are not in the macro, but the beauty of the single spreadsheet is that it is an easy reference point for the entire team to think about the larger vision of the project.

In Figure 14.7, you can see the design macro for Uncharted 2, which includes descriptions of each of the levels, the "look," time of day/mood, NPC allies, enemies, gameplay, the "flow" of the level, mechanics that will be used, the gameplay theme, weapons, vehicles, cinematic sequences, vistas and more. This document is the only deliverable for Naughty Dog's preproduction phase, because by completing it fully, they know they will have thought through many of the issues they will face during production. Game designer Richard Lemarchand discusses the use of Game

UNCHARTED 2 Macro Design

LEVELS	LOOK DESCRIPTION	TIME OF DAY/ MOOD	ALLY-NPC	ENEMY MODELS	MACRO GAMEPLAY	MACRO FLOW	Free Climb/Dyno	Wall Jump	Free Ropes	Pendulum	Monkey Bars	Monkey Swing	Balance Beams	Carry Objects Heavy	Carry Objects Light	Traversal Gunplay v.1	Forced Melee	Puzzle	Stealth	Swim	Moving Objects	Push Objects	Binoculars	GAMEPLAY THEME (FOCUS)	Trap-gun	Pistol-semi-a	Pistol-semi-b
Warzone																											
war-1-market	Nepalese city broken & burning	High Noon - War-torn & smokey		Laz Army HOT Freedom Fighters	Explore Traverse Minor Gunfights	Basic Gunplay Traversal Gunplay	X	X			X	X	X			X			X				X	Basic Gunplay Traversal Gunplay	X		
war-2-streets	Nepalese city broken & burning	High Noon - War-torn & smokey	Chloe-2	Laz Army HOT Freedom Fighters	Explore Traverse Minor Gunfights	Basic Gunplay Traversal Gunplay	X	X			X	X	X			X			X				X	Basic Gunplay Traversal Gunplay	X		
war-3-inside war-4-highrise	Nepalese city broken & burning	High Noon - War-torn & smokey	Chloe-2	Laz Army HOT Freedom Fighters	Explore Traverse Minor Gunfights	Basic Gunplay Traversal Gunplay Get to higher ground (hotel)	X	X			X	X	X			X			X				X	Basic Gunplay Traversal Gunplay	X		
city	Nepalese city broken & burning	High Noon - War-torn & smokey	Chloe-2	Laz Army HOT Freedom Fighters	Explore Traverse Minor Gunfights	Skirt close to Laz Army	X	X			X	X	X			X			X				X	Basic Gunplay Traversal Gunplay	X		
city-2	New area unlocked of City	High Noon - War-torn & smokey	Chloe Elena-1 Cameraman	Laz Army HOT Freedom Fighters	Traverse Major Fight	Basic Gunplay Traversal Gunplay	X	X					X			X		X					X	Basic Gunplay Traversal Gunplay	X		
temple	Temple complex built in the middle of the city	mysterious	Chloe Elena-1 Cameraman	Laz Army HOT Freedom Fighters Dead Expeditions	Explore Problem Solve Escape	Portable Objects use for fending off bugs w/fire Water Currents	X	X		X	X	X	X	X	X			X		X	X	X		Portable Objects use for fending off bugs w/fire Water Currents	X		
city third pass	City + Train Yard	high tension	Elena-1	Laz Army HOT Freedom Fighters	Escape/Fight Chase			X				X		X												X		
Train																											
train intro valley	Transition from warzone city to valley						X						X		X	X									X		
valley loop	Lower valley region. Chinese rice fields, bamboo forests, and distant mountains						X						X			X									X		
valley lake straight	Lake w/vista to the horizon						X						X			X									X		

14.7 Uncharted 2: Macro design

Macros at lenth in his book "A Playful Production Process," which also links to some macro templates you may want to use.

Exercise 14.6: Create a Game Macro

Your game may be much simpler than Uncharted 2, but you can still create a game macro for all of your elements. Use a spreadsheet tool like Excel or Google sheets to define your levels, description, any characters, gameplay, mechanics, features, and theme or "feel" by section of the game. You may want to use the game design macro template from Richard Lemarchand's "A Playful Production Process" as a starting point: https://www.playfulproductionprocess.com/templates/

CONCLUSION

In this chapter, you have learned techniques for communicating and documenting your original designs. You have created flowcharts and wireframes and other types of visualization for your game. You have worked with your team, if you have one, to describe both the technical and creative tasks that will need to be accomplished to make your game a reality. You have thought about both the micro level of your design and the macro level.

Design documentation can be a useful communication tool or a millstone around the designer's neck. Always remember that the purpose of your documentation is communication and articulation. A designer huddled in a cubicle writing in isolation for weeks on end will produce a document that is far less valuable than a designer who engages the team, includes them in the process, and works with them to build out each section as needed.

By working with the team, a designer will not only wind up with better design solutions but will also help focus the team on the project at hand. This is how living design documents are created, and when you have a living document, in which everyone is an acting coauthor, it becomes a force in and of itself, which serves to unite the team and give them a common platform from which to understand the game as it evolves.

Designer Perspective: Anna Anthropy

Photo credit: Mel Leverich

Independent Game Designer

Anna Anthropy is a game designer and educator whose games include Mighty Jill Off (2009), REDDER (2010), Lesbian Spider-Queens of Mars (2012), Triad (2013), Queers in Love at the End of the World (2013), and Princess with a Cursed Sword (2020). She teaches game design in Chicago.

How did you become a game designer?

I started by cutting out paper dolls and drawing little videogame levels for them to traverse. And then I found ZZT, a shareware game-making tool. And then I gave up on game making when I went to college, because it was really unclear how to do that for a living. Fortunately, I dropped out of college around the same time a dutch professor named Mark Overmars released a dinky little program called GameMaker.

What games have inspired you as a designer?

My friend, game design Amber Autumn Faebrooke, made a tweet a little while ago that really put into focus the kind of work I want to do in the role-playing space. Because I'm scared to search Twitter in 2023, I'm going to paraphrase (and probably misquote) her: "Remember looking out a car window as a kid and pretending Mario was running alongside you? That's what role-playing games are." I (mis?)remember this tweet every time I think about narrative play.

What is the most exciting development in the recent industry?

Itch.io.
It's an unspeakable den of iniquity, thank goodness, and it's a huge deal to have a marketplace for games where it doesn't cost money to be listed. Even Steam's $100 fee prices out little hobbyist weirdos and truly experimental works, and that's where the most interesting stuff is coming from.

On design process:

"Polish" and "balance" and "flow" are deeply uninteresting to me. What's been much more helpful to my craft has been cultivating a process of making and publishing lots of little things, quickly. Does a game require professional art? Does it need to be playtested? The answer isn't always yes.

On prototyping:

I don't see much of a distinction between a prototype and a finished game, if you're doing it right and not wasting your time on the parts that aren't important. For Triad—a puzzle game about fitting three people in a bed together—I cut out paper shapes and used them to figure out what the puzzle was going to be before I started making the digital game. The puzzle was the least important part; Triad is really an interpersonal drama disguised as a puzzle game.

On a difficult design problem:

In Triad, players sometimes don't realize that in addition to dragging the characters around with your mouse, you can also click on them to rotate them. So we decided that if you can't figure it out on your own—which means doing it more than once, during your first attempt—then a cat tells you during an interstitial scene. Well, the cat was just sitting there (she's part of the puzzle) and she had nothing to do.

I'm most proud of ...

My cat. She's come so far. In terms of my work: I wrote a 29-word horror game in 2023 (The Maw) that involves feeling around inside your refrigerator and I think that's one of the most perfect things I've ever designed.

Advice to designers:

Unionize. Refuse to accept crunch. Seize the means of production. Start a cooperative. Build something better than the games industry. No one should have to die for a video game.

DESIGNER PERSPECTIVE: ROB DAVIAU

President, IronWall Games and Co-owner, Restoration Games

Rob Daviau is a prolific designer of board and card games. Prior to founding IronWall Games, he was a creative director and principal game designer at Hasbro Games. His credits include Risk 2210 AD, Pandemic Legacy (three seasons), Return to Dark Tower, the Unmatched game line, Cthulhu: Death May Die, Thunder Road: Vendetta, and Risk Legacy.

On getting into the game industry:

I played games all my life and spent a lot of time fading in and out of role-playing campaigns. After five years as an advertising copywriter, I was looking for a change. I applied as a copywriter for Parker Brothers (mostly writing rules and box bottom copy) at the exact time they were looking for a game designer with a writing background. I ended up getting the designer job, and the bulk of my work initially involved copy-heavy projects. In my interview, I named two of my favorite games from childhood. It turned out that the guy interviewing me had designed both of those games.

On favorite games:

I go through all sorts of favorite games during the months and years, but it really depends on who I'm playing with and what experience I'm looking for. There are big differences between picking up an digital game to play solo versus playing a game with my kids versus playing a game with my hardcore gamer friends. I just like the act of playing. Mostly I enjoy games with a strong sense of narrative.

On inspiration:

I keep a mental list of the cool mechanic, the cool piece, the new storage tray, or different artwork in the games I play. I think of it as creating a palette to paint my own pictures. I am also inspired by the narrative potential of a. I want my games to tell a story or evoke a mood or create a moment of narrative tension. I also find inspiration from other art forms—I've been inspired by TV shows, the rules of baseball, art exhibits, books I've read, etc. I have also learned that my brain gets inspiration by talking with other people. It's why I co-design a lot of games.

On the design process:

I usually think of the feel first and then put in mechanics to evoke that feel. Do I want the game to be tense? Exciting? Dramatic? Full of twists and turns? Relentless? Do I want the players to be casually involved or intensely focused? From there I start creating a game that tries to fit the mood I am going for. This is probably backward from how a lot of people design games.

On prototypes:

Because my games live in the physical world and are made of plastics, paper, and (sometimes) electronics, it is necessary to get to a physical representation very early. My line of work has a lot of questions about board size and plastic design and piece storage issues that are unique to the board and card game world. When I was at Hasbro, I had access to a full model shop and engineering lab that could pretty much create anything I can dream up. I do spend more time these days with digital prototypes, such as Tabletop Simulator. This is a function of a remote team working on it, the pandemic, and evolving technology.

On designing Risk Legacy:

This was a crazy idea but it just stuck with me. I realized that other forms of episodic storytelling have an overall plot advancing through a season rather than a series of isolated episodes. Yet boardgames, which have all sorts of narrative between the players, constantly reset themselves to the initial state every time. I set out to design a game that allowed players to infuse the game with story, where some of the actions of one game carried on to the next.

Advice to designers:

It's very easy to hide behind a gimmick—graphics, sound, a license, nice video segments—but game players are smart. They'll figure out if it's all smoke and mirrors with no real game. What makes your game different? If it's just this game mashed with that other game then it's just a rehash. When starting a game, remember to question everything. Even if all those crazy ideas eventually are rejected or don't pan out, at least you started someplace new.

FURTHER READING

Colby, Richard and Colby, Rebekah Shultz. Game Design Documentation: Four Perspectives from Independent Game Studios. Sigdoc.acm.org, 2019. https://sigdoc.acm.org/game-design-documentation-four-perspectives-from-independent-game-studios/

Freeman, Tzvi. Creating a Great Design Document, Gamasutra.com, September 12, 1997. http://www.gamasutra.com/view/feature/131632/creating_a_great_design_document.php

Ryan, Tim. The Anatomy of a Design Document: Documentation Guidelines for the Game Concept and Proposal, Gamasutra.com, October 19, 1999. http://www.gamasutra.com/view/feature/131791/the_anatomy_of_a_design_document_.php

Sloper, Tom. Sample Outline for a Game Design, Sloperama.com, August 11, 2007. http://www.sloperama.com/advice/specs.htm

END NOTES

1. Librande, Stone. One-Page Designs. GDC Vault, 2010.

2. McInnis, Shaun. Naughty Dog designer maps out Uncharted 2 development. Gamespot.com, February 18, 2010.

Chapter 15
Understanding the New Game Industry

Unless you are a producer or an executive, you might never even see the contract or terms under which your game is produced. You might not feel the need to understand the royalty structure of the agreement or the rights assignments for the characters you create. You might want to ignore all the lengthy contract language and business mumbo jumbo and stay focused on what you love—designing games. But if you are going to be a smart, effective, and successful game designer, you might want to think again before dismissing the business side of things so quickly.

Understanding the rapidly changing structure of the game industry—the players, the market, and how business deals are structured between publishers and developers—is knowledge that can make you a better designer, especially in a commercial sense. This chapter provides an overview of the game industry, how it is changing, and how deals are structured to produce and publish games. It is not a comprehensive description, and in fact the industry is evolving so rapidly that it is impossible to give a full view, but it will give you enough understanding to participate intelligently in the deal-making process for your game if you are invited to do so. Even if you are not part of that process, this information will help you to understand the concerns of, and communicate more clearly with, the executives and marketing people who are working on your game.

My advice to all game designers is to embrace business knowledge in the same way you would embrace technical knowledge. You might not specialize in either, but understanding how the business aspects of the industry work, and how they affect your designs, will help you to be a more effective creative person and a more valuable resource on the team.

DOI: 10.1201/9781003460268-18

THE SIZE OF THE GAME INDUSTRY

The global game industry, including PC games, mobile games on smartphones and tablets, and console games, is expected to grow to $321.1 billion or more by 2026. This number is dominated by social/casual gaming on mobile devices as can be seen in Figure 15.1. The main trends, which have been in place for a number of years, are the movement toward digital revenue away from sales of physical products and the movement away from PC and console games to an industry primarily dominated by mobile games. Products delivered digitally make up 90% of all games sales in 2023, with the remaining 10% made up of all sales of physical media. These numbers make the changing face of the industry fairly clear: the industry is growing, but the growth areas are in mobile platforms and digital delivery rather than traditional retail software.[1]

Total U.S. consumer spending on video game content in 2022 was 47.5 billion. If you include hardware and accessory sales, total U.S. spending on video games in was 56.6 billion.[2] The game industry has remained strong and has grown steadily over the past decade, even as the industry has undergone major shifts in its distribution platforms and core markets.

Digital games have become a significant form of entertainment since their introduction in the 1970s. Today, 67% of U.S. households own a device that is used to play videogames. And 65% of all U.S. households are home to at least one person who plays games three or more hours a week. The split between men and women players is closing as well, with women comprising 46% of gamers. Women 18 or older make up a significantly greater portion of the game-playing population (31%) than boys under age 18 (18%), mostly due to the popularity of social and mobile games. As several generations of players have grown up with digital games, most have continued to play as they grow older, and the average age of game players is 32. Also, 45% of game players are over the age of 36, and 27% are between 18 and 35. Gaming is an activity that has become social and lifelong: 41% of gamers play with friends, 21% with family members, 17% with their spouse or significant other, and 18% with their parents.[3]

As Entertainment Software Association President and CEO Stanley Pierre-Louis, expressed during the 2020 COVID shutdowns, many people across the demographic spectrum turned to gaming for "the comfort and joy that video games provide as a source of solace, connection, community and stability." And Michael D. Gallagher, former ESA president, has said that "No other sector has experienced the same explosive growth as the computer and video game industry. Our creative publishers and talented workforce continue to accelerate advancement and pioneer new products that push boundaries and unlock entertainment experiences. The innovations in turn drive enhanced player connectivity, fuel demand for products, and encourage the progression of an expanding and diversified consumer base."[4] All of these statements point to the fact that digital games have made the transition from being a pastime to becoming an integral part of the entertainment industry.

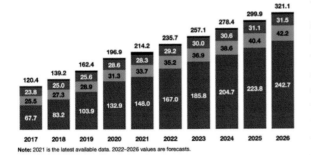

Total global video games revenue, by segment (US$bn)
■ Social/casual gaming ■ PC games ■ Console games
■ Integrated video games advertising

Note: 2021 is the latest available data. 2022-2026 values are forecasts.

15.1 Global game sales projected

Source: PwC's Global Entertainment & Media Outlook 2022-2026, Omdia.

This phenomenon is worldwide, with Asia-Pacific making up 47% of the global market to North America's 27%. Europe, the Middle East, and Africa combined are 22%, and Latin America is 4%. In all of these sectors, the major growth is in mobile and tablet gaming, which makes up 70% of the global market as of 2022 and is projected to be 75% of the market by 2026.[5]

PLATFORMS FOR DISTRIBUTION

One way to understand the changes happening in the game industry today is to look at the rapidly expanding number of platforms on which games are distributed. Consoles, which have historically dominated the sales of the industry, are still a force, but they are being rapidly challenged by mobile platforms such as phones and tablets. In 2023, two of the top ten market leaders in the video game industry were Google and Apple, neither of which is traditionally thought of as a video game company, but they have major control over the distribution channels for mobile games.[6] Also, as the latest generations of consoles have been released, their focus has extending beyond the core game market to streaming delivery of movies, television, and music. For example, both PlayStation 5 and Xbox Series X have support for up to 8K resolution and frame rates of up to 120 fps, making them incredible media players for games and other forms of entertainment.

As can be seen in Figure 15.2, 64% of players use mobile devices for gaming. Note that in this figure, many gamers use multiple devices to play games, which is why the numbers add up to more than 100 percent. Console play and PC play are still strong in terms of device usage, even though their share of the market revenues are shrinking.

advances meaning new platform releases every three to five years. The console machines of today have astounding processing power and graphics capabilities. This enables designers to create dramatic experiences with production

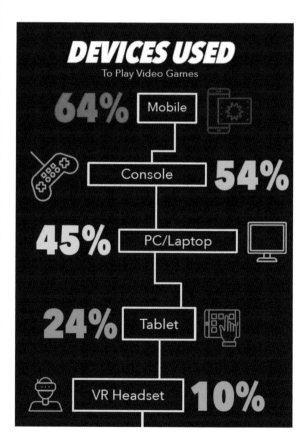

Consoles

Within the console market, there are multiple competitors. Historically, the console market has always been dominated by one or two players, with cutthroat competition and technological

15.2   What devices to players use to play video games?

Source: ESA Essential Facts about the U.S. Vodeo Game Industry 2023

values rivaling television and film. Here's a breakdown of today's top console platforms.

Sony PlayStation 5

As of April 2023, 38.5 million PlayStation 5 consoles had been sold worldwide, following its best year on the market. The PS5's GPU is roughly eight times more powerful than its predecessor, the PlayStation 4, and while it isn't as powerful as the Xbox Series X, it is a significant upgrade over the popular PlayStation 4.[7] The PlayStation 5 includes backwards compatibility for most PS4 games and its PlayStation Plus service includes access to an extensive game catalog at the higher levels of the service.

Microsoft Xbox Series X

As of June 2023, an estimated 21 million Xbox Series X consoles had been sold worldwide.[8] The Series X has a more powerful GPU than Sony's PlayStation 5, making it the most powerful game console currently available. It also includes backwards compatibility back to the original Xbox. With its Xbox Game Pass service, players can access an impressive catalog of games across console, PC, and mobile devices.

Nintendo Switch

As of June of 2023, Nintendo's Switch has sold 129.53 million consoles since its launch in March of 2017. This makes it the third-best-selling video game console of all time, behind only the Nintendo DS and the PlayStation 2. The innovative Switch is a handheld-console hybrid, which offers a completely different play experience from either of the other two major consoles. Players can take the console with them anywhere for mobile play or use it like a traditional console hooked up to a television. It was a fairly big gamble, combining the best of the company's 3DS handheld with the learnings

from the Wii U, but the gamble has paid off in a big way.[9]

Computer (PC and Mac)

The computer game market is segmented between the PC and Mac operating systems and among standalone games, online games, and social network games. For standalone games, there are still a few traditional brick-and-mortar sales points, but these are quickly being replaced by digital distribution methods such as Steam and the Epic Games Store, which offer games from small independent developers as well as larger companies. In the online game space, free-to-play dominates the market, with 24.5 billion in revenues in 2023. The incredible success of Epic's cross-platform game Fortnite is a model for many games trying to enter this area.

Mobile (Phone and Tablet)

The mobile market is also segmented, primarily by the iOS and Android operating systems. Each system has its own content store and each has varying specs as to screen size and computing power. Most developers will focus on one platform to try to make a splash with a game before porting to the wider field. As of Q3 2022, Google Play was the largest app store, with 3.55 million apps. The Apple App Store was the second largest store with 1.6 million available apps for iOS.

As with the PC market, free-to-play games dominate the mobile market, reaching 83.64 billion in the U.S. in 2023. MOBA (Multiplayer Online Battle Arena) game Honor of Kings is the highest grossing mobile game of all time as of 2023.[10]

Virtual Reality and Alternate Reality

One of the emerging areas for games today is in virtual and alternate reality experiences. These experiences, which use head-mounted displays to create immersive environments, are growing in popularity even though the market has had its ups and downs. Laird Malamed of Meta talks about the promise of this field in his sidebar on page 478. Sony's PlayStation VR and VR2 has had interesting uptake and has produced some notable VR games, including Star Trek: Bridge Crew. Alternate reality headsets, such as Microsoft's Hololens and Apple's Vision Pro, do not block the player's view, but rather integrate graphics and interactivity into the real world around the player. One interesting offshoot of these technologies is their use in location-based entertainment. VR pop-up experiences, such as Dreamscape, combine fully immersive gameplay with tangible environments and props for a new kind of themed experience.

Immersive Entertainment

Beyond the idea of Beyond traditional gaming platforms, we are also seeing an interest in real world immersive experiences that combine aspects of theater, theme parks, games, art, and more. Place-based experiences like Meow Wolf's House of Eternal Return in Santa Fe, New Mexico allow visitors to freely explore its 70,000 square foot art installation of interconnected rooms and hallways filled with strange and curious artifacts, secret passages, and hidden treasures. Immersive theater experiences like Punchdrunk's Sleep No More, which reimagines

Shakespeare's Macbeth in a film noire aesthetic set in a 1930s hotel in Manhattan. Visitors, wearing white masks follow performers through the floors of the hotel at will, exploring the interconnected stories of the guilt-ridden king and his murderous queen. In an experiment in interactive role-playing, Disney created the Galactic Starcruiser experience, a two-night, immersive experience where guests boarded a "spaceship" for an elaborate Star Wars-themed adventure. Galactic Starcruiser, which, while it was only available for a year and a half, made huge creative strides in the themed entertainment industry, winning multiple awards for its design and direction.

Board Games

Despite the fact that this book deals primarily with designing and prototyping for digital play, there is also a lot of opportunity today in the growing board game industry. This market has been very strong over the past decade, growing with the increased interest in real world social play. Board game cafes, club, and tournaments have begun to appeal to a much wider section of players. Additionally, several online sites for playing board games virtually took off during the COVID pandemic, introducing many players to a much broader range of board game play styles. North America currently dominates the global board games market, accounting for a 28.9% share in 2022 and region is seeing a high demand for Euro-style board games that include social strategy and critical thinking skills. Digital and board game designer Mary Flanagan talks about her prolific work in this are in her profile on page 169.

GENRES OF GAMEPLAY

In addition to platforms, another way of looking at the game industry is in terms of game genres. You have probably noticed by now that I did not emphasize the concept of genre in any of our discussions about design. This is because I believe genres are a mixed blessing to a game designer.

On one hand, genres give designers and publishers a common language for describing styles of play. They form a shorthand for understanding what market a game is intended for, what platforms the game will be best suited to, who should be developing a particular title, etc. On the other hand, genres also tend to restrict the creative process and lead designers toward tried-and-true gameplay solutions. I encourage you to consider genre when thinking about your projects from a business perspective but not to allow it to stifle your imagination during the design process.

That said, genre is a big part of today's game industry, and as a designer, it is important for you to understand the role it plays. The top-selling genres differ between platforms and between market segments. When publishers look at your game, they want to know where it falls in current buying trends of the gaming audience. Without the benefit of genre, this would be a difficult task.

Although I do not want you to inhibit your design process by too great an emphasis on genre, designers can learn something from the publishers' emphasis on creating products for players who enjoy specific types of gameplay. To better understand some popular genres, I have briefly listed their key differentiators.

Action Games

Action games emphasize reaction time and hand-eye coordination. Action games can include titles as disparate as Battlefield 2, Grand Theft Auto V, and Tetris. Action as a genre often overlaps with other genres; for example, Grand Theft Auto V is an action game, but it is also a driving/racing game and an adventure game. Tetris is an action game and a puzzle game. Super Mario Galaxy is an action-adventure game, and Final Fantasy XII is considered a role-playing action game. Action games are, without exception, real-time experiences, with an emphasis on time constraints for performing physical tasks.

Strategy Games

Strategy games focus on tactics and planning as well as the management of units and resources. The themes tend to revolve around conquest, exploration, and trade. Included in this genre are Civilization IV, StarCraft II, and, to some extent, the mobile smash hit Clash of Clans. Originally, most strategy games drew upon classic strategy board games and adopted turn-based systems,

MOST POPULAR GAME GENRES ACROSS ALL PLAYERS

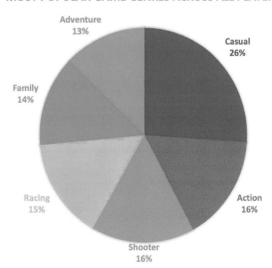

15.3 Most Popular Genres Played Regularly

Source: ESA Essential Facts about the U.S. Video Game Industry 2021.

Mobile Game Design and Zombies, Run!

by Adrian Hon and Matt Wieteska

Adrian Hon is co-founder and CEO at Six to Start, specializing in game-like stories and story-like games for the web, mobile, and real world, the latest being the international bestseller, "Zombies, Run!" Matt Wieteska is the Audio Director for "Zombies, Run!," the writer of the game's "Radio Abel" segments, and a producer on the project. Zombies, Run! has won multiple awards, including Best of Show at SXSW.

Many game designers treat smartphones as essentially identical to traditional gaming handhelds like the Nintendo DS or PS Vita. While popular games like Angry Birds, Canabalt, and Candy Crush do take advantage of new input methods such as the touch screen, the games would usually work just as well on other handheld platforms, or even on PCs or consoles. It just happens that smartphones are much more ubiquitous than gaming handhelds, and the apps are cheaper and easier to get hold of.

However, smartphones are qualitatively different from any other device out there. Let's consider the unique features they hold: constant Internet connectivity, GPS, gyroscopes, accelerometers, voice recognition, front and back HD videocameras, and Bluetooth. Billions of people keep them by their sides every hour of the day—and yet we still make Angry Birds.

The opportunities are boundless. What would a game look like that used both cameras at once? Or a game that used only voice commands? Or a multiplayer co-operative dancing game that used gyroscopes and accelerometers? Or a game tapped into your contacts and calendar and email? It can be a useful exercise to think of games that can only work on smartphones.

What's extraordinary is that technological innovation in smartphones is still continuing; in a few years' time, it's likely we will see haptic touch interfaces, bio-monitoring devices for heartbeat detection, and, of course, more wearable devices such as smart watches and heads-up displays. Games that are uniquely designed for smartphones can incorporate very different kinds of experiences, such as games that:

- Take place throughout the day and night
- Involve vigorous and outdoor physical activity (rather than being played on the sofa)

Zombies, Run! Mobile interface

- Feature new kinds of output, such as audio-only game, vibrations, augmented reality, etc.
- Feature new kinds of control, such as gesture and voice commands.

These experiences often delight new players since they force them to re-learn how to interact with the game and device.

Smartphone games are proving to be disruptive due to the extremely low bar to entry for developers and due to the massive size of the market. It is hard for other platforms like consoles to compete against free games, and it's hard to imagine that consoles will ever reach the same kind of install base or openness as the iTunes App Store or Google Play Store.

As an example, the game Zombies, Run! is a "fitness-adventure game." To play Zombies, Run!, you go running in the real world (or on your treadmill), with your headphones in and the app on your smartphone. We then use high-quality audio to immerse you in a thrilling post-apocalyptic adventure story in which you are the main character. Instead of doing just laps round the park or trying to beat your personal best in the gym, you're escaping the living dead, rescuing civilians, and gathering supplies for the people back at your home base. After each scene from the story, we'll play a track from your running playlist, which lends a cinematic tone to your run, as well as giving you some much-needed energy from your favorite songs.

On a more practical level, the game does everything you'd expect of a fitness tracker: we monitor your pace and your route (if you're using GPS) and give you a breakdown of all the vital statistics you need to track your progress and the improvement in your fitness. In addition, our optional (but highly recommended) random zombie chases will give you the adrenaline you need to push yourself further and further.

The first big step in locking down the design of the game was figuring out how long our missions (individual "episodes" of the story) should be. At first, we'd assumed that each session playing the game would have a fixed length: you choose a mission, head out for your run, and you finish running when the mission finishes. With the different levels of running experience on the team, though, we found it hard to agree on a good length. Adrian's a very keen runner, and was going to bat for longer, more challenging missions, while Matt and Naomi are both at a more novice level and wanted to make sure each mission was achievable by everyone.

Eventually, we came to the conclusion that we shouldn't be mandating any run length in particular; if you stop a mission before it's finished, you should be able to resume it on a subsequent run, and if you keep running after a mission's finished, there should be extra content to keep your experience exciting and entertaining until your run is finished. This philosophy really felt right to us as soon as we started discussing it, and resulted in our unofficial slogan: "We don't care how fast you run, we don't care how far you run, we don't care where you run, we just want you to get out there and run." We think this attitude has made the app more inclusive and more flexible, and has given it a much broader appeal than it might otherwise have had.

Zombies, Run! runner's data

Another memorable moment came when we were implementing the zombie chase mechanic. Alex, our lead developer (and only developer at the time!) was playing around with when and how often the zombie chases should be triggered. At the same time, we were breaking down the audio we'd recorded and inputting it into the game's engine for testing. In a moment of inspiration, Alex suggested that we should "force" zombie chases after certain audio segments, whenever it would be appropriate for the story. This proved to be a fantastic way of tying the story in to the gameplay experience and provides some thrilling moments when you're out running. There's nothing more exhilarating than having one of your favorite characters yell "They're right behind you! Run!" and then hearing the telltale warning noise in your headphones: "Zombies Detected, 50 meters." Pure terror.

Since the game launched, we've received an amazing number of testimonials and thanks from players who've found Zombies, Run! has helped them meet their personal fitness goals. It's always gratifying to hear from people who enjoy what you do, but there are few stories that always stand out. For us, it's the stories of people using Zombies, Run! to help them recover from serious illness or injury. Among others, we've heard from servicemen and women who were injured in the line of duty and are using Zombies, Run! to help with their rehab, people recovering from debilitating illnesses who find the game helps keep them going along the long road to recovery, and those who have made vital lifestyle changes with the help of Zombies, Run! It's hearing those stories that really makes us feel like we're doing something special.

One of the most rewarding aspects of developing an innovative game like Zombies, Run! is seeing how players interact with it in an completely different way to other games. The very act of playing the game makes walking, jogging, and running more exciting and fun, and because it's a smartphone app, it can reach an extremely wide market.

We've been continuously releasing new features and new content for over eleven years, and over that time we've had over 10 million paid and free downloads, with over 250,000 active players, many of whom credit us with helping them lose weight and keep fit where other efforts, like gyms and personal trainers, have failed. We've even had a few people tell us that Zombies, Run! has actually saved their lives. Certainly, Zombies, Run! isn't the right game for everyone—but it is the right game for a lot of people, and there are many more aspects of life and entertainment that could do with innovation.

Finally, it's worth mentioning that smartphones, and particularly Apple's VoiceOver feature, represent one of the biggest advances in accessibility technology for visually impaired people. We've designed Zombies, Run! so that it can be played by the blind and visually impaired because it was the right thing to do, and clearly that would have been much more difficult for other, more visual types of games.

giving players ample time to make decisions; however, the popularity in the 1990s of WarCraft and Command & Conquer changed this, ushering in the subgenre of real-time strategy games. Since then, there have been action/strategy games, which combine physical dexterity with strategic decision-making. Clash of Clans, with its focus on multiplayer base defense, has a simplified strategy design that has made it one of the most popular mobile games in the world.

Role-Playing Games

Role-playing games revolve around creating and growing characters. They tend to include rich storylines that are tied into quests. The paper-based system of Dungeons & Dragons is the grandfather of this genre, which has inspired such digital games as Baldur's Gate, Dungeon Siege, World of Warcraft, and the pioneering NetHack. Role-playing games begin and end with the character. Players typically seek to develop their characters while managing inventory; exploring worlds; and accumulating wealth, status, and experience. As with all genre discussions, there are hybrids. For example, games like Jade Empire and Kingdom Hearts II are typically called "action role-playing games."

Massively multiplayer online role-playing games, or MMORPGs, are a major development in this genre of gameplay that have had a great influence on the business of games. Even though the subscription market for games like World of Warcraft is quickly being replaced by free-to-play models, the most recent expansion to World of Warcraft—Dragonflight—has enjoyed the highest player retention rate of any other WoW expansion. The design for this genre of games requires a deep understanding of social play and game economies in addition to classic role-playing mechanics.

Sports Games

Sports games are simulations of sports like tennis, football, baseball, soccer, etc. Since the success of Pong, simulations of sports have always made up a strong segment of the digital game market. Some of the most popular sports games today are Madden NFL, FIFA Soccer, and NBA Jam, as well as Sega Bass Fishing and Tony Hawk Pro Skater. Many sports games involve team play, season play, tournament modes, and other modes that mimic sporting conventions.

Racing/Driving Games

Racing/driving games come in several different flavors: arcade style, with game series like Mario Kart and Burnout, and racing simulators, with games like NASCAR 07 F1 Career Challenge and Monaco Grand Prix Racing Simulation. The arcade style appeals to a broader audience overall, whereas the simulations go into more depth and tend to appeal more to enthusiasts. One thing that all of these games have in common is that you are racing and you are in control.

Simulation/Building Games

Simulation/building games tend to focus on resource management combined with building something, whether it is a company or a city. Unlike strategy games, which generally focus on conquest, these games are all about growth. Many simulation/building games mimic real-world systems and give the player the chance

to manage her own virtual business, country, or city. Examples include: Stardew Valley, The Sims series, SimCity, and RollerCoaster Tycoon. One of the key aspects of simulation games is the focus on economy and systems of trade and commerce. Players tend to be given limited resources to build and manage the simulation. Choices must then be made carefully because an overemphasis on developing one part of the simulation results in the failure of the entire system. The popular genre of "cozy games" often have a simulation aspect to them.

Flight and Other Simulations

Simulations are action games that tend to be based on real-life activities, like flying an airplane, driving a tank, or operating a spacecraft. Flight simulators are the best example. These are complex simulators that try to approximate the real-life experience of flying an aircraft. These cannot be put squarely in the action camp because they are not focused on twitch play and hand-eye coordination, but instead they require the player to master realistic and often complex controls and instrumentation. Good examples include Microsoft Flight Simulator, X-Plane, and Jane's USAF. These types of simulations usually appeal to airplane and military buffs who want as realistic an experience as possible.

Adventure and Action Adventure Games

Adventure games emphasize exploration, collection, and puzzle solving. The extended genre of action adventure games adds combat, stealth and other action mechanics. The player generally plays the part of a character on a quest or mission of some kind. Early adventure games were designed using only text, their rich descriptions taking the place of today's graphics. Early examples include the text-driven Adventure and Zork, as well as graphic adventures like Myst.

Today's action adventure games include the Uncharted series, The Last of Us, and God of War series. Shigeru Miyamoto, the creator of the Zelda series of adventure games, summed up the nature of the adventure game in his comment that "the state of mind of a kid when he enters a cave alone must be realized in the game. Going in, he must feel the cold air around him. He must discover a branch off to one side and decide whether to explore it or not. Sometimes he loses his way."[11] Although characters are central in adventure games, unlike role-playing games, they are not a customizable element and do not usually grow in terms of wealth, status, and experience. Some action-adventure games, like Ratchet & Clank, do have the concept of an inventory of items for their characters, but most rely on physical or mental puzzle solving or action and combat, not improvement and accumulation, for their central gameplay.

Educational Games

Educational games combine learning with fun. The goal is to entertain while educating the user. Topics range from reading, writing, and arithmetic to problem solving- and how to-games. Most educational titles are targeted at kids, but there are some that focus on adults, especially in the areas of acquiring skills and self-improvement. Emerging serious games, which I discussed in Chapter 2 on page 51, often include games that both teach and entertain.

Examples of kids' educational games include Motion Math, DragonBox, and Gamestar Mechanic, and for adults, Brain Age and Foldit.

Children's Games

Children's games are designed specifically for kids between the ages of 2 and 12. These games might have an educational component, but the primary focus is on entertaining. Nintendo is a master at creating these games, though its franchises such as Mario and Animal Crossing are also loved by adults. Other examples include the hit online games Fortnite, Minecraft, and Roblox.

Casual Games

Casual games are typified by the fact that they are meant to be enjoyed by everyone: male and female, old and young. This means they eschew twitch play, violence, and complex gameplay in favor of attracting the broadest possible audience. Most of the time these are simple games, like those found on the App Store, where you will see everything from Threes to Monument Valley to Ridiculous Fishing. A number of break-out hits in the casual game space, including Angry Birds and Robot Unicorn Attack, have made it a quickly growing area for innovative game designers and the reason why "casual games" are the top genre of play across all players as seen in Figure 15.3. games like Candy Crush Saga, a free-to-play tile-matching game is one of the top grossing games worldwide.

Casual games often incorporate puzzle elements into their play mechanics. Tetris is probably the most famous casual game ever made, and it is an action puzzle game. Puzzle games might emphasize story, as in Puzzle Quest Challenge of the Warlords, or action, as in Tetris. They might also include elements of strategy, as in Scrabble or solitaire, or construction, as in the famous The Incredible Machine series. Designer Scott Kim discusses puzzles and puzzle games on page 43.

Experimental Games

While not technically a "genre" of play, experimental games are nonetheless a growing category of interest. Games such as Braid, Journey, Super Meat Boy, Dear Esther, and Everyday Shooter, among many others, are games that stand outside either the traditional publishing model or the traditional conception of games. These "experimental" games are often independently financed and explore new territory creatively. See Richard Lemarchand's sidebar on experimental games on page 209 for more on games like these.

See Richard Lemarchand's sidebar on experimental games on page 209 for more on games like these.

Exercise 15.1: Your Game's Genre

What genre does your original game fit into? Why does it fit this genre? Given this information, what platform should your game be released on, and who is your target audience?

PUBLISHERS

The publishing landscape has changed dramatically over the past decade. Finding a publisher for your game is more difficult than ever due to the explosion of developers out there. However, there are more avenues than ever for publishing if you include the opportunities afforded by online-only publishers and new "indie" publishers like Annapurna. In a recent report from Metacritic, the top publishers were ranked and analyzed as to their percentage of products with good reviews, percentage of products with bad reviews, and number of "great" titles (Metascore over 90).[12]

The top ten publishers as ranked by their average Metascores based on 2022 releases were:

- Sony (85.6)
- Paradox Interactive (81.8)
- Activision Blizzard (76.5)
- Focus Entertainment (80.0)
- Take-Two Interactive (78.9)
- Capom (78.6)
- Sega (79.3)
- Annapurna Interactive (79.2)
- Humble Games (76.8)
- Devolver Digital (78.3)

Of course, we expect to see powerhouse publishers like Sony and Activision Blizzard at the top of such lists, but it is also interesting to see indie publishers like Annapurna and Humble Games get such high rankings. What we can take away from this ranking is that smaller and newer publishers are just as able to release highly rated titles. Though the market reach of larger publishers is clearly greater, considering the reputation of a publisher for releasing great games is equally important.

As Tristan Donovan from *Game Developer* magazine points out, "Awareness of a publisher's general attitude toward external development, its treatment of other developers, and what genres it concentrates on can be highly valuable when dealing with a publisher."[13] I encourage you to research publishers before approaching them. Knowledge of their products, their business focus, and trends they seem to be a part of can help you present your own game in the context of their goals and plans.

Exercise 15.2: The Right Publisher

Do some research of your own and find a publisher you think would be right for your original game idea. Do not just choose the biggest or the most well-known publisher; find a company that is a match for your game in terms of focus, market, and other games they have published.

PLAY BEYOND SCREENS

By Tracy Fullerton

One of the most interesting new opportunities for designers of play is in the realm of immersive experiences. Immersive experiences may be found in site-specific installations, theater, theme parks, museums, and more. The qualities that distinguish them are the way in which the audience is encouraged to interact with the performers, role-play, move around and play within the environment, and otherwise take on an active role in the experience. Because of the interactive nature of these experiences, a new type of "game" designer is emerging with skills that go beyond design for screen-based interactivity. Designers who work in immersive experience design may have backgrounds in traditional theater, themed entertainment design, as well as game design.

An example of a very successful and well-known immersive theater experience is Punchdrunk's Sleep No More, a loose adaptation of Shakespeare's Macbeth. But rather than sitting in a theater, in Sleep No More visitors explore the evocative, maze-like floors of the McKittrick Hotel in New York City on their own, encouraged to disengage from the groups they arrived with and have unique individual experiences. Each floor of the building is a set designed to have numerous hallways, rooms, and staircases that visitors can move around in. The densely art directed space represents the entire world of the play – so there is a forest, a ballroom, bedrooms, shops, and more. The audience is encouraged to follow whichever characters strike their fancy, as well as to investigate mysterious objects and rooms they find as they wander. Sometimes performers will draw individual audience members into private interactions, but mostly groups of guests follow characters as they go about enacting the various scenes of the play, performing the intensely dramatic situations. In one scene, Lady Macbeth is found in a bathtub, naked and shrieking as she tries to wash off blood. Guests, who are required to wear ghostly white masks to distinguish them from the performers, hover around the scene curiously and the effect is striking. In each dimly lit area of the set, groups of guests flit around the performers like eerie wraiths, watching and following the action from behind their identical masks. No two visits to Sleep No More ever feel the same, since following different characters will reveal different parts of the story and different locations, making this immersive theater experience feel deeply interactive.

Another very successful immersive entertainment experience is Meow Wolf's House of Eternal Return in Santa Fe. This sprawling interactive world is a permanent exhibit features more than seventy rooms of immersive art that tells the story of a family's mysterious disappearance. There are secret passages, strange humming noises, and trans-dimensional wonderlands hidden behind unassuming closet doors. It is a surreal and interactive experience sitting within the confines of an abandoned bowling alley. Meow Wolf's designers are a collection of artists from many different backgrounds and disciplines. The playfulness and wonder that permeate their creations speak to the potential for these kinds of wildly creative experiences to enhance opportunities for site-specific public play. Based on the success of the House of Eternal Return, Meow Wolf has opened exhibits in Denver, Grapevine mills (just north of Dallas-Fort Worth International Airport), and Las Vegas.

One of the largest, most-expensive experiments in immersive entertainment has no doubt been Disney Imagineering's creation of the Star Wars-themed lands of Galaxy's Edge at Disneyland and Disney World as well as their ambitious and short-lived Galactic Starcruiser experience, in which guests boarded a "spaceship" for a two-night adventure where they became part of their own Star Wars story. Guests were invited to interact with characters, taking on quests to help the rebels or First Order forces, training to operate the ship's navigation and defense, learning how to wield a lightsaber, eating and drinking Star Wars-style food, and playing games like Holo-Sabacc in the ship's lounge. The cast members also played roles and at no point during the "journey" was the illusion of being onboard a luxury starcruiser within the Star Wars universe intentionally broken. Even a "shore excursion" to the planet of Batuu was part of the experience: guests boarded a "shuttle" that "flew" them to the "planet's surface" and back to visit Batuu, otherwise known as Galaxy's Edge, part of Disney's Hollywood Studios at Walt Disney World Resort, as a day trip for guests. On Batuu, they could engage in more role-playing experiences, as well as go on Star Wars themed rides such as Smuggler's Run and Rise of the Resistance. Star Wars: Galactic Starcruiser opened in March of 2022 and closed in September of 2023, and while it was short-lived, it was also one of the most incredibly ambitious and innovative examples of immersive entertainment yet created. It won the Thea Award for Outstanding Achievement in Brand Experience from the Themed Entertainment Association in 2022 and was widely praised by many creatives across the games and interactive industries for the significance of its achievements. However, it was also critiqued for its high price tag and lack of flexibility in terms of visitor experience. It remains to be seen how the learning from this experiment will affect the wider industry for immersive experiences.

The Nest: from prototype to live experience

You might wonder how such detailed immersive experiences are designed and playtested. Interestingly enough, there are many aspects of this field that are very similar to the process I've described for game design. For example, paper prototypes are often made to block out both the physical layouts and to mockup interactive components. In the images above, you can see the step-by-step planning stages of a unique immersive experience called The Nest. The Nest, created by former Disney Imagineers Jeff Leinenveber and Jarrett Lantz, is an intimate immersive experience for one or two audience members at a time. It combines elements of immersive theater, narrative video games, themed entertainment, and escape rooms to tell a touching story about a young girl, Josie, growing up in the 1960s who begins documenting her life with personal audio journals when she is given a cassette recorder for her birthday. The audience members are invited to explore an abandoned storage space filled with all the personal effects of Josie's life, from girlhood to young married woman, motherhood, and beyond. What begins as a dusty crawl through piles of vintage junk, soon unlocks a mysterious journey through time, space, and memory that is both unexpected and deeply moving.

As can be seen in the images, the storage space for The Nest was envisioned as a maze-like environment, but it was important that guests be able to find their way back to a central hub several times during the experience. The hub contained a typewriter and a phone, which would ring at certain point in the scenario. It also was a focal point for several branch points and puzzles, so needed to be accessible, but not give away too much too early about what players were going to eventually notice about the area. The team laid out the entire maze using cardboard boxes as can be seen in the two images on the left. This layout was used to run very early playtests, developing story points and plans for the interaction. The entire space was then mock-up in a rough 3D layout as shown on the top right, so that more detailed plans could be made for how areas and interactable elements would be implemented. And finally, the space was art directed with real vintage objects as seen on the bottom right. Technology for sound, lighting, locking, and unlocking available areas of the set could all be designed, prototyped, playtested, and iterated on alongside the story and interaction designs in this way.

Beyond fully live immersive experiences, there are also those that combine virtual reality and augmented reality with site-specific designs. As Laird Malamed discusses in his sidebar in Chapter 14 on page 478, location-based entertainment combined with virtual reality in experiences such as Dreamscape VR can be both powerfully dramatic and interactive. One of the best experiences I have had in location-based VR was in Wevr's The Blu: Deep Rescue at Dreamscape VR. In this beautiful multiplayer experience, you take on the role of a diver, descending into an underwater research station to help a family of whales who are in desperate trouble. Interacting with both physical and virtual objects, you power up an underwater AquaScooter and steer it through shipwrecks, ravines, and circling marine life – all in the company of your family and friends. The experience is breathtaking and inspiring and uses the best of both themed entertainment and virtual reality design.

Each of these examples show different ways that game design is being used in immersive experiences and this field is growing all the time. With the proliferation of new technologies that can be embedded in physical objects and sites, the boundaries of what can be done creatively and playfully are nowhere in sight. So, if you are an aspiring game designer who also loves the idea of designing for theater, theme parks, museums, and live entertainment, the world of immersive entertainment might be a good path to investigate.

DEVELOPERS

There are so many game developers, large and small, that it would be unhelpful to list them all. In general, there are three types of developers: independent studios, wholly owned studios, and partially owned studios. Most developers start out small. Many times, it is a group of friends who have either worked together in the past or perhaps have gone to school together. Like starting a band, starting a development studio is a usually a labor of love.

Many start-up developers never make it past the ideation phase. Perhaps they build a demo and shop it around. Only a few very lucky teams actually sign a deal to produce a game. And even fewer wind up producing a hit. Being a game developer is a very risky business. Many small developers produce one or two games, but they do not have the financial cushion to deal with a dry spell or a spate of unexpected costs. These companies go out of business, but the talent always seems to reemerge at another company under a new name.

Some developers might make a series of successful games for a publisher who decides to invest in them or to buy them outright and make them an internal development group. Whatever the case, every game development company is filled with people who love games, and no matter what their level of success, are trying to find a way to balance managing a business and staying true to their artistic vision while staying alive and in the game.

The founders of thatgamecompany have spoken candidly about the fact that while producing Journey, a game which went on to win multiple game of the year awards, they nearly ran their company bankrupt because they wanted to get the game just right, and wound up taking an extra year to do so. They learned a lot during this process and now that they are self-publishing their own games, such as Sky: Children of the Light, they have been able to raise significant private investment, as well as retaining the rights to their own games. That game company has been very lucky and successful, but even successful developers are vulnerable to the business reality of the industry, which is risky even in the best of situations.

THE BUSINESS OF GAME PUBLISHING

From a business perspective, designing a game is just one small part of the elaborate process of producing the game. Producing is also a smaller part of the lengthy process for publishing a title. Game publishing involves all the steps needed to get a game from the glimmer of a concept to a polished product that is distributed to players. This section explains the four key elements of publishing: development, licensing, marketing, and distribution. Game publishers are the primary source of funding in the game industry, so understanding these elements of how they work will help you interact with them more effectively.

Development

The basic task of development involves financing a team to create a title and then managing that process so that a high-quality game is delivered on time and within the budget.

Industry Trends

The average cost of game development has risen steadily since the 1980s. Today, it typically costs $100 to $300 million to produce a high-end console title, and that number continues to rise. Call of Duty: Modern Warfare 2 cost $250 million to produce, and Grand Theft Auto 5 cost $265 million and Red Dead Redemption 2 cost a record-breaking $540 miillion. The reason for the increase is simple: Customers expect games to have more media of better quality to utilize the features of newer, better hardware systems. Back in the days of the Sega Genesis, for example, a game cartridge could hold 4 MB of data. A standard DVD can hold 4.7 GB. A 4K UHD disc such as those used by the PlayStation 5 can hold 66-100 GB. That is about a two million percent increase in capacity since the days of the Sega Genesis, and the next generation of consoles will likely see even greater media budgets. Historically, more capacity equates to greater customer expectations and to more costly production of graphics, sound, music, gameplay, etc. Of course, as I've also noted, there is an equally strong trend toward smaller development teams and costs in the mobile and indie space. 2012 Game of the Year Journey only cost approximately $5 million to produce and yet was a critical hit. An independently produced mobile game may only cost in the $500,000 range.

In addition to the new range of development costs, there is also a range of price points for games. Small indie titles for consoles might be as low priced as $4.99, while the launch price for AAA titles has remained fairly steady over the years at about $70. With the cost of AAA development rising and the price of each title remaining static, the traditional game publishers have been forced to adopt a "fewer, bigger, better" strategy. Many industry experts expect the AAA market to contract even more, while the mobile and downloadable market will continue to expand.

This is why, if you are a designer, you might find it difficult to find a publisher for a truly amazing, original AAA design that appeals to only a niche market. Diversity and innovation in the market are going to come in the area of smaller, cheaper-to-produce titles; the economics make it difficult for anything else to happen.

For this reason, a number of truly innovative game designers can be found working independently today. Designer Randy Smith talks about this in his Designer Perspective on page 57. Mobile games, like those Smith has published since forming Tiger Style, offer both innovation and good gameplay at a lower risk for both developer and purchaser.

Developer Royalties

Typically, publishers pay development costs to a developer as an advance against the royalties generated by the title. A royalty is a percentage of the overall revenue earned by a publisher that is paid to a project participant. The following is a basic explanation of how a publisher developer deal often works.

Base Deal

In most basic development deals, a publisher advances development costs to the developer in the form of milestone payments. This means that if the budget is $10 million, the publisher pays the developer a percentage of the total after each stage of development: ideation, preproduction, production, and testing.

These milestone payments are treated as an advance against future royalties. Typical royalty rates for a developer range from 10% to 18% of a publisher's net sales revenue after deductions. The publisher starts paying royalties after the development costs have been recouped via sales. In our example, this means that the publisher keeps 100% of the revenues generated by a title until the royalties reach $10 million.

After the royalties reach the amount advanced, the publisher shares the revenues with the developer according to the royalty schedule. If the agreed-upon royalty rate was 15%, from this point onward, the publisher would give the developer 15% of the net sales revenues earned and keep 85% for itself. Developers can ask for royalty rates to "step up" when certain sales goals are met. For example, the royalty rate might be 10% until 60,000 units are sold, then 15% until 120,000 units are sold, then 20% until 240,000 units are sold, etc.

First-time developers are a risk for the publisher, so their royalty rates are low. Established developers, who have proven that they can deliver hits, can negotiate for a higher rate because they represent less risk.

Royalty Calculation

Royalties are calculated on net sales revenue or adjusted gross income, meaning the developer gets paid after the publisher makes deductions, such as sales tax, duties, shipping, insurance, returns, manufacturing, and platform fees. This can open the door for creative accounting. A developer is wise to ask that these deductions be narrowly defined and that the publisher not include its overhead costs.

As we'll see below, under distribution, the costs for manufacturing physical games create a great deal of risk for the publisher in the form of up-front costs. This is the primary reasons for the move that the industry has made over the past decade or so into primarily digital sales.

Affiliate Label Deal

In an affiliate label deal, the developer shares in development and marketing costs. This reduces the publisher's risk, and thus the royalty percentages tend to be much higher—typically 65%-75%.

Licensing

There are two basic kinds of licensing in which publishers engage: content licensing and console licensing.

Content Licensing

Many publishers rely heavily on licensed properties for game titles. By licensing recognizable characters, personalities, music, or other entertainment properties and integrating them into a game, publishers can increase its exposure and sales, thereby decreasing their risk of investment. The following are examples of games based on licenses: Tony Hawk's Pro Skater, Hogwarts Legacy, Madden NFL series, The Lord of the Rings: Battle for Middle Earth 2, and Pokémon Go.

When a game uses a licensed property, the publisher pays the rights holder a fee for use of the property. In the case of the Madden NFL series, EA pays a license fee to John Madden and the NFL. With video games pulling in record profits, licensors of content are holding out for higher and higher prices. Because of this, some publishers, like Sony Computer Entertainment and Microsoft Game Studios, are actually quite aggressive about developing original game concepts, or intellectual property, as it is called.

Nevertheless, it is not uncommon for large titles to spend hundreds of thousands of dollars on a license, in addition to giving away anywhere from 1% to 10% of net revenues to the rights holder. The bottom line in terms of licensing is that it helps reduce publisher risk. Branded products have proven to be strong sellers time and time again, whether they have good gameplay elements or not.

Console Licensing Agreements

When you produce a game for the PC, you do not have to pay Microsoft, Apple, or the hardware manufacturer a royalty for distributing on their system. However, when publishers distribute a game on a console system or via a mobile app store, they must enter into a strict licensing agreement with the console maker or store, in which they agree to pay a licensing royalty for every unit sold. For digital downloads, console and mobile alike, this is typically 30% of every download sale.

Here is how the responsibilities for a typical third-party console licensing deal break down.

Publisher's responsibilities (in collaboration with developers):
- Come up with game concept
- Develop the game
- Test the game
- Market the game
- Distribute the game

Console maker's or app store's responsibilities:
- Approve the game concept
- Test the game
- Review and approve the final game
- Manufacture the game (if it is for physical distribution) or make the game available for download

Console licensing agreements as well as app story publishing agreements generally give the console maker the right of final approval, which means that if they do not approve of the game or its content, they can prevent it from being released. The testing and approval process can be quite rigorous for consoles. The console maker wants to ensure that the game works under all conditions and that it meets their quality standards. If they find flaws that they deem significant, they can send the game back to the publisher and demand that it be fixed before release. For app stores, the testing process is usually not as rigorous; however, they do check for content.

Changes at this stage of development, as I discussed in Chapter 13, can be very costly and can also impact the release date, potentially missing important market schedules. If and when the publisher finally gains approval to release the game, it must pay the console maker the royalty fee for every unit manufactured up front. Only after this payment are the games delivered to the publisher and then redistributed to retailers. In the case of digital stores, the royalties are taken off the top of revenues before the earnings are released to the publisher.

Of course, these days, it is technically possible to be your own publisher. If you can get through the process of setting up a publishing account on a console, or with a digital distributor like Steam or an app store, you can manage the sales of your game with the distribution partner directly. You won't have access to the kind of marketing that a larger publisher allows, but you will keep all the royalties yourself.

Marketing

A big part of the publishing task is marketing the game. A marketer's job is to make decisions that will result in maximum sales. The marketing department is typically involved in a game's entire life cycle, from conception through to the bargain bins. Only when the game is no longer saleable does the marketing team stop working. The marketing department handles everything from idea approvals and setting system specs through to buying up advertising on local radio stations, as well as coordinating in-store promotions and publicity. Marketing budgets may be up to double the development budgets. For our example of a $10 million game, the marketing budget could come in at up to $20 million. In the example of Grand Theft Auto 5, $128 million of that budget was in marketing costs.

Distribution

As already discussed, the majority of game sales today are digital, which would lead you to believe that anyone can publish a game digital. This is somewhat true: you can, as an indie developer or indie publisher, get your games into the distribution platforms for consoles and mobile devices. But how will players find your games in the glut of other games out there?

The major publishers have strong relationships with the digital platforms, and spend a great deal of marketing money to get good placement in their virtual storefronts, in special sales, and promotions. Think about what games you see when you open up the digital store on any platform. Is it the tiny indie game you just launched today? Probably not. Just like the brick and mortar sales environment, the big titles are what you see first. These titles have been placed by publishers to get as many eyes on them as possible, and to translate those eyes into sales.

These kinds of marketing and distribution relationships are why most developers would rather work with a publisher than go it alone and self publish their game, even though it is technically possible to do so. And, as already mentioned, the fact that digital stores do not require up-front manufacturing costs, is why publishers greatly prefer this form of distribution. In some ways, digital distribution has opened up many possibilities for developers to self-publish, but in other ways, the control of "shelf space," or in this case virtual shelf space, remains in the hands of those who can pay for it.

Consider the difference in cost to distribute between digital stores and physical stores. In the case of the digital store, the console or app store will take 30% of the price for digital downloads. 70% goes to the publisher, from which they will take their production and marketing costs until they meet the amount of the developer advance. After that, they will play the developer royalties on the 70%. So, if the price of a game was $70, the publisher's 70% would be $49. If the developer had a 15% royalty rate, they would make $7.35 per sale, leaving the publisher with $41.65 per sale. If we compare that to the costs and royalty rates of physical game sales, you will see why publishers have been so eager to move to digital distribution.

When a game is distributed physically, there are a great deal more costs to be considered. Here is a breakdown of costs for a physical console game: Let's imagine a retail price of $70:

- Wholesale price (the amount retailers pay publishers for the title) = approximately 64% of the retail price, or $44.80 per unit
- Cost of goods incurred by publisher (including the console licensing fee and manufacturing costs) = approximately 20% or $14

- Co-op advertising costs incurred by publisher = approximately 15% of wholesale price, or $6.72 per unit
- Marketing costs incurred by publisher = approximately 8% of wholesale price, or $3.60 per unit
- Return of goods contingency estimated by publisher = approximately 12% of wholesale price, or $5.38 per unit

If you subtract the cost of goods ($5.00), the coop advertising costs ($4.80), the marketing costs ($2.56), and the return of goods contingency ($3.84) from the wholesale price ($32.00), you'll find that the publisher reaps about 15.10 per unit sold or approximately 21.6% of the retail sale price. And remember, the developer doesn't get royalties until their advance is recouped from this. Once that occurs, the developer will get 15% of that 21.6%, or about $2.27 per physical game sold. This is less than most people imagine.

Even if a title is fortunate enough to be sold on the shelves of a large chain store like Wal-Mart, there's no guarantee it will stay there for long.

If the product doesn't sell right away or in sufficient quantity, retailers reserve the right to return product, which means that the publisher can wind up with a warehouse full of unsold games.

Even for larger publishers, who have a rich pipeline of games that the retailers desire, there are a lot of risks involved in producing physical games. The shelf life for most physical games is three to six months—not very long. And if you look at the publisher's other expenses, including production budget overruns, high return rates, approvals being withheld, schedules slipping, etc., you will understand why so many of the smaller publishers go out of business or are bought by larger companies. It is not easy to make a profit in the games industry unless you can control costs, produce the best products, and have the right relationships to make sure that your products get placed on the shelves and stay there.

These daunting numbers for retail distribution have been the driving forces pushing publishers and developers to move so rapidly toward complete digital distribution of games.

Conclusion

To the game designer entirely focused on gameplay and production, the business aspects of publishing games might seem to be a confusing cutthroat environment, best left to producers and executives. But as in all things, knowledge is power, and the more you know and understand about the industry you work in, the better equipped you will be to deal with the ups and downs of getting your original game ideas produced and published.

Creative people should not shy away from understanding the issues presented in this chapter. Understanding the needs and goals of all the parties involved in the publishing process, from the executives at the publishing company, to the representatives of the console makers, to the salespeople at the retail outlet, will help you make better decisions and will pay off over and over again in your career.

Think of yourself as a creative businessperson as well as a game designer, and educate yourself at every opportunity about the industry. Read marketing research, ask questions about contracts, understand the deal structure for your game, and treat each opportunity to deal with the business aspects of the industry as a chance to learn and expand your skills. The respect you show for this process will improve your relationships with the businesspeople involved in your game, and it will make you a better designer in turn.

DESIGNER PERSPECTIVE: NEIL JONES

Founder, Aerial_Knight
Neil Jones, known by his alias Aerial_Knight is a Detroit based Games Developer, Designer and Artist. His growing frustration with the games industry's lack of opportunities for people of different backgrounds at the time led Neil to start development of his own games. Offering different takes on classic mechanics Neil aims to create interesting short story games for an underserved market. Starting with his first solo-developed indie game Aerial_Knight's Never Yield. Neil was honored with Black in Gaming Foundation Award in 2021 in recognition of the achievements of top Black executives, creators, and developers who have made a significant impact in the video gaming industry. Project credits include: Aerial_Knight's: Never Yield (2021), Murder The Reaper (2018), Clique, Jett (2021), Dot's Home (2021), Bloom (2014)

How did you become a game designer?

The road to becoming a game designer for me has been a long and complicated one. I started off wanting to only do 3D art, but quickly learned that if I wanted to make games I would have to learn and be capable of much more than 3D modeling. Over the years, I grew inspired by the games like No More Heroes, Sleeping Dogs, and many of the offbeat double A games at the time. They made me want to tell stories and design more than just focus on the art side of things. Those were always the games that interest me the most as you could really feel the hand of the creators you got a lot of their personality and what they found fun out of those games. Coming into the game industry, I wanted to make games like those.

Unfortunately, I ran into a lot of trouble finding space for myself within the industry. I spent years improving my skills while looking for job placement, only to come up empty-handed. When I turn 29, I had yet to make any real progress in the game industry. I was about to give up and move on to some boring job working at a desk or a factory just so I could finally make money. But before I gave up, I figured I should put all the years of experience to use and make something that I really enjoyed. It wasn't about anything more than me wanting to make something cool, so I didn't feel like I wasted so much time. So, I created this game called Ashes to Ashes, which I later retitled Aerial_Knight's Never Yield. It was a cool experiment where I just took all the things that I loved and try to put it into one game, one short experience that anyone could play.

The game was something I worked on in my free time while also working my two part-time jobs, it had no funding outside of a porting grant I received close to the end of development with the game being mostly finished. When the Never Yield finally launched, it was already profitable as it didn't have many costs that needed to be recouped. I did everything from cutting all the trailers to managing the game's Discord. The game did really well, being part of many subscription services makes the final number of copies sold /downloaded difficult to estimate but with the low cost of development, it only needed to repay me for the time I put into it, which it has returned tenfold. My goal was just to make something that was cool, fun, and genuine, I think people really gravitated towards that and it's why it succeeded. That last-ditch effort is how I became a game designer. I was always a game designer but making that game for myself is what made others see me as one.

On games that have inspired him:

The games that inspired me the most are the games with a clear vision. The fact that there is a clear vision and it sticks to its message or non-message — those games are the ones that inspire me. I'm a person who is willing to try anything once, even if I know it's going to be bad. So, I very much enjoy games that try something different. I mean different in a sense of story, or different in the sense of a new take on a classic mechanic. I just like it when designers mix things up and think outside the box. That's what keeps our industry interesting and creative. I truly believe if we continue down that road of constantly trying new things, with fresh characters and perspectives there will always be room for new games.

On exciting developments in the industry:

One of the most exciting developments in the game industry recently has been the interest in updating classic games for new audiences. I appreciate that people can always revisit the original, but it's also great to play an updated version that might contain changes and updates that are more inclusive to a larger audience. Updated classics, like Tomb Raider, Destroy all Humans, Final Fantasy 7, and many fighting games, are often created with a more diverse team that reflects multiple backgrounds and fixes some of the oversights that the classic games might have. It's interesting to see how today's designers can take a blueprint of a classic game and polish them into something new. The changes that they choose to make — or not make — can sometimes be more interesting than the game itself.

On design process:

My design process is rather long and convoluted. I keep a notebook with me pretty much at all times, because during the day I might randomly think of a cool mechanic, theme, or overall concept for a game, and I'll just jot it down in my notebook. The game ideas that linger in my mind for months and that I keep wanting to revisit and add notes to are the ones that I pull from when I'm available to start a new project. At that point, I pitched the idea to friends and other designers to get their thoughts. If the people I trust the most think that it's a good idea, then I go into creating a game design doc, breaking down the mechanics and how they all work together. Then I like to pull back from it for a few weeks as I know I can become over-attached to things rather quickly. If I'm still as excited about the idea after not touching it for a few weeks and it's still on my mind, then I know it's something I can really commit to.

One of the major signs that this game that I'm concepting is a good idea is when I start dreaming about the levels and even the trailer and music for the game. It's almost a form of paper prototyping in my mind, and I've killed a few projects that just weren't fun to me before I even really started building it because of this. I think all designers do this in some way, shape, or form. That's how we have this relentless belief that something can be good without any real proof.

On prototyping:

When I do get to the stage where I'm ready to make an actual digital prototype that other people can play, it will be very blocky in the most basic form of the mechanics. I always fully model texture and rig the main character, but everything else in the prototype is basically blocks. I like to create my games in Lego-like pieces. I try to design my game systems so they can interact with each other but are removable without breaking the entire game. This makes it easier to not only create levels, but also to redesign the entire concept of the game if needed. After the core Lego pieces are built, my prototype process is pretty much piecing things together until it is as fun as I imagined. Also asking myself: Who is this for? Would others enjoy this? Do I enjoy this? For me the prototype is the most important thing — even more than the launch of the game. That's because prototyping is where you really understand the scope of the game, and how long things will actually take to build, how realistic it is if you're doing it yourself, and truly understanding if it's something interesting or not. Many developers have already decided that they will move forward with a game before the prototype is even built, which to me is a mistake. It should be seen as a chance to backout of a game, if it isn't working, more than a commitment to have to complete it.

On a difficult design problem:

Accessibility to me has always been a difficult design problem, particularly for the Indie space. I think every developer wants to make a game that anyone can play but there are a lot of design challenges around many of those aspects. From music cues to even the colors that you use to warn a player that something is going to happen. All these choices affect accessibility. I always struggle with how far to go with accessibility, as I might be putting a lot of work into something or some aspect of the game that might never be used, and that time could be spent designing or adding another feature that would be enjoyed more directly. But I also hate the idea of people who really want to play the things that I create not being able to, or having to wait for an accessibility update that makes it more available to them specifically. I would hate for a game that I was really interested in to only add Black characters in an update down the road after it was more convenient for the developers. That would make me feel terrible and I wouldn't want anyone else to feel that way. I haven't really thought of a solution to this problem. I'm hoping technology will solve it for me eventually, but it's something I struggle with when setting priorities.

What are you most proud of in your career?

The thing I'm most proud of in my career so far are the emails I get from parents talking about how much their kid enjoys the game or how they're inspired by my personal story. Black people really haven't had the opportunity to see themselves in developer roles, and when we have been, we've been pushed so far behind the scenes that we almost didn't exist to the public. Many others and myself are trying to change that narrative and be seen for the first time ever and I'm really proud to be a part of that.

Advice for designers:

Whenever aspiring game developers or designers or artists ask me for advice, I always tell them the best advice is to follow your own path. That's what you're going to end up doing anyway. Most advice-givers give the same advice to everyone, but if you talk to ten people in the games industry and ask them how they got in or what their path was you'll get ten different answers. Throughout the years, I've received a lot of advice when I was trying to find my way into the industry. Most of it end up doing more harm than good. So overall I would say, don't take people's advice. Look at what people do, listen to their stories, and take from that what applies to your story and what you want to do.

DESIGNER PERSPECTIVE: GRAEME BAYLESS

Executive Producer at NetherRealm Studios (WB Games)

Graeme Bayless has been directing computer game development for over 25 years. His long list of credits includes Battles of Napoleon (1988), Star Command (1988), Secret of the Silver Blades (1990), Kid Chameleon (1992), MissionForce: CyberStorm (1996), CyberStorm 2: Corporate Wars (1998), NFL Street (2004), NFL Street 2 (2004), Injustice 2 (2017), and Mortal Kombat 11 (2019). Prior to NetherRealm, he was Production Director at Fireforge.

On getting into the game industry:

I started by working on paper-game design from an early age (I did my first paper game design when I was about 12, and actually had published work at the age of 14). Long before I was in video games, I contributed to numerous paper games in a design capacity. This was driven from a strong passion for games, and a deep desire to understand what made them tick.

Through this passion, I eventually stumbled my way into the game industry, landing a job as a game developer back in 1987 for a company called Strategic Simulations (now defunct, sadly). I worked on over 20 titles for them in my four-year tenure, most in some form of design capacity.

On games that have inspired you:

- *M.U.L.E.*: This was a superb title published by Electronic Arts in 1983. It was simple yet one of the most elegant game designs ever. It was groundbreaking in several ways... the cooperative/competitive model is one that even today designers are learning from, and the trading/bidding system still stands alone today as a unique feature. The game was deeply multiplayer, with excellent AI players when humans weren't available. For me, the inspirational part was the example of simplicity in design. The game had very simple, highly accessible concepts. It didn't over-load with extraneous things; it focused on the fun. That is a lesson for any designer, and is something I still look at in design today.

- *Daisenryaku*: This was a Sega Genesis game series that spawned dozens of versions and became the inspiration for the entire series of Panzer General games that kept Strategic Simulations going for years. This game was incredibly original, with a simple war game style that made war games accessible for the broader market. The genius in this game was the fact that it took the highly complex subject (WWII conflict on land) and boiled it down to the pertinent parts. Major concepts like vulnerability of ground units to bombers, vulnerability of bombers to fighters, vulnerability of tanks to infantry on defense or in cities, requiring of infantry to capture territory, power of tanks in the open terrain, etc..., all core concepts of such conflict were deeply represented. Yet, the game required a minimal learning curve, and was deeply playable with RPG-like upgrade paths for units (to represent all the vari-ants of units that manifested during the war). This game was a deep inspiration for me in many of my game designs.

- *EverQuest*: The first true 3D MUD, this game opened the way for a new genre of game... the MMORPG. This genre requires little explanation to any reader of this book, but EQ deserves a nod as the true champion that broke MMORPGs out into the mainstream. While the subsequent World of Warcraft from Blizzard far exceeded (and eventually killed) EverQuest, EQ remains the game that broke this ground... taking a concept originated by predecessors like Meridian 59 and Ultima Online, and making it viable for the broader market. From a designer perspective, the lessons to learn from EverQuest revolve around the concept of a game as a service, not as a single delivery. EQ was the first game to truly fulfill this promise, with constant updates, expansions, and living content that made players truly feel that the world was THEIR world... THEIR game. This game certainly changed the way I look at games, and did so for millions of others as well.

- *X-Com*: Another foundational strategy game, now beautifully revived by 2K, X-Com represents a perfect storm of turn-based gameplay allowing the thoughtful players, not the dexterous player, to dominate, of unlimited replayability due to procedurally generated maps and challenges, and of a tactical game with a meta-game behind it which gave the player effectively two layers of game to play. The genius of X-Com lies in the meta-game, where decisions you make on the strategic level really set up success in the tactical, but the tactical then fed back to the strategic. This, on top of what I learned about the value of procedurally generated gameplay, made X-Com deeply inspirational to me as a designer.

- *Plants vs. Zombies*: Arguably the most successful tower defense game of all time, this game set the standard for what a casual strategy game could be. While the gameplay is very simple, it is deeply engaging. Moreover, this game showed the tremendous power of just having good graphics and audio that were thematically connected with the experience. Plants vs. Zombies shows what one can do with a modest budget and strong design.

On exciting developments in the industry:

Honestly, I think it's exciting that the industry has come full circle. When I began developing games back in the 80s, I worked on games designed and programmed by one person... often the sole artist as well. These games were great... often deeply engaging... and showed that amazing graphics or hyper technology are *not* required to make a great game. Yet, through the years, we saw an ever-increasing spiral of expectations... driven by consumer amazement at the power of these devices. As a result, games had to be bigger and more amazing to sell. Teams went from 1 to 10 to 100 to more, and budgets went from tens of thousands to hundreds of millions.

Now, we've come full circle. The independent developer is again resurgent, and devices are easy to develop for. Great games are again being built by tiny teams with tiny budgets. While there will always be a place for massive and amazing games like Call of Duty or World of Warcraft, I'm thrilled to see the quality coming from small developers again.

On design process:

There are many methodologies for developing games, but in the end I find that good design benefits from pieces of them all. One cannot focus entirely on the mechanics without losing the larger meta that can take your game idea to the next level. Likewise, one cannot build a story and world around a game with poor mechanics. In order to ensure you never lose sight of the "forest" while looking at the trees, it also is critical to take a disciplined approach to construction and design... but you also must spend time truly blue-sky brainstorming.

Coming up with game ideas for me is rarely an "event"... rather, it is a constant, organic process. Literally *anyone* can generate a great game idea... I once did an experiment to test that theory, and found that the most atypical sources could come up with stellar game ideas. The hard part is the implementation, not the idea generation. The industry is littered with thousands of "great ideas" that were not well executed or implemented... or that got lost in the "trees" along the way.

My methodology consists of the normal steps... concept development and brainstorming, prototyping to validate assumptions, more prototyping to flesh out while planning is ongoing, then build out of a focused "slice" of the game, showing all of what the game will be when done... and only then actually engaging a full team against development. Add in liberal amounts of testing and validation all through development, and you're unlikely to end up with a train wreck at the end.

As for polish... well... as the saying goes, "the last 20% is 80%." Plan a substantive chunk of time for polish and revision. Iterate, test... iterate, test. Put the game in front of as broad an audience as you can, as often as you can. Pay attention to the feedback, but temper it with the knowledge of the lens through which the players are seeing the game.

On rapid prototyping:

Rapid prototyping early on allows for validation of key concepts or mechanics. Build your game level in Legos... create a paper game for the mechanics... make physical miniatures of your models... these prototyping techniques will save you tenfold later on.

I tend to do rapid prototyping early for small components, then more substantial code prototypes for testing assumptions about interface, playability, etc. Finally, the "vertical slice" containing a full subset of the game represents the final "prototype." Once you're done there and like what you have, you're on your way to a good, complete game.

Advice to aspiring designers:

That can be summarized pretty simply... and anyone who's heard me speak at conferences, schools, or any other gathering knows I'm rarely this succinct!

- Don't join this industry unless you cannot imagine doing anything else. You will work harder, for less money, than you would in any other competing industry. You must be passionate to survive in this field... deeply passionate about the work and the craft.
- Assuming you have the passion, then show it. Start building things on your own... learn how... use the myriad of tools available and show your stuff. You can do this with modding other games, or by creating things from scratch. Either way, don't just hope that school + interview = job. I am easily ten times more likely to hire someone who shows me what they have built and what they learned from the process than someone who just has school learning on their resume.
- Play everything you can... learn from every game you can. The more you expose yourself to the gems of brilliance out there, the better you will become.

FURTHER READING

Chaplin, Heather and Ruby, Aaron. *Smartbomb: The Quest for Art, Entertainment and Big Bucks in the Videogame Revolution.* New York: Workman Publishing, 2005.

Daglow, Don. Indie Games: From Dream to Delivery. Sausalito: Sausalito Media, 2019.

Fils-Aimé, Reggie. *Disrupting the Game: From the Bronx to the Top of Nintendo.* New York: Harper Collins, 2022.

Kenney, Mary. *Gamer Girls: 25 Women Who Built the Game Industry.* Philadelphia: Running Press Teens, 2022.

Michael, David. *The Indie Game Development Survival Guide.* Boston: Charles River Media, 2003.

Polfeldt, David. The Dream Architects: Adventures in the Video Game Industry. New York: Grand Central Publishing, 2020.

Schreier, Jason. *Blood, Sweat, and Pixels: The Triumphant, Turbulent Stories Behind How Video Games Are Made.* New York: Harper, 2017.

Vogel, Harold. *Entertainment Industry Economics: A Guide for Financial Analysis.* 10th Edition. Cambridge: Cambridge University Press, 2020.

END NOTES

1. PwC's Global Entertainment & Media Outlook 2022-2026, Omdia.
2. Entertainment Software Association, "Essential Facts about the U.S. Video Game Industry," July 2023.
3. Entertainment Software Association, "Essential Facts about the Computer and Game Industry," June 2017.
4. Entertainment Software Association, "Essential Facts about the Computer and Game Industry," June 2013.
5. Newzoo. "2022 Global Games Market Report." April 2022.
6. ibid.
7. Lennox, Jesse and Yaden, Joseph, "PS4 vs. PS5" Digitaltrends.com, March 18, 2023.
8. Owens, Timothy. "Unit Sales of Microsoft Xbox Series X worldwide 2021-2023" Statista.com, June 2023.
9. Sirani, Jordan, "Where Switch, PS5 Rank Among the Best-Selling Video Game Consoles of All Time," IGN.com. August 2023.
10. Ceci, L. "Number of apps available in leading app stores Q3 2022," Statista.com November 2022.
11. Sheff, David. *Game Over: How Nintendo Conquered the World.* New York: Vintage Books, 1994. p.52.
12. Dietz, Jason. "Metacritic's 13th Annual Game Publisher Rankings." Metacritic.com. March 23, 2023.
13. Donovan, Tristan. "Game Developer Reports: Top 20 Publishers." *Game Developer.* September 2003.

Chapter 16
Selling Yourself and Your Ideas to the Game Industry

There is no one way to get into the game industry. If you have been reading along with the designer perspectives throughout this book, you have probably noticed that each individual designer has a unique story to tell about how they got a start designing games. No two took the same path, and you too will have to find your own way. But in this final chapter, I'll provide you with a number of strategies for selling yourself and your vision to the game industry. The three basic strategies I discuss are:

1. Getting a job at a publisher or developer
2. Pitching and selling an original idea to a publisher
3. Producing your ideas independently

Most game designers do not start out by selling original concepts; they get a job at an established company and work their way up the ladder. When they have some experience, they might break off to start their own company or pitch ideas internally to the company they work for. But how do you find your first job in the game industry? What are the qualifications? What should you bring to an interview? These are questions that do not have easy answers. Unlike many career paths, game design does not have an established route to success. The ideas I suggest are ways to maximize your chances in a very competitive arena.

GETTING A JOB AT A PUBLISHER OR DEVELOPER

Getting a job at an established company is the most practical way to start off in the game industry. You will gain knowledge and experience, meet and work with other talented people, and see the inner workings of game production firsthand. But even at the entry level, the game industry is very competitive. Aside from the obvious routes of responding to job postings and contacting the HR departments of game companies, I have several strategic recommendations that might help you get your first job.

DOI: 10.1201/9781003460268-19

Educate Yourself

When contacting companies and going on interviews, the most important thing you bring with you as a beginning game designer is a solid knowledge of games and the game industry. Being able to articulate concepts in gameplay and mechanics, knowing the history of games, and understanding how the companies you are speaking to fit into the business of games are all important ways to show your skills.

Academic Programs

Many colleges around the country offer degrees in game design. This includes top-tier universities, like USC, NYU, Georgia Tech, and Carnegie Mellon, which have established curricula and game design research labs. There are also trade schools, like DigiPen and Full Sail, which specialize in placing people in the game industry.

These days, major game companies like Electronic Arts, Sony, Microsoft, and others look to academic game programs first for new hires. They hire mostly from top game design, computer science, and visual design schools and tend to hire applicants who are strong in both digital production and development skills and people skills. The majority of their new hires start at the company as summer interns and are offered full-time jobs after graduation.

If you choose to attend a game design school, keep in mind that a well-rounded program might better prepare you for a career in game design than a curriculum focused only on tools and techniques. Additionally, studying subjects outside the field, such as history, psychology, economics, literature, film, or other topics you are passionate about will stimulate your mind and imagination and give you interesting perspectives from which to design games.

That said, there is one bias that game companies do have: They are more likely to hire people with technical skills. If you take courses in engineering or computer science, it will give you an edge over the competition and will introduce you to industry standards such as C++ and C#. If you are able to become in involved in a student game course, you may gain experience in using a game engine like Unity 3D, Unreal, or Source. While you should not make tools your learning focus, you should also become familiar with the applications used to make games. In addition to the game engines discussed in Chapter 8, page 284, programs like Adobe Photoshop, Illustrator, 3D Studio Max, Maya, and Microsoft Excel are all important nonprogramming tools that you might want to become familiar with. Most game programs will offer some training in these tools.

There is a sense on the part of hiring managers in the industry that there are only a small number of academic programs they can recruit from successfully. According to a study by the International Game Developers Association (IGDA), game companies see a mismatch between many university graduates and their needs. They are looking for students who have practical experience developing games as well as technical and soft skills. Also, attitude counts! Many hiring managers stressed the fact that university applicants don't know enough about the practical roles of game design production, did not demonstrate that they could apply traditional computer science backgrounds to build games, and did not showcase their abilities with a robust portfolio. Overall, hiring managers are looking for discipline-focused technical skills — concept art, production, design, programming, etc. But soft and interpersonal skills mattered as well because game production needs people with the ability to deconstruct complex ideas. Recruiters also stressed the importance of applicants with high emotional intelligence.[1]

Portfolio

A good game portfolio will showcase your skills, creativity, and allow hiring manager to get a good sense of the role you played on each project you were part of. It goes without saying at this point that your game portfolio should be available online, easily accessed by hiring managers. You want to showcase, in as clear and visual a manner as possible each of your projects, what your role was, and provide screenshots, a demo video, and link to download the final version of your games. If you've won awards for your projects, be sure to highlight these! Also, if you have process documentation – such as sketches, design documents, or even playtesting documentation, you can provide these if they give clarity to your contributions. Don't muck up the page with too much detail, however. Only include items that give a better sense of your skills and process.

You can be selective when creating a portfolio – you don't need to include every piece of art you've ever made or game project you started but didn't finish. Organize your portfolio in a way that is easy to navigate and allows managers to grasp your talents as quickly as possible. Not everyone will have time to download your games, so be sure they can get a sense of them through quality video trailers and demos. If you've published to a store, that's great, include the link so they can see your follow through, but don't expect them to purchase or download your game. Recruiters are likely going through many applicants and you don't want technical glitches or a clumsy site navigation to cause them to move past your work. These days, many people look at websites on mobile devices, so also make sure your site looks good on a small screen. One way to keep your site clean is to use a basic portfolio-building template on a site like Squarespace.com or Wix.com.

Overall, here is basic list of what you should include on your site:

- 1-3 of your best projects where you played a significant role.
- At least one example of a team project
- Documentation of your process: concept, design, playtesting, etc.
- A demo or trailer video of the final game
- Download links or store links for your game
- Easy to read and print copy of your resume, preferably as a PDF

- Good clean, response design and navigation that works across desktop and mobile devices
- Contact info

Play Games

You can teach yourself about design by playing as many games as you can, reading about their history and development, and analyzing their systems. I assume you love games, so playing them a lot is probably something you do already. But just playing is not enough. Get in the habit of analyzing the games you play. Challenge yourself to learn something new from each game you play. Be active in online game communities like Gamedeveloper.com/blogs, GameDev.net and blog.unity.com. As I discussed in Chapter 1, develop a sense of game literacy, which can help you to discuss games at a deep system level and communicate your ideas about them with concrete examples.

Design Games and Levels

If you are following along with the exercises in this book, you should have designed at least one original game prototype by now. This experience is one of the most valuable tools you have in your search for a game design job.

Good solid paper game prototypes and well-written concept documents can form the basis for a great beginning portfolio. If you have the skills to turn your designs into software prototypes as well, you should do so. Even if you do not plan on pitching your ideas to a publisher at this point, polish your prototype and concept document anyway. During that crucial moment in a job interview when they ask you what experience you have, you will be able to show your work and discuss the process of design, playtesting, and revision in detail. This will differentiate you from other applicants because even though you are a beginner, you will be able to display actual experience of the development process, even though your games have not yet been published.

In addition to making physical and digital prototypes of original games, you can demonstrate your game design skills by building levels for existing games. As I discussed in Chapter 8, many games ship with level-editing and mod-building tools that are both powerful and flexible. There are also mod and level-making competitions that you can enter, which might help give you the visibility and recognition you need to secure that first job. One strategy for getting in the door at a game company is to make levels or mods of that company's games, then submit these examples of your work along with your résumé.

Know the Industry

As I discussed in the previous chapter, it is important to stay informed about the industry you want to be a part of. Read websites that can help you find out the latest news and trends. Having a grasp on the latest industry news when you go into an interview or meeting is a good way to show your knowledge of the space, and it will allow you to take advantage of opportunities that might arise with the latest announcements.

Networking

Networking is a powerful tool for people at all levels of the game industry. By networking, I simply mean getting out and meeting people within the industry. You can do this by going to industry-related events, attending conferences and conventions, reaching out to people in the industry via the Internet, and getting introductions via friends and relatives who know people in the industry.

You'll want to create a personal business card. Don't get too fancy or cute with this, but make a card that exhibits good, clean design and includes your name, phone number, email address, and portfolio website. The purpose of having a business card with you is so that you can trade cards with people that you meet at events and get their info. Then, you'll be able to follow up with them later.

Organizations

Joining organizations related to the industry is one way of meeting people. One of the best to consider joining is the International Game Developers Association, or the IGDA. The IGDA is an international organization of programmers, designers, artists, producers, and many other types of industry professionals that fosters community and action for the furthering of games as a medium. The organization has local chapters in many geographic locations; you can find out if there is one near you by going to www.igda.org/chapters.

Chapters often hold networking events, lectures, and other opportunities to meet people who are working in the industry. There are membership fees for this organization, but if you are a student, you can get a reduced rate.

Other organizations you might look into joining include WIGI (Women in Games International), G.A.N.G. (Game Audio Network Guild), SIGGRAPH (Special Interest Group on GRAPHics and Interactive Techniques), and SIGCHI (Special Interest Group on Computer-Human Interaction).

Conferences

Another great opportunity for networking is at conferences. Two of the top conferences in the United States are the Game Developers Conference and South by Southwest. Developers and publishing executives attend these events en masse, and you will have the opportunity to meet people from all levels and areas of the industry. There are lectures and seminars on any number of topics, and you might be surprised at how accessible some of the top talent in the industry is at these events. Other conferences you might attend include E3, DICE, PAX, IndieCade, the Global Game Jam, Games for Change, Casual Play, and more. There are a tremendous number of conferences each year and some are likely to be local to your area.

Game Jams

Game jams are one of the best ways meet and work with people at all levels. There are game jams on all sorts of topics these days, but the biggest worldwide jam is the Global Game Jam: globalgamejam.org. This is generally held in January each year and developers from those with many years experience to those just starting out get together in locations around the world to "jam" game ideas over the course of a weekend. Locations are searchable online, and are generally open to anyone in the area who'd like to take part. You can search the website and find a local jam site to join in. Who knows who you might find yourself working with over a weekend? Many other local jams can be found through university programs or online communities like Games for Change, who often organized themed jams open to a wide range of participants.

Exercise 16.1: Networking

Make it your goal to attend at least one networking event per month. This can be a conference, a party, a meeting, a game jam, or any other opportunity in which you can meet people in the game industry. Start a database of the contacts you make at these events.

Internet and E-mail

Another networking resource is the Internet. You can meet many people in the industry in online communities, such as the forums on IGDA.org, or you can find internships or positions in the jobs and projects sections of Gamasutra.com or WorkWithIndies.com. E-mail is a very efficient tool for reaching out to people, but it is not necessarily the most powerful or persuasive way to introduce yourself. You can find lists of developers and publishers in the companies area of Gamasutra.com, and you can go to their websites and contact them via a "cold" (i.e., unsolicited)

e-mail, but do not be surprised if you do not get a response. Game companies are flooded with e-mail from people who want to work in the game industry, and the chance of your e-mail getting to the right person without an introduction is slim. That does not mean you should not try, but do not be dismayed if the response to your carefully written e-mail is silence.

One problem is that HR departments are often not the best way to reach the decision makers for project hiring. I recommend searching for the individual addresses of people inside the company. Find out who is the producer or line producer on a particular game title, and then try to get an introduction to this person. Do you know someone in the industry, or otherwise, who knows them? If so, get a personal introduction. If not, try to find a contact e-mail address from press releases or postings on the web and contact the person directly.

Before sitting down to write your e-mail, research this person's background and the games they have worked on. Personalize your e-mail based on your research. A little knowledge and a well-written introduction of yourself and why you are writing can go a long way. If you are lucky, your e-mail will get a response. Even if there is no job at the moment, you will have made a contact, and you can introduce yourself in person at the next industry event or conference.

Good research and writing notwithstanding, do not expect too much from each message that you send. Professionals working in the game industry receive a lot of unsolicited inquiries. If they do not write back, do not be surprised or upset. They are probably in the midst of production and too busy to answer their mail. But if you continue to persevere, your odds will increase with every message you send.

Exercise 16.2: Follow-Up Letter

Write a follow-up letter to a person you have met via your networking efforts to talk about job opportunities in her company or to show her your original game idea. Try to make your letter both persuasive and courteous. Be sure you are prepared for the meeting should they respond. The next few exercises will help you to do that.

An important note about networking is to not expect too much from each activity you do. If you go to an event and do not meet anyone who can help you, do not consider it to be a failure. Networking is a cumulative endeavor. It is seldom that a single meeting will result in a job opportunity. Usually, you will have to meet people several times at events and follow up with them each time before opportunities open up. Even if a networking event opens up no opportunities, you will still learn a lot by simply mingling and interacting with the people there.

Starting at the Bottom

What jobs should you be trying to get in your quest to enter the industry? If you are an artist or a programmer, there are entry-level positions in these tracks at most companies. You will need to have a good résumé/portfolio. These positions are competitive, but demand is high for this type of talent. As the size of game teams has grown, the largest percentage of new jobs has been created in the art and programming groups.

If you want to produce games, there might be production assistant or coordinator jobs (or internships) that you can apply for. But if you want to design games, the outlook is a bit more complicated. The best job you could get would be as an assistant designer or level designer. Truthfully, however, these positions are difficult to come by unless you are experienced or already working within a game company. Many people who become game designers do so by starting in another track and jumping over into design when they have gained experience in the industry. For example, many game designers first work as programmers or producers.

Exercise 16.3: Résumé

Create a résumé focusing on your game design experience. Even if you do not have much professional experience, make sure to include references to all the design work you have done in the exercises throughout this book, courses you have taken, or organizations you belong to, such as the IGDA.

Interning

A good way to get into the industry in any career track is by interning. Game companies, especially publishers, bring on summer interns from colleges regularly. These are a mix of paid and unpaid positions, and they are not as hard as getting a fulltime job. But before you take an intern position, make sure the company is serious about letting you become involved in actual projects. A company that takes on interns but has no structure for involving them in the work the company is doing can turn out to be a difficult situation for both the intern and the professionals they are assigned to. A good internship will allow you to learn about some aspect of the business. Interns often do research, testing, or assist producers or executives. It is a great way to get to network and to increase your knowledge.

Exercise 16.4: Internship

If you are a student, an internship is a good place to start. Go to the career center on campus or visit their website and look for postings. Another option is to approach game companies directly and ask them if there are any internship openings.

QA

A common paid entry-level job is as a QA tester. The pay is usually low, and the hours can be long, but it is a decent way to start your career because QA testers are exposed to the whole development team. You will be writing bug reports that go directly to the programmers, artists, and producers. Managers might take note of talented QA testers because many of them started in QA themselves. When production teams are being built for new projects, some companies will give a good QA tester, who has paid their dues, consideration over an outsider. More importantly, QA testing gives you front-row seats to the development process. You will get to see games evolve and come together from early builds to the final release.

Pitching Your Original Ideas

Once you have built up some experience by working in the industry, you might want to try to develop and pitch your own original ideas to publishers. This is a difficult process, and the truth is that most publishers don't accept external pitches. They develop ideas within their own organizations. But, even if you are part of a larger company, you will still need to learn how to present your ideas clearly. So understanding how to pitch is an important skill for designers at all levels and at all types of development studios.

Let's assume that you have been able to get a meeting to pitch your idea – either to an internal executive, or someone like a funder or small publisher who is interested in developing new talent. What do they expect to see? How will the process unfold? The following section explains some industry practices for pitching ideas. Even if you are not yet at that stage of your career, it is worth understanding the process so that you can anticipate what you will have to do when you do get to that point.

Pitch Process

Game publishers and funders hear pitches from hundreds of developers every year. Many of these are immediately rejected for a variety of reasons, including inadequate submission materials. Only a small number of submitted ideas are actually funded or published. Of the ones that become products, only one or two become hits. Do not be discouraged by these statistics, though, because the odds of rejection are similar in all creative industries.

As a developer, you can increase your chances of getting past the first step with a publisher by making great pitch materials. Good pitch materials will identify your team as experienced professionals, and they will convey your ideas in an exciting way. When you are pitching to a publisher, one of the questions they will ask themselves is: Can these people be trusted to deliver what they are pitching?

The first step in pitching is getting to someone at a funder or publisher who is interested in hearing your pitch. This is where networking pays off. If you meet someone at a Game Jam or Conference who is looking for new talent, follow up and see if they are open to new pitches. Don't be surprised if you don't hear back right away. Keep following up – be courteous, but also be persistent.

When you eventually get a pitch opportunity, you should be prepared to sign a submission agreement or confidentiality agreement. This document will basically say that whatever idea you are going to present might already be in development at the company or has been presented to them by another developer. In any case, you will have no recourse if they end up producing a similar idea without you. Despite the one-sidedness of this document, you should sign it. Refusing to sign will show that you are not familiar with the process. Submission agreements are standard practice in every creative industry including books, film, and television.

It is best to pitch in person. However, sometimes publishers will request to review the materials on their own first And these days, you may be asked to pitch virtually via a video call. Whatever the situation, present yourself and your materials in as professional a manner as possible. You do not need to wear a suit, but ripped jeans and an old T-shirt are not appropriate.

Depending on how aggressive you are, getting through the pitch process can take weeks to months. Make a checklist or spreadsheet of every publisher you contact. It is okay to present the same pitch to multiple companies, but dealing with publishers that have multiple individuals evaluating your project can get confusing, and you do not want to lose track of your progress.

Pitch Materials

The package you present has to instill confidence in different types of people within the publishing company. They will be evaluating your team first, your creative materials second, and your project plan third. Make your materials easy to understand in a very short time frame because not everyone at the publisher is going to read them in their entirety. Here are some materials that I recommend preparing:

1. Sell sheet
2. Pitch deck
3. Game demo
4. Gameplay video
5. Concept document
6. Gameplay storyboards
7. Technical design overview
8. Competitive analysis

1. Sell sheet

This is a "short attention span" document that explains your idea as well as the target market. The sell sheet should include: game title, genre, number of players, platform, ship date, two-paragraph description, bullet point list of features, and some game art.

2. Pitch deck

This is the heart of your presentation. A great pitch deck leads you through your pitch naturally, engaging the funders. answering their questions, and piquing their interest. It will include a top-level description of your game, key art, trailer or gameplay demo, unique features and selling points and player experience, target audience, comparable games, budget, milestones, and team information.

Decks are generally built in Microsoft Powerpoint or Google Slides. Don't get too fancy — you want to be able to leave your deck behind easily so that potential funders can share with colleagues or other excecutives during the decision-making process.

3. Game demo

A playable demo is one of the most important submission materials you can produce. Demos can be built in differing degrees of completeness. The important thing is that the publisher can get to evaluate the final gameplay.

4. Gameplay video or trailer

If you cannot produce a standalone playable demo, then a gameplay video is the next best thing. It is a video file that shows the characters and gameplay. The most credible video will be one created using your game code. However, some established developers make them using just storyboards and narration. If you create a trailer, don't go overboard with self-praise or silly "reviews." Remember that the point is to show gameplay in action so that executives can judge the potential of the game.

5. Concept document

This is a brief game design document written without excessive details. If a publisher is interested, they will want to see that you have thought through the whole project, but they will not want to read every last detail. Ideal contents include:

game story, game mechanics, level design outline, controls, interfaces, art style, music style, feature list, preliminary milestone schedule, and a list of team members with short bios.

6. Key art

This is concept art that tries to capture the essense of your game. These can be in sketch form or final art or both. They are nice to include in a leave behind link because an executive might want to review and share your documents after the meeting. Ideal key art includes: character concepts, gameplay in action, and key locations.

7. Technical design overview

This is a technical design document without excessive details. It describes how your technology works as well as the intended development path. It should include complete explanations while being accessible for nonengineers. Ideal contents are: general overview, engine description, tools description, hardware used (development and target), history of code base, and middleware used, if any.

8. Competitive analysis

This identifies titles you are competing against. It shows that you understand the market and your relative position within it. Ideal contents are: summary of your concept's market position and reason for success and pro and con descriptions of competitive titles with sales figures, if you can get them.

Exercise 16.5: Preparing Your Pitch Materials

Go over the preceding list, and with your team members, prepare as many of the pitch materials as you can, prioritizing the pitch deck. Make sure to include all of the work you have done on your original game prototype, your design document, and your project plan.

Exercise 16.6: Pitching

From your networking database and the research you have done, target a list of funders or publishers to whom you can pitch your original game. Use all the methods described previously to find a contact within the company and set up a pitch. Even if this exercise does not result in the sale or funding of your idea, this is a great way to network and will help you to meet more people in the industry and possibly get a job.

What Happens after the Pitch

Before leaving your pitch meeting, you should ask when you should expect a preliminary response to your pitch. This will set both your own expectations for a response as well as the funder or publisher's expectations that you intend to follow up.

Prompt follow-up on the developer's part is important, but over-eagerness can quickly wear on a publisher. A good guideline is to follow up with a short "thank you" e-mail immediately after your pitch, and provide any supplemental materials or copies of documents that were requested during the meeting.

If a funder or publisher is interested, they will likely get back to you quickly, but if you do not hear from them immediately, it might just mean that your contact is traveling or busy in other meetings. If you do not receive a response after 7-10 days, you should contact the individual who set up your meeting with no more than one e-mail per week to check on the status of your pitch. Contacting the person more than this will be seen as bothersome and is unlikely to help your cause.

What will likely be happening at the company during this time is an internal review process among multiple people. It is unlikely that one person will be empowered to make a decision. Most publishers are organized around three groups:

1. Sales and marketing
2. Production
3. Business/legal

Within each group are decision makers who have input on funding decisions. The people you pitch to will likely be from the business/legal group. If they like it, they will take it to the other internal groups and try to build consensus. These groups often have competitive relationships because of their differing roles in the company. Ideally, someone will feel strongly about your idea and fight to convince the other groups that it will be successful. If these groups like it, the publisher might ask a technical executive to dig deeper into your project. It is a great sign if the publisher starts asking for technical details.

In essence, the final decision will be based on a combination of many possible risks versus the potential opportunity. These risk factors can include: time to market risk, design risk, technology risk, team risk, platform risk, marketing risk, cost risk, etc. If the funder or publisher goes through their process and decides that your project is worth the risk and has a strong opportunity for success, they will prepare a detailed return on investment (ROI) analysis that will determine profit potential for the title.

If the decision makers deem all risks and the projected ROI to be acceptable, then they might send you a letter of intent for the project. This is a great day, but your pitch process is still not over. As a final step, the funder or publisher will want to execute a full contract. Or they might unexpectedly kill the project at this point for internal reasons. As a rule of thumb, do not believe you have a deal until you see a signature from the publisher on the final contract. And do not spend any of the money you expect to see from the publisher until it is actually in your company bank account.

If your pitch does not make it to this stage, know that you are not alone: You are in the company of many other pitches that publishers have reviewed and passed on that year. Each time you go through this process, you will learn more about how to pitch your ideas, and you will have more and better contacts to pitch them to.

INDEPENDENT PRODUCTION

As I have mentioned before, there are more opportunities these days for independent development. This is a hard route to take, and scraping together the money to support a team through months or years of production can be an arduous process. Some independent developers have other jobs, some do work for hire to support their original game development, some are able to run successful Kickstarter campaigns, and some use credit cards and loans from friends and family. Like independent films and underground music, independent games are a long shot for their creators. More often than not, they are never finished or never find significant distribution. But independence has its privileges as well—the ability to experiment with truly original concepts, the freedom to change ideas midstream, and the knowledge that you own your ideas and their implementation. I have taken this route myself for several independently published projects and I know the joys and heartaches of being a truly independent creator!

For some independent developers, the goal is to produce a game that will be picked up and distributed by a major publisher. If this happens, the developer will be able to negotiate a fairly good deal in terms of ownership and royalties, and the publisher will be taking much less risk in terms of advances.

For other independent developers, the goal is to self-distribute via one of the digital distribution systems available on consoles, PC, or mobile. In most cases, these digital stores will take a cut of the revenues. As already mentioned, the Apple App Store, the PlayStation Store, and the Xbox Store, each take 30% of the revenues. This is about average for other digital stores. Also, in-game micro-transactions are sometimes required to go through the distributor's proprietary system. If you are able to produce a great game at a low cost by going independent, you may make a relatively large amount of revenue, however, you will need to do a lot of marketing and publicity yourself to get the word out about your game. Indie game developer Asher Vollmer, whose Designer Perspective is on page 539, produced a quirky puzzle game called PuzzleJuice while still an undergraduate student. The game was featured at PAX and named one of the "Must-Have iPhone Games" by Yahoo.com and went on to make enough money for the tiny team that they could continue on with their independent game designs. It's not a millionaire story, but a good solid outcome for a small independent developer.

The edges of industries are where innovation often thrives, and your independent game might turn out to be exactly what the game-playing public did not know it was looking for. One way to get your independent game into the spotlight is to submit it to festivals such as IndieCade or the IGF. A number of success stories have come out of such events. See the sidebar on page 463 by Sam Roberts on opportunities for indie gamemakers for more info on these venues and the games that have come out of them.

CONCLUSION

As you can see, there are many ways to become a game designer and to get your ideas produced. Whether you get a job in the industry and you work your way up the ladder, try to get a deal to develop an original game for a publisher, or strike out on your own and produce your ideas independently, what really matters is not the path you choose but that you find a way to realize your dreams and make the type of games you truly believe in.

Whether you find yourself working at a large company, wind up producing independent games on a shoestring, or just wind up designing games as a hobby, never lose sight of your own personal vision, and keep in mind that the only way to fail is by not making games at all.

DESIGNER PERSPECTIVE: ERIN REYNOLDS

Manager of Game Design and Narrative, Disney Consumer Products, Games and Publishing

Erin Reynolds is most well known as the creator of the critically acclaimed game Nevermind. She has diverse experience spanning the past 15+ years in developing games within a variety of environments, including as a developer, publisher, academic, indie studio founder, and a two-time TEDx speaker. Erin is passionate about the potential games have to empower, educate, and inspire players of all kinds and is always seeking new ways —big and small— to help make the world a better place. She is currently working as a Manager of Game Design and Narrative at Disney Consumer Products, Games and Publishing.

How did you become a game designer?

Despite always being a gamer, I actually took a bit of an indirect route into games. As someone who had always been passionate about art and technology, I knew I'd end up in a field where I could leverage my interests in both. This initially led me to pursue 3D computer animation—which brought me to the University of Southern California. There, I immersed myself in art, cinema, and computer science courses while also becoming involved with SCFX, a student organization dedicated to visual effects and the entertainment industry. It was through these interdisciplinary courses and the opportunities made available through SCFX that I realized that I could—in fact—make games for a living!

I love playing games, but I found that I love designing them even more!

On games that have inspired her:

This is going to sound strange, but there are three games that perhaps had the most influence over me as a designer—Ecco the Dolphin, Dance Dance Revolution, and Eternal Darkness.

Ecco the Dolphin was one of my favorite games growing up. The sense of awe and wonder it imparted upon me was so deeply impactful that it inspired me to become a dolphin fanatic and I even almost became a marine biologist because of it! Knowing that games can have that level of impact on an individual is something I always keep in the back of my mind at all stages of game design and development.

Dance Dance Revolution also had a profound impact on me. It was a game that I adored playing for hours on end. Experiencing joy like that is truly important and valuable in and of itself but, additionally, the very act of playing helped to make me a healthier person. To be perfectly honest, I wasn't particularly keen on exercise up until I started playing DDR. However, that joy it brought me changed my perspective on physical activity – something that has had lasting, positive effects on my habits and mental and physical wellbeing ever since. How amazing is that?!

In fact, my experience with these two games (and many others since) is a large part of why I feel so strongly about the potential games can have to make a significant and positive impact on anyone. I am a living testament to how they can inspire players to broaden their interests and push beyond their own perceived boundaries.

Finally, Eternal Darkness taught me the importance of breaking the rules. This was a game that took many risks—often breaking the fourth wall and having the player walk the path of a wide variety of playable protagonists (not all of whom were "good guys" with happy endings). To this day, Eternal Darkness serves a reminder to challenge creative expectations and to be unafraid to (strategically) break design rules from time to time.

On exciting developments in the industry:

The breadth of ideas across the industry has flourished over the past decade or so. With game creators having more access than ever to the tools and distribution methods necessary to craft and share their ideas, so many unique perspectives from around the world are being expressed through games. This development in and of itself is fantastic, of course, but the implications are what I find most exciting. With more people playing and making games and—more importantly—different *types* of games, more ideas can flourish. Every year, we are finding new ways to play, new stories to tell, and new technologies to inspire our imagination for what's possible. In some ways, it has become completely overwhelming to keep track of all the new developments happening in the industry — both as a gamer and game creator. However, I think it is also an amazing time to be playing and making games because the possibilities truly do feel endless now more than ever.

On design process:

The ideation process is a bit different for every game and circumstance. Historically, I have found that most of my best ideas emerge when listening to music on a walk. Perhaps it's because while I'm in that day-dreamy state, the part of my brain that is wont to veto impractical (but potentially fantastic!) ideas isn't paying attention - so some of the best ideas have a better chance of slipping through to the surface.

From there, the process looks different depending on the nature of the idea and goals at the time. In some cases (if it's appropriate to do so — respect those NDAs!), I'll bounce the idea off of trusted friends —both those who are in the industry and those who are not. Different and even challenging perspectives are often a gift! Sometimes, I'll sketch the idea out, leveraging my visual art background to think about it in a different way. Other times, I'll write it out to see how things connect "on paper." Or I'll digitally prototype it (as long as I'm confident I won't get too distracted by getting the technology to work). From there, iterate iterate iterate and repeat!

On prototyping:

My prototyping process depends on the game, feature, and timeline available to me. I prefer an iterative approach that allows for the flexibility of a prototype but also, hopefully, informs the implementation process for the 'final' game itself. In other words, within a prototype I can test certain hypotheses about whether an idea will work the way I want it to. I can learn from that prototype and subsequent iterations to build an infrastructure that, little by little, gets me closer to completing the game one "experiment" at a time. In all my years of game design and development, I have learned that almost nothing will work or feel the way you initially imagine it will. So, I've found that this approach helps me discover ways to make the original idea even better while I'm creating the game (and not afterwards, when it's likely too late to make meaningful changes).

On a difficult design problem:

The core mechanic in Nevermind, a biofeedback-enhanced adventure horror game, presented a bit of a design conundrum in and of itself. Using biofeedback technology, a key goal of the game was to help players become aware of their anxiety levels by challenging them to "keep their cool" within intense and uncomfortable situations. We did this by "punishing" players for becoming stressed and frustrated by making the game even harder in response to that perceived anxiety. In most cases, game designers want to keep players in a "flow state"—challenged but not too frustrated. If you over-frustrate a player, they'll stop having fun and possibly rage-quit your game forever which, generally, isn't ideal. However, instead, we made the risky decision to actually double-down on players' frustrations in Nevermind.

We of course wanted Nevermind to be fun and engaging. However, it was important that players experienced motivation and agency in learning how to resolve their feelings of stress and anxiety within the game. So, simply making the game simply easier in order to accommodate their discomfort could indeed help keep them in "flow," but it would ultimately be counter-productive to the game's goal.

The team and I explored many potential solutions and, at times, even considered abandoning this key goal when it felt like an impossible design problem to solve. However, instead of giving up on the core mechanic, we ended up simply altering the *perception* of punishment and danger. In other words, we presented the threat of punishment in a way that would encourage players to certainly want to avoid it, but the actual punishment (the "in game death") was really only a fairly mild setback. We found that this approach, in most cases, created moments of high anxiety for players as intended, but rarely passed the threshold at which the game became unbearably frustrating.

Furthermore, the mere fact that this is a non-traditional design choice that "goes against the grain" of established best practices is actually one of the ways in which Nevermind has been able to intrigue players and establish itself as a unique experience. Sometimes breaking the rules is the only way you can establish them anew.

What are you most proud of in your career?

What gets me out of bed every morning is the thought that I might be able to make the world a better place through games. My work on Nevermind (a game intended to help players learn how to better manage their stress levels) is an obvious example, of course. However, less obvious examples include a music creation feature in Ultimate Band DS that encouraged young players to learn more about music-making or successful charity campaigns in Zynga Poker that I had the opportunity to be a part of designing.

And, at the end of the day, just getting to be involved in the creation of experiences that will bring joy and wonder to people is just such an incredible privilege – and it's something that makes me so proud of all the games I've had the opportunity to be a part of throughout my career.

Advice to designers:

Enjoy life and challenge yourself to constantly test your comfort zones – in big ways and small. As a game designer, your responsibility is to take others on amazing adventures and journeys! But how can you do this if you've never been on any adventures yourself? In any well-designed game, a player's failure is simply a chance to try again– more practiced and informed than they were last time. Life is like that, too. So, run toward those challenges head-on. The worst case is failure, after which you'll be able to tackle it again ...more practiced and informed than you were last time! You never know what treasures you may be passing up if you never take the risk of simply "pressing start."

DESIGNER PERSPECTIVE: MATT KORBA

Creative Director, The Odd Gentlemen

Matt Korba is a game designer and entrepreneur who has designed games for over 40 titles and has partnered with 2K Games, Disney, Activision, Microsoft, and Sony. His credits include The Misadventures of P.B. Winterbottom (2010), Flea Symphony (2012), and King's Quest (2015–2016).

How did you become a game designer?

I graduated from film school in 2005, and immediately rolled into USC's fledgling Interactive Media program to pursue my M.F.A. My goal was to tell stories through film and maybe learn some website designing on the side. Instead, I was exposed to a medium that was quickly evolving and had the potential to explore stories more deeply than films. I discovered that games are a powerful tool to create the feeling of empathy for players. This is something I will continue to explore for the rest of my career.

While in school, I created The Misadventures of P.B. Winterbottom as my graduate thesis project, which ended up winning a Student Showcase slot at the 2008 Independent Game Festival and garnered awards at IndieCade, E3, and Tokyo Game Show. This led to a publishing deal with 2K Games and the founding of The Odd Gentlemen. It was a whirlwind Cinderella-story of a student's first game project becoming an award-winning independent video game. Looking back now, that story seems very surface level and saccharine. There has been a ton of sacrifice, luck, hard work, and growth to continue to live that "Cinderella" story and maintain the studio for the last 15 years.

On games that have inspired him:

Games that inspire me are games that tell personal and intimate stories and explore their mechanics deeply and fully. I used to say "innovative" mechanics inspire me, but in the past years we have seen a lot of quirky mechanics. Mechanics, even innovative ones, can seem gimmicky if they are not purposeful, deeply explored, and well-balanced. If a creator pours their own emotional journey into the story, gameplay, and art of a project, the game will be forced to be innovative, because no two people's experiences are alike. When a team believes in and is passionate about a project, their enthusiasm and personal touches can be felt in the shipped game. A color-swapping match 3 game could be personal and heartfelt which would inspire me more than an 'innovative' one.

What exciting developments do you see in the industry:

The thing I am most excited about is the push for inclusiveness and accessibility in video games. The Odd Gentlemen creates games with positive messaging and universal themes that appeal to gamers of all ages and backgrounds. Accessibility and universal design allow us to reach a wider audience. And by broadening inclusivity and collaborating with underserved communities as a narrative game company, we are able to shine a light on personal and unheard stories. Game creation tools are in a place where we can create highly polished and intimate experiences with a relatively small team and that allows us to explore new experiences that can have a deep impact.

On design process:

The golden triangle for me is gameplay, art/animation, and narrative all working together to create experiences that can only happen in games. If I can't design with those three things holistically together then perhaps the idea is better served as a comic book, short film, or board game. My strongest ideas come from experiences I have had outside of games: The joy of my children and wife, growing up as a juvenile diabetic, struggling with infertility, a teenage side hustle in prestidigitation, or even just taking a simple hike. The more personal and deep I can go, the more engaging experience I can create. When I design, I stare at a blank page until my eyes hurt. I live inside my imagination. I talk through concepts with my team and collaborators. We brainstorm and improv and try to make each other laugh. I dive deeply into research. I wrestle, struggle, and bleed over ideas until they all fit together like an intricate puzzle in my mind. Once I have completed that oftentimes grueling process, it's one of the best feelings in the world. Then I am able to quickly write-up detailed and clear design documentation to share that the team can rally around.

On prototypes:

Prototyping is a huge part of our process. We start out all games with non-digital prototyping techniques. Good prototyping is an art form in itself. Very creative solutions are designed to get the game idea out as quickly as possible. There is no set way to tackle a non-digital prototype. Sometimes we use Lego, other times we use paper dolls or board game pieces. After the non-digital phase, we do a quick digital prototype and iterate on that. Oftentimes we will do a quick animation or PowerPoint to try to tackle the feel of the game. Game production is very expensive and time consuming, so when possible it is always best (and often more fun) to figure out the game first on paper.

On a difficult design problem:

When I was first learning about universal design and accessibility I had to change the core of how I thought about game design. I was mostly a puzzle-based designer in my early career. What I would want to design for was the aha moment. This is where you can't quite figure out a puzzle, then sleep on it, and have an amazing epiphany with the solution. This type of design is very much rooted in the idea that the player must play the game as intended otherwise they are "ruining" the experience. Looking up a puzzle solution on GameFAQs would be terribly offensive to the designer. However, this type of design is inaccessible to a lot of players. My goal is to make games that everyone can enjoy, however they want to enjoy them. That doesn't mean I can't design difficult puzzles, but giving players an easier or alternate path, or optional hints, or even a skip option won't "ruin" the game for anyone. Options in controls, UI, and gameplay open the game up for players that couldn't play—or worse, would have to stop playing—the "intended experience." As a designer I no longer care if players are having the exact experience that was intended, as long as they are having *an* experience.

I'm most proud of ...

Still being able to make the games that I am passionate about with the team I love after all these years. To survive we've had to be agile, not shy away from contract work that keeps the lights on, and just keep persevering through the ups and downs of this crazy industry. But, at the end of the day we are still pushing forward with passion-making games that we feel are important and have something to say.

Advice for designers:

Don't wait; make games. Make games with whatever you can get your hands on: marbles, thimbles, little pieces of string. Don't be afraid; just create. Your journey will be different from mine but if you continue to make games that bring in your vulnerable, raw, and personal experiences, whatever they may be, you will make good art and the rest will fall into place.

DESIGNER PERSPECTIVE: ASHER VOLLMER

Founder & Game Director, Sirvo Studios

Asher Vollmer is a game designer and entrepreneur whose credits include Threes! (2014), Puzzlejuice (2012), and The Misadventures of P.B. Winterbottom (2010). Puzzlejuice was a successful iOS project that was self-published while Vollmer was still a university student. Threes! was released to critical acclaim, winning an Apple Design Award and Apple's Best iPhone Game of 2014.

How did you become a game designer?

I was taught how to program at computer camp when I was around seven years old, during my critical period. Instead of acquiring a second language, I learned how to think like a computer, which has enabled me to turn my ideas into interactive experiences with relative ease. It started with simple command-prompt text adventures, but it wasn't long before I started experimenting with other experiences like multiplayer chatbot RPGs and artsy stick-figure platformers. It didn't occur to me that I was a "Game Designer" until I applied to USC. I always thought I was just a programmer who enjoyed screwing around.

On games that have inspired him:

There are two kinds of game experiences that are near and dear to my heart, but they couldn't be more disparate from one another. Adventure games and simulation. Adventure games like Monkey Island, Space Quest, and Grim Fandango defined my youth and gave me a love of narrative. The carefully crafted sense of place, character, and style in these games is overwhelming. I love to lose myself to these worlds that have sprung directly from the designer's brain. On the exact other side of the spectrum, I have lost thousands of hours of my life to intricately complex simulation games like Civilization, Rollercoaster Tycoon, and X-COM. These games downright flaunt what computers are best at: systems. You are presented with the challenge to build a complex machine that follows a very specific, but very expressive, set of rules. You will probably fail, but along the way you will learn, iterate, and every success will fill you with an overwhelming sense of pride.

On exciting developments in the industry:

I'm excited about the future of augmented reality. Once the devices are comfortable enough to wear for daily use, it opens up a whole new world of possibilities. I'm ready to play 3D games that fully challenge my spatial comprehension, but don't have to force me into an isolating void like most virtual reality devices do.

On design process:

Ideas show up with time. They come from dreams, friends, or sometimes just watching TV. But when an idea shows up and I'm excited about it, it is my responsibility to jump on the idea and make it into reality as speedily as possible. Speed is essential because I always run out of raw excitement in a matter of days and have to race myself to finish a working prototype before that happens. From there, I show off my prototype to as many people as possible. If a significant number of them have a good time, it means I'm onto something. And by essentially outsourcing my excitement-production to others, it gives me enough drive to take the game from prototype to finished product.

On prototyping:

Before you even start typing code or building assets, it is essential to figure out what is the minimum amount of work that will convey your unique and interesting idea. Your time and energy is precious, so it's important to spend it on tasks that will directly contribute to people's enjoyment of the game. It's okay to have some out-of-scope ideas, but just keep them in the back of your mind. Polish early and polish often.

On self-publishing Puzzlejuice:

Publishing and releasing Puzzlejuice on my own has always felt like a no-brainer. The game was small enough that I knew I could design and program it entirely on my own. I was in school at the time, so I didn't have any looming financial pressure. On top of all that, the App Store is incredibly supportive of self-publishing game developers. My goal was to release a game that would give me the freedom to release more games, so the idea of handing over a huge chunk of my profits (a.k.a freedom) to an outside entity was unattractive at best.

FURTHER READING

Bay, Jason. *Start Your Video Game Career: Proven Advice on Jobs, Education, Interviews, and More for Starting and Succeeding in the Video Game Industry*. Middletown: Game Industry Career Guide, 2017.

Gershenfeld, Alan, Loparco, Mark and Barajas, Cecilia. *Game Plan: The Insider's Guide to Breaking in and Succeeding in the Computer and Video Game Business*. New York: St. Martin's Griffin, 2007.

Mencher, Mark. *Get in the Game: Careers in the Game Industry*. Indianapolis: New Riders Publishing, 2002.

Rush, Alice, Hodgson, David and Stratton, Bryan. *Paid to Play: An Insider's Guide to Video Game Careers*. Roseville: Prima Publishing, 2006.

Saltzman, Mark. *Game Creation and Careers: Insider Secrets from Industry Experts*. Indianapolis: New Riders Publishing, 2003.

Steele, Craig. *Ultimate Gamer: Career Mode: The Complete Guide to Starting a Career in Gaming*. London: Kingfisher, 2021.

END NOTE

1. Nour, Nika, Wells, G., and Steinkuehler, Constance. Hireability Gaps and Frictions Between University Game Programs and Industry Hires.. https://igda.org/resources-archive/hireability-gaps-and-frictions-between-university-game-programs-and-industry-hires-2023/, 2023

Conclusion

If you have been following along with the exercises in this book as you read the text, you have not only broadened your understanding of games and game structures, but you have learned to conceive, prototype, playtest, and articulate your own game ideas.

You have thought through what it will take to produce at least one of your original game ideas by creating an Agile production plan with goals, priorities, a schedule, and a budget. You have a draft of your game's design document or macro and presentation materials such as a concept document, a pitch deck, and perhaps a working demo of your game. You might even have a list of contacts in the industry to whom you can pitch your idea. In other words, you are well on your way to working as a game designer.

It has been my goal throughout this book to empower you with the knowledge and skills to go out and work as a game designer, either by getting a job at an established company, by getting your game ideas funded, or by producing your ideas independently. If you feel confident in your ability to do this, then I have accomplished our goal.

Alongside this confidence, however, should exist the knowledge that "becoming" a game designer is a lifelong process that is never finished. Hopefully, you will continue growing and learning as a designer for the rest of your career, and the ideas I have presented in this book will just be the first step in a very interesting journey—the first level of your life as a game designer, so to speak.

Now you are ready to move on to tackle more challenging concepts in design, more professional responsibility, or perhaps to refine your focus to a particular field, such as visual design, programming, producing, or marketing. Wherever your future path in game design directs you, I hope you take with you a sense of the infinite possibility that exists for game design today, the potential for developing an entertainment form with the ability to move people to involvement and action far beyond traditional media.

The future of game design rests not only in the ever more immersive qualities of technological devices we read so much about today but, more importantly, in the ability of those technological wonders to serve some deeper sense of play and interaction. The potential is wide open to bring richer emotional qualities to the experience of games we know and to create new and unique mechanics for games we have yet to play. The game designers of the next few decades will show whether this medium will live up to that promise or not. I believe that you are up to the challenge.

Thanks for playing!

Index

Note: *Italic* page numbers refer to figures.